To Steve

Just so you don't need Ben's help with your new place.

Merry Christmas
Santa x

DIY

KNOW-HOW WITH SHOW-HOW

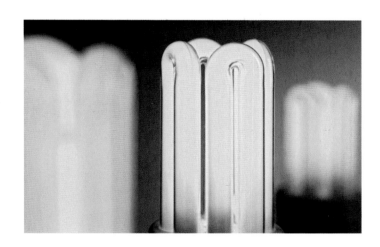

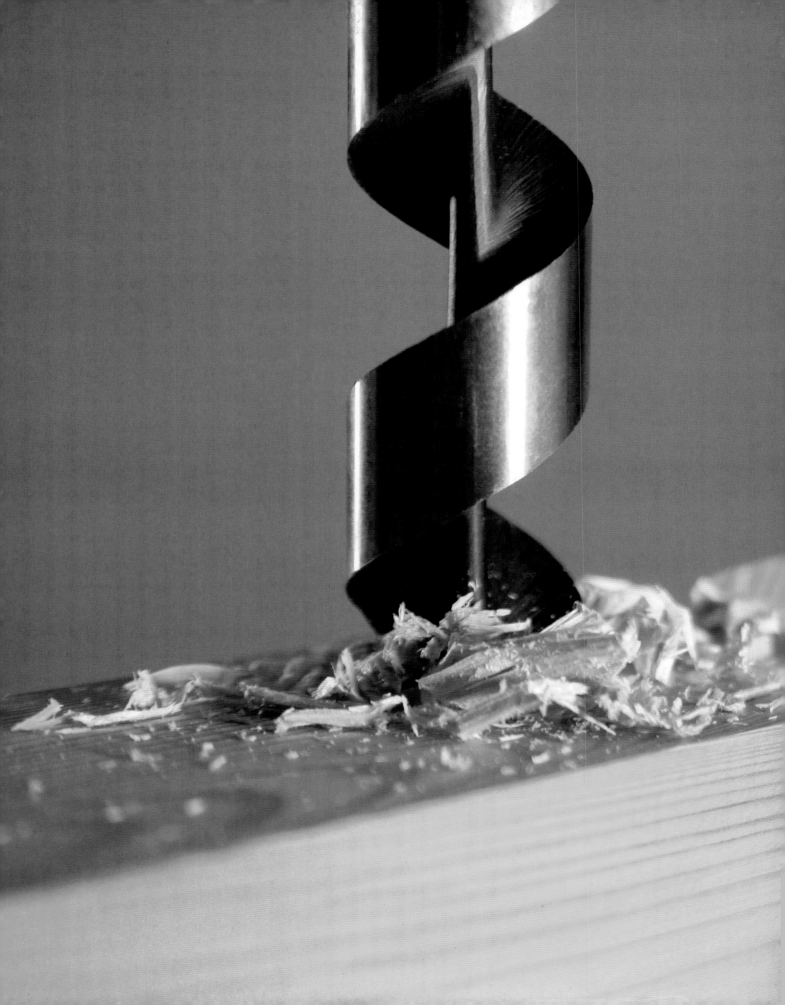

DIY

KNOW-HOW WITH SHOW-HOW

JULIAN CASSELL   PETER PARHAM

LONDON, NEW YORK,
MUNICH, MELBOURNE, DELHI

REVISED EDITION

Project Editor Bob Bridle
Senior Art Editor Sharon Spencer
Editor Ed Wilson
Production Editor Tony Phipps
Production Controller Rita Sinha

Managing Editor Stephanie Farrow
Managing Art Editor Lee Griffiths

ORIGINAL EDITION

Senior Editor Peter Jones
Senior Art Editor Susan St. Louis
Project Editors Becky Alexander, Suzanne Arnold, Miranda Harrison,
Letitia Luff, Giles Sparrow, David Summers, Andrew Szudek
Project Art Editors David Ball, Michael Duffy, Sunita Gahir,
Phil Gamble, Marghie Gianni, Philip Gilderdale, Sharon Spencer
DTP Designers Karen Constanti, Vânia Cunha
Jacket Designer Nicola Powling
Special Photography Gary Ombler, Steve Gorton
Electrical and Heating Consultant Mike Lawrence
Senior Production Controller Heather Hughes
Publishing Manager Linda Martin
Managing Editors Stephanie Farrow, Adèle Hayward
Managing Art Editors Lee Griffiths, Karen Self
Art Director Bryn Walls
Operations Publishing Director Jackie Douglas

This revised edition published in Great Britain in 2009 by
Dorling Kindersley Limited, 80 Strand, London WC2R 0RL

Original edition published in Great Britain in 2006 by
Dorling Kindersley Limited, 80 Strand, London WC2R 0RL

A Penguin Company
4 6 8 10 9 7 5 3
005-DD518-Mar/09

A CIP catalogue record for this book is available from the British Library.

ISBN 978-1-4053-3707-6

Reproduced by Colour Systems Ltd, UK
Printed and bound in China by Toppan

IMPORTANT
Neither the authors nor the publisher take any
responsibility for any injury or damage resulting from
use of techniques shown or described in this book. The
reader is advised to follow all safety instructions carefully,
wear the correct protective clothing, and, where
appropriate, follow all manufacturers' instructions.

Discover more at www.dk.com

CONTENTS

TOOLS, EQUIPMENT, AND MATERIALS   22

KITCHENS AND BATHROOMS 234

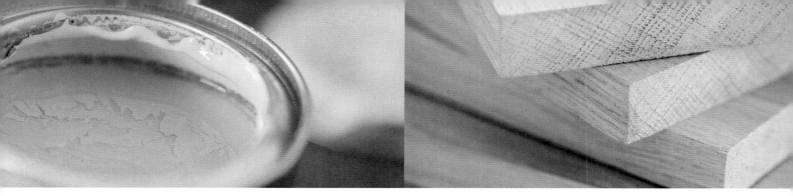

HOW TO USE THIS BOOK

The unique photographic approach of *DIY* shows you every step of every task, while a wealth of back-up information shows you how to prepare and plan for the best results. Nine major sections cover every aspect of DIY within the home. These are broken down into smaller subsections. Before trying any of the tasks shown in the step-by-step sequences ensure that you have read the relevant preparation spread and that you have all the tools and materials listed in the brown tools and materials checklist box. These checklists are in addition to the basic toolkit shown on pp.24–25.

Introduces whole subsection

Each section is colour-coded

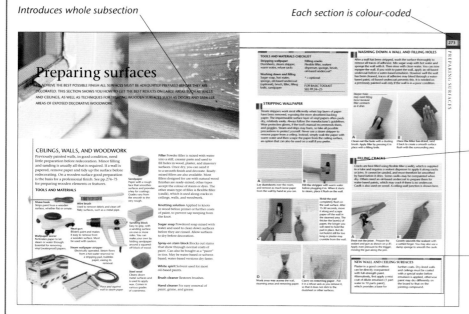

SUBSECTION OPENER
Each section is divided into several subsections that cover distinct areas of the home or of DIY. The opener introduces the spreads that follow.

Practical technique denoted by coloured square with stripe

Information box
Identified by a coloured panel across the top of the box, these provide additional information or advice on other techniques.

PREPARATION SPREAD
The spreads give advice on techniques, planning, and the tools and materials that you will need to complete the tasks that follow.

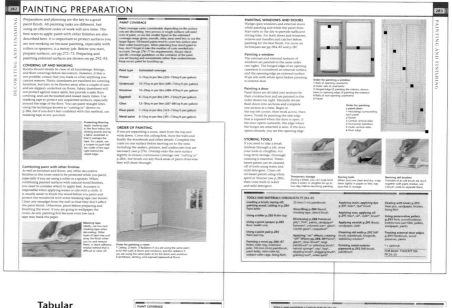

SAFETY BOX
Highlighted in red, these boxes cover important information about safety- or health-related matters. Ensure that you read this information before completing any task shown on the spread. Some of these boxes also contain information on planning and building regulations that you need to consider before commissioning or carrying out certain types of building and electrical work.

Tabular information box
Systematic layout gives an at-a-glance view of quantities, materials, and methods used.

Tools and materials checklist
Gives the tools needed for the tasks on the pages that follow. You will need these tools in addition to the basic toolkit, shown on pp.24–25.

HEALTH AND SAFETY
If the hot cylinder is in the bathroom, the circuit to the immersion heater must be protected by a high-sensitivity residual current device (RCD). The double pole (DP) switch controlling it must be at least 600mm (2ft) away from the bath or shower. If this is not possible, install a 20-amp ceiling-mounted, cord-operated switch and run cable on a flex outlet plate next to the cylinder to supply the heater.
An unvented cylinder must comply with both the Building Regulations and the water byelaws. Installation must be carried out by a qualified fitter.

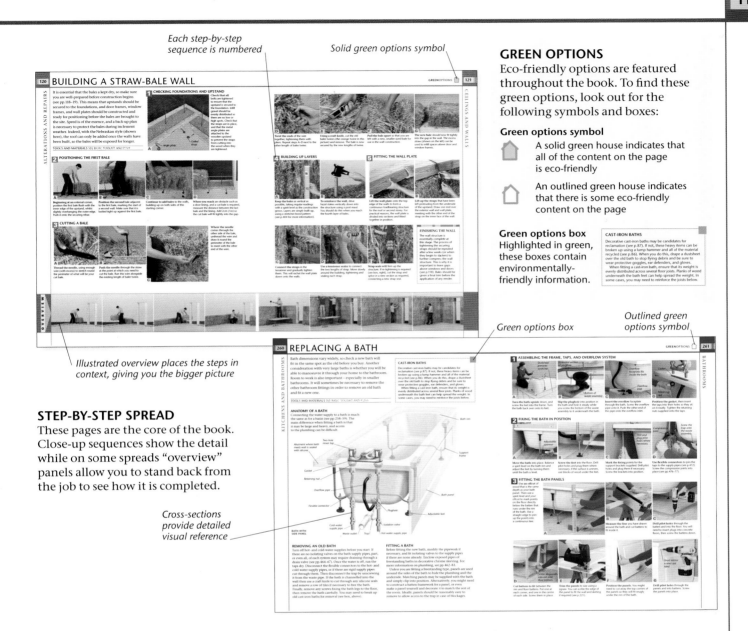

Each step-by-step sequence is numbered

Solid green options symbol

GREEN OPTIONS

Eco-friendly options are featured throughout the book. To find these green options, look out for the following symbols and boxes:

Green options symbol

A solid green house indicates that all of the content on the page is eco-friendly

An outlined green house indicates that there is some eco-friendly content on the page

Green options box

Highlighted in green, these boxes contain environmentally-friendly information.

CAST-IRON BATHS

Decorative cast-iron baths may be candidates for reclamation (see p.87). If not, these heavy items can be broken up using a lump hammer and all of the material recycled (see p.86). When you do this, drape a dustsheet over the old bath to stop flying debris and be sure to wear protective goggles, ear defenders, and gloves.

When fitting a cast-iron bath, ensure that its weight is evenly distributed across several floor joists. Planks of wood underneath the bath feet can help spread the weight. In some cases, you may need to reinforce the joists below.

Illustrated overview places the steps in context, giving you the bigger picture

STEP-BY-STEP SPREAD

These pages are the core of the book. Close-up sequences show the detail while on some spreads "overview" panels allow you to stand back from the job to see how it is completed.

Cross-sections provide detailed visual reference

Green options box

Outlined green options symbol

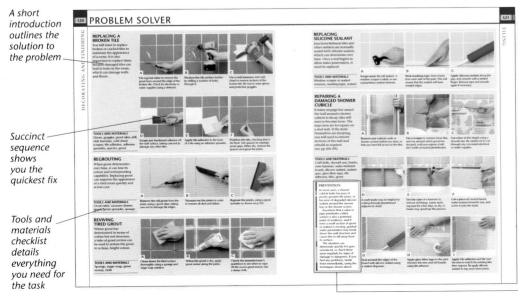

A short introduction outlines the solution to the problem

Succinct sequence shows you the quickest fix

Tools and materials checklist details everything you need for the task

PROBLEM SOLVER SPREAD

These stand-alone spreads contain one-stop, quick-fix solutions to problems, which you can carry out around the home. They fall at the end of each subsection.

Hints and tips

Provide additional hints and tips related to the main subject or task. Identified by a coloured bar down the left-hand side of the box.

INTRODUCTION

This book is aimed at showing you both how your home is constructed and functions, and how you can make repairs or changes. Once you have browsed the magazines and watched the makeover programmes, the book will both tell you, and show you, how the job is done.

In this edition, we have also included practical advice on eco-friendly DIY options, such as renewable energy sources and the use of sustainable materials. As well as combining new and old technologies, we look at the characteristics of raw and recycled building materials, examine their ability to insulate and store energy, and recommend how they may best be used.

Although "eco", "green", and "sustainability" are undeniably the buzz words of the moment, this is not simply an issue of environmentalism – shifting the focus of your home towards sustainability makes good financial sense as well. Achieving this change is easier than ever before, whether you are refitting an old house or starting anew. A sustainable house should be cheaper to run than a more conventional one, and there is a DIY solution for every circumstance that will almost certainly save you money.

One of the most rewarding aspects of writing this book was combining the benefits of traditional methods and materials with the advantages of cutting-edge technology. After all, a home constructed from straw bales and powered by alternative energy from solar panels is both an environmentally friendly and economically sound alternative to a more orthodox building.

The ideas outlined in this book present some rigorous but enjoyable challenges for DIY enthusiasts. We wish you luck with them, and hope you find satisfaction in the worthwhile and exciting projects ahead.

JULIAN CASSELL   **PETER PARHAM**

For all of us, there are tasks in which we have no interest or where we need professional help. Whatever your needs, these pages provide some guidelines for employing professions and trades, as well as outlining the differences between them. Finding good tradespeople can be difficult. Only ever go by personal recommendations, and preferably view their previous work before seeking to employ them. Always insist on a "price". As with a price in a shop, that should be the figure you pay for the job specified: no less and no more. The only reason a price should change is if you change the specifications of the particular job.

Architects

An architect will draw up any plans or drawings required for building work, if you are seeking planning permission, for example. Architects generally charge a flat fee for drawings, and then extra to oversee work being carried out (normally a percentage of the final building bill). If the architect is going to oversee work, check what that entails and get this in writing.

Bricklayers and masons

Whereas bricklayers tend just to lay bricks and blocks, a mason will also build natural stone walls and construct stone features such as window mullions. Their charges are normally based on every 1,000 bricks laid or they will provide a price for a specific job, such as building a chimney stack. If you engage a bricklayer for some work, specify brick type and insist on seeing samples.

Builders

Large companies will have their own teams of tradesmen in their employ. Small companies may consist of only one or two general builders who then subcontract aspects of work to other trades. A general builder will normally have a trade himself, such as carpentry or bricklaying, but he may also become the project manager for part or all of the work being carried out. The builder may include this cost in the submitted price, or charge a further percentage on top of the final cost. Agree this in writing before work starts.

Carpenters and joiners

Joiners assemble custom-made, wood-based items such as doors and windows, whereas carpenters will fit these items into your home, and tackle construction jobs, such as stud walls. There are overlaps between the two. In most cases a joiner will make something that a carpenter will fit. A good carpenter can be invaluable in complex tasks, such as calculating cut-roof structures. With a joiner, be clear on specifications for any items that you have commissioned him to make. If he is making windows, for example, make sure that he specifies the type of wood. The difference in quality, and price, between a good hardwood window and a standard softwood one is considerable.

Electricians

An electrician will carry out all types of electrical work, and usually the wiring for phones, televisions, and computers. Check certification before you engage an electrician. NICEIC and ECA are two of the main certifying bodies.

Floor layers

General flooring firms can tackle any floor requests, ranging from initial screeding to waxing a hardwood floor, for example. However, ensure that they have the relevant experience in all areas. You can also employ carpet fitters, wooden floor specialists, or floor tilers.

Groundworkers

Before a building starts to go up, groundworkers dig and sometimes lay foundations, dig routes for drainage and services, and generally do all the preparatory work. Many are employed by a building firm, but some work independently. It can save time and money to employ a groundworker and his digger for the day, simply to carry out all the heavy earth-moving requirements on a project.

Labourers

Skill and experience in this trade vary hugely. Good labourers are skilled at helping another trade to finish a job. A good labourer, for example, must know how to produce perfect mortar mixes. General labourers will price themselves on knowledge and experience, and hourly rates will therefore vary widely. Personal recommendation is essential.

Painters and decorators

A good decorator will carry out all aspects of decorative coatings including painting, papering, and in some cases tiling. Specialist tilers sometimes tile both walls and floors as a full-time occupation. Good decorators can provide very high-quality finishes – a preferable option when looking to hang expensive wallpaper, for example. Make sure that the number of coats, type of paint, and general quality of materials is specified in any painting job. Decorators can be an excellent source of ideas for new effects and finishes.

Plasterers

As well as internal and external rendering and plaster finishes, plasterers will fit plaster accessories and textured coatings. Pricing is usually based on meterage. Check that the price includes all coats required. They may also be able to offer "tacking" services – cutting and fixing plasterboard before plastering. Some plastering firms offer all these services, but other specialist firms only deal with cornice, cove, and textured coatings, for example.

Plumbers and heating engineers

There is often an overlap in expertise between plumbers and heating engineers. When installing, servicing, or maintaining a gas- or oil-fired boiler, they must have the relevant GAS SAFE certification. Ask for their membership number and check with GAS SAFE by calling them directly. For general plumbing work such as installing baths or toilets, the law is less exacting. Plumbers may also undertake gutterwork and any leadwork or flashing on your home.

Project managers

A general builder may be the best choice for project management. He can schedule the job, co-ordinate the various trades, and liaise between you and all other people involved on the project. If you are employing an architect, or even surveyor on new building work, it may be a best for them to project manage. If the size of job warrants a professional project manager, be certain of their credentials based on proven experience.

Roofers

Normally, roofers only deal with roof coverings, such as tiles, battens, felt, and finishing any mortarwork on the roof. A carpenter will deal with any structural elements. Large firms have carpenters working full time with the roofers. Smaller firms subcontract out structural carpentry. Roofing quotes or prices can be complicated. If weather delays work, this can have knock-on effects such as increasing the price of scaffolding hire. On large jobs, a roofer may actually scaffold over the top of the house and provide a "tent" (waterproof covering) so that work can continue in most weather. This increases cost and is only worthwhile on larger jobs. Check samples of materials such as tiles and felts before they are bought and make sure your choices are agreed in writing.

Specialist fitters

This category includes all those trades and services that offer a product with their own fitting service. This can be anything from new windows, to garage doors, to blinds, to fully fitted kitchens. Check that the product you receive is the same as the specification you were sold to avoid problems with your fitters. The more specialist fitters a project involves – for fitting a kitchen, for example – the more vigilance is required to ensure the job runs smoothly. Make sure that you specify each fitter's individual responsibilities. For example, a firm that fits blinds only has to supply what you ordered and use relatively basic fixing skills to fit them. A firm that offers a kitchen-fitting service needs to supply carpenters, plumbers, electricians, possibly heating engineers, decorators, tilers, and so on.

Structural engineers

As their name suggests, structural engineers assess the structural and loadbearing issues of a building and provide specifications. For example

they can calculate requirements for lintels and for foundations. They are often consulted by architects when plans are being made, and generally charge a flat fee.

Payment and extras

On small jobs, never pay any money up-front. Pay when you are satisfied that work has been completed to specification. On larger projects, it is usual to stagger payments through the course of the project. Link these to clear stages, such as the completion of groundwork, for example. On large projects a builder may require some money up-front. This acts as a deposit and allows the builder to order and buy materials. Schedule larger payments towards the end with the largest payment on completion of all work. Any extra payment to that originally estimated, or quoted, should be backed up by reasoning agreed between both parties, in writing.

Planning permission and building control

As health and safety, environmental protection standards, and building materials change, so too do planning and building regulations. Local authorities deal with most planning issues, under an umbrella of national policy and rules. Further rules apply to listed buildings and conservation areas. If you are considering structural work, always contact the local planning office first. They are there to help, not hinder. A quick phone call can often put your mind at rest about what does or does not need permission. Building practice is supervised by a Building Control Officer (BCO) or Inspector. Again, a quick phone call can often solve many problems. If you are carrying out work, the BCO will often need to inspect various stages to ensure that regulations are being adhered to. Insulation, ventilation, electrical wiring and installation, and how water supply and drainage systems work have all recently become more stringently regulated. Use these highly trained professionals as allies. They offer excellent advice and help.

...and finally, if you find good tradespeople, look after them, and pay them on time.

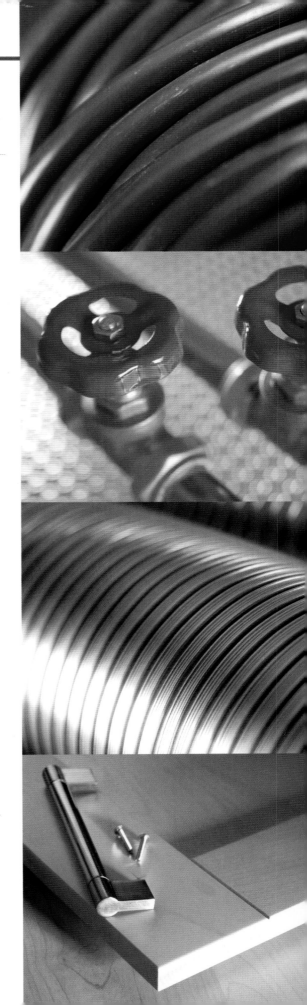

ASSESSING YOUR HOUSE: EXTERIOR

The exterior of your house has to withstand the elements all year round. An annual inspection is important to ensure that all aspects of exterior structure are maintained. It pays to be vigilant in checking for any potential problems, because this may prevent them escalating into something more serious. Some problems worth checking for are shown here and in the photographs below, though not all will apply to your home. You should also inspect the interior of your home for evidence of external problems (see pp.18–19).

WHAT TO DO NEXT?

Whenever you find evidence of a problem, consider these key issues before taking any action. First, assess the physical extent of the problem, and check whether it is symptomatic of a larger issue. For example, a loose tile may simply need refixing, or may be symptomatic of an underlying problem. Consider whether it is something you can fix yourself, or if you need to call in a professional for advice or to carry out the work. Once you know what you are dealing with, assess whether the problem needs tackling at once, or whether it can wait until you have the funds and the time to deal with it more easily. Problems such as leaking pipes or constantly running overflows are damaging and wasteful, and if you have a water meter they will be costing you a considerable amount of money. If the problem is a seasonal one, such as leaves blocking a guttering, it is worth planning for annual maintenance work. Remember that if you are hoping to sell your home, any problems with the exterior can seriously affect first impressions, and therefore the price you can expect to receive for your property.

DRAINAGE

Many external maintenance tasks involve ensuring smooth and efficient drainage from your home and into underground drainage systems. In modern homes, rainwater and waste water are kept separate. Waste water is directed into the mains sewer through a network of underground pipes. Inspection chambers, situated below manhole covers, allow access to the pipes should problems occur. Rainwater is channelled into a separate soakaway, or may run into the sewer via separate pipes. In older homes, both rainwater and waste water may drain into the mains sewer through the same network of pipes. You should update old systems when possible.

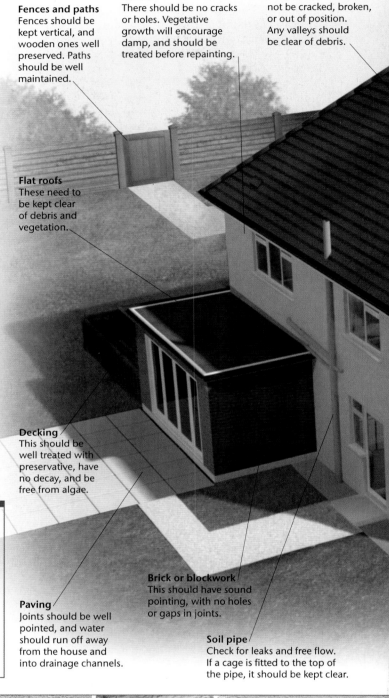

Fences and paths
Fences should be kept vertical, and wooden ones well preserved. Paths should be well maintained.

Render
There should be no cracks or holes. Vegetative growth will encourage damp, and should be treated before repainting.

Roof tiles
Slates or tiles should not be cracked, broken, or out of position. Any valleys should be clear of debris.

Flat roofs
These need to be kept clear of debris and vegetation.

Decking
This should be well treated with preservative, have no decay, and be free from algae.

Paving
Joints should be well pointed, and water should run off away from the house and into drainage channels.

Brick or blockwork
This should have sound pointing, with no holes or gaps in joints.

Soil pipe
Check for leaks and free flow. If a cage is fitted to the top of the pipe, it should be kept clear.

1 Guttering and downpipes should be free of corrosion and leaks, and water should run easily. Remove blockages immediately.

2 Hoppers must be clear of any vegetation and old leaves to ensure that water drains away efficiently.

3 Boiler flues must be clear of obstruction. This should be included as part of your boiler service schedule.

4 Air bricks should be clear, with no vegetation or garden equipment blocking any holes.

5 Flashing along abutments must be properly fitted to ensure that water cannot penetrate the roof.

Chimney
Pointing and flashing should be sound.

Cladding
Boards should be sound, with no flaking paint or varnish.

Aerials and satellite dishes
Ensure these are firmly secured.

Bathroom and kitchen waste
Pipes should have no leaks at joints, and water should flow easily into drainage systems.

Gullies
Check for any signs of blockage and keep free of debris.

Manhole
Cover should not be cracked or broken. Raised manholes suggest blockages in the drainage system.

Doors
These should have a protective or preservative finish. UPVC should be kept clean.

Outside lights
Cables, sockets, switches, and lights must be specified for exterior use. Corroded parts must be replaced.

Ridge tiles should all be in place, and their mortar must be in sound condition, with no cracks or holes.

Windows must have a protective coat of paint or finish; UPVC should be kept clean.

Trees close to the house may occasionally cause subsidence, and their leaves may block gutters.

Fascia board should be in sound condition and show no sign of decay.

Drives should be free of holes, craters, and standing water. Vegetation should be cleared from the surface.

Many parts of your home's interior can be affected by the external problems described on pp.16–17. For example, a damp area on the inside can be a result of exterior issues that need addressing. When carrying out an internal inspection, always bear this in mind. Many other internal problems relate to aesthetics and safety. The photographs below highlight common issues. Poor paintwork won't affect the structure of your house, but it will certainly detract from its look. Other issues, such as leaking taps, require more urgent attention.

WHAT TO DO NEXT?

Since you cannot physically do everything at once, prioritize the most important tasks. Tackle problems related to safety first. For example, ensure that all smoke and heat alarms function correctly. Be certain that you have regular servicing schedules for items such as boilers and any other gas- or oil-fired appliances. Aside from these more obvious items, appliances such as water softeners also require regular checking and in many cases periodic servicing. Also, if you have air-conditioning systems, be sure to check the manufacturer's recommendations on servicing. Remember that many problems will require professional help, particularly those involving gas. With all such items, servicing may not only ensure safe operation, they may also avoid costly breakdowns and repairs or replacement. Make schedules and budgets for improvements to decoration and/or permanent fittings and make sure you follow them through. Also consider whether the improvements you make would be appreciated by anyone buying your property.

HOUSE FILE

It is a good idea to keep a record of checks, important phone numbers, service schedules, and general information about your home and its appliances, but organization is key. One good way to keep track is to have a house file where all such information is kept. People often buy notebooks with a plan to transfer all the important details into them, but a ring binder is an easier alternative as scraps of paper, schedules, and instructions can simply be clipped into place. At the very least, keep a drawer in your home that is the sole place for accumulating household maintenance, repair, and improvement information.

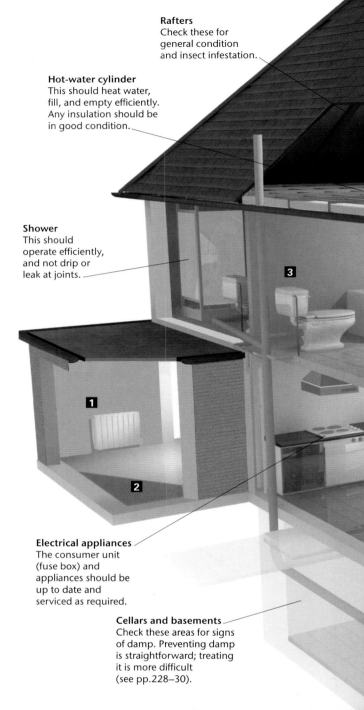

Rafters
Check these for general condition and insect infestation.

Hot-water cylinder
This should heat water, fill, and empty efficiently. Any insulation should be in good condition.

Shower
This should operate efficiently, and not drip or leak at joints.

Electrical appliances
The consumer unit (fuse box) and appliances should be up to date and serviced as required.

Cellars and basements
Check these areas for signs of damp. Preventing damp is straightforward; treating it is more difficult (see pp.228–30).

1 Radiators should heat up correctly and have no cool spots, leaking valves, or broken thermostats.

2 Concrete floors should be dry. If wet, you may need a new damp-proof membrane.

3 Toilets should flush easily. If not, replace the relevant valves (see pp.490–91).

4 Taps should operate efficiently and not leak at joints or drip.

5 Roof space insulation should be checked for general condition and depth.

Smoke detectors
Place units in open spaces. Make sure the batteries are working.

Joists
Floorboard supports should be firm; check ceilings for sags or cracks.

Water pipes
Corroded pipes should be replaced. Check that pipes in roof spaces are insulated.

Staircases
Safety is a priority. Creaking treads or risers should be attended to. Balustrades (bannisters) must also be secure.

Locks
Check these regularly for smooth and efficient operation.

Woodwork
Ensure that both structural and decorative woodwork is in sound condition.

Windows
Check that these open and close freely.

Cables and flexes should be in good condition, with no signs of fraying or damaged sheathing.

Boiler must work efficiently and must be serviced regularly as per schedule.

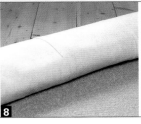

Floorboards should be checked for signs of rot or infestation.

Walls and ceilings must be sound, with no cracks or holes. Plaster should be smooth for decorative purposes.

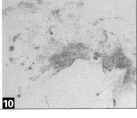

Damp can be caused by poor brickwork or by the failure of the damp-proof course. Treat it immediately (see pp.228–30).

When assessing the green credentials of your house, or investigating where green improvements could be introduced, there are a number of areas to explore. Many green solutions are relatively straightforward, while some will involve major upheaval and may be more suited to a new-build project than a retrospective fit. Use the information given here as a link to more detailed analysis later in the book. You will see that there are greener options for nearly all aspects of DIY.

GREEN RESEARCH

There are advantages and disadvantages with any building technique or material, and eco-friendly options are no different. If possible, it is always important to substantiate a manufacturer's claims with hard evidence. As in any aspect of life, manufacturers are concerned primarily with selling goods, so it is necessary to compare products, research different ideas, and make sure they meet your own needs. The areas covered here deal with most aspects of what is currently available in terms of making your home a greener place to live. Using the relevant page references, you can refer to various parts of the book for more in-depth information – and to learn how to carry out green projects yourself.

1. **Wind power** Wind turbines can produce electricity to supplement the mains supply (see pp.382–83).
2. **Green living roof** Generates oxygen, provides good insulation, and offers a habitat for wildlife (see p.93).
3. **Heat pumps** Various different designs offer a green alternative for space and water heating (see pp.510–11).
4. **Biomass boilers** A carbon-neutral option that offers a viable alternative to conventional boilers (see p.511).
5. **Insulation** This is key for energy efficiency. Try using natural or recycled materials (see pp.352–59).
6. **Passive solar power** Sunlight can be used with good house design to provide heat and light (see pp.378–79).
7. **Active solar power** Solar energy collectors can generate hot water and electricity (see pp.380–81).
8. **Paint** Natural, eco-friendly paints are readily available or can be produced at home (see pp.278–79).
9. **Green blocks** Both old and new technologies offer green solutions (see pp.84–85, 92–93, 98–99, 118–21).
10. **Rainwater** The rainwater that falls on our homes can be harvested on a small or large scale (see pp.386–87).

THE PAY-OFF WITH GREEN LIVING

If all houses featured many of these ideas, the energy usage of the population as a whole would be significantly reduced. However, the initial financial outlay must always be considered. With low-energy lightbulbs, for example, the initial cost is low, so the pay-off is fast – in terms of saving both energy and money. But with larger, more expensive projects, such as installing solar panels, the energy-saving pay-off may be quick, but it will take far longer to recoup the initial costs. The best advice is to address the key options first (insulate well, use low-energy electrical goods, and recycle), leaving the more complex projects to form part of the decision-making process of any future home improvements.

Compost Making compost is the ultimate expression of green living (see pp.400–01)

Wooden patio doors Double-glazed windows need not be UPVC or aluminium – wood is a greener option and will last just as long if well looked after (see pp.144–45)

Recycling bins A good system of sorting materials for recycling is essential for every home (see pp.246–47)

Roof tiles
Consider using wood shingles or reclaimed tiles (see pp.86–87)

Low-energy lighting
A small investment can have a large impact on saving electricity (see p.437)

Rafter insulation
In a lived-in roof space, ensure the ceiling is insulated sufficiently (see pp.358–59)

Render
Lime renders are far greener than those that are cement-based (see p.99)

White goods
Be sure to choose energy-efficient models (see pp.376–77)

Natural flooring
Flooring from sustainable sources is an eco-friendly option (see p.326)

Double glazing
Double or even triple glazing will always make your home more energy efficient (p.150)

Grey water
As well as using collected rainwater in the home, you can also recycle water from sinks, baths, and showers (see p.385)

Cavity walls
Insulating cavity walls can help to further reduce your energy requirements (see p.360)

Sustainable wood
Make sure that any wood you use in your home comes from a sustainable source (see p.75)

Reclaimed slabs
It is not always necessary to buy new – consider using reclaimed materials (see pp.86–87)

TOOLS, EQUIPMENT, AND MATERIALS

HAND TOOLS
POWER TOOLS
MATERIALS

BASIC TOOLKIT

A good toolkit is something every home should have, but you do not need to buy a lavish kit all at once. Most people will need a screwdriver, torch, or spanner from time to time, and it is worthwhile accumulating individual items as and when you need them, and adding to these when you are able to afford it. Tools can be expensive and as a general rule it is best to invest in quality, as a well-made item will last a lifetime for most household needs. Invariably, cheaper tools will break or fail to do the job they are intended for, so buy the best you can afford.

THE TOOLBOX
Sturdiness and an adequate capacity are the most important factors to consider when choosing a toolbox. Most toolboxes come with many compartments that help to keep tools organized.

Compartmentalized tray may be lifted out

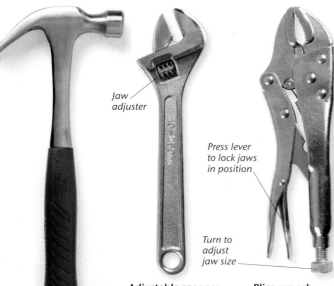

Jaw adjuster

Press lever to lock jaws in position

Turn to adjust jaw size

Flat steel blade

Claw hammer
This most versatile of hammers can be used for driving in nails and levering them out.

Adjustable spanner
A spanner suited to many tasks, as its jaws may be adjusted to fit nuts and bolts of different sizes.

Plier wrench
A multi-purpose gripping tool, with size-adjustable jaws, ideal for gripping nuts, pipes, and fittings.

Combination pliers
A gripping tool that you may use to hold, turn, or pull out different types of fixing or fitting.

Scraper
Useful for removing old decorative coverings or scraping down loose, flaky surfaces.

Torch
A vital tool when the power is off, and for viewing in dark, secluded areas.

Pencil
A sharp pencil is essential for marking off accurate measurements.

Nail punch
Used for knocking in nail heads below surface level.

Slot-headed screwdrivers
A selection of slot-headed screwdrivers of different sizes will enable you to deal with a variety of sizes of slot-headed screw.

Cross-headed screwdrivers
A set of Pozidriv screwdrivers, and ideally also a set of Phillips screwdrivers, will allow you to deal with most cross-headed screws.

Bradawl
Useful for marking and starting off fixing points. Also used for detecting uprights or noggings in studwork, or joists in ceilings.

Electrical detection screwdriver
This combines a small slot-headed screwdriver with a power detector, and has an indicator light located in its handle.

Craft knife
A sharp knife used for many precision and general cutting purposes.

Bevel-edged chisels
The most multi-purpose type of chisel.

Panel saw
A panel saw is the most versatile member of the saw family as it can be used for cutting a large variety of different materials.

Junior hacksaw
A small, fine-toothed saw that is designed to cut through metal and other materials such as UPVC.

ADDITIONAL ITEMS TO COMPLEMENT YOUR TOOLKIT

Electrical tape
This insulating tape is used in many electrical tasks.

A selection of fixings
Keep a good selection and number of general-purpose fixings so that you always have a ready choice available.

Cordless electric drill with drill and driver bits
A multi-purpose, battery-powered drill and screwdriver that can be used for a large number of fixing tasks.

Bucket
Used either as a mixing vessel or to move fluid and solid materials.

Compartments help to separate fixing types and sizes

PTFE tape
This lightweight, thin tape is part of every plumber's toolkit. PTFE tape is used on threaded connections to prevent leaks.

Small size means it will fit in a toolbox

Stepladder
A sturdy stepladder provides a good access platform for a variety of tasks.

Mini spirit level
Provides horizontal and vertical guide lines when positioning fixtures and fittings.

Tape measure
Essential for providing accurate measurements. Retractable, lockable tape measures are easy to use and space-saving.

Retractable metal tape

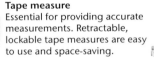

Made of lightweight aluminium

Cable, stud, and pipe detector
Can help to find pipes, wires, and studs below surfaces.

Fuses
You will find fuses of varying capacities in most household electrical appliances. Always have a variety to hand.

Dust masks
Essential when sanding or sawing to prevent you inhaling harmful substances.

Calculator
Always useful for quantity and measurement calculations and estimations.

Extension cable
Allows you to take a power supply to any area inside or outside your home.

Safety glasses or goggles
Essential for any toolbox as eye protection is vital for many DIY tasks.

Work gloves
Invest in a good-quality pair of work gloves to protect your hands when handling building materials and using heavy tools.

Portable workbench
This makes an ideal workstation for many DIY tasks. It can be easily moved from area to area in the home, and may be folded away for easy storage.

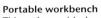

When gaining access to an area that is otherwise out of reach, ladders, in their various forms, are still the most versatile type of access equipment. However, your primary concern must always be to ensure that your equipment is set up safely, and used in the correct way. When purchasing a ladder, check that your choice meets national safety standards. Find out the maximum load that it can support. Store ladders horizontally and out of reach of children and potential burglars. Other types of access equipment, including platforms and scaffolding, are discussed opposite.

WORKING SAFELY

■ Never use a ladder near overhead electrical cables or equipment.
■ Never use a ladder in front of a doorway unless someone else guards it.
■ When positioning a ladder against a wall, make sure that the height of the top of the ladder is four times (4:1) the distance between the wall and the ladder's base. Many ladders have an angle guide printed on the side to help with this.

■ Inspect a ladder thoroughly before use, to ensure that there are no cracks or breaks. Check a wooden ladder for rot, and a metal ladder for corrosion. Never paint a ladder: paint may hide any damage to the structure.
■ Check ladder feet. A metal ladder should have rubber, slip-resistant feet.
■ Check that the ladder is sturdy enough to support your weight.

LADDERS

Most modern ladders are made from lightweight metals such as aluminium, although it is still possible to buy more traditional wooden designs. Shown here are the modern ladder types, but there are many variations on all these designs. Unlike other ladders, stepladders can stand alone and do not need to be rested on a surface. There are also many types of accessories for use with ladders, such as ladder stays that hold the top of a ladder away from a wall surface, or tool trays that clip onto ladder rungs.

Bottom section can clip onto top section

Top platform

Strengthening ribs

EXTENDED POSITION

Cleat

Unused rungs

COLLAPSED FOLDAWAY LADDER

Stepladder
A sturdy stepladder is an essential piece of household equipment because of its versatility and portability. Open it to its full extent for safe use, and never stand on the top platform or step.

Combination ladder
This can be used as a stepladder or as a conventional ladder, depending on how it is set up. Designs vary considerably: follow the manufacturer's guidelines carefully when setting up a ladder.

Extension ladder
These have two or three sections. For storage and moving, the sections are retracted. Brackets attached to each ladder section allow sections to slide over each other up into an extended position. Cleats fixed at the lower level of the upper section secure the ladder in an extended position.

Foldaway ladder
The stiles of the "telescopic" ladder shown here collapse into the ones below. Other foldaway ladders fold down into a very small, compact area. Whatever the particular design, the aim is to produce a ladder that is space-saving when stored.

PLATFORM LADDERS AND TRESTLES

The advantage a work platform has over a ladder is that it leaves your arms free to work. Various designs are available, and each provides a stable and level raised surface.

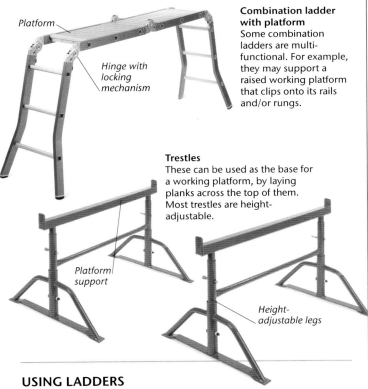

Platform

Hinge with locking mechanism

Combination ladder with platform
Some combination ladders are multi-functional. For example, they may support a raised working platform that clips onto its rails and/or rungs.

Trestles
These can be used as the base for a working platform, by laying planks across the top of them. Most trestles are height-adjustable.

Platform support

Height-adjustable legs

HIRED PLATFORMS AND SCAFFOLDING

Mechanized platform
A number of designs are available for hire, and these differ according to the surface on which they can be used and the height they can operate. Some you can operate yourself; for others, you will need to hire an operator. The hire company should be able to advise you as to the platform that best suits your requirements. Platforms are expensive to hire, and therefore might be used only when there is no other option or if the amount of work and time saved by using a platform is of clear benefit.

Scaffold tower
This provides a safe platform for one or more people, depending on its specifications, and is useful for work that would be too arduous on a ladder. Most towers have several sections that slot and clip together in stages, building up to the required height. They are best used on solid ground; where a tower is built on soft ground, place sections of board under its feet to spread the weight, and ensure that it is level. Fit stabilizers at the bottom to secure the tower in position, and tie it in to the building on the upper level. Some towers have wheels, and can be moved to different working positions, if resting on solid, level ground. Never move a tower when people, tools, or materials are on any part of it.

Fixed scaffolding
The access provided by fixed scaffolding is essential for some jobs, such as roofing. It can also offer an opportunity to carry out exterior maintenance. For example, if the scaffolding is erected for roofing work, use the access to check the gutters, and refix any loose downpipes. Erecting fixed scaffolding is a job for professionals, but check that the firm you employ has the correct certification or licence, and insurance.

USING LADDERS

Many of the safety issues involving ladder use have been identified opposite. However, aside from these standard guidelines, there are many other factors to consider.

Whether using an extension ladder (below, left) or constructing a working platform in a stairwell (below, right) safety must always be the most important concern.

Securing a ladder before climbing
The top of the ladder must rest against a solid surface. If possible, tie the top part of the ladder onto a solid structure on the wall, securing rope around the stiles rather than the rungs. It may also be possible to tie it to a strong batten braced across the inside of a window, with padding to protect the inside walls.

Aim to work on dry, solid, and level ground. On a soft surface, use a strong board underneath the feet to prevent them from sinking, and hammer stakes into the ground and tie the stiles to the stake with rope.

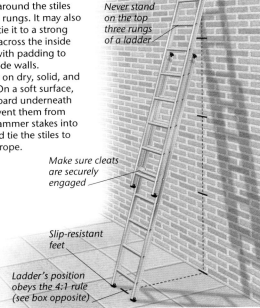

Both stiles must touch the wall surface

Never stand on the top three rungs of a ladder

Make sure cleats are securely engaged

Slip-resistant feet

Ladder's position obeys the 4:1 rule (see box opposite)

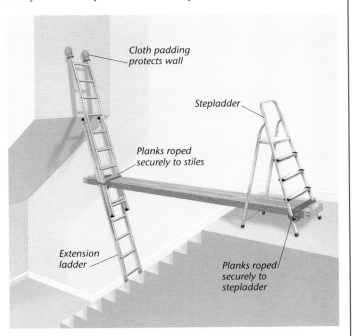

Cloth padding protects wall

Stepladder

Planks roped securely to stiles

Extension ladder

Planks roped securely to stepladder

Using two ladders and a scaffold board
Shown here is an example of how to gain safe access to a stairwell. You should use two scaffold planks tied together and secured at each end. The stepladder position shown here is very secure, but you may also reverse its orientation. Make sure the ladder obeys the 4:1 rule (see box opposite).

TOOLS, EQUIPMENT, AND MATERIALS

There is a large range of tools and equipment that you may hire for home improvement tasks, and many hire firms have a good variety of both hand tools and power tools. The degree to which you will rely on hiring tools will depend on the equipment you own, but however extensive your tool collection, there are some items that are so expensive that it would be uneconomical to own them unless you used them very regularly.

DRILLS AND BREAKERS

A power drill is essential for many tasks (see pp.54–57) but you may need to hire a heavy-duty drill for large projects. It is possible to burn out a drill's motor if it is not sufficiently powerful for the task. Some large drill bits, such as a core drill bit, require a large drill to house them. Breakers are designed for breaking up thick beds of concrete, general masonry, or tarmac.

Removable handle

Diamond-encrusted cutting edge

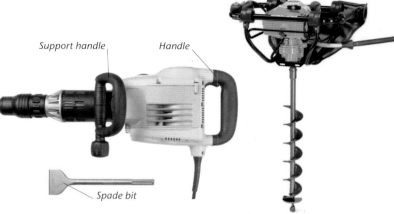

Support handle — *Handle*

Spade bit

Heavy-duty drill
A household drill (see pp.54–57) will be sufficient for most domestic tasks, but a heavy-duty drill will cope with greater demands, such as drilling a large number of holes in concrete and masonry.

Core drill bit
Use this to cut holes for ducting or pipework. The best core drill bits are diamond-encrusted for effective and efficient cuts. Hire companies may charge extra for each 1mm (1/32in) of diamond coating used.

Breaker
Choose from pneumatic (operated by compressed air) and hydraulic (operated by pressurized fluid) breakers. Smaller breakers called chipping hammers are ideal for removing plaster and render coats.

Post-hole borer
Mechanical borers make excavating deep holes much easier than if working by hand. Their sizes and designs vary, and some will require two people to operate them.

SUPPORTS

Required during major structural renovations, there are two main support designs, either used with "needles", or with proprietary supports (see below). Check that the props and supports can support the weight requirement.

Hammer-in supports
This proprietary design enables you to use a prop support on only one side of a wall, rather than on both sides.

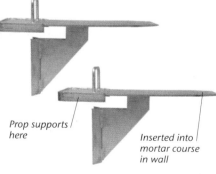

Prop supports here

Inserted into mortar course in wall

Props
These are used for medium-height support work, and are ideal for internal domestic building (see pp.102–03). Props are used in combination with needles and proprietary supports such as those shown above.

STONE CUTTERS

For cutting different types of masonry, specially designed stone saws or slab-and-block splitters are a good option. Splitters are used for cutting block paving by hand, and do not require a power supply.

Heavy-duty stone saw
Extra-thick slabs require a heavy-duty stone saw to cut them accurately and efficiently. Depending on the model of saw, slabs can be dry or wet cut.

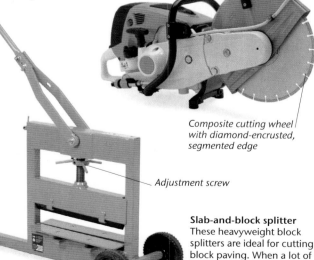

Composite cutting wheel with diamond-encrusted, segmented edge

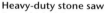

Adjustment screw

Slab-and-block splitter
These heavyweight block splitters are ideal for cutting block paving. When a lot of cutting is required, it can be well worth hiring a splitter.

ROLLERS, SCREED MACHINES, AND COMPACTORS

These are used for flattening and compacting areas of soil, hardcore, tarmac, and concrete. Rollers, screed machines, and compactors remove air pockets in material to reduce the risk of future settlement and provide a solid base for construction. Machines with vibrating mechanisms are the most effective, but you must follow advice about taking breaks during use.

Pedestrian roller
Self-propelled with vibration mode for improved compaction.

Diesel-powered motor

Weighted rollers

Petrol-powered motor

Hand grips

Fold-down handle

Power screed
This petrol-driven screed machine vibrates to remove air from concrete to increase its strength. Vibrating pokers are also available. Finish with a power float for a strong, dust-free surface.

Ride-on roller
Heavy-duty "ride-on" rollers are only really needed for work on drives or where large areas of compaction are required.

Petrol-powered motor

Plate compactor
A more common option than a roller for domestic situations, a plate compactor is ideal for compacting hardcore and sand.

EARTH MOVERS

You will need special training before attempting to use a digger. Models vary so get a hire company operative to train you. Check whether fuel is supplied as part of the deal, or if it is your responsibility, and always be sure of the particular type of fuel required. Check also if delivery is included in the hire price, and consider insurance.

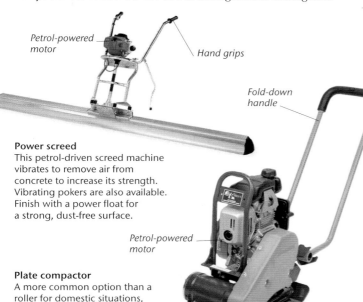

Canopy

Claw and bucket for scooping and lifting materials

Track

Mini digger
This can make major ground excavation considerably easier. Some training will be required for safe operation.

WORK CLOTHING

Work clothing falls into a number of categories. These include those items that are essential for a specific type of protection, those that aid a particular task, and those items that can be considered to be sensible options for a working environment.

BODY PROTECTION

Look for hardwearing materials that allow you to move freely. Overalls and gloves can be taped together at the sleeve when complete cover is required (see pp.356–57).

Overalls
Choose long-sleeved overalls made from tough fabric to protect your clothing while working. Many include pockets and loops for carrying tools, such as hammers and screwdrivers.

WORKING SAFELY

Make time before you start a job to consider your clothing, footwear, and headgear. Most building materials and tools are now supplied with specific manufacturer's guidelines on what sort of safety equipment should be worn when handling or using that product. These guidelines should always be followed carefully. All protective equipment will have a certain working life. Filters on face masks will specify this life, but on other equipment, such as helmets and goggles, it will be up to you to inspect them to make sure they are in good condition. This not only applies to clothing, but to tools and equipment as a whole.

Work apron
Useful to keep a number of tools to hand. Do not use to carry sharp tools that could pierce the apron. Leather aprons are more hardwearing.

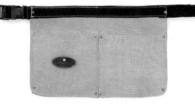

Knee pads
Protect knees when kneeling down for work. They usually attach to the knee using Velcro straps.

Nail pouch
Designed to carry small fixings such as nails and screws. May also have side loops for tools.

GLOVES AND FOOTWEAR

When choosing hand protection, consider whether you need gloves for avoiding knocks or scrapes, or to protect skin against contact with harmful substances. Good-quality footwear that covers the feet entirely will protect against falling objects or sharp or abrasive materials. Choose boots with a firm sole rather than trainers.

Rigger gloves
Heavy-duty gloves offer some protection against knocks and scrapes, and also provide some padding support.

PVC gloves
Protect against some chemicals and substances that cause skin irritation. Wearing PVC gloves reduces the need for harsh hand-cleansers.

Latex gloves
Tighter-fitting and thinner than PVC, these are useful for fiddly tasks. They protect against some chemicals, but are normally used to keep hands clean.

Boots
Good work boots are important to offer protection from falling objects, and when using tools close to your feet. Those with steel toe caps provide best protection.

HEADGEAR

Protective headgear must be worn when working at a height or in an area where items may fall on you. You also need to apply a certain amount of common sense. Wearing protective goggles or glasses is essential when you may be exposed to flying debris, but they may also be useful when painting or sanding a ceiling, for example.

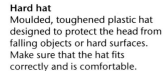

Ear plugs
A disposable, inexpensive alternative to ear defenders. Take care not to push the plugs too far into the ear.

Safety goggles
Offer all-round eye protection, creating a tight seal completely around the eye area.

Choose wraparound for maximum protection

Safety glasses
Offer eye protection from debris, but the gaps around the edges make them less effective than goggles.

Hard hat
Moulded, toughened plastic hat designed to protect the head from falling objects or hard surfaces. Make sure that the hat fits correctly and is comfortable.

Ear defenders
These provide effective ear protection when using noisy power tools.

Visor

Ear defenders

Machinery helmet
Combines eye, ear, and head protection. Visor and ear defenders clip onto a hard hat. Helmets may be supplied ready assembled, but if assembling it yourself, follow the instructions carefully so that the helmet functions correctly.

HARNESSES

When working in raised areas, you may need a harness to safeguard you from falling. Harnesses vary in design, so check for fit before buying one. A harness must be checked and serviced regularly to ensure it is in sound and safe working order. Designs will vary between different manufacturers, and even subtle differences may change the way in which one type of harness is worn compared to another. Harnesses may be attached to fixed scaffolding via a connecting lanyard with a specially designed hook.

MASKS

Protective masks are designed for use with different products. Some are designed to stop large particles such as sawdust, whereas others can protect against the inhalation of fumes and small particles. Check the type of mask recommended for use – failure to heed guidelines can compromise health and safety. Many masks have a limited effective lifespan and need to be replaced often. Others are designed for use with disposable cartridge filters. When working with paint, chemicals, and/or dust, make sure the area is well-ventilated with open windows. Ensure that you take regular breaks in fresh air.

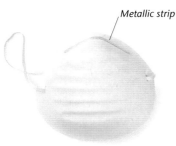

Metallic strip

Dust mask
Offers some protection against large particle inhalation. Choose a design that fits tightly. A metallic strip over the bridge of the nose keeps the mask in position and makes it as airtight as possible.

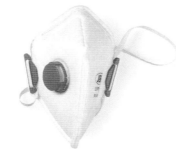

Valved mask
This is more comfortable than a dust mask as the exhalation valve helps to reduce humidity inside the mask. It may also offer a slightly higher level of protection.

Cartridge filter

Respirator mask
Fitted with cartridge filters and exhalation valves. Filters can be changed to protect against the particular substance you are working with.

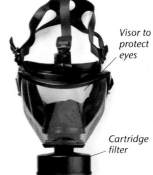

Visor to protect eyes

Cartridge filter

Face mask
Required when working with toxic substances, where a manufacturer specifies use. Regular correct cleaning and inspection of parts are essential.

Hand tools

ALTHOUGH POWER TOOLS HAVE TRANSFORMED DIY, HAND TOOLS REMAIN ESSENTIAL TO A HOUSEHOLD TOOLKIT. DESPITE THE ADVANCEMENT OF POWER TOOLS, THERE ARE SOME CIRCUMSTANCES IN WHICH HAND TOOLS ARE MOST SUITABLE. DESIGNS ARE ALWAYS IMPROVING, SO AS WELL AS LOOKING FOR QUALITY, LOOK FOR FEATURES SUCH AS ERGONOMIC DESIGNS THAT MAKE A TOOL EASY TO USE.

SCREWDRIVERS

Screwdrivers vary according to the type of screw that they are designed to drive. Different sizes correspond with screw sizes, so always use a screwdriver of the correct size to avoid damaging the tool or the screw head. Subtle variations in screwdriver design reflect the many different jobs for which they are used. For information about screws, see pp.76–77.

TYPES OF SCREWDRIVER

Screwdrivers are usually classified as slot-headed or cross-headed. While slot-headed screwdrivers have flat heads, cross-headed screwdrivers have cross-shaped tips. The most common types are Phillips and Pozidriv. Take care to use the correct type, as a mismatch may damage the head of the screw or the screwdriver. Other types of screwdriver made for specific screw designs are available, but these tend to be more associated with electric drivers (see opposite).

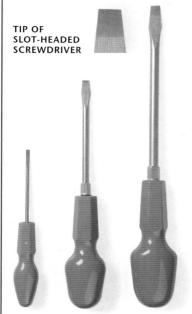

TIP OF SLOT-HEADED SCREWDRIVER

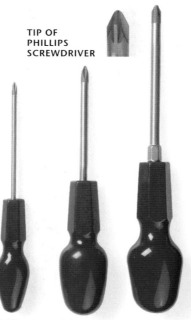

TIP OF PHILLIPS SCREWDRIVER

TIP OF POZIDRIV SCREWDRIVER

Slot-headed screwdriver
The shaft has a flattened, often tapering head and straight tip that fits into the head of a slotted screw.

Phillips screwdriver
With a cross-shaped head, the tip may be pointed or flattened. Small ones tend to be pointed; larger ones are often flat.

Pozidriv screwdriver
This is similar to the Phillips, except that between each cross-projection is a smaller projection that provides greater grip.

USING A SCREWDRIVER

Be sure to select an appropriate screwdriver to match the size and type of screw. Hold the screwdriver at right angles to the screw head, then ensure that the tip of the screwdriver is fully inserted into the head of the screw before turning it. Turn the screw clockwise to tighten it and anticlockwise to loosen it. Depending on the length of the screw, it may be necessary to adjust your grip several times.

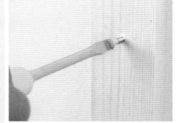

To insert a wood screw without damaging the wood, first you may need to bore a hole or drill a pilot hole, depending on the screw's size.

SPECIALIST SCREWDRIVERS

Some screwdrivers are designed to enable you to fix screws in inaccessible areas, while others have been developed to make the task of driving screws easier.

Stubby screwdriver
As the name suggests, this screwdriver is very short and is designed for use in areas that a regular screwdriver will not fit into.

Short shaft

Jeweller's screwdriver
This type of very fine screwdriver is designed for particularly intricate tasks. To use it, apply pressure to the revolving head with your index finger, and use your other fingers and thumb on the middle section of the handle to revolve the shaft.

Grooved grip

Narrow shaft

Revolving head

Electric screwdriver
An electric screwdriver can make working with screws much quicker. It is usually powered by a rechargeable battery and comes with a selection of interchangeable bits that fit into the neck of the shaft. In this model a central switch sets clockwise or anti-clockwise rotation, and a button next to the handle activates the shaft's turning mechanism. In many ways, cordless drill-drivers have taken over from the simple electric screwdriver shown here. However, these still have a function for lightweight work.

Turning shaft holds bits

Direction switch

On/off button

UNDERSTANDING A SCREWDRIVER

The tip
Flared tips are common on slot-headed screwdrivers. The flare makes the tip stronger, and therefore allows you to apply extra torque. By contrast, parallel tips align with the width or diameter of the shaft. This is important when a screw needs to be driven in below surface level – the edges of a flared tip would wedge in the fixing hole. Phillips and Pozidriv cross-headed tips enable the screwdriver to fit into the head of a screw more securely than a Slot-headed tip, enabling you to apply greater rotational force. Tips are often hardened and coated with rustproof materials.

SLOT-HEADED   PHILLIPS   POZIDRIV

The shaft
Screwdriver shafts can be either round or square in cross-section. Square sections in shafts allow a spanner or pliers to clamp on, which can make it easier to apply greater torque to drive in or remove a screw. High-quality shafts are usually made of a hardened steel and chrome vanadium alloy.

Square section

The handle
Traditionally, screwdriver handles have a bulbous section designed to fit comfortably in the palm of the hand. Modern designs place emphasis on a soft grip with a bulbous but less exaggerated section. Fluted handles are much thinner, and the fluted section along the handle shaft provides finger control of the screwdriver.

BULBOUS HANDLE   **SOFT HANDLE**   **FLUTED HANDLE**

ASSORTED SCREWDRIVER BITS

Ratchet screwdriver
You can use a ratchet screwdriver to drive in or take out a screw without having to readjust your grip. A three-position switch selects different functions. With the switch in the central position, the screwdriver operates like any other. With the switch to one side, the handle will rotate in one direction but lock when turned the opposite way. This enables you to simply rotate the handle one way and then the other to screw in or unscrew a fixing. Some ratchet screwdrivers have a spiral action in the shaft which turns the bit as you apply downward pressure.

Although traditionally associated with cutting wood, many different types of handsaw are now available for cutting through a great variety of building materials including metal and even stone. Shown here are the most common types of handsaw, but you will also find other design variations. Owning one of each kind will equip you to tackle most cutting tasks.

CUTTING WOOD WITH A SAW

Draw a guide line across each face of the wood, marking where you will cut. Use a carpenter's square to ensure that the line is accurate.

Use a craft knife to score along the guide line. This will enable you to get a clean cut through each side without splintering the wood.

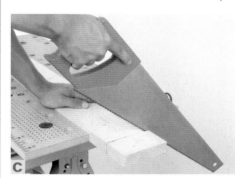

Hold the saw with your index finger pointing towards the blade. Place the blade just to the offcut side of the guide line. Start the cut by making two or three backward strokes across the corner of the wood.

Once you have cut a shallow groove, begin to saw through the wood, back and forth, using long, deliberate strokes.

Use the whole length of the saw to ensure teeth wear evenly. Support the offcut piece as you come to the end of the cut.

CUTTING WOOD LENGTHWAYS

Having begun to cut the wood lengthways, prevent the saw's blade sticking as you progress by wedging the cut edge open.

Continue with your cut. When you near the end, the scored line will enable you to finish the cut cleanly without splintering the wood.

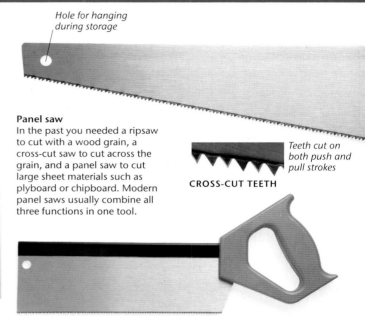

Hole for hanging during storage

Panel saw
In the past you needed a ripsaw to cut with a wood grain, a cross-cut saw to cut across the grain, and a panel saw to cut large sheet materials such as plyboard or chipboard. Modern panel saws usually combine all three functions in one tool.

Teeth cut on both push and pull strokes

CROSS-CUT TEETH

FINE TEETH

Regular, fine teeth make accurate cuts in wood

Tenon saw
Used for detailed woodworking, or when cuts need to be extremely accurate, a tenon saw makes fine cuts in wood. It has a relatively short but deep blade, and the fine teeth provide a clean cut and edges that require little sanding or smoothing. For this reason, a tenon saw is excellent for making mitred cuts, which need an accurate join.

Use point to break through material and start cut

Drywall saw or padsaw
This saw can cut irregular shapes, and is used to make holes in plasterboard, for example, when making way for power sockets. The blade is narrow, and tapers away from the handle to a point.

UNDERSTANDING SAW TEETH

The size, shape, and frequency of teeth on a saw's blade dictate the kinds of materials that the saw is able to cut. Teeth along a blade are measured in points per inch (PPI). The larger the PPI figure, the finer the cut, but the longer it will take. A saw with a high PPI is designed for precise cuts. Conversely, a low PPI saw is designed to cut quickly but less accurately.

A saw's teeth are slightly offset, so the groove cut by a saw is slightly wider than the blade. This groove is called the kerf, and it enables sawdust to leave the cutting area, helping the saw blade to move easily through a cut.

Body of blade

Tooth offset from body of blade **EDGE OF SAW TEETH**

The angle and design of teeth vary according to the uses for which a saw is designed. Saws that cut metal have very fine, forward-facing teeth, whereas a rough, general-purpose saw has larger teeth. Some manufacturers have patented tooth designs aimed at greater efficiency and ease of cut, and some make "hardened" teeth, designed to stay sharp for longer than traditional stainless- or tempered-steel blades.

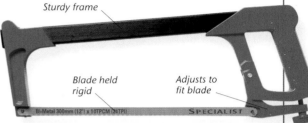

Stone saw
Although cutting through hard stone is a job for power tools, a stone saw will cut through lightweight concrete blocks. The saw's blade is very long and has large, deep teeth.

Sturdy frame

Blade held rigid

Adjusts to fit blade

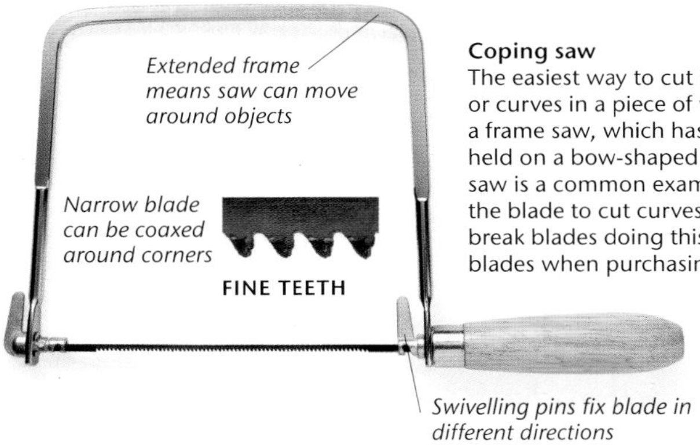

Coping saw
The easiest way to cut irregular shapes or curves in a piece of wood is to use a frame saw, which has a thin blade held on a bow-shaped frame. A coping saw is a common example. Manoeuvre the blade to cut curves. It is easy to break blades doing this, so buy extra blades when purchasing the saw.

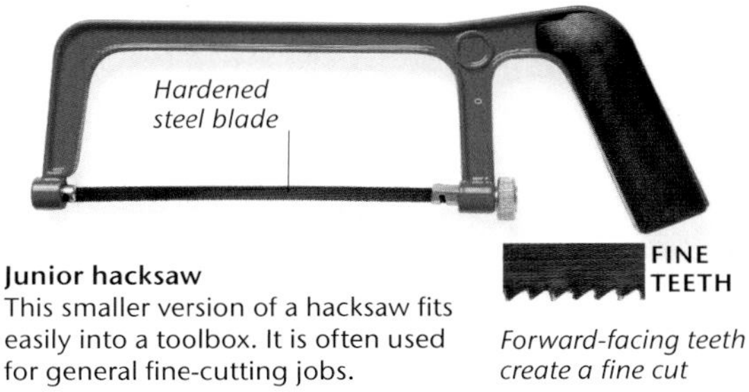

Extended frame means saw can move around objects

Narrow blade can be coaxed around corners

FINE TEETH

Swivelling pins fix blade in different directions

Hacksaw
Use a hacksaw to cut metal. Like the coping saw and fret saw, its blade is housed in a frame. However, it has a deeper blade that is not designed for cutting curves. A hacksaw's teeth are very fine, and cutting through metal is always a slow process. Renew blades at regular intervals, and always fit the blade so that its teeth are facing forward.

Hardened steel blade

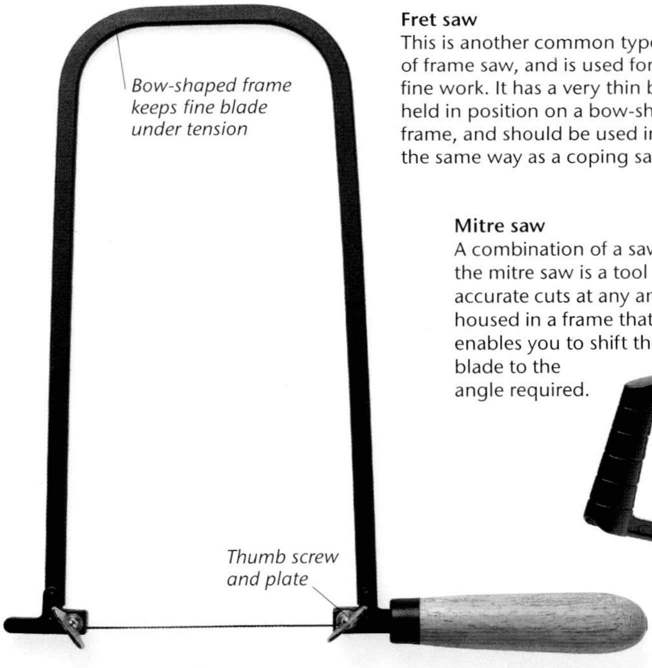

Fret saw
This is another common type of frame saw, and is used for very fine work. It has a very thin blade held in position on a bow-shaped frame, and should be used in exactly the same way as a coping saw.

Bow-shaped frame keeps fine blade under tension

Junior hacksaw
This smaller version of a hacksaw fits easily into a toolbox. It is often used for general fine-cutting jobs.

FINE TEETH

Forward-facing teeth create a fine cut

Mitre saw
A combination of a saw and a mitre block, the mitre saw is a tool that can make accurate cuts at any angle. The saw is housed in a frame that enables you to shift the blade to the angle required.

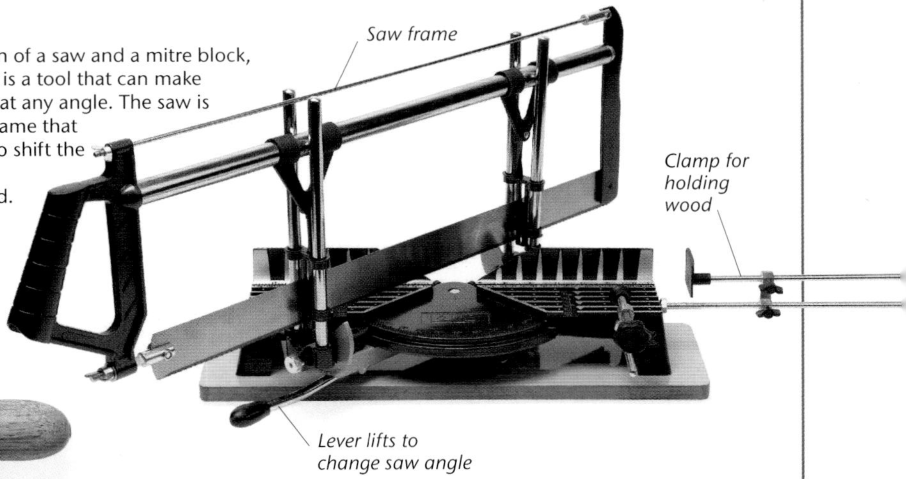

Saw frame

Clamp for holding wood

Lever lifts to change saw angle

Thumb screw and plate

CARE AND MAINTENANCE
It is now comparatively inexpensive to replace a saw, so sharpening handsaw blades is becoming a thing of the past. However, rather than throwing away a panel saw that is becoming blunted, use it to cut softer materials such as plasterboard or insulation sheets. When a coping saw, fret saw, or hacksaw is blunted, the removable blades are easy to replace.

Channels at 45 degrees to the block

Mitre block
A mitre block has channels to guide a saw (usually a tenon saw) through a material at precisely the correct angle for a mitred joint – 45 degrees.

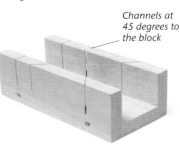

A hammer is a particularly versatile DIY tool. As well as positioning and removing nails, it can be used as a driving tool to knock in posts, or as a wrecking tool to remove a construction. The descriptions here will help you to decide which type of hammer you need for different types of job. A selection of robust fixing removers, including pliers, pincers, and pry bars, is an essential part of any toolkit.

NAIL PUNCH

This tool enables you to site a nail just below the surface. Punches are available in several sizes and weights to suit the varying nail sizes. See p.79 for how to use a nail punch.

The nail punch is made of steel, and is about 100mm (4in) long

The end of the tip may be pointed, flat, or cupped

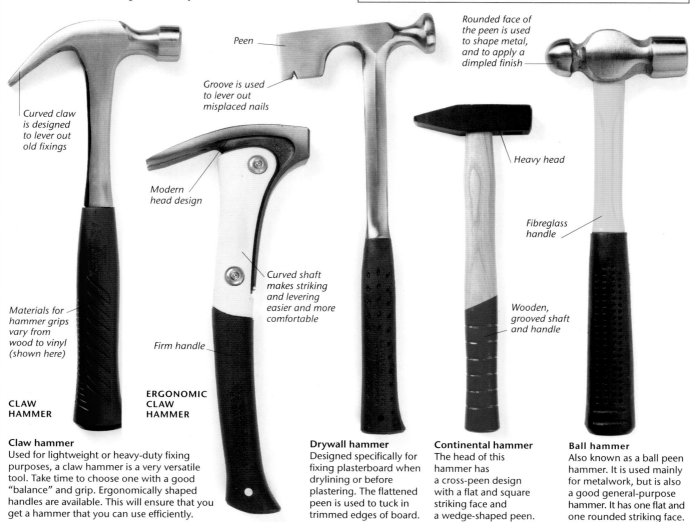

Curved claw is designed to lever out old fixings

Peen

Groove is used to lever out misplaced nails

Modern head design

Curved shaft makes striking and levering easier and more comfortable

Firm handle

Materials for hammer grips vary from wood to vinyl (shown here)

CLAW HAMMER

ERGONOMIC CLAW HAMMER

Rounded face of the peen is used to shape metal, and to apply a dimpled finish

Heavy head

Fibreglass handle

Wooden, grooved shaft and handle

Claw hammer
Used for lightweight or heavy-duty fixing purposes, a claw hammer is a very versatile tool. Take time to choose one with a good "balance" and grip. Ergonomically shaped handles are available. This will ensure that you get a hammer that you can use efficiently.

Drywall hammer
Designed specifically for fixing plasterboard when drylining or before plastering. The flattened peen is used to tuck in trimmed edges of board.

Continental hammer
The head of this hammer has a cross-peen design with a flat and square striking face and a wedge-shaped peen.

Ball hammer
Also known as a ball peen hammer. It is used mainly for metalwork, but is also a good general-purpose hammer. It has one flat and one rounded striking face.

▮ USING A HAMMER

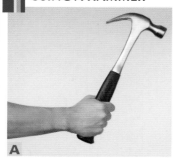

A

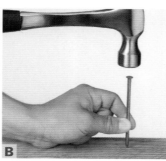

B

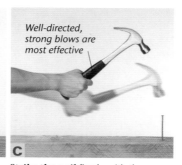

Well-directed, strong blows are most effective

C

Grip the hammer so that the end of the handle farthest from the head is only just visible.

Hold a nail in place and set its position with a few gentle taps.

Strike the nail firmly with the centre of the hammer's face. The face should be at a right angle to the nail to ensure a straight strike.

SOFT HAMMERS

Some jobs require the use of a hammer, but without the hard impact of a metal striking face. Soft hammers include wooden and rubber mallets. Wooden mallets are designed for use with chisels (see opposite) or for tapping wood joints into position. Rubber mallets are commonly used on blockwork, pavers, and slabs (see p.49).

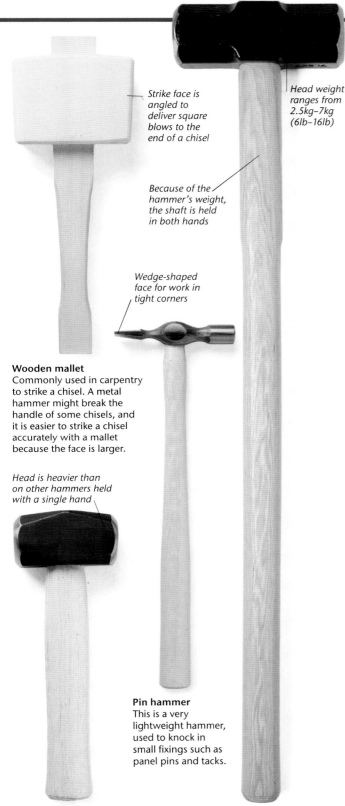

Strike face is angled to deliver square blows to the end of a chisel

Head weight ranges from 2.5kg–7kg (6lb–16lb)

Because of the hammer's weight, the shaft is held in both hands

Wedge-shaped face for work in tight corners

Wooden mallet
Commonly used in carpentry to strike a chisel. A metal hammer might break the handle of some chisels, and it is easier to strike a chisel accurately with a mallet because the face is larger.

Head is heavier than on other hammers held with a single hand

Pin hammer
This is a very lightweight hammer, used to knock in small fixings such as panel pins and tacks.

Club hammer
Also called a lump hammer. It is the heaviest hammer that can be used with one hand. It has a large striking face, and is commonly used with a bolster chisel or a cold chisel to split bricks (see p.39). In addition it is useful for driving large masonry nails into walls.

Sledgehammer
A larger type of club hammer that can be used to break up masonry surfaces such as old hardcore or paving. It is also a driving tool, and may be used to knock in posts, for example. Wear a hard hat, steel toe-capped boots, gloves, and goggles when working with a sledgehammer.

HAMMER CARE AND MAINTENANCE
It is important that you keep a hammer's striking face clean, to prevent it slipping during use and therefore striking inaccurately. The easiest way to keep your hammer in good condition is to rub its face from time to time with a piece of sandpaper.

FIXING REMOVERS
These tools are related to hammers. Some can be used as an alternative to the claw hammer, for removing nails from a surface, while others are used for more heavy-duty jobs such as breaking up masonry.

Pliers
These are very useful for small-scale work, as they enable you to get a good grip on the fixing. The toothed jaws have a curved section for gripping, and side cutters for cropping wire.

Scissor-like arms help to grip the fixing

Curved jaws assist rocking lever motion

Pincers
Use these to remove lightweight fixings such as panel pins. Grip the shaft of the fixing with the pincer jaws, and rock the pincers to lever the fixing free.

Hooked end enables large items to be levered out

Flattened, chiselled end can be positioned in narrow gaps

Pry bar
You can use a pry bar to remove heavy-duty fixings. Use the same technique as with a claw hammer. A pry bar is also suitable as a wrecking tool, to lever out or to break down masonry or woodwork.

▌ REMOVING A NAIL

A

Lay an offcut of wood next to the nail. Resting on the offcut, slide the claws of a hammer around the nail.

Offcut of wood protects surface

B

Keeping contact with the surface, pull the handle towards you. The rising claws should pull out the nail.

CHISELS

Chisels are cutting and shaping tools that are essential to many carpentry jobs. Heavy-duty chisels are also available, for use on masonry. Blade shape and size and handle design all contribute to the function of a chisel and how easy it is to use. A vast range of chisels is available for the serious woodworker, but a small selection should enable you to tackle most DIY tasks. All the chisels shown here have straight blades, but it is also possible to buy chisels, known as gouges, that have curved blades. These are used to cut out curved sections of wood and rounded corners – jobs that are more associated with wood carving.

WOOD CHISELS

Most wood chisels are based on one of two designs – the firmer chisel and the bevel-edged chisel. Of these, the bevel-edged chisel is by far the most multi-purpose and widely used. You can strike wood chisels with a hammer or mallet, or simply use hand pressure and your body weight. For example, you may use a paring chisel by hand to remove small amounts of wood at a gradual pace. Use only a wooden mallet when striking a chisel with a wooden handle. Hammers should be used solely on chisels with man-made, impact-resistant, or shatterproof handles.

◼ USING A WOOD CHISEL

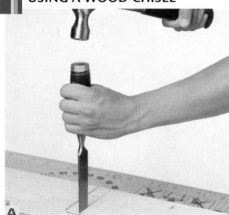

Clamp the wood securely in place, so that you can use both hands to control the chisel. To remove a depth of wood, first use the chisel to make vertical cuts along the marked guide lines. Make any cuts running across the grain first to protect the wood splitting.

A

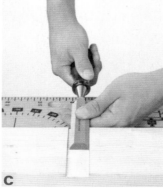

B **Place the chisel** with its bevel-edged side facing downwards. Hold it at an angle, and strike the handle squarely with a hammer or mallet.

C **Tidy the edges** of the cut using the chisel laid flat. Control the movement of the chisel by hand, gradually finishing the joint.

Firmer chisel
The blade of the firmer chisel is rectangular in cross-section, making it strong and suitable for heavy-duty work.

Cellulose acetate handle

Mortise chisel
Designed for cutting deep mortise joints, the mortise chisel is a stronger version of the firmer chisel. The deeper blade is often more square than rectangular in profile.

Bevel-edged chisel
One side is completely flat, but the other face has tapered edges. This chisel is designed for multiple uses, and provides the most accurate cuts. As well as general use, this design lends itself to removing wood in the construction of many different joint types.

Paring chisel
The blade tends to be much longer than the bevel-edged chisel, otherwise they are very similar. Paring is the gradual removal of small shavings of wood, which can be done with most chisels, but the longer blade on a paring chisel makes this tool easier to control when used by hand.

UNDERSTANDING CHISEL HANDLES
Chisel handles are struck repeatedly and so need to be exceptionally hardwearing. Traditional handles are wooden, but modern handles are often made of shatterproof and impact-resistant materials, such as cellulose acetate. These handles are so strong that most manufacturers provide a lifetime guarantee. Further protection is sometimes provided by a metal cap on the end of the handle. As well as withstanding hammer or mallet blows, a chisel also needs to sit comfortably in the hand, so some manufacturers give them a soft-touch handle, made of rubber or plastic rather than wood, which also helps with shock absorption.

MASONRY CHISELS

The nature of their work means that masonry chisels are much heavier and wider than wood chisels. They are used in conjunction with a club (lump) hammer (see p.37) to remove sections of masonry or other "hard" materials, such as wall tiles.

Guard protects hand from missed blows

Wide blade cuts bricks or blocks without shattering them

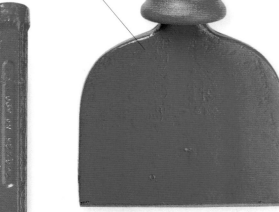

Bolster chisel
Also called a brick chisel, it has a short, broad, and flat blade, with a handle that may have a guard to protect the user's hand. You can use it to remove masonry, such as knocking off render from a wall surface, or to cut bricks and blocks (see below).

Narrow blade fits between bricks

Cold chisel
This is a narrower version of a bolster chisel (above). The blade shape is ideal for removing mortar from brick or block joints in a masonry wall.

CUTTING A BRICK

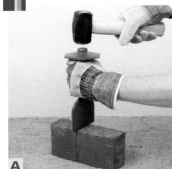

A

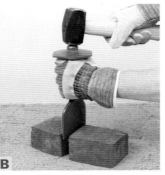

B

Use a light tap of a club hammer on a bolster chisel to mark a cutting line across each side of the brick.

Lay the brick flat, place the chisel on the guide line, and strike it with the hammer. This should split the brick along the guide line.

SHARPENING A BLADE

For chisels to work easily and effectively, they should be kept razor sharp. The best tool for this maintenance is a sharpening stone (see box, below). Chisels that are in a very poor condition, and need a lot of sharpening, may benefit from initial sharpening using a bench grinder (see p.65). It is also possible to buy a special guide that can hold a chisel at specific angles when you move it across a sharpening stone.

A

Moisten the surface of the stone with a few drops of oil or water. You may wish to secure the stone in a clamp or vice while sharpening the chisel. Use the chisel's bevel angle to guide you in getting the correct angle alignment between chisel and stone face.

B

C

Move the chisel, briskly but rhythmically, backwards and forwards across the stone to hone the blade edge to a sharp finish.

To finish off, turn the chisel over, laying it flat on the stone. Further gentle honing will remove any burrs from the cutting edge.

CARE AND MAINTENANCE

Sharpening stones
Oil stones composed of silicone carbide are the most common sharpening stones. There are other types available, such as more expensive diamond stones. Different grades of stone are available. It is best to buy more than one so that you have a coarse stone to remove large amounts of metal from a chipped blade and a smoother one for final honing. In fact, some stones are made with one coarse side and one fine side. Depending on the stone's composition, apply water or oil to the stone's face to lubricate it for sharpening.

Silicone carbide stone

Storage
Because chisels must be kept sharp, they need to be stored carefully. Chisels are often supplied with plastic covers that clip over the end of the chisel's blade to protect it. These covers should always be replaced when the chisel is not in use. The alternative is to store the chisels in a specially designed tool roll or carry case, as shown here.

Chisels held secure in individual compartments

Like chisels, planes are used to shave off fairly small sections of wood, but the broad blade of a plane is designed for use on long wooden edges. Many designs are available, but most DIY jobs can be completed with just a few. Many tasks are now carried out with a power plane (see p.62), but hand planes still have a role to play. Planes have a number of components, but are straightforward to use. Rasps and files have similar functions to planes, but remove material in a different way.

BENCH PLANES

These are generally categorized according to length. The largest version is a jointer plane, which can be around 600mm (2ft) long. It is ideal for trimming down the edges of particularly long boards, but its size makes it relatively unwieldy for more detailed work. Shown here are smaller bench planes: a jack plane and a smoothing plane.

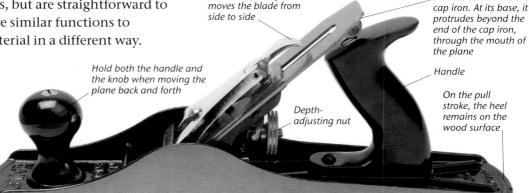

Lateral adjusting lever moves the blade from side to side

Blade is screwed to the cap iron. At its base, it protrudes beyond the end of the cap iron, through the mouth of the plane

Handle

On the pull stroke, the heel remains on the wood surface

Depth-adjusting nut

Jack plane

The most versatile of the bench plane family, you can use a jack plane for most planing tasks. It is fairly heavy-duty, and removes wood quickly and efficiently.

Hold both the handle and the knob when moving the plane back and forth

On the push stroke, place greater pressure here on the toe

The blade end emerges through the mouth in the base. The smaller the amount of blade showing, the finer the planing work will be

CLOSE-UP OF THE PLANE'S UNDERSIDE

Smoothing plane

A smoothing plane is a smaller version of the jack plane that is used for final finishing. It might be used after a jack plane, or it may simply be used for less rigorous planing on smaller pieces of wood.

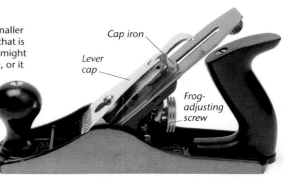

Cap iron

Lever cap

Frog-adjusting screw

SETTING AND ADJUSTING A PLANE

Lift the lever on the lever cap, and slide it out of the plane. Next, lift out the cap iron and the blade. Undo the cap iron screw.

A

B

Lift out the cap iron and blade, and slide the cap iron back until a small area of the blade is visible – up to 2mm (1/12in).

C

Retighten the cap iron screw. Do not yet replace in the plane, as the mouth settings need to be adjusted, as shown in the next steps.

D

Use a screwdriver to turn the frog-adjusting screw. Move the frog forwards to reduce its mouth size, and backwards to increase it.

E

Re-assemble the plane. Turn it upside down, hold it at eye level, and look directly along the base from the toe to the heel.

F

Turn the depth-adjusting nut until the blade protrudes from the mouth to the depth of a hair's width.

G

Finish setting the plane by moving the lateral adjusting lever to provide a uniform gap at the plane mouth, with the blade parallel to the foot.

BLOCK PLANES

Smaller than a smoothing plane, a block plane is capable of finer shaving as its blade is set at a shallow angle. The blade is positioned bevel-up in a block plane, but bevel-down in a bench plane. A block plane is normally used one-handed, but pressure can be applied with the other hand if necessary. It is particularly useful for planing the end grain on wood.

Compact plane

The compact size of a block plane makes it very easy to handle, as well as being easy to store in the toolbox. It does not have a cap iron, but the blade is adjusted in the same way as other planes.

Twist knob to move blade from side-to-side

Cutting-depth adjustor

Finger rest with mouth-adjustment lever

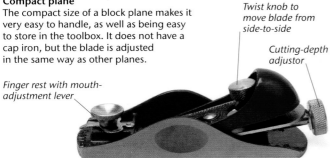

▌ USING A PLANE

Planes are best used for removing wood from relatively thin edges, such as doors or sections of prepared timber. A sound technique for using a plane is important for achieving good results. Here is the basic technique for plane use.

A **Position the plane** on the edge of the timber length. Move it forward steadily, keeping the pressure on the toe of the plane.

B **As you reach** the end, transfer the pressure to the heel of the plane. Repeat until you have removed the desired amount of wood.

▌ SHARPENING THE BLADE

Hone the blade before its first use. The corners of a straight factory edge can leave unsightly score lines in a wood's grain. The blade should be curved for general work, with corners slightly rounded for finer planing, and it should have a 30-degree bevel. Some planes are supplied with a 25-degree bevel, to avoid damage before purchase. In this instance, adjust the bevel before first use.

A **Hone the bevel side** of the blade up and down the sharpening stone to produce a bevel of about 30 degrees. Lubricate as shown on p.39.

B **Hone the flat side** of the blade to remove burrs. Work the blade across the entire surface of the stone, so that it wears evenly.

RASPS

Use a rasp for rounding edges and curves. Traditional rasps have a series of abrasive blades, varying in coarseness. Modern rasps, like those below, have holes punched across the entire surface of the blade. Each hole has a sharpened edge that shaves off layers of wood.

Two-handed surform rasp

As the surform passes across the wood, the shavings come up through the holes and clear of the blade.

Large handle leads the pulling and pushing action

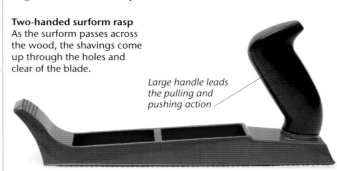

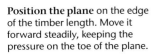

UNDERSIDE OF RASP IN CLOSE-UP

One-handed surform rasp
This has a similar cutting area to its two-handed counterpart.

FILES

Like rasps, files have an abrasive blade and are used for rounding edges and curves on wood, metal, and stone. They are often supplied just as blades, so fit a handle before use.

Handle may be removable

Curved abrasive surface

Needle file
This is a very small round file that is capable of extremely intricate filing tasks.

Flat file
Some files are also used for metalwork. The flat file is a commonly used design.

Half round file
The cross-section of this file is partly rounded, making access to curved areas easier.

Round file
This file has a completely rounded blade for accessing curved areas.

Levels are essential to many DIY jobs, as they ensure that guiding lines or marks are precisely horizontal or vertical. You can also use them to set accurate angled guides, although this is a less common function. Guide lines, which include plumb lines and chalk lines, use the tension in taught strings to determine perfectly straight lines.

SPIRIT LEVELS

Perhaps the most commonly used type of level, spirit levels come in various shapes and sizes. They usually consist of a plastic or metal straight bar containing two or more vials of liquid. Each vial contains a bubble. Hold a level against the item or surface to be checked. When the bubble in the appropriate vial rests between the two centre guide lines marked on the vial, the surface is shown to be either exactly vertical or horizontal. Some spirit levels have rotating vials that can be set at precise angles, for when you require guide lines at specific angles.

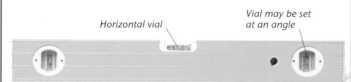

Horizontal vial *Vial may be set at an angle*

Carpenter's level

This contains three vials and is the most versatile level. The vial in the middle is used to determine the horizontal level, while the end vials determine the vertical level. One of the end vials may be adjusted when it is necessary to measure particular angles. Carpenter's levels are available in several sizes, ranging from 450mm (1ft 6in) to 1.8m (6ft) in length.

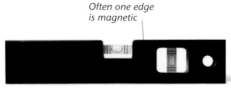

Often one edge is magnetic

Pocket level

This small level is designed to be used where a carpenter's level is too long, or unnecessarily complex. One face of a pocket level is often magnetic, so that it can be stuck to a metal surface, such as a fridge door or a cooker hood, to determine whether it is level.

Vial checks horizontal alignment

Rubber strap

Post level

A post level is a spirit level used for accurately positioning upright posts. The level can be strapped onto a post, leaving you both hands free to adjust the post's position until it is level. A post level has three vials, each positioned at right angles to the others.

Plastic casing fits around corner of post or upright

LASER LEVELS

These combine the principles of the spirit level with laser technology. They project a beam that can be set to provide an accurate guide line on any surface. A laser level can also work in the same way as a string line, helping to position things such as garden fence posts.

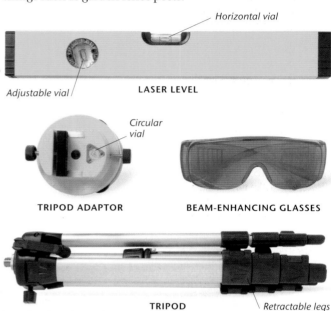

Horizontal vial

Adjustable vial **LASER LEVEL**

Circular vial

TRIPOD ADAPTOR   **BEAM-ENHANCING GLASSES**

TRIPOD   *Retractable legs*

Laser level equipment

The laser level projects a beam from the end of the level. It is used on a tripod, and the adaptor has its own levelling vial and an angle-adjusting mechanism so that its level can be adjusted without moving the tripod.

USING A LASER LEVEL

A

Set up the tripod and attach the adaptor.

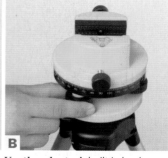

B

Use the adaptor's built-in level adjuster to centre the bubble in the vial and make sure it is perfectly horizontal.

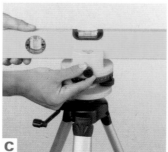

C

Clamp the laser level into position on the tripod adaptor, and check that it is level.

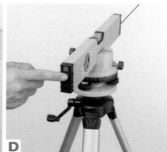

D

Turn on the beam to project either a dot or a line, as required. The beam can be projected horizontally or vertically.

Laser projector

Different vials denote different gradients

Laser gradient level

There are several vials along the length of a laser gradient level. One will be set to give a horizontal guide; the others are set to four different gradients. The laser projects a line showing your chosen gradient over several metres. This can be useful when putting up guttering (see pp.208–09), for example, or laying a patio (see pp.412–13). In both cases a slight gradient is required, and this level can provide that measurement with great accuracy.

WATER LEVEL

Although rarely used now, you can use a water level to calculate levels and gradients over long distances or around obstacles. Run water into a tube until it is nearly full. Fix one end in place so that the water level is at the required height, and take the other end to where you need to mark a guide line at the same level. The water levels at each end of the tube will always be at exactly the same height.

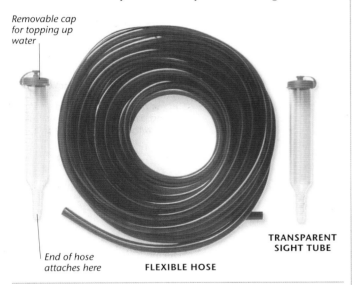

Removable cap for topping up water

End of hose attaches here

FLEXIBLE HOSE

TRANSPARENT SIGHT TUBE

GUIDE LINES

These are among the simplest and most useful elements in a toolkit. A plumb line uses gravity to ensure that vertical lines are accurate. A chalk line will enable you to mark a straight guide line on any surface. It is straightforward to make your own plumb line and chalk line.

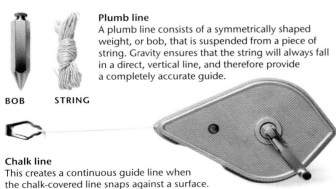

Plumb line

A plumb line consists of a symmetrically shaped weight, or bob, that is suspended from a piece of string. Gravity ensures that the string will always fall in a direct, vertical line, and therefore provide a completely accurate guide.

BOB   **STRING**

Chalk line

This creates a continuous guide line when the chalk-covered line snaps against a surface. A manufactured chalk line has a chalk reservoir in its body, so that the line is chalked whenever it is extended or wound back in.

USING A CHALK LINE

A chalk line is a quick and accurate way to mark a guide line without using a pencil and straight edge. When you no longer need the chalk line, you can simply rub it away. Make sure that the line is taut and that when you lift the chalk line before snapping it, you lift it at right angles to the surface. If you lift the string inaccurately, it may snap down and mark a line in the wrong position. You can use a length of string and some chalk to make your own chalk line.

A

Make the required measurements to work out where you need your guide line, and mark both ends. Knock in a temporary fixing – you can use nails or screws – at each end of the planned guide line.

B

Hook the chalk line over the fixing at one end.

C

Unroll the line, and wrap it around the other fixing, ensuring that the line is held taut.

D

Grip the line at its midpoint, and pull it vertically a small distance away from the surface.

E

Let go of the line, allowing it to snap onto the surface. It will leave a chalk guide line where it has hit the surface. Remove the line and fixings.

CARE AND MAINTENANCE

Checking accuracy
It is wise to check the accuracy of a spirit level from time to time. Hold it against a wall and draw a line that it indicates is horizontal. Turn the level around 180° and draw a second horizontal line beneath the first. Measure the gap between the two lines at several points. If the gap is uneven, the level is no longer accurate and should be discarded. Use the same principle to test the vertical accuracy of the spirit level, by measuring the gap between two lines that the level considers vertical.

Accurate measurements are often the key to successful home improvement tasks. Whether you are measuring a length many metres long or creating millimetre-tight guide lines for precise cuts, there are many different measuring tools available to you. Tools such as squares and gauges are often used in conjunction with these, especially when working with wood. They convert your measurements into accurate guide lines.

MEASURES

Devices for measuring distances range from traditional metal rules and tape measures to hi-tech machines using invisible ultrasonic sound waves. Their varied forms and functions reflect the great variety of DIY tasks for which they are used.

Ultrasonic sound waves are projected to calculate distance or volume

Digital estimator
This measures distances using ultrasonic sound waves. Some may also be used to calculate areas and volumes.

Easy-to-read digital display

Locking button fastens the tape in position

Case

Hooked end is lipped over an object for external measurements, or pressed against the end of the tape for internal measurements

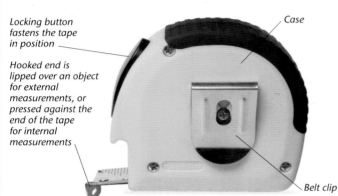

Belt clip

Retractable tape measure
This is the most commonly used measuring tool. Sizes vary, as do the calibrations along the sides of the tape, but 3-m (10-ft) and 5-m (16½-ft) tapes are popular. The first 10mm of the tape is 1mm short to accommodate the width of the metal hooked end.

Digital screen can display measurements in metric and imperial units

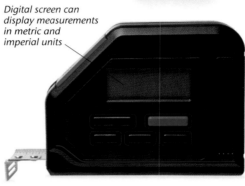

Digital tape measure
Technology has taken the traditional retractable tape measure to another level. A digital display provides a measurement once the tape is locked in place. Laser measures are also available, although they are a more expensive option.

High-visibility case

Fast-rewind handle

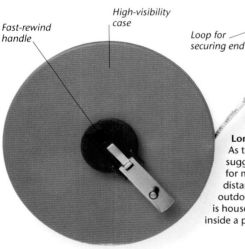

Loop for securing end

Long tape
As the name suggests, this tape is for measuring long distances, often outdoors. A fibre tape is housed on a reel inside a protective casing.

MEASURING WHEEL FOLDED DOWN

Gear-driven counter, in a weather-resistant case

Button illuminates counter

Telescopic handle

INTERNAL MEASURING

Place the tape measure inside the space. Note the reading at the point where the tape enters the case. Measure the length of the case, then add the two measurements together.

Measuring wheel
This tool is used for measuring very long distances. The user walks along holding the handles, with the wheel out in front. The machine calculates distances by counting wheel rotations. Allow for a small degree of user error when guiding the wheel, especially when measuring over uneven surfaces.

SQUARES

The main function of a square is to provide an accurate right-angled guide that can be used in any variety of applications. This simple design has been adapted into a number of tools for different types of guide line. Some, such as measuring rules and spirit levels, have additional features.

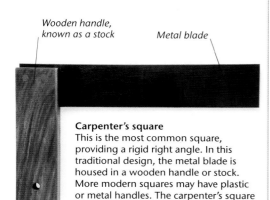

Wooden handle, known as a stock

Metal blade

Carpenter's square
This is the most common square, providing a rigid right angle. In this traditional design, the metal blade is housed in a wooden handle or stock. More modern squares may have plastic or metal handles. The carpenter's square is a simple and reliable tool that is straightforward to use (see box below).

Framing square

Generally a larger square that sits flat on a surface and combines the right-angle guide line function with calibrations along the square's edges. Very large framing squares are ideal for exterior tasks.

Combination square

Features include a steel rule that slides within the stock of the square. As well as determining a right angle, other functions of the combination square include scribing (marking a material to fit exactly against a wall or ceiling) and finding levels. It is also ideal for measuring a small rebate or grooved cut.

Combination set

This takes the combination square one stage further, adding increased functions such as a 180-degree protractor for producing angled guide lines, and an external try square for producing accurate external 90-degree guide lines.

▌ USING A SQUARE

Position the stock against the edge of a section of wood. The blade will form a right angle. Using a carpenter's pencil, draw along the edge of the blade to create your right-angled guide line.

BEVELS AND PENCILS

Two useful items for making guide lines are a bevel and a carpenter's pencil. A bevel provides a guide line for angled cuts; the carpenter's pencil is designed for marking rough surfaces.

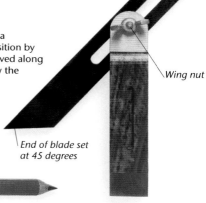

Adjustable bevel

The metal blade is first set at an angle using a protractor or other guide, then locked in position by a screw or wing nut. The handle may be moved along the blade to find the required position. Draw the guide line along the edge of the blade.

Wing nut

Carpenter's pencil

This is a thicker version of a regular pencil. The lead is usually wide and flat to enable it to mark rough wooden surfaces.

End of blade set at 45 degrees

GAUGES

These are used to score guide lines on pieces of wood. They comprise two main sections of wood – the stem and the stock. One or more marking pins is positioned on the stem. These pins score guide lines (see below).

Marking pin

Retaining nut

Stock

Stem

Marking gauge

Here, the marking pin is positioned close to the end of the stem. The stock is moved into the appropriate position, and locked in place with a retaining nut. The pin scores a guide line when the gauge is drawn along the edge of a piece of wood.

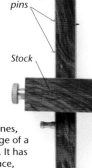

Marking pins

Stock

Mortise gauge

This version can score two parallel lines, and may be used to mark off the edge of a door for a mortise lock, for instance. It has two pins – the top one is fixed in place, and the lower is adjustable – and is used in the same way as the marking gauge. On some models, one fixed pin is provided on the reverse, so that the tool can also serve as a marking gauge.

▌ USING A MARKING GAUGE

A

B

Move the stock into the desired position, corresponding with the area to be marked off. Turn the nut to lock the gauge in place.

Draw the gauge along the the wood, holding the stock against the edge. The marking pin will score a guide line to the set measure.

CARE AND MAINTENANCE

Storing a gauge
When storing a gauge for any length of time, position the stock near the pins to protect them. Keep the gauge in a dry place. If the gauge gets damp, the stem may swell and stick in the stock.

When working on any material, if it is not already fixed in position, you will need to hold it firmly in place. This will enable you to work accurately and safely. You will need to use a workbench and additional vices or clamps, depending on the material involved and the task at hand. Clamps are very versatile tools that come in a great variety of designs.

WORKBENCHES

A workbench provides a stable surface for marking, cutting, and general construction tasks. Several types of bench are available. Fixed or freestanding, they vary in size, weight, and accessories, each designed for different purposes. When selecting a workbench it is essential to consider its suitability for your DIY needs.

Broad top

Sawhorses

A pair of sawhorses can support large items, such as sheets of board or lengths of timber, which a workbench might not accommodate. Traditionally, this type of bench was made of wood but now you can buy metal or plastic versions that are height- and width-adjustable. The manufacturer will indicate the maximum weight that a particular sawhorse can support.

Plastic legs fold down for storage

Toggles

Handles turn to adjust the gap between the slats that hold materials in place

Folding legs

Integral vice

Tightening handle

Storage drawer

Handy shelf also improves stability

Portable workbench

These popular benches are good for securing materials, easy to use, and most fold away for easy storage. On some models, measurement calibrations or angle guides are marked on the adjustable slats to help with marking guide lines.

Fixed workbench

If you have the room for one, a fixed workbench provides an excellent working platform. It gives greater stability than a portable bench can, and large ones can support bulky materials. It is easy to fix vices and clamps to a fixed workbench.

USING A WORKBENCH

Clamping wood

Turning the handles on the side of the bench adjusts the positions of the wooden slats, allowing you to clamp a material securely in place. Do not over-tighten the slats.

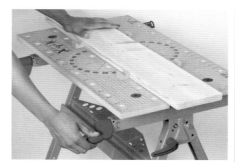

Using toggles

Another way to hold a material in place is to insert toggles into the holes in the slats and hold the material between them. Use an additional clamp if necessary.

Stabilizing the bench

If your bench has a footrest, use it not just for comfort, but also to apply downward pressure which will hold the bench in a more stable position.

VICES

A vice is a simple and solid set of adjustable jaws that holds materials in position. Unlike a clamp, a vice must be fixed to a stable surface such as a workbench before use.

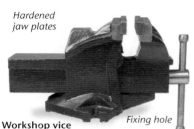

Hardened jaw plates

Plate fits to underside of workbench

Turning the threaded central bar adjusts jaws

Jaws have large surface area

Workshop vice
This heavy-duty vice grips square and cylindrical materials, such as pipes, and should be secured to the top of a fixed workbench.

Fixing hole

Woodworker's vice
This should be attached to the underside of a fixed workbench, so that its jaws sit flush with the top of the workbench. Place offcuts of wood against the jaws to protect the material you are working with.

G-clamp fixes vice to surface

Portable vice
This can be fixed to any surface, though the maximum thickness of that surface will depend on the dimensions of the vice.

CLAMPS

Also known as cramps, clamps are similar to vices in that they are gripping tools, but they are more portable and vary considerably in design, depending on their intended use. They hold materials in position for cutting, and are also useful for holding together glued joints while adhesive dries.

Corner clamp
This type of clamp is designed for use on corner sections of material. It applies pressure to each side of the right angle.

Screw tightener

Inside jaw

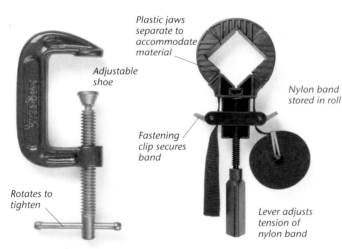

Plastic jaws separate to accommodate material

Adjustable shoe

Nylon band stored in roll

Pincer-like jaws

Soft end caps

Fastening clip secures band

Release button

Lever adjusts tension of nylon band

Rotates to tighten

Spring-controlled hinge

G-clamp
Available in many sizes, a G-clamp is a very versatile tool. Adjust the threaded bar to the required jaw size, placing offcuts of wood between the material being clamped and the jaws to protect it from being damaged.

Band clamp
Use a band clamp on awkward pieces of material. Its jaws are threaded together by a length of nylon, which is released to make the jaws separate. Once placed around the material, pulling the band tightens the jaws.

Ratchet clamp
The ratchet mechanism in this clamp offers you greater control over the pressure it applies. Once you have gripped the material, apply a little further pressure and you will feel the ratchet tighten up until it has an adequate grip.

Spring clamp
Thanks to its very simple design, this clamp can be used with just one hand. Open the jaws by gripping both handles, and release the handles to apply clamping pressure by allowing the jaws to close around the material.

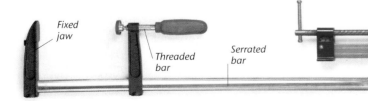

Fixed jaw

Threaded bar

Serrated bar

Movable jaw

Jaw controlled by screw mechanism

Securing pin slotted through hole

Screw clamp
Like the sash clamp, a screw clamp is another type of elongated G-clamp, with one fixed jaw and one adjustable jaw. The adjustable jaw slides along the serrated central bar, as required, and is secured in position using a threaded section with an easy-grip handle. For fine adjustments when securing the clamp, the movable jaw is fitted with a threaded bar that may be tightened.

Sash clamp
The sash or bar clamp is an elongated G-clamp that holds larger materials in place. Fix one end of the clamp in position and adjust the other as required. On some models the central bar is serrated to grip the movable jaw. On others, the bar has a series of holes through which a pin is inserted to hold the movable section in position.

BRICKLAYING TOOLS

Many of the tools used in bricklaying are actually used for other aspects of masonry work. The wide range of tools on the market can be grouped into a few basic categories: trowels, string lines, joint tools, and hammers. Each has an important role to play, and mastering a few simple techniques is the key to successful bricklaying projects.

TROWELS

Trowels are the most important bricklaying tools. Bricklayers use trowels for handling and shaping mortar and laying it between courses of bricks. Professionals use trowels of different types and shapes for specific bricklaying tasks, but a brick trowel is probably most essential. Traditional handles are made of hardwood, although modern trowel designs have softer grips designed for greater comfort and ease of use. The blade of a trowel is made from steel – hardened and tempered carbon steel is commonly used.

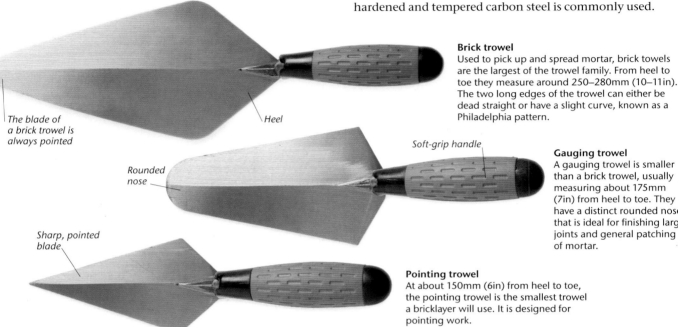

The blade of a brick trowel is always pointed

Heel

Rounded nose

Soft-grip handle

Sharp, pointed blade

Brick trowel
Used to pick up and spread mortar, brick towels are the largest of the trowel family. From heel to toe they measure around 250–280mm (10–11in). The two long edges of the trowel can either be dead straight or have a slight curve, known as a Philadelphia pattern.

Gauging trowel
A gauging trowel is smaller than a brick trowel, usually measuring about 175mm (7in) from heel to toe. They have a distinct rounded nose that is ideal for finishing large joints and general patching of mortar.

Pointing trowel
At about 150mm (6in) from heel to toe, the pointing trowel is the smallest trowel a bricklayer will use. It is designed for pointing work.

BRICKLAYING TECHNIQUE

The simplest way to set out a straight and level brick wall is to wrap string around a brick at each end of the first course. The bricks should hold the string line taut and provide an initial guide. You may then move the line up each level of bricks as you lay them. Use a spirit level to check that each course is level. Sometimes you may need to use stakes to hold the string line in place.

A Grip the handle of the trowel towards the blade end. Pick up a good scoop of mortar on the blade, and slide it onto the bricks.

B Make sure that the mortar sits on the central line of the brick course. Even off the mortar, leaving it slightly longer than brick length.

C Apply some mortar to the end of a new brick, and smooth the mortar down to each edge. This is known as "buttering".

D Position the brick, pressing it down into the mortar on the bricks below, and up against the adjacent brick on the same level.

E Use the handle of the trowel to tap the brick into position.

Remove excess mortar from the brick face with the edge of the trowel. Continue with this process along the length of the wall, and be sure to check that each brick is level, and aligned with the string line.

F

MASONRY HAMMERS

A building job may require a certain amount of reshaping of bricks and masonry, and some jobs require masonry to be knocked into position. As most bricks are fairly lightweight, use a trowel to tap them in place. Other types of masonry will require a much heavier mallet.

Round, flat striking face

Rubber mallet
Use a rubber mallet to knock blocks, slabs, or other heavy masonry materials into place. The rubber head will cause little or no damage to the surface even when a heavy impact is required.

Square striking head

Chisel-shaped peen

Fitted hardwood shaft

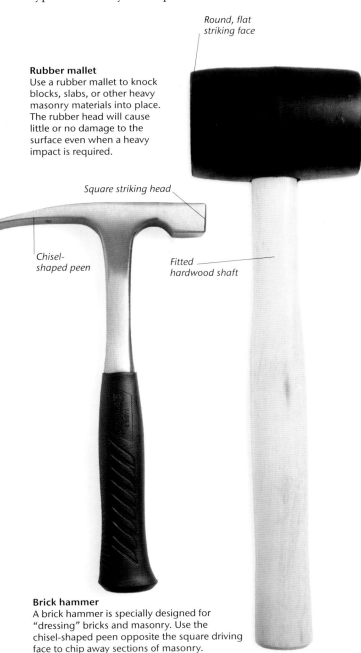

Brick hammer
A brick hammer is specially designed for "dressing" bricks and masonry. Use the chisel-shaped peen opposite the square driving face to chip away sections of masonry.

JOINT TOOLS

Joints are key components of masonry work. Not only are they integral to a wall's structure, but they also form part of the design, particularly in the case of brickwork. Usually a jointer is used only for new pointing. A raker is used for removing old mortar or producing patterned joints.

Different thicknesses cater for different joint depths

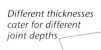

Brick jointer
These are used for finishing brick joints. This example is a double-ended brick jointer, providing options for two different joint depths.

Wingnut

Nail

Wheels straddle the joint

Joint raker
Before repointing takes place, use a joint raker to scrape out old mortar from the joints. A hardened masonry nail is positioned between the two wheels on a cast aluminium frame. A simple wingnut mechanism adjusts the depth of the nail. The raker is then wheeled across the wall surface, along the joint, allowing the nail to scrape out the old mortar.

STRING LINES

A string line is an essential bricklaying tool, enabling bricks to be laid level and straight. Usually they are held in place with line pins or line blocks.

Flat blade is inserted into mortar joints

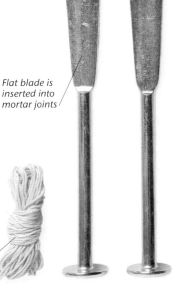

String line and line pins
Flat-bladed steel pins are pushed into drying mortar joints at opposite ends of the wall. The string is then tied between the pins, to form a guide line.

Mason's string, made of nylon

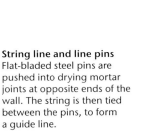

Front view of the shorter arm of the "L", which lips round the end of the wall

Line blocks
Often bricklayers use these L-shaped blocks, made of wood or plastic, to position guide lines. A continuous slot at one end of the block holds the string line in place.

FURTHER INFORMATION ON BRICKLAYING

During laying, bricks should be moist, but not wet. Too much moisture dilutes the mortar, causing the bricks to slip. Spray the bricks the day before you intend to use them, or about four hours before use if using them the same day. The correct mortar mix is essential for bricklaying (see p.71). Do not use mortar more than two hours after mixing it, as its usability will have diminished, making adhesion very poor.

GROUNDWORKING TOOLS

Many of the tools required for groundworking are very versatile, and may be used as general gardening tools. Therefore, it is well worth investing in a few high-quality tools that will last many years. Groundworking is very laborious, so know your limitations.

D-HANDLE   **T-HANDLE**   **STRAIGHT HANDLE**

SHOVELS AND SPADES

Generally, spades are lighter than shovels and have a straighter, sharper blade, which makes them better suited to digging into surfaces. The side edges of a shovel's blade are curved, making it more suitable for lifting large loads. A shovel is ideal for lifting loose material, such as aggregate, and perfect for loading cement mixers with sand and cement.

Handles and blades

Although the handles of shovels and spades are traditionally made of wood, it is now possible to buy tools with handles made of non-conductive, man-made materials such as fibreglass or polypropylene. These come in a variety of shapes and lengths, and are aimed at providing greater comfort.

Blades are generally made of some form of hardened steel. The best quality shovel or spade blades should make a ringing sound, rather than a dull thud, when tapped against a hard object.

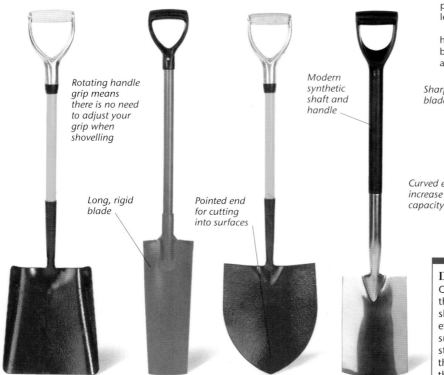

Rotating handle grip means there is no need to adjust your grip when shovelling

Long, rigid blade

Pointed end for cutting into surfaces

Modern synthetic shaft and handle

Sharp, flat blade

SIDE VIEW OF SPADE

Curved edges increase capacity

SIDE VIEW OF SHOVEL

Square-mouth shovel
This has a wide, square blade with curved edges, ideal for lifting material.

Trench shovel
Ideal for digging channels, as it has a long, narrow blade.

Round-mouth shovel
A wide, pointed blade suits both digging and lifting.

Spade
A spade's straight, sharp blade is made for digging.

DEALING WITH HARD GROUND

On hard ground grip a D-handle at the sides so that when the blade strikes, your hands can slip slightly down the sides of the D and reduce the effect of the impact. Make sure that your grip is strong enough to control the tool, but not so tight that you risk injury. Keep your wrists and forearms straight, and wear gloves or fix padding to the handle to reduce jarring.

USING A SPADE

Keep back straight

Bend knees

A **Keep the spade** vertical, with both hands on the handle, and push the blade into the ground with your foot.

B **Steadily lever** the blade backwards, pushing on the handle with both hands.

C **Slide one hand** down the handle shaft and lift the load on the blade, while keeping a straight back.

HEALTH AND SAFETY

Always wear the appropriate protective clothing when carrying out excavation work or when using these types of heavyweight hand tools.

Digging into the ground outside your home can pose a potential safety hazard due to the routing of underground cables and pipes. Use a pipe and cable detector to locate their positions. If you have no pipe and cable plans, your local authorities may be able to advise you.

OTHER GROUNDWORKING TOOLS

As well as shovels and spades, there is a large variety of other groundworking tools available for digging, carrying, shaping, and tidying earth and other materials. Some of these, such as rakes and brushes, are essential garden tools, while others, such as pickaxes or post-hole diggers, may be hired for occasional use.

Top of barrow is angled so that it is horizontal when lifted

Tubular steel frame

Inflatable tyre

Wheelbarrows

A lightweight garden wheelbarrow may be too flimsy to deal with some heavy-duty tasks. Wheelbarrows used for groundwork should be sturdy enough to deal with relatively heavy building materials and rubble.

Rubble sacks

Household refuse sacks are not hardwearing enough to deal with building spoil, as they tear easily. Rubble sacks are much stronger, and may be reused.

Pickaxe

Designed to break up ground surfaces, a pickaxe is particularly useful on rocky ground to loosen material before it can be cleared.

Long, thick handle for swinging with both hands

Heavy head with one chisel-shaped end and one pointed end

▌▌ USING A WHEELBARROW

A wheelbarrow presents the most efficient way of moving heavy materials and large volumes. However, it is important to follow a few simple guidelines to reduce the risk of injury, especially to your back. Before use, check that the wheelbarrow's wheel is sufficiently inflated, so that your passage over uneven surfaces is smooth. Be sure to keep your back straight throughout and use your legs to lift the weight of the barrow, as shown below. Most importantly, know your limitations and do not overload the wheelbarrow.

A

Bend your knees, keep your back and arms straight, and position your body between the handles, rather than behind them. Grip the handles.

B

Straighten your knees and ensure that the weight is centralized over the wheel and that the wheelbarrow is comfortably loaded.

Rammer

A rammer is a very useful tool for compacting rubble or aggregate.

Rake

Use a rake for levelling and smoothing loose surfaces.

One handle attached to each blade

Post-hole digger

This tool is used for digging deep, narrow holes for fences and gate posts. Digging this type of hole would not be possible using the broader blade of a standard spade or shovel. If you need to dig a number of post holes, consider hiring a post-hole borer (see p.28)

Long steel tubular shaft

Small surface area ensures high pressure

Curved blades for cutting cylindrical hole

Reinforced shank

Rust-resistant head

Yard brush

A sturdy yard brush is essential for keeping hard ground surfaces clear and tidy.

Rigid, densely packed bristles are very hardwearing

Power tools

POWER VERSIONS OF MANY TOOLS, IF USED CORRECTLY, CAN MAKE DIY QUICKER AND EASIER. THEY MUST BE TREATED WITH RESPECT, TO AVOID SERIOUS INJURY, AND THEY NEED LOOKING AFTER. AS WITH ALL TOOLS, QUALITY VARIES, AND COST REFLECTS THIS. MANY ARE DESIGNED FOR PROFESSIONAL USE, SO CONSIDER WHETHER IT IS WORTH PAYING FOR A TOP-QUALITY TOOL, OR WHETHER HIRING WOULD BE BETTER.

POWER NAILERS AND STAPLERS

Nailers can dramatically speed up a DIY job. Some can fix into concrete and/or steel; others are suitable only for wood. Larger nailers are more suitable for heavy-duty first-fix (construction) carpentry tasks such as erecting a stud partition wall; smaller nailers are good for second-fix (decorative carpentry) work such as positioning a skirting board. Some models can use a greater range of nail sizes than others. Staplers can be used for many fixing tasks, such as securing sheets of hardboard for a subfloor, or fixing lightweight building boards in general.

CHOOSING AN AIR COMPRESSOR

A compressor may be used to operate several tools, so if you decide to buy an air nailer, choose a compressor that will work with any other air-operated tools that you are considering purchasing. The most versatile compressors have tanks that store up a quantity of compressed air, producing a ready supply to keep your tools running. The rate at which this tank fills is usually measured in litres or cubic feet per minute. This affects the frequency at which fixings can be fired, but very few DIY tasks will need a high cfm. Air pressure is measured in bars, or in pounds per square inch (psi); make sure to match your compressor to your tools.

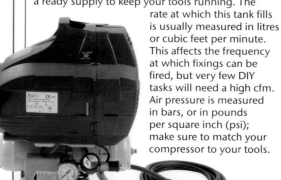

AIR TOOLS

These tools use compressed air to drive the nail or staple home. Some compressors are designed for use with one tool at a time, whereas larger ones can run two or three tools (see box at left for details).

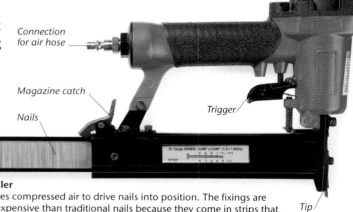

Connection for air hose

Magazine catch

Nails

Trigger

Air nailer
This uses compressed air to drive nails into position. The fixings are more expensive than traditional nails because they come in strips that feed into the nailer's rail assembly. To operate, position the nailer tip at the required point before pulling the trigger to fire the nail.

Tip

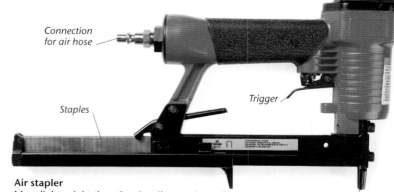

Connection for air hose

Staples

Trigger

Tip

Air stapler
More lightweight than the air nailer, an air stapler nevertheless operates in much the same way. Position the tip and then pull the trigger to fire the staple.

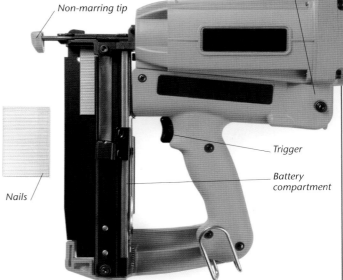

CORDLESS NAILERS
Cordless nailers are more portable than air nailers as they require no connection to a compressor. There is also no power cable, since they operate using a rechargeable battery and a gas canister.

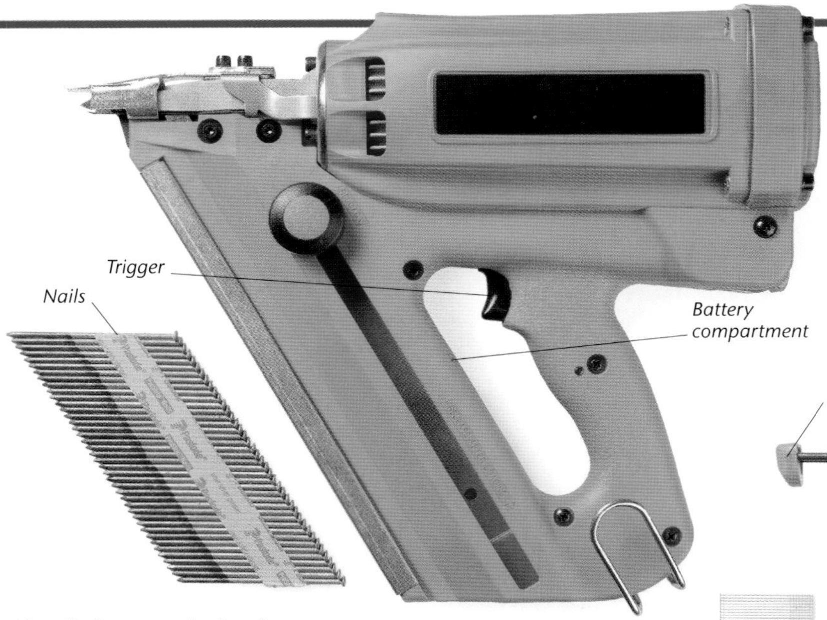

Trigger

Nails

Battery compartment

Gas cylinder compartment

Non-marring tip

First-fix (construction) nailer
This requires both a battery and a gas cell. It is the most portable nailer, because there are no leads. Despite its power, it is relatively lightweight. A metering valve, attached to the top of the gas cell, controls the amount of gas that is released for combustion.

Trigger

Battery compartment

Nails

USING A CORDLESS NAILER

A

Load the battery into the nailer's battery compartment, and press firmly until the battery locking clip engages and the battery is secure.

B

Attach the metering valve to the gas cell and insert the cell into its compartment, aligning the valve with the adapter.

Second-fix nailer
This smaller version of the cordless nailer works in the same way as its larger partner but is more suited to second-fix (decorative carpentry) work.

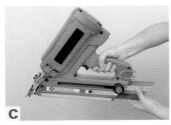

C

Load a strip of nails into the nailer's rail assembly, sliding the follower button for access.

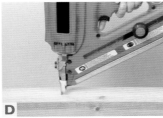

D

Press the nailer's tip onto the surface where you want the nail.

FIRST-FIX NAILER GAS   SECOND-FIX NAILER GAS   BATTERY   BATTERY CHARGER

E

Pull the trigger. The battery ignites the gas/air mixture and powers the motor to drive a nail into the surface.

F

Release the trigger. This causes the internal fan to cool the motor assembly, and to release any exhaust gases.

WORKING SAFELY
Always follow the manufacturer's guidelines carefully when using any power tools, and take particular care when loading batteries or gas cells. Wear eye protection and work in a well-ventilated area. Keep all power tools locked away from children. Some tools will require regular servicing to work efficiently, but contact your supplier to do this rather than attempting it yourself.

POWER DRILLS

Drills are very versatile tools and are necessary for many construction tasks. Competition has forced down their cost, making it possible to buy an exceptionally good piece of equipment for a very reasonable price. There are several different types of drill available; some have a screwdriving facility. The main types of drill bits and screwdriving bits, which slot into a drill's chuck, are shown overleaf.

WORKING SAFELY

Wear goggles or safety spectacles to protect against any flying debris when drilling any hole in any material. It is also a good idea if using a drill-driver as a screwdriver. Ear protection is also recommended when using a drill, especially with larger, more powerful drills, and during prolonged drill use. Wear a dust mask if you are drilling into powdery masonry. Check that any flex is not split or damaged in any way. Follow the manufacturer's recommendations on servicing any drill.

CORDLESS DRILL-DRIVER

The most versatile drill, this is both a power drill and an electric screwdriver. It is battery-operated, which makes it highly portable, and easy to use. The battery detaches so that it can be recharged from the mains. The difference between types of drill-driver are usually indicated by their level of power. The higher the battery's voltage, the more powerful the drill – most are in the range of 9.6 volts to 24 volts. Some drill-drivers also have a hammer action.

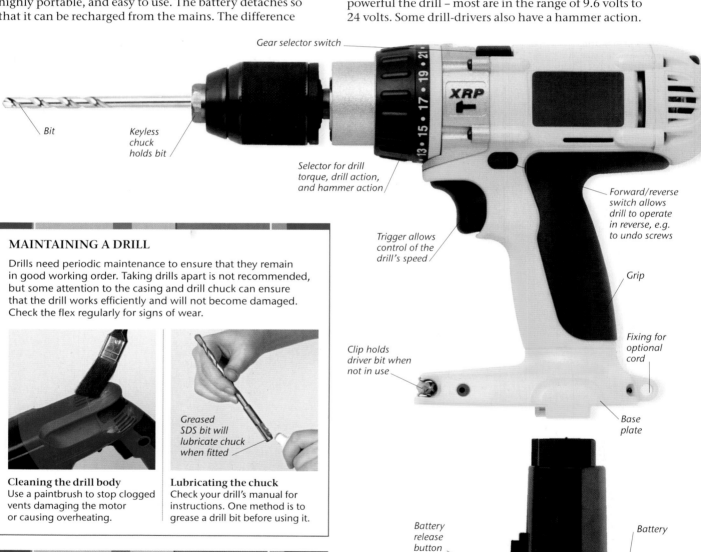

Gear selector switch

Bit

Keyless chuck holds bit

Selector for drill torque, drill action, and hammer action

Trigger allows control of the drill's speed

Forward/reverse switch allows drill to operate in reverse, e.g. to undo screws

Grip

Clip holds driver bit when not in use

Fixing for optional cord

Base plate

Battery release button

Battery

MAINTAINING A DRILL

Drills need periodic maintenance to ensure that they remain in good working order. Taking drills apart is not recommended, but some attention to the casing and drill chuck can ensure that the drill works efficiently and will not become damaged. Check the flex regularly for signs of wear.

Greased SDS bit will lubricate chuck when fitted

Cleaning the drill body
Use a paintbrush to stop clogged vents damaging the motor or causing overheating.

Lubricating the chuck
Check your drill's manual for instructions. One method is to grease a drill bit before using it.

RECHARGING A CORDLESS DRILL

Drills often come with two batteries, so that one can be recharging while the other is in use. Press the battery release button to take a battery off a drill. Invert the battery to put it in the charger. Plug the charger into the mains. Recharging may take a few hours, depending on the drill's quality and size.

MAINS-OPERATED DRILLS

Cordless drills have developed from mains-operated drill designs. These traditional designs still have an important role to play, and some are more powerful than cordless drills, so they are useful for the jobs cordless drills cannot manage. Mains-operated drills do not need recharging, so running out of power is never going to be a problem.

Speed switch

Mode selector

Keyed chuck

Variable action trigger

Switch lock allows continuous drilling without holding trigger

Holder for chuck key when not in use

Standard power drill

A mains-operated standard power drill can perform basic drill functions on a variety of surfaces, depending on its power, but its portability and ease of use are restricted by the power cable. A 550-watt drill is lighter than a 900-watt drill, which would be able to drill into more heavyweight materials such as concrete. The one shown here has a traditional keyed chuck, meaning that a key is needed to operate the chuck when drill bits are changed (see next page).

Keyless chuck

Forward/reverse switch

Switch lock

Lightweight corded drill

Fairly powerful drills are now incorporated in a very lightweight body, making them easier to use than older drills. Keyless chucks make changing bits quicker. A small drill such as this can therefore be a good toolkit companion for a cordless drill-driver. Again power is denoted by wattage.

SDS chuck

Mode selector

Switch lock

Variable action trigger

Side handle for extra control when drilling into very hard surfaces

SDS hammer drill

Heavy-duty power drills are usually SDS ("special drive system") drills with a chuck that requires a specialist bit. SDS chuck technology grips the drill bit to support the most efficient hammer action for drilling into very hard masonry. SDS drills can be mains-operated or cordless.

THINGS TO CONSIDER WHEN BUYING A DRILL

When deciding which drill to buy, think about how often you intend to use it and what you will use it for. The jobs you have in mind will influence how powerful the drill needs to be and, as with any purchase, your budget may affect your choices.

USING A DRILL

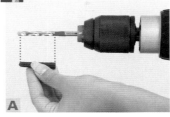 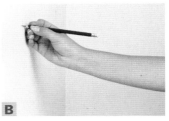

A | **B**

Position some insulating tape around the drill bit to indicate the depth to which you need to drill. Here it is the depth of a wall plug.

Mark on the wall where you need to drill a hole.

C | **D**

Use a hammer and a nail punch to make a small indent at the marked place. This will prevent the drill from slipping across the wall.

Begin drilling with a fairly low bit speed. This enables you to get the hole started easily and to keep the drill at a right angle to the wall.

Keep the drill at a right angle to the wall

E

Once the hole is established, increase the bit speed. Drill to the depth required, as marked by the tape on the bit. When the hole is finished, keep the bit rotating at a slow speed, otherwise you will be unable to withdraw it from the hole. Release the switch once the bit is out of the wall.

USING BOTH HANDS TO OPERATE A DRILL

Many drills have an extra, detachable handle. This allows one hand to support the drill's weight and keep it at the right angle while the other holds the main grip and operates the trigger.

A | **B**

First, position the handle so that it is vertical. If this is comfortable, use the drill in this posture. If it feels awkward, move on to step B.

Rotate the handle so that it is horizontal. This should give you a more comfortable working posture.

TOOLS, EQUIPMENT, AND MATERIALS

INSERTING A DRILL BIT

Tightening a keyless chuck
Insert a drill or driver bit. Rotate the chuck by hand to tighten it and hold the bit in place.

Using a chuck key
The key's serrated edge engages with the chuck's shaft to tighten it around the bit and hold it in place.

Using an SDS chuck
Push the bit into the chuck. The chuck will tighten to hold it. Pull back the chuck to release the bit.

WORKING SAFELY
Take care when changing a bit after operating a drill: the bit may be hot. Wear gloves to avoid a burn.

WOOD DRILL BITS
These are suitable for all types of wood, and come in a huge range of sizes and lengths. There are three main types of wood drill bit, which are shown here.

Spur

Brad point (dowel) bits
These are characterized by the small point at the tip of the bit. Spurs to either side of this point cut clean, straight holes.

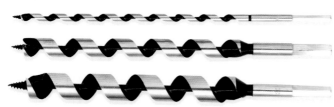

Auger drill bits
These cut large, deep, accurate holes. The spiralling shaft comes to a fine, threaded point. Carbon-steel bits are best, and can be resharpened.

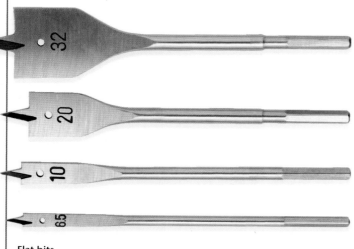

Flat bits
The pointed tip begins the hole, and the paddle-shaped blade bores a large, wide hole. The size is clearly marked on the paddle's face.

METAL DRILL BITS
These are known as HSS (high-speed steel) bits. They can also be used on wood or plastic, but they last better if reserved for metalwork.

Coatings vary

Standard HSS bits
These are characterized by their black colour. More expensive, durable ones may contain cobalt or be titanium-coated.

MASONRY DRILL BITS
These can cut into any masonry surface. The shaft spirals up to a tip that is often composed of an extra-hardened material. For instance, a chrome-vanadium shaft may be finished with a tungsten-carbide tip.

Tip often hardened

Standard twist bits
Bit colours vary, because of the different materials used. The tip may be a different colour from the shaft as well, due to the hardened coating.

STORING DRILL BITS
Most types of drill bit are available in a wide range of sizes and qualities, and often in sets, which can be economical if you do a lot of drilling. For the best results, always use the bit that is recommended for a specific job. Some sets contain many bits of the same type (those shown here are HSS bits); others contain the most common sizes of masonry, wood, and HSS bits.

SET OF BITS

OTHER DRILL BITS

In addition to the standard drill bits shown opposite, a wide range of specialist bits is available. These are made for a specific task, or to fit a particular type of chuck. The most common of these bits are shown here.

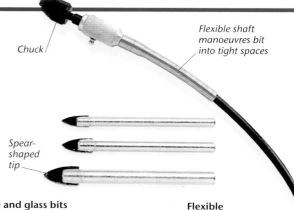

Chuck

Flexible shaft manoeuvres bit into tight spaces

Fluted end

Colour indicates hardened tip

SDS bits

Some bits are made specifically to fit an SDS chuck mechanism, and won't work with any other. The end that fits into the chuck has a fluted appearance; the drilling part of the shaft is normal.

Bit with integral countersink function

As well as drilling a hole, these bits enlarge the entrance in readiness for a screw, removing the need to use a countersink bit (see below) after drilling a pilot hole.

Spear-shaped tip

Tile and glass bits

The spear-shaped tungsten-carbide tip penetrates a tile or piece of glass, then enlarges the hole to the diameter of the tip's base.

Flexible drill shaft

This attaches to the chuck and allows a drill to be used in an otherwise inaccessible area – just insert the bit into the chuck on the end of the flexible shaft. These attachments cannot be used with the drill in reverse action.

Remove plug through the side opening

Carbon-steel tip

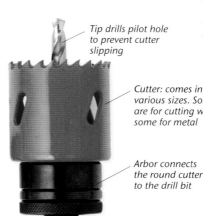

Tip drills pilot hole to prevent cutter slipping

Cutter: comes in various sizes. Some are for cutting wood, some for metal

Round shank. Some can be used in routers

Arbor connects the round cutter to the drill bit

This end goes into the drill chuck

Countersink bit
This enlarges a hole's opening so that a screw can sit flush.

Plug cutter
Cuts wooden plugs to cover screw heads and disguise them.

Hinge cutter
A tungsten-carbide tip cuts holes for kitchen unit door hinges.

Hole cutter
The drill bit cuts first, then the round cutter makes a larger hole.

DRIVER BIT HOLDERS AND NUT DRIVER

To work as a screwdriver, a drill-driver needs an attachment to hold bits in place. It is also possible to insert specialist bits into the chuck, such as a nut driver, for example.

Standard bit holder
This holds the bit and is inserted into the chuck.

Holds bit

Goes into chuck

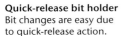

Quick-release bit holder
Bit changes are easy due to quick-release action.

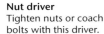

Nut driver
Tighten nuts or coach bolts with this driver.

SCREWDRIVER BITS

Some bits insert directly into the chuck, but most (such as those below) need to be put in a bit holder, which is then inserted into the chuck. Specialist bits are also available.

Flat-head bits
These are designed for use with slot-headed screws (see p.76).

Phillips bits
Screws with a Phillips head must be driven by a corresponding bit.

Posidriv bits
As for Phillips bits, these are made to drive a particular type of screw.

Allen bits
Like an Allen key, these have many uses, such as in flatpack assembly.

POWER SAWS AND GRINDERS

Used correctly and carefully, power saws are great labour-saving devices that speed up progress on a host of jobs. As with any power tools, safety is a concern. Always switch off and unplug a power saw before changing its blade, and wear protective goggles if there is a danger of flying splinters. The saws shown on these pages and overleaf are the ones most likely to be used for DIY jobs. Bandsaws and bench saws are covered, along with other bench tools, on pp.64–65.

RECIPROCATING SAWS

These are very flexible and versatile tools. The jigsaw can be used with many materials, especially wood; the more heavy-duty version shown opposite is for more arduous tasks. As well as an up-and-down (reciprocating) motion, some saws have a back-and-forth (orbital, or pendulum) action that cuts more easily and quickly, minimizes blade wear, and aids sawdust removal from the cutting point.

METAL-CUTTING BLADE

WOOD/PLASTIC-CUTTING BLADE

GENERAL WOOD-CUTTING BLADE

UNIVERSAL BLADE

HEALTH AND SAFETY

■ Always employ standard safety precautions when operating a power saw. Never change a blade, or carry out any maintenance work, with the power supply switched on.
■ All power saws generate a lot of heat when in use, so give a machine time to cool before you change a blade.

■ Always keep hands clear of the cutting blade, and keep saws away from children.
■ Wear goggles to protect your eyes from flying shards.
■ Never force a saw, and ensure that the material being cut is correctly supported and clamped firmly in position.
■ Sweep up slippery dust.

Switch lock

Trigger

Most power saws are mains powered. Battery-operated models are also available

Guides can be clamped onto base plate, for making parallel or circular cuts

Shallow blades are more manoeuvrable than deeper ones

Mitres can be cut by tilting the saw's main body. The base plate remains level

USING A JIGSAW

Guide line to cut along

A

B

Shift the SDS lever (see p.55), or whatever mechanism your saw has, to release the clamp holding the old blade.

Position a new blade against the guide roller. Release the SDS lever to secure it, or tighten according to the tool's mechanism.

C

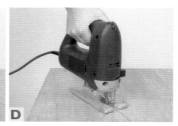

D

Rest the front edge of the base plate on the material to be cut, with the blade at a right angle to the marked guide line.

Adjust the speed and rotary action settings, if necessary, before starting up the saw. Progress along the guide line to make the cut.

Jigsaw
This cuts an accurate curved line. Blades are available in mixed packs for materials such as wood, PVC, metal sheeting, and ceramic tiles. Precision depends on a blade's qualities. Use on a high speed for wood, and a slower speed for metal or ceramic tiles. Some have a dust extraction facility.

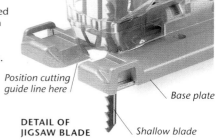

Position cutting guide line here

Base plate

DETAIL OF JIGSAW BLADE

Shallow blade

CUTTING OUT A CENTRAL SECTION

A

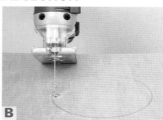

B

Drill a hole at one edge of the cut, using a wood bit with a diameter large enough to accommodate the jigsaw blade.

Insert the jigsaw blade through the hole, and make your cut. Take care to support the wood, and follow the guide line carefully.

Heavy-duty reciprocating saw

Used for more arduous tasks. As for a jigsaw, blades can be chosen for different materials, but the blades may be considerably longer than those for a jigsaw, and therefore give greater flexibility in terms of the depth of cut possible. The technique for fitting blades is similar to that for a jigsaw but, again, details may vary from brand to brand. Plunge cuts, going directly into soft materials instead of starting at an edge, can be made with a short blade.

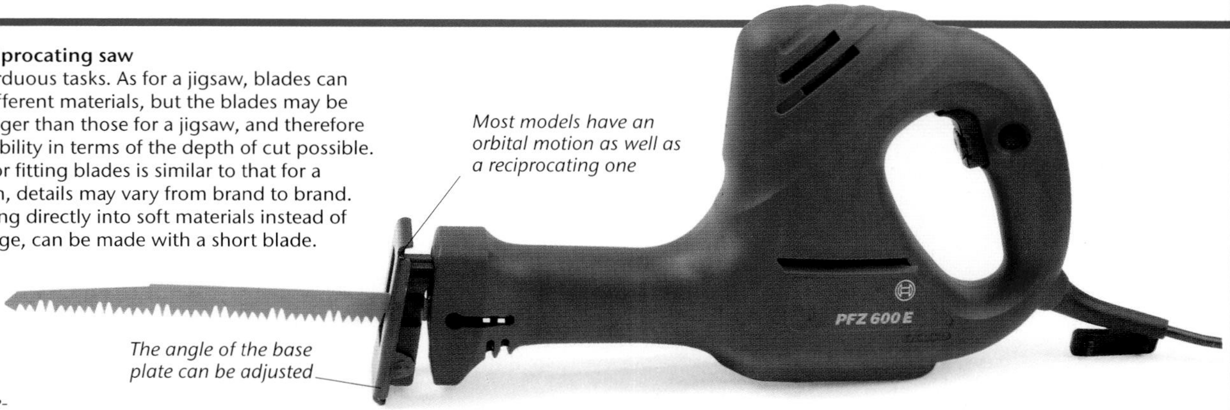

Most models have an orbital motion as well as a reciprocating one

The angle of the base plate can be adjusted

PFZ 600 E

Tungsten-carbide-tipped blade

HEAVY-DUTY BLADE

WOOD-CUTTING BLADE

METAL-CUTTING BLADE

Extra-fine teeth

CIRCULAR SAWS

These use circular blades that rotate to cut through materials. The type of material that can be cut depends on the blade; some are for specific tasks. The saw shown here, for instance, is designed for cutting wood, but will cut metal if a suitable blade is inserted.

Circular wood saw

Cuts accurate, straight lines through wood; ideal for use with large sheet materials. The blade's radius dictates the depth of cut possible. Blades are not changed often – a multipurpose blade usually copes with most cutting requirements.

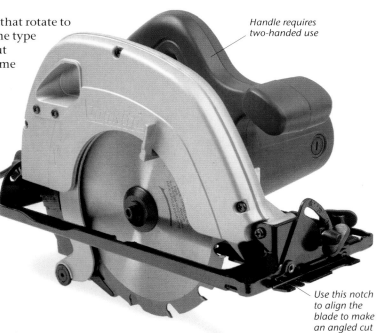

Handle requires two-handed use

Use this notch to align the blade to make an angled cut

USING A RECIPROCATING SAW

A **Insert a blade** as described by the manual. In this instance, an Allen key is needed.

B **Press the base plate** onto the material to be cut, and apply even pressure as you progress through the cut along a guide line.

Teeth can cut wood with nails in it

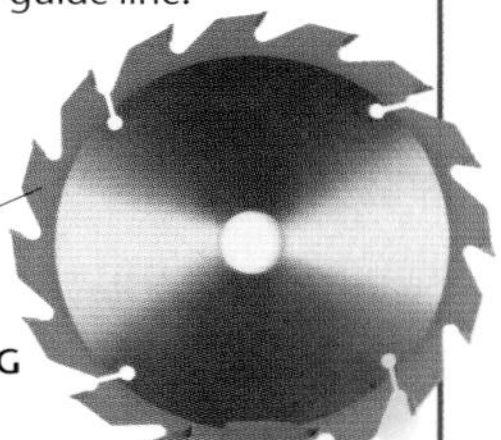

NAIL-CUTTING BLADE

Hard steel body with a tungsten-carbide tip

STANDARD BLADE

Teeth treated for smooth operation

LONG-LIFE BLADE

USING A CIRCULAR SAW

A **Adjust the depth setting,** this ensures you do not sever underfloor pipes when cutting through floorboards, for instance.

B **Hold the saw** in two hands, to enable you to control it, and switch it on. Allow the blade to reach full speed before beginning a cut.

C **Align the relevant** notch in the front of the base plate with the marked guide line, and apply even pressure as the cut progresses.

CHANGING A BLADE

A specially designed key is usually needed to remove or insert a blade; the specifics vary according to brand. Always pay close attention to your instruction manual, and follow the recommended sequence of steps to ensure that you work safely and attach a new blade securely.

Mitre saw
This housed circular saw is used for any accurate straight or angled cuts in wood – not just for mitring. Whereas a circular saw is ideal for use with large sheets, a mitre saw is more use for cutting across the grain of a length of securely clamped timber. Depth of cut is governed by blade size, and whether the saw is "compound". Compound saws have a blade on a sliding hinge so that (in addition to the downwards movement) it can cut through wood from front to back.

CHANGING A BLADE

Disconnect the saw from the mains. The method for changing blades is usually similar to that for a circular saw – a socket spanner may be required to move the bolt holding the blade in place. Make sure the blade lock is on. Follow the instructions in the manual, and use the right size and type of blade.

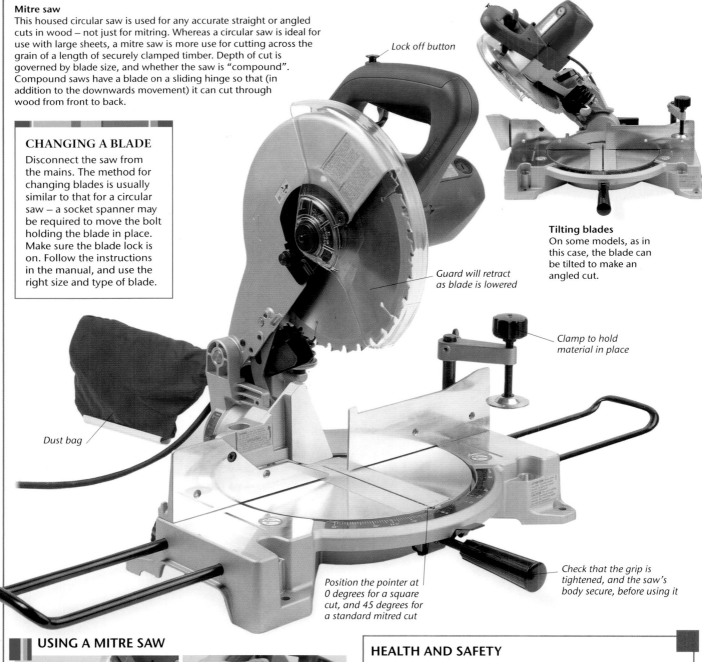

Lock off button

Tilting blades
On some models, as in this case, the blade can be tilted to make an angled cut.

Guard will retract as blade is lowered

Clamp to hold material in place

Dust bag

Position the pointer at 0 degrees for a square cut, and 45 degrees for a standard mitred cut

Check that the grip is tightened, and the saw's body secure, before using it

USING A MITRE SAW

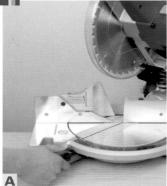

A

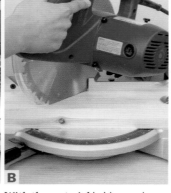

B

Adjust the saw by moving the grip until the pointer is directed at the correct angle. In this example, a 45-degree cut is being made.

With the material held securely, and the blade aligned with a guide line, press the safety button, then the start button, and make the cut.

HEALTH AND SAFETY

A mitre saw has a safety cover over the blade, which rises when the blade is lowered to cut. Never remove or tamper with this cover. To operate the saw, both the safety button and the power trigger must be pressed. Some saws have other levers or switches that must be operated to allow the saw to work. Some of these switches or levers may even be removed when the saw is not in use, so that it cannot be accidentally started. As with all safety issues, act according to the manual.

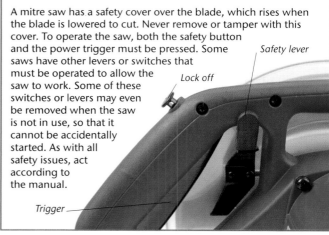

Safety lever

Lock off

Trigger

Angle grinder

This circular saw is designed for cutting metal and stone. The blades, or "cutting discs", vary according to the material they are designed to cut. A thinner disc should be used on marble than on a paving slab, for example. Angle grinders can be used for cutting and also for grinding (smoothing rough edges or areas on a heavyweight surface, such as masonry). Some discs are designed to cut; others to grind. Use the correct disc for the task. Some discs have diamond-impregnated surfaces for greater resilience. This coating is often visible around the rim. With standard discs, the surface wears away in cutting, so the disc gradually becomes smaller in diameter. Diamond blades last much longer, and so are more expensive.

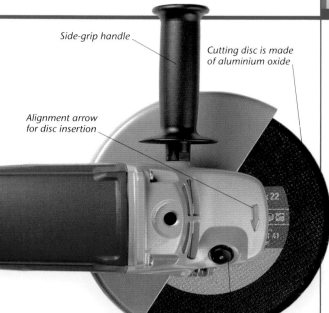

Side-grip handle

Cutting disc is made of aluminium oxide

Alignment arrow for disc insertion

Power cable

Locking button for disc insertion

Engages with clamping nut

TWO-PIN SPANNER

Some discs have segmented rims. The diamond versions of these have a diamond coating along the rim of each segment

Abrasive surface

STANDARD DIAMOND BLADE

GRINDING DISC

USING AN ANGLE GRINDER

An angle grinder is designed to operate in only one direction – upwards (an "up-grinding motion"). Pushing the angle grinder in the other direction is dangerous, and reduces control. Avoid any sideways pressure on a disc.

A

Start up the grinder and position yourself so that it can be guided away from you along a marked guide line.

B

Score an initial line in a thick material such as a slab, then make two or three further passes across it to make the cut.

CHANGING AN ANGLE GRINDER DISC

Check the manufacturer's specifications before choosing a disc for an angle grinder, and buy discs of the right size and capable of withstanding the model's operating speed. The mechanism for locking on a disc will vary according to manufacturer, so check your specification. There may be a locking button (see top) to press, which helps tighten a disc onto the angle grinder.

A

Before mounting the disc, check that it is the right way up, and that the rotation arrow on the disc matches the one on the tool.

HEALTH AND SAFETY

Protective clothing is necessary when working with an angle grinder: goggles, ear defenders, dust mask, gloves, and work boots should all be worn. Remove all combustible materials from the area before cutting metal, because showers of sparks will be produced. A large amount of dust is produced when stone is cut or ground, so use any dust extraction equipment that is supplied with your angle grinder. If possible use the angle grinder outside, to reduce mess. If the material being cut is not heavy enough to remain in position under its own weight, clamp it securely before starting.

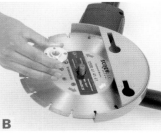

B

Mount the disc on the grinder's central spindle. Position the clamping nut on the disc, threading it over the spindle.

C

Fix it in position (often by turning a clamping nut with a special two-pin spanner). Press the locking button if there is one.

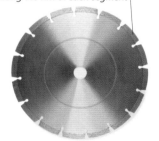

PLANERS AND SANDERS

Power planers and sanders are smoothing tools. Planers are designed for use only with wood, but some sanders can also be used on metal or masonry surfaces. Use the dust bag if your model comes with one, and make sure the machine has stopped moving before putting it down after use, to avoid accidental damage to surfaces. Unplug the machine before adjusting any settings or changing sandpaper on a sander, or adjusting or changing blades on a planer.

Trigger lock

Main depth gauge

Side limiter securing nut

FRONT VIEW

Side limiter can be used with depth gauge to cut a groove

PLANER

Planers remove sections of wood that are too small to be cut easily and accurately with a saw, but are also too thick to be smoothed down simply by using a power sander. They come in a number of sizes, and the larger, heavy-duty types are best suited to professional use. Smaller ones are fine for DIY.

Operating trigger

Dust extraction vent

Depth-gauge handle and adjustment knob

Rebate depth gauge

Motor housing

Grooved guide in underside is used to hone corners

Blade

Grooved guide for bevel cutting

Power planer
This type of planer does the same thing as a hand plane (see p.40) but with much less effort. Blades have a reasonably long lifespan, depending on usage, and replacing them is straightforward for most models. The most common reason for blade failure, or reduction in the tool's lifespan, is accidentally planing a nail or screw embedded in a wooden surface. Inspect wood carefully before planing it.

DETAIL OF GROOVED GUIDE AND BLADE

USING A POWER PLANER

Use the depth gauge to determine the amount of wood to remove, remembering that if a large amount of wood needs to be shaved off, the depth gauge should initially be set high, then reduced as you reach the full extent of the cut. Refer to your model's instruction manual for details on using the depth gauge. Most planers have a dust collection facility; use it if you have one.

A

Turn the depth gauge knob to set the required depth for planing.

B

Rest the edge of the planer on the wood with its body at a slight angle. Turn the planer on, then pull the trigger to start the blades.

C

When the planer reaches full speed, lower its body onto the wood, and sweep it evenly across the surface to remove the wood gradually.

SANDERS

Power sanders smooth a wooden surface quickly and easily. Different designs are suited for sanding large areas, smaller sections, and difficult spaces. Always wear a mask when sanding. Sandpaper is supplied in the shape needed to fit a particular type of sander. Several grades are available for all sanders, ranging from papers that sand coarsely to remove material quickly, to those that give a very fine finish. Use the grade most suitable for your task. Move to increasingly fine paper to achieve a smooth finish.

CARE AND MAINTENANCE

Maintaining a belt sander

You may occasionally need to adjust the belt tracking; see the instruction manual for your model's adjustment requirements. To change a sanding belt, first switch off the sander and unplug it. Pull the belt release lever to enable you to remove the old paper, then insert a new belt of sandpaper and push the release lever back into position.

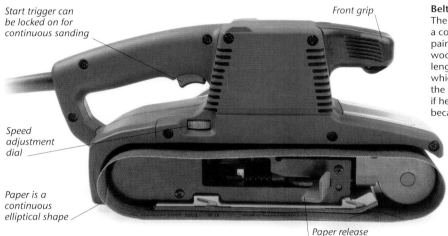

Start trigger can be locked on for continuous sanding

Front grip

Speed adjustment dial

Paper is a continuous elliptical shape

Paper release

Belt sander

The most abrasive of hand-held power sanders: takes off a considerable depth, so is good for removing layers of paint. Similar in function to a power planer, but removes wood more gradually. It is ideal for smoothing narrow lengths of wood, but can also be used on larger surfaces which a planer cannot tackle. Keep the belt flush with the wood's surface – it will cut grooves into the wood if held at an angle. Do not apply too much pressure, because it can damage the operating mechanism.

DETAIL OF SANDPAPER PARTIALLY LOADED

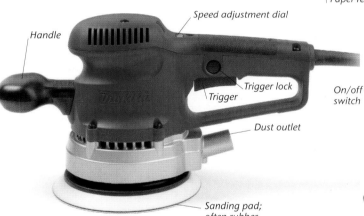

Handle

Speed adjustment dial

Trigger lock

Trigger

Dust outlet

Sanding pad; often rubber

On/off switch

Power cable

Dustbag

Sandpaper securing levers

Orbital sander

Useful for working large wooden surfaces. A large circular sanding pad vibrates with a near-circular motion, which means it can be used for a wood grain in any direction. However, a coarse paper will leave circular abrasions; use increasingly fine sandpaper as you progress for a smooth finish. The sander has a simple hook-and-loop mechanism to make changing sandpaper easy. A soft pad can also be attached to an orbital sander to turn it into a polishing tool for buffing waxed wooden surfaces. The trigger-lock mechanism keeps it switched on for continuous sanding, and speed settings control how vigorously and abrasively it sands.

Align holes in paper with those in sanding pad to aid dust extraction

SANDING DISC

Palm sander

Small tool, often with an orbital action. For use on small areas or in awkward corners, often being drawn across a surface in a circular motion. Palm sanders have limited speed settings. The paper is held in place with a lever clamp and is easy to change.

USING A PALM SANDER

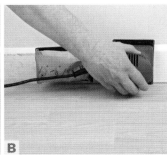

A

Position and attach the dust bag, following the instructions given in the manufacturer's manual. Switch it on and allow it to gain speed.

B

Sweep the sander across the surface to be treated. In this instance, the flat face of a length of skirting board is being sanded.

If you have ambitious projects in mind, and a home workshop is an option, consider buying some bench tools. These are heavy-duty, specialist machines, which can save a lot of time and effort when tackling certain tasks. Although such tools were once left to professionals, they are becoming much cheaper, and therefore more accessible.

JOINTERS

As their name suggests, jointers are used to make various joint types between sections of wood, and for shaping and preparing wood for jointing. Portable biscuit jointers are particularly useful for making joints in kitchen worktops.

Hand grip

Level adjustment lever

On/off switch

Cutting blade retracts into main body

Biscuit jointer
Though most often used for furniture, biscuit joints have many other applications. The jointer makes precise plunge cuts into each side of the join, then a "biscuit" (a wafer of compressed wood chips) smeared with glue is inserted, with one side in each slot (see right). Biscuits are commonly manufactured in three sizes, for different thicknesses of board or timber. Biscuit jointers do not have to be bolted to a bench before use.

Biscuits
Common biscuit sizes and shapes.

Tilting fence guides wood into blade at correct angle

Sharp blade

Blade guard

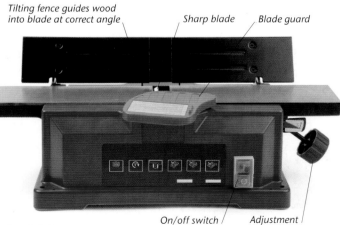

On/off switch

Adjustment knob

Bench jointer
Often used for making cabinets or other items of furniture, bench jointers shape and prepare wood for jointing. However, they are also useful for tasks such as restoring and replacing damaged sections of woodwork from all around the home. Bolt the jointer down securely and be aware of the maximum depth of material it is capable of working with before you start.

▌▌ MAKING BISCUIT JOINTS

Biscuit joints are a quick and simple way to join wood. They can be used in many situations where a strong, inconspicuous joint is required – a butt joint in a kitchen worktop is shown here. Whatever you are making, you need to judge how many biscuit joints you need for a good connection. Thickness of the biscuit should be judged on wood depth.

A

Butt the sheets together, aligned as they will be joined, and draw a pencil line across the two sheets to mark the biscuit joint's position.

B

Set the level adjustment lever according to the depth of the material, so the jointer will cut into the middle of the sheet.

C

Use the cutting depth adjuster to set how deep the biscuit jointer will cut. It should be marked with the depths needed for standard biscuits.

D

Cut a slot in each piece of board by lining up the guide on the jointer with your guidelines, and pushing the cutter into the edge.

E

Apply PVA wood glue to the biscuit. The water in this glue causes the biscuit to expand and fit tightly in its slot to give a very strong joint.

Pencil lines will marry up

F

Push one side of the biscuit into the slots in one section of material. Apply a thin bead of glue between the biscuits, down the length of the join.

G

Push the other end of the biscuit into the corresponding slot to join the two sections, and clamp. Use a damp cloth to wipe away any excess glue.

HEALTH AND SAFETY

With these large tools, the set-up and operating procedures can be complex: make sure you know how to use a machine before attempting a project. Classes to learn about bench tools are available, and it is a good idea to take advantage of professional tuition. Also, read the manual carefully and pay attention to the guidelines. Use any dust extraction devices that are available to you, and make sure you wear suitable protective clothing. On some occasions help from another person may be needed so you can work safely, such as when feeding a large sheet material through a band saw.

BENCH GRINDERS

The high-speed, rotating wheels on bench grinders are used for sharpening and maintaining tools, and other sundry metalwork tasks such as grinding off rough edges. Tools or metalwork are held ("trailed") against the wheels, which can either sharpen or abrade, according to which function is selected. Some grinders have a single wheel that can be changed as required; others have two wheels.

Dual-wheel grinder

One wheel of this grinder is suitable for rough grinding, while the second is more suited to finishing or fine grinding. Dual-wheel grinders have varying designs: some may have wet and dry grinding wheels, while in others the second wheel may be replaced by a finisher – basically a belt sander mounted in a fixed position on the grinder body. Always bolt the grinder securely to a fixed workbench.

Grinding wheel housing

Hinged plastic guard

Grinding wheel

Dust-protected mains switch

WORKSHOP SAWS

There are many different designs and types of workshop saw, some designed for specific purposes, so work out what you need before purchasing one. The two saws shown here are arguably the most multipurpose, and so the most commonly used. As with all bench tools, be sure to follow all operating instructions and safety guidelines.

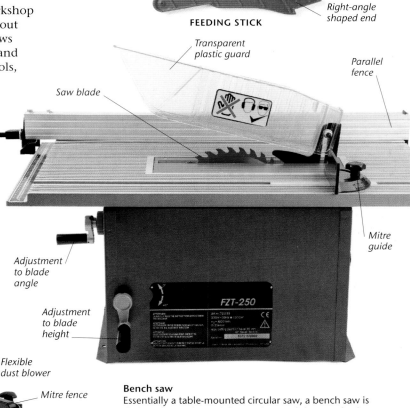

Right-angle shaped end

FEEDING STICK

Transparent plastic guard

Parallel fence

Saw blade

Mitre guide

On/off switch

Blade tension adjuster

Adjustment to blade angle

Adjustment to blade height

Flexible dust blower

Mitre fence

Saw table

Bench saw

Essentially a table-mounted circular saw, a bench saw is designed to make straight cuts in wood that you feed towards the blade. Most manufacturers supply a feeding stick with the saw. This is used to push materials across the saw table, and is most useful with smaller items rather than larger sheet materials.

Band saw

This is perhaps the most versatile of all workshop saws, and can be used to make many different types of cut – much like a fixed version of the jigsaw. Using a band saw is straightforward, but take the time to familiarize yourself with the adjustment and setting guides before you start. There is some resetting required each time you change blades – to avoid mistakes, check that everything is adjusted correctly each time you cut. Mount a band saw on either a workbench or the stand supplied by the manufacturer.

Routers use bits (cutters) to cut, mould, and rebate (cut a groove or step into) wood. Bits are available for numerous cutting and shaping tasks. A common router design is shown here. The detail of operation will vary from model to model, and there is usually a correct direction for a router to face when in use, so read your model's instruction book carefully. Routers can seem very complicated tools, but they provide professional finishes and increased options in many areas of DIY. It is a good idea to practise using a router on a spare piece of wood before beginning your project.

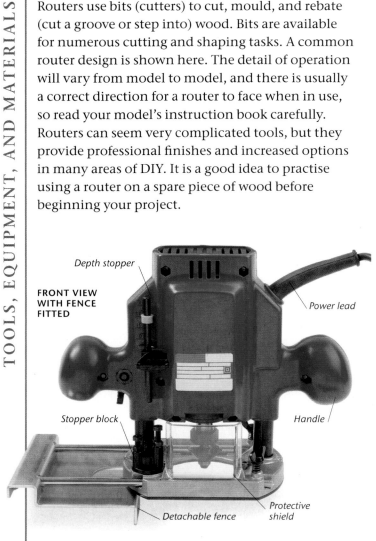

FRONT VIEW WITH FENCE FITTED

Depth stopper

Power lead

Stopper block

Handle

Detachable fence

Protective shield

BACK VIEW

Lock lever

Power switch

Collet. Check this is the right size for the bit

Baseplate

Cutting bit

HEALTH AND SAFETY

Always take care when working with a power tool. Most routers have a protective guard to shield the user from flying debris, but you should always wear safety goggles and a dust mask while using a router. Also, remember that the bit will become very hot during routing, so be careful when touching it or putting it down after use. Routing is a particularly dusty job, so use any dust extraction features that come with your router. Another option is to attach a vacuum hose, if one is recommended by your model's manufacturer, to clear away the dust.

USING A ROUTER

Check the manual for details of your model. The stopper block can store three settings at once, to save time when a job involves routing at different depths. Use an even speed when pushing the router across wood: go too fast and the cut will be rough, but go too slowly and burn marks may appear. Do not reduce the cutter speed until it is clear of the surface.

A

With the router unplugged from the mains, and resting on a steady workbench, insert a cutting bit into the collet.

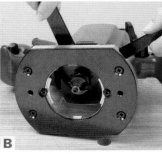

B

Tighten the collet nut with the two spanners that come with the router, securing the bit in place.

C

Place the router on a flat surface and loosen the lock lever. Press on the router until the bit touches the surface, and tighten the lock lever.

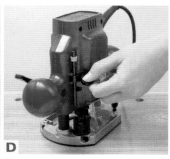

D

Set the depth stopper to the depth of the cut you want to make. Then loosen the lock lever again and allow the router to lift.

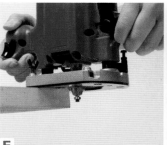

E

Start the router and let it reach full speed. Then press on the two handles to lower the bit and bring it into contact with the wood.

F

Move the router across the wood with its base flat on the surface. Judge the speed according to the cut's depth and the wood's hardness.

CUTTING A STRAIGHT LINE

You may sometimes need to use a fence (guide) to direct the cutter for an accurate straight line. Attach the fence to the base plate, then butt it against the wood's straight edge. Ensure that it remains in contact with the edge as the router moves across the wood, so that the cut is precisely straight. You will be unable to use the fence if the straight cut is not near the wood's edge. Instead, use a batten as a guide. Clamp the batten to the wood and pass the router along it, ensuring that it stays in contact with the batten. To cut out an area wider than the bit can make in one go, use two battens to provide straight guide lines.

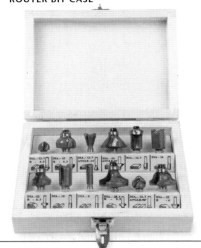

USING THE FENCE TO GET A STRAIGHT LINE

CARE AND MAINTENANCE

See your router's instruction book for information on servicing and maintenance. Make sure that you oil the machine as recommended.

Storage

Most routers are sold in sturdy boxes, which are ideal for long-term storage, if you have the space. Use a specially designed case to protect cutting bits when they are not in use.

ROUTER BIT CASE

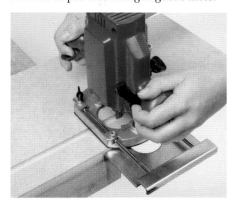

CUTTING BITS

Many different cutters are available, each suited to producing a particular effect. A number of common cutter types are shown below, subdivided into groove cutters and edge cutters. Tungsten-carbide-tipped cutters offer high quality, and some may be titanium impregnated. HSS (high-speed steel) is another common material. Cutters are often purchased in boxed sets, but can be bought separately.

Groove cutters

To create a channel through a section of wood, a groove cutter is needed. This type of bit is useful for creating joints. For example, a straight cutter can create a recess for jointing to another piece of wood (see p.393).

This end fits into collet

Straight cutter
This is used to cut straight, precise lines through a section of wood.

V-groove cutter
Use this bit to cut a groove with a sharp apex.

Dovetail cutter
This is designed to make the cuts necessary for dovetail joints in woodworking.

Edge cutters

When creating decorative profiles or rebates for joints along the side of a wooden section, use an edge-cutter bit. These cutters often have a ball-bearing in their tips that acts as a guide along the edge of the wood. This eliminates the need for a fence or other guide, while still producing a perfect, uniform cut.

Cone cutter
This bit produces a curved channel along the edge of the wood.

Rounding over cutter
This produces a uniform rounded edge with a slight rebate – a finish commonly found in kitchen worktops.

Chamfer cutter
This bit creates an angular chamfered edge. Commonly, the chamfer angle produced is 45 degrees, as shown above.

MIXING TOOLS

Mixing is a crucial part of DIY – achieving the correct consistency of mortar or plaster, for instance, can make the difference between success and failure. The tools used for mixing are therefore very important. Some are designed to blend large quantities, others for relatively small amounts. Cement mixers used to be prohibitively expensive, but if you have a lot of mortar or concrete work to do, it can be worth buying one. Otherwise, hire one when needed. Power stirrers have become a very popular and cheap option for mixing all kinds of materials.

Power stirrer

A shaped mixing paddle designed for use with a power drill that has a standard chuck. Some materials need less powerful drills than others: paint requires less power than plaster, for example. So an average-sized cordless drill-driver may be used to mix paint, provided it is not overworked. For mixing heavier materials, a high-voltage cordless drill or, preferably, an electrically operated power drill is advisable. In either case, take care not to burn out the drill's motor through prolonged use.

Clip for hanging up

Shaft

Mixing spiral

POWER STIRRER

USING A POWER STIRRER

A **Insert the stirrer** bit into the drill's chuck. Tighten the chuck.

B **Do not start the drill** until the mixing spiral is totally submerged. In this example, paint is being mixed.

C **Slowly start** the drill, and mix the paint. A slow speed is sufficient. Stop the drill before removing the mixing spiral from the paint.

Tub mixer

A smaller version of the cement mixer, offering greater portability, and ideal for mixing smaller amounts. Because the mixing receptacle is a bucket, it can be easily cleaned after use. To use the mixer, first add water to the bucket, then close the lid, and switch on the mixer. Shovel the powdered part/s of the mix onto the lid. As the lid rotates, the powder will fall from its edge into the mixer, and become evenly distributed as the mix continues.

Lid

Motor

Paddle

Handle and support stand

Mixing bucket

Wheels for easy transport

SPOT BOARD

This is used to provide a clean, defined area to hold a mix of plaster or mortar, and can be rested on trestles (for example) for a more comfortable working height. Traditionally, a spot board may have been an offcut of a building board such as plywood, but spot boards are now manufactured in PVC – strong yet lightweight, and easy to clean. Some models come with a separate stand.

Tough PVC board

SAFETY CHECKLIST

■ Never place any part of your body inside a mixer drum unless the power is off. In the case of an electrically operated machine, disconnect the mixer from the mains first.

■ Do not operate a petrol or diesel mixer in a confined space. Ventilation is vital: exhaust fumes can be lethal.

■ With a petrol or diesel model, follow the manufacturer's guidelines with particular care when handling the fuel.

■ Remember that a mixer has many moving parts, and pieces that become very hot. Take care around these parts, and never operate a machine with any guards removed.

■ Be careful to keep your tools well clear of the moving parts inside the mixer.

Cement mixer

The largest on-site mixing tool – the next stage up is to employ the services of a ready-mix lorry. Cement mixers are heavy but still fairly portable. "Tip-up" versions normally come apart, so that they may be easily moved and stored when not in use. Some are electric, while others are powered by petrol or diesel.

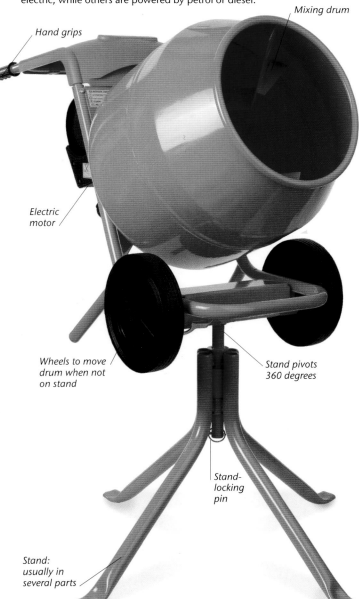

Mixing drum

Hand grips

Electric motor

Wheels to move drum when not on stand

Stand pivots 360 degrees

Stand-locking pin

Stand: usually in several parts

USING A CEMENT MIXER

When assembling a mixer from new, follow the manufacturer's guidelines carefully to ensure that the set-up is correct. When hiring a mixer, you will still need to assemble its main components. Mixers are heavy items, so it is advisable to have somebody help you. The mixer's maximum capacity will be specified in the instructions; never overload it. After using the mixer, or when finishing for the day, clean it immediately. Add clean water and some coarse gravel to the drum. Turn it on and allow this mixture to clean the inside of the mixer. After a few minutes, tip these contents away and check that the drum is clean. Wash the outside of the drum with water and a stiff brush.

A

Position the main body of the mixer on a flat, level surface, with the drum face-down.

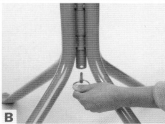

B

Assemble the stand and engage the stand-locking pin.

C

Insert the support stand into the base of the body. On some models, you will also need to engage a stand-locking clip.

D

Stand in front of the mixer and, after making sure that the ground is not slippery, tilt it into an upright position.

E

Make absolutely certain that the mixer is on solid, level ground. Tilt the drum back. It is now ready to use. Switch on the mixer.

Do not allow the shovel to enter the drum

F

Use a shovel or spade to load half of the ingredients, in the correct ratios (see p.71), into the mixer. Be sparing with water to start with.

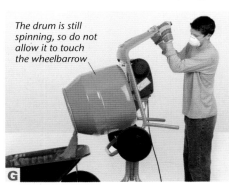

The drum is still spinning, so do not allow it to touch the wheelbarrow

G

Allow it to mix for a minute or two, and then add the rest of the ingredients to the drum. Let mixing continue for several minutes. When the mix is of the required consistency, tip it into a wheelbarrow. Keep other objects clear of the drum while it is still moving.

Materials

CONSTRUCTION MATERIALS CAN BE DIVIDED INTO THOSE FOR GENERAL USE, AND THOSE THAT ARE SPECIFIC TO CERTAIN TASKS. THE MATERIALS DETAILED OVER THE NEXT FEW PAGES ARE THE MORE GENERAL ONES. THEY INCLUDE TIMBER AND BOARDS, NAILS AND SCREWS, ADHESIVES, AND BRICKS AND BLOCKS. YOU WILL NEED TO REFER TO THESE PAGES TO SELECT MATERIALS FOR MOST DIY TASKS EXPLAINED IN THIS BOOK.

AGGREGATES, CEMENT, AND MORTAR

Aggregates and cement are mixed together to make mortar or concrete. Mortar is used as an adhesive that can hold bricks and blocks together, or hold paving slabs in place. It can also be used as an external render or an undercoat for internal plaster. Concrete, which contains coarse aggregates, is used for foundations and hard landscaping. Different kinds of mortar and concrete, suitable for various uses, can be achieved by varying the proportions of the ingredients. Aggregates and sands can be bought in bags or in bulk.

HOW MUCH DO YOU NEED?
Seek advice from your supplier on how much of each constituent you need for your project. To give you a rough idea, to lay 100 bricks with general-purpose mortar you would need: 25kg (55lbs) of cement, 100kg (220lbs) of sand, and 10kg (22lbs) of lime. In practice this is one bag of cement, four bags of sand, and half a bag of lime. The table opposite gives the proportions needed for a variety of mixes.

CEMENT
The adhesive in a mortar mix, cement binds together the components and dries to a stable, hard finish. It must be stored in a dry atmosphere and is unusable if it gets damp.

Portland Grey in colour; the most commonly used cement.

White Portland A lighter version of Portland cement.

Fast-set Sets very quickly, so is ideal for small DIY tasks.

Sulphate-resistant For cement that will be in contact with a clay-rich soil, or one that is high in sulphates.

READY-MIXED MORTAR
These are quicker to use, but are more expensive. They come in bag sizes appropriate for small-scale repair jobs.

Mortar mix A general-purpose mortar.

Slab mix For laying paving.

Concrete mix A general-purpose concrete.

Post mix For erecting fence posts.

MIXING BY HAND

A
Lay a spot board on the ground and pile your ingredients onto it (see table opposite for proportions). This mix is general-purpose mortar.

B
Use a shovel to mix the dry, powdered ingredients together.

C
Pile the dry, mixed ingredients together and make an indent in the centre. Pour in enough water to get the consistency you need.

D
Mix the water in with the rest of the ingredients until you have a mix of the necessary consistency for the job at hand (see opposite).

AGGREGATES AND SAND

Particles smaller than 5mm (⅛in) in diameter are considered a sand; anything larger is an aggregate. Both materials are used to bulk out a mortar or concrete mix. Sand varies in colour depending on where it comes from. Washed sand or aggregate contains fewer of the impurities that can weaken the adhesion of a render mix to the surface, and stain the finish.

Aggregates

Hardcore
Large stones and gravel – the coarsest aggregate. Used as a base for concrete and other hard-landscape surfacing.

Ballast
An "all-in" combination of sand and larger stones or gravel. Ideal for use in general concrete work where exact proportions of individual aggregates are not required.

Coarse aggregate
Graded stone, also known as gravel. It may be used in concrete, or as a drainage aid, or as a finished surface for a drive or path. Stones are often 10mm (⅜in) or 20mm (⅘in) in diameter.

Types of sand

Sharp sand
Coarse sand with fairly large particles. Often used in concrete mixes, but may also be used to produce a very hard, durable mortar.

Builder's and plasterer's sands
Builder's sand is fine-textured and is used in mixes for laying blocks or bricks. Plasterer's sand is similar, and is a finer grade of sharp sand used for rendering.

Kiln-dried silver sand
Very fine, dry sand, light in colour. Mainly used dry to grout exterior paved areas.

OPTIONAL EXTRAS

These can be used in all mortar mixes, according to your requirements.

Lime Cement already contains lime, but adding more makes mortar easier to work with and less likely to crack when set. Traditional mortar mixes (without cement) are based on lime. Lime retains water well, and is less likely to shrink as it dries out. Non-hydraulic lime is sold as powder or as a putty containing water. Use powder for cement-based mortar, and putty for a traditional building mortar. Hydraulic lime sets more quickly, is harder, and is less widely used.

Plasticizer Makes mortar more workable, and is used as a modern equivalent of lime. It normally comes in liquid form.

Cement pigment Powdered pigment that colours cement.

Waterproofer May be mixed with mortar, especially when render is to be applied in an area prone to damp. Some rendering waterproofers slow down the render's drying, keeping it workable for a longer period.

Frostproofer Speeds up mortar's curing time, and can be used to protect mortar while it dries if frost attack may be a danger.

GETTING THE PROPORTIONS RIGHT

The proportions given indicate ratios by volume, not weight. For most uses, proportions can be "measured out" by the shovel-load, but if accuracy is required to maintain a particular strength or colour, measure quantities by the bucket-load. The ratios given are best suited to moderate weather conditions; if the mix will be exposed to punishing weather, use more cement for strength.

Mix	Uses	Cement	Lime	Sand	Coarse aggregate	Ballast	Consistency
General-purpose mortar	Laying blocks or bricks, pointing	1	1	5 (builder's)			Should stick to an upside-down trowel
Slab mix	Laying slabs	1		4 (sharp)			Stiffer than above
Foundation concrete	Laying foundations for house or extension	1		2.5 (sharp)	3.5		Should pour easily
Alternative foundation mix	Less exacting mix for garden walls, etc.	1				5	Should pour easily
General-purpose concrete	Base for slabs, shed, oil, tank, etc.	1		2 (sharp)	3		Should pour easily
Alternative concrete	As above	1				4	Should pour easily
Render	Undercoat for plaster or exterior coating	1	1	6 (plasterer's)			Should stick to an upside-down trowel

Building boards (sheets) are used to create and/or cover large, flat surfaces. Sheet materials are usually supplied in standard sizes, 2,400 x 1,200mm (8 x 4ft) being the most common size. The main types are plasterboard and wood-based boards. These are described here to help you choose the most suitable type for your particular requirements. Some need special screws or nails to fix them in place (see pp.76–79). Eco-friendly building boards are also available (see p.85).

PLASTERBOARD

This is the most common wall and ceiling material. It is made by compressing gypsum plaster to create rigid boards, which are covered on each side with thick paper. Treated varieties are available (see below). These are often colour-coded for easy identification. Some boards have more than one quality, e.g. moisture-check and fire-check. All types are available with square edges and with tapered edges.

Choosing a sheet size

Plasterboard comes in large sheets and in laths – smaller sheets measuring 1,200 x 600mm (4 x 2ft). Laths are useful for covering ceilings, or rustic or uneven joists, or where a lot of cutting is needed, because they are easier to handle.

Choosing a thickness

Plasterboard comes in various thicknesses, 9.5mm (⅜in) and 12.5mm (½in) being the most common. Thicker board is needed if nails or screws will be far apart, for example, if there is a large gap between studs (see pp.104–05) or joists.

SCRIBING A PLASTERBOARD SHEET TO FIT

This is a way of marking where to cut a board to fit against an undulating surface, such as an uneven wall. The method shown here is the basic technique for the first sheet. Examples of when it may be needed include altering a ceiling (see pp.100–01), covering a stud wall (see p.108), and dry lining (see pp.136–37). Use the same method, if you need to, against an uneven ceiling. To cut the final sheet to fit a gap, see p.108.

Place the sheet so that it is just touching the uneven surface. Cut some wood to the length of the largest gap between board and wall (it is exaggerated for clarity in the picture, right). Then cut one end into a point. Place the pointed end against the uneven surface and, holding a pencil at the other end, run it along the surface to draw a guide line.

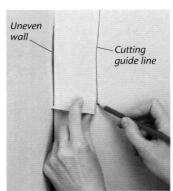

Uneven wall

Cutting guide line

Which side is which?

Standard plasterboard is pale grey or ivory on one side, and a darker grey or brown colour on the other. The lighter surface should face into the room. The other side may have manufacturers' logos on it, and visible seams down its edge.

Square-edged vs. taper-edged boards

The choice depends on how the plasterboard is to be covered. Square-edged sheets are for plastering, and taper-edged sheets for dry lining (see p.129). Laths are for plastering and are therefore square- (or round-) edged.

PLASTERBOARDS

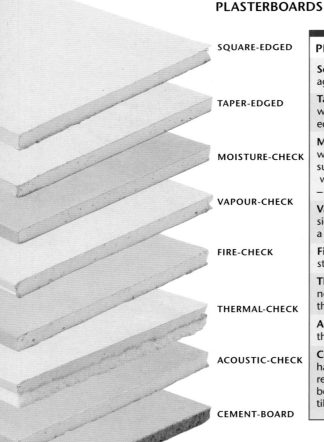

SQUARE-EDGED

TAPER-EDGED

MOISTURE-CHECK

VAPOUR-CHECK

FIRE-CHECK

THERMAL-CHECK

ACOUSTIC-CHECK

CEMENT-BOARD

PLASTERBOARDS	Uses include
Square-edged Standard plasterboard. Sheets butt against each other and should be plastered over.	Walls and ceilings to be plastered
Taper-edged Used when a surface is to be dry lined, which involves filling the gaps between the tapered edges (see p.129).	Dry lining walls
Moisture-check Core is impregnated with waterproofing materials, but is breathable so that the surface beneath the board can "breathe" through the wall's surface. Can be used in areas of high water usage – as a base for tiles in a shower cubicle, for example.	Bathrooms and kitchens
Vapour-check Has vapour-resistant paper on one side, so is less protected than moisture-check. Has a silver foil-like layer on non-decorative side.	Used for ceilings beneath loft space
Fire-check Has greater fireproofing qualities than standard plasterboard.	Integral garage ceilings, some corridors, stairwells
Thermal-check A polystyrene layer bonded to the non-decorative side provides greater heat insulation than normal. Thicker than other plasterboards.	Loft conversions, to increase insulation
Acoustic-check Has greater soundproofing qualities than other plasterboards.	Walls and ceilings in flats
Cement-board Not technically a plasterboard, but has similar properties and uses. Is a strong, moisture-resistant base board, often used as a subfloor, beneath ceramic tiles, or as a backing for wall tiles. Board thicknesses and sizes vary.	Can be used as a subfloor beneath ceramic tiles, or as a backing for wall tiles

WOOD-BASED BOARDS

Wood is the main constituent of many building boards. Some of these may be used in the main structural components of a house; others for decorative finishings.

Plywood

Thin layers of wood, with the grain of each layer at a right angle to that of the previous layer, form ply boards. Each layer is bonded tightly to the next, creating a very strong board structure, and thickness adds further strength. All plywoods are available as marine plies, which are impregnated with water-repelling chemicals.

Other boards

Boards such as MDF and chipboard are made from pieces of wood compressed together at high pressure. Water-resistant versions of these boards are also available for use in areas where humidity may be high.

CUTTING A BOARD OR SHEET

Using a hand saw
If the board is coated (with melamine, for example), mark the guide line on the side that will be visible and cut with this side facing upwards. This is because the edge of the coating on the lower face will chip during cutting; this way, the chipped edges will be invisible. Score along the guide line on all sides of the board with a craft knife, and use a fine-toothed tenon or panel saw to reduce the chances of chipped edges.

Using a power saw
The blade cuts as it rises, so to avoid chipped edges on the visible side of a coated board, mark the guide line on the rear of the board and cut with the rear side facing upwards.

Cutting plasterboard
To cut a straight line in a sheet of plasterboard, place a straight edge along the guide line, and score along it with a craft knife. Fold the board to snap it along the line, and cut through the paper backing.

PLYWOODS	Uses include
3-ply and 5-ply These common types of plywood get their name from the number of layers used in their manufacture: i.e. 3-ply has three layers.	Boxing in or decorative internal uses
Multi-ply This is composed of many layers.	Heavyweight construction, e.g. timber house frames

OTHER BOARDS	Uses include
Blockboard Not technically a ply, but shares its characteristics. Has two thinner outer layers that enclose thicker, square-cut lengths of wood. It is therefore stiff and durable. May have a decorative veneer or a finish of a lesser grade of wood.	Ideal for shelves and cupboards, and can be finished with paint
Medium-density fibreboard (MDF) Very versatile. Made up of highly compressed wooden fibres glued together. This method of manufacture means that cut edges are neater than those on other boards. It can provide a rigid structural component, or can be intricately shaped to form a decorative surface ready for paint. Available in various thicknesses. Main drawback is that it gives off a very fine dust when cut, which must not be inhaled. Wear a mask when MDF is being cut.	Cupboards, cupboard doors, boxing in, shelving
Moisture-resistant MDF A version of MDF which can resist moisture attack. Is often green to aid recognition.	Areas prone to moisture: e.g. kitchen or bathroom
Fibreboard A lightweight version of MDF. Joints between boards can be taped, and the boards decorated.	Underlay for flooring, or as an alternative to plasterboard on a ceiling
Chipboard Central core is composed of small wooden fibres. Has no decorative quality, so must be covered. Some sheets fit together using a tongue-and-groove mechanism. Available in various thicknesses.	Often used as an alternative to floorboards
Moisture-resistant chipboard is more water-resistant than normal chipboard. It is often coloured green for easy recognition.	Flooring
Veneered chipboard Has a melamine (plastic) or decorative wooden veneer.	Commonly used for shelves
Hardboard Thin, compressed fibreboard. Standard hardboard has one smooth side, and one rougher side. Different grades and a variety of finishes are available – subfloors, for example, use "flooring grade" hardboard.	Often used as a subfloor (see p.327), or for parts of kitchen units with a melamine (plastic) surface or veneer

PLYWOOD

3–PLY

5–PLY

MULTI-PLY

OTHER BOARDS

BLOCKBOARD

MEDIUM-DENSITY FIBREBOARD (MDF)

MOISTURE-RESISTANT MDF

FIBREBOARD

CHIPBOARD

MOISTURE-RESISTANT CHIPBOARD

VENEERED CHIPBOARD

HARDBOARD

Timber is a major constituent of many homes. Even a solid masonry house may contain a large proportion of timber elements, including rafters and joists, and the studs in a stud wall (see p.104). In addition to these, there are decorative aspects: doors, mouldings, and stairways. These pages deal with the different types of timber used in homes, the properties of different woods, and sourcing sustainable timber. For details of woodworking joints and how to use them, see pp.392–93.

HARDWOOD AND SOFTWOOD

Hardwood is usually harvested from deciduous trees (ones that shed their leaves), and softwood from coniferous trees (which bear cones). Hardwoods take longer to grow, and are more resilient than softwoods, so they are considered to be higher quality woods. Because of this, they are more expensive. This does not mean that softwood is a less effective building material – indeed, it makes up the bulk of all timber used in the home. It is used rough-sawn in structural components such as wall studs, and planed for mouldings such as skirting boards. Some of the more common hardwoods and softwoods used in house construction and decoration are detailed below.

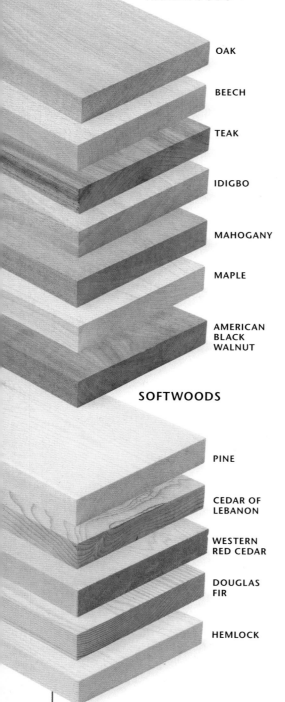

HARDWOODS

OAK

BEECH

TEAK

IDIGBO

MAHOGANY

MAPLE

AMERICAN BLACK WALNUT

SOFTWOODS

PINE

CEDAR OF LEBANON

WESTERN RED CEDAR

DOUGLAS FIR

HEMLOCK

HARDWOODS	Uses include
Oak A traditional wooden building material, oak is present in many older properties. "Green" (newly harvested) oak is still sometimes used to make timber frames for houses; when green, it is still soft, so is easily cut and shaped. As it dries, oak acquires a hardness more like concrete than like wood, making it a very strong construction material. In addition to structural elements (known as first-fix carpentry), oak can also be used for decorative elements (second-fix carpentry) to provide a high-quality, but expensive, finish.	Structure of older houses, decorative beams, kitchens, veneer on kitchen units, flooring, decorative carpentry such as skirting board and architrave
Beech A straight-grained hardwood with a fine, even texture. American beech is light or reddish brown in colour, while European beech is a lighter, yellowish-brown colour.	Kitchen worktops, floors (veneer), decorative mouldings such as quadrant, scotia, etc.
Teak Teak is a dark hardwood, sometimes used in second-fix carpentry to provide a high-quality finish.	Staircases, garden and indoor furniture
Idigbo Resilient and easily worked, idigbo is also very reasonably priced for a hardwood.	Windows, staircases
Mahogany More commonly associated with furniture than with house construction.	Furniture, panelling in period properties
Maple A highly decorative hardwood with a light, attractive appearance and hardwearing characteristics.	Flooring
American black walnut A coarse, dark hardwood used in some aspects of interior joinery.	Kitchens, veneers

SOFTWOODS	Uses include
Pine One of the most commonly used woods, sometimes called whitewood or deal. Piranha pine is similar, but the grain often contains more orange or red streaks. Also similar is redwood, which is slightly more red in colour.	First-fix (construction) carpentry, second-fix (decorative) carpentry
Cedar of Lebanon Another light-coloured softwood. Often used in internal joinery.	First- and second-fix carpentry
Western red cedar Has a red-tinged appearance. Used mainly for exterior applications.	Weatherboarding, shingles, decking
Douglas fir Has a definite reddish-brown tinge, and is commonly used in plywood. Good for exterior work.	Construction, decking
Hemlock A light, non-resinous wood.	Doors, windows

CHARACTERISTICS OF WOOD

As well as choosing a type of timber, think about the other qualities it needs. These are not mutually exclusive; a piece of timber can be both seasoned and treated, for example.

Seasoned wood

Wood has a high moisture content when it is first cut, and needs to dry out ("season") before being used. When you buy wood, it will often still have a relatively high moisture content. Wood can distort during the drying process. To overcome this, store it horizontally, above ground level, and supported evenly along its length. Before using timber, leave it to acclimatize for a few days in the environment where it will be used. Many suppliers produce kiln-dried timber on which seasoning has been accelerated, and the wood artificially dried. It is slightly more expensive, but using kiln-dried wood can prevent problems later.

Treated wood

Timber for second-fix carpentry such as skirting board or doors does not need to be treated. First-fix carpentry (e.g. rafters or a stud wall), however, does need treated wood. Pressure-treated wood is usually tanalized (impregnated with a preservative), and has a green or brown tinge. It can be placed in contact with outside surfaces, such as soil, where there is a high risk of damp attack or insect infestation. Wood that has been treated (but not pressure-treated) is less resilient. All wood, however well treated, will break down eventually, but the degree to which it has been treated will influence its working lifespan.

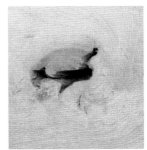

TANALIZED PLANK

BUYING TIMBER

Regardless of the type of wood, and whether it has been seasoned or treated, make sure you know whether your supplier is selling it by its rough-sawn or its planed size.

Rough-sawn wood vs. planed wood

Wood may be supplied either rough-sawn or planed (smoothed on all sides). This can make buying it confusing, because timber is usually priced and sold according to its dimensions when it is first cut into rough-sawn lengths. Rough-sawn timber is therefore close to the size stated when you buy it – although it may be slightly smaller due to shrinkage during the drying process – but planed timber is smaller than its labelled size, because it has been smoothed with a plane on all sides. However, many DIY outlets sell wood in exact, rather than nominal, size, so make sure you know which method your supplier uses.

 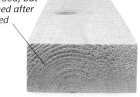

Same initial size as the rough-sawn wood, but has been planed after being measured

Rough-sawn wood
Used where it will not be visible – in a stud wall, for example. It will be close to the size quoted, because timber is measured when it is rough-sawn.

Planed timber
Used where it will be visible, such as for a skirting board. It may not be the stated size, because wood has been removed from every face to give a smooth finish.

GREEN SOURCES OF TIMBER

Sustainable wood
The most important issue when buying new wood is to know whether it has come from a sustainable source. Timber from recognized sources usually bears a stamp, such as that of the internationally-recognized Forest Stewardship Council – a not-for-profit organization that promotes the responsible management of forests.

FOREST STEWARDSHIP COUNCIL'S STAMP

Reclaimed timber
Reclaimed wood has the advantage of being thoroughly seasoned, and may look more appealing than new timber. However, some of it may be unusable, so check for damage when buying. For more on reclaimed materials, see pp.86–87.

RECOGNIZING PROBLEMS

When buying wood look out for splits, knots, and uneven grain. Splits can occur naturally in wood due to shrinkage or growth defects, but it is more likely that the wood has been dried too rapidly or the planks stored incorrectly. Softwoods damage and warp more easily when being stored. You will pay more for defect-free wood, but it is worth examining timber thoroughly before purchasing.

 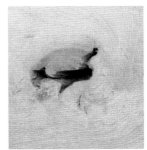

Look along the timber for signs of bowing or warping

Warped timber
Bent or twisted wood is difficult to saw accurately. Bending is usually caused by stacking or otherwise storing wood badly. Bowed or warped timber may have unseen stresses due to the twisting.

Knots
In first-fix carpentry, knots are hidden and don't matter. They may spoil second-fix carpentry by bleeding (especially on softwood) or showing through paint. Treat them with knotting solution first.

CHECKLIST WHEN BUYING TIMBER

- Make sure that the wood you are buying comes from a sustainable resource.
- Find out how it has been treated and seasoned, and how it has been stored.
- Check lengths to see if they are bowed or warped, are split, are damp, or contain excessive or dead knots.
- Find out whether the quoted sizes are nominal or actual, so that you get the correct quantity of timber.
- Check that the supplier will deliver to your home. This can be useful if you require a large quantity and/or particularly long lengths. Check timber carefully when it is delivered.

SCREW FIXINGS AND FITTINGS

Screws vary considerably in terms of size, purpose, and quality. Some are purely functional, and their appearance is of no importance; others have an aesthetic role as well as a practical one. Once you have chosen the most appropriate fixings for your project, check that you have the correct screwdriver to drive them (see pp.32–33, 56–57). Screw heads are quickly damaged by the wrong screwdriver, so always use the correct size – it also makes the job easier.

HEAD DESIGN

Screws are designed to be turned by particular types of screwdriver. You can tell which type to use by looking at the pattern of slots in the top of the screw head. Some modern screws have unusual head designs that require specialist bits rather than traditional screwdriver designs.

Dual-purpose
Some screws combine head types. This example has both a Phillips head and a slot head.

Slot-headed
Traditional design with a single slot crossing the diameter of the screw's head.

Phillips
Cross-headed, with two slots bisecting one another. The slots are deeper in the centre.

Posidriv
A cross-head screw similar to the Phillips, but with smaller divisions between the cross's slots.

Hexagonal-headed
Hexagonal (hex) screws need to be tightened with a hex screwdriver or bit.

Square-headed
These are also inserted with a special screwdriver or bit or an Allen key.

Security
Similar to a standard screw except that once inserted, it cannot be removed.

HEAD PROFILES

There are three main types of screw-head profiles, each with a different function, illustrated below. The main difference is how proud the head sits in relation to the surrounding surface.

COUNTERSUNK HEAD   PAN HEAD   ROUND HEAD

SCREW-HEAD COVERINGS

These provide decorative finishes for exposed screw heads. Some fit to the top of a fixed head; others are positioned as the screw is inserted, because it feeds through the cup.

Screw sits in cup

Top folds down

Top

SCREW CUP

Screw sits in cup

Back

INSET CUP

SNAP-ON CAP

COVER CAP

SIZE AND MATERIAL

Screws are sized in terms of length and gauge. The length measurement refers to the part of a screw that goes into the material, so it includes the head of a countersinking screw, but does not for a round-headed one. Choose a screw which is three times longer than the thickness of the smaller of the pieces being joined. The gauge refers to the shank's diameter, and is a label not an exact size. The smaller the figure, the narrower the screw. Most screws are available in gauges 2 (2.0mm; ⅛in) to 14 (6.5mm; 9⁄16in), but other sizes are available for some types, especially the most commonly used ones.

Higher quality screws usually have stronger heads, which reduces the risk of rounding off (damaging) the head with a screwdriver. Where screws will suffer exposed conditions or possible corrosion, use resistant fixings, such as stainless-steel or zinc-plated ones.

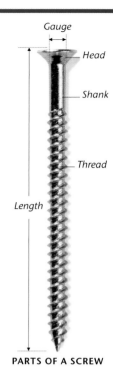

Gauge

Head

Shank

Thread

Length

PARTS OF A SCREW

PILOT HOLES AND COUNTERSINKING

Before driving a screw into wood, drill a pilot hole to guide the screw into the correct position and to prevent the wood splitting as the screw is tightened. Use a drill bit that is slightly narrower than the screw's gauge. To drill a pilot hole for a wall plug, use a bit with the same diameter as the plug's gauge. See p.54 for the drilling technique.

Before inserting a screw with a countersunk head, use a countersink drill bit to enlarge the pilot hole's opening. The bit widens towards its top, so drill a shallow hole for a small screw head, and a deeper hole for a larger one.

COUNTERSINKING A SCREW

Pilot hole has already been drilled

A

Drill a pilot hole of the correct size to take the screw, and use this as a guide for the centre of the countersink drill bit.

B

Using a countersink bit, drill a hole of sufficient depth to accommodate the screw head.

C

Insert the screw through the countersunk hole and into the pilot hole, and tighten it as usual.

D

The screw's head will sit just below the surface. Fill the hole, covering the screw, and decorate.

TYPES OF SCREW

Screw designs vary widely to suit particular tasks or materials. Some of the more specialized screws are available only in a limited range of sizes.

Drywall
Black-phosphate-coated; used to fix plasterboard to studwork.

Traditional wood
Tapered shank. With the correct pilot hole, it fits very tightly.

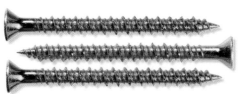

Modern wood
Untapered, less likely to split wood. Pilot hole not always needed.

Masonry
For use in masonry with no need for a wall plug, though a pilot hole is still needed. Some have a blue coating.

Decking
Long screws designed for fixing down decking boards.

Single thread   *Twin threads*

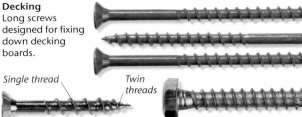

MDF
Sharp point and twin-thread perform initial penetration. Further up the shank, a single, coarser thread holds the screw tightly in position.

Coach
A coach screw or bolt is a heavy-duty fixing that is inserted by rotating the head with a spanner.

Chipboard
For fixing down chipboard flooring. Often wax-coated.

Self-tapping
Cuts its own thread. Commonly used with sheet metal. Some general-purpose screws have a self-tapping action.

Decorative dome

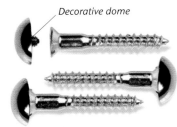

Mirror
Can also hold fittings where access may be required (such as a bath panel). Decorative dome fits over screw head.

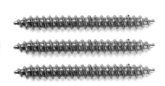

Dowel
Threaded at both ends, to join two lengths of wood (curtain poles, for example).

WALL PLUGS AND COMBINATION FIXINGS

Unless you are using masonry screws, a wall plug is required to secure a fixing that is inserted into masonry. Wall plugs are also needed to make strong fixings on hollow walls such as stud walls; these are of a different design from masonry ones. You can buy combination fixings for masonry and hollow walls, which combine a screw fixing and a plug in one product; designs vary according to function and manufacturer. Common examples are illustrated below.

MASONRY-WALL PLUGS

Common wall
Available in a range of lengths and gauges, designed for use in masonry walls.

Plug and screw supplied together

Frame fixing
Screw fixing supplied with correct size of plug. Commonly used to fix window and door frames in masonry walls. Tap it into the fixing hole, and tighten it with a screwdriver.

Hammer fixing
Similar to frame fixing except the fixing is hammered all the way into position with just half a turn given to the screw to tighten it securely.

Expanding sleeve   *Turning bolt causes sleeve to expand*

Expansion/masonry bolt
Screw fixing with bolt head and metal sleeve that expands into the masonry material as the bolt is screwed in place.

HOLLOW-WALL PLUGS

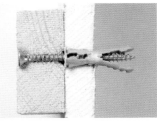

Cavity wall plug
A plug specifically designed for cavity walls. The tapering increases the plug's grip in the pilot hole.

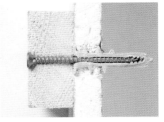

Self-drilling cavity wall plug
The tapered, threaded plug screws into wall and the screw fixing is then inserted into the plug.

Hollow-wall anchor
Combination fixing for a hollow wall, with a screw inserted with a metal sleeve.

Spring toggle
As the fixing is screwed into place, the toggle section grips the wall tightly. A gravity toggle is similar, but supports greater weights.

NAILS

The most basic of fixings, nails are essential for construction jobs where the extra strength and expense of a screw fixing is unnecessary. Common nails are for general use and are available in many sizes – choose one that is at least three times longer than the depth of the thinner material being nailed. Specialist nails, traditional nails, and pins, are designed for specific tasks or finishes and are made in sizes suitable for their purpose. Most nails are simply hammered home, although where wood is liable to split, or very close to an edge, you may sometimes need to drill a pilot hole slightly smaller than the diameter of the nail (as for screws, see p.76). For details on hammering and removing nails, see pp.36–37.

Head

Shank

ROUND WIRE NAIL

NAIL COMPOSITION AND QUANTITIES

Nails have a head to receive a hammer blow, and a longer shank to provide the fixing. Most nails are made of steel or iron, although masonry nails are of hardened zinc for strength. Many nails are galvanized (have an outer layer mixed with zinc to protect them from rust), which gives them a pale grey, mottled effect. Sherardization, a different method of coating in zinc produces a darker grey nail.

Nails are normally sold by weight rather than quantity, so a rough calculation is sufficient for purchasing. Over-buy as nails are always useful. Nail weights vary between manufacturers, and according to design and composition. As a rough guide, 175 round wire nails measuring 50 x 2.65mm (2 x ⅛in) weigh 1kg (2⅛lb).

COMMON NAILS

The most widely used nail types are shown here. They may vary slightly between manufacturers. Design differences can improve a particular aspect of fixing. Some nails are lightweight, so, where strength is not an issue, you get more for your money. Others have grooves and twists that give them a greater gripping action to create a very solid fixing.

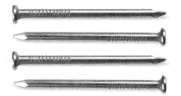

Round wire
A general-purpose nail for joining wood. Widely used where "rough" finishing is acceptable, in studwork for example. The round head provides a good point of contact for a hammer but may split wood if driven down too far.

Round lost-head wire
Similar to round wire nails, but the head is much smaller, and sits flush with the wood's surface to give a neater finish with reduced risk of splitting. It can be recessed using a nail punch (see opposite) to hide it completely.

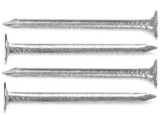

Oval wire
Similar to the round lost-head, but oval in cross-section to minimize splitting of the wood. Most of the head sits below the wood's surface without the need for punching in (see opposite).

Clout
Commonly used to fix slates, and for other roofing purposes. Smaller clout nails are used to attach roofing felt. Because they are exposed to the weather, clout nails are often galvanized to prevent rust.

Masonry
This hard, thicker nail has a small head and is usually made of hardened zinc to enable it to penetrate masonry surfaces. It is generally used to fix wood to stone or brick.

Plasterboard
Galvanized nail for attaching plasterboard to studwork. Shank design is often serrated or jagged for a better grip to hold up the heavy sheets securely.

Annular ring shank
Similar to round wire nail, but has rings all along the shank, providing greater grip in wood that results in a more secure fixing.

Square twist
Has square cross-section, twisted for greater grip. A strong general-purpose nail for fixing wood, and treated with zinc. Square twist nails are ideal for use outdoors.

PINS

Pins are designed for fine carpentry and joinery work. Their thinness makes them less likely to split wood. The small heads are designed to remain unseen. Brass pins provide a decorative detail.

Panel
General-purpose pin for use on small mouldings or thin plywood.

Veneer
These very narrow panel pins give a neat finish to detailed work.

Brass
Decorative pins for visible fixings, especially on brass door furniture.

Glazing sprig
Wedge-shaped pin used with putty to secure glazing.

SPECIALIST NAILS
Each of these is designed with features suitable for one particular purpose.

Spring head
Traditional, galvanized nail with twisted shank and large head, designed to fix board and sheet materials, particularly those used in roofing.

Upholstery
Small, decorative, dome-headed nails used for securing upholstery to furnishings. Available in a variety of finishes to suit the style of furnishings.

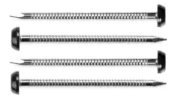

Plastic-headed
Used to hold UPVC cladding materials. The shatterproof heads are available in a range of popular colours to help disguise the fixings.

Carpet
Used to hold down carpet before the introduction of gripper rods, and still used in awkward corners, especially on stairs. Also known as carpet tacks.

FASTENERS
Although these do not look like nails, they perform the same function and, like nails, are driven into position with a hammer. The most commonly used are shown here, but a variety of fasteners are available.

Corrugated
Has a corrugated cross-section, and is usually used as an invisible connector for a mitred frame joint (see below).

Staple
The arched shape is designed to hold wire firmly in position, for example on fence posts.

▮▮ USING A CORRUGATED FASTENER

A **Position a fastener** so that it bisects the joint at a right angle, then hammer it into place.

B **Knock another fastener** across the joint, so that the wood is securely held in place by two parallel fixings.

TRADITIONAL NAILS
These simple designs predate modern nails, and are still used to provide period detail in modern homes. Their rigid, broad design makes them ideal for securing large wooden sections.

Cut clasp
An all-purpose nail, often used today for traditional-look, ledge-and-brace door construction (see p.157).

Cut floor
Similar to the cut clasp, but the head's flat design is suited to fixing down floorboards (see pp.180–81).

▮▮ PUNCHING A NAIL BENEATH THE SURFACE

You may wish to knock a nail to sit just beneath the surface of the material it is fixing. This is normally for aesthetic reasons and, in areas where people could brush past, may be needed to prevent injury or damage to clothing and other materials. The only tools needed are a hammer and a nail punch (see p.36). In many cases the hole is filled and decorated over so the fixing becomes completely invisible.

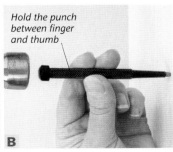

Hold the punch between finger and thumb

A **Use a nail punch** of the right size for the nail. Place its tip onto the nail head, holding the punch straight so that the nail will be driven true.

B **Lightly tap the head** of the punch with a hammer, striking it squarely. It will not take much force to knock the nail head below the surface.

C **Use a filling knife** to press wood filler into the hole, covering the nail completely. Then sand and decorate the surface.

Many projects require some kind of adhesive or sealant, and it is important to use the one most appropriate for any particular task. A vast array is available, some of which can act as an adhesive and/or a sealant. Sealants for joints between surfaces are detailed here. For details of surface sealants and primers see pp.272–77.

ADHESIVES

The most widely used adhesives are described here. Other types are designed for use with particular products, such as UPVC. Mirror adhesives, for example, do not affect mirror backings that might be stained by all-purpose adhesive.

PVA Polyvinyl acetate in concentrated form is a thick white liquid that can be used as an all-purpose adhesive. It may be used neat, as a glue, or diluted, as a surface sealer, bonding agent, or primer. Waterproof PVA is also available.

Wood glue Similar in appearance to PVA, this is designed specifically for bonding sections of wood.

Contact adhesive A very strong solvent-based adhesive, this can be used to bond a large range of materials including wood, metal, many plastics, and decorative laminates. It is not suitable for use with some materials, such as polystyrene and bitumen, or as a mirror adhesive, so check the manufacturer's instructions before using it.

Grab adhesive Used to bond surfaces that cannot easily be fixed with screws or nails, or combined with mechanical fixings to form very strong bonds. Available in tubes and sealant-like cartridges. Most (especially water-based and solvent-free types) need at least one of the surfaces being bonded to be porous.

Resin Made up of two elements that mix once they are dispensed from the cartridge, resin creates very strong bonds. Where a secure anchoring point for a wall fixing is required (on shelves, for instance), resin is injected into the hole before the fixing is inserted.

Expanding foam Supplied in an aerosol, this foam is used to fill large gaps, bonding to their edges.

▌▌ USING A RESIN ADHESIVE

A
Aim the nozzle into the hole in the wall, and discharge the resin adhesive into the hole.

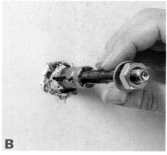

B
Immediately press a heavy-duty fixing into the resin, and allow the adhesive to set before hanging any heavy item from the fixing.

▌▌ USING EXPANDING FOAM

Polyurethane-based expanding foam can fill large gaps or holes, and bonds the surfaces in the process. Some varieties have greater heat resistance than others. This is an important feature in some situations, such as when fitting a flue. In this example, foam is being used to fill the gap around a drainage pipe.

A
Point the nozzle into the hole in the wall, and discharge the foam into the hole.

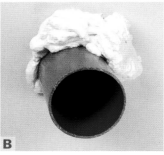

B
After about five or 10 minutes, the foam will begin to bubble and expand. It will then set.

C
Once it has set, the foam can be cut away using a saw to neaten the overall finish. Finer trimming can be carried out with a craft knife.

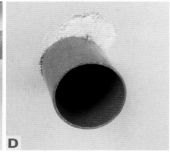

D
Holes in the trimmed area can then be filled with an all-purpose filler compound, sanded, and decorated as required.

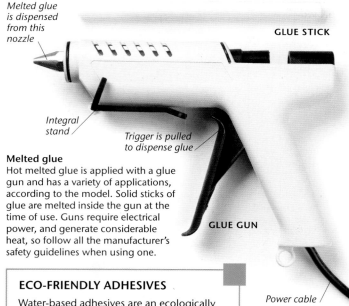

Melted glue is dispensed from this nozzle

GLUE STICK

Integral stand

Trigger is pulled to dispense glue

GLUE GUN

Power cable

Melted glue
Hot melted glue is applied with a glue gun and has a variety of applications, according to the model. Solid sticks of glue are melted inside the gun at the time of use. Guns require electrical power, and generate considerable heat, so follow all the manufacturer's safety guidelines when using one.

ECO-FRIENDLY ADHESIVES

Water-based adhesives are an ecologically sound alternative to solvent-based products. They are non-toxic and low in VOCs (volatile organic compounds). For more information about VOCs, see p.278.

JOINT SEALANTS

Some sealants prime or seal a surface (see opposite and pp.272–93), while others create a decorative, waterproof, or durable joint. Most joint sealants have a waterproofing element, often with silicone as the main ingredient. Where silicone is not specified, sealants tend to be job-specific.

Joint sealants usually come in cartridges that require a separate dispenser to apply them. Dispensers vary in size and design, so check for compatibility. Most sealants are available in an extensive range of colours, and some (though not silicone varieties) can be painted. Sealant remover is available, but can damage some surfaces.

The sealant must cope with movement, such as that caused by temperature changes, in the materials they join. "High-modulus" sealants are not very flexible, but dry to a relatively hard finish, and are recommended for use in bathrooms – however, check for resistance to mould. "Low-modulus" types are more flexible, and are used in glazing.

Curing and longevity

Most sealants form a skin fairly quickly, but take several hours, or even days, to dry or cure completely. High-modulus sealants give off strong acidic fumes while curing. A few brands are "fast cure". A sealant should never go completely hard, because of the need for flexibility. Be sure to check the cartridge for the length of guarantee. High-quality sealants may be expensive, but they are easier to work with and last the longest.

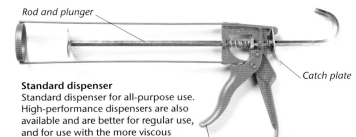

Rod and plunger

Catch plate

Trigger

Standard dispenser
Standard dispenser for all-purpose use. High-performance dispensers are also available and are better for regular use, and for use with the more viscous sealants such as grab adhesive.

▌▌ USING A SEALANT DISPENSER

A **Cut off the end** of the cartridge's nozzle, then unscrew the cartridge and cut off the tip that is revealed. Then replace the nozzle.

B **Pull back the** dispenser's plunger or rod, and load the cartridge into the dispenser.

C **Press the trigger** slowly, so that it grips the cartridge and holds it in place, but do not press it so hard that the tube starts dispensing.

D **To dispense the sealant,** apply even pressure to the trigger (see p.319 where sealant is being applied along a tiled edge).

E **When you release** the trigger, sealant will continue to dispense due to a buildup of pressure. Push the catch plate to make it stop. To store a half-used tube, insert a nail into its nozzle to prevent the channel clogging, or replace the nozzle next time you use the tube.

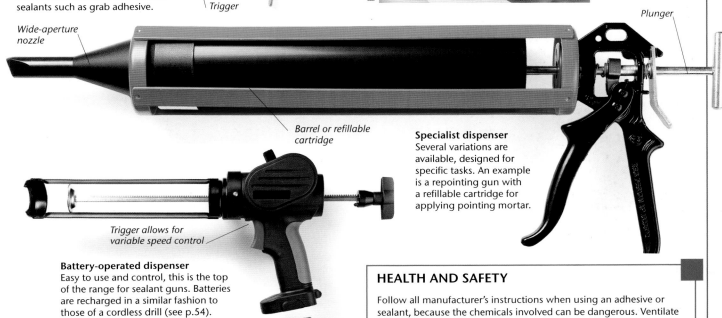

Plunger

Wide-aperture nozzle

Barrel or refillable cartridge

Specialist dispenser
Several variations are available, designed for specific tasks. An example is a repointing gun with a refillable cartridge for applying pointing mortar.

Trigger allows for variable speed control

Battery-operated dispenser
Easy to use and control, this is the top of the range for sealant guns. Batteries are recharged in a similar fashion to those of a cordless drill (see p.54).

Rechargeable battery

HEALTH AND SAFETY

Follow all manufacturer's instructions when using an adhesive or sealant, because the chemicals involved can be dangerous. Ventilate your working area and wear all recommended protective equipment and clothing.

Bricks, blocks, and stone are the main components of masonry construction, both inside and outside the home. A wall (such as a cavity wall) may contain several of these materials, or just one (as in a brick garden wall). There are several materials to choose from, including eco-friendly options (see pp.84–85). See p.46 for bricklaying tools and techniques. Interior block-wall construction is shown on pp.112–13 and garden brick-wall construction on pp.406–09.

WORKING OUT HOW MANY TO BUY
When estimating quantities, remember that the measurement of a brick or block does not usually take into account mortar joints, which will influence the eventual dimensions of your wall. However, some suppliers do quote block sizes in nominal figures including mortar joints. For brickwork, an average joint is 10mm (⅜in); it is sometimes a little larger for blockwork – 12mm (½in). To get a rough idea of how many bricks or blocks to buy, calculate the surface area of your planned structure and divide this by the nominal size of your chosen brick or block.

TYPES OF BRICKS
Many kinds of brick are available, in terms of composition, colour, and texture. The main types are shown here. Bricks are also categorized in terms of quality, referring to their resistance to such things as frost attack. This is not instantly apparent in the brick's appearance, so seek advice from your supplier.

Common
Common bricks are clay-based and general-purpose. Today they tend to be used for garden walls, and patching masonry before render.

Facing/Faced
Facing bricks have good faces on all sides. Faced bricks have one good face and one or both good ends.

Engineering
Engineering bricks are very dense and are made of clay. They are used for extra strength and resistance to weather conditions.

Calcium silicate
Made from lime and sand, these bricks come in a vast range of colours. They are also relatively smooth to the touch, and provide a very uniform finish.

Fire
Made from a special form of clay that can withstand particularly high temperatures, these bricks are commonly used in fireplaces.

Concrete
These bricks are composed of concrete and made in a large range of colours and textures.

Air
Used in a wall's structure to allow ventilation, airbricks are often used around the base of a house, ventilating the area beneath a suspended ground floor.

BRICK DESIGN
Bricks are made in different sizes, although 215 x 102.5 x 65mm (8½ x 4 x 2⅝in) is a common size. There are also other aspects of brick design that vary, such as whether they are solid, cored, or indented. These are the three most common brick designs, although many others exist, often designed for specific purposes.

Solid
Solid throughout the structure, with flat surfaces on all sides. Both fire bricks and concrete bricks are commonly solid in structure.

Cored
Have holes that extend from their upper to their lower faces, and so are not suitable for capping on top of a wall. They are laid in exactly the same way as other bricks.

Faced/Indented
Indented bricks have a wedge-shaped indentation (a "frog") in the upper face (some also have this in the bottom face). Bricks can be laid frog up, or frog down. Laying them frog up is stronger, but requires more mortar.

Speciality bricks
Less angular bricks are available for certain tasks such as capping a garden wall, creating a curved wall, turning a corner (as shown), or creating specific sill designs. Most manufacturers and suppliers will have catalogues to display their full range of specialist bricks.

BLOCKS

Blocks are a modern development, and are generally larger than bricks. Unless they are faced, blocks are normally covered over for decorative purposes – usually with render on an exterior wall, and render and plaster, or dry lining (a modern alternative to plastering), on an internal wall. Sizes vary, but blocks are often 450 x 225mm (18 x 9in). Depths also vary.

Glass
Decorative glass blocks are square in shape and may be used internally or externally, often for small features.

Rectangular concrete
Heavy, solid concrete-based block used for general construction work.

Thermal insulation
A lightweight concrete block that is thermally efficient and easy to handle. Used in loadbearing and non-loadbearing walls, depending on specification.

Concrete with cavity
Continuous cavities allow for strengthening rods through retaining walls. Cellular blocks have discontinuous cavities.

Faced building block
Concrete blocks are sometimes available with a decorative face and in various colours.

STONE

Natural stone varies widely in appearance and properties depending on its origin. Different stones are therefore suitable for different projects. When buying natural stone, quality is important. A load of undressed stone may produce a lot of waste, while dressed stone is more expensive.

Natural stone
Undressed natural stone generally requires dressing before use. Bear in mind that dressed stone needs to have a usable face, as well as the correct dimensions.

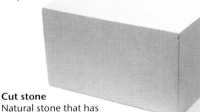

Cut stone
Natural stone that has been cut into a block, usually with all faces dressed. Cut stone is therefore very expensive and seldom used extensively.

Pitched faced (Dressed)
Stone cut to provide smooth sides for neat mortar joints, but with a rough face.

Reconstituted stone
Made from crushed stone, sand, and cement, these are moulded to mimic natural stone.

CUTTING CONCRETE BLOCKS

Angle grinder
To cut a block diagonally from corner to corner, for a gable end, use an angle grinder along a guide line. For square cuts, see p.61.

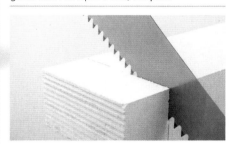

Stone saw
Use a stone saw to cut lightweight blocks by hand, following a clearly marked guide line.

WALL TIES

Wall ties are used in cavity-walls to connect the outer and inner leaves, or to connect a new masonry wall to an existing one. Designs vary according to whether a tie is for use with masonry or timber. Some common examples are shown below.

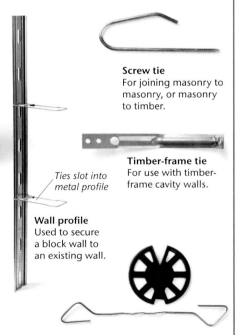

Screw tie
For joining masonry to masonry, or masonry to timber.

Ties slot into metal profile

Timber-frame tie
For use with timber-frame cavity walls.

Wall profile
Used to secure a block wall to an existing wall.

Lightweight wall tie
Stainless steel with a plastic retaining clip designed to hold insulation sheets in place.

GREEN MATERIALS

The blocks and materials used in the construction of an eco-house are key to its green credentials. There are various green options available, but it is important to consider loadbearing issues when making your decision. Ask your supplier to identify which type of block is suitable for exterior and interior loadbearing walls, as some may be loadbearing, but still unsuitable in an exterior wall. One of the best ways to help the environment is to source materials locally; transport costs are reduced and you may be able to check production methods and the sustainability of sources.

STRENGTHENING THE STRUCTURE

Laying a block flat, rather than on its edge, can make a significant difference to a wall's strength. Some compressed earth blocks, for example, have a minimum compressive strength of 3 N/sq mm (435psi) on their edge, rising to 17 N/sq mm (2,465psi) when they are laid flat. On their edge, most loadbearing concrete blocks have a minimum compressive strength of 7 N/sq mm (1,015psi).

Combining conventional bricks and blocks with green bricks and blocks in the same structure is not recommended. While conventional bricks and concrete blocks are often combined, green blocks should be used consistently. In addition, as green blocks can vary in size dramatically, complete walls should be built with cut blocks rather than alternating sizes.

Clay brick
This is an unfired clay brick, commonly used in cobwork. They can be used for non-loadbearing walls or infills in timber-frame constructions.

Hemp block
The base material of these blocks consists of fibres from the hemp plant mixed with sand and lime.

Compressed earth block
To make this block, clay, aggregates, and water are pressed into a mould and dried. Traditional blocks of this nature, such as adobe blocks, were sun-dried, but modern versions are mechanically compressed.

Extruded earth block
This block is moulded, or "extruded", into a continuous length in a machine, and then cut into smaller blocks.

Cob block
This sun-dried block is made from mud held together by straw, and is normally used to repair existing cob buildings.

Clay plasterboard block
As the name suggests, this type of block has been made from clay and recycled plasterboard. It uses a thin-joint mortar system and may be laid on its edge or on the flat for greater loadbearing strength.

Fired aerated clay block
Although these bricks are fired, their mode of manufacture uses a relatively small amount of energy, lowering their "embodied" carbon dioxide content.

Straw bale
Made from the dry stalks of cereal plants, such as barley and wheat, straw is an excellent insulator, and consequently a good material for blocks.

STORING GREEN MATERIALS

Care must be taken when storing green materials. Most do not store well outside so should be kept inside. If they must be stored in the open air, they should be covered accordingly. Although some blocks can form part of a rendered exterior wall, they will be susceptible to rain damage prior to rendering. It is important to note that most green blocks and bricks cannot be used below the damp-proof course level.

FINISHES

The most common finishes for green materials are lime-based. Lime mortars, renders, and plasters are considered greener than modern cement and gypsum-based plasters because, although their manufacture gives off carbon dioxide, it is reabsorbed as the lime sets, making it a carbon-neutral product. Lime is also recyclable and biodegradable.

It is important to ascertain the type of mortar needed for a particular green block. While it will usually be lime-based, the particular type and strength of a mortar may be crucial.

Non-hydraulic lime

This mortar is so called because it does not harden underwater. It is produced by heating a pure form of limestone to a very high temperature, burning off carbon dioxide and leaving quicklime. This is then mixed with rainwater to form lime putty – a process known as "slaking".

Lime putty
Left to mature for a number of months, lime putty is the raw material in renders and mortars that are completely lime-based. It is mixed with sand to create mortar.

Non-hydraulic hydrated lime
Sold in bagged powder form, this has had less water added to it during production than lime putty (see above). It is considered inferior to mature lime putty.

Hydraulic lime

This mortar is produced by heating up a less pure form of limestone than that used for non-hydraulic hydrated lime. The impurities found in the mix include materials such as clay.

Hydraulic lime
The manufacturing process for hydraulic lime means that it dries to a more hardened finish than non-hydraulic lime. It it is breathable, but is much less flexible than non-hydraulic lime.

Additives

Sometimes small amounts of portland cement are added to lime, to hasten the setting processs. Purists do not do this, due to the possibility of segregation occuring as the mixture dries. Animal hair – typically horse or goat – can be added, as can modern, fibrous, synthetic products. Minerals called pozzolans, which allow the mortar to harden quicker, are also used.

Horse hair
For plasterwork, horse or goat hair may be introduced to the mix. This lessens the chances of cracking in mortar that is still drying, or mortar that is prone to flexing.

WORKING SAFELY

When mixing lime and water, be sure to add the lime to the water, and not the other way round. This is particularly important when making lime putty from quicklime, as there can be a risk of explosion. Lime is a skin, eye, and respiratory irritant, so wear protective clothing.

BUILDING BOARDS

The following examples are greener alternatives to the more conventional types of building board shown on pp.72–73. They are made from natural products, so they are eco-friendly and suited for use in conjunction with the other materials shown on these pages. All these products are 100-per-cent biodegradable, avoiding the disposal problems of plasterboard, which is often left in landfill. However, recycling options are being developed, such as clay plasterboard blocks (see opposite).

Plasterboard alternatives

Clay board
The primary component of this board is clay, often bound together with reed and hessian. It offers a direct alternative to gypsum-based plasterboard. Clay board is heavier and thicker than plasterboard, and is best cut using a saw or jigsaw.

Straw board
Manufactured from straw, and free of formaldehyde, straw board can be used for flooring, or wall applications.

Reed board
This is a plasterboard alternative made from natural reeds laid side-by-side and bound together to form a rigid board structure.

Reed on a roll
A more flexible version of reed board, this is ideal for ceiling applications and walls on which the studwork may be undulating. This makes it ideal for use in restoration work on walls that have bowed over time.

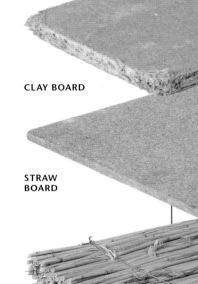

CLAY BOARD

STRAW BOARD

REED BOARD

FLEXIBLE REED BOARD

WOODEN LATH

The forerunner to plasterboard, wooden laths are nailed to studwork and used as a base for the application of lime render. They are extremely eco-friendly as they are produced from a sustainable resource. Sweet chestnut and oak laths are typically hand-made using traditional methods.

Production methods
Both sweet chestnut and oak laths have a rough key because they are made by hand. This makes them ideal for use on ceilings. In contrast, larch laths are machine-made and square-edged, which makes them better suited for use on walls.

SWEET CHESTNUT LATH

OAK LATH

LARCH LATH

When working on any project, consider where old materials may be reused. Timber, and particularly structural timber – the sort found in an old stud wall, for example – is usually suitable for reuse as long as it is sound. However, sheet materials are generally quite difficult to reuse, and plasterboard is hard to recycle. Wooden sheet materials may also be cut to shapes that make them unsuitable for a future project.

VISITING RECLAMATION YARDS

Increasingly, many old and discarded items are becoming stylish centrepieces in modern renovations. As a result, reclamation yards are now big business and, while this means bargains are harder to come by, the increased competition has led to some stabilization of prices. Positive consequences of this expansion are greater choice and the potential to compare products in different yards. When visiting a reclamation yard, it often pays to go with an open mind as they are places where inspiration can strike. However, it is also important to be as certain as you can that the products you buy fulfil their specifications.

RECYCLING MATERIALS

Recycling building materials is not only very green, in some cases, it can be financially beneficial. The most notable example of this is the current enthusiasm for old metal fittings and fixtures, such as copper pipes, brass plumbing fittings, lead pipes, and flashings. All materials of this kind can be taken to scrap yards, where they are weighed and, from this measurement, a price is calculated. Although the price obviously varies, in the current market all these materials seem to be increasing in value. It is always best to take a sizeable pile of goods to the yard, as they may only pay for items over certain weights. Try to arrange the goods by type, as the more sorted the metal, the higher the price received – the price paid for a mixed load of metal will be far less than for metal that has already been sorted into different categories. Other goods that can be recycled, but are unlikely to fetch a price, are plastics such as PVC, rainwater goods, and wood. These can be taken to a recycling centre. Remember that if you are carrying out major works, any rubble or building spoil could potentially be recycled directly as hardcore.

Copper pipe
Metal fittings and fixtures are prime recycling candidates.

▋▋ DE-NAILING TIMBER

Structural timber that you take down – such as joists – may be used in a future project, as long as it has retained its structural integrity. In many cases, the only work required is the removal of a few nails.

A

B

Use a pry bar for large nails, or a claw hammer for smaller nails, to prise them out of the surface of the wood.

Older, rusted nails may snap off on removal. Use a hammer and punch to knock the broken shaft of the nail below the wood's surface.

▋▋ DE-ROTTING AN OLD BEAM WITH AN AXE

Old timbers often have areas of woodworm or rot. However, once the worst areas are removed, the remaining timber is normally structurally very sound. The shapes produced can add great character to a project if beams are left exposed.

A

B

An axe or hatchet is the ideal tool for cutting along the edge of old beams to remove woodworm or rot.

Once the worst is removed, brush down and treat the wood to protect it and kill any woodworm. For green treatments, see p.290.

▋▋ REFURBISHING FLOORBOARDS

Old floorboards can break when lifted and, like other wood, are susceptible to infestation. Edges are especially prone to damage, so to make a board reusable you need to trim the edge back a little. Accuracy is required, so a circular saw or router is ideal.

A

B

Use a straight cutter and guide, or clamp a piece of batten to the plank to act as a guide for the router (for more on router use, see pp.66–67).

Simply run the router along the edge, trimming a few millimetres (fractions of an inch). Sanding will be required for a smooth finish.

▋▋ CLEANING BRICKS

After demolition, bricks may be reused, but in most cases they will need cleaning, as old mortar tends to stick to their surface. Soft mortar (lime-based) may scrape off with a trowel, but for persistent lumps, and cement-based mortars, a lump hammer and bolster chisel will be required.

A

B

Position the brick on a flat surface and gradually knock off the mortar. Be sure to wear protective gloves and goggles for this procedure.

Wipe off any residue with a sponge and warm water, and you will be left with bricks that are now ready for reuse.

THE RECLAMATION INDUSTRY

Reclamation is big business and, with the increased interest in environmentalism, the industry has expanded significantly. You should bear in mind that approaching a reclamation yard from a buyer's perspective is very different to approaching it as a seller. It is certainly possible to sell goods to these yards, but you are unlikely to receive as high a price as you would selling to a private buyer.

Consequently, you should not be surprised to find similar items to yours being sold for much higher prices than you are being offered. Condition of goods is also very important for both a buyer and a seller; buyers should be aware that slightly damaged items tend to be competitively priced, and may be reasonably straightforward to repair. Keep an open mind, as you are unlikely to find exactly what you're looking for.

COMMON RECLAMATION-YARD ITEMS

Reclamation yards may be specialist, or more general in their stock, but it is always sensible to expect the unexpected. Most of the larger reclamation companies now have websites, but you would be well advised to inspect the goods before purchase wherever possible. The following categories of materials frequently appear in reclamation yards.

Category of materials	Example items	Comments
FLOORING	Tiles, flagstones, floorboards	All these items are subject to a reasonable amount of waste, such as split or damaged boards and chipped tiles. Adjust your quantity calculation requirements accordingly to compensate for this
FIREPLACES	Mantelpieces, firebacks, complete fireplaces, hearths	When buying a complete fireplace, make sure all items are present. For period fireplaces, check that tiles are original and that they fit the surround. Look out for cracks or chips in stone components
STRUCTURAL MATERIALS	Bricks, natural stone, beams, joists	Condition and grade of stone or bricks is important – are there enough and are they suitable for your needs? Wooden items must be checked for condition, such as rot or insect infestation.
DECORATIVE MOULDINGS	Wooden panelling, handrails, balusters, decorative plasterwork	Condition must be thoroughly checked. Be certain of your size requirements. Reclaimed plasterwork is often very delicate and prone to damage
BATHROOM FURNITURE AND FITTINGS	Roll-top baths, basins, WCs and cisterns, shower trays, taps	These items may need lots of restoration, so think carefully before purchase. Taps will almost certainly need new washers and a general overhaul to restore to good working order
ROOFING	Clay tiles, stone tiles, slates, chimney pots, ridge and hip tiles	Check colouring, especially if trying to match with existing roof – also check that nibs have not broken off tiles. When buying a batch of roman tiles, ensure all profiles match – there are subtle variations
DOORS AND WINDOWS	Internal doors, external doors, windows, door and window fittings	Check doors and windows are "square" – old doors are often warped. Stripped doors may also be loose at the joints. Check for rot. Make sure fittings already work or are repairable
PLUMBING ACCESSORIES	Radiators, towel rails	Bear in mind that valves may require changing. There will often be size-compatibility issues with new fittings. Radiators will require thorough flushing out and possibly sand-blasting
RAINWATER GOODS	Cast-iron guttering, downpipes, hoppers, outlets	Check general condition, as old cast-iron guttering cracks and rusts – both of which can put it beyond repair. Check for correct size of fittings and brackets for installation
GARDEN ARCHITECTURE	Capping and coping stones, ornamental stonework, paving slabs	Carry out general damage inspection, and check size variations. Different slab depths will make laying them much more difficult

ALTERATIONS AND REPAIRS

The illustrations shown here demonstrate the most common types of house structure. Variations to these basic categories often arise from architectural innovation, using new materials or using established materials in new ways. Concrete and steel, for instance, are often used as alternatives to traditional masonry construction. Details for identification, construction, or repair of individual elements can be found in the relevant subsections.

LOADBEARING AND NON-LOADBEARING WALLS

The walls in any house can be divided into loadbearing or non-loadbearing. Loadbearing walls, as well as supporting their own weight, carry some of the load of other parts of the building, such as the roof and floors. Non-loadbearing walls support only their own weight, and are not structural components of the house. Always assume that all exterior walls are loadbearing (even though, in the majority of cases, it is only the internal leaf of a cavity wall that is loadbearing). It can be difficult to identify the other loadbearing walls in a house, but establishing whether a particular wall is loadbearing or not is vital when planning renovation work. The subject is discussed in more detail on pp.102–103.

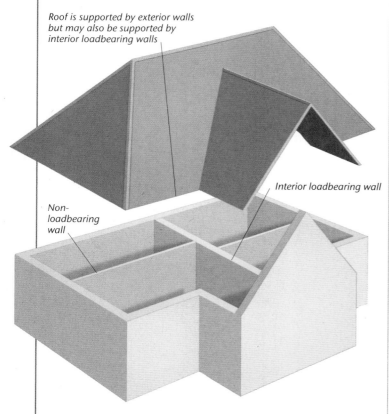

Roof is supported by exterior walls but may also be supported by interior loadbearing walls

Interior loadbearing wall

Non-loadbearing wall

Basic features of a house
Loadbearing walls transmit the weight of roof and floors to the ground, non-loadbearing walls act only as partitions. Foundations spread weight. Within these basic areas of construction there are many variations according to architectural preference and need.

TYPES OF CONSTRUCTION

Three main types of roof, four types of wall, and four types of foundation are shown here. They may be used in any combination so different foundations, walls, and roofs can appear together.

Types of foundation

Foundations are the supportive structures on which all houses are built. The type used depends on a property's age, and the type of ground on which it stands.

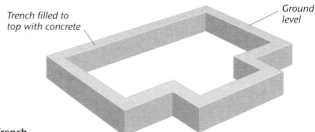

Trench filled to top with concrete

Ground level

Trench
Exterior loadbearing walls sit on channels filled with concrete. Any internal loadbearing walls may also be built up from trench foundations. The depth of the foundation will depend on the geology of the underlying ground, and the size of the building.

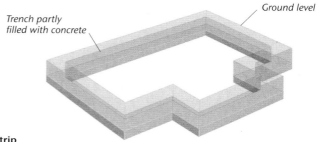

Trench partly filled with concrete

Ground level

Strip
Similar to trench foundations, but less concrete is poured into the channels, so the walls begin below what will be ground level. These walls may be constructed from the same bricks or blocks that will form the main wall, or from different blocks rising to just above ground level.

Ground level

Raft
A concrete pad, reinforced with steel, covers the area on which the house sits. In some cases the edges of the raft, directly below the exterior walls, will be thicker than the rest of the raft. Modern raft foundations are well insulated.

Ground level

Pile
The walls are built on a concrete beam. This rests on reinforced concrete, or steel beams, drilled into the ground. The depth and frequency of beams depend very much on the type of ground below the building, and the building size. Piles may also be required for internal loadbearing walls.

Types of wall

The four main types of house construction are generally defined by the way in which the exterior walls have been built. Much more detail about the many variations on these basic categories can be found over the next few pages.

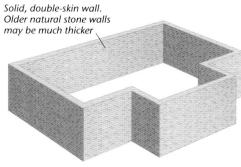

Solid, double-skin wall. Older natural stone walls may be much thicker

Traditional solid masonry

Older houses tend to have solid exterior walls. Internal loadbearing walls are usually also masonry, but may be timber. Ground floors may be concrete or suspended wood, and very old properties may have traditional floor coverings such as flagstones laid directly on a soil base. Upper floors are usually of timber. Most will not have a damp-proof course (DPC).

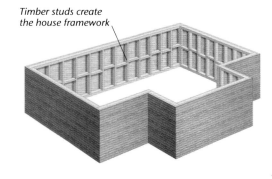

Timber studs create the house framework

Timber

Exterior walls have a timber inner leaf, and an outer leaf that may be masonry or timber. If the outer leaf is masonry, metal ties attach it to the inner leaf. Internal walls, whether loadbearing or not, are timber. Upper floors are timber, but the ground floor may be timber or concrete. Newer houses have a DPC. For more on timber-frame constructions see pp.92–93.

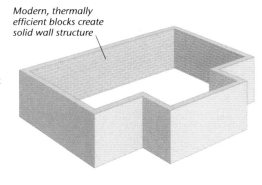

Modern, thermally efficient blocks create solid wall structure

Modern solid masonry

Some newer houses have solid exterior walls, often built with different materials to their traditional counterparts. Internal walls may be timber or masonry, or there may be some of each. Floors, on all levels, may be concrete or timber. All walls should have a DPC.

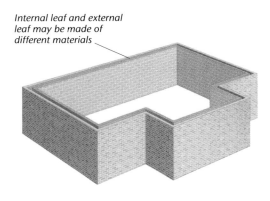

Internal leaf and external leaf may be made of different materials

Masonry with cavity

Exterior walls have an inner and an outer leaf, held together by metal ties with a cavity between them. The leaves may be made of the same or different materials. Internal walls and floors may be masonry or timber. Most will have a DPC.

Types of roof

Most roofs are angled to divert rainwater away from a house. The internal supporting frame is timber-based. The intersection between separate pitched roofs is achieved by forming valleys between each structure. Pitched roofs are commonly tiled, although other roofing materials may be used. Flat roofs can also be covered in a variety of materials. The line along which a pitched or a flat roof meets a wall is known as an abutment, and both valleys and abutments require some form of flashing to create a waterproof join. See pp.196–213 for more information on roofs.

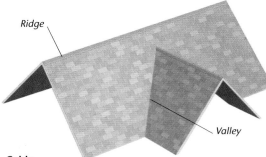

Ridge

Valley

Gable

The gable roof is characterized by the triangular wall shape formed where the pitched roof surfaces meet along an apex known as a ridge. This design creates a greater loft area than a comparable hipped roof design.

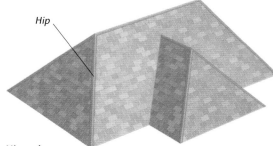

Hip

Hipped

On a hipped roof, the gable is effectively cut back at ridge level to provide a triangular sloping roof. The angled ridge that joins this section with the main roof is called a hip.

Flat

A flat roof looks level, but has a slight pitch to allow water to run off the surface. This design is often used on ground-floor extensions, but may form the main roof structure for some houses.

There are many different ways to build an eco-house, just as there are many different structures for most modern conventional houses. Determining which is the best (and greenest) option is a matter for debate, but architectural and personal preference, geographic location, current trends and, of course, cost all play an important part. Some of the most traditional materials and methods are outlined here, along with more recent developments.

AN UNGREEN MEANS TO A GREEN END

There is often a conflict of interest when it comes to determining what is and what isn't "green". While the structural elements of an eco-house may ultimately perform in an energy-efficient way, their initial production may involve the use of materials or techniques that are far from ecologically sound. A house constructed entirely from poured concrete, for example, with thick, well-insulated walls, is a green option in the long term. However, the initial outlay of energy to produce the concrete in the first place is high – and consequently very ungreen.

MIXING GREEN AND CONVENTIONAL MATERIALS

Building an entirely green house or renovating an existing structure to completely green specifications is rarely a practical option. Instead, it is more likely that a green solution is reached by combining green and conventional methods. When considering a green new-build, such as a straw-bale house for example (see pp.118–21), using a solid concrete foundation could be the best option because the risk of subsidence and egress of moisture is greatly reduced. Equally, with a renovation project, using thermally efficient blocks for an extension will improve the green credentials of a house, even though much of the existing structure may be made from less green alternatives.

TYPES OF FOUNDATION

Many green homes are built on conventional foundations (see p.90), predominantly because they offer a sound defence against subsidence and damp (see above). However, it is still possible to use less conventional foundations for a green home. The two examples shown here have been used successfully in straw-bale constructions. The use of rammed earth held in place by old car tyres, and compacted rubble reinforced with steel rods, clearly demonstrate that concrete is by no means the only material capable of providing a solid foundation for a house structure.

Rammed earth
As the name suggests, rammed-earth foundations consist of compacted subsoil. For the rammed earth to form a solid base for the structure's walls, it needs to be contained within an effective mould. A modern example of a type of mould is shown here – the compacted earth is being contained within old car tyres.

OVERVIEW OF A RAMMED-EARTH TYRE FOUNDATION

Rubber tyres filled with rammed earth

Ground level

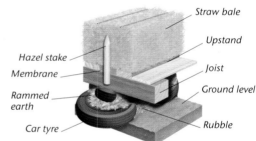

CROSS-SECTION OF A RAMMED-EARTH TYRE FOUNDATION

Straw bale
Upstand
Hazel stake
Membrane
Joist
Rammed earth
Ground level
Car tyre
Rubble

Rubble foundations
In this example, a trench is filled with compacted rubble or stone. Some blockwork or natural stone is required above ground level to provide a solid base for the structure. Rubble foundations form an ideal base for a straw-bale home, as reinforced steel bars can be buried into the rubble for extra strength and support.

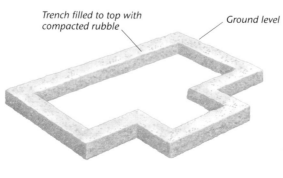

Trench filled to top with compacted rubble

Ground level

OVERVIEW OF A RUBBLE FOUNDATION

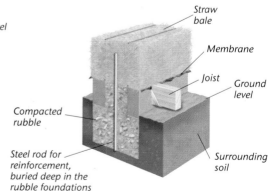

CROSS-SECTION OF A RUBBLE FOUNDATION

Straw bale
Membrane
Joist
Ground level
Compacted rubble
Steel rod for reinforcement, buried deep in the rubble foundations
Surrounding soil

TYPES OF ROOF

In a structural sense, most green roofs follow the same design as conventional roofs (see p.91), with the main difference being that any materials must be obtained from sustainable sources. Wood is the most common component and should be sourced from responsibly managed forests (see p.75). Equally, roof coverings must be green – wooden shingles are a clear green alternative to concrete tiles, and thatch is a roofing material with excellent green credentials.

Green living roof

A green living roof is a truly "green" option as the covered surface consists of plant matter. A living roof offers good insulation, retains a high percentage of rainwater (reducing stormwater run-off), and provides a habitat for wildlife. However, the main roof structure must be strong enough to support its weight – a key concern, especially if considering a retrospective fit.

Growing medium

Drainage and root barrier

Insulation layer

Sedum-planted roof surface

Structural support

Roofing membrane

Membrane protection and root barrier

Extensive green living roof
A green living roof may be described as "extensive" (see diagram above) or "intensive". An extensive roof is typically planted with sedum, which requires a low-level of maintenance for use on often inaccessible roofs. An intensive roof is similar in nature to a roof garden: it has good access and a greater variety of plants. Higher maintenance, however, is usually required.

TYPES OF WALLS

A green structure must score highly in terms of sustainability and performance – the materials should come from a sustainable source and the building should be well-insulated. Some conventional structures (see p.91), such as modern timber-framed houses, can be considered green as long as they conform to these principles. The alternative methods described below, however, arguably come closest to the ideal of a truly green construction.

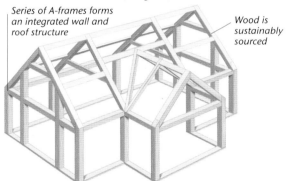

Series of A-frames forms an integrated wall and roof structure

Wood is sustainably sourced

Wood – post and beam
Large wooden members are used to create the loadbearing structure of the house. Wooden post and beam differs from a conventional timber-framed house in that the size of the members often means they form an integral part of the aesthetic finish of the house, and may be visible from the inside, outside, or both. Straw bales may be used as infill (see right).

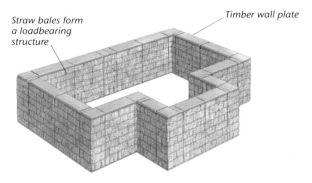

Straw bales form a loadbearing structure

Timber wall plate

Straw bale
Bales can be used as either loadbearing blocks or infill for a timber-framed house (see left). Although straw-bale constructions have been built around the globe, climate is an important consideration as it is vital that water is kept out of the structure. Straw bales are a perfect example of what is essentially a waste product being used in major construction.

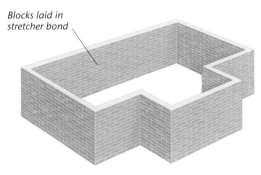

Blocks laid in stretcher bond

Earth block
After wood, earth- or soil-based structures make up the next biggest category of green structures. Compressed soil, usually in the form of blocks, is used to build the structural walls of the home. Although modern building standards question the integrity of such structures, history has shown that they can easily withstand a variety of climates.

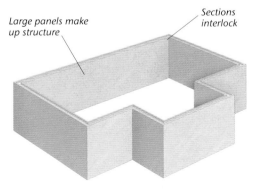

Large panels make up structure

Sections interlock

Structural insulated panel
This type of eco-house construction is an example of green building at its most developed. Highly efficient insulation is integrated into building boards to form large panels. These panels can then be clipped together in a custom-made design. Structural insulated panels may be used to form the roof structure as well as the walls of a house.

Ceilings and walls

THE WALLS AND CEILINGS OF A HOUSE ARE SOME OF ITS MOST IMPORTANT STRUCTURAL ELEMENTS, BUT ALSO OFFER CONSIDERABLE SCOPE FOR CREATIVITY. THE PAGES IN THIS SECTION WILL HELP YOU UNDERSTAND THE STRUCTURE OF CEILINGS AND WALLS, SO THAT YOU CAN WORK OUT WHICH OPTIONS ARE MOST SUITABLE WHEN UNDERTAKING REPAIR OR ALTERATION WORK.

TYPES OF CONSTRUCTION

A knowledge of how ceilings and walls are put together is important to fully understand the structure of your home. In the most general terms, ceilings either have a timber structure or a concrete one. Walls are either cavity or single-skin, and may be loadbearing or non-loadbearing. In addition, there is a variety of ways that ceilings and walls may be finished, and there are different combinations of materials that can be used to achieve these finishes.

CEILING COMPONENTS

The illustrations opposite demonstrate the basic structures of timber and concrete ceilings. Beneath these are shown the typical finishes used on their lower surfaces. Timber ceilings are traditional but still widely used. A framework of timber joists provides support for the floor above, and a surface for attachment of the ceiling finish below. Concrete ceilings can take a variety of forms. They are more often found in modern buildings, and their popularity has grown with the general use of concrete in the building industry.

Insulation and finishes

A wide range of materials can be used in finishing either a ceiling or wall – plasterboard can vary in thickness and density, and can also be purchased with useful retardant properties to make the surface more resilient, or to adhere to building and safety regulations. Different types of plasterboard are explained on p.72. Insulation is not shown in the illustrations here or overleaf, for reasons of clarity. However in reality many ceilings and walls will incorporate insulation. Choices and types of insulation are covered in detail on pp.352–63.

UNDERSTANDING BEAMS AND JOISTS

Beams and joists are essentially the same, but they tend to be called "joists" when they are relatively close together, as in a ceiling. Traditionally, they are made of wood, but modern types are often made of steel, and are known as "RSJs" – rolled steel joists. Wooden beams are often left uncovered to form part of a room's decorative aspect, although they can be clad with plasterboard and then plastered. Old beams may even be found beneath lath and plaster.

RSJs are usually boxed in with plasterboard and then covered with finishing plaster. To provide fixing points for plasterboard, wedge noggings (small vertical lengths of wood) are fitted inside an RSJ. Lintels look similar to beams, but perform a different function: they support the weight of a wall above an opening such as a window or door. They come in many materials and strengths, designed for a variety of uses.

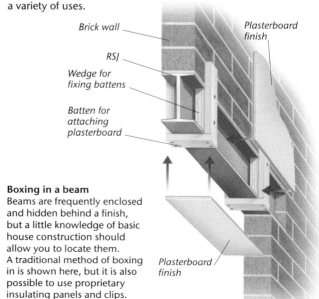

Brick wall

Plasterboard finish

RSJ

Wedge for fixing battens

Batten for attaching plasterboard

Plasterboard finish

Boxing in a beam
Beams are frequently enclosed and hidden behind a finish, but a little knowledge of basic house construction should allow you to locate them. A traditional method of boxing in is shown here, but it is also possible to use proprietary insulating panels and clips.

TIMBER CEILING

Timber ceiling and finishes
The type of wood and dimensions of joists will depend on the date of the ceiling and its functon – ceilings with a floor above must be more substantial. Noggings at right angles to the joists connect them and increase integrity.

Plasterboard and plaster
Sheets of plasterboard are fixed directly to the joists, the joints are taped with scrim, and the whole surface is covered with finishing plaster (see pp.134–35).

Tape

Fixing hole filler

Dry-lined plasterboard
The joints between sheets of plasterboard are taped, fixing holes and joints are then filled with jointing compound and sanded smooth (see pp.136–37).

Wooden cladding
Boards are attached directly to the joists, at right angles to them, to give this wooden ceiling finish.

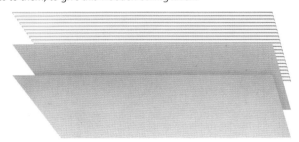

Lath and plaster
This is an old-fashioned construction. Thin, wooden laths sit closely together beneath the joists, and at right angles to them, and are covered with traditional lime plaster.

CONCRETE CEILING

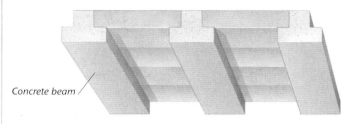

Concrete beam

Concrete ceiling and finishes
There are several ways of using concrete to create a ceiling, but this beam-and-block structure is a common system.

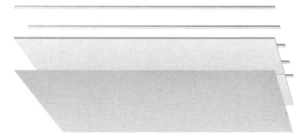

Battens, plasterboard, and plaster
Wooden battens are fixed to the concrete, and board attached. Joints are taped, and the whole plastered.

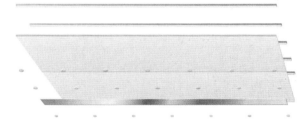

Battens and dry-lined plasterboard
Board is attached to a batten framework, and then treated like dry-lined plasterboard (see left).

Channel

Metal channels, plasterboard, and plaster
In this case, metal channels perform the same function as the battens in the previous example.

Metal channels and dry-lined plasterboard
Again, the channels perform the role of battens. The plasterboard is then dry lined.

TIMBER-FRAMED WALLS

Even if a house has masonry on the outside, its structure may be timber, as shown below. Also, a masonry house may well contain some timber interior walls, especially if these are not loadbearing.

Exterior timber-framed walls

Timber-framed exterior walls all have an internal layer made of timber, and an external layer that may be timber or masonry. There is a cavity between the two layers. The external face of the timber frame is covered with plywood sheathing for extra strength and rigidity. Most will have a DPC.

Interior timber walls

These are the walls that partition rooms. They may sometimes be filled with insulation. They may be loadbearing or non-loadbearing. These walls are a good choice in a renovation project as they are straightforward to construct. For more information, see pp.104–09.

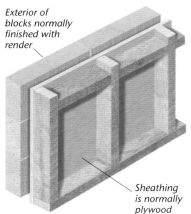

Exterior of blocks normally finished with render

Sheathing is normally plywood

Timber and block
The interior timber layer is exactly the same as that on a brick-clad wall, but the exterior layer is constructed with modern blocks instead of bricks.

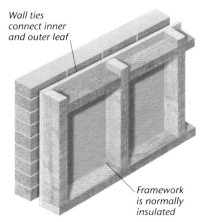

Wall ties connect inner and outer leaf

Framework is normally insulated

Timber and brick
The interior timber frame is covered on its external face with plywood for rigidity, and the exterior layer is built of brick. There is a cavity between the two.

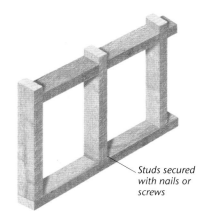

Studs secured with nails or screws

Stud wall
This is an easy-to-make non-loadbearing partition consisting of a timber framework which can take any of the finishes listed below.

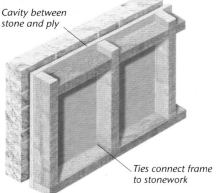

Cavity between stone and ply

Ties connect frame to stonework

Timber and stone
An exterior layer of natural stone is paired with an interior timber frame exactly like the one in all other timber-framed exterior walls.

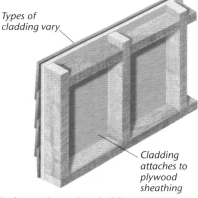

Types of cladding vary

Cladding attaches to plywood sheathing

Timber and wooden cladding
The timber exterior layer partners an interior identical to the other timber-framed walls. Cladding is normally fixed to counterbattens to create the cavity.

Studs secured with drywall screws

Metal stud wall
This modern variation of the stud wall uses metal channels instead of timber studs to form the framework.

TIMBER WALL FINISHES

All of these finishes can be used on the interior face of an exterior wall, or on either side of an internal wall. They all need a decorative layer such as paint or wallpaper, or in the case of wood cladding, perhaps a natural wood finish.

Lath, render, and plaster
In this traditional wall covering, timber laths (narrow strips of timber) are attached to the timber wall frame. They are then covered with several coats of lime plaster.

Plastered plasterboard
Straight-edged plasterboard is attached to the timber frame. Joints are taped with scrim, and the surface is plastered (see pp.108 and 134–35).

Dry-lined plasterboard
Taper-edged plasterboard is used to cover the frame. The gullies left by the tapers are taped and filled with jointing compound to create a smooth surface for decoration (see p.137).

Wooden cladding
Cladding, often in board form, is attached directly to the frame. Depending on the material used, it may or may not need decoration after fitting.

Dry partition plasterboard
Plasterboard panels are secured between studs (spaced further apart than shown above). The finish depends on whether the panels have tapered or non-tapered edges. Dry partition walls are non-loadbearing.

MASONRY WALLS

Although this information relates to houses, it also applies to outbuildings. Whereas a house may have thick exterior walls, an outbuilding may have thin, undecorated walls (blocks may be left bare in a garage, for example).

Exterior masonry walls

These are usually made up of two layers of masonry. The two layers of a cavity wall are held together by metal wall ties. The cavity may contain insulation. Some have a damp-proof course (DPC).

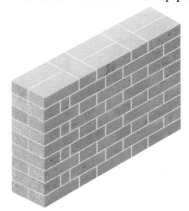

Solid brick
The internal and external layers are made of brick, with no cavity between the layers of masonry.

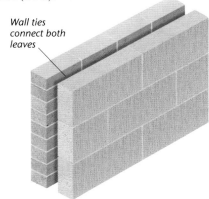

Wall ties connect both leaves

Brick and block with cavity
The external brick layer provides the finished exterior look. The internal layer is of blocks, and requires a finish (see right).

Solid block
A modern construction that uses thick, thermally efficient blocks to create a solid wall.

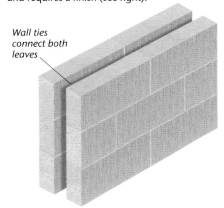

Wall ties connect both leaves

Block and block with cavity
Both layers are made of modern blocks, so both the interior and exterior faces need finishing (see right for finishes).

Solid stone
This may use one or two layers of stone – the space between layers is often filled with broken stone and mortar. Sometimes the external face is stone and the internal brick.

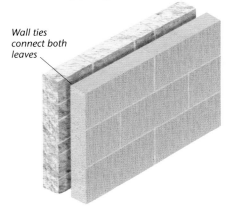

Wall ties connect both leaves

Stone and block with cavity
An external layer of natural stone provides the finished look, while the internal layer is of blocks that need finishing (see right).

Interior masonry walls

These are the walls inside a building, dividing it into rooms. They may be loadbearing or non-loadbearing.

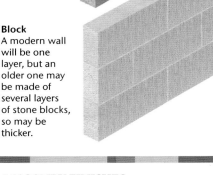

Brick
Modern ones are built of a single layer of bricks, though older ones may have two layers.

Block
A modern wall will be one layer, but an older one may be made of several layers of stone blocks, so may be thicker.

MASONRY FINISHES

Any of these finishes can go on any masonry wall, whether it is the internal layer of an exterior wall or either side of an interior wall.

Render and plaster
A coat of render or undercoat is covered with a layer of finishing plaster to give a smooth wall surface (see pp.134–35) – getting this right requires considerable skill.

Dry-lined plasterboard
Taper-edged plasterboard can be attached to a wall. The indent left between the tapers is taped, and filled with a filling compound (see p.137). The compound is applied in a number of layers before being sanded smooth with the surrounding plasterboard surface. The whole wall surface is then coated with proprietary board sealant before further decoration. The plasterboard may be attached to the wall in a number of ways (see p.136).

Plastered plasterboard
Straight-edged plasterboard can be attached to a wall, with the joints between boards taped with scrim, and then plastered. The plasterboard may be attached to the masonry using dabs of adhesive, with a timber-battened frame, or using metal channels (see p.136). This avoids the need for render or undercoat, but still demands great skill in plastering to achieve the top layer.

Wooden cladding
A frame of timber battens can be attached to the masonry, forming a base for the attachment of timber cladding.

The following pages deal with wall structure in its greenest form, although it is worth bearing in mind that, with proper insulation, the more conventional wall structures shown on pp.96–97 are generally thermally efficient. Consequently, these pages focus on environmentally friendly methods of manufacture, sustainability, and biodegradability, all of which increase a wall's green credentials. The principal types of green wall construction are shown below.

BENEFITS OF STRAW BALES

Straw bales, a waste product of the food production process, can be used to build a green and cost-effective wall. A 450-mm (18-in) thick bale has a U-value of 0.13 W/sq m (brick cavity walls have U-values of approximately 1.4 W/sq m) making straw an extremely thermally efficient choice. The simplicity with which bales can be cut and moulded into shapes makes them a usefully flexible material. Rendering will leave them as fireproof as most wooden structures, while their compactness, and the lack of any viable food supply, make it difficult for vermin to flourish in the structure.

TRADITIONAL GREEN WALL STRUCTURE

These structures return to the basics of material use; despite their simplicity, however, there is plenty of evidence to suggest that these building techniques are successful. The materials used in these constructions tend to occur naturally, dispensing with energy-hungry manufacturing processes.

STRAW-BALE WALL STRUCTURE

Straw-bale wall structures are a development of traditional techniques (see left). They do, however, still use natural materials as the main part of the wall, with very few man-made components. There are different techniques of construction, with the two main types shown here, although hybrids of these examples do exist.

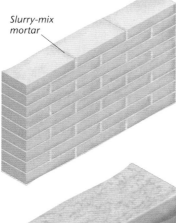

Compressed earth
Also known as adobe, blocks are laid in rows, and bonded together in a stretcher bond (running bond) with mortar constructed of a slurry mix made from the basic block material.

Slurry-mix mortar

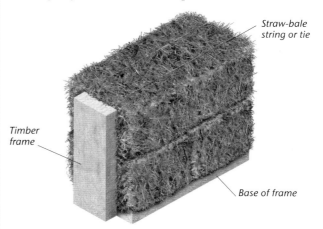

Straw-bale string or tie

Timber frame

Base of frame

Straw bale – post-and-beam structure
In this structure, straw is used to fill a loadbearing wooden frame. The frame is traditionally a post-and-beam structure, although modern alternatives include engineered-wood and planed-timber.

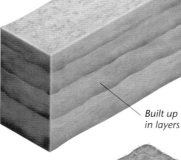

Rammed earth
Rammed earth differs from the compressed block (above) in that formwork is used to create a mould for the wall. Therefore, the wall is effectively a continuous mud form.

Built up in layers

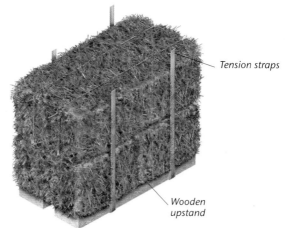

Tension straps

Wooden upstand

Cob
With a cob wall, earth is mixed with a binding product, such as straw, and is piled and moulded into a wall structure. These walls are typically much wider at the base than the top.

Wider base

Straw bale – Nebraskan
In this method, the straw itself is used as the loadbearing material and supports the roof. Metal or wooden bars are used to lend the wall solidity.

INTERIOR WALLS

The interior walls of an eco-friendly home may be constructed using similar materials to the exterior walls or – as with conventional building – alternatives can be used. For example, a solid masonry house construction may have interior metal-framed stud walls, while a straw-bale house may have internal walls constructed from wooden studwork. The choice often rests on the creation of as much internal space as possible. Some straw-bale houses do have internal straw-bale walls, but greater space can be achieved with much thinner stud walling. For internal walls, straw bales can also be positioned on their edges to provide more space.

MODERN GREEN WALL STRUCTURE

The theory behind traditional green walls has been technologically modernized, meaning that these ancient techniques are now in commercial production. In most examples, the source material is exactly the same, but there are some examples of recycled materials being used to create green blocks that are then built up in much the same way as their more ancient equivalents.

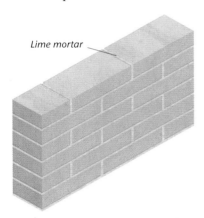

Lime mortar

Recycled block
Most closely related to a compressed earth or adobe block (see opposite), these are laid in much the same way, using a running bond, and may be loadbearing or not depending on the positioning of the block.

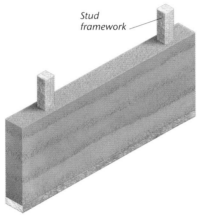

Stud framework

Green infill
Materials such as hemp are used to fill a wooden frame. Similar to a post-and-beam straw-bale structure (see opposite), the hemp may be in block form or cast in a similar way to rammed earth (see opposite).

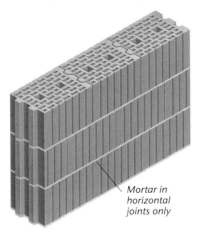

Mortar in horizontal joints only

Aerated clay block
A thin-bed mortar system is used, but only horizontally. The vertical joints interlock, which makes construction very straightforward.

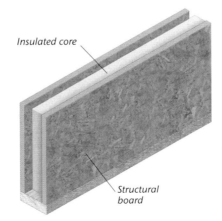

Insulated core

Structural board

Structural Insulated Panel (SIP)
This is a modern construction that uses large manufactured panels to create the wall. Insulating material is compressed between two building boards to create a thermally efficient structure. Some panel systems are made of very green components, such as compressed straw.

WALL FINISHES

The organic nature of green wall construction means it is important that any internal or external finish allows moisture to dry out through the wall surface. External coverings are most important, as they protect the structure from the elements. Lime products usually make up the main constituent of these renders or plasters (see p.85).

Applying lime finish

A three-coat system of lime render or plaster is normally sufficient, and should be applied in the following manner:

■ Apply an initial coat (the "scratch coat") roughly 10mm (⅜in) in depth. For the technique for scratching the surface, see p.133. Leave the scratch coat to dry for 2–3 days, then wet it in preparation for applying the next coat (the "float coat"). If hair is added to the mix, a longer drying time is required – especially on internal walls, which may need 4–5 days.
■ The float coat (made from the same mix as the scratch coat but with no hair added) should be slightly thinner than the scratch coat, and should provide a more even surface. Do not scratch the float coat. Leave external walls to dry for another 2–3 days, or internal walls for 4–5 days, before applying the top coat.
■ Always dampen the float coat before applying the top coat. Top-coat plaster should consist of lime putty mixed with very fine sand, rather than the coarser sand commonly used for render and interior scratch coats.
■ When applying the putty, ascertain the suction properties of the background wall – very dry block surfaces should be wetted before render is applied. In the case of some rough surfaces, such as straw, it may be best to press the scratch-coat render on by hand (wearing gloves), as traditional plastering floats can be difficult to use on such surfaces.

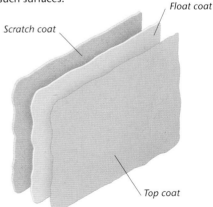

Float coat

Scratch coat

Top coat

Lime layers
For most finishes, three layers are standard, but on interior walls, the top coat may in fact be two thin coats. Some manufacturers may also have their own ready-mixed systems, which involve ready-mixed base coats and finishing coats.

You may wish to install lighting, reposition a loft hatch, or replace an old ceiling that has become distorted and unsightly. Three ways of replacing a ceiling are shown here. The method chosen will depend on your particular needs and preferences. Do not plan any change without considering its structural consequences – a structural engineer can advise on whether a bowed ceiling should be completely replaced, joists and all, for instance. You may wish to take the opportunity, while redoing a ceiling, to add insulation or soundproofing (see pp.352–63). Also plan the later decoration, and use suitable plasterboard (if relevant; see pp.72 and 128–31).

THINGS TO CONSIDER

■ Remember to use a detector to check whether there are any pipes or cables beneath a surface before inserting any nails or screws.
■ Find out whether your existing ceiling is timber or concrete. If it is timber, you need to find the joists so that you can fix into them. If it is concrete, use masonry fixings and plugs.
■ If you are lowering a ceiling that features an electrical rose with a light fitting in it, simply remove the rose, extend the wire, and re-attach the rose as shown on p.447.

CUTTING A LOFT HATCH

Loft access is important for inspection purposes as well as storage. If you need to open a new hatch, perhaps because your property does not have one, or because alterations mean it needs relocating, consider how you wish to use it, as well as the safety aspects.

Positioning the access hole

Consider the angle at which a ladder will extend through the opening, if relevant, and if it will have room to fold or slide into the roof space. Make sure there will be headroom in the loft, and do not position the hatch too close to a staircase. If possible, cut into only one joist to make the opening, because the cuts weaken the structure.

Fitting a hatch and ladder

The design of the hatch itself will depend on whether you wish to use a fixed loft ladder. If you will access the loft via a stepladder, use a simple hatch resting on a section of doorstop, as shown right. If a fixed ladder is to be fitted, you may need a hinged door; check the specifications for the hatch and ladder. Follow the manufacturer's instructions to fit them.

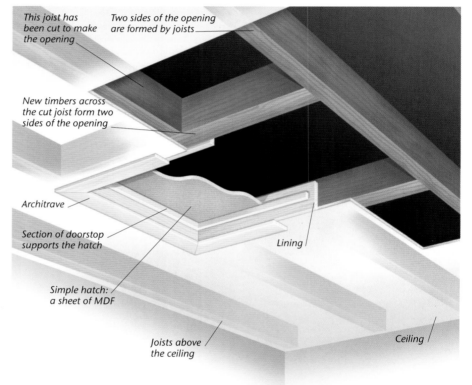

This joist has been cut to make the opening

Two sides of the opening are formed by joists

New timbers across the cut joist form two sides of the opening

Architrave

Section of doorstop supports the hatch

Simple hatch: a sheet of MDF

Lining

Joists above the ceiling

Ceiling

A simple loft hatch
This method cuts only one joist, to minimize structural weakening. The loft is accessed with a stepladder, and the hatch rests on a ledge. More information on bridging gaps is shown on p.177.

REPLACING A LATH-AND-PLASTER CEILING

If an old ceiling has become unsightly, either replace it as described here, or choose one of the options opposite (see pp.104, 108, 128–31, and 136–37 for details of plasterboard options, and pp.268–307 on decorating). Removing a ceiling creates a lot of dust and debris, so empty the room and spread dustsheets. Wear protective clothing, including a respiratory mask (a simple dust mask is not sufficient).

Removing the ceiling

Use a hammer to break away some of the plaster, and then pull away chunks by hand or with a pry bar, working your way across the ceiling. Once all the plaster is cleared, prise out any remaining nails or screws from joists with a claw hammer or pry bar. Then inspect the joists to see if they are in sound condition before applying plasterboard.

RE-ROUTING CABLES AND PIPES

Any services that run through a ceiling need to be protected from damage and supported while the ceiling is removed. They may well need to be re-routed to suit your new ceiling, but you may be unable to plan this very far in advance.

Locating services for re-routing

Switch off the electricity supply at the consumer unit and water supply at the rising main. Use a detector to locate pipes and cables, or cut a small inspection hatch and look inside the ceiling to see where services run. When removing a ceiling, proceed carefully – removal may expose some services that you hadn't previously found. Support all pipes and cables. Once the ceiling is gone and all services are clearly visible, work out the best way of dealing with them in accordance with your plans for the new ceiling and its fittings.

LOWERING A CEILING

One way of replacing an unsightly ceiling is to create a new one below the old ceiling. This avoids the mess involved in removing old plaster.

Technique

Using a spirit level, draw guide lines on the walls for the new ceiling. Fix 100 x 50-mm (4 x 2-in) rough-sawn timber along these lines, and attach joist hangers to two of these wall plates. Screw joists, also of rough-sawn timber, into the hangers. Attach noggings (strengthening timbers) between joists, to provide fixing points for plasterboard. A large span will need more noggings than a narrower span. Then attach plasterboard (see p.108).

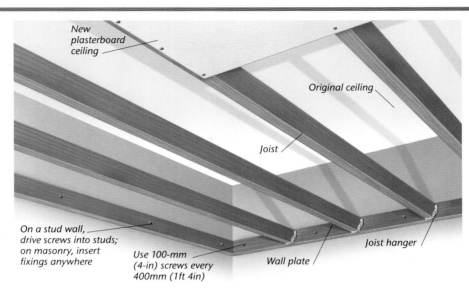

New plasterboard ceiling

Original ceiling

Joist

On a stud wall, drive screws into studs; on masonry, insert fixings anywhere

Use 100-mm (4-in) screws every 400mm (1ft 4in)

Wall plate

Joist hanger

A LOWERED CEILING

LEVELLING A CEILING WITH METAL CHANNELS

If joists sag slightly, but not enough to be replaced, achieve a level ceiling by removing the old one, and attaching a metal frame to the exposed joists. Then cover it with plasterboard.

Technique

Mark guide lines on the wall at the height that you want the ceiling, as described above (Lowering a Ceiling). Attach wall channels along the guide lines, then fix brackets to the joists, at intervals of 400mm (1ft 4in) for 2,400 x 1,200-mm (8 x 4-ft) boards. Attach channels to the brackets, and then apply plasterboard as shown on p.108, and dry line as on p.137.

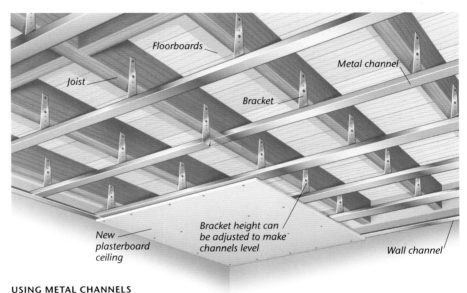

Floorboards

Metal channel

Joist

Bracket

Bracket height can be adjusted to make channels level

New plasterboard ceiling

Wall channel

USING METAL CHANNELS

FITTING A SUSPENDED CEILING

This gives a different look from other ceilings, and offers other options for lighting, as well as acoustic and thermal insulation. It involves hanging a wooden or metal grid from the ceiling, and filling it with panels.

Planning and technique

The grid may not fit exactly, so you may have to cut panels to fit around the edges. Work out the best position for the ceiling to keep even cuts on all sides. Mark a guide line on the walls (see Lowering a Ceiling, above). Attach wall angles, and insert tees (the main channels) and cross tees. Suspend tees from the ceiling above using wires that can be adjusted to keep the framework level. Then insert panels.

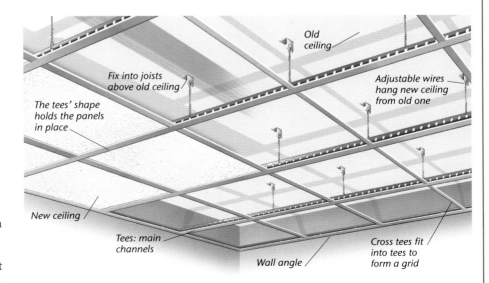

Old ceiling

Fix into joists above old ceiling

Adjustable wires hang new ceiling from old one

The tees' shape holds the panels in place

New ceiling

Tees: main channels

Wall angle

Cross tees fit into tees to form a grid

A SUSPENDED CEILING

MAKING AN OPENING IN A WALL

Before you can remove a wall or knock an opening through it, you need to know whether it is loadbearing or not. If a wall is not loadbearing, it can be removed without any need to support the structures above – though support will be needed if you remove only part of a masonry wall. If it is loadbearing, however, the structures above the wall need to be supported both during the work and afterwards with either a beam or a lintel. Take advice from a structural engineer about the level of support needed. If any pipes or cables run through the wall, think about how your plans will affect them. See p.100 for advice on re-routing services.

ASSESSING WHETHER A WALL IS LOADBEARING

A loadbearing wall is one that contributes to a house's structure, supporting the weight of floors and ceilings, and sometimes part of the roof as well. A non-loadbearing wall is merely a partition, and plays no structural role. Whether a wall is constructed of masonry or timber is irrelevant: both can be loadbearing or non-loadbearing. If floor or ceiling joists run at right angles to a wall, the wall may be supporting their weight, although this is not necessarily the case. Also, a wall on the ground floor that is directly below a wall on an upper floor suggests that the wall is loadbearing. In a loft, check whether any hangers from the roof direct weight to the top of any internal walls (see p.196). To eliminate any doubt, consult a structural engineer.

THINGS TO CONSIDER

■ These alterations are slow work, especially if you need to allow mortar to dry. Allow several days for the job.
■ Remove any doors, architraves, and skirting board, and chip off coving or any other junction coverings, before taking down a wall.
■ Remove skirting to do the work, and re-fit it after cutting the opening.
■ Removing a wall or cutting an opening is messy work. Clear the rooms affected, spread dustsheets, and cover doorways to prevent dust and debris spreading throughout the house.
■ Wear gloves, goggles, and a dust mask to cut into a masonry wall.
■ Ventilate a room by working with all the windows open, to disperse dust.
■ Some lintels are heavy, so you may need help lifting and positioning one.
■ Consider recycling the materials you remove. For instance, timber lengths taken out of a stud wall can be kept and used for other projects.

MAKING AN OPENING IN A TIMBER WALL

If you want to cut into a loadbearing wall, get a structural engineer's advice on the type and strength of lintel needed. For a non-loadbearing wall, these precautions are not necessary.

Cutting into a loadbearing wall

Props (as shown, right) are needed either side of the wall to support the ceiling, and must run at a right angle to the joists. If the joists run in the same direction as the wall, seek advice on propping from a structural enginer.

Use an existing stud to form one edge of the opening. Remove some plasterboard with a drywall saw, so that you can see into the wall to locate cables and pipes. Saw through studs and noggings, and remove them; use a hacksaw on nails and screws. Cut through the sole plate in the opening (see pp.104–05) with a panel saw, and remove the unwanted section. Fit the lintel beneath the sawn-through studs above the opening, supporting it on "cripple studs" (new studs fitted at each end), to a size and specification calculated by your structural engineer.

Cutting into a non-loadbearing wall

Props are not necessary. Cut out the required area, and insert rough-sawn wood between the cut-off studs above the opening. Insert a new stud if one is needed to frame the opening.

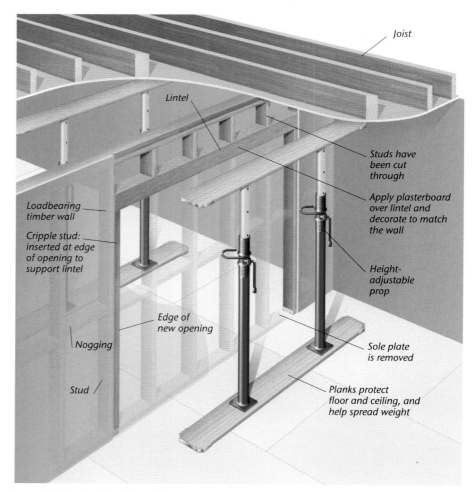

Cutting into a loadbearing timber wall
This image shows props set up, before cutting into a wall, to support the weight of the structure above. It also shows the lintel and cripple studs, which are positioned after the opening is cut.

Joist

Lintel

Studs have been cut through

Apply plasterboard over lintel and decorate to match the wall

Height-adjustable prop

Sole plate is removed

Planks protect floor and ceiling, and help spread weight

Loadbearing timber wall

Cripple stud: inserted at edge of opening to support lintel

Edge of new opening

Nogging

Stud

MAKING AN OPENING IN A MASONRY WALL

Get a structural engineer's advice on the beam specification, which will be needed whether the wall is loadbearing or not. Use a club hammer and bolster chisel to knock out holes for "needles" every 1m (3ft), or as advised by your engineer. Once the props are in place, use the hammer and chisel to remove just enough masonry to make space for the lintel. Bed the beam (or RSJ in this case) on padstones and mortar, and check its positioning with a spirit level. If the wall is very thick, let this mortar dry, then cut a hole in the other side of the wall, and insert a second lintel next to it. When the mortar is dry, remove the props and needles. Cut the rest of the opening, either with the hammer and chisel, or using an angle grinder to cut straight down the sides.

Temporary support for masonry
Use this propping method when cutting any large opening, whether the wall is loadbearing or not. Allow the beam mortar to dry, to support the wall, before making the main opening.

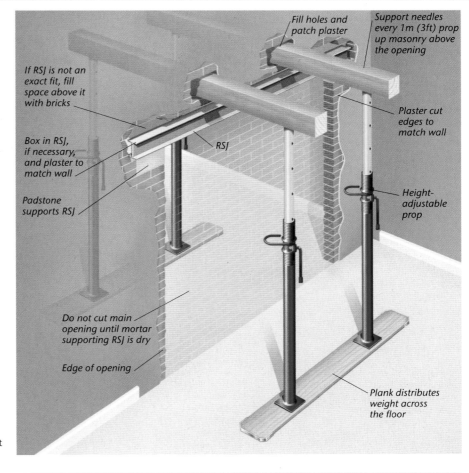

Fill holes and patch plaster

Support needles every 1m (3ft) prop up masonry above the opening

If RSJ is not an exact fit, fill space above it with bricks

Plaster cut edges to match wall

Box in RSJ, if necessary, and plaster to match wall

RSJ

Padstone supports RSJ

Height-adjustable prop

Do not cut main opening until mortar supporting RSJ is dry

Edge of opening

Plank distributes weight across the floor

CREATING AN ARCH

Use an arch former to give an opening rounded edges instead of square corners. Arch formers are made of galvanized steel wire mesh, and can be used on masonry or timber walls. Decorative plaster ones are also available, for use on stud walls. Formers are positioned after beams or lintels. Attach the sections of arch former to the wall, ensuring that the arch's peak is central in the opening. The edges of the former will give sharp edges to the arch. If the opening does not have matching sharp corners, you can achieve them by attaching angle beads to the wall from arch former to floor (see pp.128–35). Plaster and decorate.

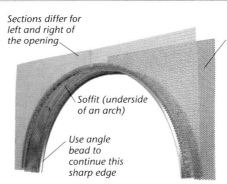

Sections differ for left and right of the opening

Former fits to both faces of the wall

Soffit (underside of an arch)

Use angle bead to continue this sharp edge

Wire-mesh arch formers
Arch formers come in four sections, shown here fitted together, so they can be easily adjusted to suit any size of opening. If you need to span a wide gap or thick wall, insert another section (called a soffit piece) between the main segments of arch former.

REMOVING AN ENTIRE WALL

Complete removal of a loadbearing wall is a job for professionals. Removing a non-loadbearing wall, however, is a much easier task and can be undertaken by a DIYer.

To remove a block wall, use a lump hammer and a bolster chisel to weaken the mortar joint between the wall and ceiling. Knock out a brick or block from the top course. After this initial breakthrough, a solid tap on adjacent blocks will loosen their mortar and enable you to remove them. Remove the wall row by row from top to bottom.

To remove a stud wall, pull away sections of plasterboard, removing fixings using a pry bar if necessary. Then remove any insulation. Cut through studs and noggings, and move them back and forth to ease them out of the wall. Finally, use a pry bar to prise away the head, sole, and wall plates.

MAKING GOOD AFTER REMOVING A WALL

Damage	Solution
Visible fixing holes	Fill holes and repair decoration.
Gaps in plasterboard ceiling or wall	Fix strips of plasterboard in the gap, patch plaster, then sand and decorate.
Broken block edges in side wall	Patch plaster to cover edges.
Blocks embedded in floor, sitting below floor level	Chisel back blocks so that upper surface sits below floor level. Apply self-levelling compound to blocks to bring them up to the surrounding floor level.

PLANNING A STUD WALL

A stud wall is the most common way to divide a room. Its framework is constructed of timber or metal verticals (studs) strengthened by horizontal lengths (noggings) fixed between them. Cables, pipes, and blanket insulation can sit within the cavity between the plasterboard sheets, which cover both sides of the frame. The wall can be plastered or dry lined (see pp.136–41) and decorated as normal.

FIRST THINGS TO CONSIDER

Even a minor internal alteration may need local authority approval. When planning a stud wall, check the regulations governing lighting, ventilation, and electrical circuits, and get any necessary permissions before starting work.

If you need water or electricity in your new room, locate existing pipes and circuits. Work out where to put fittings such as radiators or basins, so that pipes or wiring are sited where you need them (see pp.430–31 and 474–75).

CHOOSING PLASTERBOARD AND TIMBER

Choosing plasterboard
Decide how the wall is to be finished, and choose board that is suitable for your plans (see pp.72–73). The sheet's thickness affects how far apart studs should be positioned: they should be no more than 400mm (1ft 4in) apart for a board that is 9.5mm (⅜in) thick, or 600mm (2ft) if it is 12.5mm (½in) thick. If you want to plaster the wall, use square-edged boards; use taper-edged ones if you intend to dry line it (see pp.136–41).

Sheets should be slightly shorter than the walls to allow you to manoeuvre them. Fit the boards against the ceiling and leave a small gap at the floor, to be hidden by the skirting board.

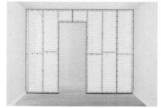
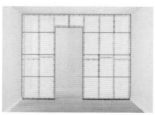

Standard sheet plasterboard
Sheets cover a wall quickly but are harder to cut and position.

Lath plasterboard
Smaller sheets are easier to handle but cannot be dry lined.

How much plasterboard to buy
1. Calculate the wall's area: multiply its height by its width.
2. Divide this by the area of one sheet of your chosen plasterboard to find out how many sheets to buy. The result will not be exact and, depending on how many cuts you need to make, you may need to buy a little extra to cover the wall, because board edges need to run down the centres of studs, so that fixings can be inserted into the studs.

Choosing timber
Choose rough-sawn lengths of softwood (see p.75) measuring 100 x 50mm (4 x 2in) or 75 x 50mm (3 x 2in). Narrower timber can be used, but tends to be rather flimsy. Check that the wood you buy is not misshapen: straight lengths are easier to work with. See pp.74–75 for more information on wood.

How much timber to buy
Measure the length of each stud, plate, and nogging, and add these together for a total length. Remember that timber lengths will not divide exactly into the lengths that you need.

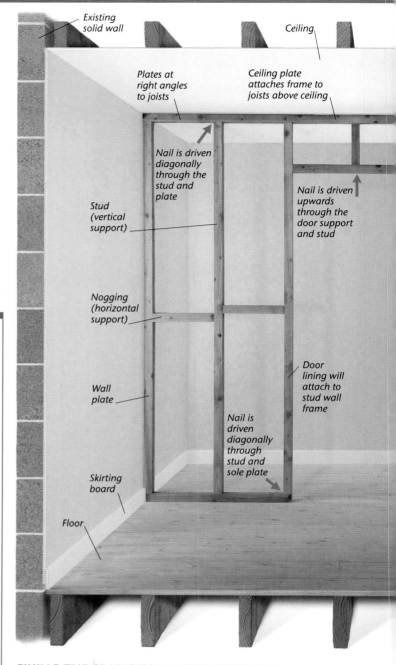

Existing solid wall

Ceiling

Plates at right angles to joists

Ceiling plate attaches frame to joists above ceiling

Nail is driven diagonally through the stud and plate

Nail is driven upwards through the door support and stud

Stud (vertical support)

Nogging (horizontal support)

Door lining will attach to stud wall frame

Wall plate

Nail is driven diagonally through stud and sole plate

Skirting board

Floor

FIXING THE FRAME TO AN EXISTING WALL
A stud wall must be carefully positioned so that it is stable. Fixing it to masonry should be possible at any point, but it is harder to make secure fixings to another timber wall.

Ideally, a new wall should be fixed to studs in the old wall. Use a stud detector to find the stud nearest to your ideal location. If you must put a wall between studs, place fixings at top and bottom, into the ceiling and sole plates, and into a central nogging.

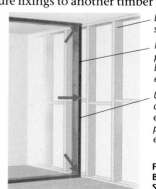

Existing stud wall

New wall position between two existing studs

Use adhesive along the entire wall plate for extra strength

FIXING BETWEEN STUDS

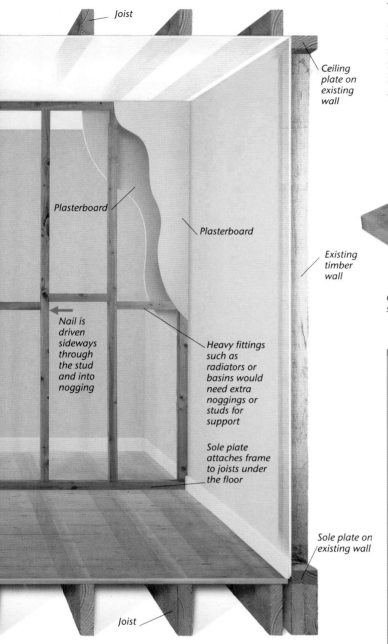

Joist

Ceiling plate on existing wall

Plasterboard

Plasterboard

Existing timber wall

Nail is driven sideways through the stud and into nogging

Heavy fittings such as radiators or basins would need extra noggings or studs for support

Sole plate attaches frame to joists under the floor

Sole plate on existing wall

Joist

FIXING THE FRAME TO THE FLOOR AND CEILING

Ideally, plates should cross joists (as shown above). If they run in the same direction, build the wall on a floor joist. There may not be a ceiling joist aligned with this, but the ceiling plate must be attached to a solid fixture, not just to plasterboard. If you can't fix it directly to a joist, fit noggings every 600mm (2ft) between two joists. Fix the ceiling plate to these. This method can also be used on the floor, for instance, if you cannot access ceiling joists from above.

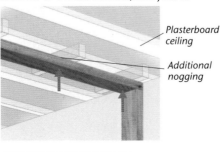

Plasterboard ceiling

Additional nogging

ATTACHING CEILING PLATE TO SUPPORT NOGGINGS

TURNING A CORNER

A corner is two walls butt-joined. However, on one wall, an extra stud is added close to the corner. This provides strength, and is the fixing point for plasterboard on the inside of the corner, because the main stud is inaccessible from that side. Ensure that the corner forms a precise right angle. Site all sole plates on, or at a right angle to, joists.

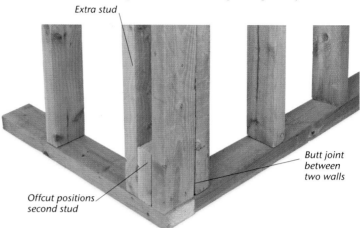

Extra stud

Butt joint between two walls

Offcut positions second stud

PLANNING A METAL STUD WALL

Metal is a modern alternative to timber studs. Systems differ between manufacturers, but the basics are the same: metal channels and sectional pieces slot together to form a frame. Metal studs may be thinner than wooden ones, but they are just as strong. Preparation and marking out for a metal stud wall is the same as for a wooden one. Plasterboard is screwed onto the metal channels, in the same way as it fixes to timber. See p.109 for the steps needed to build a metal stud wall.

Channels and tracks
Channels form all the verticals. They slot into the tracks (head and sole plates) and are easily positioned as required.

Channel

Tracks

Drywall screw
Fixes the sole plate without risk of piercing pipes or cables in the floor. A plasterboard screw is shown on p.77.

Tin snips
Use these to cut tracks and channels to size.

TOOLS AND MATERIALS CHECKLIST PP.106–09

Building a stud wall (pp.106–07) Plumb line or spirit level and chalk, try square, pry bar*

Applying plasterboard (p.108) Board lifter*, drywall saw, timber offcut, trowel, undercoat plaster

Building a metal stud wall (p.109) Tin snips, lengths of timber, spirit level

* = optional

FOR BASIC TOOLKIT
SEE PP.24–25

BUILDING A STUD WALL

Before you start, you need to decide where you will position your partition (see pp.104–05). The technique shown here uses guide lines to mark where the centres of studs will sit. If you want them to mark the edges (as shown on p.109), draw them to one side of the joists or studs into which you will drive fixings. If your stud wall is to have a doorway, lay a full sole plate as shown, and later cut away a section of it to make the doorway (see step 5B). You may need somebody to hold the ceiling plate in position while you fix it in place.

TOOLS AND MATERIALS SEE BASIC TOOLKIT AND P.105

1 MARKING OUT

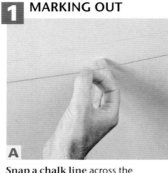

A Snap a chalk line across the ceiling (see p.43 for technique) to mark either the centre or one edge of the ceiling plate's position. Remove the chalk line.

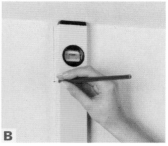

B At one end of the ceiling line, use a long spirit level and a pencil to draw a line on the wall, all the way down to the floor. Repeat on the other wall.

2 FITTING THE FLOOR PLATE

A Cut away the marked sections of skirting on both walls, taking care to saw accurate vertical lines. Lever the waste sections away from the wall with a pry bar if they stick.

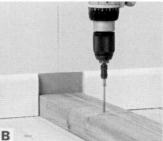

B Cut the sole plate to fit across the room where the skirting has been removed. Position it along its guide line, and secure it to the floor.

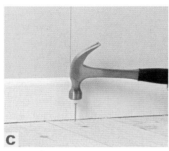

C Knock a nail into the floor at the base of each wall guide line. Attach and snap a chalk line across the floor to draw a guide line.

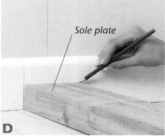

D Where the wall guide lines meet the floor, mark a section of skirting on each wall equal to the width of the sole plate.

AN ALTERNATIVE TO CUTTING SKIRTING

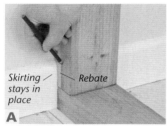

A Mark a rebate (area to be cut away) on the wall plate so that it will sit over the skirting board and lie flush on the wall.

Skirting stays in place / *Rebate*

B With the wall-facing side upwards, saw along the guide line to the depth marked by the pencil lines on the edges.

C Use a bevel-edged chisel and a hammer to remove chunks of wood, working down to the depth required.

Rebate to lap over skirting

D Position the plate against the wall and secure as normal.

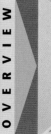

FIXING A STUD WALL TO A CONCRETE FLOOR

A Use a masonry drill bit to drill through the sole plate and into the concrete floor. This will guide your masonry fixings into place.

B Use hammer-in fixings (see p.77) through the drilled holes to fasten the sole plate securely into place.

3 FITTING THE OTHER PLATES AND DOOR STUDS

Cut the ceiling plate to length. Position it along the guide line, centred along it if necessary, and secure it to the ceiling. This will be easier if two people work together. Cut the wall plates to length and secure them to the walls.

Wall plate

A

B Mark the door position on the sole plate, allowing for the door plus its lining. Mark positions for other studs, at distances suitable for your plasterboard (see p.104).

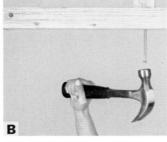

C Cut and position a stud on one side of the doorway, using a spirit level to keep it vertical and securing it as shown in the next step.

D

Keeping the stud precisely vertical, secure it to the ceiling and sole plates with 100-mm (4-in) nails inserted diagonally through the stud and into the sole plate. Use two or three nails fixed this way at the top and bottom of every stud. Position a stud on the other side of the doorway. Then position and secure all other studs.

4 FITTING THE DOOR HEAD

A Cut a nogging to the width of the doorway. Secure it to the door studs at the height required for the top of the door lining, using a spirit level to ensure it is precisely horizontal.

B Cut a stud to fit between the top of the doorway and the ceiling plate. Secure it at the centre of the doorway's width.

5 FINISHING THE FRAME

A Fit noggings about halfway up the studs. They need to be at differing heights so that you can nail into their ends. Add extra ones if they will have to support heavy fittings.

Stud at edge of doorway

B Saw through the sole plate just inside the doorway studs and remove the offcut, so that the doorway is clear. The frame is now ready to be covered (see p.108).

APPLYING PLASTERBOARD

Trim sheets so they are 50mm (2in) shorter than the walls. Before fixing plasterboard, mark on the floor and ceiling the positions of studs to help you find fixing points. If the first sheet sits against an uneven wall, cut it to fit as shown on p.72.

TOOLS AND MATERIALS SEE BASIC TOOLKIT AND P.105

1 POSITIONING THE FIRST SHEET

Measure from the centre of the doorway, if there is one, to the wall against which the first plasterboard sheet will sit, and cut the sheet to fit this space (see p.72). If there is no doorway, cut the first sheet to end at the centre of a stud. Have somebody help move the sheet into place, and use a board lifter to push it firmly against the ceiling.

B

Get the board correctly positioned before you start securing it. Its edge should run down the centre of the stud above the doorway to reduce the risk of cracking.

2 COVERING THE FRAME

A

Apply fixings every 150mm (6in), driving their heads just below the sheet's surface. Fix into noggings and studs in the middle of the sheet as well as those at the edges.

B

Use a panel saw to remove the section of plasterboard that overhangs the doorway. Begin with the horizontal cut, using the edge of the door head nogging as a guide.

C

Use the point of a drywall saw to help you turn the corner, and make the vertical cut. Carry on down to the floor and remove the plasterboard offcut. Position the next sheet and cut around the doorway. The last sheet will need cutting to fit against the wall, which may be uneven. To do this, first loosely fix the final sheet precisely on top of the penultimate one.

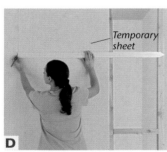

Temporary sheet

D

Cut a batten to the width of a sheet, and cut one end into a point. Run the point down the wall, using a pencil at the other end to mark a guide line on the board.

E

Remove the sheet from its temporary fixings, and cut along the guide line with a panel saw. The sheet should now fit cleanly against the wall, so fix it in position.

3 FINISHING OFF

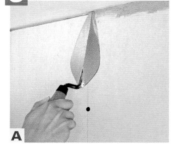

A

Attach plasterboard to the second side of the frame. Then use undercoat plaster to fill any cracks or gaps between the plasterboard and the walls or ceiling.

FIXING TIPS

Although nails are cheaper, you are less likely to damage plasterboard sheets if you fix them with screws. Use the speed controls on a cordless screwdriver to get the fixings flush with the surface, but avoid pushing them in too far, as this weakens the joint. When joining sheets at external corners, let one overlap the edge of the other, giving a sharp edge.

BUILDING A METAL STUD WALL

Measuring and marking up is the same as for a timber-framed stud wall (see pp.106–07). Adjust the steps shown here to allow for any techniques recommended by the manufacturer. Then attach plasterboard as shown opposite.

TOOLS AND MATERIALS SEE BASIC TOOLKIT AND P.105

1 POSITIONING THE TRACKS

Measure and mark on the floor, walls, and ceiling where to fix the wall channels and ceiling and floor tracks. If there is going to be a doorway, mark where it should go. Also mark where all the vertical channels will go. Use tin snips to cut channels and tracks to length.

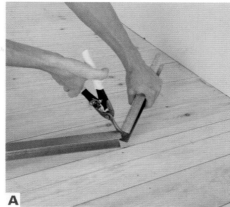

A

Gap large enough for door and lining

B

Screw the floor tracks into position, placing fixings no farther than 600mm (2ft) apart. You do not need to drill fixing holes in the metal tracks; just drive in the screws.

2 COMPLETING THE FRAME

C

Twist the wall tracks into position in the floor plates, and secure them with fixings placed no more than 600mm (2ft) apart.

D

Fit the ceiling track, again inserting fixings no more than 600mm (2ft) apart. This may be easier if somebody helps you.

A

Slide a length of wood into a channel. Insert it at one side of the doorway to provide a fixing point for the door lining. Repeat on the other side of the doorway.

B

Position a channel for the door head. This will have extensions at right angles to the main body, for fixing to the upright channels.

C

Secure the door-head channel to the uprights with drywall screws. Use a level to keep it horizontal.

D

Position the first vertical channel, twisting to fit it inside the ceiling and floor tracks.

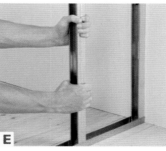

E

Twist the channel to face the correct direction once it is inside the floor and ceiling tracks. Repeat for all other verticals and the small, central stud above the doorway.

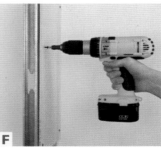

F

Fix noggings if you will need them to support heavy fittings, or to act as fixing points for joints between laths. Then attach plasterboard to both sides of the wall.

OVERVIEW

Choosing to build a block partition wall instead of a timber stud partition (see p.104) may depend on several factors. A block partition will give greater acoustic and thermal insulation than an uninsulated stud wall, and may feel more "solid", though a stud wall has a similar level of structural strength. Even if the rest of the house is of block-wall construction, there is no need to build new walls of blocks. There will be little difference in terms of cost, but building a block wall requires greater skill than a timber one.

THINGS TO CONSIDER

Think about why you are dividing the room and what you will use the new room for. Also consider whether a block wall is suitable. If the existing walls are timber, you would be better off building a stud wall (see p.104). Plan how to provide elements such as ventilation, lighting, and heating, and whether you need power sockets or water. See the relevant chapters for details on installing these features and work out how to do them and the most logical working order before starting to build the wall. Also think about building regulations in your area. Even a minor internal alteration to a building may require local authority approval. Make sure you have any necessary permissions before starting work.

Positioning the wall

Think carefully about where to build the wall. It will have considerable weight, so make sure that the surface you plan to build on can support it. The ideal scenario is to build on a concrete floor at ground-floor level, and between existing masonry walls. Masonry gives good fixing points for wall profiles, which hold the new wall securely to existing stuctures. If you choose to build against a stud wall, attach wall profiles to studs.

Building off a wooden floor

Check first that the floor will be strong enough to support the wall's weight (see p.174 for information on floors). Use a stud detector to locate joists, and position your wall across joists or above a reinforced joist (see p.177). To spread the weight, build off a timber sole plate, as for a stud wall or a glass-block wall (see pp.104, 114).

Planning a doorway

You may well need to leave space for a doorway in your block wall. Work out roughly where you want to place it, and how wide it will be. Remember to include the width of the door lining in your calculations (see p.158). Have these measurements to hand when you start building (see next page). You will need a lintel to support blocks above the doorway. A basic concrete one will suffice, because the wall is not loadbearing.

How long will it take?

Building a concrete-block wall is at least a two-day job. Blocks are heavy, so mortar needs to dry overnight after five or six courses, otherwise the wall may collapse. However, if you use lightweight thermal insulation blocks, you can build from floor to ceiling in a day.

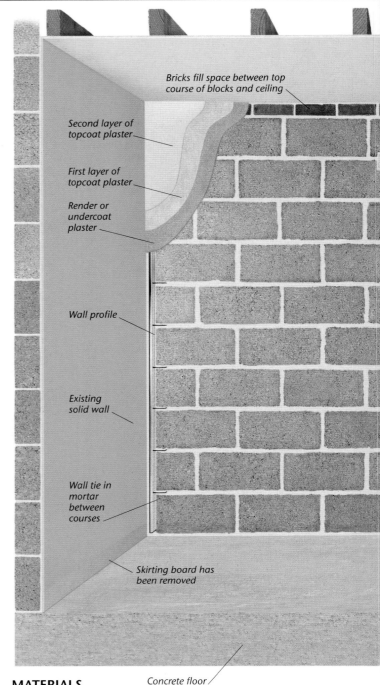

Bricks fill space between top course of blocks and ceiling

Second layer of topcoat plaster

First layer of topcoat plaster

Render or undercoat plaster

Wall profile

Existing solid wall

Wall tie in mortar between courses

Skirting board has been removed

Concrete floor

MATERIALS

Wall profiles
These "tie in" a wall to adjoining walls. Design varies, but profiles usually have holes through which fixings can attach them to walls.

Profile wall ties
These strengthen a wall's structure by "keying in" to the adjoining walls. Use one at each end of every row of blocks, linking it in to the wall profile and embedding it in mortar along the top of the blocks.

Concrete lintel
This supports blocks above a doorway. You may need help to lift it into position.

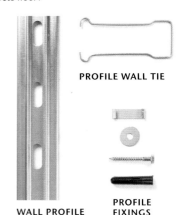

PROFILE WALL TIE

WALL PROFILE

PROFILE FIXINGS

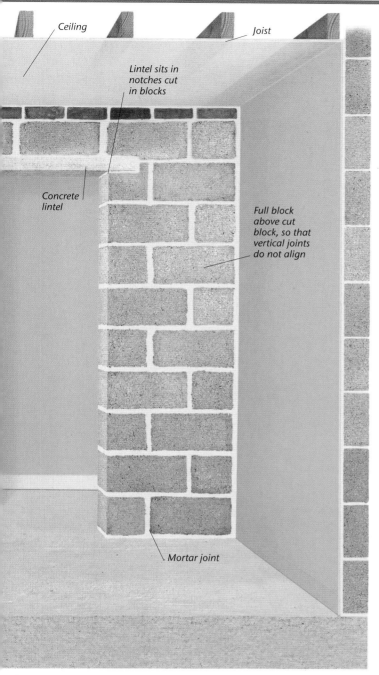

Ceiling

Joist

Lintel sits in notches cut in blocks

Concrete lintel

Full block above cut block, so that vertical joints do not align

Mortar joint

TECHNIQUES

See pp.82–83 for more information on working with blocks, and pp.48–49 for bricklaying techniques and information on using mortar.

Cutting blocks

Lightweight thermal blocks can be cut with a panel saw (p.34). Sturdier concrete blocks can be split apart using a bolster chisel and a club hammer (p.113), or cut with an angle grinder (p.61). The cut does not need to be precise, because the cut end will be invisible in a mortar joint. If it comes up a bit smaller than expected, a slightly larger than normal mortar joint will not show on the finished wall.

Running services through the wall

In contrast to building a stud wall, you cannot leave space for cables or pipes in a solid block wall. If these services are needed, you will have to channel out spaces for them after the wall has been built and the mortar dried (see p.442).

Building up courses and keeping them level

In the steps over the page, we lay the lower row of blocks first, and build up the wall course by course, because it is easier to demonstrate the principles this way. However, professional builders may "rack" the blocks – stack a few at each end of the wall, then fill in the rest (see pp.406–407). The steps show how to use a string line to keep blocks straight; adjust it for the string to come off the top or bottom of a block as needed at any moment.

Turning corners

When turning a corner with blocks or bricks, ensure that the two elements of the wall are set at a precise right angle. Also take care to use the correct pattern of blocks (bond).

Quarter block

End of block

The bond
To keep the mortar joints staggered, use a quarter block in alternating rows on one side, next to the block-ends from the first row.

CHOOSING BLOCKS AND USING MORTAR

Choosing blocks
If the floor is strong enough, you can use concrete blocks or lightweight thermal insulation ones (see p.97). For eco-friendly materials see pp.84–85.

How many blocks to buy
1. Find the surface area of a block by multiplying its height by its width.
2. Then multiply height by width to find the surface area of the planned wall.

3. Divide the wall's area by one block's area to find out how many blocks you need.
4. Buy roughly 10 per cent extra, to allow for cut blocks, breakages, and damage.

Buying and mixing mortar
Seek advice from your supplier on the quantities needed. Use a general-purpose mortar mix (see p.71). Mix only as much as you can use before it dries so much as to be unworkable.

TOOLS AND MATERIALS CHECKLIST PP.112–13

Building a solid block wall
Mortar mix (see p.71), spot board, shovel, spirit level, wall

profiles, wall ties, string line, bricks, brick trowel, bolster chisel, club hammer, lintel

FOR BASIC TOOLKIT SEE PP.24–25

BUILDING A SOLID BLOCK WALL

Plan carefully where to site a new wall, taking into account the existing structure (see pp.110–11). The steps shown are suitable for a wall with or without a doorway, as long as you keep blocks straight and level, and joints staggered. For clarity, the steps here begin each course to the left of the doorway. After laying five or six courses, let mortar dry overnight before you build any higher. When the wall is complete and dry, either render and plaster the wall or dry line it before decorating it (see pp.136–41 for finishing options and instructions).

TOOLS AND MATERIALS SEE BASIC TOOLKIT AND P.111

1 PREPARING THE AREA

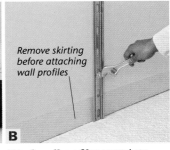

A

At your chosen position, mark the new wall's location and check that there are no pipes or cables at that point in the existing wall. Do the same at the opposite end.

B

Remove skirting before attaching wall profiles

Attach wall profiles securely to the walls at the marked positions, using a hacksaw to cut them to the right height if necessary. Check they are truly vertical with a level.

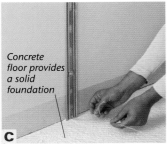

Concrete floor provides a solid foundation

C

Attach a taut string line between the two wall profiles at floor level; the new wall will lie along this line.

Use a pencil to mark the doorway

D

Measure and mark the position of the doorway, if you need one, allowing space for the door lining as well as the door. Draw a guide line from the doorway to the wall.

The string acts as a guide for the back of the wall

E

Remove the string line and tie it between two blocks. Sit each block next to a wall profile, keeping string taut. This string line will help you lay the first row of blocks evenly.

F

Use a brick trowel to butter one end of the first block. Then lay a bed of mortar, about the same length as the block, along the line of the new wall next to the profile.

2 LAYING THE FIRST BLOCKS

Place the block with its buttered end hard against the wall profile and tap it firmly with the trowel handle to bed it in. Once compacted, the mortar should be 10–12mm (⅜–½in) deep. Position the next block. Use the trowel's sharp edge to remove excess mortar seeping from beneath and between blocks. Then use a spirit level to check that blocks are straight.

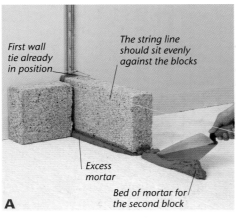

First wall tie already in position

The string line should sit evenly against the blocks

Excess mortar

Bed of mortar for the second block

A

Use one or two taps from the trowel handle to bed in blocks

B

Continue laying whole blocks until you reach the doorway, bedding in all the blocks firmly as you go by, using the end of the trowel handle to tap them down.

Keep checking that blocks are straight and level

Remember to use a wall tie

C

Lay a whole block at the far end of the wall, on the other side of the doorway. Lay all the whole blocks in a course before you measure for any cut blocks needed to complete it.

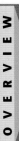

3 CUTTING A BLOCK

If you need a cut block to fit the doorway, measure and mark on the block where to cut. Lay it on a bed of sand to stop it slipping, and use a club hammer to tap a bolster chisel along the guide line. When you have made an appreciable indent all along the line, apply some stronger blows to the chisel. The block will eventually break along the indented guide line.

Wear protective gloves

A

4 LAYING A CUT BLOCK

Adjust the amount of mortar at cut end if necessary

A

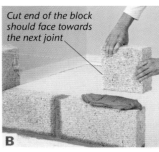

Cut end of the block should face towards the next joint

B

Butter the cut end of the block. Place the block with its square end exactly at the marked door position. Check it is level and tidy the joints.

Raise the string guide by sitting it on the first course. Lay the second course, starting at the doorway with a cut block on top of a whole one so the mortar joints are staggered.

5 BUILDING UP LAYERS

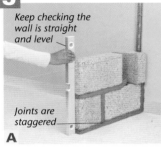

Keep checking the wall is straight and level

Joints are staggered

A

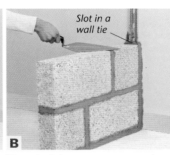

Slot in a wall tie

B

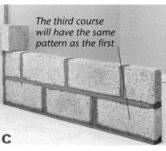

The third course will have the same pattern as the first

C

D

Mortar the top of the first course on the other side of the doorway. Place a full block on top of the half block. Then cut a block to fit in the remaining space, and place it.

Keep the joints neat as you work. Remember to slot wall ties into the wall profiles when you finish each course. Bed them into the mortar for the next course.

Move the string line up and start the third course at the doorway. Lay the whole blocks first, working towards the wall, then finish the course on the other side of the door.

Keep building, remembering to let the mortar dry after five or six courses, until you reach the height at which you need to place the lintel above the doorway.

6 BUILDING FROM THE LINTEL TO THE CEILING

If the required lintel height does not fall neatly at the top of a whole block, use an angle grinder to cut notches in blocks for the lintel to sit in. Position it across the opening, bedded in on mortar at either end. The lintel must be accommodated in the course above, which must be level, so cut notches in blocks to fit above it.

Check lintel is level

Notches can be used to adjust lintel height

A

B

Carry on laying blocks. Check that they are in line and are level, then remove excess mortar.

C

Whole blocks may not fit to the ceiling exactly, so fill the gap with bricks or cut blocks. Butter their tops and slide them in on mortar. Let the completed wall dry overnight.

BUILDING A GLASS-BLOCK PARTITION

A glass-block wall divides a room without shutting out light. It cannot be loadbearing, but it will be a sturdy structure, thanks to metal reinforcing rods that are positioned in the mortar. Blocks sit with the mortar joints aligned and, because the blocks form the wall's decorative finish, white mortar is normally used to give a neat result. (An alternative to using mortar is briefly described opposite.) Glass blocks can also be used to build a screen across part of a room, as shown here, or (with no timber frame) as a shower cubicle. Do not build any higher than six courses without stopping to let mortar dry overnight, otherwise the wall may collapse.

1 CONSTRUCTING THE FRAME

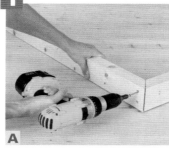

A **B**

Make a wooden frame to fit your chosen wall dimensions. Use timber struts of 100 x 50mm (4 x 2in) or 75 x 50mm (3 x 2in), with the same width as the blocks.

Fix the frame in place at your chosen location for the wall (see pp.104–07). Remember to use a cable detector to check that it is safe to insert fixings into the floor.

PLANNING AND PREPARATION

Most glass blocks measure 190 x 190 x 80mm (7½ x 7½ x 3⅛in). They cannot be cut to size, so base your calculations on how they best fit into the space. Half-blocks and corner blocks are available. Use wooden plates to fill any gaps left between blocks and a wall or ceiling. These will be inconspicuous when painted.

Designing a partition
■ Lay out a single row of blocks to judge a screen's extent into the room.
■ A full wall may need a doorway. Its position will depend on how blocks fit across your room. The opening will need suitable ties inserted through the door lining into the mortar.
■ Building within a wooden frame gives clean edges, but the mortar method can be used without a frame, provided you consider your floor surface (see below).

The floor surface
■ Mortar can be laid directly onto a concrete floor.
■ With a wooden floor, lay the first row of blocks on a wooden sole plate, even if you are not building in a frame.

Calculating quantities
■ Multiply the length of the wall by its height to find its surface area. Divide this by the area of one block for a rough

idea of the number of blocks needed, not allowing for mortar joints. Buy 10 per cent extra, in case any get broken.
■ White mortar (ready-mixed) is available in 12.5kg (27½lb) bags – enough to construct a small shower enclosure.
■ Spacers give even joints. Allow 1½ per glass block, and buy 10 per cent extra. The spacer shape can be modified from X-shaped to T- or L-shaped as required.
■ Allow two reinforcing rods per row of blocks. Buy more if you wish to push rods into the vertical joints for extra rigidity.

Sealing the partition
■ Use white mortar and white grout. Use waterproof grout and silicone sealant in a humid room, such as a bathroom, and use silicone sealant on the joint between the glass-block wall and the existing wall.
■ Some manufacturers supply expansion strips for the wall's perimeter in a humid area or one with temperature change.

2 LAYING THE FIRST BLOCKS

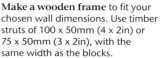

Nail white expansion foam to the inside of the wooden frame. This foam is a spongy material that allows the wall a small amount of movement without any danger of damage – for instance, if materials expand slightly when the temperature changes. Make sure the foam sits centrally on each length of wood.

A

B **C**

Position spacers inside the floor of the wooden frame, ready to hold the glass blocks. Check that they are level and accurately spaced to fit the dimensions of the blocks.

Trowel white mortar onto the frame's floor, between the spacers. "Butter" mortar onto one side of a glass block. Try not to get any on the block's face.

TOOLS AND MATERIALS CHECKLIST

Timber, expansion foam, spacers, white mortar, bricklaying trowel, spot board, plasterer's hawk, metal reinforcing rods, wall ties, white grout, grout shaper, silicone sealant*, paint*, paintbrush*

The "dry" method Wooden frame pieces, clips, brackets

* = optional

FOR BASIC TOOLKIT
SEE PP.24–25

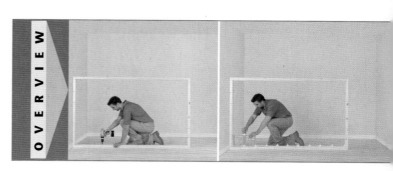

3 BUILDING UP ROWS

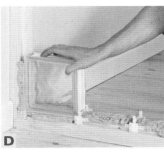

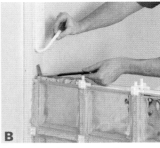

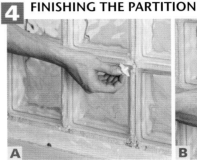

D

Place the first block onto the spacers, pressing the buttered side firmly into position against the frame and bedding the block into the mortar along the floor.

E

Lay more blocks and spacers to finish the row, checking that they are level. Wipe off any excess mortar with a damp sponge; dried mortar is hard to remove from glass.

A

Apply mortar along the top of the first row. Drill holes in the wall plate and fit the reinforcing rods. Press them down into the mortar. Carry on laying blocks on top.

B

After every two rows, cut through the foam on the wall plate, just above the top edge of the course. Apply mortar to the end block, ready to bed in a wall tie.

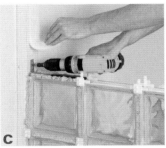

4 FINISHING THE PARTITION

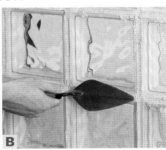

C

Screw the wall tie to the wall plate, behind the foam, and bed the tie into the mortar. Then lay mortar and reinforcing rods, and carry on laying blocks.

D

Keep checking as you build up the height that blocks are level and vertically aligned. If you are going higher than six courses, let mortar dry overnight before finishing.

A

Once all the glass blocks are in place, twist the spacers' faceplates to remove them.

B

Allow the mortar to dry, and then grout the joints (see p.315). Wipe off excess grout from the glass-block faces as you go, because grout is difficult to remove once it has dried.

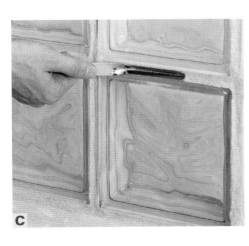

C

Smooth the grout using a grout shaper, or brick jointer as shown here. Apply silicone sealant around its perimeter if required to make the junctions waterproof, and wipe down the wall to give it a polished look. Paint the wooden frame if you wish.

THE "DRY" METHOD

The alternative to using mortar is to buy a wooden frame to house blocks and support the structure. Interlocking wooden sections are assembled at the same time as blocks are placed within them. Each row sits on a rebated wooden strip, with shorter vertical strips around the blocks. The rebates in the wooden strips prevent blocks falling out, and the frame is held together by clips and brackets. The entire wall is housed within a rectangular wooden frame.

CREATING A DOORWAY

When planning to cut an opening in a wall, whether masonry or timber, establish whether it is loadbearing or non-loadbearing. For advice on this, and on supporting the upper levels of a wall or structure while cutting openings, see p.102. The techniques needed for cutting smaller openings such as a doorway or serving hatch are those shown on p.102. If a door is to be placed in the opening, you do not need to be exacting in making good the cut edges, because the door lining will cover them. In calculating how large to make the opening, allow for a door lining, and get lintel specifications calculated by a structural engineer.

BEFORE YOU START

■ Internal alterations may not always need planning or building permission, but check with your local council, because regulations vary. External changes such as adding a new window often have to be authorized.

■ If the wall has a skirting board, remove it before starting work, and re-fit it after making good the walls around the new doorway.

■ Seek professional advice if you have any doubts about carrying out structural improvements to your home.

MAKING AN OPENING IN A TIMBER WALL

If you are cutting into a loadbearing wall, use temporary props, a lintel, and cripple studs, even for a small opening. Use the techniques shown on p.102.

Cutting an opening in a non-loadbearing wall

Use an existing stud as the hinging edge of the doorway. After cutting the opening, fit noggings between the sawn studs above it, and insert a new stud in the open edge of the doorway. Then either attach a door lining and door (see pp.156–63) or, if the gap is to be an opening with no door, apply plasterboard and an angle bead, then plaster (see pp.128–35). For a serving hatch, cut an opening in the same way. Insert a nogging across the bottom edge before lining, and fitting architrave (see p.218).

Creating an opening in a loadbearing exterior wall

This is a job for professionals. A structural engineer will give specifications for the lintel and supports (see p.102). Supporting the frame is possible only on the inside. If the wall is brick- or block-clad, masonry is removed slowly, and angled props placed, until it is possible to insert the lintel.

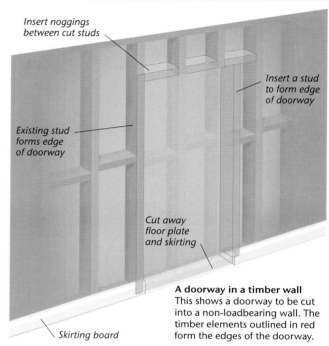

Insert noggings between cut studs

Insert a stud to form edge of doorway

Existing stud forms edge of doorway

Cut away floor plate and skirting

Skirting board

A doorway in a timber wall
This shows a doorway to be cut into a non-loadbearing wall. The timber elements outlined in red form the edges of the doorway.

MAKING AN OPENING IN A MASONRY WALL

A lintel is needed for any opening in masonry, no matter how small the span. It will probably need to be concrete or a metal box lintel; take advice from a structural engineer on the type and strength you need. Some tips specific to small openings are given here, but the techniques for supporting the wall and cutting the opening are those shown on p.103.

Cutting into a non-loadbearing wall

For small openings in brickwork – no wider than 1m (3ft 3in) for example – it may be possible to cut the opening without temporary support. If any bricks fall out of their positions, they can be replaced after the lintel is set in place. With blockwork, however, it is almost always necessary to use a temporary support.

Cutting into an exterior cavity wall

If you need to cut into an exterior cavity wall for a new window or a doorway, use a cavity wall lintel. These will provide support while retaining the cavity wall's damp-proofing function. They direct any moisture in the cavity out though weep holes in the wall. Your structural engineer will specify the strength to use. Close off the cavity at the sides of the new opening, either using cavity closers or by laying blocks with a DPC.

SUPPORT NEEDED WHEN CUTTING AN OPENING

This table gives general guidance on the support needed when cutting into a wall. Consult a structural engineer for advice on the size, material, and strength of lintel needed. Also get advice on temporary support if you wish to cut into a cavity wall.

Wall type	Temporary support	Lintel required?
Non-loadbearing timber	Not needed	No
Non-loadbearing masonry	If masonry above opening exceeds two rows of bricks or blocks, use a proprietary support or needle centrally, or every 1m (3ft 3in); if it is one or two rows, no support is needed – if blocks fall out, just re-insert them above the lintel	Yes
Loadbearing timber	Props on ceiling	Yes, with cripple studs
Loadbearing masonry	Needle or proprietary support centrally, or every 1m (3ft 3in)	Yes

Filling in an unwanted doorway can be done either with a timber stud frame or with blocks. It is best to fill in a stud wall with studs and a block wall with blocks, because these materials have different reactions to environmental changes such as fluctuating temperatures or humidity levels. Using timber is easier, and can be done on a block wall if using blocks seems too difficult. But because the materials used do not match, cracks may later appear at or near the position of the old doorway. These can be filled and painted, but may reappear. By using matching materials, you reduce the risk of having these settlement or movement cracks appear.

PREPARING THE AREA
■ Remove the old door, architrave, and door lining before starting work on the wall. Lift a door off its hinges or unscrew them from the doorjamb. Prise away the architrave and door lining with a claw hammer or pry bar.
■ When removing old woodwork, keep damage to the surrounding wall to a minimum, but bear in mind that any loose plaster can be removed and made good along with the doorway area once the opening has been filled in.

USING TIMBER STUDS
This method for filling in a doorway uses the techniques shown on pp.106–07 (Building a Stud Wall). Use lengths of rough-sawn timber 100 x 50mm (4 x 2in) to line the doorway. In a block wall, use wall plugs and masonry screws to attach the studs to the blocks. In a stud wall, simply attach the new studwork to existing studs with wood screws. Insert more studs and noggings, to strengthen the frame: depending on the dimensions, a central stud (vertical) and two noggings (horizontals) may be sufficient. Cut some square-edged plasterboard to fit the gap, and attach it to the wooden frame. Tape the joint between the new plasterboard and the surrounding wall with self-adhesive scrim, and apply finishing plaster (see pp.134–35), feathering in the join between the new and the old wall surfaces.

Finishing off
When the plaster has dried, sand it to a smooth finish. Fill any holes with an all-purpose filler, and sand again, if you wish to for the smoothest possible finish. Attach skirting board (see pp.220–21), and then decorate the room. You can either use a short section to fill in the gap and match the adjoining boards, or replace the skirting board along the whole wall.

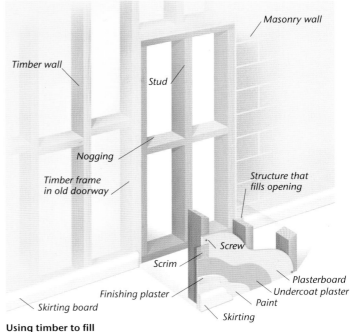

Using timber to fill
This method is easier than using blocks. It is normally used in a timber wall, but can also be used in a block wall. Both wall types are shown here.

USING BLOCKS
Blocks can be laid in the opening, using screw-in ties to secure them to the existing blocks, or you can remove blocks at alternate levels from either side of the opening, in which case the new blocks will automatically be securely fitted into the existing wall. Both methods are shown to the right.

Once the wall has dried, remove any loose material and apply a coat of PVA solution (5:1 water to PVA) before applying undercoat plaster (see pp.132–33). Apply PVA to the dried undercoat, then apply finishing plaster (see pp.134–35), feathering in the edges with the existing wall edge. When the plaster has dried, sand it, paying particular attention to the join between the old plaster and the new. Decorate, and attach a piece of skirting board across the old doorway, or replace the full length (see pp.220–21).

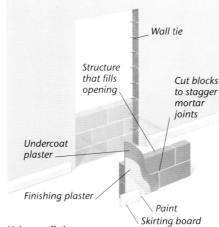

Using wall ties
Build a small block wall using the principles shown on pp.110–13. Match the depths of mortar beds to those on the existing wall, so that wall ties inserted in the old wall's mortar align with the new mortar courses. The blocks will not be an exact fit across the doorway: work out where cuts will be needed.

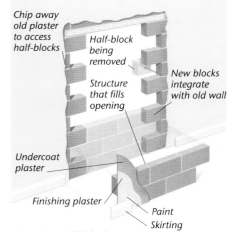

Removing half-blocks
This method takes longer than the wall-tie one. Use a club hammer and bolster chisel to take out half-blocks from the edge of the doorway. Chip away any hardened mortar. Then insert new blocks (see pp.110–13). If they are not an exact fit, make cuts, or add slightly more mortar, to fill the space appropriately.

PLANNING A STRAW-BALE WALL

There are several ways to build a straw-bale wall (see p.98). The main consideration is whether the straw bales themselves will be loadbearing or whether they will act as infill for another loadbearing structure, such as post and beam (see p.93). The method shown here is for a type of loadbearing wall known as the "Nebraskan style". While there are alternative techniques within this style, all of the key steps are shown, with alternative materials suggested where relevant.

CONSTRUCTION CONSIDERATIONS

These techniques apply to an exterior wall, so you will first need to choose a suitable foundation. There are a variety of options available (see p.92), but here the walls are being built on concrete. While concrete is not the greenest or most sustainable option, it is one of the best for reducing the risk of moisture egress. In fact, the most successful straw-bale structures incorporate many features to guard against damp. Wrapping the first course of bales in a damp-proof membrane, for example, protects the structure at this crucial level. Designing a roof with a large overhang to deflect rainwater away from the wall surfaces is also important. While the exterior wall will be clad in a protective skin – usually lime render (see p.99) – it is still best practice to keep as much water as possible away from the walls.

Upstands

It is essential that the bales are raised off the immediate surface of the floor. This is achieved by laying a wooden upstand, or frame, on the foundation wall and bolting it to the floor. The upstand must be slightly narrower than the width of the bales. Treated timber measuring 100 x 50mm (4 x 2in) is ideal for use in constructing an upstand. Here, reinforcement bars are set in the foundations and extend upwards through the centre of the upstands to secure the first layer of bales in place. Upstands also allow you to accurately position doorways in the wall.

Wall plates

Similar in design to an upstand, a wall plate is a wooden framework that sits on top of the bale wall to ensure that the structure is loadbearing. The upper and lower surfaces of a wall plate are strengthened by attaching structural ply or orientated strand board (OSB). This board should be 18mm (¾in) thick and, like the upstands, made from 100 x 50mm (4 x 2in) lengths of treated timber.

Cross-section of the wall plate

Layers of lime plaster to finish wall surface (see p.99)

Wire mesh acts as key for plaster

Wall plate provides support for roof timbers or floor joists

Wooden upstand

Bales laid stretcher bond

Reinforced bar

Concrete raft foundation

Damp-proof membrane

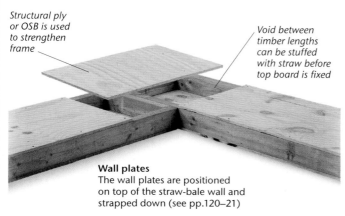

Structural ply or OSB is used to strengthen frame

Void between timber lengths can be stuffed with straw before top board is fixed

Wall plates
The wall plates are positioned on top of the straw-bale wall and strapped down (see pp.120–21)

Doorways and windows

When planning doorways and windows, keep in mind that the height of these openings may decrease during the build. This is because the bales will compress as the walls are built upwards and the roof is added. Consequently, the area above a door or window head should be left open until the wall plate (see left) has been tied down. A box frame for the opening (within which the door or window frame itself will sit) can be made from a framework of structural ply and treated timber lengths. Once any compression of the bales has occurred, any gaps can be stuffed with straw.

There is usually no need for an extra lintel above the door or window in a single-storey building as the wall plate should be able to support the roof. Equally, if a second storey is planned, the wall plate should be able to bear any joists for the next floor. However, always make careful structural calculations regarding loadings, especially with two-storey structures.

Fixing points

The bale structure alone does not offer suitable fixing points for screws or nails, so you will need to use wooden dowels. If, for example, fixing points are required for clipping a cable to a wall, drive wooden dowels into the straw-bale structure and

Tensioning Strap

Door lining-box frame construction

Infill above doors and windows after compression of walls

Half bales rebound with baling wire

Gravel infill

fix the cable to the end of the dowel. This procedure is relatively straightforward during construction, before any finish is applied to the walls. However, when hanging heavy objects, such as kitchen units, more planning is necessary. Sturdier wooden fixing points need to be introduced into the bale surface. One way of doing this is to drive threaded bolts through the wall, bolting them to blocks of wood on the outside surface of the wall, and to lengths of wood on the inside surface, to provide a secure fixing rail.

CABLES AND SERVICES
Electrical cables can be run through the structure of a straw-bale wall, or surface-mounted to the bales and covered with lime render and plaster. In either case, it is important to enclose the wires in plastic conduit. Avoid burying water pipes in the walls as any leak could have a devastating effect on the integrity of the structure. If you have no option but to pass water pipes through a wall, keep the pipework continuous (i.e. don't bury a joint in the wall) and aim to position them in internal walls wherever possible.

Temporary bracing and framing
Due to the lack of framework associated with the Nebraskan style, it is advisable to construct some temporary bracing as the wall develops. This is especially important at corners, where a temporary framework makes it easier to maintain a vertical structure prior to the wall plates being attached. It is also best practice to fix door and window frames in place during the build rather than after the walls have been completed.

Tools
Although many tools required for straw-bale construction can be found in a standard toolbox, certain items are specific to this building technique.

Baling wire Tightens cut bale structure.

Bill hook Multi-purpose cutting and trimming tool.

Shears Ideal for trimming bales.

Baling needle Used for threading wire when cutting bales.

Tensioner sealer Used to fix strap seals.

Angle plate Protects wood where straps are tightened.

Strap seal

Hazel stake

Tensioner Tightens up straps.

Reinforced bar Stabilizes structure. In some cases, hazel stakes are used.

Strap Made from polyester or metal.

Post maul Used for knocking in stakes.

TOOLS AND MATERIALS CHECKLIST PP.120–21
Building a straw-bale wall Angle plates, baling needle, baling wire, bill hook, reinforced bars, hazel stakes, post maul, strap, tensioner, strap seals, tensioner sealer, shears

FOR BASIC TOOLKIT SEE PP.24–25

BUILDING A STRAW-BALE WALL

It is essential that the bales a kept dry, so make sure you are well-prepared before construction begins (see pp.118–19). This means that upstands should be secured to the foundations, and door frames, window frames, and wall plates should be constructed and ready for positioning before the bales are brought to the site. Speed is of the essence, and a back-up plan is necessary to protect the bales during inclement weather. Indeed, with the Nebraskan style (shown here), the roof can only be added once the walls have been built, so the bales will be exposed for longer.

TOOLS AND MATERIALS SEE BASIC TOOLKIT AND P.119

1 CHECKING FOUNDATIONS AND UPSTAND

A

Angle plate   Coiled strap

Check that all bolts are tightened to ensure that the upstand is secured to the foundation. Infill gravel should be evenly distributed so there are no low or high spots. Check that the straps are in place, and that the metal angle plates are attached to the wooden upstand to prevent the straps from cutting into the wood when they are tightened.

2 POSITIONING THE FIRST BALE

A

B

C

D

Beginning at an external corner, position the first bale flush with the inner edge of the upstand, whilst slightly overhanging the outer edge. Push it onto the securing rebar.

Position the second bale adjacent to the first bale, marking the start of a second wall. Make sure that it is butted tight up against the first bale.

Continue to add bales to the walls, building up on both sides of this starting corner.

When you reach an obstacle such as a door lining, and a cut bale is required, measure the distance between the last bale and the lining. Add 2cm (1in) so the cut bale will fit tightly into the gap.

3 CUTTING A BALE

A

B

C

Where the needle comes through the other side of the bale, unthread the wire and draw it round the perimeter of the bale to meet with the other end of the wire.

Thread the needle, using enough wire (with excess) to stretch round the perimeter of what will be your cut bale.

Push the needle through the straw at the point at which you need to cut the bale. Run this wire alongside the existing length of baler twine.

D Twist the ends of the wire together, tightening them with pliers. Repeat steps A–D next to the other length of baler twine.

E Using a craft knife, cut the old baler twines (the orange twine in this picture) and remove. The bale is now secured by the new lengths of twine.

F Pull the bale apart so that you are left with a new, smaller-sized bale for use in the wall construction.

G The new bale should now fit tightly into the gap in the wall. The excess straw (shown on the left) can be used to infill spaces above door and window frames.

4 BUILDING UP LAYERS

A Keep the bales as vertical as possible, taking regular readings with a spirit level as the construction grows. Layers are simply built up, using a stretcher-bond pattern (see p.404 for more information).

B To reinforce the wall, drive hazel stakes vertically down into the structure using a post maul. You should do this when you reach the fourth layer of bales.

5 FITTING THE WALL PLATE

A Lift the wall plate onto the top edge of the walls to form a continuous loadbearing structure for the roof or second storey. For practical reasons, the wall plate is divided into sections and fitted together in position.

B Lift up the straps that have been left protruding from the underside of the upstand. Draw one end over the exterior wall and wall plate, meeting with the other end of the strap on the inner face of the wall.

C Connect the straps in the tensioner and gradually tighten them. This will rachet the wall plate down onto the walls.

D Use a tensioner sealer to connect the two lengths of strap. Move slowly around the building, tightening and sealing each strap.

E Strap seals will firm up the structure. If re-tightening is required (see box, right), cut the strap and splice in a new section as required, connecting a new strap seal.

FINISHING THE WALL

The wall structure is essentially complete at this stage. The process of tightening the securing straps should be repeated after a few weeks (or when they begin to slacken) to further compress the wall structure. This is why it is important to leave gaps above windows and doors (see p.118). Bales should be given a final trim before the application of any render.

Sometimes an external wall's structure provides the decorative finish, and sometimes extra coverings are required for decorative or weatherproofing purposes. For example, a brick-built wall forms structure and finish, but a block-built wall needs to be rendered or clad to cover unsightly blocks. For most householders, the systems and techniques for these coverings become relevant only when they need to carry out repairs (the most common repair jobs are shown on pp.126–27). However, you will need to understand how these coverings are created if you want to match them on an extension, or if you wish to refurbish an entire section of wall.

REGULATIONS AND PERMISSIONS
The rules covering external alterations vary from area to area, and according to whether the building is listed or in a conservation area. Before your plans advance too far, check with your local authorities as to whether you need permission to render or clad your home. It may also be necessary to get permission to use certain paint colours. In all cases, a quick phone call can normally confirm any local guidelines or requirements.

RENDER
This can be applied directly to blocks or bricks, or onto metal laths (sheets of wire mesh that help adhesion) to provide a decorative, weatherproofing coat that protects a wall's structure. There are several finishing options, the most common of which are shown to the right (for green renders, see p.99). Some topcoats have extra features, such as enhanced damp-proofing properties, or suitability for finishing with exterior-quality paint. Investigate your options with your builder or supplier, who will also be able to advise you on the quantities needed, and any waterproofing measures that may be necessary.

Planning to render
Rendering large walls is not a job for an amateur – advanced plastering skills are required, as is experience in achieving the chosen finish. Unless you are very experienced, hire somebody to carry out the work for you. It may need several coats – usually an initial scratch coat followed by one or more further layers of render. Avoid application at times of extreme weather conditions, which can seriously affect the way render adheres, and may therefore reduce its lifespan. A Tyrolean gun (see below), which sprays a rough finish (Tyrolean) onto a rendered wall, may be used by an amateur, but it takes practice and is hard work. However, Tyrolean is applied after a scratch coat and a render coat, so you will need professional help even for this option.

Smooth render
The smoothest of render finishes will still have some slight texture.

Patterned render
Smooth render can be tooled to produce various patterns if needed.

Tyrolean
A uniform rough finish that is applied over smooth render.

Pebbledash
Achieved by throwing pebbles onto damp render.

Tyrolean gun
The Tyrolean is held in a reservoir within the gun. The paddles inside turn when the handle is turned, to spray out the Tyrolean. It is hard work turning the handle and holding a gun steady. If you decide to apply your own Tyrolean, practise on a rough area first, which will not be visible. Build up layers of Tyrolean slowly.

Paddles spray Tyrolean

CLADDING
Also called weatherboard, cladding is often found on timber-framed houses, forming the outer layer of a cavity wall. However, it can also be used with masonry. Some homes are partially clad for decorative effect – boards can be placed horizontally or vertically – but cladding also performs a vital weatherproofing function. Boards are usually timber, so as long as the wood comes from a sustainable source they can be considered eco-friendly. Man-made options such as cement board, UPVC, and metal-based boards are also available. These need less maintenance than wood, and some can be painted. Metal-based boards are called siding, and are usually attached to the house with special clips and channels, bought with the boards.

Cladding should be fixed on top of either building paper (a moisture barrier) or a breather membrane (which stops water entering a wall, but allows vapour within the wall to escape). A series of battens must be fixed over the paper or membrane, to provide fixing points for the nails or screws used to attach the cladding itself.

Using battens
Horizontal cladding goes onto vertical battens (see right), which provide a cavity for drainage channels between boards and wall. To maintain channels behind vertical cladding, which attaches to horizontal battens, fit vertical battens first. Chamfering the top edges of the horizontal battens directs water away from the wall. Battens must end 150mm (6in) above the ground, so that cladding does not touch damp earth. Use treated softwood measuring 25 x 50mm (1 x 2in); see pp.136–37 and 222 on fitting battens. Some manufacturers will produce cladding systems that incorporate an insulation layer between cladding and the wall. Take professional advice, as it is important to use the correct insulation in order to avoid problems with condensation.

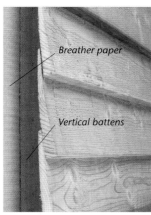

Breather paper

Vertical battens

FEATHER-EDGE BOARDS

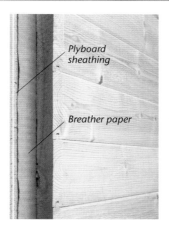

Plyboard sheathing

Breather paper

TONGUE-AND-GROOVE BOARDS

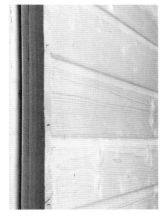

SHIPLAP BOARDS

Vertical battens beneath horizontal

SHINGLES

Cladding in use

This example shows the effect that can be achieved with cement boards. Plan how to fit boards around windows and doors, and whether they will fit beneath a guttering downpipe. Joints with other surfaces need to be finished with corner strips (see below) and/or silicone sealant. Butt-join the lengths of board, and overlap layers of breather paper by at least 150mm (6in). You can nail just the tops of the boards, or both the tops and the bottoms. Use the method most suitable for your chosen boards. Tongue-and-groove boards can have hidden nailing, as shown on p.222.

APPLYING CEMENT-BOARD CLADDING

Having attached breather paper and battens at 400-mm (1ft 4-in) intervals, you can start building up rows of cladding. You will need the following: nail gun and nails, corner strips, boards, kicker strip, silicone sealant, and dispenser.

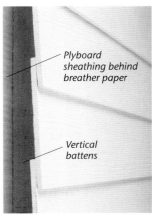

Plyboard sheathing behind breather paper

Vertical battens

CEMENT-BOARD CLADDING

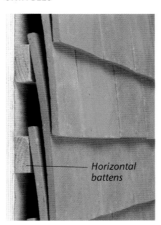

Horizontal battens

TILES

A Apply corner strips with a nail gun, taking care to use the tool safely (see pp.52–53).

B Attach a kicker strip to the bases of the battens. This will push out the boards to a slight angle, helping with positioning and water run-off.

C Apply boards, inserting fixings into every batten. Build up rows, overlapping the previous layer each time by at least 25mm (1in).

D Use silicone sealant at corners and where boards meet another surface. Another option for a corner is to use a covering strip.

GREEN CLADDING OPTIONS

Consider green alternatives when choosing cladding for your external walls. Try using reclaimed wood, for example, or make sure that any new timber you use comes from a sustainable source (see p.75).

Aluminium cladding produced from recycled aluminium – rather than a virgin source – is another viable option. For clay tiles, visit a reclamation yard, as reuse is the most eco-friendly option and may save you money (see pp.86–87). While cement board is not the greenest option, if you are determined to use it, find manufacturers that use high quantities of recycled material.

PATCH PLASTERING

Use this technique on an area of flaky or missing plaster, either on a wall (shown here) or on a ceiling. Use undercoat plaster on a semi-porous surface and bonding coat on a non-porous one (see p.138). If old plaster is unstable in a number of areas, whether on a masonry or a timber wall, remove all plaster and render, and re-plaster. Most plaster will come away relatively easily, but use a club hammer and bolster chisel on any difficult areas.

TOOLS AND MATERIALS
Brush, paintbrush, PVA solution, trowel, hawk, undercoat plaster, finishing plaster, plasterer's trowel, sandpaper

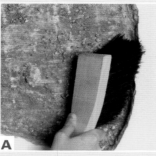

A Brush out any loose debris from the damaged area, paying particular attention to the edges.

B Apply a coat of PVA solution (5:1 water to PVA), overlapping the surrounding wall. This aids bonding for new plaster.

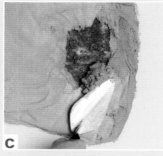

C Apply undercoat plaster or bonding coat.

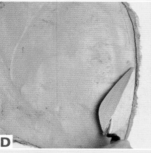

D Smooth the plaster to a level slightly shallower than that of the surrounding wall's surface.

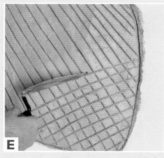

E Score the plaster with the edge of the trowel to provide a key, which will aid bonding, for the top coat of plaster.

F Once the undercoat is dry, apply finishing plaster. Feather in the join with the surrounding wall. When it is dry, sand the area until smooth.

REPAIRING A SMALL HOLE IN A STUD WALL OR CEILING

A small area of damaged plasterboard can be filled in with a plasterboard offcut. Use the same technique when repairing a hole in a plasterboard ceiling. Make sure that you do not cut through any supply cables or pipes when enlarging the hole.

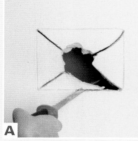

A Trim off loose pieces around the hole to create a rectangular space. Cut a piece of plasterboard that is slightly larger than the hole.

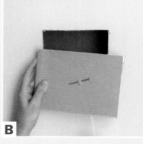

B Make a small hole in the centre of the small board. Thread a piece of string through the hole, knotted or tied to a nail on one side.

C Apply PVA adhesive around the edge of the board on the opposite side to the tied-off end of string.

TOOLS AND MATERIALS
Craft knife, string, nail, PVA adhesive, offcut of wood, filler, scraper, sandpaper

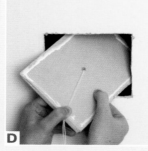

D Post the board through the hole, making sure you hold onto the piece of string.

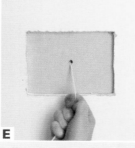

E Pull the board into position using the string. To hold it in place as the adhesive dries, tie an offcut of wood to the string, spanning the hole.

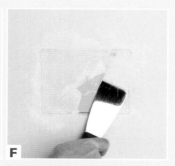

F Once the PVA is dry, remove the string and apply filler to the hole. When dry, sand the filler. You may need another layer for a level finish.

REPAIRING A LARGE HOLE IN A STUD WALL OR CEILING

If a hole is too big for the quick fix shown opposite below, cut out the damaged section of plasterboard, insert new noggings (timber fixing points), and replace the plasterboard. As with other repairs shown on these pages, this technique is suitable for use on a wall or a ceiling. Be careful not to cut through any hidden supply cables or pipes.

TOOLS AND MATERIALS
Stud detector, spirit level, pencil, drywall saw, craft knife, noggings, piece of plasterboard, drywall screws, self-adhesive scrim, finishing plaster, plasterer's trowel, sandpaper

PATCH PLASTERING LATH AND PLASTER

The best technique to use when patching damaged lath and plaster will depend on whether the laths are broken or damaged. In some cases, a repair can be made by fixing plasterboard to bare laths and skimming, or undercoat plaster followed by a layer of topcoat plaster can be applied to undamaged bare laths. Badly damaged areas or gaps between broken laths can be patched with wire mesh first. Make sure that the laths are cleaned down and primed with a PVA solution before the plaster is applied.

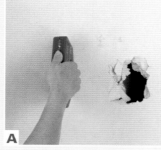

A **Find the stud** on either side of the damaged area by feeling into the hole, or by using a stud detector.

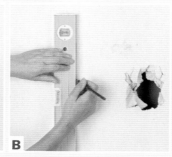

B **Use a spirit level** to draw a pencil line on the wall to indicate the centre of each stud. Draw it so that it extends to just above and below the damaged area.

C **Add horizontal lines** to join the vertical pencil lines and create a rectangular guide line.

D **Cut out the rectangular** area with a drywall saw and a craft knife and remove the damaged section of plasterboard.

E **Attach two noggings** to the studs, one above and one below the hole. These will provide fixing points for screws.

F **Measure and cut a section** of plasterboard to fit the hole and fix it across the hole, driving drywall screws into the studs and noggings.

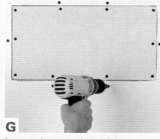

G **Secure the cut edges** of the original plasterboard onto the noggings and studs.

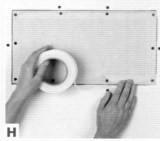

H **Tape the joints** between pieces of board with self-adhesive scrim.

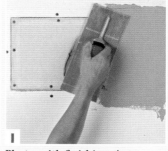

I **Plaster with finishing** plaster, allow to dry, and sand to smooth.

REPAIRING LOOSE JOINTING TAPE

The joints between boards in a dry-lined ceiling or wall are secured with tape (see pp.136–37). This sometimes loses adhesion and comes away from the surface, but is easily fixed.

TOOLS AND MATERIALS
Craft knife, jointing tape, jointing compound, taping knife

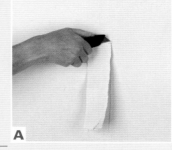

A **Cut away the loose** strip of tape with a craft knife.

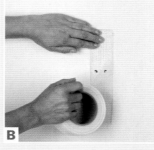

B **Re-tape the joint** using jointing tape or self-adhesive scrim.

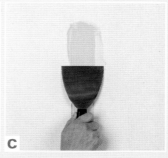

C **Re-seal the area** with jointing compound (see p.137).

REPAIRING A CORNER ON INDOOR WALLS

Corners are susceptible to wear and tear, but they are straightforward to restore. A small repair can be carried out with all-purpose filler using the technique shown here. To restore a larger area or the full height of a corner, use a piece of angle bead to renew the corner's apex and then apply finishing plaster to provide a sharp profile (see pp.133 and 135).

TOOLS AND MATERIALS
Hammer, nails, batten, filler, fillling knife, sandpaper

A **Fix a length of batten,** longer than the area that needs repairing, along the edge of the corner.

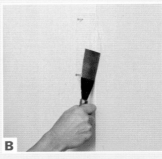

B **Use all-purpose filler** and a filler knife to fill the damaged area, using the batten to provide a straight edge for the repair.

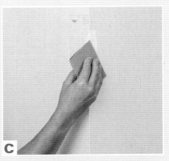

C **When the filler** has dried, sand it down to provide a smooth surface.

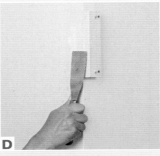

D **Repeat these steps** on the other side of the corner's edge so that the repair is even and the corner sharp.

E **Remove the batten** and fill the holes made by the fixings.

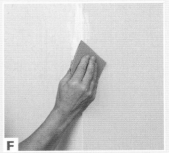

F **To complete the repair ,** sand all the repaired areas, smoothing off all the filler to the surrounding wall's level. Then decorate as required.

REPAIRING VERTICAL TILES ON AN EXTERIOR WALL

Because layers of tiles overlap each other, a new tile cannot be nailed into the support batten below. Instead, use adhesive to secure a new tile. If you need to replace several tiles, you will be able to nail all but the last one, which will need to be fixed using the method shown here. A slate ripper can be used as an alternative to a hacksaw blade. This technique can also be used to repair tiles on roofs.

TOOLS AND MATERIALS
Gloves, masking tape, hacksaw blade or slate ripper, grab adhesive, new tile, heavy-duty tape, sealant dispenser

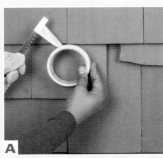

A **Wrap some masking** tape or similar around one end of a hacksaw blade to enable you to hold the blade without injury.

B **Holding the wrapped** end, slide the saw blade under the broken tile and cut through the fixings that hold the tile in place.

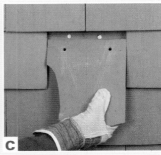

C **Slide out the** broken tile.

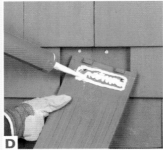

D **Apply some all-purpose** grab adhesive to the back of a new tile, at the top and bottom, where it will sit on the batten and the tile below.

E **Slide the new tile** into position, ensuring that its top edge lies on the batten and its lower edge rests on top of the tile in the row below.

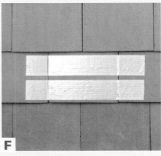

F **Tape the new tile** so the surrounding tiles hold it securely in position while the adhesive dries. When it is dry, remove the tape.

REPAIRING SPLIT CLADDING BOARDS

Boards are difficult to remove so aim to repair, not replace, them. If you do have to remove boards, cut through joints, or lever boards out and cut through fixings with a hacksaw, as appropriate to the boards.

TOOLS AND MATERIALS
Chisel, adhesive, hammer, nails, nail punch, filler, paint

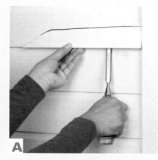

A

Lever away the split section of board and remove it.

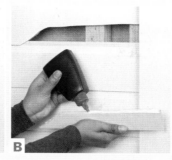

B

Apply a water-resistant wood adhesive along the edges of the removed piece of board.

Hide new fixings with filler and points

C

Re-apply the broken piece to the board it came from, and use fixings to hold the repair securely together.

PATCHING CRUMBLY EXTERIOR RENDER

After this repair, apply whatever decorative finish is on the surrounding area (see p.122). A chipping hammer can be hired to remove a lot of render; get guidance from the hire shop on using it.

TOOLS AND MATERIALS
Club hammer, bolster chisel, gloves, goggles, PVA, render, gauging trowel, sponge

Pay attention to the edges when applying PVA

A

Remove loose render with a club hammer and a cold chisel. Dust away debris and apply PVA solution (one part PVA to five parts water).

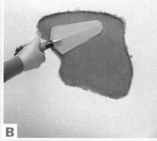

B

Apply a first coat of render, pressing it firmly into the hole and allowing it to sit slightly lower than the surrounding wall surface.

A damp sponge will feather in edges with existing wall

C

When the first coat is dry, use a trowel to score it so that a second coat will bond. Apply another layer of render flush with the wall.

REPOINTING MORTAR

If old mortar has cracked or deteriorated, get advice from a structural engineer about whether it is a sign of serious structural problems or simply due to settlement. If settlement is the cause, mortar can be repointed (shown here) or "stitched" (a technique involving special "stitching rods" and an epoxy resin). If the problem is more serious, follow your engineer's advice on tackling it.

A

Use a joint raker to remove any loose, crumbly bits of old mortar.

B

Use a club hammer and cold chisel to "peck" out the more obstinate, solid chunks of mortar from between the bricks.

C

Dust out the old mortar joints to remove all debris.

D

Use a spray to wet the bricks and mortar joints. This prevents bricks soaking up the new mortar and ensures that it will adhere.

E

Use a pointing trowel and a brick jointer to press new mortar into place. Use the jointer to mimic the profile of existing mortar joints.

F

Use a dry brush to remove any excess mortar and to tidy up joints.

TOOLS AND MATERIALS
Gloves, joint raker, club hammer, cold chisel, brush, misting spray, pointing trowel, brick jointer, small paintbrush

Plastering

INTERNAL MASONRY WALLS USUALLY NEED PLASTERING BEFORE DECORATING, THOUGH NATURAL STONE OR BRICK CAN BE LEFT EXPOSED. FINISHING (TOPCOAT) PLASTER CANNOT BE APPLIED DIRECTLY TO MASONRY: IT REQUIRES A "BACKGROUND" OF CEMENT-BASED RENDER, UNDERCOAT, OR BONDING PLASTER. THESE PAGES DEAL WITH INTERNAL WALL PLASTERING AS WELL AS DRY LINING (AN ALTERNATIVE TO PLASTERING).

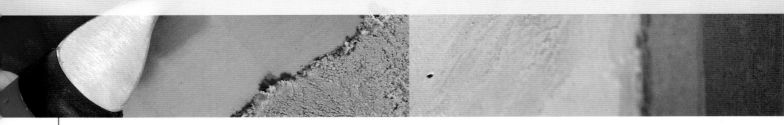

PLASTERING AND DRY LINING

The traditional way of covering walls, plastering is useful for large repairs or when matching existing plastered walls. It can also be more cost-effective than buying large quantities of plasterboard. If covering a whole room, consider dry lining, whereby plasterboard itself is used as the decorative surface and the joints between boards are filled with jointing compound, and sanded smooth. Dry lining is easier to master, and is a good option if you are not confident about plastering. It can be used on both stud walls and new or existing masonry. For information on greener finishes for internal walls, see p.99.

BEFORE YOU START
■ Plastering is a particularly messy job, and it is important to cover or mask any surfaces that need to be protected from splashes or drips during application.
■ Sanding even small areas of plaster or dry-lining compound creates dust that can spread across a wide area.
■ Take as many moveable objects as possible out of the room, and cover any remaining items with dustsheets.

PLASTERING AND DRY LINING OPTIONS

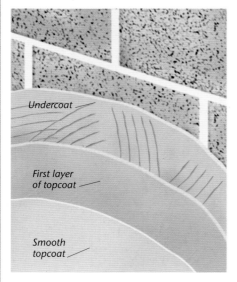

Undercoat

First layer of topcoat

Smooth topcoat

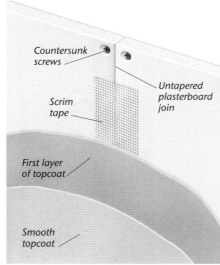

Countersunk screws

Scrim tape

Untapered plasterboard join

First layer of topcoat

Smooth topcoat

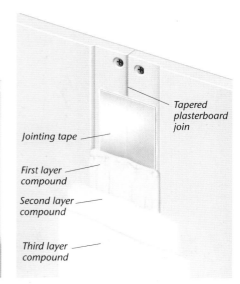

Jointing tape

First layer compound

Second layer compound

Third layer compound

Tapered plasterboard join

Option 1: Plastering a masonry wall
A cost-effective method for preparing a large area of wall, ready for decorating.

Option 2: Plastering a stud wall
A smooth finish over untapered board, achieved by plastering across the entire surface.

Option 3: Dry lining (masonry or a stud wall)
Layers of compound fill the gully, which is then sanded to provide a smooth finish.

CHOOSING TO PLASTER

One-coat plaster can be applied directly to masonry but, despite the name, two coats will give a better finish. However, the smoothest finish on masonry is achieved by applying a layer of either undercoat or render, and then following it with finishing plaster. It is difficult to achieve good results without practice, though, so consider your level of skill when deciding your approach. See p.130 for the types of plaster. For a stud wall, your options depend on the plasterboard (see p.104). If the wall has boards with tapered edges, you should dry line (see below). Boards with non-tapered edges must be plastered. If you are building a new stud wall, consider which method best suits before buying and applying plasterboard.

Choosing render or undercoat plaster

The choice between render and undercoat plaster depends on a number of factors. Undercoat plaster cannot be used if a wall shows any signs of damp, whereas render – to which damp-proof additives can be added – can be used. Information on treating damp walls is on pp.228–30. Undercoat plaster provides better insulation than render, but will not give such a hard-wearing finish. Undercoat plaster is also easier to work with and easier to apply, making it a more attractive proposition for a DIY project.

CHOOSING BETWEEN PLASTERING AND DRY LINING

When choosing between plastering and dry lining, remember that plastering is more difficult. If there are pipes or cables across a wall, the battening-out method of dry lining can hide them, but if you are about to install services, run them through the wall (see pp.104–105 and pp.442–443) and dab out.

Wall	Finish required	Method
Masonry	Plaster	Use render or undercoat plaster, followed by finishing plaster
	Dry lining	Use dry-wall adhesive to dab out, then apply tapered plasterboard and dry-lining compound
		Use battens (timber or metal), tapered plasterboard, and dry-lining compound
Stud wall	Plaster	Use untapered plasterboard followed by finishing plaster
	Dry lining	Use tapered plasterboard and dry-lining compound

CHOOSING TO DRY LINE

This is an alternative to plastering which uses the plasterboard itself as the decorative surface. The joints between sheets, and all holes for nails or screws, are filled with joint compound. The compound is then sanded smooth to create a flat surface that is suitable for decoration. After sanding the board, prepare its surface using proprietary board sealant.

Dry lining uses plasterboard with a tapered edge, the ivory-coloured edge uppermost. It is suitable for internal brick, block, or stud walls.

Problems can arise when sheets have to be cut to fit, and so have no gap left by a joint of two tapered edges. Apply jointing compound to flush joints; it may be slightly proud of the overall surface, but will not be noticeable.

Insulation – thermal or sound (see pp.352–63) – can be added behind a dry-lined surface. Another option is to use thermal-check plasterboard (see p.72). Most types of metal-framed wall or ceiling coverings have their own systems for insulation.

There are three options for attaching plasterboard to masonry, shown below.

COVERING A CEILING

Plastering a ceiling is really a job for professionals, but dry lining offers an alternative for the DIY enthusiast.
■ Ceilings should be covered with large taper-edged sheets, not small laths.
■ Problems may be encountered where the flush cut ends of the boards (with no tapered edge) join, and there is no taper to fill with compound.
■ In this area, tape the joints, but feather out the compound to make a very gradual hump along the join. Once sanded and painted, this will become unnoticeable.

Option 1: Dabbing out
This technique involves using dabs of adhesive to secure sheets of plasterboard directly to a wall. It is not suitable for use on external walls that are prone to damp or water penetration, because the wall surface should be as stable as possible, with no flaky paint or loose surface material. In any case, damp problems should be addressed as soon as possible, to prevent them getting worse (see pp.228–30).

Option 2: Battening out with wood
This option involves fixing wooden battens to the masonry, and then nailing or screwing plasterboard onto the battens. Any unevenness in the wall surface can be taken up by packing out behind the battens as required. This system is ideal when a wall has pipes and cables running on its surface, because they can easily be concealed in the cavity behind the plasterboard itself.

Option 3: Battening out with metal channels
A third option is to use metal wall channels. These are modern, metal versions of wooden battens. They can be easily cut to size, slot together, and are attached to the wall using masonry fixings or adhesive. If using adhesive to attach them, you can add a little extra in some places to "pack out" the channels, accounting for uneven surfaces and ensuring that the channels are level. Plasterboard is then screwed onto the channels with drywall screws.

BEFORE YOU START

When considering whether to attempt a plastering job yourself or to employ a professional, assess the scale of the task, your own abilities, and whether you will be able to achieve the finish you want. Also factor in the cost of buying or hiring equipment.

Consider the required finish; topcoat plaster gives the best finish, yet it requires considerable skill to achieve the right look. If using plasterboard, check that you are

purchasing the right product for your job (see p.72). Taper-edged plasterboard (not untapered) is essential for dry lining.

You can use either taper-edged or non-tapered plasterboard for lining a stud wall, but you will need to plaster over untapered boards. Most manufacturers recommend that you plaster or seal on the ivory side of the board only – not on the reverse side.

Types of plaster

Several types of plaster are available, as a powder to be mixed with water, or ready-mixed, which is more expensive. Professional plasterers tend to use gypsum-based plaster, which needs to be mixed to the correct consistency and has a fast drying time. An amateur may have more success with ready-mixed products. Two main types of plaster are needed for a job: undercoat (basecoat) and topcoat (finishing coat). Quantities are based on area covered and thickness of layer. An alternative to using undercoat plaster is a cement-based render. When coating the inside of an exterior wall, a plaster containing fungicide may prevent damp. See p.85 for information on greener finishes.

ESTIMATING QUANTITIES

Material	Usage	Coverage
Bonding coat	10kg (22lb) for 8mm (⅓in)	1.5sq m (16sq ft)
Undercoat plaster	10kg (22lb) for 10mm (in)	1.5sq m (16sq ft)
Render	10kg (22lb) for 12mm (½in)	1sq m (12sq ft)
Finishing plaster	10kg (22lb) for 2mm (½in)	4.5sq m (48sq ft)
One-coat plaster	10kg (22lb) for 10mm (⅜in)	0.7sq m (7½sq ft)
Decorative plaster	10kg (22lb) for 3mm (⅛mm)	2sq m (22sq ft)

CHECKLIST WHEN USING PLASTER

■ Ready-mixed plaster is supplied in plastic, resealable tubs and lasts well between applications if resealed.
■ When purchasing dry plaster, check that it is within its sell-by date.
■ Store plaster in dry conditions. Once opened, seal between usage to protect from moisture.
■ Wear a dust mask when mixing and sanding plaster to avoid inhalation.
■ Take care not to allow dust or other contaminants to fall into the plaster while you are mixing it. If plaster does become contaminated, it will be more difficult to apply and to smooth.

UNDERCOAT	Uses include
Bonding coat An undercoat plaster suitable for a non-porous background. It can be used over PVA sealant. Best applied when PVA is still tacky (i.e. not completely dry).	Patching old masonry, engineering bricks, patching old laths
Undercoat plaster An undercoat suitable for use on a semi-porous background. Use as a complete basecoat for finishing plaster.	Bricks and building blocks
Render A sand and cement mixture suitable for internal masonry walls. An alternative to undercoat plaster, but more difficult to apply. Additives can be used to increase waterproofing capability.	Bricks and building blocks

ONE-COAT AND TOPCOAT	Uses include
One-coat plaster No undercoat plaster is needed with a one-coat plaster. It can be applied and finished in a similar way to topcoat plaster. Suitable for amateurs or when some degree of surface undulation or imperfection is acceptable.	Internal walls and ceilings. Can also be used over undercoat plaster or plasterboard
Finishing plaster Topcoat plaster that forms the final surface to be decorated. It is a finer product, and is applied about 2mm (¹⁄₁₆in) thick. Best finishes achieved by applying two thin coats, the top one being added before the first is completely dry.	Internal walls and ceilings without an undercoat
Lime plaster The most common wall covering before the advent of gypsum-based plaster. It is still used for repairs in period properties. Lime plaster allows the wall surface to "breathe" more than a gypsum-based plaster; modern properties have damp courses, so tend not to suffer as much from damp. Lime plastering is a complex job, and best left to a professional.	Period properties, renovation projects
Textured coating This is not a plaster in the traditional sense, but has similarities in that it is a commonly used ceiling – and occasionally wall – covering. Used as a topcoat, it creates a textured, rather than smooth, finish.	Mainly ceilings, occasionally walls
Decorative plaster This is a professional finish and requires a great deal of practice to master. Made from ground marble, the plaster coat itself provides a matt, coloured finish, and can be polished.	Decorative topcoat

PLASTERING TOOLS AND MATERIALS

Darby
Use to smooth large areas of plaster.

Handle (one at each end)

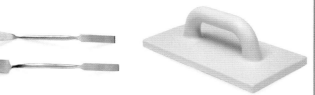

Hawk
A hand-held platform to hold small amounts of plaster. Scoop plaster onto the hawk with a trowel and hold near wall for easy application.

Plastering trowel
Use to scoop all types of plaster from a hawk onto a surface, and to spread on wall or ceiling.

Feather edge
Removes excess plaster and smooths surface.

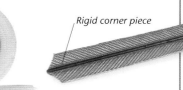

Plasterer's brush
An all-purpose brush to apply PVA sealant, dampen surfaces, or to clean trowels and equipment.

Finger edging trowels
Finish awkward areas such as around windows and doors with this small plastering trowel.

Plasterer's spatulas
Small, shaped steel spatulas, use these for finishing off plaster at joints and on decorative mouldings.

Polyurethane float
Traditionally made of wood, but now commonly available in plastic, this tool is for finishing render coats.

Rigid corner piece

External corner trowel
Shaped to finish plaster on external corner edges. Hold the handle and draw downwards.

Internal corner trowel
Shaped to finish plaster inside internal corners. Hold the handle and draw downwards.

Types of scrim
Covers joins between boards. Bed traditional scrim (left) in place with a band of plaster. A self-adhesive version (right) is also available.

Angle bead
Fix this right-angled metal bead to external corners to make a sharp, neat finish. Plaster up to and flush with the edges.

DRY LINING TOOLS AND MATERIALS

Caulking blade
Use this broad-bladed spatula to smooth a width of jointing compound when dry lining.

Jointing sponge
Use to smooth jointing compound over scrim and joint tape when dry lining a wall.

Joint tape
Use this tape to fill gaps between taper-edged sheets of plasterboard when dry lining.

Corner joint tape
Contains metal bands for strength. Used mainly when dry lining on external corners.

Taping knives
Use to press tape into plasterboard joints and joint compound. Available in several sizes.

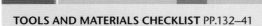

TOOLS AND MATERIALS CHECKLIST PP.132–41

Applying undercoat or render (pp.132–33) Timber battens, drill, mister, power stirrer, hawk, plastering trowel, feather edge, wooden float, angle bead*

Applying finishing plaster (pp.134–35) Scrim, power stirrer, spot board, plasterer's trowel, hawk, small paint brush, angle bead*, corner trowels*

Dabbing out (p.136) Taper-edged plasterboard, spirit level, chalk line, plumb line, dry-wall adhesive, plastering trowel, darby or feather edge

Battening out with wood (p.136) Timber battens, spirit level, chalk line, timber offcuts, taper-edged plasterboard

Battening out with metal battens (p.137) Chalk line,

metal battens, tin snips, spirit level, taper-edged plasterboard

Dry lining (p.137) Joint compound, joint tape, taping knife, caulking blade, jointing sponge, sandpaper, board sealant, paintbrush

* = optional

FOR BASIC TOOLKIT
SEE PP.24–25

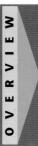
APPLYING UNDERCOAT PLASTER

First, decide whether you need to use render (see pp.128–30), or undercoat plaster (shown here). You can follow the steps below for either option. Plastering to a consistent depth is difficult, so fix temporary battens to the wall. These divide the wall into manageable sections, or bays, and provide a useful depth gauge. Before applying topcoat or finishing plaster (see pp.134–35), allow the undercoat to start "going off" (drying out). If it dries too fast, use a mister. This is a messy job so protect all vulnerable surfaces.

TOOLS AND MATERIALS SEE BASIC TOOLKIT AND P.131

1 PREPARING TO PLASTER

Saw battens to fit the height of the wall to be plastered; you need one for every 1m (3ft 3in) of wall. Battens should be 10mm (⅜in) deep as this will be the final depth of plaster.

A

Fix the battens temporarily and use a spirit level to ensure that they are vertical. The battens divide the wall into bays for ease of plastering. You will need to remove the battens later so use screw fixings for easy removal; masonry screws are ideal.

B

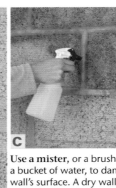

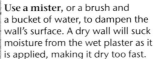

C

Use a mister, or a brush and a bucket of water, to dampen the wall's surface. A dry wall will suck moisture from the wet plaster as it is applied, making it dry too fast.

D

Mix the undercoat plaster according to the manufacturer's instructions. You need a smooth, yet stiff, consistency. Mix in a bucket using a power stirrer (see p.68).

2 FILLING THE FIRST BAY

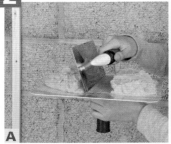

A

Transfer some plaster to a hawk. Use a plastering trowel to cut away a section of plaster, then tilt the hawk so you can pick up plaster onto the face of the trowel.

B

Press the plaster onto the wall within the first bay, and distribute it as evenly as possible. Aim to achieve a uniform depth of 10mm (⅜in) by using the battens as guides.

C

Pick up more plaster from the hawk, press it onto the wall, and smooth it out, monitoring depth carefully as you go. Continue until the first bay is filled.

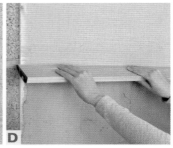

D

Run a feather edge down the battens to remove any excess plaster from the bay. Fill any areas with more plaster to bring the surface level to the top of the battens.

3 FILLING FURTHER BAYS AND REMOVING BATTENS

A Move on to the next bay, and follow the same steps to fill it with undercoat plaster, applying plaster and smoothing it until the entire bay is filled to the batten level.

B Carry on filling bays until they have all been plastered and levelled. The process will speed up as you get used to loading the trowel and achieving the right depth of plaster.

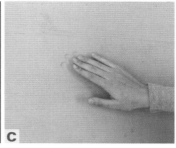

C Allow the undercoat to just begin to go off – it should be firm, but still give to gentle fingertip pressure. How long this takes will depend on the conditions in the room.

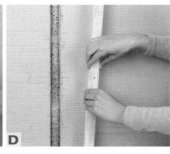

D Unscrew and remove the battens. Work quickly before the plaster dries completely, but take care not to damage the plaster you have already smoothed.

4 FINISHING THE UNDERCOAT

A Fill the channels left by the battens with more undercoat plaster. Use the trowel to smooth the plaster to the same depth as the existing plaster.

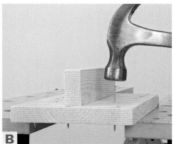

B Undercoat plaster needs to be scored to provide a key for the top coat. Make a tool for this by driving several nails through a wooden float so their tips protrude from the face.

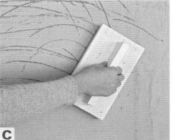

C Score the undercoat by drawing the modified float across its damp surface so that the nails produce fine channels. Press down lightly: you do not want deep gouges.

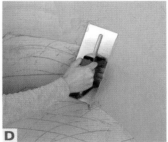

D Leave the undercoat to go off, but not to dry out completely. Drying time is about two hours, but check progress regularly. Apply finishing plaster (see pp.134–35).

PLASTERING EXTERNAL CORNERS

A Dab some undercoat plaster onto the wall at approximately 300-mm (1-ft) intervals to act as an adhesive for an angle bead.

B Cut the angle bead to the required length. Press into the undercoat plaster, taking care that it lies straight and is held firmly in place.

C When the angle bead plaster has dried, apply undercoat plaster so that it lies level with the angle bead. Let this plaster begin to go off.

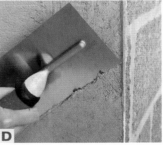

D Scrape back the plaster next to the bead by 2mm (½in) to allow room for the finishing plaster to lie level with it. Score as above.

APPLYING FINISHING PLASTER

Finishing (skimming) with topcoat plaster is an art that takes practice to get a smooth finish. No batten guides can be used. The technique is the same whether you skim over plasterboard sheets (as here), render, or an undercoat, though the surface preparation varies (see p.129). An undercoat should be slightly damp when plaster is applied; use a mister to dampen it, if necessary. Practise using plastering techniques on a small area before tackling a whole wall.

TOOLS AND MATERIALS SEE BASIC TOOLKIT AND P.131

COVERING BOARD

Plasterboard has to be skimmed with plaster before the surface will be suitable for painting or papering. Use scrim to cover the joins between boards. Apply a layer of plaster across the entire surface, including the scrim. Then follow the steps below to achieve a smooth surface. The same type of plaster should be used for each layer.

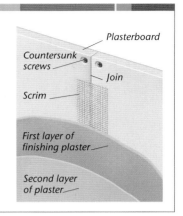

Plasterboard

Countersunk screws

Join

Scrim

First layer of finishing plaster

Second layer of plaster

1 SMOOTHING PLASTERBOARD JOINTS

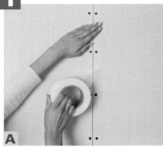

A

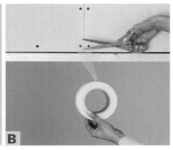

B

Use adhesive scrim to cover joints between plasterboard sheets, or use non-adhesive scrim, attaching it with a little prepared plaster.

Trim scrim with scissors to get a neat edge. Fill any gaps greater than 3mm (⅛in) with pre-mixed plaster (see p.108).

2 PREPARING PLASTER

A

B

Half-fill a bucket with clean tap water, and slowly add the plaster, following the manufacturer's instructions. Mix more as you need it.

Use a power stirrer to mix the plaster. Submerge the stirrer before starting the drill and use at a low speed. You can also mix manually.

C

D

Keep adding plaster and mix until it has a creamy consistency. Run a trowel around the edge of the bucket to incorporate all the dry plaster.

Pour the plaster onto a spot board. It should be thick enough to spread evenly over the board without running over the edge.

3 APPLYING THE PLASTER

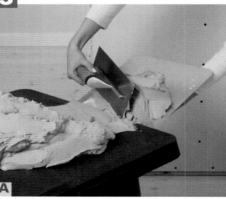

A

Use a plastering trowel to cut away a section of the mixed plaster, and transfer it to a plastering hawk. Use a small amount at first to get used to handling the hawk.

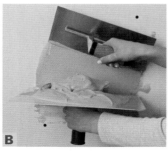

B

Holding the hawk in front of the wall, cut away a section of plaster, using the plastering trowel. Push the plaster up and onto the wall surface.

C

Spread the plaster across the wall surface, pressing firmly and distributing it as evenly as possible. Work from the top of the wall to the bottom, in broad, vertical and horizontal strokes. Aim to work quickly to cover the surface before the plaster starts to dry.

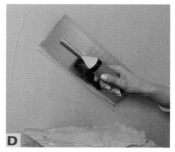

D

Continue to add more plaster, building up a rhythm of loading the hawk and transferring the plaster to the wall surface.

4 SMOOTHING THE PLASTER

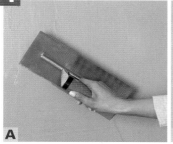

A

Once the surface is covered, go back over it, smoothing the plaster to an even thickness. Do not try to achieve perfect smoothness yet.

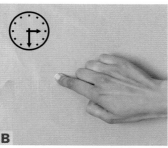

B

Leave the plaster to dry for at least half an hour, until the surface is firm enough to touch without moving the plaster, but is still damp.

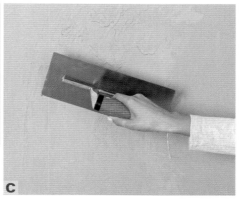

C

Sweep a clean, dampened trowel blade across the entire surface, smoothing the plaster and redistributing any excess to fill small indents. Hold the blade at a slight angle with only one edge on the plaster to achieve a smooth finish.

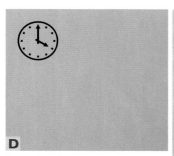

D

Leave the plaster to dry for another half hour, until it is harder, but still slightly damp.

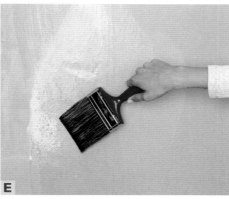

E

Repeat the smoothing process, again using any excess surface plaster to fill small depressions. If necessary, use a wet brush or garden spray gun to dampen the plaster as you work. Aim for a smooth finish at this final stage; it is more effective than trying to sand rough plaster when dry.

F

Use a small, damp brush to finish edges and corners neatly.

5 FINISHING AN EXTERNAL CORNER

To produce a sharp, straight edge when plastering an external corner on plasterboard, use an angle bead. This acts as a guide for the finishing plaster, but is covered by the plaster to give a clean finish. Saw the angle bead to the length you need using a junior hacksaw or tin snips (see p.105).

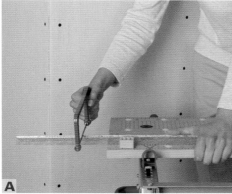

A

B

Fix the bead to both walls at the corner ensuring that the bead is tight against the corner.

C

Apply plaster over the top of the angle bead, allowing the plastering trowel to rest on the apex of the bead to give you a good finish.

APPLYING A SECOND LAYER

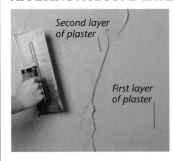

Second layer of plaster

First layer of plaster

An alternative to smoothing off the first layer of plaster is to apply a second, thinner layer, giving two topcoats. If you want to follow this option, do it between steps 4A and B. Most professional plasterers do this to achieve the flattest, highest quality finish. Once the second layer has been added, follow steps 4B onwards to smooth the plaster.

FINISHING AN EXTERNAL CORNER

An alternative to using an angle bead on an external corner is to smooth the plaster with a corner trowel. This gives a more rustic finish, rather than a clean, straight line. A corner trowel is not suitable for achieving a high-quality finish; angle beading gives better results. A similar finish is achieved on an internal corner by using an internal corner trowel.

DRY LINING A WALL

Plasterboards can be used to line large areas of wall. Dry lining can be used to cover pipework and insulating material. There are three ways of fixing plasterboard to masonry: dabbing out with dry-wall adhesive; battening out with wood; and battening out with metal. To achieve a smooth finish, fill the joints between boards (see below right). Dabbing out is not suitable for external walls prone to damp. For cutting plasterboard to size see pp.72–73 and p.108. To attach plasterboard to a stud wall, see p.108.

TOOLS AND MATERIALS SEE BASIC TOOLKIT AND P.131

▌ DABBING OUT

A

Hold a sheet of plasterboard in place against the wall, and mark roughly where the edge will be using chalk. Aim to reach as high as possible to get close to the ceiling. This will guide where to position the dabs of dry-wall adhesive. Measure and cut the boards for the whole wall before you apply any adhesive.

B

Use a spirit level to add vertical guide lines at marks. Also add guide lines at intervals of 400mm (1ft 4in) between these.

C

Pin a chalk line across the ceiling. The chalk line position should be the thickness of the board plus 10mm (⅜in) away from the wall. Snap a chalk line on the ceiling to mark where the front edge of the plasterboard will be.

D

Hang a plumb line from the ceiling chalk line, and mark a further line on the floor surface as an extra guide for board position.

Apply dabs of dry-wall adhesive using a plastering trowel. Dab inside the chalk lines to coincide with the board edges and along the other chalk lines through the central area of the "board". Also apply a continuous channel of adhesive around the perimeter of the wall. Each dab should measure about 75mm (3in) wide and 300mm (1ft) long.

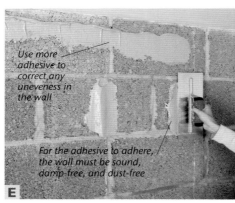

Use more adhesive to correct any unevenness in the wall

For the adhesive to adhere, the wall must be sound, damp-free, and dust-free

E

Use the chalk lines as a guide

F

Press the board in place. Use a wedge underneath to hold it flush, and use a straight edge or darby to tap the board into position.

G

Repeat for the remaining sections of wall. Mix only the amount of adhesive you require for each board, and work quickly.

▌ BATTENING OUT WITH WOOD

A

Measure and mark chalk guide lines for the battens around the wall perimeter, and with vertical battens 600mm (2ft) apart.

B

Cut the battens to the required length. Use masonry fixings and a drill to attach battens securely around the wall's perimeter.

C

Fix vertical battens to the guide lines. Alternate battens will provide fixing points for sheet edges, and for support in the centre of the boards.

D

Pack out battens if they do not lie flat, by placing wooden or sheet offcuts behind them. Then attach the plasterboard (see p.108).

BATTENING OUT WITH METAL BATTENS

A

Measure and mark chalk lines as in step A of Battening Out With Wood (opposite). Cut battens to length with a hacksaw or tin snips.

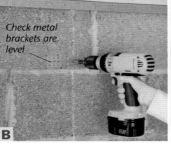

B

Attach the ceiling and floor battens. Fasten the wall brackets using masonry fixings. Drill the fixings in the centre of the metal brackets.

Check metal brackets are level

C

Position the vertical battens on the brackets, using the guide lines. Fold the bracket edges around the tracks and fix into position.

D

Attach all other battens. Bend any bracket edges back using pliers. The battens must be flush, so the boards will form a flat surface.

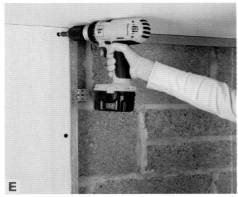

E

Position the first plasterboard so that it overlaps half of the vertical batten. Fasten on both edges and at the top and bottom. Place the next board so that it overlaps the vertical batten, until no metal remains visible. Fix into position. Repeat with the remaining boards.

JOINING BOARDS

Before you decorate a wall that has been lined with taper-edged plasterboard, you will need to cover the boundaries between boards using jointing compound. All compound must be sanded smooth before a proprietary board sealant is applied.

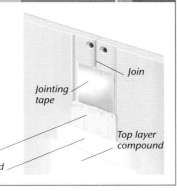

Join
Jointing tape
Top layer compound
First layer compound
Second layer compound

DRY LINING

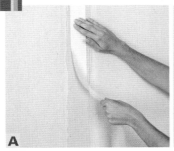

A

Apply joint compound to the first joint between plasterboards, and press the jointing tape into it. Allow to dry until it hardens.

B

Apply another thin layer of compound over the tape using a taping knife or trowel. Fill any screw holes with compound.

C

Leave the compound to dry until hard, and apply another layer on top. Feather its edge just beyond the edge of the previous layer.

D

Allow to dry, then apply a final layer using a caulking blade. Feather beyond the earlier layer.

E

Use a dampened jointing sponge to smooth the compound. Leave the compound to dry fully, and then sand to a smooth finish.

F

Prepare the entire wall for decorating by painting with proprietary board sealant.

PROBLEM SOLVING: EXTERNAL CORNERS

A

Apply a thin strip of joint compound onto both sides of the corner. Position a strip of corner joint tape onto the corner.

B

Smooth the tape using a taping knife and a thin layer of compound. Feather the edges. Sand smooth when dry.

Plaster has uses other than providing a base for decoration, and can be decorative itself. Ready-made accessories can be attached to walls and ceilings with little trouble. Some common examples are shown to the right. A plaster-like coating can also be used to create a textured effect on a ceiling or wall. The steps for fitting coving and fitting a ceiling rose are on p.140, and those for textured coating are on p.141.

PLASTER ACCESSORIES IN USE
The picture to the right shows how these items are used. See below for further details on preparing to buy and install these plaster accessories.

Planning to apply coving
In order to fit coving, you will need to know its depth, which is indicated on the packaging. Use the depth to draw guide lines (as shown on p.140) around the room, to ensure

Coving mitre
Provides a guide to cutting when placed on coving's profile.

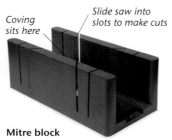

Coving sits here

Slide saw into slots to make cuts

Mitre block
Makes it easy to cut mitred ends on lengths of coving for corners.

Keep upright

Holding coving in block
Ensure coving sits with its back edges flush against the block.

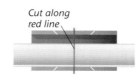

Cut along red line

Making a straight cut
Use the centre slots to make a 90-degree cut in coving.

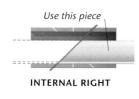

Use this piece

INTERNAL RIGHT

Use this piece

EXTERNAL RIGHT

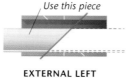

Use this piece

INTERNAL LEFT

Use this piece

EXTERNAL LEFT

Internal corners
Different cuts are needed for internal and external corners. The diagrams above show how to place coving in a mitre block for the correct cuts for an internal corner. The white part represents waste.

External corners
As for internal corners, coving will neatly fit an external corner only if it is cut in the correct direction. Copy the cuts shown above. Again the white part in each diagram represents waste.

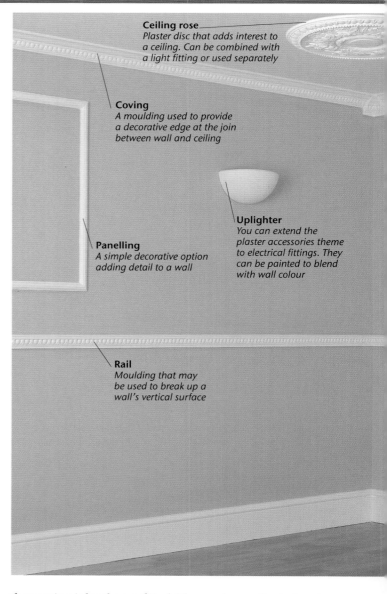

Ceiling rose
Plaster disc that adds interest to a ceiling. Can be combined with a light fitting or used separately

Coving
A moulding used to provide a decorative edge at the join between wall and ceiling

Uplighter
You can extend the plaster accessories theme to electrical fittings. They can be painted to blend with wall colour

Panelling
A simple decorative option adding detail to a wall

Rail
Moulding that may be used to break up a wall's vertical surface

that coving is level once fitted. The most complicated part of fitting coving is dealing with corners. If you are not using moulded corner pieces (as shown in the picture above), cut coving for the corners using a mitre block, a mitre template, or a coving mitre. All three work well, and the choice of which to use is entirely down to personal preference and/or what may be supplied by the manufacturer.

Planning to fit a plaster ceiling rose
Decide where you want the rose in the room; you will fix it to the joists nearest that point (see p.140, and p.95 about joists). If it will incorporate a light fitting, drill a hole through the centre of the rose and thread the wire through it when positioning the rose. Once the adhesive is dry, wire up the light fitting and fix it in place (see pp.450–51). The number of fixings and amount of adhesive needed will depend on the rose's weight. Larger ones can be very heavy, and you may need help to fit one. It may even be necessary to position a working platform below the fixing position – trestles and planks for example, or even one or two levels of a scaffold tower.

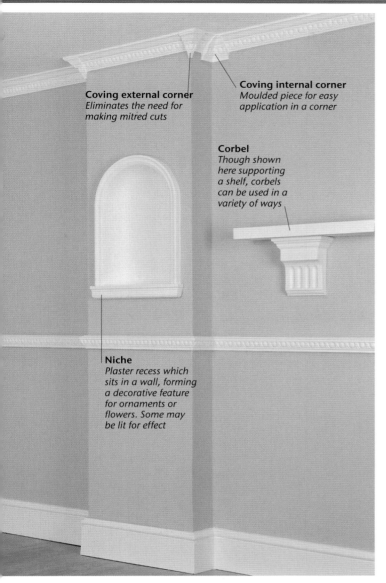

Coving external corner
Eliminates the need for making mitred cuts

Coving internal corner
Moulded piece for easy application in a corner

Corbel
Though shown here supporting a shelf, corbels can be used in a variety of ways

Niche
Plaster recess which sits in a wall, forming a decorative feature for ornaments or flowers. Some may be lit for effect

Examples of accessories in a room
The room above shows a selection of plaster accessories as they are used. Plan your order of work before embarking on fitting any of them. It is always best to work from the ceiling down.

Choosing and fitting a niche

Before buying a niche, check that the wall is deep enough to accommodate it. If you want to light the niche, work out how to supply it (see pp.426–51). Most manufacturers provide a template for marking the wall. Using this, cut a hole for the niche (see pp.102–03; on a stud wall, position the niche between studs and fit a nogging at the base to support it). Apply coving adhesive to the back of the niche, and position with even pressure to the edges. A large niche may require extra, temporary support while it dries.

Fitting the other features

Fit panels with coving adhesive, mitring the corners. Fit rails as for wooden ones (see p.219), and support them while the adhesive dries. Also use coving adhesive for corbels, adding screws if necessary, and support them until set. Uplighters are fragile; handle them carefully. They normally have pre-drilled holes for screwing to the wall.

USING A TEXTURED COATING

Textured coating can be applied to a new surface or a stable old surface. Switch off heating during application to prevent it drying too fast. If possible, work with another person – one applying the coating, the other texturing it.

Preparing the surface

Tape the joints on a new plasterboard ceiling (see pp.136–37) and fill fixing holes with textured coating. Then apply primer sealer to the ceiling.

If the ceiling is old, remove any wallpaper, scrape off flaky paint, and make good any holes with a stiff mix of textured coating or filler. Then sand the surface, and apply primer sealer across it.

If there is old texturing, knock off the spikes, and apply primer sealer. Apply one or more layers of textured coating (use a caulking blade or plastering trowel) to give a smooth surface as a base for the textured layer.

Mixing the coating

Mix textured coating in accordance with the manufacturer's instructions, until it is smooth and creamy. The stiffer the mix, the more heavily textured the ceiling. Allow it to sit for 10 minutes and then stir it again to get an even finish.

Texturing tools

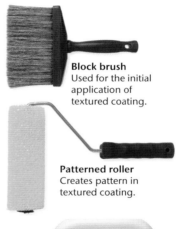

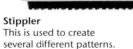

Block brush
Used for the initial application of textured coating.

Standard comb
Draw this across and through coating for decorative effect.

Patterned roller
Creates pattern in textured coating.

Lacer
Softens textured effect by smoothing it.

Stippler
This is used to create several different patterns.

UNDERSIDE OF STIPPLER

TOOLS AND MATERIALS CHECKLISTS PP.140–41

Fitting a ceiling rose
Coving adhesive, countersink bit, filling knife, filler*, sponge, sandpaper

Fitting coving
Coving adhesive, filling knife, countersink bit, mitre saw, block, or template, filler, sandpaper

Creating a textured ceiling
Chosen texturing tools, power stirrer, block brush or roller, 12.5-mm (½-in) paintbrush

* = optional

FOR BASIC TOOLKIT
SEE PP.24–25

PLASTER ACCESSORIES AND FINISHES

Use these steps in conjunction with the information on pp.138–39, where you will find details such as how to combine a ceiling rose with a light fitting, and the cuts needed to mitre coving for external or internal corners. Coving fixings can be temporary, to support it while adhesive dries (method shown), or driven through the coving, punched in, and covered with filler. They should be permanent if the coving is heavy. See pp.76–77 for suitable fixings. If the wall is timber-framed, drive them into studs (see p.96).

TOOLS AND MATERIALS SEE BASIC TOOLKIT AND P.139

FITTING A CEILING ROSE

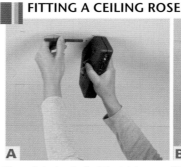

A Use a detector to find the joists nearest your chosen point for the rose. Mark their position and the direction in which they run.

B Hold the rose in position, and mark where the joists cross it. Also draw a pencil guide line on the ceiling around the rose's circumference.

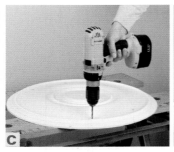

C Drill holes for fixings in the areas that will align with the joists. Use a slow drill speed with no hammer action to avoid cracking the rose.

D Enlarge the entrances to the fixing holes with a countersink bit. Again, be sure to use a slow drill speed.

E Withdraw the countersink bit when a hole is large enough to accommodate the heads of your chosen fixings.

F Mix up some coving adhesive and use a filling knife to apply a good covering of adhesive across the back of the rose.

G Position the rose on the ceiling, inside the edge guide line and with fixing holes in line with the joists. Apply light, even pressure.

H Use wood screws to fix through the holes in the rose and into the joists. Do not over-tighten them, or the rose may crack.

I Use adhesive or filler to fill the fixing holes. Fill around the edge of the rose, and smooth with a damp sponge. Once filler is dried, sand the filling holes and around the edge of the rose if necessary to achieve a smooth, even finish.

FITTING COVING

A Use the measurement given on the packaging to draw a horizontal guide line on the wall to mark where the lower edge of the coving will sit.

B Use the same measurement and an offcut of coving to mark a mirroring guide line on the ceiling, for the top edge of the coving.

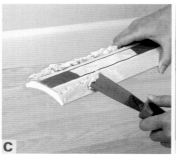

C Mix the adhesive according to the manufacturer's instructions, and apply it to the rear upper and lower edges of the coving.

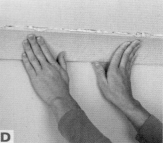

D Press the coving into place, aligning its edges with the guide lines to get it level.

E

Excess adhesive may squeeze out from behind the coving. Wipe this away with a damp sponge.

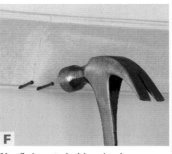

F

Use fixings to hold coving in place while it dries. This is especially important where lengths meet, which can be butt-joined (above) or mitred.

G

Continue adding lengths until you reach a corner. Carefully measure the length of coving required, and work out which cuts you need (see p.138). If several corners are close together (as in this example), make all cuts at once, for a smooth workflow. A mitre block is being used here, to cut for the left-hand part of an internal corner.

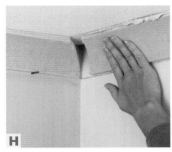

H

Carefully place the two mitred pieces, ensuring that they sit on the guide lines and that they fit neatly in the corner (here, an internal one).

I

Treat an external corner in the same way, making the cuts first and checking that the fit is exact as you secure the coving in place.

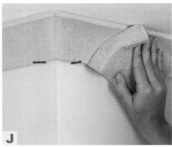

J

Continue placing coving, adding fixings to support it and wiping away excess adhesive as you go. Work around the room until it is all done.

K

When the adhesive is dry, remove all temporary fixings and apply filler to the holes.

CREATING A TEXTURED CEILING: STIPPLING

A

Mix textured coating (see p.139), and use a block brush or roller to apply a band 0.5m (1ft 8in) wide across the ceiling's narrowest width.

B

Apply the stippled pattern to the wet coating by repeatedly pressing the stippler into its surface.

C

Once the band is stippled, run a slightly damp 12.5-mm (½-in) paintbrush around the edge where the texturing meets the wall.

D

Apply another band of coating, feathering in its edge with that of the previous band. Stipple and brush it. Repeat across the ceiling.

CREATING OTHER TEXTURES

Bark
Run a bark-patterned roller across the wet coating to get this effect (see p.139).

Scroll
Push and pull a stippler through the textured coating in overlapping figures of eight.

Swirl
The swirl is created in a similar way to the scroll, but moving the stippler in overlapping circles.

Broken leather
Place a stippler in a plastic bag and move it at random from left to right across the wet coating.

Windows

WINDOWS ARE AVAILABLE IN A VARIETY OF DESIGNS AND SIZES. THERE ARE DIFFERENCES IN OPENING MECHANISMS AND STRUCTURE, AS WELL AS THE TYPE OF GLASS THEY CONTAIN. THE FOLLOWING PAGES CONTAIN INFORMATION ON REPLACING AND RENOVATING WINDOWS, AS WELL AS FITTING CATCHES, SHUTTERS, AND GLAZING. COMMON MINOR REPAIRS FOR WINDOWS ARE SHOWN ON PAGES 154–155.

TYPES OF WINDOW

There are several different types of window. Traditionally, most windows were side-hinged windows, referred to as casements, and sliding sash windows. New opening mechanisms such as friction and pivot hinges (opposite) are increasingly popular. Window materials, shapes, and sizes vary considerably (see p.144), as does terminology so you should read your manufacturer's literature carefully. Replacement windows often need to be custom-built to your requirements.

CHOOSING WINDOWS

Commonly the material and mechanism of a replacement window is chosen to match up with the originals. There are some exceptions – new sash windows, for example, will often be fitted with modern spiral balances, although they look the same as original lead counterweight versions (see opposite and p.147). If you are replacing all the windows in your property, or embarking on a new-build, then take time to consider energy-efficient products such as double and even triple glazing. Frames may have a sill attached, an optional sill, or none at all. If your old frame has a sill attached, make sure your replacement has one.

Parts of a casement window

Casement windows are widely used. Many of the terms used to describe the parts that make up a casement window also apply to other windows.

The window is made up of one or more opening casements, hinged along one side. Top-hung and side-hung casements are available. The metal casement shown here combines opening, non-opening, and side- and top-hung casements.

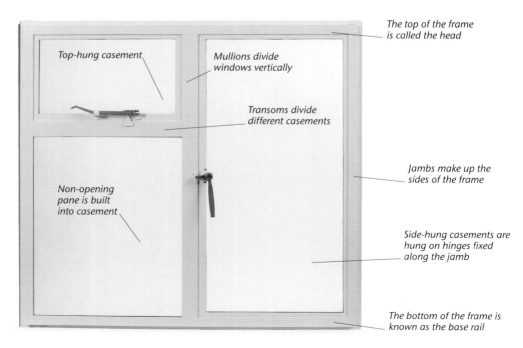

Top-hung casement

Mullions divide windows vertically

Transoms divide different casements

Non-opening pane is built into casement

The top of the frame is called the head

Jambs make up the sides of the frame

Side-hung casements are hung on hinges fixed along the jamb

The bottom of the frame is known as the base rail

Common types of window

Side-hinged casement and sliding sash windows are still very popular, although pivot and awning windows are becoming common. There are variations on these themes, with each type of window made in many different sizes, shapes, and styles.

Casement windows

As well as the metal casement shown opposite, UPVC and wood casements are also common. See p.144 for information on the properties of different materials.

UPVC CASEMENT WINDOW

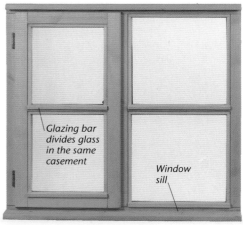

Glazing bar divides glass in the same casement

Window sill

WOODEN CASEMENT WINDOW

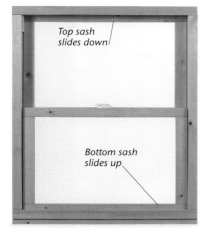

Top sash slides down

Bottom sash slides up

Sash window

A distinctive, traditional design with two vertically sliding sashes (see p.147). Modern sashes are made of wood or UPVC, and some versions allow tilting of sashes for easy cleaning.

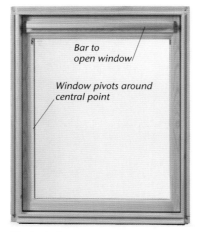

Bar to open window

Window pivots around central point

Pivot window

The window swings around a central pivot mechanism (see below). This allows access to both exterior and interior surfaces for easy cleaning.

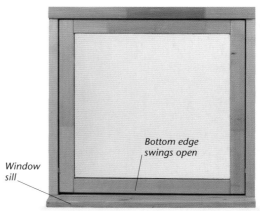

Bottom edge swings open

Window sill

Awning window

Butt hinges are used along the top edge of older designs, newer awning windows use friction hinges at either end of the top edge (see below). Both arrangements allow the bottom edge of the window to swing open.

TYPES OF MECHANISM

There are several different mechanisms used to open windows. How a window opens can have implications on how space in a room is used – clearance may be needed to enable you to open some windows. Some types, known as "tilt-and-turn windows" have combination hinges and can open vertically or horizontally, depending on how the handle is operated. The opening mechanism of an existing window cannot normally be changed.

Butt hinge

This is the simplest opening mechanism. Hinges are attached down one side, or along the top edge on a "top-hung" casement.

Spiral balance

Weights and balances

Vertically sliding sashes use lead weights or modern spiral balances to hold them in position. Horizontally-sliding windows run on tracks, similar to those for patio doors (see pp.156–57).

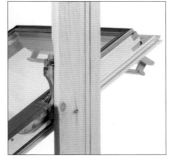

Pivots

Tilting casements pivot halfway down each side, or midway along the top and bottom of the frame. The pivots are designed to hold the window in any position.

Friction hinge

These are used on awning and casement windows. The hinges are fitted at either end of the hinged edge, rather than along the edge itself. The 'friction' holds the window in any open position.

WINDOW MATERIALS

Most styles of window are available in a number of different materials. Each material has advantages and disadvantages in terms of maintenance and appearance.

Wood

Windows were traditionally made of wood, and it is still popular because it is so versatile. If old windows are draughty then you can fit draught excluders (see p.361). Hardwood is expensive, but is durable and only needs the protection of oil (see p.290–91). You can also paint hardwood windows or give them a natural finish. Softwood windows need to be protected by paint or a natural wood finish, and regularly maintained, see pp.290–93.

UPVC

Double-glazed, UPVC windows offer excellent heat and sound insulation. Old windows are often replaced throughout a house by new UPVC windows. As well as white, other finishes are available, such as wood-grain. UPVC requires little maintenance.

Steel

Where maximum light is required, steel windows can be an excellent option – the strength of steel means a thin frame can support a large expanse of glass. However,

BUILDING REGULATIONS
■ Check with Building Control before replacing windows. New windows will often require double-glazed units.
■ Check with Building Control before replacing windows in listed buildings and conservation areas.
■ Consider fire safety – glass in non-opening upstairs windows must be breakable to provide an emergency escape route. Ideally windows should open – see p.375.

steel conducts heat out of the home and is prone to condensation. Double-glazing may be required by building regulations to reduce heat loss. Old steel windows were prone to rust, but modern versions are coated during manufacture and are durable and low maintenance.

Other materials

Windows can be made from a combination of materials. Aluminium windows, for example, often have a wooden core, and steel casements can be housed in wooden frames to reduce heat loss. Frames with decorative real wood on the inside, and maintenance-free fibreglass or UPVC exteriors are also available. Traditional lead lights are made up of small pieces of glass held between strips of lead within a wood frame. Other types of windows are available with lead-light effect double-glazing.

SHAPE DIFFERENCES

Although most windows are square or rectangular, many shapes and architectural variations exist. Round windows and arched windows are often used above doors, for example. Windows that project out together with, or proud of, the walls of a house are referred to as bay windows, or bow windows if their profile is rounded. These are generally composed of a number of casements that are joined by a larger and more substantial frame. Large windows with a single, non-opening pane of glass are often referred to as picture windows because of the way they frame the view.

When replacing a window with an uncommon shape you will usually need to go to a specialist supplier, who will often measure up and fit the window for you, as well as manufacture it. If you want a wooden window, then consider employing a joiner.

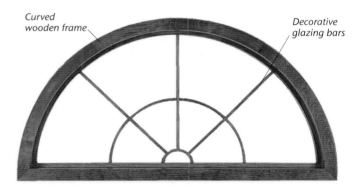

Curved wooden frame

Decorative glazing bars

Curved windows
Decorative, curved fixed windows are often used above square or rectangular windows, or sometimes doors. Their frames are fixed in place using the same method as for other types of window (see opposite).

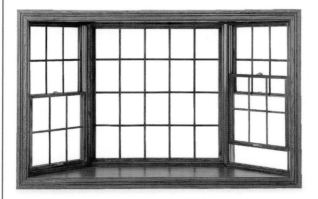

Bay windows
This period design is made up of a combination of fixed and opening sashes or casements. Large windows may help support the walls above so seek professional advice before replacing them.

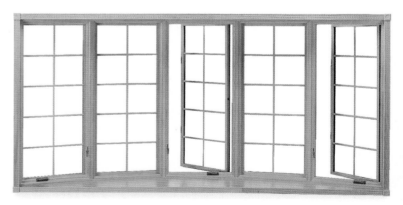

Bow windows
Despite their curved profile, a bow window is usually made up of flat casements. Always seek professional advice before replacing very wide windows – they may have reinforced mullions with a structural role.

Replacement windows usually need to be made-to-measure, so measure up carefully before ordering. Once your window has arrived, check it is the right size. Remove the old window before fitting a new frame (see p.146). Seek professional advice before removing large windows – they may be structurally important. Consider the wall structure before removing old windows (see box, right). You may wish to consider fitting triple glazing (see p.378).

> ### WALL STRUCTURE
> Determine whether your walls are solid masonry, cavity, or timber-framed (see pp.94–97 for wall construction). You may have to chip away some mortar, or prise off beading or cover strips around the window. Buy timber or masonry frame fixings appropriate for the material you will be fixing into. The wall above the window is supported by a concrete or wooden lintel. If you can gain access, check wooden lintels for rot. Seek advice if it is present (see also pp.226–33).

MEASURING FOR A REPLACEMENT WINDOW

Take vertical and horizontal measurements of the window opening (not the existing frame) in at least three places. If there is any variation use the shortest. Then, deduct 10mm (½in) from each to give you the frame size for the new window. Take these measurements to your supplier. If you have timber-framed walls, in addition to the window opening, you should also measure the thickness of the walls. If the house is masonry-clad, the height and width of the opening in the masonry must be noted in addition to the dimensions of the window opening itself.

Measuring up
Mistakes made while measuring up can be costly so take time to measure accurately.

Edge of aperture

Take three measurements in both directions

Jambs of frame

Only include the sill in your measurements if it is also being replaced

REMOVING THE OLD WINDOW

Don't remove the old window until the new one has arrived and you have checked that it is undamaged and the correct size. Otherwise you could be left with a hole in your wall for months while you wait for a replacement frame. Before removing the old frame itself, take out any glass. If all the casements or sashes are removable, simply unscrew or lever them away with the glass intact. Carefully remove glass from fixed panes as shown on p.155. You can then begin to remove the frame itself. Expect to find most, if not all of the fixings through the jambs of the frame. While you are removing the frame, take care not to damage any damp-proofing around the edges of the opening – you will have to replace it if you do.

Removing a wooden-framed window
Use a panel saw to cut through the top and the bottom of one side. Angle your cuts towards the centre of the side to create a wedge-shaped section that you can lever out easily. Lever away the side using a pry bar, taking care not to damage the wall (although in some cases a bit of damage is inevitable). Once you have removed the first section it should be easier to remove the other sides. Remove any "horns" that protrude into the wall, and any fixings. Finally, clear away loose debris with a dusting brush.

Removing a metal-framed window
Use the same technique as for a wooden frame, but use a hacksaw or an angle grinder fitted with a metal cutting blade (disc). When using an angle grinder, watch out for flying sparks, which can be a fire hazard (see p.61 for technique and safety information).

Checking the window opening
If you have damaged any damp-proofing around the window opening, it should be replaced. If you find an open cavity under the old frame, or if it is a new-build, consider using cavity-closers. As well as closing the gap, they have a wedge of insulation that extends into the cavity on the side and lower edges of the window.

With the lintel now fully exposed, double check for any rot in wooden lintels (see also wall structure, top). If you suspect rot (see pp.226–33), seek professional advice.

This is a much easier job when tackled by two people. You should pre-order the replacement window and check its size on arrival. Having removed the old window and prepared the opening using the techniques described on p.145, you will usually be able to fix a window directly through the frame into the wall. Fixing brackets are another option provided by some manufacturers. Always fit the new frame at the same depth in the wall as the one you have removed.

FITTING A WINDOW

How you fit a window depends on your wall type and window design. Always follow any specific instructions that come with the window you purchased. However, the general technique is always similar. If you need to fit a new window sill, fix this into the bottom of the frame before you fix the window. In a new window, glass will normally be loosely fixed in place and should be removed during fitting. Glass may already be secured in place in the opening casements of UPVC windows, but access to the frame can be gained by simply opening the casements.

Positioning the new window

Place the window in the rough opening in the same position that the old window occupied. Drive wooden wedges beneath the sill or frame to get it level and tight against the lintel. Use a spirit level to ensure that the frame is horizontally and vertically straight. Gently insert wedges down either side of the frame to hold it in position, not so tightly that they distort the shape of the frame. Measure the distance diagonally between opposite corners, and make sure both measurements are the same. Adjust the wedges if necessary.

Fixing the frame

Open the casements to provide access to the side of the frame. Drill pilot holes for 100-mm (4-in) frame fixings through the frame and into the wall below. Fixings every 300mm (1ft) should be sufficient. Hammer the fixings in until the plugs sit flush with the frame. Use a cordless drill-driver to screw them so that they countersink into the frame and hold it securely in position. Avoid over-tightening as this can distort the frame. If possible, fix through the top of the frame, but in many cases this will be impossible because of the lintel. Fix the bottom edge of the frame if the sill and frame depth allow. Bottom fixings are not recommended by some window manufacturers.

Finishing the job

Saw off or chisel away any protruding wedges. Fill any large gaps around the frame with expanding foam. You will need to protect UPVC window frames with low-tack masking tape if they have no protective film because the foam may damage the finish. Once the foam is dry, trim it neatly using a craft knife. Apply a thin, neat line of cement (a fillet) around the joint with the wall to hide the foam. On timber-framed or clad homes, use wooden mouldings, or for UPVC windows use the cover strips supplied. Create a final seal with a continuous bead of silicone around the edge of the window frame. Glaze windows where necessary (see pp.150–51).

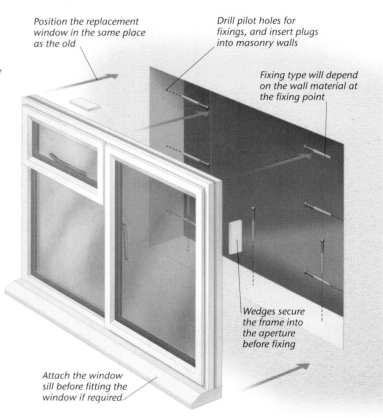

Position the replacement window in the same place as the old

Drill pilot holes for fixings, and insert plugs into masonry walls

Fixing type will depend on the wall material at the fixing point

Wedges secure the frame into the aperture before fixing

Attach the window sill before fitting the window if required

Fitting a window frame
Inserting a frame into all types of wall is similar – position the new frame in the same place as the one you removed and fix it in position. Use suitable fixings for the window, and the point to which you are fixing it (see below).

OTHER FIXING SYSTEMS
Bracket fixings
An alternative to fixing through the frame is to fix brackets around the edge of the frame before fitting. The window is then positioned just as above, but fixings are made through the brackets and not through the frame. Sealant must be used to cover the exterior bracket fixings. If fixing is done inside the house, cover the brackets with plaster to provide a neat finish.

Fixing windows in timber-framed walls
The same technique is used, but the framework fixings do not require plugs. Some window manufacturers produce windows with fixing flanges around the edge of the window specifically designed for use in timber-framed buildings.

A replacement sash window is fitted in much the same way as any window frame. However, the cord, pulley, and weight-operating mechanism of sash windows means that repair is often necessary. Commonly the cord breaks and needs replacing. This is a straightforward task once you understand how a sash window fits together. Even if only one cord has broken, it is worth replacing them all.

REPLACING A BROKEN SASH CORD

Work from the interior. Use a chisel to lever away the beading holding the inner sash in the frame. Cut any unbroken cords attached to the sash so that you can lift it out. Remove the central staff beads and repeat the process to remove the outer sash. Undo the knots or remove the nails holding the old cords to the sashes. With the sashes removed you should be able to lever the four weight covers out of the frame to expose the weights.

Threading in the replacement cords

The easiest way to thread the new sash cord over the pulley mechanism is to use a piece of string with a small weight tied to one end – a small screw or nail is fine. Tie a length of sash cord to the other end of the string. Then, push the nail over the pulley, so it drops down next to the weight. Use the string to pull the new cord over the pulley, taking care not to pull the whole length over. Tie the cord to the weight – you may need to remove the weight from the frame to do this. Repeat for the other three cords.

Replacing the sashes

Hold the outer sash up to the frame in the fully open position. If your sash cords are knotted in place, pull the cord taut, and mark the cord where it reaches the hole. Lower the sash, then thread the cord through the retaining hole, and knot it at the marked-off point. If your cords are fixed with nails, the technique is similar but you should mark the position of the top of the sash on the taut cord. Lower the sash, realign your mark, then nail the cords in place along the sash edge. Check the sliding mechanism is still fitting well. Fix the staff beads in position and refit the inner sash. Finally, replace the weight covers and beading.

OTHER SASH MAINTENANCE

If the sliding mechanism is stiff, try oiling the pulleys. Paint in the runners can also hinder movement – you will have to strip back to bare wood (see pp.274–75) and repaint carefully (see below). If you have the window disassembled for any maintenance or repairs, take the opportunity to fit brush seals to reduce draughts (see p.361).

PAINTING SASHES

■ Lift the inner sash up and pull the outer sash down. Paint the bottom of the outer sash.
■ Lift the outer sash up, pull inner sash down so they are both slightly open. Paint the rest of the outer sash,

the inner sash, and the frame, apart from the runners.
■ When the rest of the window is dry, apply a thin coat of paint to the runners. See pp.276–95 for more on paint types and techniques.

REPLACING SASH WINDOWS

■ You might not be allowed to replace sash windows with any other kind in a conservation area or listed building. Check with your local Building Control Office.
■ Even if you are not in a conservation area, be aware that original windows can

sometimes add value to your property.
■ If your old windows are draughty, try fitting draught excluders (see p.361) before considering replacement.
■ Old, sticking sashes may only require old paint to be stripped off and new cords fitted to works perfectly.

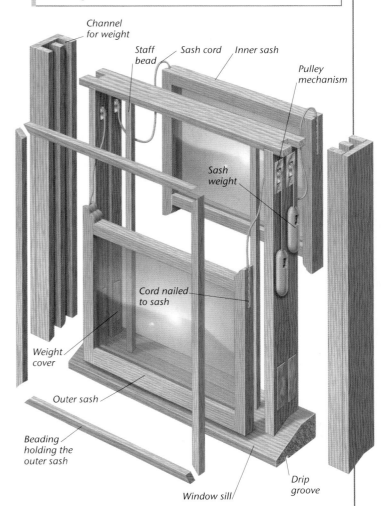

Parts of a sash window
Working with sash windows is relatively easy as long as you understand how all the parts fit together. You may find it useful to label and number parts as you remove them, so you can replace them in the reverse order.

SPIRAL BALANCES

Unlike the traditional sash with its counterweights and cords, modern sashes use spiral balances. If the tension in the balances is wrong it is easy to adjust by unscrewing the channels and rotating them – one direction increases the tension and the other reduces it. If a spiral balance system completely fails, it is easily replaced like for like. You can fit modern spiral balances in old sash windows – weigh your sashes so you buy the right size of balance. Follow the fitting instructions for the system you choose.

FITTING WINDOW FURNITURE

Window furniture is used to secure opening sections, as well as being decorative. Most items are available in a choice of traditional brass, a coated alloy, or chrome. A selection of the styles available is shown here. Hinged casement windows use different fastening systems to sliding sash windows. Although these catches will hold your windows firmly closed, for security you also need window locks (see pp.368–69). UPVC windows tend to come with closing and locking mechanisms attached.

UPVC FASTENERS

- UPVC windows normally come with fasteners, but they may need fixing in place.
- Most UPVC window fasteners also have an automatic locking mechanism. As the handle is moved into the closed position, bolts (called Espagnolette bolts) lock the window into the frame, around the opening edge.
- Further security is offered by lockable handles. Some manufacturers now use this design on wooden windows.

CASEMENT FURNITURE

Choose casement window furniture that will work with your window type and style. There are three main types of casement fastener used to hold windows shut. Stays can either keep a window closed, or can fasten it in an open position to stop it slamming. Both a fastener and stay may be fitted to the same window.

Casement fasteners

A wedge or mortise type fastener is used when a casement closes against the frame, a hook fastener when the closed casement and frame sit flush. Some fastener sets include both mortise and hook options.

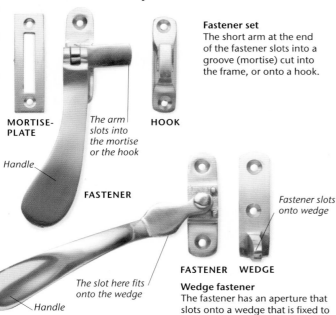

MORTISE-PLATE

Handle

The arm slots into the mortise or the hook

HOOK

Fastener set
The short arm at the end of the fastener slots into a groove (mortise) cut into the frame, or onto a hook.

FASTENER

The slot here fits onto the wedge

Handle

FASTENER   **WEDGE**

Fastener slots onto wedge

Wedge fastener
The fastener has an aperture that slots onto a wedge that is fixed to the window frame.

Casement stays

Stays are long bars with holes in them that are fitted to the opening casement of a window. Separate "pins" are positioned on the window frame. The holes on the stay can be slotted onto both pins to hold the window tightly closed. Alternatively any hole can be slotted onto either pin to keep the window open the desired amount.

Sliding stays are a different design that move within a bracket. A screw mechanism is tightened to hold the casement in the required position.

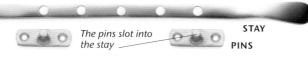

The pins slot into the stay

STAY

PINS

SASH FURNITURE

As well as fasteners, sashes are also often fitted with some kind of grip to open and close the window. Several traditional styles are available.

Sash fasteners

These hold the two sliding sections of a sash window together. They all work as two-part mechanisms, with one part fixed to each sash.

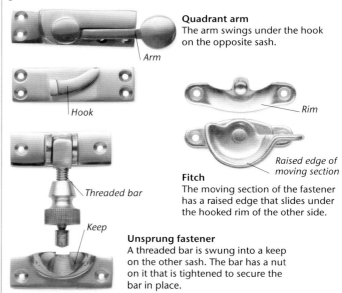

Quadrant arm
The arm swings under the hook on the opposite sash.

Arm

Hook

Rim

Threaded bar

Keep

Raised edge of moving section

Fitch
The moving section of the fastener has a raised edge that slides under the hooked rim of the other side.

Unsprung fastener
A threaded bar is swung into a keep on the other sash. The bar has a nut on it that is tightened to secure the bar in place.

Sash handles

These are attached to the sashes to aid lifting and lowering. Several styles are available including knobs, handles, and rings.

SASH LIFT

Two handles are fixed to the bottom of the lower sash

SASH HANDLE

TOOLS AND MATERIALS CHECKLISTS P.149

Fitting a stay and pins
Wood filler, sandpaper

Fitting a mortise casement fastener Wood filler, sandpaper

FOR BASIC TOOLKIT SEE PP.24–25

FITTING A STAY AND PINS

Position a stay and pins in the middle of the bottom rail of each opening casement. This includes top-hung casements. The fixing bracket of the stay can be positioned near the opening edge or the hinged edge of the casement.

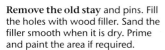

A

Remove the old stay and pins. Fill the holes with wood filler. Sand the filler smooth when it is dry. Prime and paint the area if required.

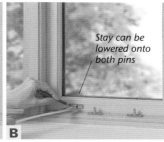

Stay can be lowered onto both pins

B

Hold the stay in position. Place the pins on the frame and use them to get the stay at the correct height. Mark the fixing points for the stay.

C

Drill pilot holes at the marked fixing points. Reposition the stay and screw it into the casement.

D

With the window tightly closed, position the pins to correspond with the holes at each end of the stay.

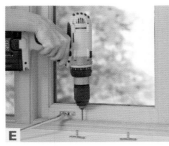

E

Gently lift the stay clear. Mark the two fixing points for each pin. Remove them and drill pilot holes.

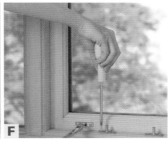

F

Reposition the pins and screw them in place. Check that the stay fits securely over the pins.

G

Positioning the stay fixing bracket closest to the opening edge of the casement allows greater leverage and security when closing the window.

FITTING A MORTISE CASEMENT FASTENER

Most side-opening casements require one fastener, although larger ones may need two, as will large awning windows. Fitting fasteners is a straightforward procedure that simply requires accuracy in positioning. For hook or wedge fasteners follow steps A-C, then pilot and screw the hook or wedge in position on the window frame.

A

Remove the old fastener. Fill the holes with wood filler. Sand the filler smooth when it is dry. You can buy coloured fillers that are almost invisible in wood with a natural finish. If your window is painted then you will need to prime over the filler before touching up the paint.

B

Hold the fastener in position and mark the fixing points.

C

Drill pilot holes in the casement frame at the points you have marked. Screw on the fastener.

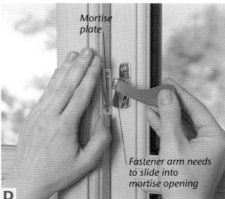

Mortise plate

Fastener arm needs to slide into mortise opening

D

Close the casement. Swing the fastener towards the window frame. Position the mortise-plate so the arm touches the frame in the middle of the opening. When you are happy with the position, use a pencil to draw round the edge of the mortise-plate and its central opening. This will provide a guide for chiselling out the mortise (slot).

Rebate for the plate

E

Chisel out the mortise and a rebate for the plate. The mortise depth should be slightly greater than the length of the arm.

F

Mark and drill pilot holes at the fixing positions. Reposition the mortise-plate and screw it in place.

GLAZING A WINDOW

There are many types of glass and several fixing techniques to consider when fitting and replacing it. Modern manufacturing techniques have produced glass to meet a number of specific needs. Some types of glass are required by law in certain situations so check the building regulations. For example, wired or fireproof glass needs to be used in fire doors, and laminated or toughened glass in floor-to-ceiling windows. To fix the glass in wooden frames, you can choose between putty or glazing beads. Metal and UPVC frames often have special fixing systems built into them.

BROKEN WINDOWS

It is unlikely that you will be able to replace a broken pane immediately, so do one of the following in the meantime:
■ Patch small cracks with clear glazing tape.
■ Fix masking tape across badly cracked glass then fix polythene over the window, using battens to stop it tearing. This will keep the weather out until you can re-glaze.
■ If security is an issue, cut a sheet of plywood or hardboard to size and screw it to the frame.

TYPES OF GLASS

Standard glass

Float glass
Clear, "normal" glass. The perfectly flat finish is created by floating the hot, liquid glass on top of molten tin.

HEAT-EFFICIENT GLASS

Double-glazed unit
Two sheets of glass have a layer of inert gas sealed between them to provide heat and sound insulation. For information about triple-glazing, see pp.378–79.

Low-emissivity glass
A special coating lets heat from the sun in, but prevents warmth escaping back through the glass. A common component of double-glazed units.

Solar control glass
Excessive heat from the sun is blocked from passing through the glass. This reduces heat build-up in buildings with large expanses of glass.

Strong glass

Laminated glass
Clear plastic bonded between layers of glass produces a very strong product. If it does break, the plastic prevents shards flying.

Toughened glass
This glass is strengthened against impact, and shatters into granules rather than shards. It is commonly used in glazed doors.

Wired glass
The wire stops glass shattering in high temperatures, so it is used in fire doors.

Fire-resistant glass
New fire-resistant glass is not strengthened by wire but is just as strong, although expensive.

Speciality glass

Mirror glass
To make household mirrors, normal float glass is "silvered". A reflective layer is applied to the back of the glass.

Self-cleaning glass
This glass has a special coating on its exterior surface that makes sunlight break down dirt. Rainwater washes any debris away.

Reduced visibility glass

Privacy glass
Allows light in but distorts the view through the glass. Commonly used in bathroom windows and front doors.

Etched glass
Also known as "frosted" glass, this is similar to privacy glass, but does not distort outlines. Patterns can be etched, instead of the whole surface.

BUYING GLASS

It is best to get glass cut to size or, in the case of sealed double-glazing units, made to size by your supplier. They will be able to do a more accurate job with less wastage. Float glass is the only type of glass you can attempt to cut at home. You should wear protective gloves and goggles. Draw a glass cutter across the glass to score it. Position matches under each end of the scoreline, then simply apply pressure either side of the line to snap it in two.

Measuring up

Take careful measurements of the aperture of the window you are glazing, horizontally and vertically from edge to edge. You need to measure to the farthest edge of each glazing rebate. Then deduct 4mm (¼in) from your figures for single glazing. Take these dimensions to your supplier and they will cut the glass to size. For double-glazed units, give the exact measurement from edge to edge of the rebate to your supplier. They will make any deductions, depending on how their units

are constructed. For more unusual window shapes, including curved glass, make an accurate cardboard template for your supplier.

Lead lights

Modern lead lights are fitted as a single pane, using a method for single or double glazing, as appropriate. See p.155 for how to repair traditional lead lights.

TOOLS AND MATERIALS CHECKLIST FOR P.151

Using putty Putty, powder filler, glass, putty knife, pin hammer, glazing sprigs or pins, cloth, white spirit

glazing bead, pins

Fitting double-glazed units Packers, UPVC glazing beads

Using beads Glazing silicone sealant, sealant dispenser,

FOR BASIC TOOLKIT SEE PP.24–25

REMOVING BROKEN GLASS

Wear thick gloves, work boots, and goggles when working with glass. Preferably, fix masking tape over the glass to prevent shards falling, then remove the putty or beading and tap out the pane in one piece. If this is not possible, you will have to break the glass to remove it and dispose of the glass carefully. Clean the rebate before you reglaze. For detailed information on how to remove glass, see p.155.

FIXING GLASS

Glass is traditionally held in place by putty or glazing beads. However, aluminium and UPVC windows often use systems such as gaskets and cover strips to form a watertight seal, although other variations exist. If you purchase windows with a proprietary fixing system, use it as instructed.

▌▌ USING PUTTY

Clean the rebate before you start, as shown on p.155. Cut some putty from its container with a putty knife. If it is particularly sticky, spread a small amount of powder filler on your hands, and coat the putty itself with more filler to make it easier to handle. Work it in the palms of your hands so that you achieve a malleable, smooth consistency before you begin.

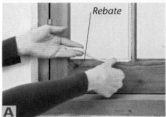

Work from the outside. Roll the putty into strips about 10mm (⅜in) in diameter. Press the strips into the rebate.

Manoeuvre the glass into the rebate. Press gently around the edges of the pane.

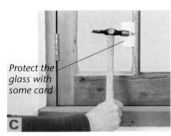

Hammer glazing sprigs or pins into the rebate, not quite touching the glass. Their heads will be hidden by the finished putty.

Press more strips of putty into the junction created by the glass and the rebate using your thumb.

Use a putty knife to trim excess putty from behind the glass, then draw the knife along the external putty to create a smooth seal.

Remove smears from the glass with white spirit. Before painting, let the putty dry until a hard skin has formed on its surface.

▌▌ FITTING WOODEN BEADS

Wooden glazing beads (see pp.214–15) are attached to the exterior of the frame to secure panes of glass. They can be used to glaze a window that was previously puttied. A snug fit is essential to ensure that the glass is secure and weatherproof. Glazing silicone is used to seal the join.

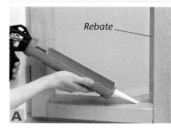

Apply glazing silicone around the rebate to one-third of its depth. Press the pane gently into position to create a seal.

Nail each bead in place on the silicone. The inner edge of each bead should sit flush against the glass. Wipe off any excess silicone.

▌▌ FITTING DOUBLE-GLAZED UNITS

Double-glazed units are most often factory-fitted into specially made windows. They can be fitted into other types of window but unless a casement or sash is draught-free, the insulating glass will be rendered useless. Often, double-glazed units cannot be fitted in old windows because the depth of rebate is not large enough to accommodate them. Some manufacturers produce units with a stepped edge that allows the extra depth to extend over the inner window rebates.

If the seal around a double-glazing unit fails, condensation builds up inside. Check if the unit is covered by a manufacturer's guarantee before replacing it yourself, the guarantee can be invalidated if you don't follow the fitting instructions. When you buy new UPVC windows, check they are guaranteed and keep the paperwork in a safe place. If you want to fit double-glazed units yourself then follow the manufacturer's guidelines on what, if any, fixing system is suitable – UPVC windows often have their own glazing system built in.

Place two packers along the bottom of the glazing rebate. UPVC glazing systems vary, so follow guidelines specific to your system. Further packers may be required around the edge of the unit to ensure that it is positioned centrally and securely within the frame.

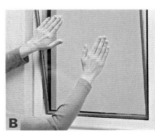

Position the unit on the packers and push it into the rebate. Take care not to crease the waterproof seal or gasket as you push.

Clip the glazing beads and gaskets into position to hold the unit securely.

FITTING SHUTTERS

Window shutters can be fitted internally or externally and are available in a variety of traditional and modern styles. Most shutters are decorative, as well as providing increased security and privacy. Protect windows from weathering with external shutters. Internal shutters can be used instead of curtains–they take up less room and don't become damp in steamy bathrooms and kitchens. Shutters are easily cleaned and allergy sufferers often find them preferable to curtains.

SECURITY SHUTTERS
Exterior roll-down security shutters are available. These are often motorized and can be easily operated from inside the home. The modern, unobtrusive designs also offer excellent heat and sound insulation. If you wish to fit security shutters, then seek advice from a manufacturer. They will usually measure up for you, then make and fit them to your exact specifications.

CHOOSING SHUTTERS

Once you have decided whether you want internal or external shutters, choose what style you prefer. Solid or louvre panels are most common – some louvre designs are adjustable so you can control the amount of light that you let in. Manufacturers may offer a range of other options such as tongue-and-groove, solid panels with designs cut out of them, or shutters that only cover the lower half of the window. Shutters can be made of traditional wood, as well as aluminium, UPVC, and a range of other materials. Wooden shutters require more regular maintenance than other materials such as aluminium and UPVC. Whatever material you choose, it is worth buying pre-finished shutters – louvred shutters are very time-consuming to paint. Shutters are usually supplied with catches to hold them closed and tie-backs to secure them in an open position.

CLOSED　　　　　**OPEN**

Adjustable louvre shutters
These are an excellent choice if shutters are being used instead of curtains. You can vary the amount of light (and air) you let into the room by swivelling the louvres, and angle them to increase privacy.

MEASURING UP

Shutters are usually custom-built for your windows or recesses. Before placing an order for shutters, take note of any mechanisms and fitting procedures and check they are compatible with your window. If you are fitting the shutters into a window recess, then make sure there is enough room to fit them without blocking out light. You will need to measure up carefully. Most companies will provide specific guidelines on how and where to take the crucial measurements. When you are measuring a window recess, make sure that you take at least three measurements for the width and height of the opening. Use the smallest of the three, because walls are rarely dead straight. This is a similar technique to that used for measuring for a new window frame (see p.146).

MOUNTING OPTIONS

When you have decided on the style of your shutters, there are two main options for fitting them. Frame-mounting is the most straightforward technique. The shutters are built into a two-, three-, or four-sided frame, which is then fixed around or into the window recess. Alternatively, the shutter hinges can be attached directly to the existing window frame or jamb. This is known as hinge-mounting. With either option you need to decide whether the shutters are going to be mounted within the window recess or around the opening. Internal shutters are often fitted in the recess. External shutters are usually fitted so that they are flush with, or just proud of the wall when they are closed.

Interior shutters
You can maximize the feeling of space and light that shutters give an interior by fitting them inside the window recess. The frame of the window will need an adequate depth to accommodate the shutters and their fixings without cutting out light. Large shutters are available that fold like a concertina to rest neatly against the wall surface.

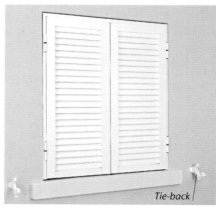

Tie-back

Exterior shutters
These can be mounted to open out flat against the wall on either side of the window. This requires free wall space, and room for them to swing into position. You can use offset hinges to allow the shutters to shut into the mouth of the window recess when closed (shown here). Alternatively you can mount the shutters on the wall around the window.

TOOLS AND MATERIALS CHECKLIST FOR P.153

Fitting interior shutters
Spirit level, wooden offcuts, moulding strip*, filler*

Fitting exterior shutters
Spirit level, wooden offcuts

FOR BASIC TOOLKIT SEE PP.24–25

* = optional

FITTING INTERIOR SHUTTERS

Here, shutters are being frame-mounted into a window recess. The shutter frame is fixed to the window frame so the shutters take up as little space as possible when they are open or closed. Most types of shutter are fitted in a similar way, but you should follow the assembly and fitting guidelines specific to those you purchase precisely.

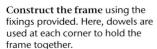

Tap dowels into position with a hammer

A

B

Construct the frame using the fixings provided. Here, dowels are used at each corner to hold the frame together.

Position the shutter frame in the recess and check that it slides neatly into place against the window frame.

C

Use a drill-driver

D

Use a spirit level to check that the frame is precisely square. Wedge wooden offcuts between the frame and recess if any packing is required.

Drill pilot holes, then screw through the shutter frame and into the window frame at the top, bottom, and centre of each member.

E

F

Position the shutters. Align the two sections of the loose-pin hinges. Follow specific instructions if your shutters use different hinges.

Insert the pins into the hinges. Check that the shutters open and close smoothly – try adjusting the frame packing if they don't.

G

Clip or stick lengths of moulding over the frame to cover the fixings. If there are gaps between the frame and the wall, you can fit more lengths of moulding to hide them. Alternatively, mask the shutter frame with low-tack tape while you fill the gaps, then paint the filled areas to match the wall.

FITTING EXTERIOR SHUTTERS

Exterior shutters are often mounted on a three-sided frame so that there is no frame member along the window sill. This type of design is neater, and allows rainwater to run off the sill easily to prevent problems with damp. Because exterior shutters are exposed to the elements, make sure you choose hardwearing or factory-coated materials.

A

B

Construct the frame as specified, unless it is supplied ready-made. Position the frame at the front of the recess. Check the fit.

Use a spirit level to check the frame is square. If packing is required, get help to hold the frame while you make any adjustments.

C

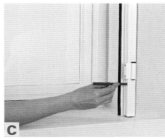

You might distort the frame if you over-tighten fixings

D

Mark the pre-drilled fixing hole positions on the wall. If holes are not pre-drilled, then fix each member at the top, bottom, and centre.

Remove the frame and drill the pilot holes using a suitable bit. Plug the holes if necessary, then reposition the frame and fix it in place.

E

Lower the hinge sections on the shutter onto the hinge sections secured to the frame. The shutter should easily slide into place when the hinges are correctly aligned. Check that the shutters open and close smoothly.

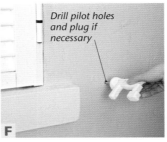

Drill pilot holes and plug if necessary

F

G

Position the tie-backs. Open the shutters to get the right level, then make sure you will be able to reach them from inside. Screw into place.

Check that the tie-backs operate smoothly and make any adjustments as required.

FREEING STUCK WOODEN WINDOWS

Wooden windows can swell in wet weather. Try rubbing candle wax along the sticking edge of the window. If that does not work then plane away some wood as shown here. For protecting exterior wood, see p.293.

TOOLS AND MATERIALS
Plane, hammer, screwdriver

Sticking opening edge
You can plane the opening edge of a casement in situ. Take off enough extra wood to allow for decoration.

Tap a screwdriver with a hammer to free painted-in screws

Sticking top or bottom edge
Unscrew the casement from its hinges so that you can plane the sticking edge.

REPOSITIONING FASTENERS

Movement of wood due to damp weather can also make fasteners difficult to close, or lead to loose, rattling windows. Fix the problem by adjusting the fitting positions, as if you were fitting from scratch (see p.149). If adjustment only requires minimal movement, you may have to move the fastener so you can fix into solid wood.

MAINTAINING UPVC WINDOWS

UPVC windows need little maintenance, apart from washing to keep them clean (see box, right). Hinges may sometimes need lubricating, and occasionally you might need to replace a catch.

TOOLS AND MATERIALS
Screwdriver, oil

The screw is often covered

Broken catch
Lever off the fixing cover with a screwdriver then remove and replace the catch.

Stiff friction hinges
Lubricate metal hinges with low-viscosity oil. Spray plastic hinges with polish containing silicone.

CLEANING UPVC

With warm water, remove as much dirt as possible. Use a mild detergent on stubborn marks, then rinse well, especially the seals. Some cream cleaners can be used on UPVC, but keep them off the seals and rinse very thoroughly. Some cleaners are only suitable for smooth, white UPVC, not wood-grain effect types. Never use an abrasive cleaner on UPVC.

ADJUSTING A MORTISE-PLATE

If the mortise-plate for a mortise-type catch (see pp.148–49) is poorly fitted, it makes the catch difficult to use and can prevent it holding the window closed securely. Remove the mortise-plate and re-fit it properly.

TOOLS AND MATERIALS
Screwdriver, pencil, chisel

A Unscrew the mortise-plate from the window frame.

B Reposition the mortise-plate. Draw around the outside and the inside of the mortise-plate with a pencil.

Rebate
Mortise

C Use a chisel to adjust the rebate, and to widen the mortise if necessary. Re-attach the mortise-plate and check it fits snugly.

REPAIRING A ROTTEN SILL

If a small area of a wooden sill is rotten, but the rest of the window is sound, you can just replace this part of the sill. For protecting exterior wood, see pp.292–93.

TOOLS AND MATERIALS
Pencil, saw, router, wood, screws, drill-driver, plane

Prime cut edges

A Cut back the sill to sound wood. Use it as a template for the patch. Mark the position of the groove under the sill (the drip groove).

Countersink screws to allow plane clearance

B Cut the patch slightly larger than the rotten section you removed. Rout out the drip groove. Screw the patch in place, and plane it smooth.

OTHER WOODEN FRAME REPAIRS

■ Another option for fixing loose joints is to strengthen them with dowel.
■ If a whole section of your window is rotten, then prise the piece out and fashion a replacement, using the old section as a template. For woodworking joints, see pp.392–93. If rot is more widespread, you should replace the entire window.

REMOVING GLASS SAFELY

Broken glass can cause serious injury. Always wear protective gloves, work boots, and goggles when you are removing glass from a window. Remove the glass safely and clean old putty and fixings from the rebate as shown here, before reglazing (see pp.150–51).

The technique for glass fixed with glazing beads is similar. Tape the glass before prising off the beads (you can reuse them). You should be able to free the pane from any glazing silicone fairly easily by cutting around the silicone with a craft knife. With the glass removed, scrape out the old silicone, prime any bare wood, and reglaze.

TOOLS AND MATERIALS
Goggles, gloves, masking tape, hammer, hacking knife/old chisel, pliers, paintbrush, exterior primer

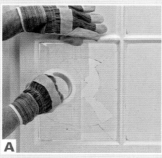

A **Apply strips** of masking tape over the surface of the window pane to prevent shards falling when you remove the remaining glass.

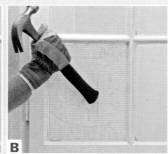

B **Protect surfaces below** the window with dustsheets to catch broken glass. Tap the glass with the butt of a hammer to loosen it.

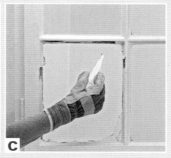

C **Carefully remove** the loose, large sections of glass first, then pick out the smaller shards. Dispose of °broken glass safely.

D **Use a hacking knife** or old chisel to remove the old putty and stubborn pieces of glass from around the glazing rebate.

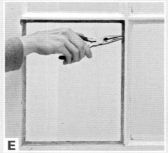

E **Remove any old** pins or glazing sprigs using pincers or pliers.

F **Dust off surfaces.** Use an exterior wood primer on any bare wood before fitting a new pane of glass.

REPLACING GLASS IN LEAD LIGHTS

You can repair single-glazed lead lights using silicone sealant. Take a cardboard template to a specialist supplier to buy replacement glass. Silicone can also be used to repair old putty.

TOOLS AND MATERIALS
Putty knife, silicone glazing sealant, sealant dispenser, replacement glass, cloth

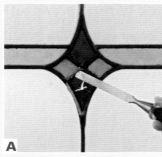

A **Carefully fold up** the lead around the broken pane using the end of a chisel. You may find this easier if you run a craft knife under the lead first.

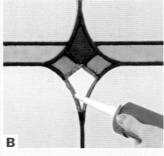

B **Apply a continuous bead** of silicone sealant, using a dispenser (see p.81), around the folded lead.

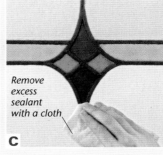

Remove excess sealant with a cloth

C **Position the new** pane. Fold the lead back in place and smooth its edge flush with the glass surface.

REMOVING UPVC BEAD FIXINGS

With beaded and double-glazed units try to remove the fixings carefully so they can be reused. Only carry out DIY work on old double-glazed units – if they are still under guarantee then get the manufacturer to repair them.

TOOLS AND MATERIALS
Scraper, packers

A **Work a scraper** blade under the edge of the first bead.

B **Prise up the bead** so you can position a packer underneath, beside the scraper. Insert another packer on the other side of the scraper.

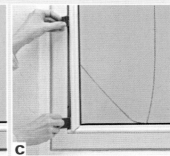

C **Move the packers outwards** to unclip the bead from the frame. Repeat for all beads. Remove the double-glazing unit carefully.

Doors

BOTH EXTERNAL AND INTERNAL DOOR SYSTEMS NEED TO SUIT THE ARCHITECTURAL STYLE OF YOUR HOME. EXTERNAL DOORS ARE OFTEN THICKER AND MORE DURABLE TO WITHSTAND THE ELEMENTS. WHEN BUYING A NEW DOOR, REMEMBER THAT ALL DOOR FURNITURE – HINGES, HANDLES, LOCKS, LATCHES, AND SO ON – IS USUALLY BOUGHT AND FITTED SEPARATELY. A RECLAIMED DOOR IS A CHEAPER, ECO-FRIENDLY OPTION (SEE PP.86–87).

TYPES OF DOOR

The simplest way to categorize the wide range of doors is to consider if they are for external use, such as a front door or a shed door, or for internal use within the home.

WOOD   **UPVC**   **FIBREGLASS**   **SLIDING PATIO**   **STEEL**

EXTERIOR DOORS

A wide range of exterior doors is available, the most common of which are shown here. The material of the door is an important indicator of its durability, and will also determine if a finish is required. The age of the building will affect your choice – a panelled design is more appropriate for an older building, for example. The manufacturer should supply details of recommended security fittings. Many exterior doors are supplied as part of a doorset (i.e. with, or already fitted in, a frame). If you are replacing a door that also needs a new frame, see opposite.

COMMON EXTERIOR DOOR TYPES

Type	Information	Finish
Wood	Hardwood is most durable. Softwood is cheaper, but higher maintenance.	Use a varnish or paint suitable for exterior work
UPVC	Thermally efficient, and low maintenance. Always supplied as part of a doorset.	Factory-finished. No need to paint after fitting
Fibreglass	Made of a wooden framework with large areas of insulation. Often pressed or moulded for a wood-grain effect.	May be supplied pre-finished. If not, finish with varnish or paint
Sliding patio	Supplied in sections, with a frame. Some have both doors on runners; others have only one door sliding and opening.	Door shown left is UPVC in a UPVC frame
Steel	May comprise a wooden core, covered with steel; or may have a steel internal frame with wooden covering.	May be factory-finished. Handles and locks may be factory-fitted

INTERIOR DOORS

As with exterior doors, there is a wide range of interior doors on the market – the most common are shown here. Internal doors are lighter, and tend to cost less than external doors. Flush doors are generally cheaper than panelled ones. Again, choose a design appropriate to the age of your home. The manufacturer should supply details such as whether the door is fireproof or has soundproof capabilities.

FRAMES, LININGS, AND DOORSETS

To hang your door, you will need a frame or a lining. Or you may choose to buy an all-in-one doorset.

Door lining
The door is hung on the door lining. Usually comes as a kit. Will require cutting down to fit.

Door frame
Frames a rough opening. Made of softwood or hardwood. Made in set sizes, relating to door sizes.

Doorset
Used for hanging a door without having to build or insert a door lining first. Labour-saving system, but more expensive.

| PANEL | GLAZED | LOUVRE | BI-FOLD | LEDGE-AND-BRACE | FRAMED LEDGE-AND-BRACE | FLUSH |

COMMON INTERIOR DOOR TYPES

Type	Information	Finish
Panel	Two types: solid and pressed. Solid is of hardwood or softwood; sometimes made of knot-free wood. Pressed version mimics the grain and panels of solid, with moulded hardboard, making it cheaper and lighter.	Solid may be painted, or finished using a natural wood system. Pressed is only suitable for painting
Glazed	Glass is not often supplied. When buying glass, ensure it is toughened and that it complies with internal glazing regulations. Ideal door for a room requiring light.	Prime and undercoat door before fitting glass
Louvre	Angled slats for ventilation/decoration. Ideal door type for wardrobes or airing cupboards. Fitted with hinges, or used in a bi-fold or sliding door set-up.	May be painted, or finished using a natural wood paint or finish
Bi-fold	Fitted to the door lining with butt hinges. Butt hinges also connect the sections. May have a sliding rail mechanism at the top.	May be painted, or finished using a natural wood paint or finish
Ledge-and-brace	Made up of tongue-and-groove sections, braced with horizontal and diagonal timber. Softwood or hardwood. Ideal for cottage-style home.	May be painted, or finished using a natural wood paint or finish
Framed ledge-and-brace	Ledge-and-brace construction, in a frame for extra strength. Sometimes used as an external door. Stable doors are based on this design, cut horizontally in two.	May be painted, or finished using a natural wood paint or finish
Flush	Cheaper than panel doors. Two types: solid and hollow. Better-quality versions have solid timber core, with a softwood frame for hinging and latch fitting. Hollow flush doors are cheaper.	Solid may be pre-finished with a wooden veneer. Hollow versions are mostly designed for a paint finish

DOOR ANATOMY

External doors are generally heavier than internal doors and there are also differences in the frames in which they are hung. Internal wooden doors are typically hung in a door-lining frame, which is then attached to a rough frame opening, whereas exterior doors are hung directly onto a doorframe. When a door is being replaced, the new door will fit in the same place as the old one. When fitting a new door in a cavity wall, the frame should be aligned with the external skin of the wall and then recessed to form a rebate between the frame and exterior wall surface.

CHOOSING SIZE AND NUMBER OF HINGES

Once quality and finish has been decided, the number and size of the hinges required relates directly to the weight and function of the door. Internal doors may have two or three hinges. A third hinge, positioned centrally, may be necessary for heavy internal doors. A minimum of three or four hinges are used on external doors. Large hinges with four or more fixing holes are normally used on external rather than internal doors. Also, remember that hinges should be oiled after fitting (they rarely come ready-oiled). Finally, if a hinge is used on a fire door, make sure that it has the required resistance rating (for fire doors see p.375).

INTERIOR DOOR

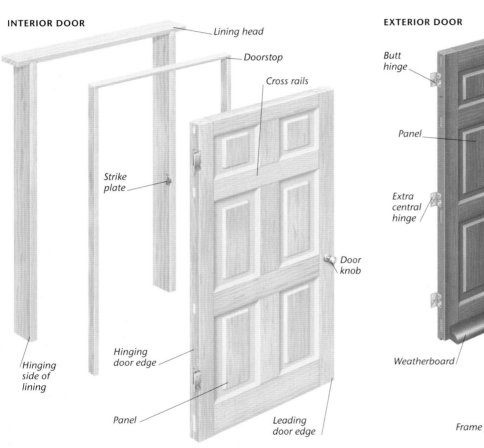

Lining head
Doorstop
Cross rails
Strike plate
Door knob
Hinging side of lining
Hinging door edge
Panel
Leading door edge

EXTERIOR DOOR

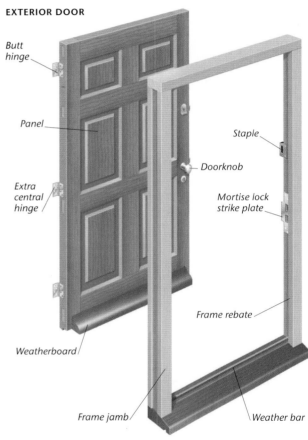

Butt hinge
Panel
Staple
Doorknob
Extra central hinge
Mortise lock strike plate
Weatherboard
Frame rebate
Frame jamb
Weather bar

LATCH ANATOMY

Doors normally require a latch mechanism so that they can be securely closed. Internal doors tend to have a simple mortise catch, but external doors may have a mortise lock combined with the catch design. With either latch type, the main body of the latch is fitted to the closing edge of the door. The catch then engages with a plate that is fitted to the door lining or doorframe.

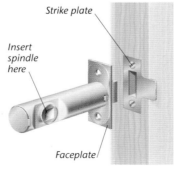

Strike plate
Insert spindle here
Faceplate

Mortise latch
Used on internal doors where security is not an issue (see p.162 for fitting). See opposite for handle design.

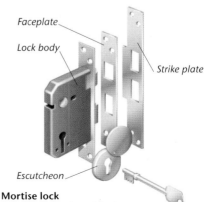

Faceplate
Lock body
Strike plate
Escutcheon

Mortise lock
Suitable for back or side doors, mortise locks can also be fitted to front doors for added security (see p.168 for fitting).

When choosing door furniture, ensure that it is in scale with the door itself. Two hinges are usually sufficient for internal doors, but use three or four on external doors. The heavier weight of external doors generally calls for more durable fittings. Choose locks according to the amount of security you require (see p.168 for more on locks).

HANDLES

Latches require a handle that turns, moving the internal mechanism, whereas with catches (see below right) a simple pull knob or handle is sufficient.

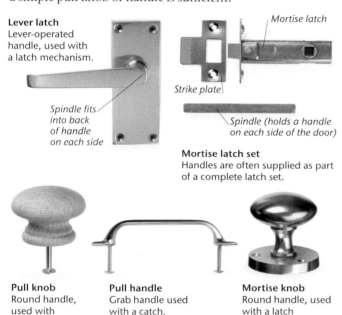

Lever latch
Lever-operated handle, used with a latch mechanism.

Spindle fits into back of handle on each side

Mortise latch

Strike plate

Spindle (holds a handle on each side of the door)

Mortise latch set
Handles are often supplied as part of a complete latch set.

Pull knob
Round handle, used with a catch.

Pull handle
Grab handle used with a catch.

Mortise knob
Round handle, used with a latch mechanism.

HINGES

Butt hinges are the most common form of hinge. Good-quality hinges come in brass and stainless steel. Some have extra features such as washers and ball bearings. Oil hinges once they have been fitted.

Standard butt
Has three or four fixing holes on each leaf, and a fixed pin in the hinge barrel.

Rising butt
Lifts the door upwards as it is opened, to allow for a sloping floor.

Parliament
Extended leaf allows a door to open fully, where the frame might otherwise prevent it.

Doorset
Specific hinge for a doorset.

Strap/Tee
Used on a ledge-and-brace door, or a door needing extra support.

Ball bearing
Fitted like butt hinge. Ball bearings give smooth action.

Loose pin
The pin allows you to detach the door without removing the hinge.

Flush
Surface-mounted, so no need to cut into the door edge when fixing.

UPVC
Specific hinge for a UPVC door.

DOOR CLOSERS

There are two main types of closer: a hydraulic closer, surface-mounted on and above the door, and a concealed closer, fitted on the hinging edge of the door. Door closers are always used on fire doors.

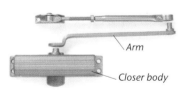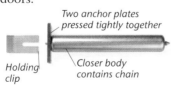

Two anchor plates pressed tightly together

Arm

Holding clip

Closer body contains chain

Closer body

Hydraulic door closer
For heavier doors. The hydraulic mechanism in the closer body pulls the door into a closed position.

Concealed door closer
A sprung chain is attached to two anchor plates. The outer anchor plate is attached to the door lining, and the inner plate to the door.

CATCHES

Catches are either screwed directly to the door and door lining, or they may need recessing. This is the case with ball catches, for example. Catches are commonly used on cupboards and wardrobes (see p.394).

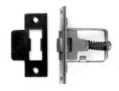

Magnetic
Often used on glass doors. Made of high-impact plastic.

Ball
Used on cupboards. The ball pushes into the strike plate.

Roller
A quiet alternative to the clicking sound of a magnetic catch.

TOOLS AND MATERIALS CHECKLIST PP.160–69

Fitting a door lining (p.160)
Wooden batten, wooden mallet, wedges, spirit level

Hanging a door (p.161)
Hinges, combination square, plane

Installing door fittings (pp.162–63)
Combination square, auger or flat bit

Fitting an internal doorset (p.164)

Wood for wedges, spirit level, timber strips, wood adhesive, architrave

Attaching a door closer (p.165)
Spirit level, auger or flat bit

Making external doors secure (pp.168–69) Auger or flat bit, lock, combination square

FOR BASIC TOOLKIT SEE PP.24–25

FITTING A DOOR LINING

An internal door is not fitted directly into the rough frame of the opening in a wall. A wooden door lining is fitted first, to provide a fixing point for hinges as well as creating a "finished" internal framework to the opening. Door linings are supplied as cut timber lengths. These are then adjusted to the required size for the specific doorway, and the three sections assembled before being fitted into the opening. To ensure that the door hangs correctly, it is very important that the lining is fitted exactly square.

TOOLS AND MATERIALS SEE BASIC TOOLKIT AND P.159

1 ATTACHING THE FIRST BATTEN

Lay the three sections of the door lining out on the floor. Line up the factory-cut grooves of the head section with the side section ends. Use a wooden mallet to hammer together the three sections. (The butt end of a hammer could also be used.)

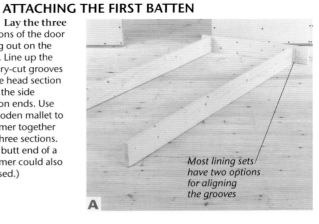

Most lining sets have two options for aligning the grooves

A

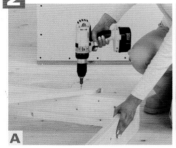

B

Screw down through the top of the head section into one of the side sections. Two screws will be sufficient.

C

Repeat for the other side section. Saw off the excess wood protruding from each end of the head section.

MAKING THE DOOR LINING SQUARE

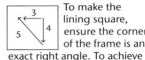

To make the lining square, ensure the corner of the frame is an exact right angle. To achieve this, a basic principle is used – a right-angled triangle is formed when the lengths of the three sides are in a ratio of 3:4:5.

■ Mark off a length of your own chosen measurement, along the head section of the lining. Mark a second length, in ratio to the first, along the adjoining vertical section.

■ Calculate the length of the third side (it will be the third part of the ratio).

■ Measure between the two pencil marks, across the corner.

■ Add 150mm (6in), and cut a batten to the resulting length.

■ Angle the batten across the corner until the measurement of the third side is achieved.

2 MAKING THE FRAME RIGID

A

Having calculated the precise right angle for the batten, screw each end over the pencil marks.

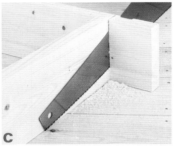

B

Measure the exact width at the top. Cut a length of batten to a little wider than the resulting measurement.

C

Nail the batten across the frame, about 150mm (6in) up from the bottom. Saw off excess wood, flush with section sides, for both battens.

D

Measure the height each side of the rough opening. Transfer these measurements to the side sections of the door lining, and cut to size.

3 FITTING THE DOOR LINING

Lift the lining up from the floor, and position it in the opening. It is likely to fit well in some places but not in others, due to the unevenness of the opening. Use wedges of wood to fill any gaps. Knock them in tightly. Be careful not to distort the lining shape.

Use a spirit level to assess where the lining is not straight

A

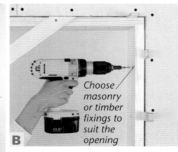

B

Choose masonry or timber fixings to suit the opening

Position fixings along the inside edge of the lining and the lining head. Screw through the lining (and any wedges) into the opening's sides.

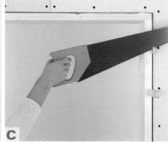

C

Once the lining is fixed, remove the battens. Saw off any excess wood from the wedge, flush with the edge of the door lining.

HANGING A DOOR

It is usual for the door to require some height and width adjustment for a perfect fit. Th is is achieved by temporarily holding the door in place and measuring for fit. Get someone to help you lift the door, or else use a board lifter. Once you are satisfied with the fit of the door, the next task is to attach the hinges. For information about hinge choices, and deciding on the number required, see p.159. In the example shown here, standard butt hinges are being fitted.

TOOLS AND MATERIALS SEE BASIC TOOLKIT AND P.159

1 ADJUSTING THE DOOR TO FIT

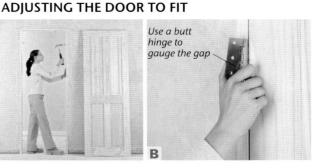

Use a butt hinge to gauge the gap

A **Knock two temporary** nails into the lining head and two in the sides, to the exact door depth. Position the door against the nails in the lining.

B **There needs to** be a gap of 3mm (⅛in) between the hinging edge of the door and the lining. (This is the thickness of most butt hinges.)

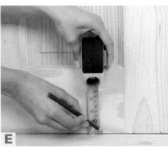

Always plane from the outer edge inwards, to prevent wood splitting

C **Move to** the closing edge. Measure a second gap of 3mm (⅛in) between the door and the lining. With a spirit level, draw a line down the door.

D **Remove the door** from the lining. Place it on the floor, with its closing edge facing upwards. With a plane, take the wood down to the line.

E **Reposition the door** to check that the sides fit with the clearances of 3mm (⅛in). Repeat the measuring process for the base of the door.

F **With a level floor,** 3mm (⅛in) is needed, but any undulations may require more. Plane off the required amount and check for clearance.

2 FITTING THE HINGES AND HANGING THE DOOR

Place the door on the floor, hinging-side up. Make a pencil mark 150mm (6in) down from the top of the door. This is for the top hinge. Place the hinge below the mark, and pencil around it. Repeat for the lower hinge, but this time position it above the mark.

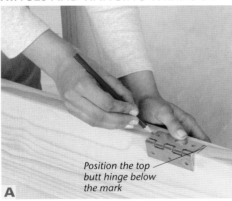

Position the top butt hinge below the mark

A

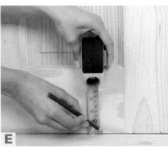

B **At each hinge position,** mark the thickness of the hinge onto the door's front edge. Use a chisel to remove the marked-off depth of wood.

C **Cut across** the grain first, so that you do not split the wood at the next stage. Make cuts every 3mm (⅛in).

D **Now use the chisel** blade along the guide line on the door's front edge. Gently remove the cut wood from inside the hinge guide lines.

E **Holding a hinge** in each hinge area, mark off the screw holes. Pilot drill and test a hole with one screw to make sure of the fit.

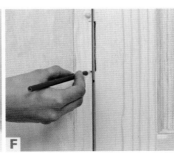

F **Repeat the marking-off** process on the door lining. Repeat steps A–E on the lining and screw the hinges to the door.

G **Wedge the door open** and screw the hinges to the lining. The latch and handle can now be fitted.

INSTALLING DOOR FITTINGS

The main task here is that of fitting a door handle with a latch. This can be broken down into three stages – firstly the latch is fitted in the door, then the handles are fixed on the door surface, and finally the strike plate is fitted on the door lining. The second task shown here is that of fitting the doorstop. This is fixed onto the door lining, to enable the door to close rather than swing out the other side. Although a simple technique is used, accuracy is essential to ensure that the door closes securely.

TOOLS AND MATERIALS SEE BASIC TOOLKIT AND P.159

FITTING A MORTISE LATCH AND HANDLE

A

Mark the top, bottom, and end of the latch case at the required height on the door. Continue guide lines around the edge and the other side of the door.

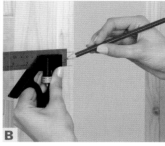

B

Measure the width of the door edge, draw a vertical guide line through the horizontal guide lines.

C

Measure the distance from the centre of the spindle's position on the latch to the latch plate.

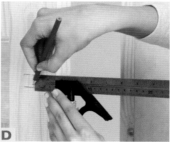

D

Mark, on the appropriate line, the distance from the front of the latch plate to the centre of the spindle position on the door.

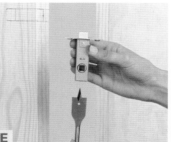

E

Select an auger bit or flat bit that is slightly larger than the latch casing (in this case a flat bit is used). Mark off the latch depth with tape.

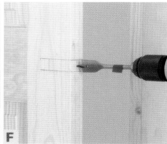

F

Position the point of the bit on the vertical guide line between the horizontal guide lines showing width.

Start drilling slowly. It is essential that the drill bit enters the door at a precise right angle to the door edge. If it does not, the latch will not sit flush in position. You may also split the door face if the bit is misaligned.

G

H

Drill to the depth of the latch. Push the latch into the hole, positioned precisely vertical. Draw a guide line around the latch plate.

I

Remove the latch and chisel out the wood from inside the guide line, to a depth equal to that of the latch plate.

J

For the marked-off spindle position, gently drill into each face of the door, taking care not to split the wood surface.

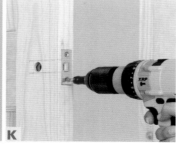

K

Push the latch into position. Drill pilot holes for the screw positions on the latch plate. Secure it with retaining screws.

L

Insert the spindle and fit a handle on it. Mark through fixing holes with a bradawl for the screw positions.

M

Repeat the marking process on the other door face, then screw the handles into position.

FITTING A STRIKE PLATE

A Rest the door in an almost closed position. On the edge of the door lining, mark off above and below the latch.

B Open the door, and continue the guide lines round onto the inner face of the lining, using a combination square.

C Measure the exact distance between the front edge of the door and the front face of the latch. Mark it on the lining.

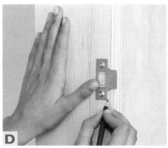

D Using the guide line, hold the strike plate in position and draw a further line inside the plate and around its outer edge.

Use a chisel to remove the wood from the central marked-out area, at a depth to accommodate the latch. Follow the external guide line for the strike plate, to remove wood to a depth equal to that of the strike plate.

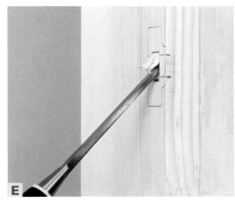

E

F Hold the strike plate in position and mark the screw holes.

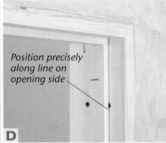

G Remove the strike plate and drill pilot holes. Reposition the plate and screw it in place.

FITTING A DOORSTOP

A Close the door, and draw a guide line around the lining at the point where it meets with the door edge.

B Cut a section of doorstop for the door head. Place it on the guide line. Hold in position with three nails — lightly knock them in.

C Measure and cut two lengths of doorstop for each side of the lining. Position one length on the door hinging side of the lining.

Position slightly back from line on hanging side

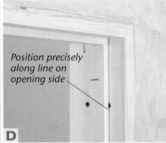

D Position another length on the lining opening side. Again, do not hammer fixings all the way in.

Position precisely along line on opening side

E

Check that the door opens and closes smoothly, and adjust doorstop positions if needed. Then firmly knock in the nails.

FURTHER INFORMATION

Pull knob/handle
A pull handle is used when a catch holds the door closed, rather than a latch mechanism. Pull handles are most commonly found on cupboards, and should be fitted before the doorstop.

Fixing a pull handle
At the required place on the door, drill a hole for the handle-retaining screw or bolt. Hold a wood offcut on the opposite side of the door, to prevent the wood splitting. Position the retaining screw and screw on the handle. Washers may be used to strengthen the fixing. If screws or bolts are too long for the depth of door, cut them to the correct size using a hacksaw.

FITTING AN INTERNAL DOORSET

An alternative to buying and fitting a door and a separate lining or frame is to buy a doorset. This is supplied with the frame and door pre-assembled. You will still need to make adjustments to ensure a good fit.

TOOLS AND MATERIALS CHECKLIST SEE P.159

1 ENSURING THE DOORSET FITS

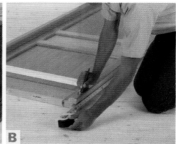

Fix one or two braces across the frame if it is not supplied pre-braced. This keeps the frame rigid during the fitting process.

Measure the dimensions of the doorset – and the rough frame where it is to be installed – to ensure that the doorset will fit.

Trim frame jambs as required, so that the doorset will fit in the rough opening.

2 POSITIONING THE DOORSET

Hammer in some nails around the rough opening, so that the back of the doorset can temporarily rest against them.

It is easier to place the doorset into the rough frame with two people, as you need to ensure that it goes in flush against the wall.

Make some wooden wedges from offcuts, and knock them along the joint between the doorset frame and the rough frame. This is to hold the doorset in position. (Do not knock in the wedges so hard that they distort the frame of the doorset.) Use a spirit level to ensure that the doorset is positioned precisely vertical.

3 FIXING AND FINISHING THE DOORSET

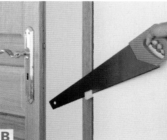

Attach your chosen handle and the strike plate, following the steps shown on p.162.

Saw off any protruding wedge pieces, so that the wood lies flat in the gap between the doorset and the rough opening.

On the other side of the door (where it is supported by the temporary nails), fix through the doorset frame into the rough frame.

With timber strips, fill in the gap between the back of the doorset and the rough frame. Use wood glue to attach the strips.

Return to the front of the door. Remove any braces you may have added for support. Open the door to check that it is functioning correctly, then finish adding fixings to secure the frame in its final position. Keep checking the door position with a spirit level and that it opens and shuts properly.

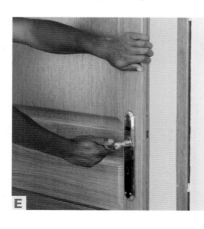

To finish off, glue architrave strips around the doorset. (If you prefer to fix the strips, hide fixings with pelleting; see p.217.)

On the other side of the door, repeat your chosen method of attaching architrave.

ATTACHING A DOOR CLOSER

Two closers are shown here. A hydraulic door closer is fitted on and above the door. A concealed door closer is fitted on the hinging edge of the door and door lining. Two or more are used for heavy doors.

TOOLS AND MATERIALS
CHECKLIST SEE P.159

FITTING A HYDRAULIC DOOR CLOSER

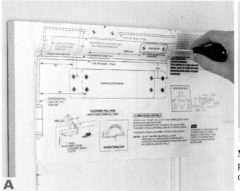

The manufacturer of the closer will supply a template for its installation. With the door closed, tape the template to the door face as shown. Here the closer will be fitted to the "pull" side of the door; some closers have the option of being fitted on the other side. Through the template, mark the fixing positions with a bradawl.

A

B

Make pilot holes for the fixing points, and secure the main body of the door closer in position.

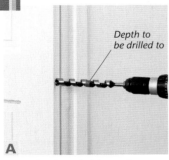

C

Position the first arm of the closer, using the template hole guides. Draw a pencil guide line around the fixing end of the arm.

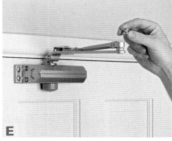

D

Attach the arm to the doorframe, on the pencil guide lines. It may help to swing it out of the way as you screw in the fixings.

E

Attach the other arm to the main body of the closer. Join it to the first arm with the supplied nut and bolt. Open the door, and let it swing shut.

APPROPRIATE HINGES

Because a door closer relies on a smooth hinge action, some manufacturers specify that the hinges to be used in conjunction with the door closer must be of a specific type. This usually means a heavier duty hinge, and one that operates with a ball-bearing mechanism. For further information on choosing hinges, see p.159.

FITTING A CONCEALED DOOR CLOSER

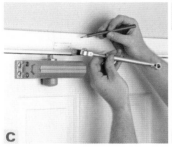

Depth to be drilled to

A

Mark the closer height on the hinging side of the door. Mark the depth of the closer cylinder on the drill bit, and drill to that depth.

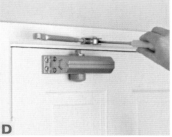

The two anchor plates are tight together here

B

Insert the cylinder into the hole, pushing it in until the outer anchor plate sits flush with the door surface. Draw a pencil line around the plate.

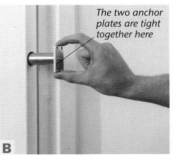

C

Pull out the cylinder. Chisel inside the pencil guide line. Remove the wood to the depth of the outer anchor plate.

D

Re-insert the cylinder. Slowly close the door so that the back edge of the outer anchor plate marks the door lining. Pencil around the plate.

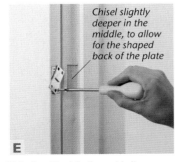

Chisel slightly deeper in the middle, to allow for the shaped back of the plate

E

Chisel out inside the guide line to the depth of the anchor plate. Screw down the inner anchor plate, to secure the cylinder in the door.

With a pair of pliers, pull the outer anchor plate away from the inner anchor plate. Once a small section of chain is exposed, place the holding clip on to it. Now that the chain is held in its extended position, you can pull the outer anchor plate round onto the chiselled-out area on the door lining.

F

G

Drill pilot holes for the outer anchor plate's fixing points, and screw in place. Remove the holding clip. The closer will now work.

Fitting an external door is similar to fitting an internal door (see pp.161–63). The main difference is that some external doorframes have a weather bar along the bottom. If this is the case, the bottom edge of the door will need to be rebated so that it closes neatly. External doors often have three or even four hinges, which is an additional fitting requirement to most internal doors. There are various door materials to choose from; a popular choice is UPVC, which is both strong and easy to maintain. UPVC doors are usually sold as a doorset.

FITTING A UPVC DOORSET

UPVC doors are normally supplied as part of a doorset, so the installation procedure is similar to that shown on p.164. The main difference is that many UPVC doorsets come with an integral threshold and so do not require temporary braces. If the threshold is separate, or not required, some form of bracing will be needed to hold the door and frame components in position.

Fixing the hinge side

Wedge the doorset in position. If a threshold strip is required, this should also be cut and fitted. Start by inserting two or three fixings along the hinging side of the frame; if fixing into masonry, drill directly through the internal edge of the lining into the masonry below. Insert fixings and tap into place with a hammer, then insert screws to the correct depth and allow to bite firmly into the fixing holes; overtightening distorts the frame profile.

Fixing the opening side

With two or three fixings in place, check that the door is level, then start on the opening edge of the frame; insert two or three more fixings using the same technique. Recheck the levels, then add a further two fixings on each side of the frame. For frames that include a threshold, two or three further fixings may be inserted through the threshold. Fixing through the head of the frame is not required in most circumstances; this process can often be difficult because of the lintel above.

Finishing the job

Saw off any wedges around the edge of the door, or remove if appropriate. Where substantial gaps are found between the edge of the doorset frame and the rough frame, expanding foam may be used to fill this gap, and add further rigidity to the frame position. Once dry, the foam may be trimmed back flush with the frame. Silicone sealant or covering strips can be used internally or externally to provide a neat and weatherproof finish; the combination of these will depend on the exact door design and the nature of the frame opening. Most UPVC doorsets are supplied with door furniture fitted, or at least with factory-cut fixing holes in position. Fit if required, and make any adjustments to ensure that the door opens and closes smoothly. UPVC door hinges are usually adjustable to aid final positioning.

MORE INFORMATION

■ For wooden-hinged patio doors opening in a wooden frame, the fitting procedure is the same as for a regular door. Sliding patio doors are slightly different; they are generally supplied with a frame that will need to be assembled before fixing into the wall.

■ When building a new wall the doorframe can be placed during the construction process. In masonry walls, ties are fixed to the outside of the frame; in timber-framed walls the frame is simply screwed into place as part of the wall assembly.

■ Removing an old wooden frame can be a tricky process, especially if it is original and was built into the wall structure at the time of construction. Try to remove any fixings with screwdrivers before using a pry bar to lever the frame free.

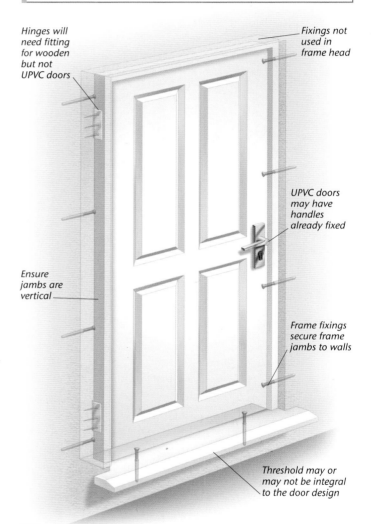

Hinges will need fitting for wooden but not UPVC doors

Fixings not used in frame head

UPVC doors may have handles already fixed

Ensure jambs are vertical

Frame fixings secure frame jambs to walls

Threshold may or may not be integral to the door design

Fitting an external door
The fixing process for an external door is fairly straightforward. Take time to ensure that frames are precisely vertical before fixing them in place. Frame fixings are used whatever the type of frame material.

DAMP-PROOF COURSES

When an old doorframe is being removed some consideration needs to be given to the DPC. If a UPVC door is being fitted, it is not necessary to fit a new DPC below the threshold. For a wooden frame, inspect the existing DPC, which if undamaged may be left in place and the frame fitted. However if it is damaged, replace this section with a new piece before fitting the new frame.

There are a number of tasks that apply only to external doors, to resist weather conditions and to provide reliable security for the home. Wooden frames and doors can rot at the base where moisture penetrates the end of the grain of the wood. Small areas of damage can be repaired. One way to prolong the life of an external door is to fit a weatherboard, which deflects water away from the base of the door. Replacing a threshold may also become necessary.

REPLACING A THRESHOLD

■ It may be necessary to cut out a new threshold by sawing through the joint between the doorframe stiles and the top surface of the threshold. It should then be possible to ease it out of position.
■ Apply wood preservative to all surfaces before fitting.

Apply several coats to the underside as this can't be accessed once fitted.
■ The new threshold will need to be cut to fit. It may be necessary to rebate each end so that it fits in the opening rebate of the door.
■ If necessary, replace the DPC below the threshold.

REPAIRING A ROTTEN DOOR AND FRAME

Wooden doors and frames tend to rot at the base where moisture has penetrated the end grain of the wood. As long as penetration has not reached too far up the wood, sections can be cut out and replaced with new pieces of timber.

Repairing the frame

Make an angled cut through the stile of the frame 50mm (2in) above the rotten area. The angle of this cut should be as close to 45 degrees as possible. Depending on the frame design, more than one section of timber may be required (e.g. one piece for the stile and one for the doorstop). Cut the new timber to size, using the old section of wood as a template if possible; if not, use a bevel to determine the exact angle of cut. Apply wood preservative to all the surfaces of the new section of wood and to the end grain of the angled cut in the frame. Once dry, pre-drill some fixing holes into the new timber. Apply wood adhesive to the angled cuts of the new timber and to the frame. Position the new timber, allowing it to sit slightly proud of the frame. Fix through pilot holes using the appropriate fixings; the addition of these will pull the joint flush with the doorframe, creating a neat, tight joint.

Repairing the door

Rot can cause the complete failure of the corner joints of panelled doors. If this happens, the bottom rail and the affected stile can be replaced. This involves cutting back to sound wood and using the cut sections as templates for new ones. Make sure that all new wood is coated with preservative. With ledge-and-brace doors it is essential to catch the rot early. A small amount of wood can then be removed from the bottom edge of the door. A weatherboard can be fitted to the exterior, and a rebated section of wood fixed to the inside; the latter should overlap the underside of the door. Again, new timber must be treated with preservative; apply wood hardener to the end grain of the tongue-and-groove boards to prevent further rot. Where large areas of rot have spread up the boards the entire board can be removed and replaced. Use a padsaw to cut through the existing tongue-and-groove joints, and a tenon saw to make angled cuts above the rotten sections. When a new board is positioned, joints should be made on the horizontal rails of the door. Craft knifes and chisels can be used for final trimming.

FITTING A WEATHERBOARD

A weatherboard can be fitted into the doorframe or cut to fit against the frame's profile. This decision often depends on the design of the door. If you choose to cut the weatherboard into the frame of the door, use an offcut section to draw a profile on the edge of the frame. The unwanted wood may then be removed, using a chisel.

A

B

At the base of the door, measure the distance between the stiles of the frame. Cut the weatherboard to this length.

Draw a line along the top of the weatherboard. Pre-drill some holes in the front of the board and countersink them.

C

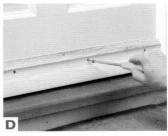

D

Apply wood preservative to the underside of the board. Once dry, apply wood adhesive along the back edge of the board.

Screw the board, in place. Test by closing the door; plane off any parts that catch the frame. Fill any holes, then sand and decorate as required.

Peeling door paint
Paint that is peeling is a sign that moisture is penetrating the structure of the door. If action is taken quickly, only redecoration will be required. Delay may lead to bracing or replacing parts of the door.

When fitting a front door or entrance door, the two most common locks are a mortise lock and a cylinder rim lock. A mortise lock has a key that opens and closes it from inside and outside the door – it is therefore referred to as a deadlock. A cylinder rim lock has a key for the outside, and a knob for the inside (the knob may be operated by a key). With the internal key, this provides the cylinder lock with a deadlocking option, so it cannot be opened by breaking the door's glass to turn the knob.

TOOLS AND MATERIALS SEE BASIC TOOLKIT AND P. 159

CHOOSING A LOCK

When choosing a mortise lock, bear in mind that the higher the number of levers, the more difficult it is to pick. Mechanisms vary between two and seven levers. A front door should have a minimum of five levers. For cylinder locks, check the "anti-drill/pick resistance". Although deadlocks provide excellent security, they should not be used when somebody is left inside the house – in an emergency it would be impossible to undo the door unless another key was readily available.

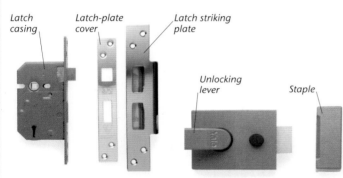

Latch casing | Latch-plate cover | Latch striking plate

Unlocking lever | Staple

FIVE-LEVER MORTISE LOCK

Mounting plate | Connecting bar

CYLINDER RIM LOCK

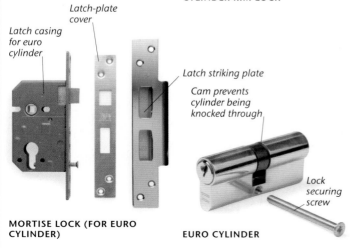

Latch casing for euro cylinder | Latch-plate cover | Latch striking plate

Cam prevents cylinder being knocked through

Lock securing screw

MORTISE LOCK (FOR EURO CYLINDER) | **EURO CYLINDER**

FITTING A MORTISE LOCK

A

B

On the door, measure off the main points for the latch mechanism – the top and bottom edge of the latch, spindle height, and keyhole height.

Continue the guide lines around the edge of the door onto the other face. Draw a central vertical guide line for the latch on the edge of the door.

Mark both door faces

C

Tape marks depth needed

D

Measure off keyhole depth and spindle depth from the latch mechanism. Transfer measurement onto the guide lines on the door.

Choose a flat drill bit or auger bit with a diameter very slightly larger than the width of the latch mechanism.

E

Carefully drill overlapping holes down the central guide line on the door edge. Drill the holes in stages, so that the bit is kept at right angles. Next, drill through the door face, with a flat drill bit or auger bit, to provide access holes for the latch spindle and keyhole. Drill into both faces so that your holes meet in the middle, to avoid splitting the wood.

F

G

Use a chisel to neaten edges of drilled holes so that the latch can slide easily into the recess.

Fit the latch, handles, and strike plate, as shown on p.162. Here, two holes are required (one for the latch and one for the lock).

REPLACING EURO OR OVAL CYLINDERS

With the door wedged open in position, unscrew the lock securing screw on the edge of the door.

Put the key in the keyhole and turn to the open position.

Pull out the cylinder, and replace with the new cylinder. Then reverse the process, turning the key to a closed position and refixing the lock securing screw on the edge of the door.

FITTING A CYLINDER RIM LOCK

Draw a horizontal guide line from the internal face of the door, around the edge and continuing on to the front face of the door.

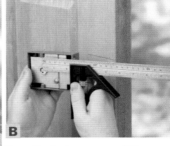

From the lock, measure off the distance from its edge to the hole that will accommodate the connecting bar of the cylinder.

Drill from both sides to avoid splitting wood

Drill through the door face, with a flat drill bit or auger bit, to provide access holes for the cylinder.

On the door's exterior, position the cylinder according to the supplier's instructions. Extend the bar through the hole to the door's internal side.

Fit the mounting plate on the inside. Cut down the connecting bar using a hacksaw to the correct length for fitting into the rim lock.

Slide the rim lock into position on the mounting plate, and secure it with the retaining screws.

With the door in a closed position, mark off the level requirement for the staple on the doorframe.

Open the door, and pencil an outline around the staple to mark its position.

Chisel out the depth required for accommodating the staple.

Secure the staple in place. Then test that the lock clicks into place properly when the door is closed.

GARAGE DOORS

When choosing a garage door, it is important to consider the appearance, material, construction, and method of operation (manual or automatic). Your decision will also depend on budget, and the structure of the garage itself – you may need more than one door in a double garage. A selection of styles is illustrated below, but since garages vary widely in dimensions, a suitable door is seldom available off-the-shelf, so be sure to leave plenty of time between ordering and installation.

FRAMES

The vast majority of garage doors are positioned in wooden or steel frames. These frames are far more substantial than normal doorframes or door linings, as they have to support the weight of both the door and its opening mechanism. In some cases, frames may be reused, but they should always be checked to ensure that they are strong enough to support any new door. Many doors come ready-framed, which makes installation easier. There can be a considerable difference in price, depending on whether you are just buying a door, or a door and frame. Also check that the manufacturer's quoted price includes any hinges or other mechanisms required.

TYPES OF DOOR

Garage doors, traditionally made of wood, are now available in various materials. Steel is commonly used, as is glass-reinforced polyester (GRP). The latter is particularly popular, because it is lightweight, strong, and easy to maintain. Weight is an important consideration; a lightweight door is particularly desirable if it is large, or if an automatic system is being installed. If you plan to fit doors yourself, even lightweight ones will be difficult to handle alone, so make sure you have help at hand during installation. Also remember to think about your old doors. They are not small items, and you may have to make special arrangements for their disposal.

STYLES AND MATERIALS

GRP up-and-over
This type of canopy door is made of lightweight material, and has a pivot mechanism allowing for easy opening and closing by hand.

Steel side-opening
These doors are often sold as "doorsets", already mounted and hinged within a steel frame for ease of fitting.

Wooden up-and-over
Whether side-opening or up-and-over, wooden doors are sometimes pre-treated, although re-treating will be necessary to maintain their looks.

Steel up-and-over
Although not as light as GRP doors, steel canopies still provide a relatively lightweight feel, and are easy to open and close by hand.

OPENING AND CLOSING MECHANISMS

Garage doors have a wide variety of opening and closing mechanisms. Some are similar to those used by other entrance doors, and some are used only with garage doors. The four examples above rely on the two most popular operating principles – simple hinges and a pivoting canopy. Each can be constructed in various ways, and alternatives such as roller doors are also worth considering. Almost any type of door can be automated (see opposite).

Up-and-over: canopy
Canopy up-and-over doors have a pivoting hinge mechanism that allows the door to be lifted upwards and slid back at ceiling level into the garage. A portion of the base of the door protrudes from the garage, providing a small overhang or "canopy". This is the simplest up-and-over mechanism, and the system is secured to the sides of the frame, saving space.

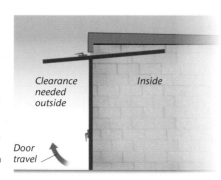

Clearance needed outside

Inside

Door travel

Up-and-over: retractable
A retractable up-and-over door operates in a similar way to a canopy door except that the door retracts fully into the garage at ceiling level; it is suspended on a framework independent of the doorframe, and therefore occupies a little more space than a canopy mechanism.

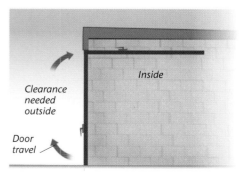

Inside

Clearance needed outside

Door travel

Sectional

Subdividing a door into a number of horizontal sections provides the basic structure of a sectional garage door. The divisions in the door allow it to roll straight up into a retracted position so there is no need for door clearance outside the garage. The sections slide through channels fixed to the doorframe, which keep the door rigid when shut.

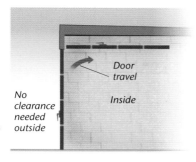

Door travel

No clearance needed outside

Inside

Roller

This type of door is also sectional, but with much narrower horizontal sections than the type shown left. The narrow sections allow the door to wrap around a roller at the top of the frame. As a result, this system takes up minimal room inside the garage.

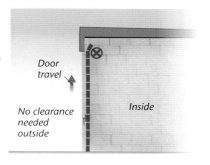

Door travel

No clearance needed outside

Inside

ELECTRIC DOOR OPERATION

An automatic garage-door operation system is now an affordable option for many home-owners. Most systems are based on a ceiling-mounted electric motor, linked to the door through a mechanism that pushes or pulls the door into a closed or open position. Some systems can be fitted to existing doors, in which case it may not be necessary to purchase a new door. However, there may still be a need to modify the opening mechanism of the existing door in order to incorporate an electric opener, so if you are fitting the electric system retrospectively, take time to choose a design of opener that best suits your existing door. Although the systems illustrated here are for use with up-and-over doors, there are other types available that work equally well with side-opening doors.

Motor

The motor is electrically operated and secured to the ceiling. A belt or chain held in the rail mechanism connects the motor with the door. Most motors are operated by remote control, and have safety devices that prevent the door trying to close when obstructed. In the event of a power cut, manual operation should still be possible.

Automated retractable door

A typical installation for automating this type of door involves a central rail fitted with a motorized belt or chain. This moves an arm, which in turn pulls the door up or pushes it down.

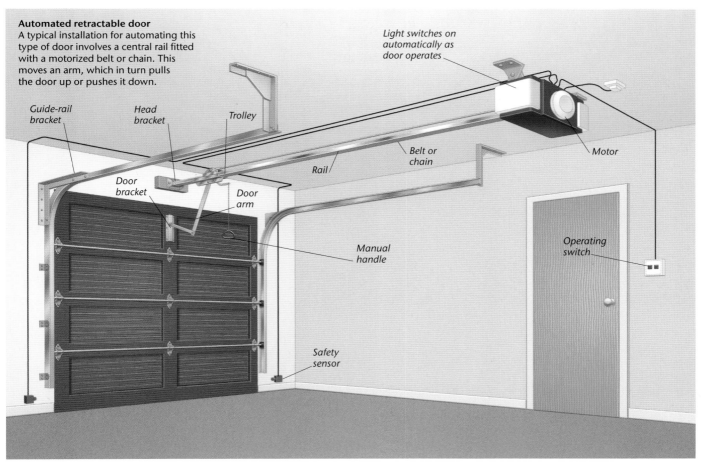

Light switches on automatically as door operates

Guide-rail bracket

Head bracket

Trolley

Belt or chain

Rail

Motor

Door bracket

Door arm

Manual handle

Operating switch

Safety sensor

STICKING DOORS: PLANING SIDES

Doors can stick when part of the door edge is binding against the frame or floor. Gently removing wood from these areas will return the door to an easy opening and closing action.

TOOLS AND MATERIALS
Pencil, plane

A

Mark on the door edge, with a pencil, where it touches the frame. For elongated areas, draw a pencil guide line along the door edge.

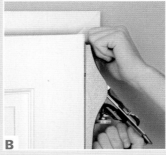

B

Open the door and plane along the edge, down to the marked-off guide line. Check that the door fits; re-plane if necessary.

AWKWARD AREAS

■ **The sticking area is very close to the floor.**
If there is not enough room for a plane, remove the door from its hinges.
■ **The sticking area is very close to the latch.**
Do not risk damaging the plane on the metallic latch surface. Remove the latch before planing, and/or recess the latch in the door slightly farther in.

STICKING DOORS: SCRIBING BOTTOM

Doors can also stick when the entire bottom edge binds against the floor.

TOOLS AND MATERIALS
Measure, panel saw, wood, pencil, block plane

A

Measure the exact height needed to clear floor level. Cut a small offcut of wood to the height that you have just measured.

B

With a pencil on top, move the offcut across the floor to trace an exact line on the door.

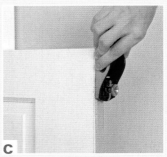

C

Remove the door from the frame and plane down the guide line. If a large amount of wood needs to be removed, use a panel saw.

RATTLING DOORS: MOVING THE STRIKE PLATE

Doors that fit too loosely in their frame rattle in a draught. This is often due to the strike plate being in the wrong position. Measure the area accurately and move the strike plate.

TOOLS AND MATERIALS
Combination square, pencil, screwdriver, drill-driver, chisel

A

Measure the gap between the door latch and the closing edge.

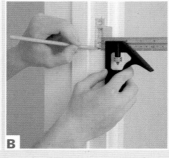

B

Transfer this measurement to the area between the frame edge and the strike-plate opening. Move the strike plate to this position.

C

Pilot hole the fixing points. Chisel out any further wood from the door lining to accommodate the strike plate's new position.

RATTLING DOORS: MOVING THE DOORSTOP

The other reason a door rattles in a draught is that the doorstop has been wrongly positioned. Moving the doorstop to the correct place should fix the problem.

TOOLS AND MATERIALS
Chisel, hammer, nails

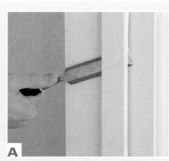

A

Lever off any doorstop sections that do not fit properly against the door when closed.

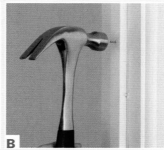

B

Re-fix the removed sections, making sure they touch the door edge along their full length when the door is closed.

LATCH PROBLEMS

■ **The latch does not catch when the door closes.**
The strike plate may be too far forward in the frame. Filing the plate's inner edge may be all that is needed.
■ **The latch does not catch in the strike plate.**
The plate may be too far recessed in the frame. Pack out the plate, in the same way as shown for packing out a hinge (opposite).

STRENGTHENING HINGE FIXINGS

A door may not close properly because the hinge fixings are loose. You can fix this by drilling out the old holes and plugging them with wooden dowels. New fixing points are then drilled in the surface created by the dowels. Begin by unscrewing the leaves of the hinges attached to the lining.

A Use a large wood drill bit to bore out a hole in the lining at each existing fixing hole.

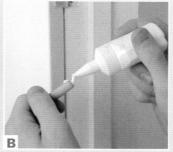

B Apply wood adhesive to the end of a cut section of dowel.

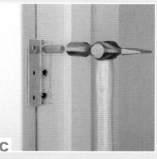

C Tap the dowel into the hole.

D Continue adding dowels into the holes as required. Allow the glue to dry.

E Cut off the exposed dowel ends with a chisel.

F Re-drill pilot holes for fixings into the dowels, and re-hang the door.

TOOLS AND MATERIALS
Drill-driver, dowels, hammer, chisel, wood adhesive

FILLING OLD HINGE POSITIONS

If you are moving the door to the other side of the frame, you will need to fill in the old hinge rebate holes.

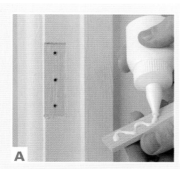

A Cut a piece of wood with the exact dimensions of the former hinge position.

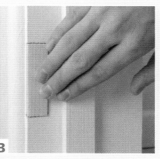

B Glue the wood in position, with the offcut sitting proud of the surrounding surface.

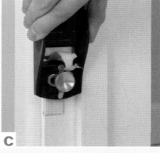

C Once dry, plane the offcut down to the exact level of the surrounding wood, then fill and decorate as required.

TOOLS AND MATERIALS
Wood, adhesive, block plane

PACKING OUT A HINGE

"Packing out" can help a door to open and close if it is binding on its hinges. It is also a good solution if too much wood has been removed from the frame or door to fit a hinge.

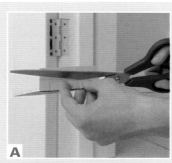

A Remove the door. Cut out pieces of cardboard to the exact shape of the hinge recess.

B Position the cardboard in the hinge recess. Re-hang the door.

C Test the door, adding more pieces of cardboard if required. Repeat for other hinges on the frame.

TOOLS AND MATERIALS
Scissors, cardboard, drill-driver

Floors

IF YOU NEED TO BUILD OR REPLACE A FLOOR, CONCRETE AND WOOD ARE THE MOST WIDELY USED BASES ON WHICH TO LAY DECORATIVE FLOORING. ALTERNATIVELY, YOU MAY LEAVE A STRUCTURAL FLOOR EXPOSED. BARE, WOODEN-PLANKED FLOORS ARE VERY POPULAR. CONCRETE FLOORS, SUCH AS A GARAGE FLOOR, MAY BE PAINTED. FURTHER INFORMATION ON INSULATING FLOORS IS PROVIDED ON P.360 AND P.362.

CONCRETE FLOORS

Ground floors made with concrete have been common for many years, but the use of concrete for upper floor construction has become more popular recently. If you lay a new concrete floor, you may need to add a damp-proof membrane and insulation. Older properties may have a concrete floor laid directly onto a hardcore base on the existing subsoil. Upper floor construction uses the two methods discussed here: beam-and-block or planked concrete. It is also worth bearing in mind that when using concrete as a building material you may need to consider the fact that although it is a strong and long-lasting material, it is environmentally "unfriendly" to produce.

CONSULTING A STRUCTURAL ENGINEER

If you are replacing an old wood floor with new beams, there is no need to consult a structural engineer or a Building Control Officer (BCO). If you plan to replace a wood floor with a concrete floor, or want to lay a new concrete floor, check with your local BCO for local regulations and guidelines. If you are removing a load-bearing wall, when joining two rooms, consider structural implications for the floor.

CONCRETE FLOOR CONSTRUCTION

The construction of concrete floors is divided into two basic methods: the traditional use of poured concrete that sets to form a large slab, and the modern use of pre-cast beams and planks. Both methods have their advantages and disadvantages. The pre-cast system, involves a very quick "dry-build" technique, but may be unsuitable for some renovation projects. The poured concrete method is versatile but requires considerable drying time before floor coverings can be added.

CONCRETE PLANKS METHOD

As their name suggests, concrete planks are plank-shaped sections of concrete that are laid between supporting walls to form a floor's basic structure. A screed is then laid over the top of the planks to provide a surface for floor coverings. There is a large variation in the size of concrete planks, and the size required will depend on a project's design needs. This method is particularly favoured in the construction of modern flats, where huge planks can be craned into position to provide a quickly assembled, yet extremely solid floor structure. As with concrete beams and blocks, concrete planks will need to fit the individual specifications of your home. It is not possible to buy them off the shelf, and they will have to be ordered through manufacturers, who will specify the plank type and size that best suits your needs. This fact alone is important for any renovation project, as there can be a considerable length of time required when ordering a pre-cast floor system.

CONCRETE BEAM   CONCRETE BLOCK

BEAM-AND-BLOCK METHOD

This method uses concrete joists filled in with concrete blocks to form the base structure of the floor. At ground level, beam-and-block is used much like a traditional suspended wooden floor: the beams are supported at each end on the outer wall structure. The strength of the beam-and-block materials allows wide spans of floor to be made without additional support. Depending on the particular manufacturing design, the blocks are laid dry between the beams, the joints are grouted, and then a screed is applied.

First floor
Builders use a similar method to ground-floor construction, except battens are required on the underside to help create the ceiling surface.

Concrete beam

Concrete block

Batten or track

Plasterboard

Ground floor
In its basic construction a concrete beam-and-block ground floor is, in many ways, very similar to a suspended wooden floor (see p.176). You will still need to consider ventilation beneath the floor, and the beams are supported well above ground level.

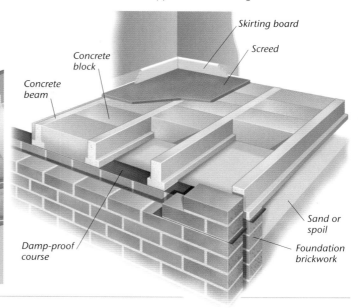

Skirting board

Screed

Concrete block

Concrete beam

Damp-proof course

Sand or spoil

Foundation brickwork

SOLID CONCRETE FLOORS

When building a new property, laying a new concrete floor is relatively straightforward. There is good access around the edges of the floor to float and level the concrete. It is more difficult to replace an existing internal floor because you must work within the confines of the room's walls. Pouring in the concrete and levelling it off by "eye" is possible, but it is far more accurate to create some shuttering within which a level floor can be laid (see p.178). To achieve a smooth subfloor, concrete floors are usually covered with a topcoat of screed. Screed is a 3:1 mix of flooring sand and cement. Ready-mixed screed can be bought, and has the advantage of being quick-drying so that it can be walked on relatively quickly after laying. If an old concrete floor needs smoothing, a self-levelling

product is normally the best option (see p.328). Where a significant level needs to be built up, screed may become the preferred option.

Floor alignment

When altering floors – for example, in a renovation project where two rooms are to be knocked into one – you may need to align the floor level. To level between two concrete floors, adjust the screed using mortar or self-levelling compound, depending on the degree of change. Rather than levelling across a large area, you may need to build a small step. If there is only a small height difference, it may also be possible to simply create a small slope across the floor surface.

Solid concrete floor
The structure shown here is suitable for renovating or replacing an old wooden suspended floor (see p.178). However, this type of structure is also used in new-build properties. In this case the damp-proof membrane would be lapped into the main wall structure.

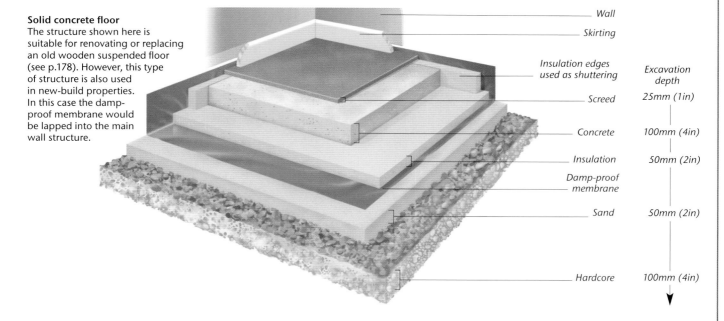

Wall

Skirting

Insulation edges used as shuttering

Screed

Concrete

Insulation

Damp-proof membrane

Sand

Hardcore

Excavation depth

25mm (1in)

100mm (4in)

50mm (2in)

50mm (2in)

100mm (4in)

A suspended wood floor is the most common way of constructing a floor above ground-floor level. The floor is constructed using timber beams called joists. The method of securing these in place is dependent on a floor's age and local building practices.

WOODEN FLOOR CONSTRUCTION

Floor joists are supported by exterior walls (the interior section in cavity walls) as well as internal load-bearing walls. Smaller sleeper walls are often used to add support below suspended timber floors at ground level. The floor surface is constructed by laying wooden boards or chipboard sheets across the joists.

Sawn timber joist
These are made out of treated timber and vary in size. They are typically 225 x 50mm (9 x 3in) in cross-section.

I-beam
Modern versions of sawn timber joists, I-beams are made of laminated layers of wood, and are lighter than timber joists.

Wooden boards
These are the traditional covering for joists and are available with flat edges and with tongue-and-groove edges.

Chipboard floor sheet
This is available with tongue-and-groove edges and in moisture-resistant forms.

Chipboard sheet 18mm (¾in) thick

Face-fixing hanger
Joist hanger that fixes directly to the wall face.

Straight-flange hanger
This hanger's top section is fitted into the mortar.

I-beam hanger
This type of hanger is designed for use with I-beams.

Lateral restraint straps
Used for bracing joists and floor structures.

Timber joist connector
Used to connect two joists together in order to give greater support.

Wooden herringbone strut
Used to brace floor joists by adding diagonal support.

Metal herringbone strut
Modern version of a wood strut. Used to brace floor joists.

SAWN TIMBER JOISTS METHOD

In this traditional floor construction, the ends of joists or beams are built into the walls of a building, and are therefore directly supported by the wall structure. Sometimes joist ends rest on wooden wall plates fixed to the wall surface. Old timber joists secured within a wall may eventually become damp, and might need replacing over time. Joist size can vary according to the floor span, and this is an important consideration when building a new house or creating an extension.

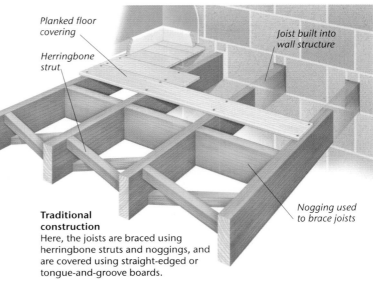

Planked floor covering

Herringbone strut

Joist built into wall structure

Nogging used to brace joists

Traditional construction
Here, the joists are braced using herringbone struts and noggings, and are covered using straight-edged or tongue-and-groove boards.

JOIST HANGING METHOD

In modern buildings, metal joist hangers are often used to support the joists. Joist depths, widths, and designs vary, so there is a wide range of hangers available to match. It is also an option to use joist hangers when renovating an old floor as these do not require you to make large holes in walls, and are straightforward to fix.

Metal lateral joist straps are used to brace joists in position. One end of the strap is fixed to the external wall, and the other end is fixed to joists (either across or in line with them), to secure their position. Lateral joist straps are mainly used in new-build projects.

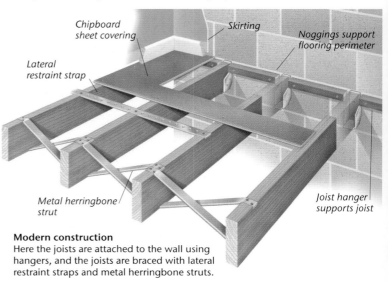

Chipboard sheet covering

Skirting

Noggings support flooring perimeter

Lateral restraint strap

Metal herringbone strut

Joist hanger supports joist

Modern construction
Here the joists are attached to the wall using hangers, and the joists are braced with lateral restraint straps and metal herringbone struts.

I-BEAM METHOD

The modern version of a traditional sawn timber joist, I-beams are made from laminated wood layers. They are strong and lightweight joists, and are less likely to warp or go out of shape compared to traditional timber. The name is derived from the cross-section shape. The upper and lower surfaces of the beam consist of separate laminated sections called flanges.

As well as I-beams there are many other types of wooden joist and beam constructed from what are known as engineered wood products. These types of products are now commonly used in many areas of construction, such as roof structures and other designs that use lintels or structural supports.

SECURING AND STRENGTHENING JOISTS

If you are dividing a room, and a new wall is being built in an area that was not part of original house design, you may need to strengthen the joists. A stud wall built across the joists in a house does not normally require any strengthening. However, if the wall is built parallel to existing joists, you may need to double the width of an existing joist to provide better support for the stud wall.

Timber connectors are used to join the joists, and joist hangers are used at the wall surface. Use a joist of a similar dimension to the original, and sandwich the original in place.

BRIDGING GAPS

Most timber joists that span between supporting walls are called bridging joists. Where an opening is necessary in a floor, for a staircase or loft hatch, for example, the joists need to be cut to accommodate it. Cut joists that run parallel with main bridging joists are called "trimmed joists". The ones that run at right angles to make the opening are "trimmers". The bridging joist that houses the trimmers is a "trimming joist". Joist hangers are commonly used to support openings.

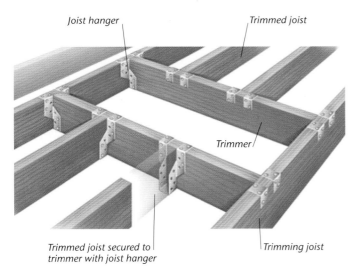

Joist hanger

Trimmed joist

Trimmer

Trimmed joist secured to trimmer with joist hanger

Trimming joist

Openings in floors
The arrangement of joists surrounding floor openings is shown above. Always take professional advice when making these openings in an existing structure. There will certainly be some structural issues that need to be considered. For example, a double width of trimmer is often needed to increase strength.

DETERMINING SPAN AND DIMENSIONS OF A JOIST

A joist's depth and width is determined by its span and the weight it has to support, as well as where it is supported along the span. This is a building regulation specification, requiring professional advice.

Type of floor	Support required
Suspended wooden ground floor	Joists are supported at each end in the wall structure, and sometimes by "sleeper" walls midway along their span.
Between ground and first floor	Joists may be supported by an internal load-bearing wall.
Extension	Joists may span from one external wall to the other. In this case, there will be a crucial length where joist depth and strength will need to be increased depending on the span.
Renovation project	Where a joist needs changing, simply replace with a joist of the same size and length.

VENTILATION AND INSULATION

Suspended ground floors must be ventilated adequately with airbricks positioned in the external walls. Many of the problems associated with damp in old floor joists at ground level are related to the lack of adequate ventilation and the failure or lack of a damp-proof course. Joist ends should sit on the inner leaf of the external cavity wall above the damp-proof course level. Before any replacement or renovation work is carried out on joists, ensure that the ends of the joists are adequately treated, and, in the case of cavity walls, that they do not extend into the cavity.

Airbricks must be kept clear of vegetation, or any other materials or items that will obstruct a free flow of air.

Replacing one floor in a property can impact on the ventilation of a nearby existing floor, so consult a Building Control Officer for advice before commencing work. When replacing or building a new floor, add a layer of insulation to retain heat and reduce draughts (see p.178 and p.360).

TOOLS AND MATERIALS CHECKLIST PP.178–81

Preparing to lay a concrete floor (p.178) Pry bar, chalk, rammer, shovel, hardcore, sand, damp-proof membrane, waterproof tape

Laying insulation board (p.178) Insulation board

Laying concrete (p.178) Concrete, straight-edged plank, float, trowel, battens

Laying a "floating" floor (p.179) Insulation boards, damp-proof membrane, boards, wood glue, cloth, skirting board

Fixing down floor battens (p.180) Damp-proof

membrane, battens, heavy-duty drill, spirit level, wood offcuts

Laying square-edged boards (p.180) Wood boards, offcut wedges or floor clamp, extra hammer, jigsaw*

Laying tongue-and-groove boards (p.181) Wood boards, jigsaw*

Laying tongue-and-groove chipboard (p.181) Chipboard, wood glue, sponge, jigsaw*

* = optional

FOR BASIC TOOLKIT
SEE PP.24–25

LAYING A CONCRETE FLOOR

Laying an internal concrete floor is usually a renovation project that results from the failure of a suspended timber floor. Here an old wood floor is removed and a base is prepared on which concrete can be laid. It is possible to pour the concrete and level it off by eye, but it is far more accurate to use shuttering. Here insulation is used as shuttering and as a levelling guide. However, you could use wood offcuts to make a temporary frame around the floor edge, which you would remove after use.

TOOLS AND MATERIALS SEE BASIC TOOLKIT AND P.177

PREPARING TO LAY THE FLOOR

A Remove the skirting boards by prising them away from the wall using a pry bar.

B Use a pry bar to lever out the floorboards one by one. Once the floor is out, chalk a line to mark the required height of the floor.

C Excavate to the required level (see p.175 for calculating the excavation depth). Draw chalk lines to indicate infill layer levels.

D Infill to the height of the appropriate marked-off level, with hardcore. Compact using a rammer.

E Cover the hardcore with sand, up to the height of the next guide line. Move the back of a shovel in a circular motion, to smooth the sand.

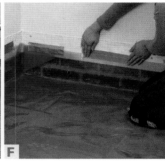

F Lay the damp-proof membrane on the sand. Take it up the wall above the finished floor level. Tape it to the wall to hold it in place.

LAYING INSULATION BOARD

Place the insulation foam board across the sand and membrane, cutting sections to fit as required. Cut 100-mm (4-in) widths of insulation board and lay them around the edges of the room. The insulation provides a guide for the height of the concrete pad, as well as a rest for a levelling plank as you lay the concrete.

A

LAYING CONCRETE

A Shovel the concrete over the floor, starting at the wall farthest from the door. See pp.70–71 for mixing concrete.

B Scrape a straight-edged plank across the concrete to level it, using the top edge of the insulation as a guide.

C Fill in any gaps or indentations using a trowel as you work backwards. You may need to go over the area more than once.

D Use a plastering trowel to smooth any rough areas, right to the edges of the insulation foam. Leave the concrete to dry for two to three days.

E Place battens on the dry concrete. Apply a screed layer, levelling it to the top of the battens. Remove the battens and fill the gaps.

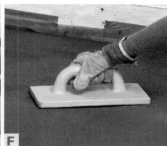

F Level the screed using a float. Work to the edges and back towards the door. Leave for another two to three days to dry completely.

PREPARING TO LAY FLOORING

The decision to lay a boarded floor on a concrete base is often made when a decorative natural wood floor is to be created. Another reason is to create a warmer, insulated floor (see opposite and p.360), on which you can lay various types of flooring. In the first sequence, chipboard panels are laid "floating" on top of insulation board. In the second sequence, battens are secured to the floor, on top of which wooden floorboards may then be fixed. This method is demonstrated on pp.180–81.

TOOLS AND MATERIALS SEE BASIC TOOLKIT AND P.177

LAYING A "FLOATING" FLOOR

Position insulation board directly onto the concrete base, then lay a damp-proof membrane over the insulation board. Cut the corners to allow it to lap up the walls. Make sure it laps up to higher than the depth of the floor. Overlap the joints in the membrane sheets by at least 300mm (1ft), and tape using waterproof tape.

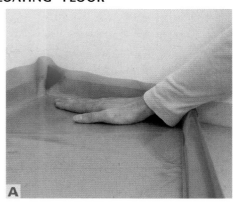
A

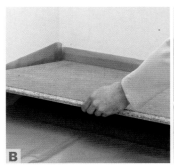
B Lay a chipboard panel directly on top. Making sure you leave an expansion gap of 10mm (⅜in) around the edge of the floor.

C Glue then interlock the tongue-and-groove joints. There will be no need for screws or nails.

D Wipe away any excess glue, then lay the remaining boards using the same method.

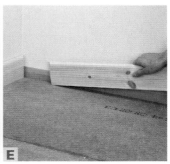
E You can then fit the skirting board. For fitting skirting board, see pp.220–21. It will hold down the board edges, and cover the gap.

FIXING DOWN FLOOR BATTENS

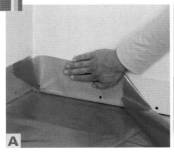
A Lay down the membrane, as shown for a floating floor, cutting the corners to enable it to lap up the wall about 100mm (4in).

B Position the first batten against the wall, and drill pilot holes down through the wood, the membrane, and into the concrete floor.

C Use 100-mm (4-in) frame fixings, including plugs, to secure the battens. Initially, hammer the screw and plug in place.

D Once knocked in, use a cordless drill-driver to tighten the screw. As an alternative, use hammer-in fixings for steps C and D (see p.77).

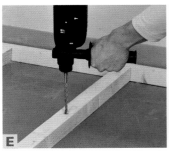
E Fix battens around the edge of the room, then place battens across the floor, at intervals of 500mm (1ft 8in), in parallel lines. Drill pilot holes.

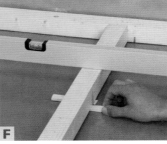
F Where necessary, insert wedges underneath the battens to ensure that they are at the correct floor height. Use a spirit level to check they are level.

G

Once the correct height has been achieved, screw through the batten, down through the wedge, and into the floor. Repeat for all battens, making sure you screw down through all wedges where necessary. Lay insulation boards between the battens. The battens are ready for wooden boards to be laid on top (see pp.180–81).

LAYING SQUARE-EDGED BOARDS

When laying a new boarded floor, there should be no skirting board on any wall surfaces. Therefore, on a floor renovation project, existing skirting needs to be removed at the same time as the old boards. For a new-build, the floor boards are laid first. New floor boards should be left in the room in which they are to be laid for a few days, so that they acclimatize to the room's specific temperature and humidity. When laying the floor, place chipboard across the joists to form a safe working platform.

TOOLS AND MATERIALS SEE BASIC TOOLKIT AND P.177

1 FIXING THE FIRST ROWS

A

Position the first board across the joists, parallel to the wall. Leave a 10-mm (⅜-in) gap, for expansion. Use wedges to maintain the gap.

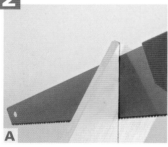

B

Nail the board in place. Use two fixings at each point where the board crosses a joist, 25mm (1in) from each edge of the board.

C

Use a nail punch to ensure that the nail heads are recessed just below floor level. Continue laying boards along the row.

D

When joining boards, cut lengths so that the joins occur midway across a joist. Having fixed the first row, loosely fit the next five rows in place.

E

Leave a gap, then temporarily fix the next board. You should then clamp the first five boards using one of the methods below.

2 CLAMPING USING TRIANGULAR WEDGES

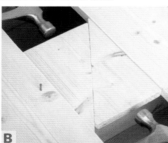

A

Cut through an offcut of board, at a diagonal, to make two wedge-shaped sections.

B

Position the wedge sections in the gap, so that they slot together. Knock the wedges together using hammers to tighten.

C

You may choose to use more than one pair of wedges in the gap, so that you tighten the full lengths of the boards.

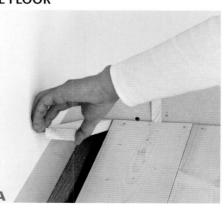

D

Fix the boards in position using nails or screws. Loosely position the next five boards, and repeat the wedging and fixing process.

CLAMPING USING A FLOOR CLAMP

A

Attach the clamp to a joist, and position the grip on the edge of the nearest board.

B

Turn the bar to tighten the grip of the clamp. This will create a tight joint between the boards.

3 FINISHING THE FLOOR

It is likely that the final row of boards will need to be cut down to fit. Measure the desired width, and saw to fit. Since there will be no room for clamping, tap the boards in place with a hammer. A jigsaw is ideal for trimming the back edges of this final row of boards.

A

The technique for laying tongue-and-groove boards is similar to that used for square-edged boards. Boards may be surface-fixed with the same clamping and nailing technique shown opposite, however, secret nailing is mostly used to conceal fixings. For this you may simply use a hammer, nails, and a nail punch, or you may decide to hire a floor nailer. This fires a nail at precisely the correct angle through the tongue of the board and into the joist below, securing it below the floor surface.

TOOLS AND MATERIALS SEE BASIC TOOLKIT AND P.177

▌▌ LAYING TONGUE-AND-GROOVE BOARDS

Position the first board in the way described opposite for laying square-edged boards (step 1A). Check that the board is the right way up. The tongue should be facing you. The following steps show you how to fix tongue-and-groove boards using secret nailing.

A

Position nail at 45-degree angle

B

Place the nail where the board's tongue meets the vertical edge. Using a nail punch, tap it in place, until it sits below the surface.

C

Place the groove of the next board over the nailed tongue, covering the nails. Make sure that you join boards together over a joist.

D

Continue to position rows of boards across the floor. Use secret nailing, in the way shown, as you progress.

E

On reaching the final board, scribe and cut to fit as required. A jigsaw is ideal for this. Surface-fix with lost-head wire nails.

▌▌ LAYING TONGUE-AND-GROOVE CHIPBOARD

Flooring-grade chipboard is usually made with tongue-and-groove edges, including the board's shorter sides. Supporting noggings should be placed around the room's perimeter. Position the first board across the joists. Insert wedges between the board and the wall, to create an expansion gap of 10mm (⅜in).

A

B

Screw the board in place, using chipboard screws. These should be inserted at 150-mm (6-in) intervals, positioned along a joist.

C

Apply wood glue along the tongue of the fixed board. Then slot the next board in place.

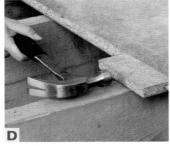

D

To create a tight joint, tap the boards in place, using an offcut of chipboard as a knocking block.

E

As you tighten the boards, you will probably need to wipe away excess glue with a damp sponge.

F

Continue to lay the chipboard. At the edge of the room, mark and cut the boards to fit the remaining space and fix them with screws.

ACCESS PANELS

Gaining access underneath a tongue-and-groove floor is difficult, due to its interlocking structure. Note where access may be required. Remove the tongue from the board, and screw the board down. It can then be unscrewed and lifted easily. Fix extra noggings to support the edges of the access hatch.

REPLACING TONGUE-AND-GROOVE BOARDS

The interlocking design of tongue-and-groove boards means that it is necessary to cut through the board joints to release them from their position. A circular saw is ideal for this purpose. Take care to avoid damaging any supplies below floor level.

TOOLS AND MATERIALS
Metal cutting blade, circular saw, pry bar, chisel, replacement board, lost-head nails, hammer, nail punch

REPLACING CHIPBOARD FLOORBOARDS

Replacing a section of chipboard floor is similar to replacing tongue-and-groove boards. A circular saw is the best tool to use. Any superficial damage caused to other boards is not important, as the floor will be covered.

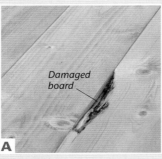

A Use a metal cutting blade to cut through any concealed nails. Set the circular saw to the exact depth of the damaged board.

Damaged board

B Run the saw down the entire length of the board on either side of the damaged area where possible.

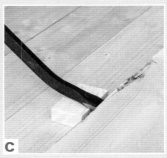

C Pry out the damaged board using a pry bar. Rest the bar on a wood offcut to prevent the bar damaging adjacent boards

D Remove the tongue from the new board, using a sharp chisel. If the boards are very thick, you may need to use a saw.

E Reposition the board and fix it in place. As secret nailing is not possible, use lost-head wire nails and fill the holes.

CUTTING ACROSS THE GRAIN

An alternative way to cut the damaged board is to cut it across the grain, along a joist. In this way a smaller section of board can be removed. However, the adjacent boards would also have small cuts on their edges. For an exposed floor these would have to be disguised with an appropriate filler.

REPLACING SQUARE-EDGED BROKEN BOARDS

It is simpler to replace square-edged boards than tongue-and-groove boards, as they do not have interlocking edges. Take care to avoid damaging cables and pipes below floor level.

TOOLS AND MATERIALS
Pencil, ruler, pry bar, replacement board, nails, hammer, offcuts

MATCHING BOARD DIMENSIONS

It may be difficult to buy replacement boards with matching dimensions.
■ If the new boards are too wide, reduce the width with a power plane.
■ If an exact depth match is not possible, buy boards that are slightly less deep than the desired depth. Position pieces of hardboard on the joists below to level the boards.

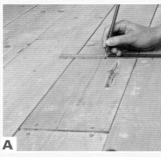

A Mark a pencil line on the damaged board over the nearest joist. If the damage is central, mark lines on joists either side of the damage.

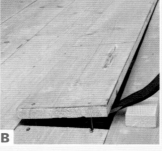

B Lever up the broken board, using a pry bar. Rest the pry bar on a wood offcut to avoid damaging the floor.

C Once the board has been raised high enough, place wood offcuts underneath to hold it in a secure position.

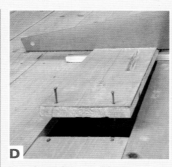

D Saw along the pencil lines to remove the damaged section of board. Protect the floor with a spare piece of board.

E Using the damaged section of board as a template, mark the new board and cut it to size.

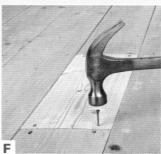

F Position the new section of board in the gap, and nail it in place.

FIXING LOOSE BOARDS

Loose or creaking boards are a common problem, particularly in older buildings, but they are straightforward to fix. Take care to avoid damaging cables and pipes below floor level.

TOOLS AND MATERIALS
Drill, nails, hammer, nail punch

A

On one side of the loose floorboard, drill a pilot hole down through the board and into the joist below.

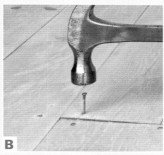

B

If the floor is exposed, hammer a nail into the hole. If appearance is not important, use a screw, which will provide a more secure fixing.

C

Use a nail punch and knock nail heads (if using nails) just below the surface. If required, repeat on the other edge of the board.

FILLING GAPS BETWEEN BOARDS

Gaps between boards look unsightly and can cause draughts. This is not normally a problem with tongue-and-groove boards. For square-edged boards, large gaps should be filled.

TOOLS AND MATERIALS
Sliver of wood, wood glue, hammer, block plane

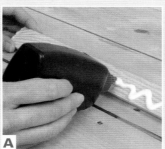

A

Cut a strip of wood to fit in the gap. Apply wood glue to both sides of the strip.

B

Insert the wood strip into the gap, knocking it in with a hammer for a tight fit. Allow it to sit slightly above the floor surface.

C

After the glue has dried, use a block plane to remove the excess wood, and to create a smooth finish flush with the floor.

MENDING HOLES IN CONCRETE FLOORS

If only a small area is damaged, patch the hole only and level it off. For large holes, patch with a strong mortar mix before applying a screed or self-levelling compound.

TOOLS AND MATERIALS
Dusting brush, paintbrush, PVA solution, mortar, gauging trowel

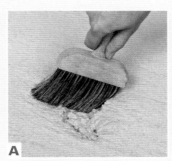

A

Dust out any loose material or debris from the hole using a dusting brush.

B

Dampen the hole with some PVA solution made up of four parts water to one part PVA.

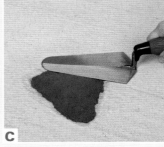

C

Once the PVA is tacky, press some mortar into the hole and use a gauging trowel to smooth it over.

EXPOSED BOARD SOLUTIONS

If floorboards are exposed, finding a replacement board that matches the existing boards is an issue.
■ Use an original board from a less visible area of the room, such as under a sofa. You can then use a new board in the less conspicuous area.
■ If you are replacing more than one or two boards, try reclaimed or seasoned boards.

Often their dimensions are more likely to suit, and a certain degree of wear on replacement boards may better match the existing floor.
■ If you have no alternative but to use a replacement board made of a different type of wood, you may be able to treat the wood with wood dye or stain. There are many different types available.

CONCRETE FLOOR SOLUTIONS

■ It is possible to improve a rough floor surface by adding a self-levelling compound or new screed (see p.178). You can buy screed ready-mixed.
■ After removing an old floor covering, such as cork tiles, use floor scrapers and proprietary solutions to remove adhesive remains and bitumen-based products

before laying a new floor covering. Otherwise, most self-levelling materials laid over a bitumen base will fail to adhere properly and may cause further problems.
■ To protect a new concrete floor, seal it with PVA sealant or a concrete sealer.
■ If you suspect damp in an existing concrete floor, see pp.226–31.

Staircases

THERE ARE THREE MAIN TYPES OF STAIRCASE – STRAIGHT, SPIRAL, AND ALTERNATING TREAD. NEW STAIRCASES ARE AVAILABLE AS KITS, OR ARE MADE TO MEASURE. HOWEVER, AN EXISTING STAIRCASE IS OFTEN INTEGRAL TO THE LAYOUT OF A HOUSE. THIS MEANS THAT IT IS MORE COMMON TO REPAIR THE STAIRS (SEE P.186), AND REPLACE ONLY THE BALUSTRADE IF A CHANGE OF STYLE IS DESIRED (SEE PP.188–89).

TYPES OF STAIRCASE

Staircases are complicated constructions. Traditional straight flights are most common, although in new-builds and refurbishments other designs, such as spiral and alternating tread stairs, are often used. If you want to change the style of your existing staircase then you can get a new one made to measure. However, it is much easier to purchase a kit to renew the balustrade (see opposite).

STAIRCASE CONSTRUCTION

A staircase may be composed of one material or a combination of several – wood, concrete, and metal are most commonly used. Modern boards, such as MDF, are increasingly popular. Methods of construction vary depending on the materials. Standard designs are between 800mm and 900mm (2ft 7½in and 2ft 11½in) wide.

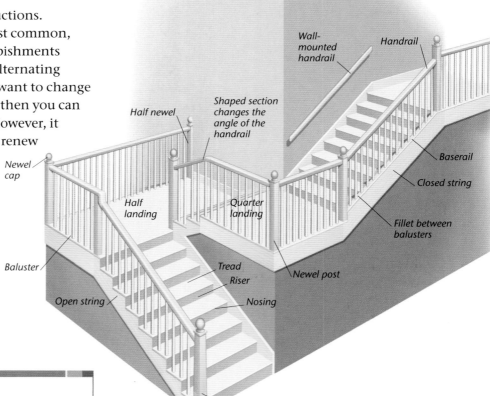

Parts of a staircase
There are many specialist terms associated with a staircase and balustrade and it is important to understand what they describe, and how the parts relate to each other. The staircase shown here has a traditional design with landings, but an alternative is to use winders – kite-shaped treads that turn a corner in a similar way to a section of spiral staircase (see opposite top). Many of the terms used here also apply to other designs of staircase, such as spiral and alternating tread stairs.

CONCRETE STAIRCASES

Most of the terminology used for a wooden staircase is also relevant for a concrete one, the differences being in construction and installation.

A concrete staircase can be built on site to your requirements and is a professional job. A plywood mould is created, steel bars are inserted to strengthen and reinforce the structure, and then concrete is poured in. Once the concrete is dry, the ply mould is removed.

STAIRCASE DESIGNS

Traditional staircases are based around a straight flight or flights of stairs. Spiral stairs have long been used as an alternative, and modern designs are popular in open-plan spaces. "Space-saving" or alternating tread stairs are often used to access loft conversions. The steps are wider at alternate ends so your foot can always rest on a deep tread. Both spiral and alternating tread stairs are available in kit form.

TRADITIONAL STAIRCASE

Components slot together on site

SPIRAL STAIRCASE

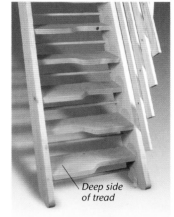

Deep side of tread

ALTERNATING TREAD STAIRCASE

BALUSTRADE MATERIALS

Staircases are not usually replaced, although a balustrade can be updated using a kit (see below and pp.188–89). Several styles are available, modern and traditional, and may have solid wood or metal balusters. Newel posts and handrails are usually made of wood. If you want to replace the whole staircase then you will probably need to get one custom-built, although ready-made straight flights are available in standard sizes, and can be fitted with a balustrade kit.

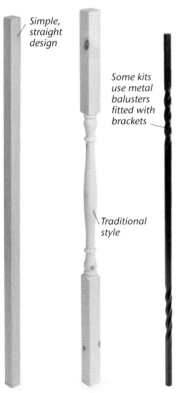

Simple, straight design

Some kits use metal balusters fitted with brackets

Traditional style

STRAIGHT BALUSTER

TURNED BALUSTER

METAL BALUSTER

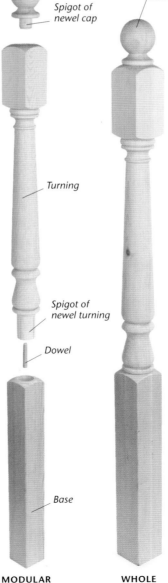

Cap

Spigot of newel cap

Turning

Spigot of newel turning

Dowel

Base

MODULAR NEWEL

Constructed from one section of timber

WHOLE NEWEL

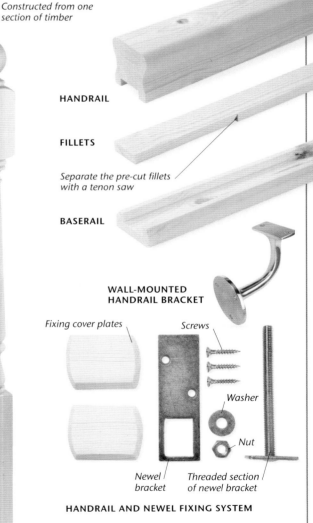

HANDRAIL

FILLETS

Separate the pre-cut fillets with a tenon saw

BASERAIL

WALL-MOUNTED HANDRAIL BRACKET

Fixing cover plates

Screws

Washer

Nut

Newel bracket

Threaded section of newel bracket

HANDRAIL AND NEWEL FIXING SYSTEM

Balustrade kit
All of the components needed for the new balustrade should be supplied – handrail, baserail, newel posts, balusters, and specialist brackets and fixings. Newel posts may come whole, or be made up of several pieces (modular). Modular newels are better for fitting to an existing staircase.

STAIRCASE PREPARATION

The layout of your home is generally designed around the staircase so it is unusual to replace it unless it is unsafe. Staircases are bought in standard sizes or more often custom-built. Fitting a staircase is a complex job and may be best left to a professional who will measure for, order, and fit the stairs. Renewing the balustrade can update a staircase, and with a kit it is quite a straightforward task (see pp.188–89). Staircases are the subject of several building regulations (see box, right).

REPLACING A STAIRCASE

Most specialist manufacturers will measure and fit a new staircase for you, and ensure it complies with building regulations (see box, above right). If you are measuring up yourself, always read your chosen manufacturer's instructions – they will explain where and how to take the crucial measurements. Generally you will need to measure from floor to ceiling to get the "rise" – the height of the staircase. Remember to take the finished floor level into account. The advance of the staircase across the floor is known as the "going". It is measured as the distance between the face of the first riser and the face of the last riser. If you are fitting a staircase between two walls, measure the width of the gap in several places and work with the smallest figure.

REPLACING A BALUSTRADE

You may wish to replace a balustrade if it is broken, or purely for cosmetic reasons. Traditionally, balustrades are jointed into the staircase, and require considerable expertise to replace (see pp.392–93 for woodworking joints). An alternative is to purchase a kit that includes newels, balusters, rails, and fixings (see p.185). These are easy to use and can be adapted to fit around most stairs and landings. Make sure you buy the right kind of kit for your stairs – the fixing system will vary depending on whether the staircase is closed- or open-string (see parts of a staircase p.184). Fitting a kit for a closed-string staircase is shown on pp.188–89. If your stairs have an open string, then metal balusters are ideal because they can be fixed directly to the treads with brackets.

STAIRCASE REGULATIONS

The staircase should comply with these rules:
■ The handrail must be at least 900mm (2ft 11½in) above the pitch line and landings.
■ It must not be possible to pass a 100-mm (4-in) sphere through any gap.
■ Staircases wider than 1m (3ft 3in) must have a handrail on both sides.

■ If a staircase has tapered treads then there must be a handrail on their widest side.
■ The maximum tread height and width is 220mm (8½in) to give a pitch of 42 degrees.
■ Ceilings should be at least 2m (6ft 6in) above the pitch line of the staircase.
■ Newel posts should be fitted every 2.4m (7ft 10in).

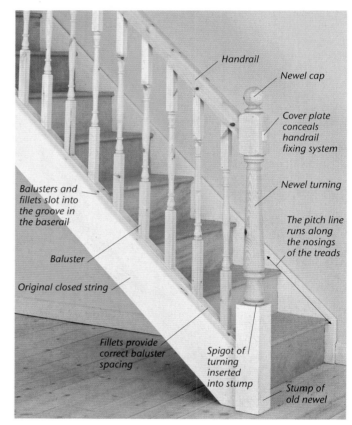

Handrail

Newel cap

Cover plate conceals handrail fixing system

Newel turning

The pitch line runs along the nosings of the treads

Balusters and fillets slot into the groove in the baserail

Baluster

Original closed string

Fillets provide correct baluster spacing

Spigot of turning inserted into stump

Stump of old newel

Fitting a replacement balustrade
Your kit should comply with building regulations (see above) and you should fit it using the instructions supplied. It is particularly important to cut the old newel at the right point to avoid weakening the structure.

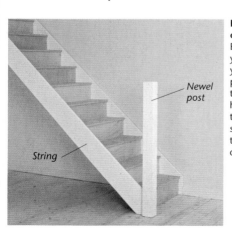

Removing the old balustrade
Before you can fit your balustrade kit you need to use a pry bar to remove the old balusters and handrail. Strip back the baserail. You should be left with the bare string and old newel post.

Newel post

String

TOOLS AND MATERIALS CHECKLIST PP.187–89

Repairing creaking stairs from below (p.187) Wood glue, new wedge, block of wood

Repairing creaking stairs from above (p.187) Basic toolkit only

Replacing a broken baluster (p.187) Replacement baluster, pin hammer, panel pins

Replacing a balustrade (pp.188–89) Balustrade kit,

spirit level, pry bar, hole saw bit, straight edge, try square, wooden mallet, adjustable bevel, tenon saw, wood glue, pin hammer, panel pins

Fitting a wall-mounted handrail (p.189)
Handrail, brackets, chalk line, spirit level

FOR BASIC TOOLKIT SEE PP.24–25

Staircases are exposed to a lot of wear and tear. Small amounts of damage are not uncommon, but can be dangerous so you shouldn't put off fixing them. Check your staircase regularly for any minor problems. Joints can loosen over time, or wood may crack, but the affected parts can almost always be easily fixed or replaced.

TOOLS AND MATERIALS SEE BASIC TOOLKIT AND P.186

CREAKING OR DAMAGED TREADS OR RISERS

Treads and risers are usually wedged tightly in position. The wedges can loosen so the stair moves and creaks. If this happens then you should carefully check all the stairs (see box, below right), and carry out any repairs necessary, from below the stairs if possible, or from above if not.

If the treads or risers split they can be easily replaced in an open-string staircase (see p.184). Remove the balusters and the fixings from the damaged tread or riser (fixings are under the stairs). Slide out the broken part and use it as a template to cut a new one. Slip the new part into place and replace the fixings and balusters. You will need professional help to replace treads or risers into a closed-string staircase.

If the nosing of a tread is damaged, it can often be fixed without removing the whole tread. Cut away the damaged area and use it as a template to cut a new section. Then glue and screw the patch in place. This is a similar method to that used for window sills (see p.154).

LOOSE-FITTING NEWEL POST

Take the loose joint apart, clean it, then refix it with glue and screw fixings. Adjust the fit of a modular newel turning into the newel base by using wedges and dowels (see p.188) if required. Resin can also be used to form a strong joint.

REPAIRING CREAKING STAIRS FROM BELOW

   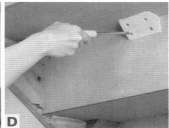

A **If a wedge is loose** under the squeaking stair, remove it. Use it as a template to cut a new wedge, and apply wood glue to its sides.

B **Knock the new,** glued wedge back into place firmly. The wedge needs to fit tightly to prevent any movement in the joint.

C **Once the wedges are tight,** glue a reinforcing block across the join between the tread and riser.

D **Drill pilot holes** through the block and into the stair, taking care not to penetrate the outer surface. Screw the block tightly into place.

REPAIRING CREAKING STAIRS FROM ABOVE

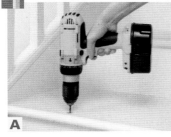 

A **Drill pilot holes** through the squeaking or moving tread and into the edge of the riser below.

B **Screw tightly into the riser.** The screw head should recess into the tread. Fill the hole when you have finished. Repeat along the riser edge.

CHECKING THE STAIRS

The treads and risers of the staircase are exposed to the most damage. Many problems aren't obvious so it may be worth checking the condition of old stairs occasionally, and certainly if you detect any movement when using the stairs. If you can get under the stairs then this is the easiest way both to inspect for damage and fix it – especially if the stairs are carpeted. Ask someone to walk up and down the stairs while you check for any movement in the joints underneath. Mark any that need attention then strengthen them using the technique above. If you have no access underneath the stairs, you will have to fix them from above (see left).

REPAIRING A BROKEN BALUSTER

If you have a closed string staircase (see p.184), simply replace the broken baluster as shown here. If the baluster is jointed into the tread of a step it may be necessary to remove beading around the step in order to replace the spindle. If lots of spindles are damaged, you can replace the whole balustrade (see pp.188–89).

 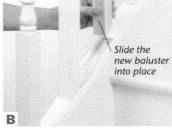 

A **Lever up the fillet** below the broken baluster using a chisel.

B **Take the damaged** baluster out and use it as a template to trim a replacement.

Slide the new baluster into place

C **Replace the fillet** and pin it into place using a panel pin. You can then decorate to hide the repair.

REPLACING A BALUSTRADE

These sequences show you how to replace a balustrade using a kit. Remove the old handrail and balusters before you start, using a pry bar where necessary (see p.186). In most cases the newel post is jointed into the string to provide structural strength (see p.184 for anatomy). This means it is better to cut the old post off above the string and fit only the top sections of a new newel, as shown here. Get professional help to replace the whole post unless a fixing specified for the job is provided in your kit.

TOOLS AND MATERIALS SEE BASIC TOOLKIT AND P.186

1 PREPARING TO TRIM THE OLD NEWEL BASE

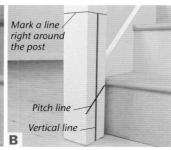

Hold level against nosings

Newel post base

Mark a line right around the post

Pitch line

Vertical line

A Use a level to draw a vertical pencil line up the centre of the newel post. Mark the pitch line by holding the level against the steps.

B Measure the distance specified up from where the two lines cross. Use a try square and pencil to mark a line around the post at this level.

2 FITTING THE NEW NEWEL POST

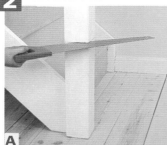

Keep the drill precisely vertical

Knock dowel into this hole

A Use the guide line you have marked around the post to make an accurate cut through the old newel post with a panel saw.

B Make a hole in the top of the stump to house the spigot of the new newel turning. A hole saw bit for a drill-driver is the ideal tool.

C Measure the length of the new newel-turning spigot. Then use a chisel to remove waste wood to this depth in the stump.

D Keep checking the depth of the hole. If the spigot seems to be loose you can knock dowel into the hole in the base to expand it slightly.

Tap the new newel turning into position using a wooden mallet. You will need to remove it again later so do not use any glue at this stage.

3 CUTTING THE BASERAIL AND HANDRAIL TO FIT

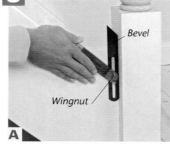

Bevel

Wingnut

Guide line for cutting

A Hold an adjustable bevel against the string and the newel base. Tighten the wingnut to set the angle (see also p.45).

B Measure the length of baserail needed. Mark each end, using the bevel so that the rail will fit neatly. Trim it with a tenon saw.

C Drill pilot holes through the baserail into the top of the string at intervals of 300mm (1ft). Then glue and screw it into position.

Remove baserail to apply wood glue to the top of the string

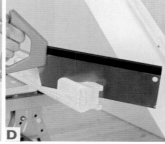

D Measure the length of handrail needed. Mark guides at each end, using the bevel as for the baserail. Trim the handrail with a tenon saw.

4 FIXING THE HANDRAIL IN POSITION

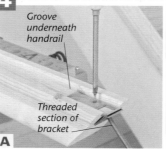

Groove underneath handrail

Threaded section of bracket

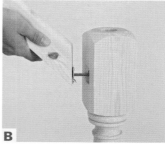

A Screw the handrail fixing bracket supplied with the kit into place.

B Feed the threaded section through the hole in the top of the newel turning.

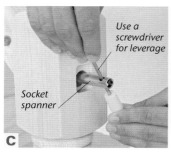

C On the other side of the newel turning, tighten the nut onto the threaded section of the bracket, using the socket spanner provided.

Socket spanner

Use a screwdriver for leverage

D Check the newel is held vertically by the handrail. Remove the newel, apply wood glue to the spigot, then replace it. Recheck the level.

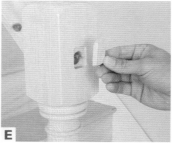

E Glue the cover plate in place to hide the fixing system.

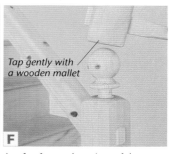

Tap gently with a wooden mallet

F Apply glue to the spigot of the newel cap then tap it into position. Leave the newel and handrail to dry for 24 hours before continuing.

5 FITTING THE BALUSTERS

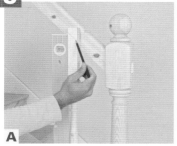

A Hold a baluster against the handrail and baserail. Mark cutting guides, allowing for the groove depth in the baserail and handrail.

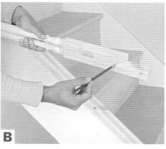

B Check the fit of the cut baluster. Make any adjustments necessary, then use it as a template for cutting the rest of the balusters.

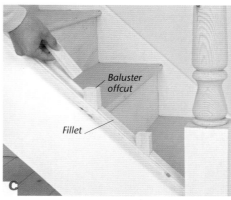

Baluster offcut

Fillet

C Lay baluster offcuts and fillets alternately on the baserail. The fillets are pre-cut to ensure the balustrade will comply with building regulations (see p.186). The last fillet will be too long for the remaining gap. Measure the length of the gap and divide it by two to give you the required lengths of the first and last fillets. Then remove all the offcuts and fillets.

Use the bevel you set to cut the baserail and handrail to mark angled cutting lines on four fillets to trim them to the length you have just calculated. Take two of these measured fillets and pin one into the baserail and one into the handrail. They should be positioned in the grooves, hard against the newel post.

D

Apply wood glue to each end of the baluster

Fillet

E Slide the first spindle into place against the fillets. Pin diagonally through each end into the baserail and handrail.

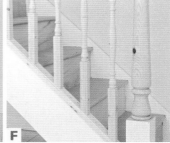

F Carry on fitting full-size fillets and spindles until you reach the top. Complete the balustrade with the two fillets you have cut to size.

FITTING A WALL-MOUNTED HANDRAIL

A Measure up from the pitch line at the top and bottom of the flight to 900mm (2ft 11½in) to comply with regulations (see p.186).

B Position a nail at each point and use a chalk line to snap a straight guide line between them (see p.44).

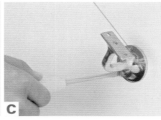

C Fix brackets in place along this guide line - one at the top, one at the bottom, and at equal intervals at least every 1m (3ft 3in) between.

D Cut the handrail to length, then fix it to the brackets, screwing up into the underside of the rail.

Fireplaces

FIREPLACES CAN BE DECORATIVE, HOUSE A HEAT SOURCE, OR MAY BE DISUSED. FIRES BURN SOLID FUEL OR GAS. ELECTRIC FIRES ARE ALSO AVAILABLE. WHAT KIND OF FIRE YOU CAN HAVE DEPENDS ON YOUR FLUE TYPE (SEE P.192). INSTALLING A FIRE IS A JOB FOR A PROFESSIONAL, BUT YOU CAN FIT A FIRE SURROUND (SEE PP.194–95) OR BLOCK UP A FIREPLACE (SEE P.193) YOURSELF.

TYPES OF FIREPLACE AND FIRE

Several types and styles of decorative fireplace are available. A fireplace can simply be a display area or it may contain a "real" (solid fuel), electric, or gas fire. Each fuel has advantages and disadvantages, and some areas have restrictions on burning particular fuel types (see opposite). What kind of fire you choose will be influenced by hearth size, and flue size and type (see p.192).

TYPES OF FIREPLACE

If you have an original fireplace designed to burn solid fuel then it will be one of two types. The most simple is little more than an opening at the bottom of the chimney. Alternatively, the opening may have a fireback, which can be decorative and will often improve how the fire burns because the smaller opening (throat) creates a stronger draw of air up the chimney (see p.192).

FIRES AND FIREPLACES
Your options when changing to a different fuel type, or installing or renovating a fire depend on your starting point. If you already have a chimney and fireplace then you can put any sort of fire in the opening as long as the flue conforms to regulations, or you may prefer to close it up and decide on a wall-mounted design. If you don't already have a fireplace then you can still construct a false opening and install a "real-effect" fire, or choose a contemporary style.

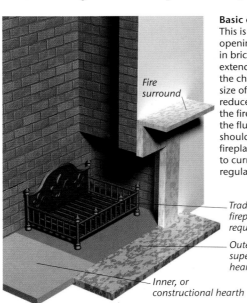

Basic open fireplace
This is simply an opening, often formed in brick or stone, that extends upwards from the chimney or flue. The size of the opening may reduce at the throat of the fireplace as it enters the flue section. You should check that old fireplaces conform to current building regulations (see p.193).

Fire surround

Traditional fireplaces normally require a grate

Outer, or superimposed hearth

Inner, or constructional hearth

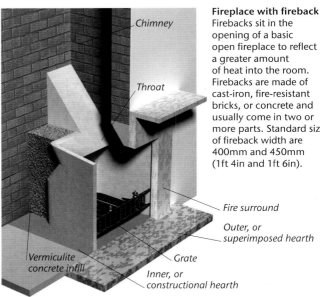

Fireplace with fireback
Firebacks sit in the opening of a basic open fireplace to reflect a greater amount of heat into the room. Firebacks are made of cast-iron, fire-resistant bricks, or concrete and usually come in two or more parts. Standard sizes of fireback width are 400mm and 450mm (1ft 4in and 1ft 6in).

Chimney

Throat

Fire surround

Outer, or superimposed hearth

Vermiculite concrete infill

Grate

Inner, or constructional hearth

TYPES OF FIRE

Your choice of fire types will be narrowed down by what fuels are available to you (see also pp.498–99), the construction of your chimney, and whether it has a flue liner. If you have no chimney, you can install an electric fire, a flueless gas fire, or a gas fire designed for use with a balanced or power flue (see p.192).

Solid-fuel open fires

A real fire burns wood or coal, or some can burn a range of solid fuels. The most efficient fires have a grate so that a good flow of air can get to the fire. Real fires may be in an open fireplace or one with a fireback. Canopies can be used over large fires that do not draw well. The canopy helps to direct combustion gases up into the flue.

Solid-fuel stoves

A woodburner or stove burns solid fuels. They are installed on the inner hearth of an open fireplace, or project onto the outer hearth. The flue may connect directly to a flue liner that either continues all the way up the inside of the chimney, or finishes on the other side of a so-called register plate fitted across the bottom of an unlined flue.

Gas fires

These are fuelled by mains natural gas or bottled gas. Running off the mains gas supply, they are very clean and convenient. Manufacturers will specify flue requirements – they commonly use balanced or power flues (see pp.192–93), so a chimney is unnecessary.

Traditional and modern designs are available, including stove and open-fire styles. Contemporary designs that don't mimic real fires, such as fires containing pebbles are also available. Wall-mounted types are also popular.

Electric fires

Real-effect electric fires can mimic traditional fires with a fireback, woodburner styles, and contemporary and wall-mounted designs. No flue is necessary.

FIRE SURROUNDS

Traditionally, a fire surround is made up of a mantel, a back panel, and an outer hearth. These items are sold separately or as part of a kit. Reclaimed period and reproduction fire surrounds are popular, especially for older properties (see pp.86–87). Modern styles are also available. Existing surrounds may require refurbishing. For example, a period cast-iron surround may need to be stripped of old paint layers, and its tiles, or the whole surround may need replacing. Although installing a new fire is a job for a professional, you can change a fire surround yourself. See pp.194–95 for more information.

Traditional fireplace
Stone, cast-iron, and wood are popular materials for traditional fire surrounds. Traditional styles are available for all fuel (see above) and flue types (see p.192). For use with "real" fires, reproductions of antique designs, as well as old reclaimed fire surrounds, are available.

Stoves in fireplaces
A stove or woodburner positioned in a basic open fireplace (see opposite) provides a traditional look. Doors can be opened on most fires, except for those with a balanced flue (see p.192). With a real, solid-fuel burning fire, remember the flue will require periodic sweeping.

Contemporary fireplace
This type of surround is popular in modern homes, and used to update period properties. They are available for all fuel (see above) and flue types (see p.192)

Freestanding stoves
These often have a contemporary design. They are usually electric, flueless, or use balanced or power flues (see p.192). Those that are electric or flueless need not be positioned anywhere near a wall.

Wall-mounted fireplace
This is a modern, space-saving option. Electric and flueless types can be extremely thin and need no flue – they can be fitted almost anywhere in the home. Other types need a flue and so are more disruptive to fit. See p.192 for more information on flue types, and see above for more on fuels.

There are several things you need to consider when choosing a new fire or reinstating an old one. You may need to fit a new flue, or have an existing chimney lined or re-lined – the main types of flue are shown here. If your current flue does not need renovating or replacing, it will be easier to choose a fire that is suitable for it. Unless you have a balanced flue, you need to consider ventilation because fires require a good supply of air to burn well. A lack of wall space can make it desirable to block up a fireplace, either leaving the recess or blocking it flush with the wall.

GAS SAFETY

Gas-fired appliances must be installed, then serviced according to manufacturer's specifications at least once a year, by a CORGI-registered engineer. It is illegal to undertake work yourself. All gas fires, apart from those with a balanced flue, must be fitted with an oxygen depletion system (ODS). This is a safety device that cuts off the gas supply if high levels of the deadly gas carbon monoxide build up in the fire. Gas fires may also have a flame supervision device (FSD) that turns off the gas supply if the pilot light fails.

FLUES

As fires burn they give out combustion gases, which are carried out of the home by a flue. The main types of flue are discussed below. As the gases are carried out of the house, they must be replaced by fresh air. In older houses, natural draughts were relied upon to provide this constant airflow. In modern, well-insulated homes it is unlikely that a natural airflow exists, so ventilation must be provided. Some flues (balanced flues) have a built-in air intake, otherwise airbricks can help to provide a good air supply or vents can be built into suspended floors. Ventilation requirements should be specified for particular fires. See pp.364–65 for more on providing ventilation. Fires and flues need to be checked occasionally by a professional to ensure that they are working safely and efficiently.

Flues without chimneys

There are several types of flue that do not need a chimney. Two common designs are shown below and flueless fires (right) are also available. The type of flue you need will normally be specified by the fire manufacturer. Some fires only radiate heat, but the fires shown here also warm air from the room by circulating it inside of the body of the fire, separately from the combustion process.

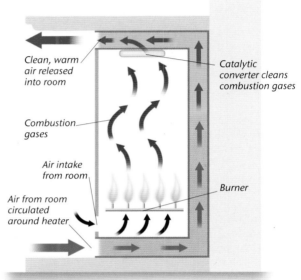

Flueless
The combustion gases are cleaned by a catalytic converter and released into the room, making flueless fires efficient because no heat is lost via the flue. Flueless fires can only be installed in larger rooms. The minimum room size varies, so carefully check the manufacturer's specifications.

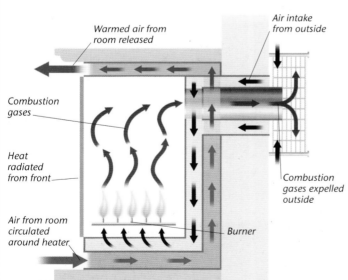

Balanced flue
This kind of flue is built into the fire and runs straight through the wall behind. It takes fresh air in and lets combustion gases out. A balanced flue is used with glass-fronted fires so there is no contact between the fire and the air in the room.

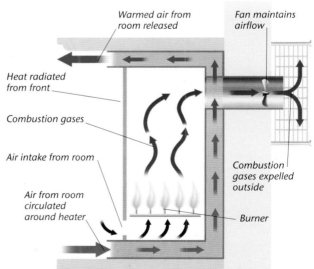

Power flue
This type of flue has a fan to suck combustion gases through the flue and expel them outside. Power flues can be extended so it may be possible to fit a fire away from an external wall. An electric supply is required for the fan.

FIREPLACES

Flues in chimneys

Modern chimneys are built fully lined with a corrosion-resistant, rectangular, pre-cast concrete flue suitable for any fire. If you have an older chimney it will be a class one unlined flue, or a class two lined flue. If a class one flue has smoke or condensation problems, seek advice from a professional – they may recommend fitting a concrete or metal flue liner compatible with your fuel type.

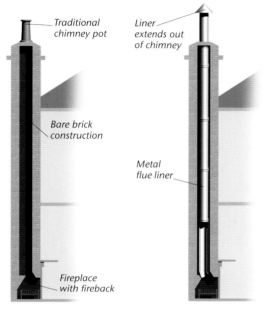

Traditional chimney pot

Liner extends out of chimney

Bare brick construction

Metal flue liner

Fireplace with fireback

Class one flue
Basic chimney constructed of brick or stone. If it is in good condition, it is suitable for any type of fire.

Class two flue
A class two flue is a chimney with a concrete or metal liner in it.

CHIMNEY COWLS

Chimney pots provide a decorative finish and raise the top of the chimney above the roof line, where the airflow draws combustion gases out. A cowl is often attached to the top to improve ventilation and keep out rain and animals. If any damp problems are associated with a chimney, check that the flashing and pointing are intact, and that a cowl has been fitted. Different cowl designs are used with different fire types so make sure you have the right cowl. If you are opening up an old fireplace you should enlist professional help to check that the top of the chimney has not been blocked, and is fitted with the right type of cowl. They will also check the chimney is in good repair, and possibly fit or replace a flue liner (see above).

Coating resists corrosion

Cowl is tied to the chimney pot

Basic cowl
If your chimney is well-situated and has no significant downdraught problems, a basic cowl will prevent entry of rain, hail, animals, and birds.

OLD FIREPLACES

Closing up a fireplace

If you are blocking up a fireplace it is important to ensure that the chimney is capped at the top to stop rainwater and birds entering, but you need some ventilation to prevent damp. Cowls are available that are specially designed for this purpose. Inside the house, the fire surround can normally be unscrewed or prised away from the wall surface, and any hearth area that sits above floor level can be levered up. The opening can then be boarded or bricked up. Be certain to place an airbrick or static vent in the centre of the blocked-up area that will still allow airflow into the chimney flue, otherwise there may be damp problems. It is then simply a question of repairing and decorating the walls and floor to match the surrounding surfaces.

Opening up an old fireplace

Exposing an old fireplace is a journey into the unknown – there is no way of knowing what you will discover behind the boarding or blockwork. There might be an intact period fireplace, or little more than debris. If the latter is the case, you will need to get a new or reclaimed surround, and a grate and a fireback installed.

If you plan to use the fireplace, then notify your local building control office. A previously blocked-off chimney must be tested before reuse to ensure that it is sound, gas-tight, and free from blockages. An old hearth must also be checked to ensure that it complies with current building regulations.

If the fireplace looks like it was blocked off recently there may be little to do once it is uncovered, other than getting the fire and chimney structure checked and swept. Get professional advice on how to proceed when unblocking very old hearths because you may need to get the integrity of the structure checked before removing any rubble or brickwork. You will then probably need to get some work done on the chimney and fireplace before you can safely use it.

Uncoated cowls are only suitable for some types of fire

Pins secure the cowl to the chimney pot

Multi-purpose cowl
This type of cowl can be adjusted to fit most terracotta chimney pots. It is designed to prevent downdraughts blowing smoke and fumes back into the house, and to prevent entry of rain, hail, animals, and birds.

Fins catch the breeze

Hinged versions are available to make chimney cleaning easier

Revolving cowl
Cowls that revolve are designed to encourage airflow in chimneys that don't draw well and are prone to downdraughts.

The technique for installing a fireplace surround is straightforward. As long as it is for a false or blocked up fireplace you will not require any professional checks. If you are replacing a surround for a working fire then you need to make sure that it is compatible with your fire type – check the manufacturer's instructions. If you are reinstating an old fireplace, you need to follow all the guidelines and make sure that Building Control have been informed (see p.193).

INSTALLING A FIRE SURROUND

If you are replacing an existing surround for a working fire, check that the new fire surround is compatible with the fire type. Some surrounds are designed for ornamental use and may not be heat-resistant. Building regulations state that fire surrounds for working fires need a superimposed, or outer hearth (see right), which is at least 48mm (2in) thick, and extends at least 300mm (1ft) from the front of the fire. Before purchasing a new fire surround, check the dimensions of your opening and make sure new items will fit. Depending on the fireplace type you have, the inner hearth may also need to be built up to bring it to the same level as the outer hearth that you have installed.

If you want a purely ornamental fireplace, you can fit a surround around a blocked opening, or even on a flat wall. A kit designed for a decorative purpose will usually be cheaper than a fireproof surround.

Fitting a wooden surround

This is normally a very straightforward task that simply requires bracket fixings. The order of work for installing the mantel, back panel, and hearth may vary, but a typical procedure is shown here. Wooden surrounds often incorporate a stone (marble, for example) back panel. Or, the back panel area can be tiled.

Fitting a stone surround

Because of the weight of a stone surround, it needs to be broken down into more sections than a wooden surround, which in turn means that assembly involves joining these sections together. Hearths are likely to come in a number of pieces, as are the mantel and back panel. In this example, a typical stone fireplace surround is shown but the order of work may well need modifying according to the particular design you have chosen. Some manufacturers will recommend using a stone sealer on the surround to prevent staining when using the fire.

FIREPLACE REGULATIONS

Regulations govern the structure of fireplaces (see pp.190–93) so seek professional advice if you are unsure of any installation. New installations and previously disused fireplaces that you have worked on yourself will need inspecting by your local Building Control Officer who will issue a certificate of approval. Without certification some insurance companies may invalidate your policy, and it can cause problems if you wish to sell your home. It is illegal to work on any gas-fuelled appliance unless you are GAS SAFE registered. An authorized installer will certify a new fireplace and there is no need to contact Building Control.

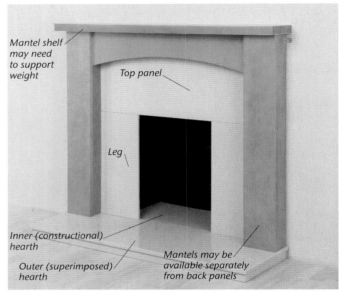

Surround kits
This type of surround is normally sold in kit form. Manufacturers generally offer a range of mantel shelves, back panels, and hearths, so you can choose which combination you prefer.

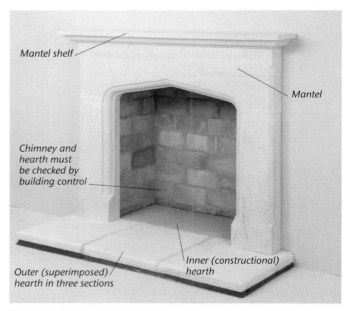

Stone fireplaces
Some manufacturers sell standard sizes and styles of stone surround, but more often they are custom-built. The components are very heavy so you will need help with installation.

TOOLS AND MATERIALS CHECKLIST P.195

Fitting a marble hearth and wooden fire surround Spirit level, dustsheet, adhesive spreader, white mortar*, fire cement*

Fitting a stone hearth and fire surround Spirit level, slab mortar* trowel, corner braces,

white mortar*, threaded bolts, resin

* See pp.70–71 for cement and mortar mixes

FOR BASIC TOOLKIT SEE PP.24–25

FITTING A MARBLE HEARTH AND WOODEN FIRE SURROUND

A Apply a thin bed of white mortar to the constructional hearth. Position the marble hearth and check it is central and level.

Dustsheet protects hearth

B Apply white mortar to the legs. An adhesive spreader is the ideal tool to texture the surface of the mortar to increase grip.

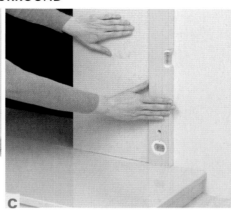

C

Position the upright, using a spirit level to get it vertical. Don't worry about getting mortar on the wall because it will be covered by the surround, but make sure you keep the marble clean. Check the two legs are level, then allow the mortar to dry.

D Spread white mortar across the top panel and place it by resting it on the legs to get the bottom edge level before pressing it into the wall.

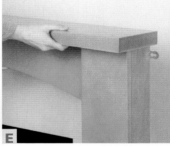

E Position the mantlepiece and mark the fixing points. An option is to draw round the brackets, then cut rebates in the wall surface for them.

F Remove the surround. Drill pilot holes in the wall at the marked off points. Reposition the mantlepiece and screw it in place.

G Carefully fill any gaps between the surround and the fireplace using fire cement.

FITTING A STONE HEARTH AND FIRE SURROUND

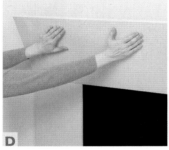

A Mark out the exact position of the hearth and lay a 20-mm (¾-in) bed of slab mortar (see p.71). Roughen the surface with the trowel.

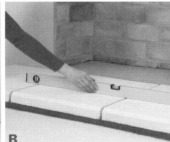

B Position the slabs that make up the hearth. Adjust the mortar until the slabs are precisely level. Point them with white mortar (see pp.70–71).

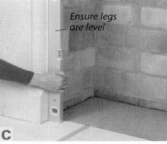

Ensure legs are level

C Position the legs. Mark the fixing points of the corner braces on the wall and upright. Remove the legs and drill pilot holes.

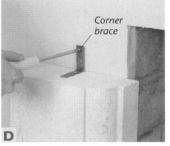

Corner brace

D Spread a thin bed of white mortar underneath the legs. Re-position them and screw them into place.

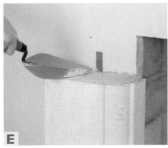

E Apply a thin layer of white mortar to the tops of the legs.

F Place the mantle and check it is level. You will need help to lift it. Screw the corner braces into the wall.

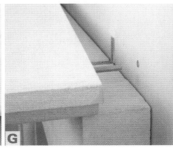

G Place the mantel shelf and mark the position of the bolts. Drill holes at the marked points. Fill them with resin, then re-position the shelf.

H Tidy up all the joints in the hearth and surround with a pointing trowel, then clean any excess mortar from the stone faces.

Roofs

ROOFS MAY BE PITCHED (ANGLED), OR "FLAT" (WHICH IS ACTUALLY VERY SLIGHTLY ANGLED). A NEW ROOF IS ALMOST CERTAINLY A JOB FOR A PROFESSIONAL. BUT YOU CAN TACKLE MINOR REPAIRS YOURSELF, SO LONG AS YOU ARE CONFIDENT WORKING HIGH UP. THE NEXT FEW PAGES DETAIL TYPICAL REPAIR JOBS – INCLUDING REPAIRING OR REPLACING GUTTERING – AS WELL AS A STRAIGHTFORWARD WAY OF COVERING A FLAT ROOF.

PITCHED ROOFS

Most house roofs are pitched. This kind of roof has evolved to suit different situations. As a result, there are many variations on the basic design and numerous combinations of design elements with construction methods. Flat roofs are shown and discussed on pp.204–05.

TYPES OF PITCHED ROOF

Three main designs of pitched roof are shown here. There are many variations on these themes, one common example of which is also shown. Roofs are usually defined according to their shape. Each type can be built in different ways, and from different materials.

Gabled
The roof slopes around a triangular extension of the end wall. This piece of wall is the gable.

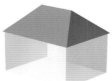

Hipped
A hip is the joint between two adjacent slopes of a roof. Some complex roofs have several hips.

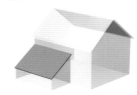

Mono-pitched
This simple roof has only one slope. It is commonly used on lean-to structures, such as extensions.

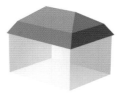

Mansard
A modified version of the pitched roof that creates a spacious living area in the roof space.

PITCHED ROOF FRAMES

A pitched roof has a network of timbers to support the structure and its covering. There are two main types of wooden frame – a cut roof and a trussed roof – which are sometimes combined to achieve more complex roofs. Both types of construction will support any coverings (see pp.200–01).

Cut roof frame

Traditionally, all roofs were "cut"– carpenters would cut rafters on site during construction. To cover greater spans, some of the roof's weight may be transferred onto internal loadbearing walls using purlins (beams that brace the rafters; shown right). This forms a "double" roof. Although they are labour-intensive, single- and double-cut roofs are still constructed.

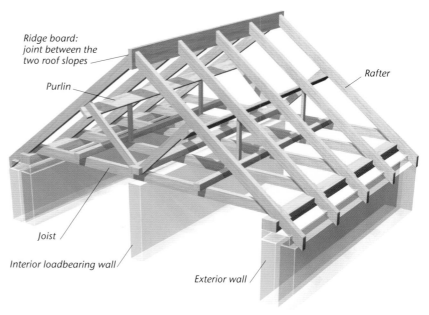

Ridge board: joint between the two roof slopes

Purlin

Rafter

Joist

Interior loadbearing wall

Exterior wall

Trussed roof frame

Commonly referred to as A-frames because of their shape, modern trusses (timber frames) are manufactured off site by specialist companies. The A-frame combines rafters, joists, and struts. A roof is made up of several A-frames. Because of technological advances in calculating the stresses and loading requirements of roof timbers, trusses can be made slimmer than the timbers in a cut roof. Trusses are manufactured in a number of different shapes and sizes to suit the needs of various types of roof. For example, some trusses are designed to leave a lot of open space in a roof, so that it can be used as a room. Lean-to, or mono-pitch, trusses are commonly used for extension roofs.

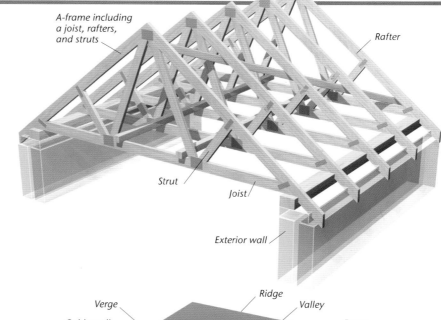

A-frame including a joist, rafters, and struts

Rafter

Strut

Joist

Exterior wall

ROOF DETAILING

Ridges, hips, and valleys are the corners or joints where a roof changes direction; they are the points at which pitched roofs meet. Verges, abutments, and eaves are the "edges" of a roof. The eaves are horizontal joints between a roof and a wall, whereas the verges are angled joints between a roof and a gable wall. Not all roofs feature all of these details, and some of them can be constructed in a number of ways. The main kinds of eaves and verges are shown below; valleys are shown on p.203.

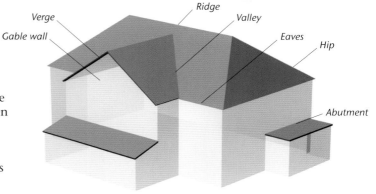

Verge

Gable wall

Ridge

Valley

Eaves

Hip

Abutment

Eaves

The point at which rafters and joists meet an exterior wall is called the eaves; it is the horizontal lower edge of the roof. There are several ways of constructing eaves, with differences mainly due to age or architectural style. Three common types of eaves are shown, without a roof covering above them for ease of understanding.

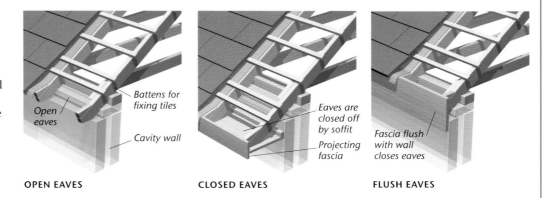

Open eaves

Battens for fixing tiles

Cavity wall

OPEN EAVES

Eaves are closed off by soffit

Projecting fascia

CLOSED EAVES

Fascia flush with wall closes eaves

FLUSH EAVES

Verges

The joint between a roof and a gabled wall is known as the verge; verges are therefore at an angle, whereas eaves are horizontal. There are two ways of constructing a verge: it can be flush with the wall; or, if the roof overhangs the wall, a gable ladder forms part of the construction. Like the eaves, verges must be waterproof.

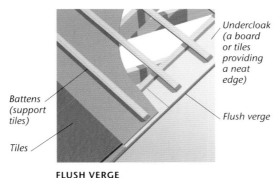

Battens (support tiles)

Tiles

Undercloak (a board or tiles providing a neat edge)

Flush verge

FLUSH VERGE

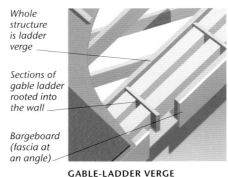

Whole structure is ladder verge

Sections of gable ladder rooted into the wall

Bargeboard (fascia at an angle)

GABLE-LADDER VERGE

ROOF STRUCTURE

Before you can carry out any work on a roof, you need to understand how its elements combine to create a waterproof layer. This varies according to design, age, type of covering, and whether the roof space is used as a room. Some roofs have all the elements shown; others have only some. However, the principles tend to remain the same. They are illustrated here on pitched roofs. All the elements described are shown in at least one of the pictures. They can be used in combinations other than those shown.

BUILDING REGULATIONS

Check your local regulations regarding roofs. There may well be requirements for almost every detail, including materials, ventilation, and fixings. The regulations are much stricter with regard to listed buildings, for which certain styles have to be maintained, and loft conversions, for which stringent safety rules must be followed.

THE PARTS OF A ROOF COVERING

The features described here may be expected to appear on most roofs. Further information on roofing felt, tiles, and other roof coverings is on pp.200–01.

Tiles or other coverings

Most roofs have some kind of tile, or tile-like covering (see p.200) to provide the waterproofing. Two ways of overlapping tiles are shown below and opposite.

Battens

These provide fixing points for tiles, and hold down felt. They are evenly spaced to give the correct overlap between rows of tiles. The spacing (gauge) depends on roof pitch, tile type and fixing (see p.200), and prevailing weather. Vertical counter battens sometimes lift the horizontal ones for ventilation, usually if a roof is sheathed (see right). Asphalt shingles do not need battens (see p.203).

Roofing felt

Felt, or another kind of underlay (see p.201), is laid below tiles to create a waterproof barrier. It is now required by building regulations, but it may not be present on older buildings. It is laid over the ply sheathing, if there is any, or directly over the rafters, in overlapping horizontal strips.

Sheathing

Boarding laid on top of the rafters in some designs of roof (see opposite) is known as sheathing. It is normally used on slightly pitched roofs, and in some areas it is required by building regulations. Sheathing is sometimes spaced out towards the apex of a roof to allow for greater ventilation. If you need sheathing, nail sheets of ply every 150mm (6in) along the rafters, staggering the joints between sheets.

Timbers

Even if a new roof covering is to be fitted, it is normally laid on the existing timbers. Some repair may be needed – and you may wish to treat the wood – but timbers need replacing only in cases of decay. If new timbers are needed, make sure the wood has been treated. Rough-sawn or planed wood can be used (see p.75). Do not store wood directly on the ground, and minimize storage time.

ATTACHING TILES

Tiles and shingles are laid with either single or double overlaps, shown here and opposite, top. The edges of single-lap tiles usually have a "tongue-and-groove" connection mechanism (see p.200). Flat tiles, slate tiles, and wood shingles are usually laid double-lap.

Rafter
Batten
Joist
Wall plate
Cavity closure
Exterior cavity wall
Eaves (closed in this example)
Roofing felt
Full tile on lower row
Joints between flat tiles can be aligned or staggered
Interlocking ridge prevents water seeping between tiles

Single-lap tiles

These can be laid on ordinary battens (shown here) or with counter battens (see opposite top). Each row of tiles only slightly overlaps onto the row below. With flat tiles, the joints can be staggered (shown). With some, joints will be aligned and valleys will run all the way down the roof (see roman tile on p.200).

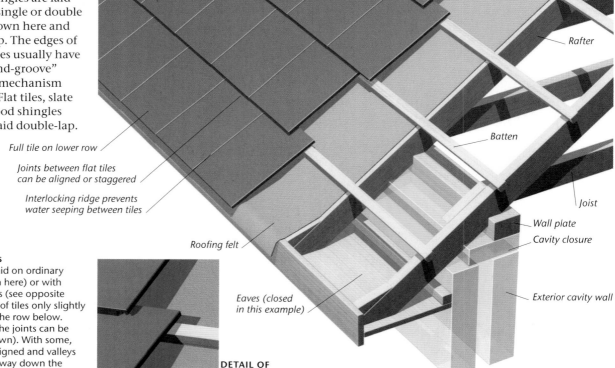

DETAIL OF OVERLAP

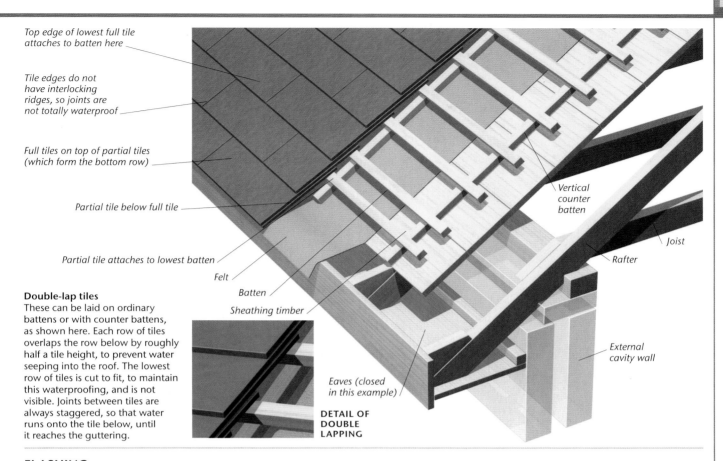

Top edge of lowest full tile attaches to batten here

Tile edges do not have interlocking ridges, so joints are not totally waterproof

Full tiles on top of partial tiles (which form the bottom row)

Partial tile below full tile

Partial tile attaches to lowest batten

Felt

Batten

Sheathing timber

Vertical counter batten

Joist

Rafter

External cavity wall

Eaves (closed in this example)

DETAIL OF DOUBLE LAPPING

Double-lap tiles
These can be laid on ordinary battens or with counter battens, as shown here. Each row of tiles overlaps the row below by roughly half a tile height, to prevent water seeping into the roof. The lowest row of tiles is cut to fit, to maintain this waterproofing, and is not visible. Joints between tiles are always staggered, so that water runs onto the tile below, until it reaches the guttering.

FLASHING

Where a lean-to roof meets a wall or other structure, the abutment needs to be waterproofed with "flashing". Many materials can be used for this, including lead, zinc, tin, or a proprietary membrane (see p.201). In order to fit flashing, a channel must be cut. The flashing is inserted and held in place with small rolls of lead or clips, then pointed with mortar or lead mastic. This holds it securely and keeps it watertight. An angled abutment, where a pitched roof meets a wall or a chimney stack, for example, is slightly more complex. It needs several overlapping sections of flashing to cover the joint (see below). On flat roofs, flashing can take a different appearance (see pp.204–05).

Chimney

Front flashing

Lead apron

Flashing strips jointed into brickwork

Each section of flashing overlaps the next

Lead soakers

Tiles overlap soakers

Flashing
Strips called "lead soakers" cover the joint between the roof and the chimney. They are overlapped on one side by the edges of tiles, and on the other by the flashing, which is jointed into the chimney's brickwork. A lead "apron" along the front of the chimney is in effect an extra-large soaker.

STRIPPING A ROOF

A roof may need to be stripped for any number of reasons. In order to carry out the work, you will need secure scaffolding and a roofing ladder. Hard coverings such as tiles do not easily break down, so they can often be reused. New asphalt tiles can sometimes be laid over old ones, to avoid stripping a roof; ask for your supplier's advice.

If you are considering changing the type of roof covering, find out first whether the new roof can be supported by the existing structure. You can get advice on this while hiring a professional builder to replace the roof.

ROOFING MATERIALS

Roofs are composed of many different materials but, generally, there are four main components common to most roof systems: a timber framework (shown on the previous pages), felt underlay, a roof covering, and flashing (waterproofing at joints). The options in these four areas are shown and explained here, along with some supplementary items used with the materials shown. You may find it helpful to read this alongside pp.198–99. For information on reclaimed roofing, see pp.86–87.

FIXINGS

The specifications for fixings such as nails and/or screws used in roof construction can vary according to local building regulations. Stainless steel, copper, and galvanized fixings are often used. They provide the best protection, because they are anti-corrosive. The most commonly used are clout nails, such as those shown on p.78.

ROOF COVERINGS

Seek advice from manufacturers when deciding how to fix tiles or shingles to a roof. Although it may seem easy to replace like with like, new regulations may require a different fixing method. If you are planning a new roof, the fixing method will be influenced by the pitch of roof, chosen tile type, and prevailing weather conditions. For example, some tiles have "nibs" on the back that hook over battens to hold tiles in place. However, in an area prone to driving winds, it may be necessary to nail down some or all of the tiles. Specialist tiles for ridges and hips are usually fixed with mortar, as are verge details. However, many new properties have ridges, hips, and verges finished using waterproof gaskets and screw fixings.

Specialist tiles
Tile manufacturers now produce tiles shaped specially to finish different roof details (see p.197).

Cloaked verge tiles
These lap over the edge of a gable to finish the roof line neatly, and eliminate the need for any mortar to finish the verge.

Clay tiles
Give a traditional look, but cost more than concrete.

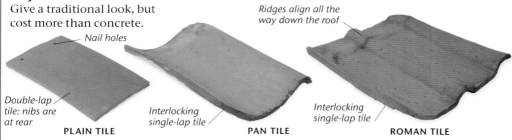

Nail holes

Ridges align all the way down the roof

Double-lap tile: nibs are at rear

PLAIN TILE

Interlocking single-lap tile

PAN TILE

Interlocking single-lap tile

ROMAN TILE

Concrete tiles
Mimic clay designs and are made to interlock easily.

PLAIN TILE

PAN TILE

ROMAN TILE

Hip tile and hip iron
Also known as bonnets, hip tiles are fitted along the hip of a roof. Ridge tiles can be used instead, with a hip iron at the eaves to support them.

Slate tiles
Strong and durable, slate provides long-lasting roofing and is more lightweight than tiles. Cheaper synthetic slates are another option.

SYNTHETIC SLATE TILE

NATURAL SLATE TILE

Valley tile
Shaped tile used in valleys in place of a flashing system.

Shingles
Another type of tile. Wooden shakes are similar to shingles, but are handmade so have a rougher appearance.

Usually cedar or redwood

May be reinforced with fibreglass for strength and fire resistance

WOODEN SHINGLE

Machine-sawn for smoothness

ASPHALT SHINGLES

Come in sheets of several shingles

Ridge tile
Arched tile used to cover a ridge. May also be used along a hip, depending on the roof design.

ROOFING FELT

For a small repair, choose felt to match that already on the roof. If you need to lay all-new felt, think about whether you need it to be breathable, for instance, because the roof space is insulated and/or ventilated in a particular way (see pp.354–55).

Often coloured

Normally black

Sheets should overlap to the dotted line

Breathable felt
Allows moisture inside the roof to escape, but prevents moisture that is outside getting in.

Bitumen-reinforced felt
A very effective waterproof barrier.

Plastic "felt"
Alternative to bitumen-reinforced felt. Both types are non-breathable.

STRAPS AND PLATES

Metal straps and plates are used to hold timbers together in roof structures – especially in modern truss constructions. These types of joint and plate make fitting much more straightforward, as there is no need to cut complex wooden joints. Since roof structures have so many joints, they can be a considerable timesaver.

Restraint strap
There are several designs of restraint strap made for various uses and roof types. The example shown here fits across the end rafters next to a gable and attaches to the wall.

Small holes for fixings

Fixes to joist

For deeper joists

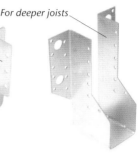

Timber connector
Used at joints in trusses to hold together roof parts.

Truss clip
Used to connect trusses to a wall plate.

Heavy-duty truss hanger
More robust.

FLASHING TOOLS AND MATERIALS

The waterproofing materials used in valleys, abutments, around chimneys – or at any other joint between different parts of a roof – are known as flashing. Metal flashings such as tin and lead are the most traditional type, and are still widely used despite modern alternatives.

Handle

Curved side

Flat side

Lead flashing
A traditional flashing material, lead is hardwearing, waterproof, and malleable, so it can be easily moulded into the desired profile.

Self-adhesive flashing repair
Applied over damaged flashing for a repair. Primer may be needed before application.

Glass-reinforced polyester (GRP)
GRP flashing is now commonly used as an alternative to lead flashing for valleys and abutments.

Lead dresser
For shaping lead along abutments and over different shaped tile profiles. Has curved and flat faces to suit all roof shapes.

VENTILATION MATERIALS

Poor ventilation in a roof is a major cause of damp. There are a number of different options for ventilating a roof. Ridge and tile vents can be joined with ducting to soil pipes or devices such as a bathroom extractor fan (see p.365), but they must not be used instead of a flue for extracting hot combustion gases unless this use is specified by the manufacturer. Insulating a roof is discussed in detail on pp.352–59.

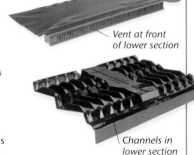

Vent at front of lower section

Channels in lower section

Tile vent
These tiles have an integrated vent. They are often plastic, and need to be fitted with an underlay seal.

Ridge vent
Offer direct ventilation channels through the ridge. This may be as part of ridge-tile structure (as shown here), or in the form of channels that are fitted along the lower edge of the tiles as they are laid in place.

Fascia vent
Clips onto fascia. The channels in the lower section allow for airflow through fascia and into loft space.

Reroofing is a major project, and should usually be carried out by a professional contractor. DIY work on a roof usually involves carrying out a small-scale repair, rather than total replacement – and that is what these pages deal with. Common problems with tiled roofs are broken tiles (or slates, or shingles), missing tiles, and damage to a valley; they may be due to natural wear and tear, or as a result of storm damage for example. These pages show how to replace a few types of tile, and three common valley structures. See pp.86–87 for information on reclaimed materials.

TOOLS AND MATERIALS CHECKLIST PP.202–03

Replacing a tile
Access equipment (e.g. ladder or scaffolding)*, timber wedges*, bound hacksaw blade*

Replacing a slate
Access equipment (e.g. ladder or scaffolding)*, bound hacksaw blade*, slate ripper*, lead strip or proprietary clips

Replacing a wood shingle
Access equipment (e.g. ladder

or scaffolding)*, bound hacksaw blade*, silicone sealant, sealant dispenser

Replacing an asphalt shingle
Access equipment (e.g. ladder or scaffolding)*, pry bar

* = optional

FOR BASIC TOOLKIT
SEE PP.24—25

REPLACING A DAMAGED TILE OR SHINGLE

The method needed for replacing a roof covering will depend on the type of tile or shingle in use. For instance, the steps below show a simple way of replacing a tile, but you may need to alter them slightly, as described alongside the steps. To remove a slate, you may prefer to use a slate ripper rather than a hacksaw blade (as shown). Slate rippers are specially designed to remove fixings that are under a row of slates, but they are specialist tools and probably not worth buying unless you are likely to replace a lot of slates. With wooden shingles, the problem may be to do with waterproofing rather than breakages: damp shingles may buckle or rot. Replace any split or misshapen shingles so that they do not allow moisture to penetrate into or

through the roof. Replacing asphalt shingles is easier because they are flexible, so they can simply be lifted up to give access to the fixings beneath them.

Cutting a tile or shingle

Wooden shingles and shakes can be cut with a saw, and asphalt shingles can be cut with a craft knife. Clay and concrete tiles are best cut using an angle grinder (see p.61, paying attention to the safety issues involved, and wearing all suitable protective clothing). Slates can be scored by running a sharp nail along a guide line, and then snapped along that line, or they can be split apart by tapping the scored line with the edge of a trowel.

REPLACING A TILE

Tiles with nibs may be nailed in place, so fixings may need to be cut free as shown in Replacing a Slate (below). Otherwise, just lift the old tile free of the batten, and lip the nib(s) of a new one over the batten. With interlocking or single-lap tiles, wedge up the tiles next to the damaged one, as well as those above it as shown here, to undo the interlocking joints.

A

Wedge up the tiles above the broken one, so that you can access it. Unhook its nibs from the batten and lift out the broken tile.

B

Position the new tile, hooking its nibs over the batten and ensuring that it is securely attached. Remove the wedges from the adjoining tiles, and check that the new tile is sitting flush with the neighbouring tiles.

REPLACING A SLATE

A

Remove any loose pieces of slate, then cut away the fixings with a hacksaw blade wound in tape at the "handle" end.

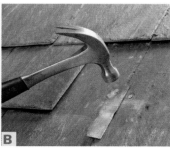

B

Nail a strip of lead over the exposed vertical joint between slates, fixing into the batten below. You can use clips instead.

C

Position a new slate to replace the old one, ensuring that it fits well.

D

Bend the lead or clip up over the new slate to secure it in position.

REPLACING A WOOD SHINGLE

A Use a hammer and chisel to split and remove the broken shingle. It may be possible to reclaim some of this material (see pp.86–87).

B Wind tape around one end of a hacksaw blade to form a "handle" by which to hold it. Use the blade to cut through the shingle's fixings.

Slide the new shingle into position and fix it in place with nails as close as possible to the row above. Seal along the edges of the shingle, and across the nail heads, with a silicone sealant (see p.81).

REPLACING AN ASPHALT SHINGLE

A Use a pry bar to lever up the fixings in the damaged strip of shingles. Then remove it.

B Loosen the fixings at the top and bottom of the strip of shingles above, so that you can slide the new strip of shingles in underneath it.

C Slide the new strip of shingles up and into position.

D Hide nails by placing the end of the pry bar over them, and hitting it farther down the shank of the bar with a hammer to knock them in.

REPAIRING A VALLEY

A valley can be constructed from lead or other metals such as tin, from plastic, or from special valley tiles or shingles. Repairing a leaking valley will normally involve stripping back the tiles, slates, or shingles from along the valley edge to expose the structure, and then replacing the damaged part. Tiles or similar coverings may well have been cut to the right size to follow the valley course. Chalk numbers on them as you remove them, so that you can put them back in the right order. Not all valleys have flashing on them; some are made with shaped tiles or even with shingles cut to fit across the valley. Assess your repair requirements according to the type of valley you have. Three common types of valley are shown here.

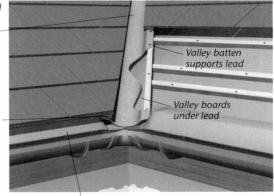

Lead moulded to fit using a lead dresser

Valley batten supports lead

Mortar fills gap between tiles and lead

Valley boards under lead

LEAD VALLEY *End cut to shape to point water into gutter*

Pre-shaped valley will weaken if bent

Valley is nailed to valley battens

Valleys are available in different profiles to suit tile types

Felt is normally lapped under valley

GRP (GLASS-REINFORCED POLYESTER) VALLEY

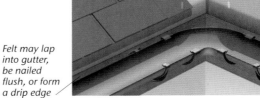

Sometimes extra felt strip or tin flashing is laid below shingles

Felt may lap into gutter, be nailed flush, or form a drip edge

SHINGLE VALLEY *Felt laid on sheathing*

FLAT-ROOF STRUCTURE

The definition of a flat roof is one that has a pitch of less than 10 degrees. Traditional flat roofs are made of wooden decking covered with felt and bitumen, but a number of more straightforward construction methods can provide a weatherproof flat roof. A typical modern structure is shown below, and one of the most common ways of covering a flat roof is demonstrated opposite. Systems vary, however, so always read the manufacturer's instructions carefully before starting to lay proprietary roofing systems.

A TYPICAL ROOF

This illustration shows a modern flat-roof structure. Like pitched roofs, flat roofs may be "warm" or "cold" (see pp.352–55). All flat roofs should be insulated. A cold roof is insulated between joists (which are below the roof deck), so ventilation has to be allowed around the joists to prevent condensation. Because of the condensation risk with cold roofs, most new roofs are warm. A warm roof is insulated above the joists (as in the example shown below), lessening the potential for condensation problems. Systems such as that shown below are actually constructed using the insulation as the deck. Traditional decks, however, are normally made of ply.

SHEET ROOFING

Materials such as corrugated metal or plastic, UPVC, or polycarbonate sheeting are often used to cover lean-to roofs. These structures are usually left open to the elements on one or more sides — porches and carports are examples. Fix your chosen material to the joists using nails or screws. Some specialist sheet-roofing screws have large heads to cover the hole they make and prevent water penetrating the roof. **SHEET-ROOFING SCREW**

TOOLS AND MATERIALS CHECKLIST

Covering a flat roof
Access equipment (e.g. scaffolding or ladder)*, brush, straight edge such as metre rule, primer*, brush*, heat

gun, flat roofing seam roller, timber battens, silicone sealant, sealant dispenser

* = optional

FOR BASIC TOOLKIT SEE PP.24–25

The layers in a flat roof
Joists form the core of a flat roof. The ceiling of the room below is attached to them, while the roof itself sits on top of them. Depending on the type of roof, insulation can be laid on top of the ceiling between the joists, or can sit above the joists themselves. In the warm roof shown here, insulating panels are laid across the joists, but there are other methods. Joints between panels, and the nails or screws attaching the panels and joists, are covered with tape. Overlapping sheets of waterproof roof covering lie across the panels, lapped over the edge of the roof so that rainwater drips off rather than running down the walls.

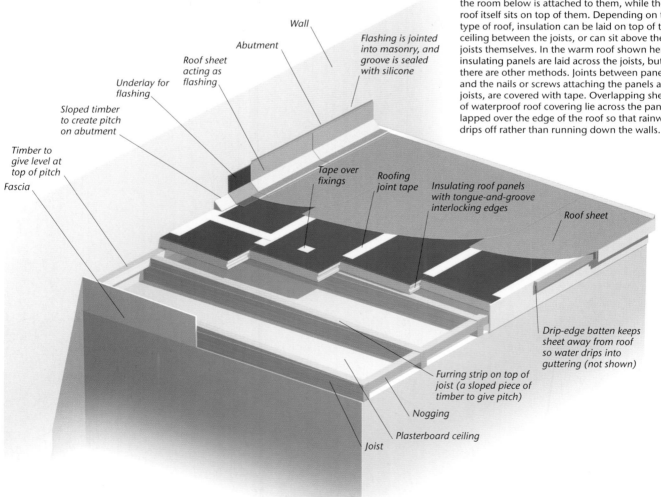

Wall

Abutment

Flashing is jointed into masonry, and groove is sealed with silicone

Roof sheet acting as flashing

Underlay for flashing

Sloped timber to create pitch on abutment

Timber to give level at top of pitch

Fascia

Tape over fixings

Roofing joint tape

Insulating roof panels with tongue-and-groove interlocking edges

Roof sheet

Drip-edge batten keeps sheet away from roof so water drips into guttering (not shown)

Furring strip on top of joist (a sloped piece of timber to give pitch)

Nogging

Plasterboard ceiling

Joist

COVERING A FLAT ROOF

Rubber sheeting is a durable choice for covering a flat roof. The technique for fitting a typical system is shown here. Ensure that you can access and work on the roof in safety, and if possible get somebody to help you.

TOOLS AND MATERIALS SEE BASIC TOOLKIT AND P.204

1 LAYING THE RUBBER SHEETS

Clean down the roof thoroughly, removing any loose material, and checking that the surface is completely dry. Remove any guttering if possible. Then have somebody help you lift the self-adhesive rubber roofing rolls up to the roof.

A

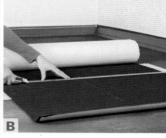

B

Cut the rubber to length. Allow for the sheets to overlap each other, the roof edge, and any abutment by at least 50mm (2in).

Unroll the cut lengths to check that they fit correctly. Then remove them from the roof. Apply primer to the roof surface in accordance with the manufacturer's instructions. Leave the primer to dry for at least an hour before continuing.

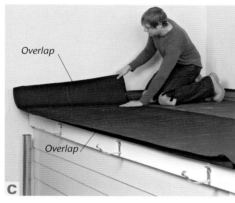

Overlap

Overlap

C

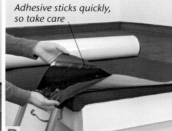

Adhesive sticks quickly, so take care

D

Start to peel the backing away from the first sheet. You will now have to move quickly, taking care to position it correctly along the roof edge.

Lap roofing over edge

E

Carefully unroll the sheet, removing the backing as you progress across the roof. Smooth out any wrinkles immediately.

F

Overlap by 50mm (2in)

You will probably need to use a heat gun with a fishtail nozzle to bond together the joints between individual sheets.

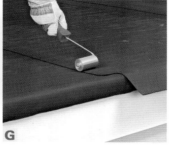

G

Use a flat roofing seam roller to ensure that the seam lays flat and – if a heat gun has been used – is completely bonded.

2 SEALING THE EDGES

A

Cut a length of roofing to attach to the fascia (above any guttering brackets) and lap onto the flat roof. Position a batten to hold it in place.

B

Nail the batten onto the fascia, securely holding the sheet of roofing rubber in place.

Guttering bracket

C

Fold the sheet up, over the batten, and stick it onto the roof. Smooth it carefully to remove any wrinkles.

D

Use the heat gun and seam roller to seal and finish the seam.

3 SEALING AN ABUTMENT

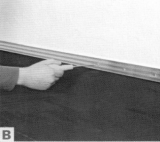

A

Where there is an abutment, use the heat gun and seam roller to make a tight seal between the roofing and the wall.

B

Screw a metal cover strip over the joint between the roofing and the wall, and apply silicone sealant along the top joint of the cover strip.

TYPES OF GUTTERING

A correctly installed guttering system will increase the efficiency of water transfer from roof to drainage system. This helps to maintain house structure by eliminating damp problems often caused by leaking or badly positioned gutters. Guttering does not need replacing often. Clear guttering regularly of debris, refix any loose joints as soon as you notice them, and remember that some materials – cast iron, for example – require painting.

RECYCLING WATER

Rainwater is usually directed into underground drainage systems, but it can be recycled. This can be done by collecting it in a water butt positioned below a guttering downpipe, or with a system of water recycling for use in the household plumbing system (see p.384–87).

MATERIALS

Guttering is made from a variety of materials, each with different strengths, appearances, and costs. There may be regulations in conservation areas about replacing gutters, so check these if they may apply to you before you buy new guttering.

UPVC
Lightweight, and easy to work with. Sections clip together. Requires only minimal maintenance.

Aluminium
Lightweight. Joining systems vary. Continuous guttering (without joints) can be made on site by specialists to suit your requirements.

Cast iron
Traditional and hardwearing, but extremely heavy. Iron needs painting. Sections are joined with mastic, nuts, and bolts.

Copper
Durable and easy to install. With time, the bright finish weathers to an attractive verdigris.

PROFILES

Most guttering has a rounded or a squared shape, but several profiles are available (see below). The decision in this regard is purely one of preference. If you are replacing a whole guttering system, your main concerns will be appearance, cost, and ease of installation (if you are planning to carry out the work yourself).

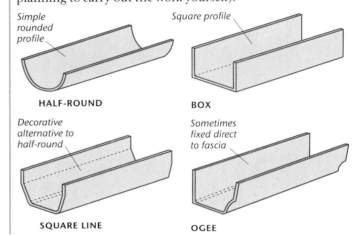

Simple rounded profile

HALF-ROUND

Square profile

BOX

Decorative alternative to half-round

SQUARE LINE

Sometimes fixed direct to fascia

OGEE

A GUTTERING SYSTEM

Several different sections fit together to drain rainwater quickly and efficiently. Although the method of joining these elements varies depending on the guttering material used, the components are similar. Shown here is a basic UPVC system. The system you fit may need some or all of the components shown here.

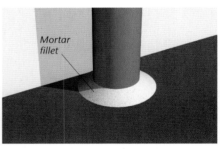

Mortar fillet

Direct drain connection
Downpipes may connect directly to underground drainage. For a new system, an adapter socket may be required.

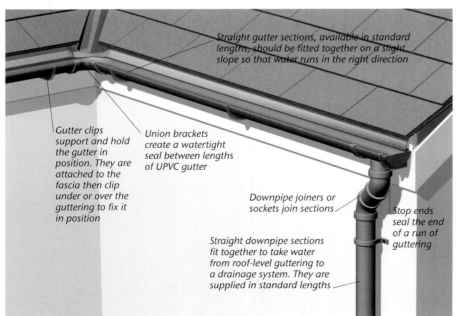

Straight gutter sections, available in standard lengths, should be fitted together on a slight slope so that water runs in the right direction

Gutter clips support and hold the gutter in position. They are attached to the fascia then clip under or over the guttering to fix it in position

Union brackets create a watertight seal between lengths of UPVC gutter

Downpipe joiners or sockets join sections

Stop ends seal the end of a run of guttering

Straight downpipe sections fit together to take water from roof-level guttering to a drainage system. They are supplied in standard lengths

LAYOUT OF A GUTTERING SYSTEM

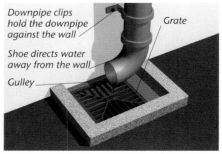

Downpipe clips hold the downpipe against the wall

Shoe directs water away from the wall

Gulley

Grate

Gulley
For gulley drainage, the downpipe may feed down into the gulley grate or have a shoe attached at the base of the downpipe.

Installation is a simple, methodical process, but the technique will vary slightly depending on the type of guttering. Plan thoroughly the layout and components needed. In most cases it will simply be a case of replacing like with like, so it may be worth making a sketch of how the components of the old system are arranged. Familiarize yourself with how to assemble the joints used with your system, and see pp.26–27 for how to position a ladder and information on scaffolding. Arrange to have somebody to help you do the work.

REMOVING OLD GUTTERING

Whether it is difficult to remove old guttering depends on what material it is made of, and how easy it is to gain access to it. Aim to carry the guttering down the ladder with you, rather than allowing it to drop to the ground. If the guttering is very high, or it is difficult to put up a ladder, get a professional to take down the old guttering and replace it. If you are removing metal guttering, bear in mind that it may be heavy. Make sure the area below where you are working is clear. Another alternative to ladders or fixed scaffolding is to hire either a scaffold tower or a mechanized platform. For more information on these options, see p.27.

MEASURING FOR NEW GUTTERING

Guttering needs to slope towards a running outlet to ensure that water drains away efficiently. The gradient needed is very slight – only 1:500, which amounts to 25mm (1in) in every 15m (50ft). In practice, you do not need to work it out precisely, but just make sure that the guttering slopes all the way down to the running outlet (as shown on p.208) – and that it slopes even while turning any corners. On a particularly long run of guttering, the fascia board may not be deep enough to accommodate the gradient required. In this case, a running outlet may be positioned centrally along the length of a fascia board, with lengths of guttering on either side running downhill towards it. The number and position of downpipes will therefore be very much dependent on the length of a gutter run, and also where the downpipe can direct water to underground drainage. In most cases, these routes will be well established, but on new-build projects, some more detailed planning will be required.

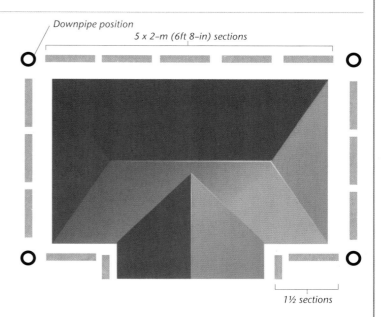

Downpipe position

5 x 2–m (6ft 8–in) sections

1½ sections

Typical guttering arrangement
A diagram of your property provides the easiest way of working out requirements. It is then possible to calculate how many standard lengths will be required, and how many will need cutting. It also makes it straightforward to calculate joints (and the requirements for union brackets), corner sections, and the number of running outlets needed.

ESTIMATING QUANTITIES

Basic estimate	If possible, measure lengths of old guttering and the downpipes. Otherwise, measure around the building at ground level, and measure its height. Feed a rigid tape measure up a wall to find the height for the downpipe.
Wastage and trimming	Buy about 10 per cent extra. Guttering tends to come in standard lengths, which you will have to cut to fit, so some will be wasted.
Clips	The number of clips needed per length may be specified by the manufacturer. Otherwise, aim for one every 2m (2yd) on metal guttering and every 1m (1yd) on UPVC guttering.
Union brackets	If you are using UPVC guttering, work out how many joints there will be between lengths: you will need a union bracket for each joint.

TOOLS AND MATERIALS CHECKLIST PP.208–09

Installing UPVC guttering (pp.208–09) Ladder or scaffolding*, string line, file, spirit level or gradient spirit level

file, spirit level or gradient spirit level, hacksaw, sealant dispenser*, sealant*, nuts*, bolts*

* = optional

Installing metal guttering (p.209) Ladder or scaffolding*, string line,

FOR BASIC TOOLKIT SEE PP.24–25

Lightweight UPVC can be assembled by one person but, because most work involves handling long lengths up a ladder, it is best to enlist a helper if you can. Move your ladder to each new working point; do not reach across. See p.207 for details on choosing an appropriate gradient for guttering. The steps show how to fit a straight run of standard 2–m (6ft 8–in) lengths of UPVC guttering. If you need to turn corners, simply use the same principles but attach corner sections at the appropriate places.

TOOLS AND MATERIALS SEE BASIC TOOLKIT AND P.207

1 ESTABLISHING THE GRADIENT

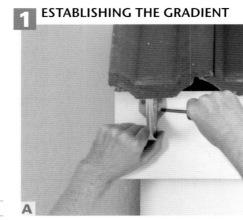

Fix a support clip high up on the fascia board, at the opposite end from where the running outlet will be. You will probably find it easier to tighten screws near the roof covering with a hand-held screwdriver rather than a power drill-driver.

A

B

Position a clip at the other end of the eaves, lower than the first and at the correct height to give the necessary gradient.

C

Tie a string line between the two clips, to form a guide line.

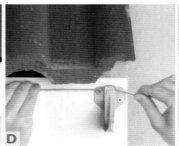

D

Make sure the string line is taut and is not caught anywhere, especially if it has to travel round a corner.

E

Check the gradient with a spirit level. If it is not as you want it, adjust it by slightly repositioning the lower bracket.

2 ATTACHING CLIPS AND THE RUNNING OUTLET

Fix a third clip 1m (3ft 3in) away from the first one, with the string line just touching the top edge of the bracket.

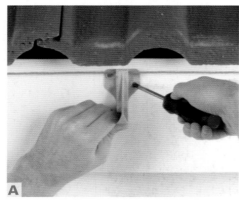

A

B

Fix a union bracket 1m (3ft 3in) along from the third clip. Then fix alternate clips and brackets until within 1m (3ft 3in) of the end.

C

Remove the string line. Then clip the running outlet into the last, lowest support clip.

3 FITTING THE GUTTERING

A

Position the first whole length of guttering by snapping one end of it into the highest clip.

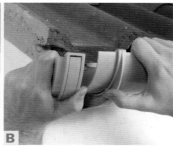

B

Snap a stop end onto the guttering before moving the ladder to clip the rest of the length in place.

C

Snap the guttering into the next clip, and then fit its end into the first union bracket.

D

Snap the next length into the union bracket. Continue fixing whole lengths until near the end.

4 CUTTING TO FIT

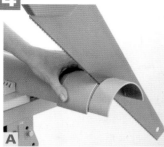

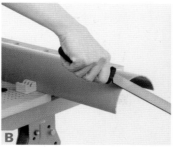

A Mark where you need to cut the last piece of guttering to fit. Use an offcut of guttering to guide you for a straight cut with a panel saw.

B File the cut end of the guttering to remove burrs.

C Position the last piece of guttering and clip it into the running outlet. Clip a stop end onto the running outlet if it needs one. If the roof overhangs the edge of the house by a long way, you may need to attach a short length of guttering the other side of the outlet, angled down from the eaves into the running outlet.

5 FITTING THE DOWNPIPE

Assemble a bend to connect the guttering with the downpipe, using two offset bends with a length of downpipe between them. Adjust the middle section of downpipe so that the main downpipe will lie against the wall.

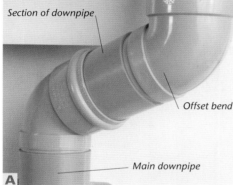

Section of downpipe

Offset bend

Main downpipe

A

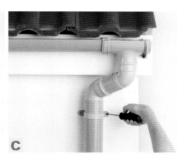

B Push the bend into the bottom of the running outlet to fix it in place. Then push the downpipe into the offset bend.

C Use a spirit level to check that the downpipe is vertical. Also make sure that it enters the gully at ground level in the correct place.

6 FIXING THE DOWNPIPE BRACKETS

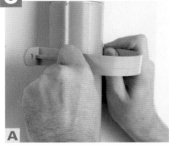

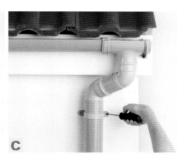

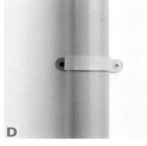

A Hold a bracket in place at the top of the downpipe and draw through the fixing holes to mark the wall.

B Use a masonry bit to drill pilot holes at the marked points. Insert wall plugs into them.

C Screw the bracket into position over the downpipe.

D Secure more brackets every 1m (3ft 3in) along the length of the downpipe.

INSTALLING METAL GUTTERING

Set up a string line for metal guttering just as shown left for UPVC. Cast-iron guttering will not have union brackets, but lightweight aluminium, shown right, does. Some systems have standard running outlets. The system shown here involves using a hole cutter to make holes in gutter lengths, allowing running outlets to be positioned as required.

Joining lengths
The union bracket has a rubber gasket to create a watertight seal.

Attaching a stop end
The stop end has a rubber seal, and clips into place.

Using a running outlet
The running outlet clips over and around the gutter profile, where the hole has been cut.

Some roof spaces are constructed from the first to be used as additional rooms in a house. Even those that are not can often be converted, adding extra space to the home. Roof windows bring natural light into these areas and come in a range of designs. Most are made to fit into a pitched roof, although domes and other openings for flat roofs are available. Broadly speaking, there are two types of design that are used – dormer windows, and tilting pitched roof windows.

BUILDING REGULATIONS
Converting your loft space into a habitable area is certainly something that requires planning permission. Apart from standard regulations, a Building Control Officer will be particularly interested in ventilation, insulation, and access to and from the loft. There are also strict regulations on fireproofing and the provision of fire escape routes.

TILT OR PIVOT WINDOWS
Tilt or pivot windows are fitted at the same pitch as the roof, so no other roof structure needs to be built in order to accommodate the window. Access for maintenance is also easier with a tilting design. Because of the ease of fitting and upkeep, you can install pivot windows when you renovate other areas of the roof space. The success of this type of window design has expanded product ranges. In addition to standard tilting windows, it is now possible to buy top- or side-hung variations, as well as specially designed blinds and shutters. These may attach to the inside of the window, or sit between two panes of glass inside the window itself.

Planning and permissions
Standard sizes of tilt window are available, or several windows can be fitted alongside each other to make a larger window space – although this may have implications for the

structural integrity of the roof. Before buying the window, take professional advice to ensure that any required cuts in roof timbers will not weaken the roof structure. Planning permission is sometimes required to fit this type of window, and there may be local regulations governing a window's size, its position in the roof, and even its design.

Fitting a tilt window
Illustrated below are three different designs of window, all of which are fitted using much the same technique. One major advantage of tilt windows is that the fitting process can be carried out entirely from inside the roof space. Unless you are fitting a very small window that can sit between rafters, at least one rafter will need to be cut to make room. To ensure this does not weaken the roof, support members called false rafters and trimmers will have to be inserted to strengthen the opening you create.

Waterproofing
Tilting roof windows are fitted in conjunction with flashing kits to make sure the window is waterproof. Flashing kits vary not only with window size and design, but also according to the type of tiles.

The way in which rafters are cut and trimmers are inserted is very much dependent on window size and positioning. The three examples below are aesthetically quite different, but structurally similar.

Tilt window
This is a variation on a straightforward design. The window opens from an upper hinge instead of tilting around the central window axis.

Speciality tilt window
The aperture needed for this window is the same as at left and right, but an extension to the lower part creates a "larger" opening.

Escape window
By hinging the window along its side, it can easily be "thrown" open, for use with an emergency ladder (see p.375) if required.

WORKING FROM INSIDE

Tilting roof windows are designed so that the entire installation process can be carried out from inside your roof, which is one of their major advantages. However, make sure that the area below is cordoned off while you work, to protect passers-by from the risk of falling debris. Fitting the window should be a quite straightforward procedure, and the unit should be supplied with detailed instructions from the manufacturer. However, this is still probably a job for the more experienced home improvement enthusiast, rather than a beginner.

DORMER WINDOWS

The actual casement or sash used for a dormer window can be of the same design as any other window – the distinguishing feature is that a projection from the main part of the pitched roof is built to accommodate the window. This can be a smaller pitched roof, or in some cases a simpler flat roof.

The addition of a dormer window to an existing roof is a complex job, and you will almost certainly need professional help with design and construction. Maintenance of existing dormer windows can also be difficult, because access to them will often require fixed scaffolding.

Pitched-roof dormer
A pitched-roof dormer window is a miniature roof construction in its own right, with a ridge, valleys, verges, and eaves. Installation of such a window is quite a major undertaking.

FLAT ROOFS

Windows can also be added to flat roofs to provide more light. These are often built up on a frame above the main roof deck, and tilted to allow for good runoff. The actual window design is the same or similar to that in other roof windows, and again the weatherproof flashing is an essential part of the design. Because of the location, fitting is straightforward – you can simply work directly from the roof deck.

Light chutes

An alternative to roof windows are light chutes. These are often smaller, non-opening windows that draw natural light down into darker areas of the home. The lining of the chute is often made of reflective material in order to maximize the amount of light it transmits.

FLAT ROOF WINDOW

LOFT CONVERSIONS

There are a number of factors to consider when converting a loft space. One of the most important issues is how much structural work will be required. If the existing joists are not substantial enough to support a floor, they will require strengthening. If roof-support struts cross the area you want to use, you may have to alter the roof's structural framework to remove them. Other important considerations include the number and type of windows, and where the stair access will enter the loft from below. You may need to re-tile parts of the roof before or during conversion, and will certainly need to re-route some electrical supplies, and possibly plumbing as well. Plan how you will heat the loft space. Your boiler may not be able to support new radiators, and may have to be upgraded. One other major thing to consider is how you will move the building materials into your roof space, and access it while working.

CONVERTED LOFT INTERIOR

Tilting windows are a good option for loft conversions

Make sure the roof is properly insulated

Insulated dwarf wall provides best shape to room

PATCHING A FLAT ROOF

Small holes in a flat roof can be patched with a specially made primer and patching system. The technique will vary slightly according to manufacturer; that shown here is typical. Carry out this repair in dry conditions.

TOOLS AND MATERIALS
Primer and patching system, brush, scissors, flat-roof roller

A Dust off any loose material from the damaged area. Apply primer to the area, overlapping it onto the undamaged part of the roof.

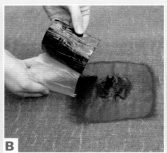

B Allow primer to dry if instructed to. Cut some self-adhesive patching material to cover the hole and overlap onto the sound roof.

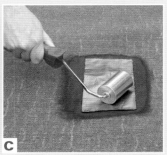

C Apply the patch to the primed area, and smooth it by hand. Then smooth it with a flat-roof roller, ensuring a good seal.

RE-BEDDING A RIDGE TILE

Fix a loose ridge tile or one with cracked pointing to stop damp from penetrating. If the tile is well bedded but has cracked pointing, rake out the mortar and replace it. If the tile is loose, re-fix it as shown here.

TOOLS AND MATERIALS
Lump hammer, cold chisel, gloves, dusting brush, mortar mix, spot board, bricklaying trowel, spirit level

A Use a lump hammer and cold chisel to loosen the mortar. Remove the ridge tile.

B Remove hardened mortar with the lump hammer and cold chisel. Dust away any loose material with a dusting brush.

C Apply a fresh bed of mortar on either side of the apex.

FIXING OTHER SYSTEMS
■ Dry-fix systems can be unscrewed and the gaskets and/or tile replaced.
■ Cut an asphalt shingle to overlap a damaged ridge shingle by 75mm (3in). Bend it over the ridge, cement in place, and nail the corners. Dab cement over nail heads.
■ Wooden ridge shingles can be replaced in a similar way to other wooden shingles (see p.203). Cut new shingles to match old, if necessary.

D Carefully reposition the tile, lowering it into place on the fresh mortar.

E Check that the tile is level with the ridge tiles to either side of it. Adjust the mortar level if necessary to make it sit higher or lower.

F Point in the tile with some more mortar, ensuring that no gaps are left through which water can penetrate.

REPAIRING A LEAK IN FLASHING

Leaks are most likely where lead flashing is bedded into masonry. The repair shown here can be used if lead is channelled into a wall. Lead wedges can be used instead of clips.

TOOLS AND MATERIALS
Dusting brush, screwdriver, flashing clips, lead sealant, sealant dispenser

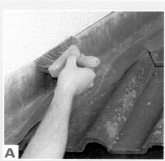

A Dust any debris from the joint, removing any old mortar or sealant as required.

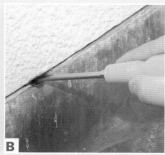

B Use the end of a screwdriver to push flashing clips into the joint to hold lead firmly in place.

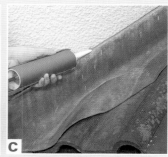

C Run a continuous bead of lead sealant along the joint (see pp.80–81 for more information on sealants).

REPAIRING A LEAKING GUTTER

Gutter joints, whether sealed with a rubber gasket or sealant, will deteriorate over time and leak. This can cause damp problems and needs to be fixed. The repair shown here uses silicone sealant. Otherwise, gaskets can be replaced.

TOOLS AND MATERIALS
Cloth, silicone sealant, sealant dispenser

OTHER CAUSES OF LEAKS
■ The gutter might be blocked and overflowing. Unblock it to fix the problem.
■ Insecure fixings may cause sagging and overflowing. Fix them using the method for a leaking downpipe (below).
■ Guttering needs a slope to drain away efficiently. Check whether it needs adjusting to the correct angle (see p.207).
■ Cast-iron guttering may rust and leak. Paint it often to avoid this (see p.292).

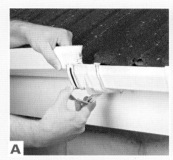

A **Disassemble the gutter** joint by unclipping the gutter length from the joint clip.

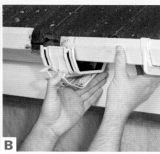

B **Remove the adjacent** length of guttering to give you clear access to the internal profile of the joint clip.

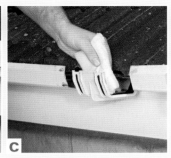

C **Dust out the joint,** making sure that it is clean and dry.

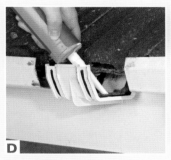

D **Apply silicone sealant** around the edge of the gutter's profile.

E **Reassemble the joint,** fixing the clips securely back in place.

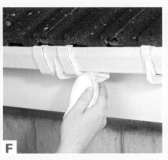

F **Wipe away any excess** sealant with a cloth.

FIXING A LOOSE DOWNPIPE

If downpipe brackets become loose, joints in the pipe may fracture and cause water to run down the side of the building. This would cause problems with damp, so loose pipes should be re-fixed immediately.

TOOLS AND MATERIALS
Drill, suitable fixings and wall plugs (see pp.76–79)

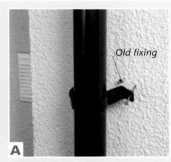

A **Slide the loose** downpipe bracket to slightly above or below its previous position.

Old fixing

B **Hold the bracket** in place, and mark where the new fixings will need to go. Then drill pilot holes.

New fixing position

C **Fix bracket in place** with the appropriate fixings. Use wall plugs on masonry.

REPOINTING A LEAKING VERGE

The drawback of a pointed verge is that the cement fillet sealing the edge of the tiles may become cracked. This leaves an opening for damp penetration, but is easily fixed, as shown here.

TOOLS AND MATERIALS
Cold chisel, mallet, mortar mix, spot board, pointing trowel, small paintbrush

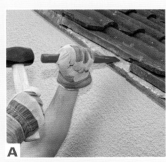

A **Rake out loose** mortar carefully, using a cold chisel and mallet, taking care not to dislodge or damage any of the tiles.

B **Mix up some mortar** (see p.71), and use a pointing a trowel to press it into the joint below the tile.

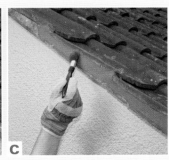

C **Use a dry paintbrush** to brush lightly along the edge to tidy the joint and provide a neat finish.

Decorative woodwork

WOODEN MOULDINGS PROVIDE A DECORATIVE FINISH TO MANY AREAS OF THE HOME. SKIRTING BOARDS AND DOOR ARCHITRAVES ARE THE MOST NOTICEABLE EXAMPLES, ALTHOUGH FINER MOULDINGS ARE OFTEN USED FOR DETAILING ON WARDROBES AND BOOKCASES, AND TO CREATE PANELS ON DOORS OR WALLS. THIS SECTION CONSIDERS THE USES OF THIS TYPE OF WOODWORK, AND TECHNIQUES FOR APPLYING IT.

TYPES OF MOULDING

Mouldings usually need either painting or a natural wood finish (e.g. paint or varnish; see pp.282–95) after they are fitted. Some ranges need no finish. Skirting board and architrave, for example, may be made in the same colour and style as a doorset (see p.164). This saves time, but needs careful fitting: mistakes are not easily covered with filler or paint.

SKIRTING BOARD AND ARCHITRAVE

Probably the most common moulding, skirting board forms a decorative, protective edge at a wall and floor junction. Architrave creates a decorative join between a door lining and wall. Architrave usually has less depth than matching skirting board. For example, 100–mm (4-in) skirting is often used with 50-mm (2-in) architrave. Provided you measure carefully, (see pp.218–21), both are straightforward to fit.

MDF mouldings

A common alternative to wood, MDF mouldings are normally primed and moisture-resistant. MDF is not prone to splitting, and has no knots. It also has some flexibility, making it easier to fix into slight contours across a surface. A tighter fit to an undulating wall surface will also reduce the need to fill gaps between the moulding and wall.

Green colour indicates moisture-resistant MDF

SKIRTING BOARD

ARCHITRAVE

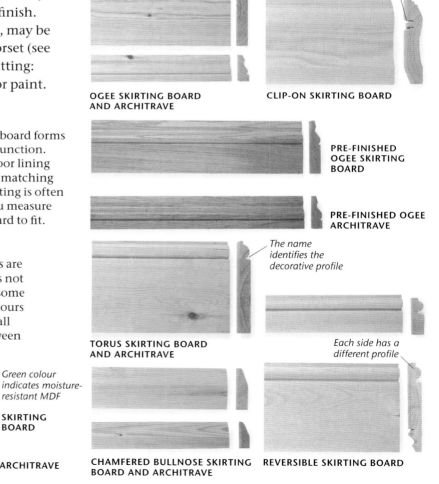

Skirtings and architraves

Clip attaches to wall, eliminating need for fixings

Slots in skirting snap onto clips

OGEE SKIRTING BOARD AND ARCHITRAVE

CLIP-ON SKIRTING BOARD

PRE-FINISHED OGEE SKIRTING BOARD

PRE-FINISHED OGEE ARCHITRAVE

The name identifies the decorative profile

TORUS SKIRTING BOARD AND ARCHITRAVE

Each side has a different profile

CHAMFERED BULLNOSE SKIRTING BOARD AND ARCHITRAVE

REVERSIBLE SKIRTING BOARD

DECORATIVE WOOD MOULDINGS

These mouldings provide the finer decorative detailing in a room, such as around a bookcase or along the edges of shelving. Mouldings such as quadrant and scotia are commonly used to fill the expansion gap around the perimeter of wooden flooring (see pp.338–39). A greater range of profiles is available than for larger mouldings such as skirting board and architrave. It is also more common to find smaller mouldings in a range of soft- and hardwoods. Profiles range from the simple to the highly ornamental. The selection shown to the right features the most commonly available mouldings, but some manufacturers produce much wider ranges that can accommodate most decorative preferences.

DECORATIVE RAIL AND CORNICE

Rails may be decorative (to break up a wall surface) or practical (to hang pictures or to protect a wall from chairs). Cornice is used in the same way as coving (see pp.138–41) and comes in two sections. As an alternative to wood, MDF and plaster rails and cornices are available (see pp.138–39).

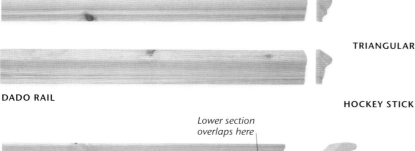

DADO RAIL

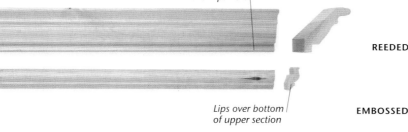

Lower section overlaps here

Lips over bottom of upper section

USING DECORATIVE BLOCKS

Lengths of architrave are usually mitre-joined at the top of a doorway, and butt-joined to matching skirting board at the bottom of a doorway. Decorative blocks, however, create a more traditional look.

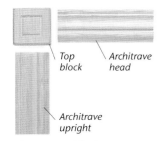

Top block *Architrave head*

Architrave upright

Architrave top block
Available in many designs. This butt-joins with the upright and head lengths of architrave to give a traditional appearance.

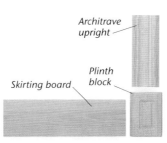

Architrave upright

Skirting board *Plinth block*

Architrave plinth block
Butt-joins with skirting board and forms the base on which upright lengths of architrave are placed, again with butt-joins.

SQUARE

HALF ROUND

QUADRANT

DOWEL

SCOTIA

STAFF BEAD

TRIANGULAR

HOCKEY STICK

REEDED

EMBOSSED

CARVED

ORNAMENTAL

GLAZING

ANGLE

DOUBLE D

FLAT D

USING MOULDINGS

This page shows some of the ways in which mouldings can be used, and the effects that can be achieved with them. It addresses some of the reasons for using mouldings, and highlights issues to consider when planning to fit them. It also shows you how to cover fixings so that they do not blemish the appearance of your mouldings.

MOULDINGS IN USE

Whereas the previous pages show examples of mouldings, the image to the right depicts them in use and gives more information on how to use them.

Picture rail

Originally, picture rails were used to hang pictures from hooks which looped over the rail, with wire or chain hung from them to support a picture. This had the advantage of allowing pictures to be moved easily without marking the wall. Today, picture rails tend to be used as a decorative feature to add greater shape or interest to a room's design.

Dado (chair) rail

These rails protect walls from chairs and other items pushed against them. The division in a wall's surface can be both practical and decorative. For example, the lower part of a wall often suffers knocks, or is marked by children. If a rail separates this from the upper wall, you need redecorate only the area below the dado rail to restore the decor.

Skirting board and architrave

These are usually of the same design and decoration throughout a room (see p.214), and are straightforward to fit provided that measuring and cutting are accurate.

Panelling

You can partially or totally cover a wall with panelling. Fielded panelling (used in period properties) is often made from hardwoods such as mahogany, and is expensive. It can be imitated with routed MDF (see below and pp.66–67), or by attaching mouldings. Tongue-and-groove panelling is also common (see main picture). Most panelling is attached to battens on the wall (which must not be damp). In a timber-framed house, these panels can be fixed directly to the timber frame if the structure is insulated and has a vapour barrier. They may also be attached to ceiling joists.

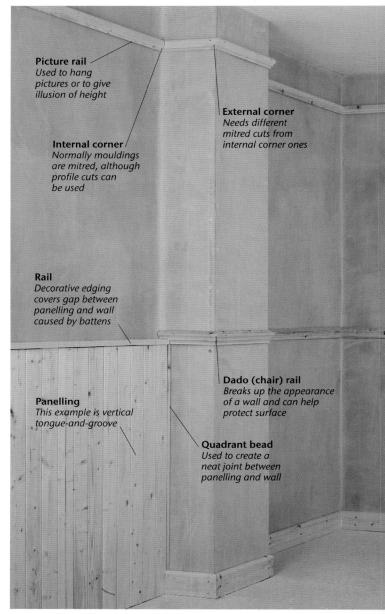

Picture rail
Used to hang pictures or to give illusion of height

External corner
Needs different mitred cuts from internal corner ones

Internal corner
Normally mouldings are mitred, although profile cuts can be used

Rail
Decorative edging covers gap between panelling and wall caused by battens

Dado (chair) rail
Breaks up the appearance of a wall and can help protect surface

Panelling
This example is vertical tongue-and-groove

Quadrant bead
Used to create a neat joint between panelling and wall

Examples of mouldings in a room
The room above shows a selection of mouldings in a typical room. The effect will vary according to whether they are painted or maintain a natural wood finish (see p.290–91).

Self-adhesive panels
Used on flush doors to create the look of a panel door, these can also be used on walls to imitate fielded panelling. Most have double-sided tape on the back.

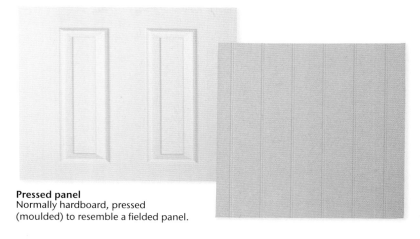

Pressed panel
Normally hardboard, pressed (moulded) to resemble a fielded panel.

Moisture-resistant MDF panelling
This has been routed (see p.66) to resemble tongue-and-groove panelling. Moisture resistance makes this panelling suitable for use in a kitchen or bathroom. Once painted, it performs well as a splashback, around baths or basins in a bathroom, for example.

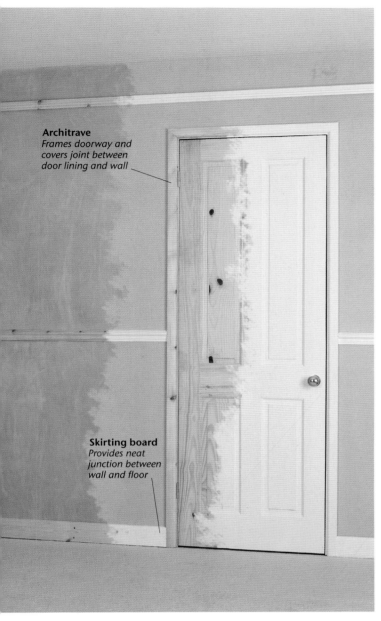

Architrave
Frames doorway and covers joint between door lining and wall

Skirting board
Provides neat junction between wall and floor

Radiator cover

This provides a decorative alternative to an exposed radiator. You can make your own, or buy a kit that can usually be adapted to fit most radiators. Covers are usually made of MDF. The grill may be metallic or wood fretwork.

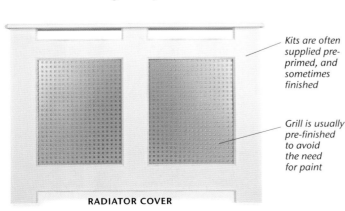

Kits are often supplied pre-primed, and sometimes finished

Grill is usually pre-finished to avoid the need for paint

RADIATOR COVER

DISGUISING FIXINGS

When fixing any type of moulding in place, you will probably want to hide screws or nails. If the moulding is to be painted, filler can be used to cover these holes. Stainable filler is also available for natural wood finishes. For pre-finished mouldings, or where expensive hardwoods have been used, the most professional finish is achieved by pelleting the holes. This involves filling the hole with a piece of wood that matches the moulding in appearance and is thus almost invisible. The technique is shown below; you will need a drill plug bit and the basic toolkit.

A

Use a plug bit to drill into an offcut of moulding, to get small pieces of dowel. Drill into the fixing holes to the same diameter as these dowels.

B

Once a fixing has been inserted, apply wood glue to a dowel, and insert it into the fixing hole.

C

Knock the dowel firmly into place with a hammer. Wipe away any excess adhesive.

D

When the glue has dried, use a chisel to knock off the end of the dowel so that it is flush with the surrounding wooden surface.

E

Use a block plane to smooth the cut end of the dowel.

F

The plugged hole will now be almost invisible. Repeat on all fixing holes across the surface.

TOOLS AND MATERIALS CHECKLISTS PP.218–23

Fitting an architrave (p.218)
Mitre saw, filler, filler knife

Fitting a decorative rail (p.219) Countersink drill bit or nail punch, mitre block, tenon saw, spirit level, grab adhesive*

Fitting skirting board (pp.220–21) Grab adhesive, masonry drill*, countersink drill bit*, mitre saw, jigsaw*, timber offcut*, spirit level*

Panelling a wall (p.222)
Timber battens, timber offcuts, rail, block plane, jemmy, quadrant or scotia*

Panelling around obstacles (p.223) Drill, mounting box, tenon saw, timber offcut

* = optional

FOR BASIC TOOLKIT
SEE PP.24–25

FITTING AN ARCHITRAVE

Before you start, cut three lengths of architrave – two for the uprights and one for the horizontal head section – to very roughly the length you need them. Cut them longer than they need to be, because the most accurate way to mark where to cut them is to hold roughly cut lengths in place and mark on them. Transferring measurements from lining to architrave is less accurate. The architrave's inner edge should be set back from the edge of the door lining by 5–10mm (⅕–⅖in); this is called the margin.

TOOLS AND MATERIALS SEE BASIC TOOLKIT AND P.217

1 ATTACHING THE FIRST UPRIGHT

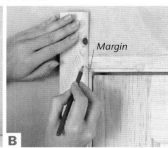

Margin

A Mark off the margin position around the edge of the lining. Join the marks at the corners to provide a right-angled guide line.

B On the left-hand side, align some architrave precisely with the margin. At the head, mark on it where it meets the right-angled margin mark.

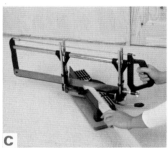

C Make a mitred cut, using the marked-off point to guide you in cutting at the correct place.

Attach securely but not permanently

D Reposition the architrave, with its inner corner at the apex of the margin's right angle. Loosely attach it with two or three nails.

2 CUTTING THE HEAD SECTION

A Make a mitred cut, in the same way, on the head section, to join with the section already fitted on the lining. Check that it fits.

B Hold the head section in position while marking off the cut for the other mitre on the right-hand end of the length. Cut the mitre.

3 CUTTING THE OTHER UPRIGHT

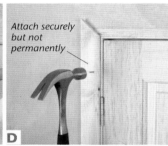

A Offer up the right-hand upright section of architrave, mark off in relation to the margin requirement, and cut this mitre.

B Fix the right-hand upright in place, securely but not permanently, so that small adjustments can be made to its positioning if necessary.

4 ATTACHING THE ARCHITRAVE

A Check that the head length of architrave fits, and nail it into position.

B Knock in all fixings firmly, and add more. Use three or four fixings on the head section and five or six for each upright.

C Use a nail punch to knock all fixings below the surface.

D To keep mitred corners tight, you will need fixings through both pieces. Prepare for this by drilling pilot holes.

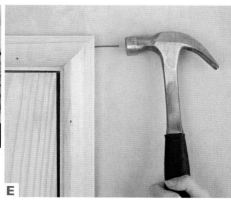

Knock a 25-mm (1-in) lost-head wire nail into each pilot hole on the mitred corners. It should run through the outer piece of architrave and into the head section, to hold the joint tightly. Then apply filler to fixing holes and sand smooth if necessary.

E

FITTING A DECORATIVE RAIL

The technique demonstrated here on a dado rail may be used to apply other decorative features such as picture rails. You may find it useful if someone else holds the rail steady while you draw guide lines. See pp.76–79 for fixings suitable for timber and masonry walls, and use a nail punch to knock fixings in below the rail's surface, giving the best possible finish. Make sure you do not fix into hidden cables or pipes below surface level. Use a detector to help check for their positions.

TOOLS AND MATERIALS SEE BASIC TOOLKIT AND P.217

1 FIXING THE RAIL

A

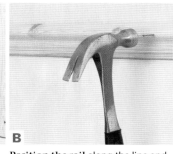

B

Draw a level guide line around the room at the height where you want the lower edge of the rail – often 1m (3ft 3in) from floor level.

Position the rail along the line and fix through its centre (into uprights of a stud wall; plugging as required in masonry). Knock nails right in.

2 MAKING MITRED CUTS FOR A CORNER

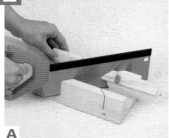

A

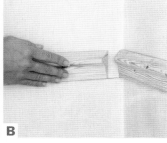

B

Use a mitre block and tenon saw to cut mitres for a corner.

Check that the mitred cuts fit neatly together in the corner before fixing the rails in place. The corner shown here is an internal one.

3 MEASURING AND CUTTING FOR A STAIRWELL

Mark where level bisects horizontal guide line

A

Original line is at base of dado rail

B

To determine where the rail must change direction, hold a spirit level upright where the skirting board meets the stairwell.

Hold a length of rail along the original guide line. Draw a line along the rail's top edge, reaching at least as far as the vertical mark.

Mark distance between rail and skirting

C

D

E

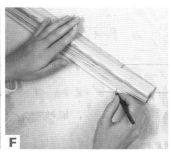

F

Higher up the staircase, make a mark the same height above the stair string as the original guide line is above the skirting board.

Join this mark to the one at the foot of the stairway to provide a guide line in the stairwell for the lower edge of the dado rail.

Position a length of rail on this guide line. Draw along its top edge, joining and intersecting with the horizontal line drawn in step 3B.

Now that clear guides are on the wall, position a length of rail and mark off on either edge to provide the correct angle for mitring the join.

G

Cut the stairwell rail at the marked angle. Then repeat the process with a horizontal piece of rail to mitre that length. Position the lengths, checking that they fit tightly together. Fix them to the wall. Use this technique each time a rail needs to change direction.

USING ADHESIVE

One way to make rails more secure is to use some grab adhesive in addition to the nails. If the wall surface is flat, you may even be able to use grab adhesive alone – provided you choose one that bonds quickly to the wall surface.

The drawback of using a quick-bonding adhesive is that your positioning must be fast and exact – repositioning the rail, even after a relatively short time, will not be possible.

On straightforward runs – between two architraves, for example – use butt joins between the end of the rail and the upright architrave, fixing the rail with adhesive. Mitred joins are best fixed with screws or nails, because they sometimes need slight adjustment to get a precise fit.

FITTING SKIRTING BOARD

Fitting skirting requires accurate measurement and precise joints, and fixing it securely and neatly can be difficult. The make-up of a wall defines the fixing method. Skirting may be joined with mitred cuts at internal and external corners; internal corners can also be done with profile cuts. Skirting may need cutting to keep it level despite an uneven floor, and this will involve scribing, a method of accurately marking and cutting a board to fit exactly the profile of the floor on which it is being positioned.

TOOLS AND MATERIALS SEE BASIC TOOLKIT AND P.217

FINDING FIXING POINTS

Before fixing skirting boards, establish whether the wall is timber, masonry, or lath-and-plaster (see pp.96–97). Use the relevant fixing method from those shown below. If you are attaching skirting to a stud wall, establish first where the studs are – you will need to secure the skirting at these points. If you are building a new stud wall (see pp.104–08) this is not a problem.

Vertical cracks in the plaster, or lines of nail heads, may indicate edges of plasterboard sheets – and, therefore, studs. Otherwise, use a stud detector, or simply pierce the plasterboard with a bradawl until you hit an upright. Once you have located one stud, look for others at (usually) 400-mm (1ft 4-in) or 600-mm (2-ft) intervals. Use a cable/pipe detector to avoid wires and services.

FIXING TO A MASONRY WALL

A

B

C

D

Apply grab adhesive to the back of the skirting board, and place in position. Use a masonry drill to make two pilot holes every 300mm (1ft).

Enlarge the openings of the holes with a countersink bit. This will allow the screw heads to sit below the wood's surface.

Insert masonry wall plugs into the holes. These provide support in the masonry for the screws.

Screw the boards to the wall. Fill the countersunk holes with filler, if necessary, and sand.

FIXING TO A TIMBER-STUD WALL

A

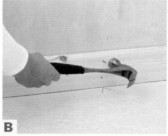

B

Apply some grab adhesive to the back of the skirting board, and place the board in position.

Fix the skirting board with two screws or lost-head nails at each stud. Uprights are usually 400mm (1ft 4in) or 600mm (2ft) apart.

FIXING TO A LATH-AND-PLASTER WALL

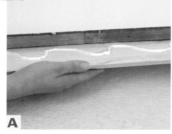

A

B

If possible, locate vertical studs and mark their positions. Apply grab adhesive to the back of the skirting board, and position the board.

Fix the skirting board to the studs at regular intervals with two screws or lost-head nails. If you cannot locate studs, fix at regular intervals.

MITRED CUTS

Mitring gives neat joints in a corner or between lengths on a straight run along a wall. A mitre block (see p.35) is an alternative to a power saw (see right) – but it is difficult to get accurate cuts, and most blocks will not hold the tallest boards.

Make sure you cut in the correct direction; mitring angles differ for internal and external corners.

MITRING FOR AN INTERNAL CORNER

The easiest way to make a mitred cut is with a power mitre saw. If the saw has the height, a board can be clamped upright and cut down through its height. In this instance (right), it is laid flat on the stage of a mitre saw. Larger boards are best cut this way. Tilt the blade and cut a 45-degree angle in the board.

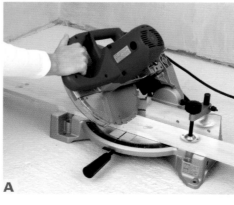

A

B

Slide into the corner

Repeat for the joining board, and fit the pieces together in the corner.

MITRING FOR AN EXTERNAL CORNER

A Cut mitres as before. Check for fit. Place one board. Apply wood glue to the cut end, position the other board, and wipe away excess glue.

B Drill pilot holes for two panel pins to fit through the mitred join and hold it together. Pin the corner.

MITRE-JOINING LENGTHS

 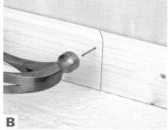

A Mitred joints are neater than butt-joined boards. Cut the ends at a 45-degree angle, checking that they will fit together when fixed.

B Glue the boards into place, and hammer in a panel pin to secure them. Fix the rest of the skirting as normal (see opposite).

CUTTING ORNATE SKIRTING

  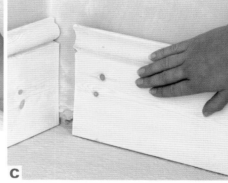

A Butt one piece of skirting against the wall and cut the other piece to fit exactly against the first.

B Using an offcut of skirting, draw around its profile on the board that needs cutting. This forms a guide line to cut along with a jigsaw.

C Having cut along the guide line (try a hand-held coping saw or a fret saw if the skirting is too ornate to cut with a jigsaw), butt the cut end against the first piece of skirting. It will exactly match the profile and give a tidy finish. Fix the skirting in place and continue fitting the skirting around the room.

SCRIBING AGAINST AN UNEVEN FLOOR

Undulations in a floor can leave unsightly gaps below a skirting board, which can let in draughts. It is always best to ensure that the top edge of the skirting is level, and to trim any necessary adjustments from the bottom edge. In some cases, a slight slope may be acceptable, as long as the joint with the floor is flush. Minor gaps at the bottom may be covered with carpeting, the edge of a laid wood floor, or a decorative moulding.

Cutting off a section from the base of a length of skirting may mean that neighbouring sections also require trimming, even if they sit flush with the floor, otherwise they may be taller. Therefore, cut all pieces to length and loosely position them all (as shown in step A, right) to find the right height for all boards.

SCRIBING SKIRTING

A Position skirting against the wall, and use a spirit level to check if it is level at the top and flush with the floor. If not, scribing is needed.

B Wedge the skirting so that it is completely level – check this with the spirit level. Use a temporary fixing to hold it if required.

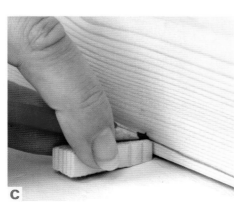  

C Cut a small piece of wood that is slightly taller than the biggest gap between the skirting and the floor. You can use this as a scribing block. Place a pencil on top of it, and slide the block and pencil across the floor surface, so that the pencil leaves a guide line on the skirting, matching the profile of the floor.

D Use a jigsaw to cut away the excess skirting board, following the pencil line carefully.

E Fix the length of skirting board in place. It should be flush with the floor and level along its length.

PANELLING A WALL

Tongue-and-groove panelling is attached to a battened frame. Vertical boards need horizontal battens, as shown here. For the battens needed in horizontal panelling, see dry lining on p.136. This example fits panels to dado rail height.

TOOLS AND MATERIALS
SEE BASIC TOOLKIT AND P.217

1 FIXING BATTEN FRAMEWORK

Fix horizontal battens around the perimeter of the area to be panelled. They should be at the floor and ceiling (or at top and bottom of the area to be panelled), and also at equidistant intervals between these extremes, ideally 400mm (1ft 4in) apart, taking care not to fix into cables or pipes.

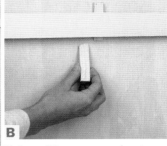

B If the wall is uneven, pack out battens as required to get them level, using wedges or offcuts of ply.

2 FIXING TONGUE-AND-GROOVE PANELLING

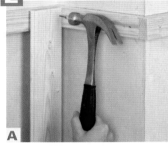

A Position the first length at one end of a wall. Fix it into the batten below with lost-head nails, placing nails at the edge nearest a wall.

B Using a spirit level, ensure that the first length is precisely vertical before proceeding any further.

C At a 45-degree angle, nail through the tongue side of the board into the batten below. Use a nail punch to knock the nail head in completely.

D Overlap the groove of the next board onto the tongue of the first.

E Use an offcut of board as a knocking block. Tap the board once or twice with a hammer to make a tight joint between the boards.

F Continue across the wall surface. Nails through the boards' tongues at each batten are all that is needed to secure the boards in place.

3 DEALING WITH CORNERS

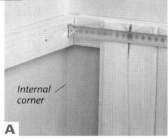

A Internal corner

A Eventually you will need to cut a board to fit the space into a corner. Measure the space and cut a board to slightly smaller than this.

Partial board

B Position the cut board, fixing its groove over the previous board's tongue. With the board a little short, you will have space to manoeuvre it.

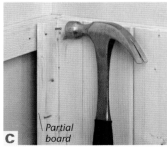

Partial board

C Finish the internal corner by butting the other piece of the cut board against the panelling. Then carry on across the wall as normal.

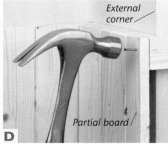

External corner

Partial board

D Deal with an external corner by cutting a board to fit. Fit the other cut piece on the other side of the corner, for a balanced appearance.

Partial board

E The corner will seem unsightly because the cut edge is visible. Neaten it by using a block plane to tidy the edge.

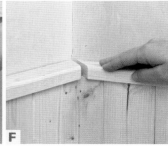

F When all panelling is in place, fix a rail along the top. This covers the gap caused by the battens between boards and wall. Mitre it in corners.

PANELLING AROUND OBSTACLES

Sometimes you need to cut a panel to fit around an item on the wall or to end a run. A wall may be uneven, so rather than measuring and cutting to fit a board against it, use the method shown below (called scribing) to get a neat fit.

TOOLS AND MATERIALS
SEE BASIC TOOLKIT AND P.217

WORKING SAFELY

Switch off the electricity supply at the consumer unit (see p.432) before removing the face plate from any fittings such as a socket or plateswitch. Pay attention to all safety advice for working with electricity, and check terminal connections before refixing a plateswitch and turning the electricity back on (for details, see pp.430–45).

CUTTING AROUND A SOCKET OR LIGHT SWITCH

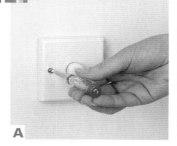

A Deal with fittings as you come to them. Remove the plateswitch, remembering that wires are still connected to it.

Remove mounting box from wall

B Remove the wires from the back of the plateswitch and tape the cores separately before taping the wire as a whole to protect it.

C Position battens around the perimeter of the hole, and fix them in place.

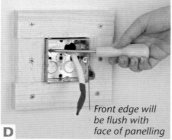

Front edge will be flush with face of panelling

D Feed the cable into a mounting box suitable for the kind of wall you have (see p.436). Secure the box in place.

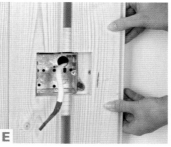

E Cut carefully measured sections out of the panelling to sit around the fitting. Position and secure panelling in the normal way.

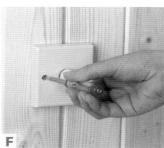

F Rewire the fitting, reposition the plateswitch, and screw it back on. Then switch the electricity on again.

FITTING A PANEL AGAINST A WALL

A Temporarily position a new board exactly on top of the last placed complete board.

B Cut a small section of the width of a board. Holding one end against the wall, run it down the wall, using a pencil at the other end to draw a line.

C

Fit the board with the aid of two chisels, as shown, or a pry bar (see p.37). Depending on the fit, you may need to trim slightly more from the cut edge of the board in order to manoeuvre it into position for a tight fit.

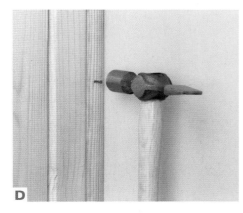

D Surface fix along the edge of the board. There is no tongue for secret nailing at an angle, as shown opposite, so you must fix through the face of the board into the batten below. Then neaten the join between the panelling and wall by pinning some quadrant or scotia in place, mitring any joins between lengths if required.

COPING WITH OTHER OBSTACLES

Doors and windows
Fix battens around the perimeters of all doors and windows, and attach boards to them. Panelling will sit higher off the wall than the door lining; cover the gap with a decorative moulding. The external corner formed at windows will also require a moulding – an external wooden angle bead is ideal.

Radiators
These must be temporarily removed while panelling is fitted. Rigid pipes may need to be moved away from the wall to align with the newly hung radiator (see pp.502–05).

Ceilings
On concrete ceilings, use battens; on wooden ones, fix panelling directly to the joists.

REPAIRING TONGUE-AND-GROOVE PANELLING

Boards interlock, making it difficult to repair a small area: releasing one damaged board would mean releasing all the boards. Instead, use this method to replace just the damaged board.

TOOLS AND MATERIALS

Drill, new board, drywall saw, chisel, workbench, claw hammer, nails, filler, sandpaper, paint or finish as required, paintbrush

FURTHER INFORMATION

■ Where the damaged board crosses battens on the wall, it may be easier to use a hammer and chisel to cut through the board.
■ If the board is very thick, it may be easier to remove the tongue with a saw.
■ If you want a natural-wood finish, consider using grab adhesive to fix the board in place rather than nails.

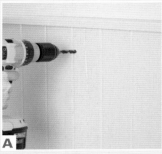

A

Drill a hole close to one edge of the damaged board, towards the top, and large enough to take the point of a drywall saw.

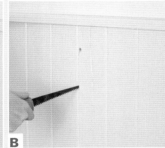

B

Insert a drywall saw into the hole and cut all the way down the joint between the boards.

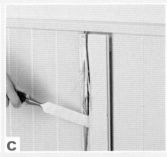

C

Use a chisel to lever out the damaged section of board.

D

Cut a new section of board to fit. Secure it in a workbench and use a hammer and chisel to remove the tongue so that you can position it.

E

Fix the new board in place, fixing through its face ("surface fixing") because there is no available tongue for angled secret fixing.

F

Fill the fixing holes, and sand when dry. Then decorate the board to match the surrounding surface.

REPLACING A DAMAGED SECTION OF SKIRTING BOARD

If a short run of skirting is damaged, replace it all; for longer runs replace only the damaged area. See pp.86–87 for reclamation possibilities.

TOOLS AND MATERIALS

Pry bar, wooden blocks, pencil, spirit level, mitre block, panel saw, nails, hammer, wood glue, grab adhesive, skirting, filler, sealant dispenser, paint, paintbrush

MATCHING OLD SKIRTING BOARD

■ For an entire room, a close match to that in the rest of the house will pass unnoticed because the two designs are not sitting side by side.
■ One way to get a match is to cut MDF to size and use a router cutter to create the profile (see pp.66–67).
■ Another option is to pin decorative mouldings to the top of timber (see opposite).

A

Pry the damaged section away from the wall. Place wooden blocks between the skirting and wall, either side of the damaged area.

B

Draw pencil guide lines vertically down the skirting board on either side of the damaged area, marking the section to be cut away.

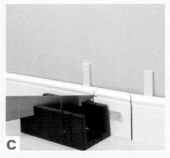

C

Using a mitre block and panel saw, carefully cut down each guide line, using short, accurate strokes. Cut at the angles shown here.

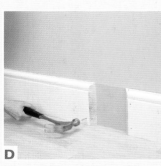

D

Remove the blocks from behind the skirting board and re-fix the existing skirting to the wall.

E

Measure and cut a new section for the gap. Apply wood glue to its mitred ends and grab adhesive across the back.

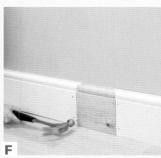

F

Position the board, allowing the glue and adhesive to adhere to the skirting board and wall. Knock in nails to strengthen the joints.

REVIVING POORLY DECORATED MOULDINGS

Where mouldings have been poorly decorated and/or paint buildup has left them in poor condition, simply sanding the area can help. You don't need to strip back all the previous layers of paint to achieve a marked change in appearance, as this example shows. This technique can be used on all kinds of mouldings. Paint buildup in the grooves of the profile often creates an unsightly effect. Filling these areas as shown here improves their appearance. Flexible caulk cannot be sanded when dry, so it must be completely smoothed while still wet.

TOOLS AND MATERIALS
Sanding block, vacuum cleaner, sealant dispenser, decorator's caulk, sponge, paint, paintbrush

A **Sand back the "flats"** on the moulding as smoothly as possible, and glance across the higher areas of the moulding with sandpaper.

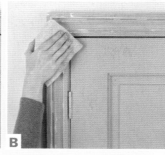

B **Use a vacuum** to remove any dust and debris, and then wipe down the area with a damp cloth.

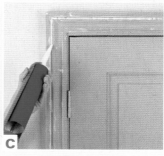

C **Using a sealant gun,** apply a bead of decorator's caulk along the moulding profile and groove details.

D **Smooth along the caulk** with a wetted finger.

E **Carefully remove** any excess with a clean, damp sponge. Smooth the caulk again with a wetted finger.

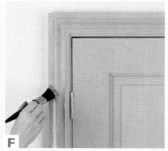

F **Once the caulk** is dry, repaint the moulding to achieve a much-improved surface.

REPAIRING AN EXTERNAL MITRE

External mitres can sometimes crack open and become unsightly. In most cases, this is because the joint was not properly glued and fixed in place when it was fitted.

TOOLS AND MATERIALS
Drill, hammer, wood glue, panel pins or thin screws, paint or finish as required, paintbrush

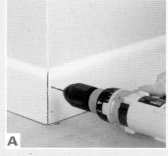

A **Drill pilot holes through** the top and bottom of the joint, making sure that you drill into both mitred edges of the corner.

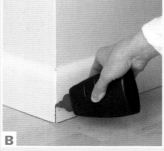

B **Apply some wood** glue to the joint, and wipe away any excess.

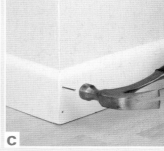

C **Use panel pins** through the pilot holes to fix the mitre in position or, for larger skirting boards or mouldings, use thin-gauge screws.

USING DECORATIVE MOULDING TO ENHANCE A PLAIN SKIRTING BOARD

Improve plain skirting with wooden mouldings. You can use this technique to match a discontinued design.

TOOLS AND MATERIALS
Pin hammer, moulding, panel pins or lost-head wire nails, filler, spatula, sandpaper, paint, paintbrush

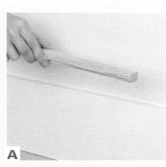

A **Cut the moulding** to size and position it on the top edge of the skirting. Joints may be mitred or butt-joined (as in this sequence).

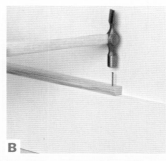

B **Fix the moulding** in place with panel pins or, for more substantial mouldings, lost-head wire nails.

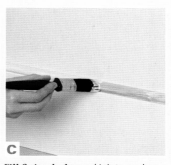

C **Fill fixing holes** and joints, and sand before painting.

Structural problems

IN THIS SECTION ALL TYPES OF STRUCTURAL PROBLEMS – THOSE CAUSED BY DAMP, ROT, AND INFESTATION OF VARYING KINDS – ARE EXAMINED IN DETAIL. IN MOST CASES, RELATIVELY STRAIGHTFORWARD REMEDIES ARE POSSIBLE. HOWEVER, INITIALLY IT IS A GOOD IDEA TO IDENTIFY WHERE PROBLEMS ARE LIKELY TO OCCUR AND HOW YOU MAY RECOGNIZE THEM.

IDENTIFYING THE PROBLEM

Structural problems can be hard to recognize because they often remain hidden in the fabric of a house. Even if there is an obvious symptom, such as a crack in a wall, initially it can look the same whether it is due to harmless settlement or dangerous subsidence. Similarly, damp caused by blocked guttering – which is easily remedied – may look like damp caused by a leaking roof. With structural problems, if you are not sure of the cause, or if a problem persists after you have attempted to fix it, then seek advice. A professional will be able to make a correct diagnosis, inform you of the right course of action, and, if necessary, carry out work with the guarantee required by some mortgage lenders.

TYPES OF ROT

There are two types of rot: wet and dry. Wet rot is most common in the wood of window sills and door bases that have been exposed to damp conditions. Dry rot starts in damp wood, usually in poorly ventilated areas, but can cause greater damage by spreading through a property, moving across both wooden and plaster surfaces.

Early treatment of both types of rot is essential. In both cases, the original cause of dampness must be addressed, and the infected areas removed, but with dry rot you must also cut back into the sound material, to make sure that all traces are removed. Extensive dry rot should be treated by a certified firm that offers a guarantee of their work.

Problems with rot are generally the result of poor maintenance or poor ventilation. Therefore it is best to improve both of these aspects of your home to prevent the presence of rot in the first place.

Damp window reveals
May be caused by condensation, or by penetrating damp due to poor seals at edges or flawed installation.

Damp floor
Generally a result of condensation, a damp covering suggests that ventilation needs improving. If the structure itself is damp, with visible patches on a concrete floor or wooden floorboards, rising damp may be the cause.

Large cracks in walls (internal or external) or ceilings
May be due to settlement or subsidence, and therefore require investigation. Cracks are commonly found along wall-ceiling junctions. Central cracks may be due to poorly fixed plasterboard. Cracks in old ceilings may be caused by sagging joists, or the plaster itself beginning to fall away from the ceiling structure.

Damp lower wall
When soil or debris piles up against a wall above the damp-proof course (DPC), water retained by the debris may gradually penetrate the wall surface and create a damp problem.

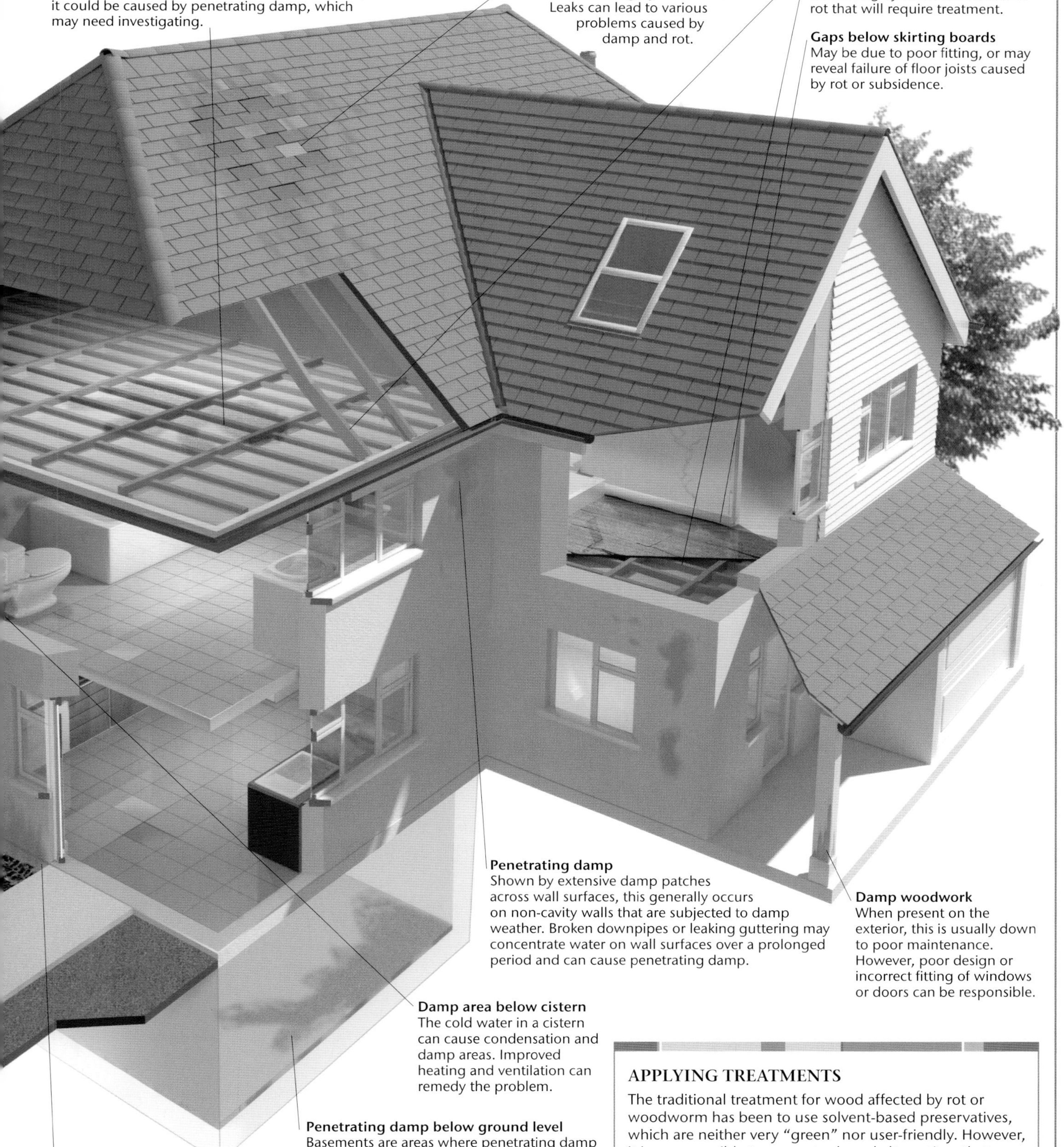

Damp ceiling areas
Often caused by a leaking pipe or roof. However, when the damp patch is close to an exterior wall, it could be caused by penetrating damp, which may need investigating.

Leaking roof
A sound roof is essential to the structural integrity of a house. Leaks can lead to various problems caused by damp and rot.

Sagging rafters and joists
These may be due to age, or weakening by insect infestation or rot that will require treatment.

Gaps below skirting boards
May be due to poor fitting, or may reveal failure of floor joists caused by rot or subsidence.

Penetrating damp
Shown by extensive damp patches across wall surfaces, this generally occurs on non-cavity walls that are subjected to damp weather. Broken downpipes or leaking guttering may concentrate water on wall surfaces over a prolonged period and can cause penetrating damp.

Damp woodwork
When present on the exterior, this is usually down to poor maintenance. However, poor design or incorrect fitting of windows or doors can be responsible.

Damp area below cistern
The cold water in a cistern can cause condensation and damp areas. Improved heating and ventilation can remedy the problem.

Penetrating damp below ground level
Basements are areas where penetrating damp is a common problem. Because it is below the damp-proof course level, some form of lining will be required. A damp smell, patches over large wall areas, and flaking paint on wall surfaces all tend to reveal the problem clearly.

Damaged DPC
An old DPC may decay over time, enabling damp to rise above it and cause problems with the wall structure.

APPLYING TREATMENTS

The traditional treatment for wood affected by rot or woodworm has been to use solvent-based preservatives, which are neither very "green" nor user-friendly. However, it is now possible to use water-based alternatives that are effective and more eco-friendly. These boron-based products are applied by spray, brush, or cartridge depending on the particular treatment required.

TACKLING DAMP

The term "damp" strikes fear into most homeowners. Left untreated, a small, easily fixed problem can become much larger and considerably more expensive to repair. The presence of damp is usually signalled by obvious visual clues such as discolouration of surfaces, mould, peeling paper, or crystallized salts on plaster. Surfaces may be damp to the touch and the smell of a damp room is always obvious on entry. There are three main types of damp – condensation, penetrating damp, and rising damp. The first two are dealt with here; for rising damp, see p.230.

for rising damp, see p.230.

CONSIDERATIONS

■ Check building regulations before attempting to convert a basement into a living space.
■ Seek professional advice if you find any signs of rot.
■ Never ignore a persistent damp smell.
■ DIY work on rot may not be accepted by mortgage lenders.
■ Get advice if damp is not caused by an obvious and simple maintenance issue; do not tank (see below) without consulting a professional.

CONDENSATION

Mould in bathrooms and kitchens, and sometimes in other rooms, is often a result of condensation. If there is a lot of moisture in the air, droplets will form on cold windows, cold water pipes, and cold external walls. Once ventilation has been improved, remove the mould stains with a fungicide or bleach solution. If tile grout has been permanently stained you may need to remove and replace it (see p.320).

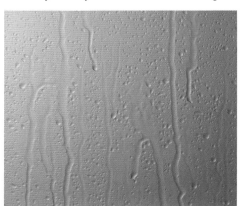

Condensation
Allowing condensation to persist in your home can lead to structural problems. Simply opening windows regularly to aerate your home can eliminate the problem.

PENETRATING DAMP

This kind of damp, which penetrates the house from the outside, can show itself anywhere on an internal wall after wet weather. This may take a long time to dry out and causes staining and damage to surfaces. If there is a single patch of damp, it can often be traced to an easily fixed problem. Leaking guttering (see p.213) can often cause penetrating damp, saturating a wall in a way that it is not designed to withstand. Soil piled up against a wall is another cause.

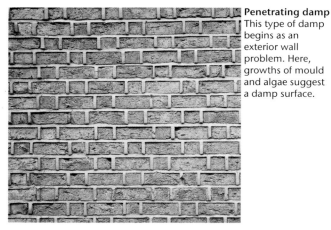

Penetrating damp
This type of damp begins as an exterior wall problem. Here, growths of mould and algae suggest a damp surface.

TREATING PENETRATING DAMP

One of the simplest solutions to penetrating damp caused by structural problems is known as "tanking". This technique involves applying a membrane to the internal wall or floor surface to hold back the damp. Tanking is most common in cellars and basements because these are the areas most prone to penetrating damp. It is often the only option in these areas because they are inaccessible from the exterior. These factors make it impossible to use other solutions, such as injecting damp-proofing chemicals (see p.230) or coating the external surface to keep moisture out. The following are two effective forms of tanking.

Applying an epoxy damp-proof membrane is the simplest solution, although particularly damp environments (e.g. those requiring pumps to remove moisture) may need a polypropylene membrane.

Applying an epoxy damp-proof membrane

Two-part epoxy coatings are now available for coating wall and floor surfaces in cellars and basements. They offer a quick and effective waterproofing measure and can be decorated over. They are easy to apply (see opposite above), provided you follow the manufacturer's guidelines. Although epoxy coating can be applied to damp surfaces, any standing water should be removed. Rather than plastering directly onto the membrane, it is possible to dab out and plasterboard, as shown on p.136.

Fitting a polypropylene membrane

An alternative to epoxy coatings is to use a polypropylene membrane (see opposite below). Although it holds back water, it may be necessary to install channels and pumping mechanisms to collect and remove water from behind the membrane. Seek professional advice on whether this is required. Measure the surface area you need to cover and make sure you buy enough membrane, clips, and tape for your needs. When finished, plaster directly onto the membrane or dab out as shown on p.136.

TOOLS AND MATERIALS CHECKLIST PP.229

Applying an epoxy damp-proof membrane
Brush, power stirrer, paintbrush, sand, protective equipment

Fitting a polypropylene membrane Mallet, clips, double-sided tape, drill, plastering trowel

FOR BASIC TOOLKIT SEE PP.24–25

APPLYING AN EPOXY DAMP-PROOF MEMBRANE

Before you start, follow any safety guidelines specified by the manufacturer, and wear all recommended safety items. Brush the wall and wash off any oil or grease. Though the coating can be applied to damp surfaces, the drier the wall, the better the finish will be. On floor surfaces, be sure to remove any standing water.

A

B

Pour one part of the coating into the other. Epoxy systems require two parts to be mixed before use.

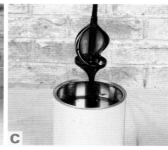

C

Mix together, ideally with a power stirrer, following all guidelines for safe use (see p.68).

D

Apply the first coat, using horizontal strokes across the surface. Use a brush or roller, making sure that the membrane is continuous.

E

When the first coat is dry, apply the second coat wth vertical strokes at right angles to the first. Again, make sure of continuous coverage.

F

The wall can be decorated once the coating is dry. Alternatively, if you need to render and plaster the surface, throw sand onto the coating while it is still wet. This will provide a good key for the render.

FITTING A POLYPROPYLENE MEMBRANE

Using a craft knife, cut the membrane roll into lengths equal to that of the floor-to-ceiling height. You will need a helper to hold the membrane in position while you fix it in place.

A

B

Drill pilot holes at 300-mm (1-ft) intervals through the membrane and into the wall.

C

Hammer clips into the pilot holes, pinning the sheet to the wall.

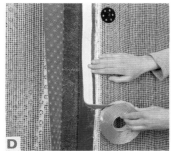

D

When the first sheet is in place, secure the second so that the two overlap. Stick double-sided tape to the edge of the first sheet.

E

Starting at the top, peel the backing off the tape, pressing the second sheet onto the first.

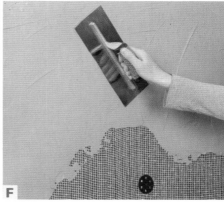

F

When the wall is covered, plaster over the membrane using the normal plastering method (see pp.134–35). Alternatively, if approved by your membrane manufacturer, it may be possible to dry line over the surface.

RISING DAMP

Rising damp enters the house from the ground and is generally caused by the damp-proof course or damp-proof membrane failing. If a floor is damaged by rising damp, you will need to lay a new one that includes a damp-proof membrane (see pp.178–79). If the problem is in the walls, you will need to install a new damp-proof course. This is best achieved using a chemical-injection system; these come in both pressurized and non-pressurized varieties.

NON-PRESSURIZED INJECTION

This system is the most straightforward DIY option and it requires no heavy-duty machinery. The manufacturer will specify how to carry out the work according to wall type and depth, but the basic principle is to drill holes in a mortar course and inject a waterproof chemical into them. This is usually carried out from the exterior. The chemical acts by following the moisture along the mortar lines. Most manufacturers recommend drilling injection holes every 120mm (4in). This roughly corresponds on a brick course to once every half brick.

PRESSURIZED INJECTION

This technique is as effective as the non-pressurized system, but requires more machinery and skill. Normally, holes are drilled into the bricks or blocks themselves from both sides of the wall. A special lance is then pushed into the holes and the waterproofing chemical is injected under pressure. The chemical then soaks into the wall and creates an impervious layer. The chemicals used in this technique are often more toxic than those used in the non-pressurized method, so be sure to use any recommended protection and to handle the materials with care. Also, when hiring machinery, adhere to any guidelines laid down by the manufacturer.

TOOLS AND MATERIALS CHECKLIST

Non-pressurized injection of DPC Sealant dispenser, sealant, protective clothing, drill, pointing trowel

Dealing with the internal wall surface Bolster chisel,

club hammer, brush, PVA, waterproofer and render, plaster, plastering trowel

FOR BASIC TOOLKIT SEE PP.24–25

NON-PRESSURIZED INJECTION OF DPC

Most non-pressurized systems simply require a heavy-duty drill to make the holes and a sealant dispenser with which to inject the chemicals. As manufacturers specify, the system need only be used on the outer side of the wall; this prevents any chemical smells being noticeable on the inside. Wear protective gloves and any other equipment specified by the system you are using.

Use a power drill to drill holes at the intervals and to the depth specified by the manufacturer.

Load the chemical cartridge into the sealant dispenser and pierce the end, ready for use (see pp.80–81).

Squeeze the dispenser trigger to fill a drilled hole with chemical. Fill to within 10mm (⅜in) of the wall surface.

Finish the end of each hole with a dab of mortar (see pp.70–71 for mixing).

DEALING WITH THE INTERNAL WALL SURFACE

Even though the injection of a damp-proof course should prevent the passage of further moisture up through the wall, it is normally the case that the interior plaster layer has been damaged by the damp action and needs to be replaced. The effects of rising damp normally do not proceed 1m (3ft 4in) above ground level, and therefore the repair job needn't go much higher than this.

Hack off the damaged plaster with a bolster chisel and club hammer. Hack off back to the masonry to a height of 1.2 m (4ft).

Dust off the wall surface, and apply a coat of dilute PVA (3:1 water to PVA).

Apply a waterproof render to the wall surface, rebating its edge slightly below that of the existing plaster (see pp.132–33).

Once dried, apply finishing plaster, feathering the join with the existing plaster (see pp.134–35).

Subsidence is the movement of land around or beneath a building, whereas settlement is the movement of the building itself. The latter occurs as a building adjusts to its foundations and to that extent it is a normal part of a building's early life. However, what appear to be settlement cracks can often be a result of poor building practice, so a thorough investigation is always necessary. Subsidence is more serious as shifts in the land can cause damage to foundations.

CAUSES OF SUBSIDENCE

Various factors contribute to subsidence. Clay expands and contracts, depending on its water content, and this can cause ground shifts large enough to affect a building's foundations. Large trees are also a problem as they suck up vast quantities of water, which can dry out the surrounding land and affect its structure. Their roots can also grow into foundations and destabilize them. Although cutting trees down is sometimes the solution, removing them can also make subsidence worse. A possible solution is to include root barriers below ground to keep the roots away from the foundations. Leaking drains and water pipes can also be responsible for subsidence, so it is vital to deal with these immediately.

Deep roots
A tree's roots tend to be as deep as its branches are high. For this reason, trees can be a major cause of subsidence. One solution is to sink barriers underground to divert the roots away from your home.

MONITORING CRACKS

It is possible to monitor the movement of a crack on a wall, floor, or ceiling surface by using a crack gauge. Proprietary designs for these vary, but each contains a pair of plates that are aligned on the crack. One plate contains a calibrated scale, while the other contains vertical and horizontal guide lines. Any movement in the crack is shown by the guide lines on one plate moving in relation to the calibrations on the other. The example below shows how to monitor a single crack in a wall surface; once the gauge is in place you can measure exact shifts accurately over specific periods of time.

▌▌ USING A CRACK GAUGE

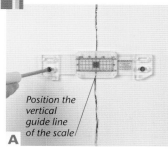

Position the vertical guide line of the scale

A

Position the gauge over the crack with both plates aligned at zero. Screw each side securely into the wall, but not tightly at this stage.

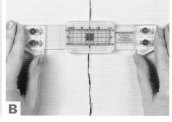

B

Move the detection scale to sit precisely vertical over the crack.

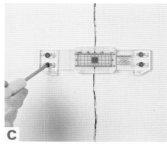

C

Tighten the screws on either side of the gauge.

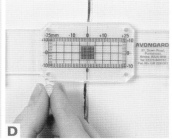

D

Remove the lugs from the detection scale to disconnect the plates. Any movement will now move the guide lines from zero.

SUBSIDENCE SOLUTIONS

Prevention is better than cure, so always get underground service leaks repaired as soon as they are identified. Also, be sure to assess the potential problem of tree and root growth next to your home and seek advice if you think there is cause for concern. If subsidence occurs and cannot be controlled, underpinning may be the only solution. This involves reinforcing the foundations with concrete, an expensive, specialist's job that should only be undertaken if absolutely necessary. It may be the case that only parts of the house need underpinning; for this reason costs for repair can vary widely depending on the extent of the problem. In all cases, if you have concerns about cracks in your home, especially if they appear suddenly, seek professional advice on what to do.

INFESTATION

Infestation by insects or animals can be little more than a harmless nuisance, or it can have serious consequences for house structure. It is therefore important to be aware of the tell-tale signs of infestation, how to recognize the particular animal or its traces, and how effectively to treat and rid yourself of the problem. The table opposite lists the most common pests and the dangers they may pose to house structure.

HANDLING POISONS

Many of the chemicals used in dealing with infestation are toxic or poisonous. For this reason, adhere strictly to manufacturers' guidelines. Make sure that all such products are stored out of the reach of children (preferably in a locked cupboard). Similarly, make sure that children cannot come into contact with poisons once they have been deployed around the house.

INSECTS AND ANIMALS

With all insect and animal infestations, the general rule is that if you find one (or evidence of one), there are likely to be more. Early identification is key to dealing with the problem before it can escalate into a far less manageable situation. Fortunately, most problems can be brought under control without professional help.

WOODWORM

A group of wood-boring beetles, commonly known as woodworm, can cause serious structural problems. Obvious signs are small flight holes in timber; dust around the holes confirms that the worm is active. Immediate treatment is essential.

Furniture beetle
This small brown beetle is generally found during the summer months. It is usually about 3–5mm ($\frac{1}{10}$–$\frac{1}{5}$in) in length.

Deathwatch beetle
This grey-brown beetle prefers old hardwoods. Up to 8mm ($\frac{3}{10}$in) long, it lays its larvae in wood; years later the larvae emerge as beetles.

House longhorn beetle
This is less common than the two above, but is equally destructive. It can be up to 20mm ($\frac{4}{5}$in) long.

Weevil
This has an elongated snout which it uses to bore into the wood. Weevils are found in a range of colours and sizes.

IDENTIFICATION

There are various ways of identifying which pests have entered your home. Some distinctive signs of common pests are shown below.

BLUEBOTTLE FLY MAGGOTS

Flies
Apart from the flies themselves, maggots are the most obvious sign of fly infestation. They may be found in decaying food or in any rotting organic matter.

WASP ENTERING NEST

Wasps
A wasp nest is the obvious source of a wasp problem in your home. It may be found in the open (e.g. in a loft space), or hidden in a cavity wall.

BEE NEST

Bees
Some bees live in nests (as shown here), while others are solitary and live alone. They tend to nest in enclosed spaces.

ROT IN WOOD

Woodlice
The presence of woodlice suggests a rot problem; they tend to live in damp areas where there is wood decay.

MOUSE

Rodents
Frayed wires, gnawed woodwork, holes in woodwork, nests in loft insulation, and rodent droppings all signify a rat or mouse infestation. Rodents cause minor structural damage, but gnawed electrical cables can cause considerable trouble.

CROW'S NEST IN WALL

Birds
Nests can be found in cracks and crevices in masonry, as well as in loft spaces, or attached to downpipes and soffits (see p.197). Bear in mind that many birds are protected, so tampering with nests and eggs can be illegal. It is best to discourage nesting before it occurs (see opposite).

Insect and animal pest	Problem	Solution
FLY	Poor hygiene can cause fly infestations. They pose no structural problems, but their body fluids can stain decorated surfaces. They also pose a general health hazard by spreading bacteria.	Keep food covered; promptly dispose of rubbish; keep dustbins away from windows; use insecticides
SILVERFISH	Silverfish can indicate a damp problem. They are nocturnal and enter the house looking for food and moisture. Among other things, they feed on paper and adhesive, and so can damage wall coverings.	Treat damp (see pp.228–30) and use insecticide on infested areas
BEE	As well as loft spaces, bees tend to nest in inaccessible areas such as wall cavities. They can enlarge holes in mortar and burrow into wall structures to gain access to a cavity. Some repointing may be necessary.	Insecticide can be injected into nests; large nests should be removed professionally
WASP	Wasps commonly nest in loft spaces. If situated above a ceiling, a nest can drip an unpleasant secretion into the plasterboard, breaking it down and staining the ceiling. Sections of plasterboard may need to be removed and replaced.	Inject special insecticide into the nest, or have the nest removed professionally
COCKROACH	Cockroaches appear when hygiene is a problem. This may be due to blocked drains, food debris on surfaces, or lack of cleaning in cupboard areas.	Poisons are available, but professional help may be necessary
ANTS	Ants are mainly attracted by food debris on work surfaces and on floors. The nest can normally be traced by following the line of an ant column.	Pour boiling water into the nest, then apply insecticide. Insecticide lacquer can be applied to thresholds
WOODLOUSE	Woodlice feed on damp wood, suggesting a damp problem. They also destroy plants, both indoors and out.	Treat damp (see pp.228–30) and use insecticide on plants and thresholds
EARWIG	Earwigs are easily recognizable by the pincers on their abdomen. Though harmless, they are scavengers and eat kitchen waste and plants.	Cut back vegetation from doorways and windows. Use insecticide spray or vapour strips
MOTH	Moths tend to feed on natural fibres, damaging clothing, carpets, and upholstery.	Clean stored clothes, vacuum all cracks and crevices, and use insecticide or mothballs
BAT	Bats are likely to be found in loft spaces or in basements that have external access. They pose no structural problems.	Bats are a protected species. Contact a professional to have them removed
RAT	Rodents, especially rats, are disease carriers and should be kept well away from the home. Rats and mice chew all manner of items, including wires, woodwork, plastic, and even metal pipes; damage to all of these can cause serious problems.	Keep food covered; promptly dispose of rubbish; keep dustbins away from windows; use traps and poisons
SQUIRREL	Squirrels tend to live in loft spaces, where they can chew pipework, cabling, and insulation.	Physical barriers are the best deterrent; various vent meshes and fillers are available
BIRD	Birds can nest in the eaves of a house or in loft spaces. The damage they cause is limited, but in large numbers, droppings can stain painted and masonry surfaces.	Like squirrels, birds are best discouraged with physical barriers

KITCHENS AND BATHROOMS

KITCHENS

BATHROOMS

Kitchens

ONE OF THE MAIN FOCAL POINTS OF A HOUSE, A KITCHEN REQUIRES CAREFUL PLANNING IF IT IS TO BE EASY TO USE AND ATTRACTIVE TO LOOK AT. MOST MODERN KITCHENS FEATURE FITTED UNITS, AND FITTED KITCHENS ARE THE MAIN FOCUS OF THIS SECTION. REMEMBER THAT FITTING A NEW KITCHEN MAY INVOLVE STRUCTURAL, PLUMBING, AND ELECTRICAL WORK COVERED IN OTHER SECTIONS OF THIS BOOK.

FITTED KITCHENS

Fitted kitchens are designed to make the best use of all available space. Attached units combine ample storage space and ease of use with a contemporary finish. Most manufacturers produce standard carcass units fitted with different styles of doors, draw fronts, worktops, sinks, and appliances.

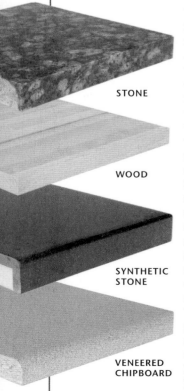

STONE

WOOD

SYNTHETIC STONE

VENEERED CHIPBOARD

WORKTOPS

Standard worktops are manufactured in lengths of 2m (6ft 6in), 3m (10ft), and 4m (13ft), and in thicknesses varying from 20–40mm (1–2in). Choose a worktop wider than you need because you will probably waste some of the width during the fitting process (see p.244–45). A worktop is commonly manufactured from solid wood or stone, veneered chipboard, and stone-effect materials. Solid wood and veneered worktops, and some stone-effect types, are sold as standard sizes and can be fitted on site. Worktops made of solid stone, such as marble or granite, are usually supplied and fitted by specialist manufacturers, who make a template of your requirement, cut the worktop offsite, and then deliver and fit it. Worktops are also a frequent object for reclamation (see pp.86–87). A worktop can be tiled. When tiling a worktop, use moisture-resistant plywood or MDF as a base. It is usual to fit walls behind the worktop with splashbacks of tiles, stainless steel, or glass.

KITCHEN UNITS

Fitted kitchens are made up of wall units and base units that house cupboards, drawers, and appliances. Units are supplied ready-made or flatpacked – the latter type require assembly before fitting. Most fitted kitchens can be viewed already assembled in a showroom. The price usually depends on the material and the thickness of the carcass members and panels. As a rule, the more substantial a unit is, the more expensive it will be.

Base unit
Most manufacturers produce these in standard widths and heights. Their depth is usually 500–600mm, (1ft 8in–2ft), although some are shallower to accommodate services.

Wall unit
These are available in standard widths that match base units, but they are typically only up to 720mm (2ft 4in) high and 300mm (1ft) deep.

FIXING PACK ACCESSORIES

Most manufacturers will supply a pack of accessories for each unit, some or all of which will be required, depending on how the unit is to be used. A selection of the most common fixing pack accessories is shown here.

Drawer runner
May be fitted on drawers and units when supplied.

Cam and cam stud
Two-part fixings for assembly of some flatpack units.

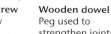

Connection screw
Two-part screw that joins units.

Wooden dowel
Peg used to strengthen joints.

Hinge
Kitchens use easy-fit hinges and usually pre-drilled fixing positions.

Jointing plate
Metal plate used to strengthen joins between units or sections of worktop.

Damper
Small pad fitted to protect surfaces when doors or drawers are closed.

Wall unit mounting plate
Shaped bracket for hanging units on walls.

Worktop fixing bracket
Attaches a worktop to base units.

Angle brace
Often used to secure units to a wall surface.

Cover cap
Decorative cap for screws and other fixing heads.

Plinth vent
Provides airflow to appliances.

Unit leg
Adjustable leg used to help support base units.

SINKS AND APPLIANCES

Freestanding kitchen appliances – fridges, washing machines, dishwashers, and cookers – are normally just under 500mm (1ft 8in) or 600mm (2ft) wide and around 820–880mm (2ft 8in–2ft 11in) in height and so should fit into standard kitchens without problems. Integral appliances are hidden behind doors that match the base units, with hobs and sinks mounted into the worktop. As well as standard sizes, many manufacturers produce both extra-large appliances for large families, and slimline models for small kitchens. Ideas and innovations are always coming on to the market, so take time to select appliances that suit your needs best.

Chimney

Hood

Extractor unit
Housed in units or the more decorative design of a hood and chimney, extractor fans either filter then re-circulate air or require you to fit ducting through an exterior wall.

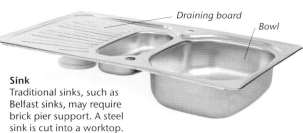

Draining board

Bowl

Sink
Traditional sinks, such as Belfast sinks, may require brick pier support. A steel sink is cut into a worktop.

Hob
These come in gas (shown here) and electric versions. Gas hobs are generally sunk into a worktop. Electric hobs can have sealed plates or ceramic tops.

Oven
An oven may be housed in a special unit that comes as part of a fitted kitchen. Fixing kits will be supplied. Cookers with an oven and hob combined slide between units.

FINISHING TOUCHES

The carcass structure of units is ultimately hidden by door fronts, drawer fronts, and a number of other decorative items. If you are happy with your kitchen's current layout but want a new look, changing the finish can be a cheap and very effective option. Finishing touches are supplied in styles to suit many different tastes.

Decorative trims
Plinths are fitted between the floor and the underside of base units. They may have a vinyl strip fitted on the under edge to stop moisture penetrating the edge when the floor is cleaned. A pelmet tidies up the bottom edge of wall units and a cornice runs along the top edge of wall units.

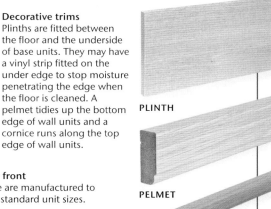

PLINTH

PELMET

CORNICE

Door front
These are manufactured to fit all standard unit sizes.

Drawer front
Made to fit standard base unit drawers. Some act as "dummy" drawer fronts.

Handles and knobs
For use on door and drawer fronts. Threaded bolts and screws secure them in position.

Planning a new kitchen requires considerable time and thought. It can be complicated fitting all the components and supplies together and, because it is an expensive investment, mistakes can be costly. An existing kitchen layout is a good starting point. If it works, then you can just update the design, often simply by changing doors and drawers rather than fitting a complete new kitchen. However, if you wish to incorporate some new appliances or additional storage, or feel the space is currently utilized poorly, you will need to design a new layout.

PLANNING YOUR KITCHEN LAYOUT

Planning a kitchen is a fairly complex task because of the many different factors that need to be considered. It is also an area in which strict budgeting is necessary as much of the cost of a kitchen is not in the units, but in the time and cost of installation. This will also depend on how much you wish to tackle yourself.

Appliances

■ Decide what appliances you are going to have in the kitchen. A kitchen should contain a hob and oven, a fridge, and a sink. Other options include a microwave, a dishwasher, a washing machine, a separate freezer, or a combined fridge-freezer. Of course, not all of these have to be in the kitchen – garages and utility rooms can often house appliances.

■ Most food preparation in the kitchen is related to the cooker, the sink, and the fridge. Generally a triangular layout of the three essentials is considered ideal — access is straightforward, and there is room for preparation or storage beside each area (see right).

■ It is best not to position your fridge next to your cooker as the fridge will have to work harder because of the warm air around it when the cooker is on.

■ If you want an island unit in your design, it is best if it does not block your route between sink, fridge, and cooker. An electrical supply for an island unit can be run underfloor easily, especially if you are fitting a new floor anyway. However, plumbing for an island unit is more difficult because the gradient of the waste pipes needs to be accommodated beneath the floor, and this is often impractical in many cases.

Storage

■ Storage for food, utensils, and cleaning products is useful in a kitchen. The greater the number of units, the more crowded a kitchen will feel, but too little storage space may be frustrating, so a compromise will usually need to be sought.

Worktops

■ Worktops are essential for both food preparation and to accommodate electrical appliances such as kettles, coffee makers, and freestanding microwaves.

■ Worktops can also provide an eating space, in the form of a breakfast bar, for example. The underside can be left open, or peninsular units can be fitted below. In the latter, a wide section of worktop provides a large overhang.

USING YOUR SUPPLIER

Once you have formulated some ideas about what design and style you are looking for, the next step is to speak to your supplier. Take accurate measurements of the room. Include existing alcoves, room height and width, and heights and widths of windows and window sills. Your supplier will produce a computer-generated design to give you a good idea of what your kitchen will look like.

Some manufacturers have kitchens in stock, but with others, orders may take weeks or even months to come through. Bear this in mind in overall planning when considering any necessary structural change requirements and re-routing of services. Coordinating the delivery of materials is crucial to your project running smoothly, so plan well ahead and confirm delivery dates.

TYPICAL KITCHEN LAYOUTS

In smaller kitchens, the size and shape of the room will often dictate the layout. In larger rooms there are more options to consider. Typical kitchen unit layouts are single run, L-shaped, or U-shaped, and may include island units, breakfast bars, and dining areas. Most kitchens are a variation on one of these examples. Typical layouts are shown below with "work triangles" indicating the possible positioning of appliances.

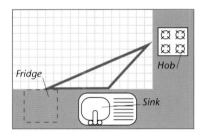

L-shaped layout
This layout has units along all or part of two adjoining walls. In a larger kitchen this may allow room for a dining area in the kitchen. This layout provides ample storage space and floor space and is therefore ideal for a busy family life.

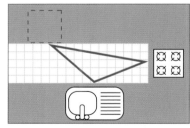

U-shaped layout
Here units cover three walls, and in a larger room one length of the U may be used as a breakfast bar. In a small kitchen, this layout provides maximum storage and appliance capacity, but standing room is limited. It is always best to keep the fridge close to the door.

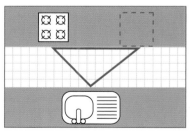

Galley layout
This design uses straight runs of units on opposing walls in a narrow kitchen. As in the U-shaped layout above, floor space may be limited, but wall space is used to its maximum potential.

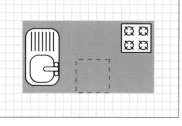

Island layout
This type of layout tends to be used either in large kitchens or as a design feature in smaller ones. When appliances are fitted in an island, the "work triangle" theory doesn't apply. Routing supplies may be tricky with this layout design.

Fitting a new kitchen
When carrying out a complete kitchen refurbishment you need to consider the order in which you complete each task. Below there is an example of a typical work strategy, but there must always be some flexibility built into the work schedule, depending on design elements.

Initially you will need to remove the old kitchen, but you should take into account such issues as how you will maintain a water supply during renovation work and how you will deal with cooking and washing needs.

Order of work for refurbishing a kitchen:
1 Re-route electrical wiring, if necessary
2 Re-route plumbing, including gas pipes, if necessary
3 Complete structural work on walls, ceilings, and floors
4 Install base units then wall units
5 Fit worktops and any infill panels
6 Fit sink and plumbing fittings
7 Install hob and oven
8 Fit extractor fan

PLANNING SERVICES

If you are going to keep the layout of a new kitchen similar to that of the old one, this will cut down on a lot of work. However, in most cases some re-routing of services will be necessary. The main issues to consider are outlined below.

Gas services

Consider whether the position of any existing gas pipework needs re-routing or adjusting. When purchasing new gas appliances, check where the connections are. In some situations the supply pipes may need converting. Only a CORGI-registered engineer is allowed to carry out any work on gas pipes or appliances.

Electrical services

Kitchens are full of electrical appliances, large and small. As well as standard sockets above the worktops for kettles, toasters, and blenders, large appliances should be connected to fused connection units (FCU's), and an electric cooker needs its own radial circuit (see p.431).

Lighting should be planned to combine general illumination with directed task lighting above areas such as sinks and food preparation areas. As well as ceiling lights, wall units and cooker hoods can have lighting installed underneath.

Once you have designed your layout, use it to plan how the electrical wiring needs re-routing. Any rewiring is most easily carried out after an old kitchen has been removed and before the new one is installed. Although you can do the rewiring yourself, it must be checked by a professional. For more information on electrics, see pp.426–61.

Plumbing services

A kitchen sink needs hot- and cold-water supplies, to be connected to its taps, and a drainage pipe. Washing machines and dishwashers also need to be plumbed in, and their supplies and drainage are often extended from the sink plumbing. Therefore it makes sense to keep them close together, if possible. Drainage pipes are particularly difficult to take any distance, because they must run at a gradient. If you alter drainage pipes you may need to notify the building control officer (BCO).

TOOLS AND MATERIALS CHECKLIST PP.241–48

Installing base units (p.241) Batten*, brackets*, G-clamp, connection screws, spirit level

Installing wall units (p.241) Mounting plate, G-clamp, connection screws, spirit level

Fitting doors (p.242) Hinge plates, hinges

Attaching a handle (p.242) Offcut of wood, G-clamp

Fitting a plinth (p.243) Clips, vinyl strips

Fitting a cornice (p.243) Mitre saw, wood glue

Fitting a pelmet (p.243) Jointing block, mitre saw, wood glue

Cutting a worktop length (p.244) Masking tape, G-clamp, block plane, straight edge

Scribing a worktop to fit (p.244) Block of wood, jigsaw

Joining square-edged worktops (p.245) Wood glue, fixing plate

Using a joining strip (p.245) Joining strip, silicone sealant and dispenser

Securing a worktop (p.245) Clamps, fixing brackets

Fitting a recycling cupboard (p.247) Screwdriver

Fitting a worktop bin for food waste (p.247) Jigsaw, silicone sealant

Cutting a recess hole (p.248) Flat or auger drill bit, jigsaw, preservative primer, paintbrush

Assembling and inserting a sink (p.248) Retaining clips, adhesive, silicone sealant and dispenser

* = optional

FOR BASIC TOOLKIT SEE PP.24–25

FITTING KITCHEN UNITS

Before you start to fit your kitchen units you should have removed the old kitchen, re-routed any services, and have the option to tile the floor, if that is part of your plan. Always check that the entire kitchen has arrived and that it is undamaged when it is delivered. Make sure that every item, right down to the fixings, is checked off, as waiting for a second delivery can hold up the entire fitting process. Fitting a kitchen is a job for two people, especially when it comes to hanging large wall units.

TOOLS AND MATERIALS SEE BASIC TOOLKIT AND P.239

PLANNING AND PREPARATION

Take time to prepare the wall surfaces and assemble the kitchen units before fitting them. Finding the right point to draw the first guide line for positioning units is essential to the whole project. Units and worktops are heavy items and you will need someone to help you lift them into position.

Marking up

■ The starting point for fitting any kitchen is a level guide line for the top of the base units. Generally a height of about 890mm (2ft 11in) above the floor is comfortable as the depth of the worktop is added later.

■ Start in one corner, using a spirit level to guide you. Floors are often uneven, so check the line's height at intervals to make sure base units and appliances will fit beneath it comfortably along the entire length.

■ Mark a second line to show the depth of the worktop. Generally wall units are fitted so that they are 450–500mm (1ft 6in–1ft 8in) from the top of the worktop, but adjust this height according to the manufacturer's specifications for positioning units around the hob. Unless it is very deep, do not include the pelmet's depth.

■ If you are fixing wall units on a stud wall you may need to provide additional support with extra noggings to ensure that fixings are solid.

Preparing the units

■ Once you have marked up the wall surfaces, you should assemble the units. Follow the manufacturer's instructions for each type of unit carefully.

■ Wall units sometimes have fixing rails across their backs that you cannot see once the

unit is held up to the wall. Note their size and position so that you can drill pilot holes directly through the inside of the unit once you have positioned it.

Fitting a kitchen

■ Providing you have measured and marked out accurately, fitting the kitchen itself should be relatively straightforward. An effective method, shown opposite, is to attach battens to the wall and fix the units into these. This leaves a gap behind each unit for service pipes, as well as providing extra support for the back edge of the worktop. Battening out is generally only practical with units less than 580mm (1ft 11in) deep, otherwise the rear edge of deeper units will require notching out.

■ Alternatively you can fix the units directly to the wall using brackets. Drill and plug pilot holes in a masonry wall, or try to find fixing points in studs for a timber-frame wall. It may be necessary to cut holes or notch out units to accommodate service pipes and supplies. You may need to cut holes in the back of units to accommodate service pipes. Wall units come with special brackets, and these need to be positioned carefully, again ensuring that they are fixed solidly to the wall surface.

▮▮ MARKING UP

A

B

Use a tape measure to mark a point 890mm (2ft 11in) above the floor level at your starting point (see left).

Use this mark to draw a horizontal guide line across the wall to indicate the top level of the base units.

C

D

Mark a point 450–500mm (1ft 6in –1ft 8in) plus the worktop height above this line, and draw a line to mark the bottom of the wall units.

Measure the width of each of your units and mark their positions across the horizontal guide lines.

▮▮ DRILLING PILOT HOLES

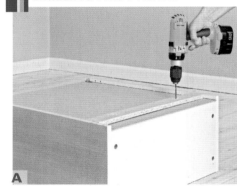

A

For all units that have fixing rails, make a pilot hole through the rail into the unit. When you are ready to fit the unit you will have the necessary fixing holes visible inside the unit. This mostly applies to units hung on walls.

▮▮ ATTACHING FEET TO A BASE UNIT

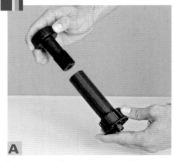

A

B

Screw together the two sections of the adjustable feet, so that their height is at a central position. This may be indicated by a small mark.

Push the feet into the pre-drilled holes in the base of the units, then secure using short wood screws.

INSTALLING BASE UNITS

A

Fix a batten measuring 50 x 25mm (2 x 1in) around the wall with its top edge aligned with the lower pencil guide line.

B

Starting with the corner unit, place each unit so that it is resting in position against the batten and flush with its top.

C

Make sure the units are level by placing a spirit level across the top of the units and adjusting the feet, where necessary.

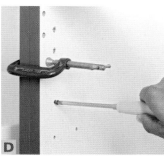

D

Hold adjacent units together using a G-clamp, then insert connecting screws through drilled holes to secure them.

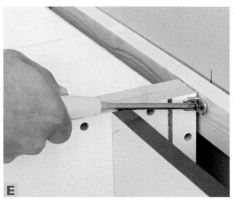

E

Attach the units to the batten. In this example, using a corner brace, one leg of the brace is screwed into the unit and the other is screwed into the face of the batten.

ALTERNATIVE TECHNIQUES

Fixing straight to a wall
This method requires good fixing points where the fixing bracket and wall surface meet.

Using a fixing rail
Some unit designs, especially housing units, are fixed through a rail directly to the wall.

INSTALLING WALL UNITS

A

Use a spirit level to mark out the positions of the ends of each wall unit, so that the corners of the units are clearly defined.

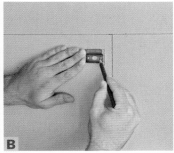

B

At each corner, measure out the exact position required for each wall bracket, corresponding with those fitted to the back of the units.

C

Fix the wall brackets in place using fittings appropriate to the structure of the wall. Continue for each of the wall units to be fitted.

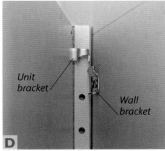

D

Unit bracket

Wall bracket

Position the unit so that the unit brackets are adjacent to the brackets on the wall.

Hang the unit by raising it up, then hooking the brackets together, so that the unit sits in place. For large units, you will need someone to help you.

E

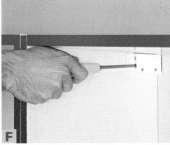

F

Make any final levelling-up adjustments using the adjuster block on the cabinet's inside top corner.

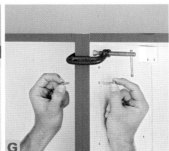

G

Clamp the units together so that their front edges are flush. Drill holes through the units and join them using the connection screws supplied.

Once carcasses have been fixed in place, the units are given their decorative finish. You will need to fit doors, drawer fronts, and any trims such as cornices. The final look of the kitchen depends on these finishing touches so it is important that the correct procedures and techniques are followed, and time and care is taken.

TOOLS AND MATERIALS SEE BASIC TOOLKIT AND P.239

UPDATING AN EXISTING KITCHEN

Replacing doors, drawers, and handles can be a great way of updating a kitchen if changing the layout is unnecessary. If you are on a tight budget then you will be amazed how much difference some paint and new handles can make to the look of a kitchen. You can paint any finish of kitchen unit, as well as tiles, but make sure you use the right paint system – special primers will often be necessary (see p.276). If you decide to change doors or drawers, make sure that the new ones are compatible with your existing units.

FITTING DOORS

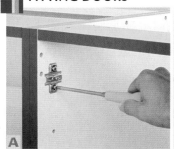   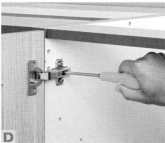

A Screw the hinge plate into its pre-drilled holes in the unit. Hinge plates often come with the screws already inserted.

B Insert the hinge into the pre-cut recesses on the doors, and screw it in place. Be sure to use the correct short wood screws.

C Position the door, with the hinges aligning with hinge plates, and use the screw already positioned in the hinge to join them.

D Tighten the central screw in the hinge plate to secure the door. Follow the instructions below to align the doors perfectly.

ALIGNING DOORS

Moving the door left and right Tightening or loosening the screw, as shown, will move the door to the right or left.

Moving the door up and down Loosen the screws in the hinge plate, as shown, and reposition the door before tightening them again.

Moving the door in and out To position the door farther away from the unit, loosen the central screw in the hinge plate and adjust the door accordingly. Re-tighten the screw to secure the door.

ATTACHING A HANDLE

Clamp an offcut of wood firmly against the front face of the door at the position where the drill bit will emerge. Using a drill bit slightly larger in diameter than the threaded screw of the knob or handle, drill through the door until you penetrate the block. This should prevent the front surface splitting.

  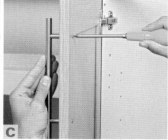

B Remove the block. You should have a perfect pilot hole, with no splintering or other damage around its edge. Insert a screw.

C Because a handle is being fitted here, a second hole is required. Position the handle against the door and secure the screw in place.

FITTING A PLINTH

A

Position a cut section of plinth face down in front of a unit run. Mark the positions of the unit legs and secure the clip attachments.

B

Attach the clips to the plinth by pushing them into place.

C

Cut the plinth seal to the exact lenth of zthe plinth. Position the plinth with its bottom facing upwards and, starting at one end, secure the seal by pushing it down onto the edge of the plinth. Seals are optional, but they prevent moisture getting into the plinth.

D

Position the plinth, pushing the clips in place onto the legs of the units. Continue to add further sections of plinth until you have covered all areas. A plinth is easy to remove, allowing new floor coverings to lap under units. Plinth height may then be trimmed to accommodate any floor-level change.

PUTTING ON DRAWER FRONTS

A

First attach the handles to the drawer using the same method for attaching door handles (opposite). Hold the front against the drawer.

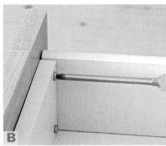

B

Insert screws through the front of the drawer from the inside, so that they are driven into the drawer fronts, and fix them securely.

FITTING A CORNICE

A

Cut the cornice to the lengths required and cut mitred joints using a mitre saw. Screw in place the piece of cornice that fits against the wall.

B

Apply some wood glue to the mitred end to add extra strength.

C

Butt the next piece of cornice against the first and press the mitred joints together firmly.

D

Secure this length of cornice using wood screws.

FITTING A PELMET

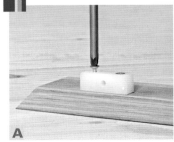

A

Cut the pelmet to the required lengths, with mitred ends where necessary. Screw joining blocks to the top inside edges of the pelmet.

B

Position the pelmet flush with the edge of the unit and screw the joining blocks into the underside.

C

Apply some wood glue to the mitred end. Butt the next piece of pelmet against the first and press the joint together.

D

Secure the pelmet by screwing the joining blocks into the underside of the unit.

FITTING A WORKTOP

Fitting a straight run of worktop is reasonably straightforward. However, joining two lengths to take a worktop round a corner requires more care, as the join needs to be perfect to create a continuous, flat finish. Corner joint strips are simple to use, but do not provide the best finish. Better joins can be achieved if you use the right techniques, and make good use of factory-cut straight edges. Joining worktop with square edges is easier than if the front edge has been finished with a curved profile.

TOOLS AND MATERIALS SEE BASIC TOOLKIT AND P.239

SCRIBING TO FIT

Any deviations in the wall surface will cause gaps along the back edge of the worktop. In these situations the best finish is achieved by scribing the worktop to fit the wall. Consider that you will lose some worktop width, so if the gaps are large, buy wider worktop and trim it as described below.

Position the worktop with the back edge touching the wall and the front edge overhanging the units by the same distance along the run.

Measure the largest gap between the worktop and the wall and cut a small scribing block of wood the same width.

Hold a pencil at one side of the block as you run the other end along the wall. This will provide a guide line for trimming.

Use a jigsaw to cut along the line. You may need to use a sander or plane where a small amount of material needs to be removed.

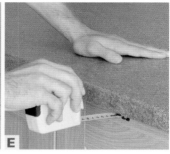

Reposition the worktop and check that you have a good fit between the wall and the worktop, and a consistent overhang at the front.

CUTTING A WORKTOP LENGTH

For a straight run, the worktop needs to be cut to the right length, including an overhang of about 25mm (1 in) at each end. Handsaws or power saws can be used. Make sure you use an appropriate blade. For a laminate worktop, place masking tape over the cutting line to help prevent any splintering of the laminate surface. See p.73 for advice on cutting a board or sheet.

Draw a pencil line across the worktop where you want to cut it, and cover the line with masking tape.

Clamp a straight edge to the worktop along the guide line (a steel rule is ideal). Using a craft knife, score down the line through the masking tape.

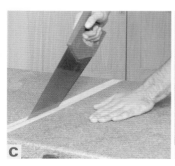

Carefully saw through the scored line using the panel saw. Make sure that the worktop is well supported on both sides of the cut.

Remove the remaining masking tape. Use a block plane to smooth the cut end of the worktop.

TRIMMING A WORKTOP WIDTH

If you have a wider worktop than you need, you can trim it at the same time as scribing it to fit the wall. With the worktop positioned on top of the base units, work out the width of material that needs to be removed to leave you with your desired overhang. Subtract the width of the largest gap at the back of the worktop from the trimming amount and cut a scribing block of this length. Use the block in the same way described above.

Deciding on what size of overhang is required at the front of the units is a matter of personal taste. Some people prefer a finish fairly flush with the drawer fronts, whereas other people prefer an overhang of 20-30mm (1–½in). The standard overhang is 10mm (⅜in). Cut through the worktop using the method shown left.

JOINING WORKTOP

If you want your worktop to turn a corner you will need to join two lengths. Options for joining worktops are limited by the material the worktop is made from, and whether its profile is square or rounded. Once a joint has been cut, it is essential that it is held tightly in position. Fixing plates can be fitted across the joint on the underside of the worktop, or a biscuit jointer will create an exceptionally strong joint. The technique for using a biscuit jointer is demonstrated on p.64.

USING A JIG

Professional kitchen fitters use worktop jigs to make accurate joins. These specially designed tools are relatively expensive, although often they can be hired. The jig provides a template for a router to cut against. With practice, it produces very accurate cuts for each side of the join required, and guides for rebated cuts to fit connector bolts to hold the join together.

Round-edged worktops

If your worktop is supplied with a curved finished edge it is not possible to create a simple right-angled butt join. The best option is to use a joining strip, or a worktop jig. Making a mitred join is possible, but will be difficult to cut accurately unless you use a worktop jig (see above, right).

Worktop joint kits

Some manufacturers provide proprietary joint kits. Basically, these are coloured fillers that may be used to neaten a less than adequate mitre or butt join. Some are epoxy-based, so you should remove any excess before it has the chance to dry.

▌▌JOINING SQUARE-EDGED WORKTOPS

Square edges mean that two sections of worktop can be easily and neatly butt joined without the need for a joining strip or worktop jig. Once the worktop is fixed in place, the front edge may then be finished using a router (see p.66).

A

Cut the worktop lengths to fit and, if necessary, scribe to fit (see opposite). Apply wood glue along one of the joining edges.

B

Push the worktop together and secure the join using a fixing plate and screws. You may need to drill pilot holes for the screws, and apply weight to the worktop as you fix the screws. Wipe away excess glue. For an even stronger join use two or even three fixing plates.

▌▌USING A JOINING STRIP

A

Use a hacksaw to cut the joining strip to the same width as the worktop.

B

Apply some silicone sealant along the edge of one section of worktop, position the strip on the edge and screw it in place.

C

Apply some sealant along the other worktop edge.

D

Butt the sections together, and use a cloth to remove any excess sealant.

▌▌SECURING A WORKTOP

Once a worktop has been fitted, it should be secured in place using screws inserted through the worktop fixing brackets that are attached to the units and fixing rail. You will need someone to apply weight to the back of the units while you fix them in place.

A

Clamp the worktop to the units along their front edge. Insert screws through the fixing rail into the underside of the worktop.

B

Apply weight from above while you secure the back of the worktop using fixing brackets.

FINISHING WORKTOPS

Laminated worktops

These often have unfinished edges that require covering with laminate strips supplied by the manufacturer. The strips can sometimes be ironed on, but others will need contact adhesive. Once the strip is fixed in place and any adhesive is dry, you can trim the edges flush using a craft knife.

Synthetic stone worktops

Sawn edges of some types of synthetic stone can be sanded smooth. Always check manufacturer's guidelines.

Solid wood worktops

These are best sanded smooth, then stain-protected using the oil recommended by the manufacturer. Paint on several coats of oil, removing any excess with a dry cloth. Extra oil may be required at intervals to maintain the finish.

GREEN KITCHEN SOLUTIONS

Recycling is a part of daily life in most homes, with food waste and packaging being the most commonly recycled items. Most recycling, therefore, occurs in the kitchen. Food waste can be composted (see pp.400–01), but here we show how a kitchen can be adapted to make recycling an efficient and simple process. The precise way in which you recycle will depend on your local authority – some materials may be collected from your home while others must be taken to a recycling centre – but a good system of sorting and temporarily storing your recycling is needed.

WHAT CAN BE RECYCLED?

Most packaging carries a symbol that states whether it can be recycled – the universal recycling symbol (pictured) means that it can be. There are, however, a number of other signs – some are country-specific and some give details of the way in which an item may be recycled. Confusion can occur over whether a product is recyclable, or whether it has been made from recycled materials, so check the packaging carefully.

UNIVERSAL RECYCLING SYMBOL

HOUSEHOLD RECYCLING SYSTEMS

The main way to sort and conveniently store your recycling material in the short term is to make use of a dedicated recycling bin. There are many different styles available, but all are designed to make the process of recycling as simple and convenient as possible. Some manufacturers produce specific designs to fit into their kitchen units, but it is also possible to buy more generic bins that will fit the vast majority of kitchen units.

A selection of different types of bin are shown here – in all cases, the aim of the bin is to make recycling easier, but also to be unobtrusive and make the best use of the available space. It helps if you compact the items for recycling before placing them in the bin, which saves space in your home, and makes it easier to transport them to a recycling centre.

Stacking bins
Some recycling bins are designed to be stacked up, to save on floor space. The stack can be disassembled for transporting to the recycling centre, or separate sections can be left for collection by your local authority.

CRUSHING PLASTIC BOTTLES

A Remove the lid and crush the bottle with your hand or foot to compact the bottle (the space taken up by empty plastic bottles consists almost entirely of air).

B Replace the lid when you have crushed the bottle to create a vacuum that prevents the bottle returning to a larger size. By doing this, a large amount of room is saved in storage and transit.

Pedal bins
These are a more stylish solution for recycling. A bin that is internally subdivided makes it easier to sort different types of recycling.

CRUSHING METAL CANS

A Place the can in the jaws of the crusher. There are many such gadgets available and a simple design allows most sizes of can to be crushed underfoot.

B Push down with your foot to flatten the can. As with plastic bottles, this saves space both in storage and transit.

Built-in recycling bins
This is a good option for keeping recycling out of view, as well as utilizing space under a worktop. Most designs are internally divided, meaning recycling can be separated. Styles vary, but the principle remains the same. For more on installation, see opposite.

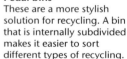

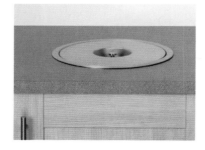

Worktop bins
Worktop bins conceal the body of the bin, which is set into the worktop. This design is commonly used for recycling food scraps or waste, such as vegetable peelings. These may then be composted domestically, or put out for collection. For more on installation, see opposite.

FITTING A RECYCLING CUPBOARD

Make sure you have chosen a bin that will fit your kitchen units. Depth is very important here, as it tends to vary more across products than the internal height. Remove any shelving from the cupboard to allow for installation of the recycling bin.

B Position the bin frame on the floor of the cupboard, so it is central to the door opening. Observe any supplier's guidelines on positioning.

C Screw the frame in place – normally into the cupboard floor, but some designs may require fixing to the back, or sides, of the cupboard.

D Fit the bins into the frame – they tend to be the same size, and usually consist of two or three separate bins.

E Fit the lid in place. Sometimes, the lid may be attached to the door to allow it to open automatically when the cupboard is opened.

F

Replace any shelving if the bin height allows (in this example, the bin is on runners and can be pulled forward to allow the lid to be lifted). If there is not enough space between the shelf and the bin, the shelf brackets can be raised to create space.

FITTING A WORKTOP BIN FOR FOOD WASTE

Draw a cutting guideline on the worktop. The bin's manufacturer should provide a template, as well as instructions for fitting, but here the lid ring is being used for this purpose. Positioning is very important with a bin of this type, as it is necessary to cut a hole in the worktop, meaning mistakes are not easily rectified.

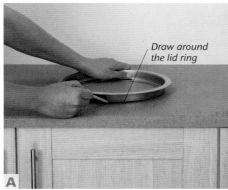

Draw around the lid ring

A

B A jigsaw is needed to cut the guideline. For more on positioning the blade for the initial incision, see p.248.

C Position the lid ring in the hole. Some manufacturers recommend fixing the ring with silicone sealant around the underside of the rim.

D Position the bin in the ring by simply placing it through the hole.

E Create a seal for the lid using an inner rubber ring. These are easily removed for cleaning.

F

Fit the lid to the rubber seal for a neat finish. Depending on the depth of your bin, it may be necessary to remove shelves below, or at least customize the cupboard design so that the bin sits in its hole.

FITTING SINKS AND APPLIANCES

Most types of sink and hob need to be recessed into the worktop, but many kitchen appliances are freestanding and slot into gaps beneath the worktop. If you have chosen integral appliances, you may need to use special brackets as well as fitting matching doors. For new kitchens, power and water services should be in place, but renovations may require some re-routing. See pp.86–87 for information on reclamation.

TOOLS AND MATERIALS SEE BASIC TOOLKIT AND P.239

FITTING A SINK

Depending on design, a kitchen sink may take up the entire top surface of a unit, or may be recessed into the worktop. To fit a recessed sink you need to cut a hole in the worktop to accommodate it. Some manufacturers will supply a cutting template with the sink, otherwise you can draw your own guidelines. It is advisable to fit the taps and waste to the sink or worktop before the sink is secured in place because access is much easier. The method for connecting taps is similar to that for a bathroom basin (see pp.258–59). In this example, a stainless steel sink is being fitted into a laminated worktop.

1 CUTTING A RECESS HOLE

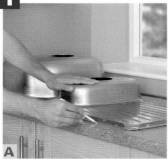

A

Position the sink face-down on the worktop, making sure that the space at the front and back is even. Draw a pencil guide line around the sink.

B

Measure the depth of the lip of the sink, then mark a second pencil line at this distance inside the first, all the way around.

C

Use a drill with a flat bit or auger bit to make a hole in each corner of the sink position, inside the inner guide line. Make sure that the drill is at precise right angles to the worktop, so that you make an accurate hole.

D

Cut around the inside guide line with a jigsaw, using the holes as starting points. Support the worktop underneath as you cut.

E

Check that the sink fits well in the hole. Seal the cut edges of the worktop with a preservative primer.

2 ASSEMBLING AND INSERTING A SINK

A

Fit the tap into the cut hole in the sink and secure it on the underside of the sink using the washers and fixing nuts supplied. Fit the tap hoses.

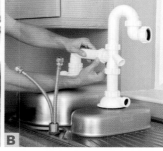

B

Fit the waste assembly and connect up the overflow section as guided by any supplied instructions.

C

Apply silicone adhesive around the hole in the worktop. This may not be necessary if the manufacturer has supplied a gasket or seal.

D

Fit retaining clips around the edge of the sink. Position the sink and check whether you have enough room to connect the taps.

E

Tighten the retaining clips to the underside of the worktop. Wipe away any excess sealant that may squeeze out from around the sink edges.

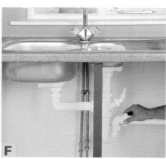

F

Connect up taps and waste as for a bathroom basin (see pp.258–59). Flexible connectors are the easiest option for taps.

FRIDGES AND FREEZERS

In some cases manufacturers will supply conversion kits that can be used on freestanding models. However, normally the fridge or freezer will have to be made specifically for integral use and require a unit door to be fitted in the same way as for a dishwasher.

INTEGRAL OVENS

Integral ovens often form part of fitted kitchens, and are usually housed in purpose-made units. Ovens normally slide into position on brackets, which you will probably have to fit. Instructions must be followed carefully according to the precise make and model being fitted. There are often differences in procedure and positioning of brackets. As with hobs, you cannot connect a gas oven yourself. You can wire an electric oven – it will need its own radial circuit – but your work must be checked by a professional. For more information, see p.431.

A **Some ovens** are fitted with their own feet, and are simply slid into position between units.

B **The only adjustment** that may be necessary is to use a spanner to adjust the oven's feet and level the oven in position.

HOBS

Hobs are recessed into worktops using a similar technique to that shown for sinks. All gas connections must be made by a CORGI-registered fitter. However, if you are fitting an electric hob you can wire a spur and fused connection unit (FCU) yourself, although all electrical work must be checked by a professional to comply with building regulations. For more information on electrics, see p.431.

Fitting a hob
To fit a hob into a worktop use the method described for fitting a sink (opposite). Hobs need to be fitted before an oven is positioned so that you can make any necessary connections under the worktop.

FITTING AN EXTRACTOR FAN

A kitchen extractor fan is often housed in a wall unit that matches the rest of the kitchen and is fitted in much the same way. There are two extraction methods. If a recirculator is being used, there is no need for any ducting to the outside of the building. However, if conventional extraction is chosen, it may be necessary to cut a hole in an exterior wall to accommodate a ducting channel. Use the method shown on p.364 to make an opening. Decorative chimneys and hoods are often secured on the wall with simple brackets. Great care needs to be taken when handling these items as they can damage and dent easily. All fans will require an electrical supply, via a fused connection unit (FCU) (see pp.434–35 for more details).

WASHING MACHINES AND DISHWASHERS

In many cases washing machines and dishwashers are freestanding. However, in some kitchen designs they are housed in integral units. With a washing machine this generally means that a unit door simply covers the front of a freestanding machine. A dishwasher is actually supplied with brackets that are used for both securing the machine in position and also for securing a unit door on the front of the dishwasher. In all cases a template and separate fixing pack is supplied, along with instructions for fitting.

If you are fitting a dishwasher or washing machine into a new kitchen, the services should all be in place for easy connection. In an existing kitchen the electricity, water supply, and drainage may need to be extended from existing services. Routing of supply and waste pipes is dealt with in greater detail on pp.474–83. You may need to use a hole cutter (see p.57) so that pipes and hoses can be threaded through the back of the units, or you may be able to run the services underneath them, depending on the unit design.

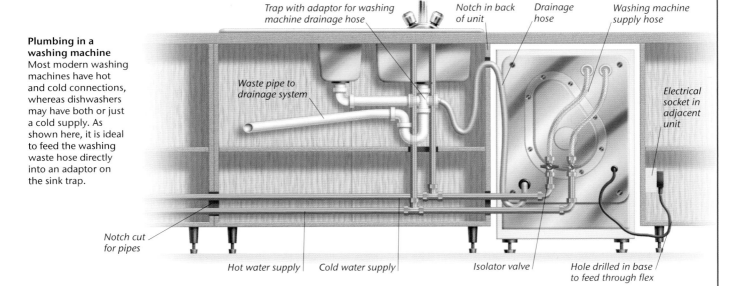

Plumbing in a washing machine
Most modern washing machines have hot and cold connections, whereas dishwashers may have both or just a cold supply. As shown here, it is ideal to feed the washing waste hose directly into an adaptor on the sink trap.

Trap with adaptor for washing machine drainage hose

Notch in back of unit

Drainage hose

Washing machine supply hose

Waste pipe to drainage system

Electrical socket in adjacent unit

Notch cut for pipes

Hot water supply

Cold water supply

Isolator valve

Hole drilled in base to feed through flex

REPLACING DOOR HINGES

Hinges themselves tend not to break – if they do, you can simply replace them. What is more likely is that the hinge plate will loosen through wear and tear. If this happens, you can re-fix the hinge or below its existing position.

TOOLS AND MATERIALS
Screwdriver, tape measure, pencil, drill, hinge-cutting bit

A **Unscrew the loosened** hinge plate and remove it.

B **Mark off a new position** where you can get a firmer fixing, slightly lower in this case, and re-fix the plate.

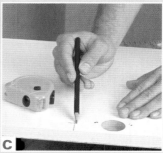

C **Measure off** the new hinge position on the door using the new plate position as a guide.

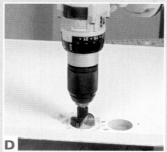

D **Use a hinge-cutting** bit to drill out the recess for the new hinge position. Take care not to drill too deeply.

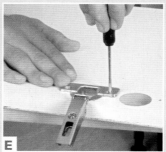

E **Screw the hinge** in place, making sure that it sits perfectly flush.

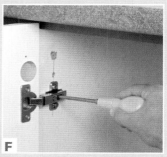

F **Re-hang the door.** The old hinge plate and hinge holes can be filled and painted if required.

REPAIRING DRAWER HANDLES

The most common problem with drawers is a loose handle. You may need to strengthen the fixings that hold the handle in position or attach the drawer front more securely.

TOOLS AND MATERIALS
Adhesive, washers, clamp, screwdriver, wood glue

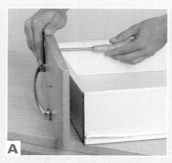

A **Unscrew the drawer** front and remove the handle from its position.

B **Apply some strong** adhesive to the thread of the handle. Position a washer on the screw before replacing the handle.

C **Spread some grab** adhesive on the back face of the drawer front before securing it back in place.

ADJUST DRAWER RUNNERS

Drawer runners may require adjustment because of wear or simply because they were misaligned when the unit was constructed. Adjustment is a straightforward process of re-fixing the runner.

TOOLS AND MATERIALS
Screwdriver, mini spirit level, bradawl

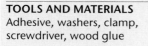

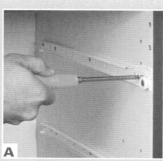

A **Unscrew the runner,** ideally leaving the rear screw in place.

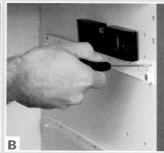

B **Position a level** on the runner and use a bradawl to mark new fixing holes.

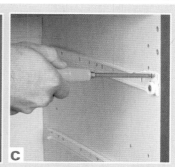

C **Screw the runner** back in place. Reposition the drawer and check for improved operation. Re-adjust if necessary.

DRILLING THROUGH TILES WITHOUT CRACKING THEM

Many installations in kitchens involve making fixings in a tiled surface. It is essential to use the correct technique for drilling through tiles so they do not crack. The dust created from drilling ceramic tiles can discolour grout and silicone sealant so try to vacuum dust from the hole as you drill it.

TOOLS AND MATERIALS
Felt-tip pen, masking tape, drill and bits, vacuum cleaner, wall plug

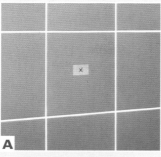

A **Mark the point** for the fixing using a felt-tip pen. Apply some masking tape over the mark – it should still be visible.

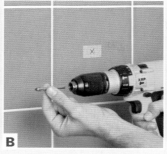

B **Fit a tile drill bit** (see pp.56–57) and switch off any hammer action.

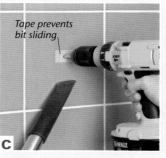

Tape prevents bit sliding

C **Position a vacuum** cleaner below the mark and switch it on. Start up the drill on a low speed, and slowly increase the speed.

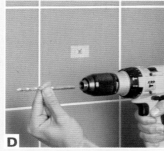

D **Once through the tile**, change the bit for a masonry bit or wood bit, depending on the surface below. Drill to the required depth.

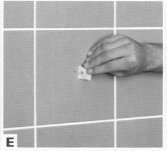

E **Once you have drilled** the hole, remove the masking tape from the tile's surface.

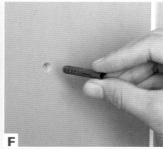

F **Plug the hole** with the appropriate wall plug and insert the fixing as required.

REPAIRING A LAMINATE WORKTOP

A repair is achieved by disguising the damage. Jointing compounds are usually supplied with a fitted kitchen and are the best option for hiding dents or scratches. Re-attach broken edging as shown.

TOOLS AND MATERIALS
Contact adhesive, masking tape, pencil or crayon

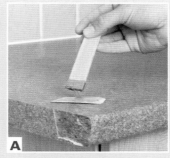

A **Apply contact adhesive** to both the worktop edge and the broken section of laminate.

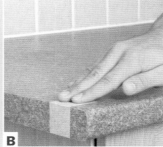

B **Wait for it** to become tacky and stick it in place – use masking tape to hold it securely.

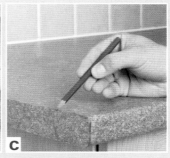

C **Once the adhesive** has dried, remove the masking tape and use a pencil or crayon to disguise any white edges along the join.

REPAIRING A WOODEN WORKTOP

Over time a worktop surface can become damaged or discoloured. In most cases you can simply sand back the damaged area. This technique can be used only for solid wood worktops, not veneered ones.

TOOLS AND MATERIALS
Sanding block, latex glove, cloths, wood oil, brush

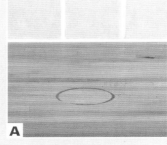

A **Singeing and staining** can look unsightly, but these problems are easy to repair in two steps, as shown.

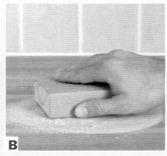

B **Sand the area back** to the bare wood, making sure not to create a depression. Then use a cloth to remove all traces of dust and debris.

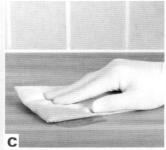

C **Brush on two** or three coats of the recommended oil, usually tung oil. Brush on a coat, then remove the excess with a cloth.

Bathrooms

WHEN PLANNING ANY BATHROOM YOU SHOULD THINK ABOUT WHAT STYLE YOU PREFER, AND WHAT WILL MAKE BEST USE OF THE SPACE AVAILABLE. HOW TO REPLACE OLD FITTINGS IS DESCRIBED IN THIS SECTION, AND WILL INVOLVE A MINIMUM OF PIPEWORK. NEW LAYOUTS OR BATHROOMS WILL CERTAINLY PROVIDE MORE DEMANDING TASKS IN TERMS OF ROUTING SUPPLY AND WASTE PIPEWORK.

CHOOSING YOUR SUITE

A huge range of bathroom fixtures and fittings is available. Most manufacturers sell matching bathroom suites, and bathroom furniture is a popular target for reclamation (see pp.86–87). A basic suite usually includes a toilet, basin, and a bath, with bidets and showers as options. For more information on showers, see pp.262–65. Most bathroom fittings are white, but other colours are normally available. Modern or traditional styles can be complemented by taps (see pp.484–89) and tiles (see pp.308–09). For ideas on planning a bathroom layout, see pp.254–55.

PLUMBING

Simply replacing existing fittings with new ones in the same position usually requires very little plumbing work. However, if you want to move fittings, or are planning a new bathroom, consider carefully if you are confident with the plumbing involved. The different types of supply and waste pipes and the systems and techniques for routing and joining them are shown in the plumbing section (see pp.462–83). However, you might prefer to choose and design the layout yourself, and then leave the plumbing to a professional.

TOILETS

A cistern and a pan make up a toilet. The cistern holds the flush mechanism and water, which empties into a pan attached to the waste pipe (see pp.490–91 for filling and flushing mechanisms). Cisterns either match the pan and sit on top of it (close-coupled), or are connected to the pan by a pipe. They are made of ceramic, acrylic, or metal. Some cisterns are designed to be hidden in the wall. Pans are usually made from ceramic with a vitreous enamel coating, or stainless steel. They can be wall-mounted or floor-mounted. All pans have an integral trap – a U-bend filled with water – to prevent bad smells escaping from the waste pipes. Toilets connect to the waste stack horizontally or vertically – adapters are available if a new toilet is differently aligned to the old. Steps for replacing a toilet are shown on pp.256–57.

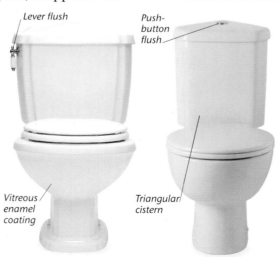

Lever flush

Push-button flush

Vitreous enamel coating

Triangular cistern

Close-coupled toilet
Modern toilets are usually close-coupled – the cistern is attached to the top of the pan and made of the same material. Wall-mounted and hidden cisterns are available.

Space-saving toilet
En suite bathrooms and cloakrooms are often very short of space. This type of toilet is designed to fit into a corner. Several space-saving designs are available.

BIDETS

There are two types of bidet available. Over-the-rim bidets are filled in the same way as a basin, and fitted in a similar way (see p.259). Rim-supply bidets have heated seats and sprays, but generally require professional installation.

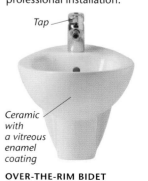

Tap

Ceramic with a vitreous enamel coating

OVER-THE-RIM BIDET

BASINS

Basins are traditionally made from ceramic, although contemporary designs made of glass, wood, marble, and other types of natural stone are available. There are several common designs – full-pedestal, half-pedestal, and wall-mounted. Basins can also be supported by fitted units with storage cupboards underneath. Steps for replacing a basin are shown on pp.258–59.

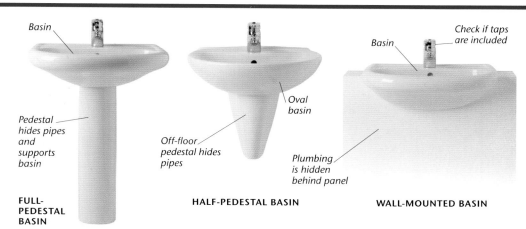

Basin

Pedestal hides pipes and supports basin

FULL-PEDESTAL BASIN

Off-floor pedestal hides pipes

Oval basin

HALF-PEDESTAL BASIN

Basin

Check if taps are included

Plumbing is hidden behind panel

WALL-MOUNTED BASIN

BATHS

Baths can be made from a variety of materials. Enamelled steel and iron baths are cold to the touch. Steel baths are cheaper but chip easily, iron baths are expensive and heavy, but are long-lasting. Acrylics are light, cheap, and warm but can be scratched, and thin acrylic can be deformed by heavy loads of water. Composite resins are sturdy, but lighter than metal and warm to the touch. Other options include baths with water jets and air bubbles. Walk-in baths are also available with improved access for the elderly and disabled. Replacing a bath is shown on pp.260–61. You can also fit a shower over a bath (see pp.262–65).

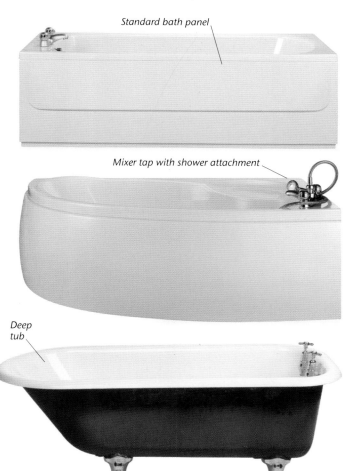

Standard bath panel

Mixer tap with shower attachment

Deep tub

Feet

FITTED BATHROOMS

Fitted bathrooms are becoming increasingly popular. They are often supplied flatpacked and are constructed in a similar way to kitchen units (see pp.240–43).

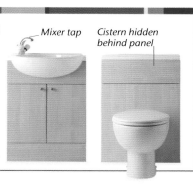

Mixer tap

Cistern hidden behind panel

FITTED BASIN AND TOILET

Traditional bath
Straight baths are the most popular choice. They are usually supplied with a matching panel, or you can make a panel yourself from MDF or ply and decorate it to match the walls.

Corner bath
Baths designed to sit in a corner can increase your layout options when planning a new bathroom. Some designs are space-saving, but others are bigger than traditional baths.

Freestanding bath
Traditionally baths were supported on feet. Original cast-iron baths can be found in reclamation yards. Modern freestanding designs are also available. Decorative chrome plumbing is often used with these types of baths.

HEATING AND VENTILATION

Even if your home has central heating, electric heaters or towel rails are often used in bathrooms to provide extra heating on demand (see p.506). If there is not one already, build a ventilation system into your bathroom (see pp.364–65) to reduce mould and mildew caused by damp air. Also, consider using paint specially formulated to cope with the humidity (see p.277).

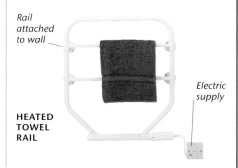

Rail attached to wall

Electric supply

HEATED TOWEL RAIL

TAPS

The final look of the bathroom depends to some extent on the taps you choose, and your choice is limited by the number of holes in your chosen fittings, although you can cut your own tap holes in some baths. Choosing taps is dealt with in more detail on pp.484–85.

BATHROOM PLANNING

Your initial bathroom design should focus on making the best use of the space available. Then consider which services would need re-routing for the new design. Decide whether you are going to tile the walls, change the floor surface, and if you will update heating and ventilation. You can then construct an order of work. If you are replacing the whole bathroom, remove all the old fittings and re-route the plumbing and wiring before fitting the new bathroom. If there is little re-routing required, you may prefer to replace each item in turn.

TYPES OF BATHROOM LAYOUT

Most homes have at least one "standard" bathroom fitted with a toilet, basin, and bath. Optional extras to this basic suite include a shower, either in a separate cubicle or above the bath, and possibly a bidet. An extra basin is a popular choice in a bathroom used by lots of people.

Fitted bathrooms

Like a standard bathroom, fitted bathrooms have a full suite of fittings. The difference is that they are totally or partially housed in units, and the final design has matching built-in storage and worktops around part of the room. If you are considering this type of bathroom, the manufacturer will help you plan the layout.

En suite bathrooms

Because of the proximity of the bedroom, noise is an issue. Often these have no windows so an extractor fan with a timer is essential – in-line fans are especially quiet (see p.365). The noise of a toilet cistern refilling can be reduced by fitting a quiet, modern inlet valve (see pp.490–91).

Cloakrooms

Space-saving designs can fit into a smaller area than standard fittings. These include narrow cisterns, known as "slimline" cisterns, and toilets and basins designed to fit into corners. A cloakroom should have a window that opens or an extractor fan.

Wet rooms

These are bathrooms that include a shower with no enclosure – the water runs away through a drain in the floor. The whole room has to be fully waterproofed.

NEW BATHROOM CONSIDERATIONS

■ Even if replacing fittings in the same position, check that supply and drainage pipes don't need to be extended or otherwise modified.
■ A new tiled floor will increase floor height, which can affect the pipe positions. Flexible connector pipes will accommodate changes.
■ Check the dimensions of new fittings; don't assume

they are the same as the old. Fittings can vary in size even if they look similar.
■ Consider improving ventilation, and fitting a bathroom extractor fan.
■ Stud walls need modifying for wall-mounted fittings.
■ Floors may need to be strengthened for a cast-iron bath. Get a professional opinion on what is required.

BATHROOM REGULATIONS

Electrical installations

Water is a good conductor of electricity so it increases the chance and severity of shocks. There are strict regulations regarding where and how you install electrical equipment in bathrooms (see p.433). Metal pipes also conduct electricity, and so the plumbing system should be earthed using earthing clamps (see p.436 and p.464).

Waste pipe installations

Changing or installing a new bathroom may involve making a new connection to your home's main soil stack or drain (see pp.480–83). Contact your local building control office should you need to check regulations regarding stack connection.

SPACE CONSIDERATIONS

All bathroom fittings require space around them so that they can be used comfortably. For example, a bath should be at least 700mm (2ft 4in) from a wall or another fitting to allow you to step in and out, and dry yourself easily. You should also make sure there is room for the door to open without scratching or chipping fittings. Try to provide space for a waste bin in your plan. Make sure you fit items such as mirrors and cupboards where they suit the height of all users when possible. Medicine cabinets should be lockable, and be out of the reach of children.

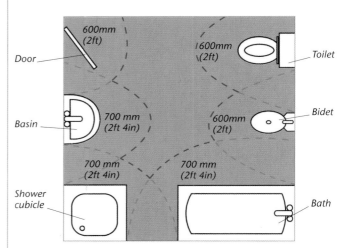

A GUIDE TO FURNISHING CLEARANCE ZONES

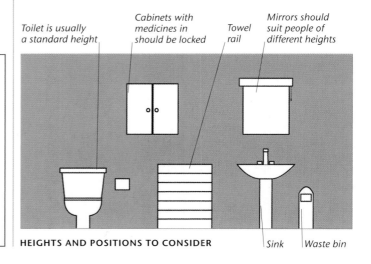

HEIGHTS AND POSITIONS TO CONSIDER

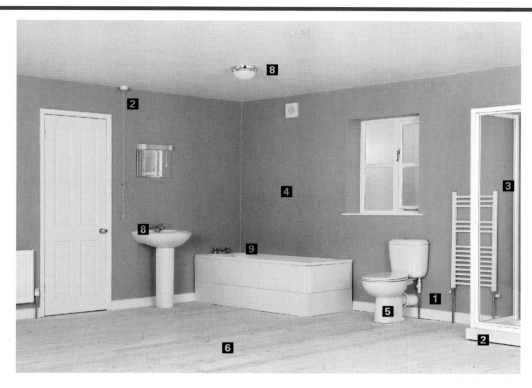

Replacing a bathroom suite
Before fitting the new bathroom you will have to remove the old fittings. If you are not replacing a tiled floor or moving fitting positions, you may choose to tackle them one at a time. If you are tiling the floor or moving any fittings, you will probably need to remove all the old fittings before you start. In tight spaces you may have to take away the toilet and basin before you are able to remove the bath.

Order of work considerations:
1 Re-route or extend pipework
2 Route wiring, but do not wire in any equipment (first fix). Replace subfloor if necessary
3 Fit bath and shower tray
4 Fit the base of the shower mixer valve into the wall
5 Complete any tiling on floors and walls, and paint if required
6 Fit the toilet and basin, and the shower and cubicle
7 Lay soft flooring
8 Fit electrical items (second fix)
9 Seal all joints with silicone

FIXING FITTINGS TO A STUD WALL

As well as modifying the plumbing, if you are attaching fittings to a stud wall you need to fit an extra nogging to fix into. Wall-mounted fittings will need double noggings, one on top of the other, or purpose-built frameworks inserted into the wall to support their full weight.

To fit noggings or frames into a stud wall, you will need to remove the plaster or cut a hole in the plasterboard at the fixing position. With the studwork exposed you can nail any extra noggings in place (see pp.104–09 for more on stud walls and how to fix noggings). Alternatively, insert the support frame. While you have access to the studwork, you might want to hide supply and waste pipes in the wall. To repair the wall, fix a plasterboard patch in place and create a neat join with the existing plaster (see p.125).

PLANNING PLUMBING IN BATHROOMS

The simplest option when planning a new bathroom is to position the new fittings in the same place as the old ones. In this way plumbing is kept to a minimum. If each item is already plumbed in with isolating valves and flexible connector pipes you can easily work on each in turn. If there are no isolating valves, then you will have to shut off the water at a nearby gate valve, or drain down the entire system if there is no other option (see p.465).

When you are repositioning a toilet, re-routing its waste pipe is complex, and in many cases may not be possible. An option is to fit a macerator behind the toilet pan. This can pump waste through small pipes to join the main stack and makes it possible to fit a toilet almost anywhere.

Showers may need to take their water supply directly from a tank or the mains, rather than from a nearby supply pipe (see p.263). This helps maintain pressure and reduces temperature fluctuations. Repositioning other fittings requires teeing off the water supply pipes and running waste pipes to the new position. See pp.474–83 for more on routing and connecting supply and waste pipes.

PLANNING ELECTRICAL WORK IN BATHROOMS

Electrical considerations are an important part of bathroom planning. Aside from obvious features such as lighting, it may also be necessary to provide power for an extractor fan, towel rail, heater, shaver point, shower pump, or electric shower. Water and electricity are a dangerous combination so bathrooms are divided into zones, each with their own wiring regulations (see opposite and p.433). For information on electrics, see pp.430–451. For installing heaters in bathrooms, see p.506.

TOOLS AND MATERIALS CHECKLISTS PP.257–65

Replacing a toilet (p.257)
Toilet pan connector, stubby screwdriver*, silicone sealant, sealant dispenser, spirit level, slip joint pliers, flexible connector

Fitting a wall-mounted basin (p.258) Brackets, spirit level, flexible pipe connectors

Replacing a basin (p.259)
Dustsheet, tap (or taps, depending on holes in basin), flexible pipe connectors, basin trap, basin wrench, silicone sealant, sealant dispenser

Replacing a bath (p.261)
Dustsheet, tap (or taps, depending on holes in bath), flexible pipe connectors, trap, panels*, spirit level, batten, wood offcuts, tenon saw, jigsaw, silicone sealant, sealant dispenser

Fitting a solid resin or ceramic shower tray (p.265)
Jigsaw, battens, PVA, mortar (see pp.70–71), trowel, spirit level, shower trap, silicone sealant, sealant dispenser

Fitting an acrylic shower tray (p.265) Spirit level, shower trap, silicone sealant, sealant dispenser

Fitting a shower or bath screen (p.265) Spirit level, silicone sealant, sealant dispenser

* = optional

FOR BASIC TOOLKIT SEE PP.24–25

REPLACING A TOILET

Replacing an existing toilet is a straightforward task because the supply and waste pipes are already in position. In this example a close-coupled toilet is shown – the most common design of toilet fitted today. Before replacing the toilet, remove the old one, taking care not to damage the outlet to the soil stack. Fitting a toilet in a new position requires more complex rerouting.

TOOLS AND MATERIALS SEE BASIC TOOLKIT AND P.255

ANATOMY OF A CLOSE-COUPLED TOILET

This type of toilet design, where the cistern sits on top of the back of the pan, is popular because it is so compact and simple to fit.

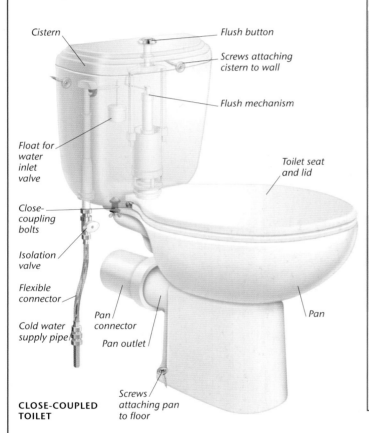

Cistern

Flush button

Screws attaching cistern to wall

Flush mechanism

Float for water inlet valve

Toilet seat and lid

Close-coupling bolts

Isolation valve

Flexible connector

Pan

Cold water supply pipe

Pan connector

Pan outlet

Screws attaching pan to floor

CLOSE-COUPLED TOILET

MOVING OR ADDING A TOILET

You may need to notify your local building control office if you are planning to modify your main soil stack and/or install a toilet (see building regulations, p.466). Routing toilet waste pipes is complicated so it is worth seeking professional advice on what the best options are. In some cases it may be necessary to fit a macerator, which chops up waste and pumps it through small pipes to provide more options for toilet position.

TOILET PAN CONNECTORS

Pan connectors are used between the entry to the soil stack and the pan outlet. Push the concertinaed end into the entry to the soil stack, then simply slide the pan outlet fully into the open end. There is no need for further fixing. A good fit between the pan, connector, and waste is essential, otherwise leaks will occur.

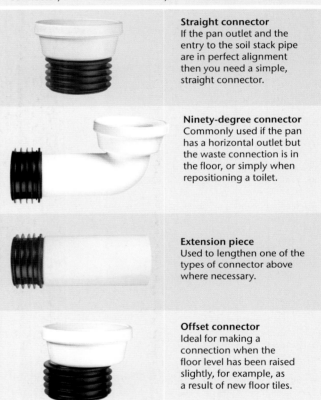

Straight connector
If the pan outlet and the entry to the soil stack pipe are in perfect alignment then you need a simple, straight connector.

Ninety-degree connector
Commonly used if the pan has a horizontal outlet but the waste connection is in the floor, or simply when repositioning a toilet.

Extension piece
Used to lengthen one of the types of connector above where necessary.

Offset connector
Ideal for making a connection when the floor level has been raised slightly, for example, as a result of new floor tiles.

REMOVING AN OLD TOILET

Turn off the water to the toilet cistern at the isolation valve on the supply pipe, a nearby gate valve, or by draining down the entire system (see p.464–67). Flush the toilet until the cistern is empty. Disconnect the flexible connector to the cold-water supply pipe from the cistern or cut through an old, rigid pipe. Then disconnect the pan from the cistern by undoing the connecting screws on a close-coupled toilet, or sawing through the connecting pipe on other designs. Remove or cut through the old cistern overflow pipe if the new cistern has an internal overflow. You should now be able to unscrew the cistern from the wall and lift it away. Undo the screws fixing the pan to the floor and, if there is a plastic pan connector (see above

right), simply slide the pan out. Keep it level because there will still be water in the trap built into the bottom of the pan. If an old pan is cemented in place, break the old toilet to release it, ensuring you don't fracture the waste pipe. Wear goggles and gloves to chisel out the remains of the pan, and any old putty or cement from the waste pipe.

FITTING A CLOSE-COUPLED PAN AND CISTERN

The steps opposite show how to fit a close-coupled toilet. Most manufacturers supply the fill and flush valves (see pp.490–91) for a cistern in the package. If you are buying valves, check they will fit. If there is no isolating valve, fit one to the supply pipe before fitting the toilet.

1 CONNECTING THE PAN AND CISTERN

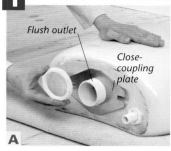

Flush outlet

Close-coupling plate

A

Fit the close-coupling plate onto the flush outlet then screw on the large plastic nut supplied. Some cisterns bolt directly onto the pan.

B

Slide the bolts into position on the close-coupling plate.

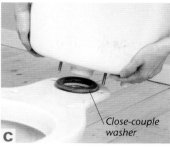

Close-couple washer

C

Position a close-couple washer over the inlet to the pan. Lower the cistern into place, inserting the bolts into the holes in the pan.

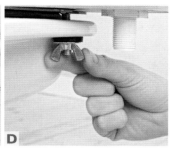

D

Slip rubber washers onto the bolts before you secure them with wingnuts. Don't over-tighten – you could crack the pan or cistern.

2 POSITIONING THE TOILET

Pan connector

A

Insert a pan connector into the waste pipe (see opposite). Slide the toilet fully into position. There is no need to fix or seal the connection.

B

Ensure the toilet is level and mark the positions of the fixing holes. A stud wall may need an extra nogging to provide fixing points (see p.255).

C

Draw around the base of the pan to make it easy to reposition. Mark the position of fixing points at the back of the pan on the floor.

D

Remove the toilet. Drill pilot holes at the marked points and plug them if necessary.

3 FIXING THE TOILET IN PLACE

Reposition the toilet using the outline you marked on the floor to guide you. The fixing holes and pilot holes should match up perfectly. Hold a washer in place, then insert screws to fix the cistern to the wall. You may find a short screwdriver provides easier access to tighten the screws. Take care not to over-tighten them.

Washer

A

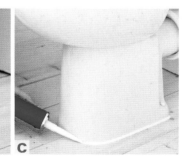

Rubber washer

B

Place a rubber washer over the fixing holes in the base of the pan. Insert screws and tighten, but again, don't over-tighten them.

C

Apply a continuous bead of silicone sealant around the bottom of the pan using a sealant dispenser (see p.81).

4 CONNECTING UP THE CISTERN

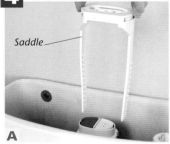

Saddle

A

Cistern valves vary, and therefore so do fitting methods. In this push-button cistern, the saddle section of the valve needs correct positioning.

B

Cut the flush button rods to fit and insert them through the cistern lid and into the flush valve body.

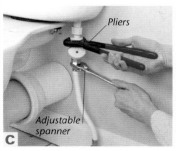

Pliers

Adjustable spanner

C

Brace the inlet pipe with slip-joint pliers as you screw on the flexible connector from the cold-water supply with an adjustable spanner.

Adjustable spanner

D

Fit the toilet seat. Insert the bolts through the pan, slip on a washer, and tighten the nuts. Adjust the seat if necessary (see p.266).

REPLACING A BASIN

Basins are straightforward to replace. Simply remove the old basin and connect the new one. If it is a new-build project or a basin is being installed in a new position, you will need to re-route water supply and drainage pipes (see pp.474–81). Bidets have similar fitting and plumbing requirements and can be replaced using the method shown here.

TOOLS AND MATERIALS SEE BASIC TOOLKIT AND P.255

ANATOMY OF A BASIN AND PEDESTAL

The pedestal helps support the weight of the basin and sits in front of the water supply and waste pipes to partially hide them.

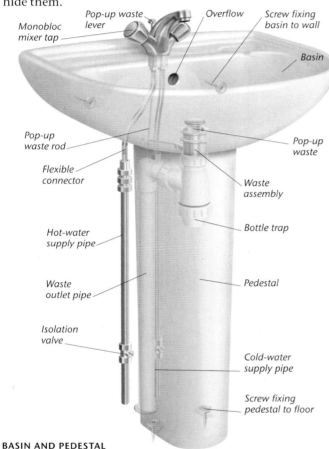

Pop-up waste lever
Monobloc mixer tap
Overflow
Screw fixing basin to wall
Basin
Pop-up waste rod
Flexible connector
Pop-up waste
Waste assembly
Hot-water supply pipe
Bottle trap
Waste outlet pipe
Pedestal
Isolation valve
Cold-water supply pipe
Screw fixing pedestal to floor

BASIN AND PEDESTAL

REMOVING AN OLD SINK

Before you start, turn off the water at the isolation valves on the hot- and cold-supply pipes. If there are no isolation valves, part or all of each system may require draining down (see p.465). With the water off, open the taps and allow them to run dry. Disconnect the flexible connectors from the taps, or on older systems, cut through rigid supply pipes. Unscrew the plastic nut connecting the trap to the waste pipe. When all the pipework is disconnected, locate the screws holding the basin to the wall and remove them, then lift the basin away. There is no need to remove the taps from the basin unless you want to reuse them. Undo the screws fixing the pedestal to the floor and remove it.

FITTING A BASIN AND PEDESTAL

When you have removed the old basin, assess whether you need to re-route the pipework. You may want to adjust the supply and drainage pipes slightly so that they run up inside the pedestal, rather than simply being hidden behind it. This isn't essential, but you might decide it is worth doing if you have a side view of the basin. If the supply pipes don't have isolation valves, fit them before you fit the new basin (see p.465). Then follow the steps shown opposite to fit a basin with a pedestal. Use any brackets and fixings provided by the manufacturer.

Fitting other styles of basin

Assembling the components of the plug, trap, and taps (shown opposite) is similar for all types, but other aspects of the fitting procedure can differ. For example, you might need to hide supply and drainage pipes in a wall. Units or worktops may need to be cut to house some types of basin – the manufacturer will generally supply a cutting template. If you are fitting a basin into a stone worktop, it will need to be cut at the factory. Wall-mounted basins (see below) rely on their fixings to support their full weight. Most manufacturers supply special brackets with wall-mounted basins. If none are supplied, seek installation advice from your supplier. When fixing a wall-mounted basin to a stud wall, you will need to insert new noggings to provide firm fixing points (see p.255 for advice). You can modify the pipework to run through the wall at the same time. If you want to hide the supply and drainage pipes of a wall-mounted basin in a solid wall you will have to chisel out grooves for them to sit in. Run the pipes through protective sheaths, then plaster over the top. This technique is known as "chasing".

FITTING A WALL-MOUNTED BASIN

Measure the fixing positions on the basin and mark them to the wall. Make sure the two fixing points are level and the supply and waste pipes are central. Drill pilot holes at the marked off points.

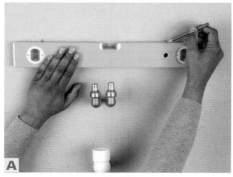

A

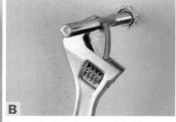

B

Screw the brackets provided into the pilot holes. If you are fixing into a masonry wall, insert wall plugs into the pilot holes first.

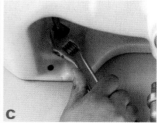

C

Hang the basin on the brackets, then tighten the nuts to hold the basin firmly. Connect the hot and cold water, and the waste pipe.

1 ASSEMBLING THE TAP AND WASTE COMPONENTS

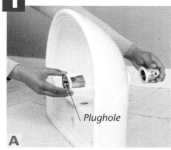

Plughole

A

Balance the basin on its back. Push the top of the waste assembly (the plughole) through the waste hole to meet the bottom section.

Pop-up waste system

B

Hold the top of the waste assembly steady while you screw the bottom on. The pop-up waste system should point towards the back of the basin.

C

Insert the washer supplied into the bottom of the tap (see pp.484–87 for more information on taps).

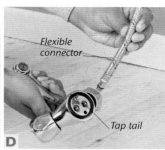

Flexible connector

Tap tail

D

Screw flexible connectors into the tap tails.

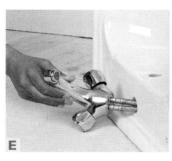

E

Insert the taps, with flexible connectors attached, through the hole in the top of the basin.

F

Slip a washer on before you tighten the retaining nut underneath the basin to hold the taps in position, but take care not to over-tighten it.

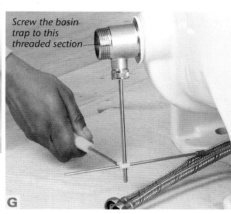

Screw the basin trap to this threaded section

G

Connect up the pop-up waste system. Insert the rod with the lever attached through the tap. Screw the other rod into the waste assembly. Connect them using the fixing supplied. See p.487 for more information on pop-up waste systems. Screw a bottle trap onto the bottom of the waste assembly.

2 GETTING THE BASIN IN POSITION

A

Position the pedestal in front of the supply and waste pipes.

B

Place the basin on the pedestal. Adjust the pedestal so that it provides good support and the basin nestling securely on top of it.

Check the basin sits level

C

Use a spirit level to make the final adjustments, then mark through the basin and pedestal fixing points with a pencil.

D

Drill pilot holes at the points you marked. Plug them if necessary.

3 FIXING THE BASIN IN PLACE

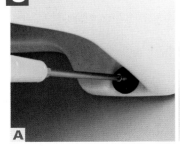

A

Reposition the basin. Place rubber washers over the fixing points then screw the basin into position. Repeat for the pedestal.

B

Screw the trap connector nut onto the waste pipe.

C

Use slip joint pliers (see p.468) to brace the supply pipe while you tighten the flexible connector pipe onto it with an adjustable spanner.

D

Position the waste plug. Apply silicone sealant across the back of the basin and around the bottom of the pedestal. Turn the water back on.

REPLACING A BATH

Bath dimensions vary widely, so check a new bath will fit in the same spot as the old before you buy. Another consideration with very large baths is whether you will be able to manoeuvre it through your home to the bathroom. Room to work is also important – especially in smaller bathrooms. It will sometimes be necessary to remove the other bathroom fittings in order to remove an old bath and fit a new one.

TOOLS AND MATERIALS SEE BASIC TOOLKIT AND P.255

CAST-IRON BATHS

Decorative cast-iron baths may be candidates for reclamation (see p.87). If not, these heavy items can be broken up using a lump hammer and all of the material recycled (see p.86). When you do this, drape a dustsheet over the old bath to stop flying debris and be sure to wear protective goggles, ear defenders, and gloves.

When fitting a cast-iron bath, ensure that its weight is evenly distributed across several floor joists. Planks of wood underneath the bath feet can help spread the weight. In some cases, you may need to reinforce the joists below.

ANATOMY OF A BATH

Connecting the water supply to a bath is much the same as for a basin (see pp.258–59). The main difference when fitting a bath is that it may be large and heavy, and access to the plumbing can be difficult.

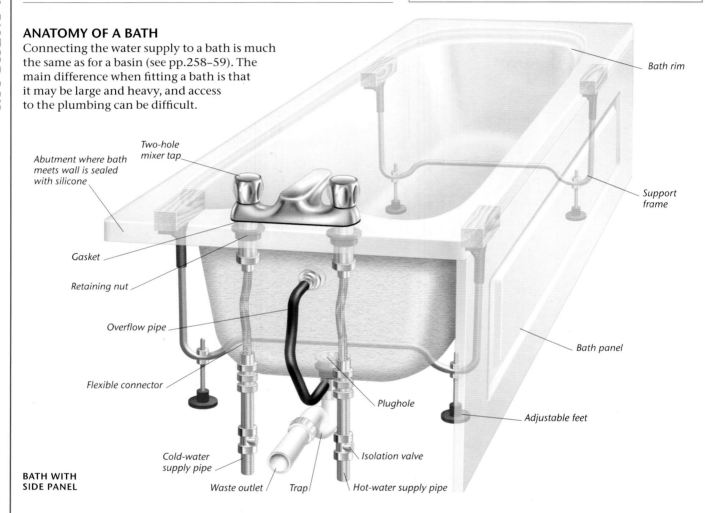

Two-hole mixer tap

Abutment where bath meets wall is sealed with silicone

Gasket

Retaining nut

Overflow pipe

Flexible connector

Cold-water supply pipe

Waste outlet

Trap

Isolation valve

Hot-water supply pipe

Plughole

Bath rim

Support frame

Bath panel

Adjustable feet

BATH WITH SIDE PANEL

REMOVING AN OLD BATH

Turn off hot- and cold-water supplies before you start. If there are no isolating valves on the bath supply pipes, part, or even all, of each system may require draining through a drain valve (see pp.464–67). Once the water is off, run the taps dry. Disconnect the flexible connectors to the hot- and cold-water supply pipes, or if there are rigid supply pipes cut through them. Then disconnect the trap by unscrewing it from the waste pipe. If the bath is channelled into the wall then use a craft knife to cut through any silicone seals and remove a row of tiles if necessary to free the bath. Finally, remove any screws fixing the bath legs to the floor, then remove the bath carefully. You may need to break up old cast-iron baths for removal (see box, above).

FITTING A BATH

Before fitting the new bath, modify the pipework if necessary, and fit isolating valves to the supply pipes if there are none already. Enclose exposed pipes of freestanding baths in decorative chrome sleeving. For more information on plumbing, see pp.462–83.

Unless you are fitting a freestanding type, panels are used around the sides of the bath to hide the plumbing and the underside. Matching panels may be supplied with the bath and simply clip into position. Alternatively, you might need to construct a batten framework for a panel, or even make a panel yourself and decorate it to match the rest of the room. Ideally, panels should be reasonably easy to remove to allow access to the trap in case of blockages.

1 ASSEMBLING THE FRAME, TAPS, AND OVERFLOW SYSTEM

Dustsheet prevents scratches

A

Turn the bath upside down, and screw the feet into the frame. Turn the bath back over onto its feet.

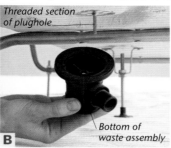

Threaded section of plughole

Bottom of waste assembly

B

Slip the plughole into position in the bath and hold it steady while you screw the bottom of the waste assembly to it underneath the bath.

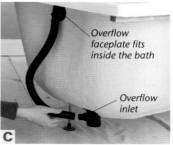

Overflow faceplate fits inside the bath

Overflow inlet

C

Insert the overflow faceplate through the bath. Screw the overflow pipe onto it. Push the other end of the pipe onto the overflow inlet.

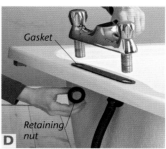

Gasket

Retaining nut

D

Position the gasket, then insert the taps into their holes so they sit on it neatly. Tighten the retaining nuts supplied onto the taps.

2 FIXING THE BATH IN POSITION

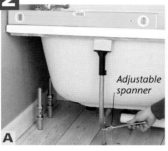

Adjustable spanner

A

Move the bath into place. Balance a spirit level on the bath rim and adjust the feet by turning them until the bath is level.

B

Screw the feet into the floor. Drill pilot holes and plug them where necessary. If the surface is uneven, use blocks of wood under the feet.

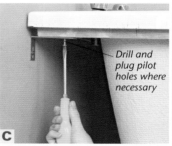

Drill and plug pilot holes where necessary

C

Mark the fixing points for the support brackets supplied. Drill pilot holes and plug them if necessary. Screw the brackets into position.

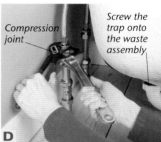

Compression joint

Screw the trap onto the waste assembly

D

Use flexible connectors to join the taps to the supply pipes (see p.472). Screw the compression joints into place (see pp.476–77).

3 FITTING THE BATH PANELS

Use an offcut of wood that is the same depth as your bath panel. Then use a spirit level and your offcut to mark points on the floor directly below the batten that runs under the rim of the bath. Use a straight edge to join up the points into a continuous line.

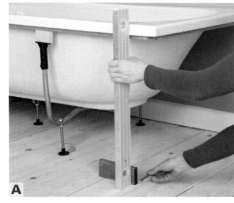

A

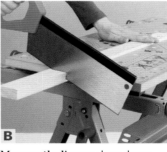

B

Measure the line you have drawn around the bath and cut battens to fit inside it.

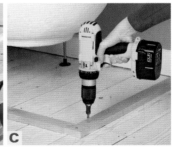

C

Drill pilot holes through the batten and into the floor. You will need to insert plugs into concrete floors, then screw the battens down.

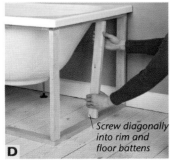

Screw diagonally into rim and floor battens

D

Cut battens to fit between the rim and floor battens. Put one at each corner, and one in the centre of each side. Screw them in place.

E

Trim the panels to size using a jigsaw. You can scribe the edge of the panel to fit the wall and skirting if required (see p.221).

F

Position the panels. You might need to cut away the top corners of the panels so they will fit snugly under the rim of the bath.

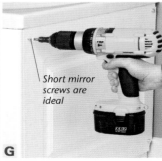

Short mirror screws are ideal

G

Drill pilot holes through the panels and into battens. Screw the panels into place.

TYPES OF SHOWER

There is an enormous selection of shower designs on offer. To add a new shower to your existing suite, one option is to construct a separate cubicle for one if there is room (see p.254 for bathroom planning). Alternatively, install a shower above the existing bath. The type of plumbing system you have will determine the type of shower you can fit (see opposite).

CHOOSING SHOWER FURNITURE

In some cases your main bathroom suite (see pp.252–53) will come with a matching shower tray and cubicle as an optional extra. If you are not buying a new suite, then separate cubicles, trays, and screens are readily available. Like other bathroom furniture, white is the most popular colour for trays, as well as screen and cubicle frames.

Shower cubicles

These are designed to fit particular sizes and shapes of shower tray. The structure of a shower cubicle usually relies on tiled areas of the bathroom walls making up one or more of its sides. Use cement board on walls that will be tiled inside a cubicle. Some manufacturers make all-in-one cubicles with a built-in shower. Alternatively you can create a walk-in shower (see p.264).

Shower trays

Acrylic, resin, and ceramic shower trays are available. Solid resin and ceramic trays need to be installed on a bed of mortar. You will need to remove a section of flooring to accommodate the trap under a solid tray. If this is impossible then build the tray up on a plinth or choose an acrylic tray. Acrylic trays usually have adjustable legs and side panels, similar to a bath (see pp.260–61). They sit higher off the floor than solid trays, which means waste connection is easier, and removing sections of the floor is rarely necessary. Fitting both types of tray is shown on p.265. There are many shape variations – make sure you buy one to match the cubicle design you have chosen.

Shower screens and curtains

Screens are used along the edge of a bath when a shower is fitted above. Some are single, fixed sheets, whereas others are constructed of a number of folding sections. See p.265 for how to fit a shower screen. Alternatively, you can fit a shower curtain. These run on straight or curved tracks to fit any shape of bath or shower, and styles are available to suit any bathroom.

BUILDING REGULATIONS

If a shower head can reach below the rim of a shower tray or bath, you must fit a double check to prevent waste water siphoning back into the water supply. These valves are sold separately as "shower check" valves, or in many cases, the valve is integrated into the shower itself. Read the model specifications carefully.

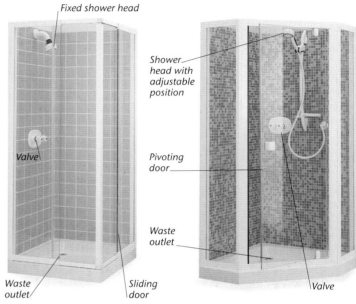

Fixed shower head

Shower head with adjustable position

Valve

Pivoting door

Waste outlet

Waste outlet

Sliding door

Valve

SHOWER CUBICLE – TWO SIDES

SHOWER CUBICLE – THREE SIDES

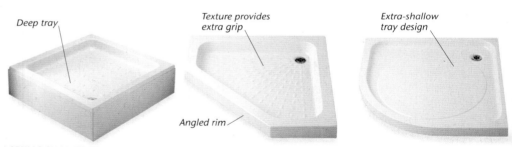

Deep tray

Texture provides extra grip

Extra-shallow tray design

Angled rim

ACRYLIC SHOWER TRAY

RESIN SHOWER TRAYS

Screen fixes to wall

Width of screen can vary

Folding screen doors

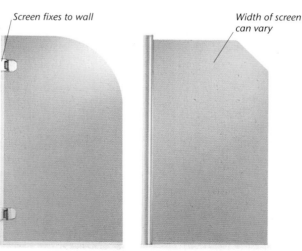

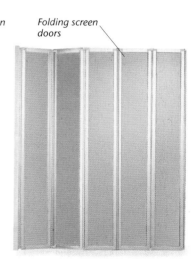

SHOWER SCREEN WITH CURVED EDGE

SHOWER SCREEN WITH STRAIGHT EDGE

SHOWER SCREEN WITH FOLDING DOORS

CHOOSING THE RIGHT SHOWER

There are several different types of shower and it is critical that you choose the right one for your plumbing system (see table below and pp.464–67). If you have a tank-fed hot-water storage cylinder or a combination boiler you can fit a mixer shower. If you don't have a cylinder, or if it doesn't store enough water, then you may choose an electric shower. The power of both mixer and electric showers can be boosted with a pump, but only if they are fed from water storage tanks. If in doubt, ask your supplier for advice.

Mixer showers

These use a mixer valve to combine hot and cold water to the temperature required. Mixers need hot water to be fed from a storage cylinder or a combination boiler. Thermostatic mixer showers have a more sophisticated valve that remains set at the required temperature when you turn the water on and off, and prevents temperature fluctuation. Many thermostatic mixer showers have an automatic shut off if hot or cold supplies fail, and on some models you can set a maximum temperature.

Electric showers

These are fed only from the cold-water supply – either from a tank or from the mains. The water is heated to the temperature required within the wall-mounted unit of the shower. Flow is dependent on mains pressure and on the power of the shower installed – more power will heat water quickly and allow it to pass through the system faster.

Pumps

You can only fit a pump if your shower is fed from a tank. Follow the manufacturer's guidelines on the exact position to locate the pump for supplying the shower. Alternatively, you can buy mixer and electric showers with integral pumps. Pumped showers are known as "power showers". Most tanks are large enough to feed one pump, but in households with more than one pumped shower, a larger or second cistern may be required. If a pump is being fitted, it requires connection to the electrical supply via a double-pole isolating switch (see p.435).

Mixer showers

Most manufacturers produce mixer showers that may be fitted in a high- or low-pressure plumbing system. However, always take care to check compatibility before purchase.

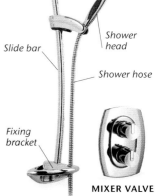

Slide bar — *Shower head*
Shower hose
Fixing bracket

FULLY ADJUSTABLE SHOWER

Shower rose

FIXED SHOWER HEAD

MIXER VALVE

Spray direction can be adjusted

DIRECTIONAL SHOWER HEAD

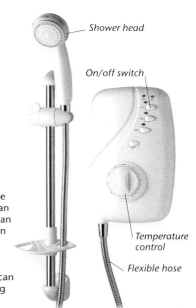

Shower head
On/off switch
Temperature control
Flexible hose

Electric shower

Because the water is heated by the shower itself, these are bulkier than mixer showers. They also require an electricity supply run on their own circuit from the consumer unit (see p.431). Basic models only have a temperature control. On more sophisticated showers you can also adjust water flow and heating power to your requirements.

SYSTEM REQUIREMENTS OF DIFFERENT SHOWER TYPES

Shower type (see above)	Water supply system	Height of cold tank	Electricity supply
Mixer shower	Hot and cold water from tanks	At least 1m (3ft 3in) above	None required
	Cold water direct from rising main; hot from combi boiler	No tank	None required
Mixer shower with a separate pump	Hot and cold water from tanks	At least 150mm (6in) above	Yes, spur to pump with a double-pole isolating switch
Mixer shower with an integral pump	Hot and cold water from tanks	At least 75mm (3in) above	Yes, spur to shower with a double-pole isolating switch
Electric shower	Cold water from rising main	Can be in any position	Yes, radial circuit to shower with a double-pole isolating switch
Electric shower with pump	Cold water from tank	500mm (4ft 8in) above (integral) 100mm (4in) above (separate)	Yes, radial circuit to shower with a double-pole isolating switch

FITTING A SHOWER CUBICLE

Unless a shower is used in a wet-room design, an enclosure is needed to prevent the surrounding area getting wet. In most cases this takes the form of a shower tray and a cubicle. Screens or shower curtains are used when a shower is above a bath. A third option is to create a large, walk-in shower using screens, or tiled or glass-block walls.

TOOLS AND MATERIALS SEE BASIC TOOLKIT AND P.255

ANATOMY OF A SHOWER
Plumbing and electrical requirements vary depending on the type of shower you choose (see p.263). A mixer shower fitted in a cubicle with an acrylic tray is shown here.

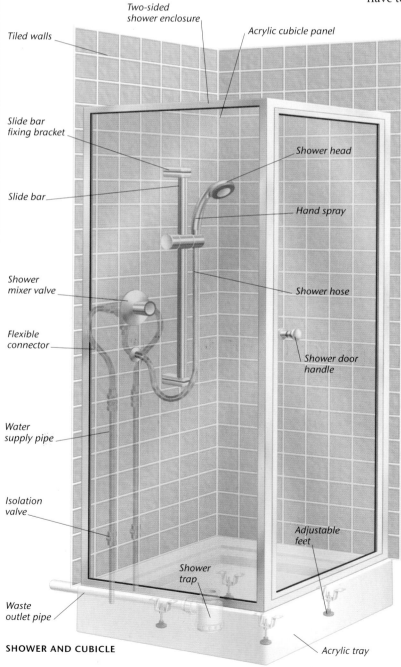

Two-sided shower enclosure

Acrylic cubicle panel

Tiled walls

Slide bar fixing bracket

Shower head

Slide bar

Hand spray

Shower mixer valve

Shower hose

Flexible connector

Shower door handle

Water supply pipe

Isolation valve

Adjustable feet

Shower trap

Waste outlet pipe

Acrylic tray

SHOWER AND CUBICLE

WALK-IN SHOWERS
This type of shower enclosure is an option in large bathrooms. A "drying area" separates the entrance and the shower, making a door or curtain unnecessary. A walk-in shower can be fitted in a similar way to a standard tray and cubicle. Alternatively, you can build one yourself. Stud walls are the easiest option (see pp.106–09). Use cement board rather than plasterboard for the internal walls of the shower. This provides the best possible surface for tiling (see pp.308–21) and gives a fully waterproof finish. Alternatively you can build a glass-block wall (pp.114–15).

FITTING A SHOWER
Plumbing and electricity requirements differ depending on the shower type – clear instructions should be supplied with your shower. As a general rule, you will have to route 15-mm (½-in) water supply pipes directly from a tank or tanks, or the rising main, using as few corners as possible. In the shower, the pipes need to be hidden in the wall in protective sheaths. Because walls inside the shower will be tiled and waterproofed, where possible provide emergency access to the shower isolation valves from the other side of the wall behind the shower. Alternatively fit the valves somewhere more accessible farther down the pipe route, but make sure you label them carefully. Waste pipes will also need to be installed. (see pp.474–75 for more on routing pipes). Wiring requirements for an electrical shower are dealt with on p.431. Mixer showers require no electrical connection, but will need power for a pump, if applicable (see p.263).

FITTING A SHOWER OR BATH SCREEN
A bath screen is required if you are fitting a shower over a bath. They are attached to the wall at the shower end of the bath. It is essential that the rim of the bath is flat to create a watertight seal. If your bath has a curved rim, then shower curtains are usually a better option.

FITTING A SHOWER TRAY AND CUBICLE
Basic instructions for fitting a tray and cubicle are given here, but you should always follow any specific guidelines given by the manufacturer. Fit the tray in place before you begin to tile the walls or lay any flooring. Choose a position for the shower that will allow you to fix the cubicle into a wooden stud or a solid wall. There are two main types of tray, each fitted using a different technique (see opposite). Once you have fitted the tray, the next step is to tile the walls within the shower cubicle (see pp.308–21). The bottom row of tiles should overlap the top of the tray rim. After tiling, fit the cubicle in a similar way to a bath screen (see opposite). Then seal the joins between the cubicle, tray, walls, and floor with silicone. Fit the shower valve, connecting up the supply and waste pipes as required.

FITTING A SOLID RESIN OR CERAMIC SHOWER TRAY

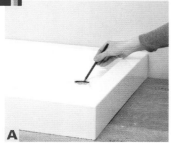

A

Place the tray with its waste outlet in a good position to connect to the waste pipes. Mark the position of the outlet and the tray on the floor.

B

Remove a section of the floor in the position you marked using a jigsaw. The hole must be big enough to house the trap (see p.480).

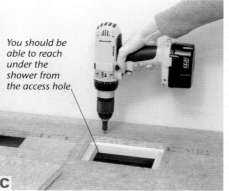

C

You should be able to reach under the shower from the access hole

Remove a second section of flooring next to the first, but outside the tray area. The drainage pipe for this type of tray runs under the floor so you need to provide access to make the connection with the trap. To create a permanent access hatch, screw battens around the edge of the hole to support the section of flooring you have removed.

D

Apply dilute PVA solution (five parts PVA to one part water) to the tray area. When it is dry, spread a thin bed of mortar over the area.

E

Neaten edges when tray is level

Screw the trap to the plughole as for an acrylic tray (below). Place the tray on the mortar bed and check it is level. Adjust the mortar if needed.

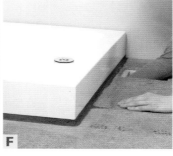

F

Allow the mortar to dry for at least 24 hours. Connect up the shower trap with the waste pipe, using the access hatch.

G

Use a sealant dispenser to apply a continuous bead of silicone sealant around the edge of the tray.

FITTING AN ACRYLIC SHOWER TRAY

Screw the feet into the frame of the tray if necessary, although many trays are sold pre-assembled. However, you will have to insert the drainage outlet into the tray and screw on the trap below.

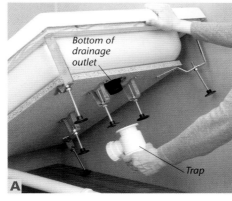

A

Bottom of drainage outlet

Trap

B

Adjust the feet of the frame using an adjustable spanner until the tray sits precisely level. Connect up the trap to the waste pipe.

Push the panels under the rim of the tray

C

Clip the side panels into position. Apply silicone sealant where the tray meets the wall and floor, and on the joins between the panels and rim.

FITTING A SHOWER OR BATH SCREEN

Hold the channel sections vertically

A

Mark the fixing points of the channel. Drill pilot holes though the tiles and insert plugs (see also p.251). Screw the channel in place.

B

Carefully slide the panels into their channels. Make sure they are vertical, and resting on the rim of the shower tray or bath to provide a seal.

C

Screw the fixings provided into the side of the channel to secure the screens in position.

D

Use a sealant dispenser to apply a bead of silicone sealant down the outside edge of the channel. Don't apply sealant on the inside edge.

UNBLOCKING TRAPS

One of the most common areas where blockages occur is in traps. A basin trap is shown here. Some traps have what is known as a "cleaning eye" on the side. This unscrews to allow cleaning access without removing the trap.

TOOLS AND MATERIALS
Bowl or bucket, old toothbrush, replacement washers

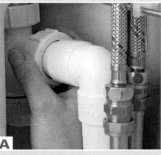

A Undo the basin trap. Position a bowl beneath it to catch any water.

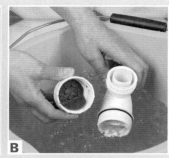

B Remove debris and wash the trap in a bucket of clean water. An old toothbrush is an ideal cleaning tool.

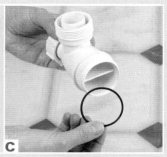

C Replace the trap. It is worth replacing worn washers while the trap is disassembled to prevent future leaks.

UNBLOCKING PIPES

If the trap is clear then the problem is probably in the basin waste system. To begin with, try shifting the blockage with chemicals. If this doesn't work, use a plunger or auger. These solutions also work for a kitchen waste system.

TOOLS AND MATERIALS
Chemical cleaner, protective gloves, plunger

Pour direct into plughole

Chemical cleaner
Follow the instructions provided. Ensure the area is well ventilated and wear protective gloves.

Plug the overflow

Plunger
If chemicals don't work, use a plunger. Put the cup over the plughole and pump up and down.

MORE INFORMATION

■ Take special care when dealing with caustic chemicals. Splashes may burn skin and clothes. Read usage and safety instructions carefully and wear any protective equipment as directed.
■ Help prevent blockages by regularly removing debris from plugholes.
■ An auger, as shown below, can also be used for unblocking basin and bath waste systems.

UNBLOCKING TOILETS

If flush water rises to the rim and then drains slowly, the toilet trap or drain is blocked. To unblock these, use a plunger or auger – the latter burrows into the blockage and loosens it up.

TOOLS AND MATERIALS
Auger

A Pull a section of the auger out of the drum.

B Tighten the retaining nut on top of the auger body.

C Rotate the drum of the auger so it burrows into the waste system to dislodge the blockage.

ADJUSTING A LOOSE TOILET SEAT

Toilet lids can be poorly adjusted and may not stay in an upright position. There is usually no need to purchase a new seat and lid; you can simply adjust the lid so that it leans back against the wall or cistern.

TOOLS AND MATERIALS
Screwdriver

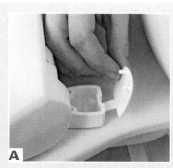

A Locate the nuts holding the seat and lid to the pan.

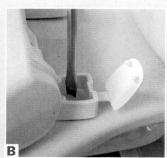

B Unscrew the nuts and slide their rubber washers to adjust the opening angle of the lid.

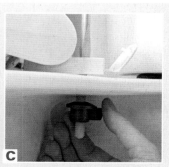

C Tighten the nuts and check that the seat and lid now open to the desired angle.

REPAIRING CHIPPED CERAMIC FITTINGS

Proprietary kits are available to repair minor damage to ceramic bathroom fittings. Instructions for use may vary slightly between different manufacturers, but the example shown here displays the common principles. Some filling compounds can also be used to glue chipped sections back together.

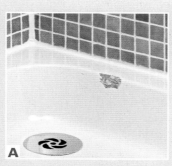

A **Dust out** the damaged area and ensure that it is completely clean and dry.

B **Mix up the two-part** filler in the ratio specified by the manufacturer.

C **Fill the chipped area,** leaving it slightly proud of the surrounding area because the filler shrinks as it dries. Repeat if necessary.

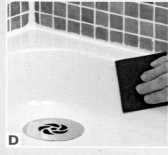

D **Sand the filled area** until it is smooth. Shape it to match the fitting.

Make sure you cover the area you sanded

E **Use the paint** supplied to cover the repair. Any excess may normally be removed with acetone.

F **The finished patch** should be invisible.

TOOLS AND MATERIALS
Ceramic filler, filling knife, mixing spatula, sandpaper, ceramic paint, paintbrush, acetone

ADJUSTING WATER LEVELS IN CISTERNS

When a cistern overflows, it is usually caused by the inlet valve being at the incorrect level. The way to correct this will depend on the type of float valve you have (see pp.490–91).

TOOLS AND MATERIALS
Screwdriver

Torbeck valve
Rotate the float clockwise or anticlockwise to move it up or down the float arm.

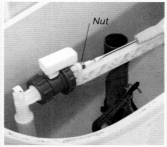

Nut

Modern plastic float arm
Simply adjust the plastic screw and nut positioned on the float arm next to the inlet valve entry point.

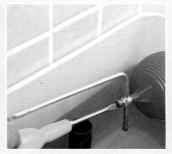

Traditional metal float arm
Either bend the arm or move the float up or down by loosening the screw holding it.

WEAK SHOWER

Reduced shower flow is usually due to limescale buildup. This can easily be removed with a descaling product.

TOOLS AND MATERIALS
Screwdriver, bowl, descaling solution

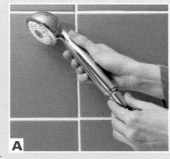

A **Unscrew the shower** head from the hose.

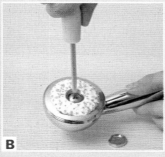

B **Unscrew the spray plate** and immerse it in descaling solution.

C **Leave it in the solution** for specified length of time. Flush any remaining scale from the pipes before replacing the shower head.

DECORATING AND FINISHING

HOME DECORATION

Architecture and design provide the framework for the look of your home, but the decoration provides the finish. Options for finishing depends very much on surface type and your personal preferences. The variety of decorative options has expanded greatly in recent years. Many aspects of the home that were once considered purely functional can today offer scope for decoration and expression of personal taste and style. This section considers many of these options, as well as the all-important preparatory steps in any decoration project, which are required in order to achieve the best finish possible.

DECORATION OPTIONS

The opportunity for decoration extends into almost every aspect of the house, including many you might not immediately think of. A huge range of products and techniques are available to enhance the decorative aspects of both interior and exterior walls, floors and ceilings, and fixtures and fittings. Lighting can also play an important part in a decorative scheme, and everything from staircases to guttering can be designed or treated to personalize the look of your home. Decorative projects may be large or small, ranging from minor enhancements of an existing scheme to full-scale refurbishment of a room or even an entire house. Whatever the scale of the job, however, advance planning is key. Work out what you intend to achieve, consider the problems you may encounter, and ensure you have all the equipment you need close at hand before beginning work.

DECORATIVE STYLE

The appearance of your home is, of course, a matter of personal taste, but there are some general issues that are always worth bearing in mind. Consider the age and style of the house's exterior, the shape and size of the rooms, the design of any fittings such as kitchen units or a bathroom suite and other aspects that you either cannot change, or do not wish to. Bear in mind the amount of natural and artificial light available, and remember that dark colours will tend to make a room seem smaller, while light colours can make it look larger. If you plan to use two or more strong colours in the same room, consider carefully whether they go together. In a period home, you may want a decorative scheme appropriate for its age, perhaps with brass fixtures and fittings. Or, if appropriate, you may want a bold modern approach with stone and stainless steel.

Carpets

Comfortable and warm underfoot, carpet is ideal for most rooms apart from kitchens, and to a certain extent bathrooms. In a bathroom, some people like the feel of carpet, but in practice it can become damp and therefore rot if the appropriate ventilation is not present. Good-quality underlay increases durability, adds soundproofing, and provides extra comfort.

Vinyl floors

Whether in tiles or sheet form, vinyl is ideal for "wet" areas in the home like bathrooms and kitchens. It is waterproof and easy to clean. Linoleum is a more "natural" alternative to vinyl that achieves a similar finish.

Bathroom and kitchen walls

Wall tiles are commonly used in kitchens and bathrooms to provide durable, easily cleaned decorative surfaces. Wallpaper used in these rooms should be of a vinyl variety. Paints that contain vinyl are also ideal as they provide a good wipeable surface. Some manufacturers will also provide paint that is recommended for bathroom and kitchen use.

Tiled floors

Ceramic floor tiles are commonly found in kitchens and bathrooms, and offer a very hardwearing, easily cleaned flooring option.

Doors (exterior)

The treatment for exterior door surfaces is much the same as for windows. Making sure that the top edge and the underside of the door are painted or treated will increase the life expectancy of the door considerably.

Render

Painted render will last for up to 10 years before it requires re-coating. Only exterior emulsion or masonry paint should be used. Other masonry surfaces, such as brick or stone, can be painted, but these are more often left with their natural finish, since paint will take to some types of brick or stone better than others.

Ceilings
Most ceilings can have paint applied directly, or be given a textured finish and then painted. You can often apply lining paper over rough ceilings to provide a smoother surface for decoration.

Wall surfaces
Internal plaster walls can be painted or covered with wallpaper depending on decorative preference. Different types of paint can provide varying durability, in terms of finish. Water-based paints such as emulsion are best suited to wall and ceiling surfaces. This is also the case for wallpaper. When wallpapering, walls should be lined first.

Natural wood floors
If the existing floorboards are used as a decorative finish in their own right, natural wood floors can be an integral part of your home. Alternatively, a natural wood floor can be laid on existing concrete, floorboards or any other type of boarded floor. In a similar way, modern laminate floors can also be laid in most areas of the home.

Drainpipes and guttering
PVC guttering only needs to be cleaned down, although it may be painted if required. Metal (ferrous) guttering requires periodic painting to prevent rust and keep it in good condition. Proprietary metal paints are ideal for this purpose.

Weatherboard
This may be painted, or, if wooden, given a natural finish. PVC and aluminium-based weatherboard only requires cleaning down, although it can be painted using proprietary systems. Cement-based weatherboard is normally supplied pre-finished, but this may also be painted if required.

Fascia
Wooden fascia boards are either painted or have a natural wood finish applied. They should be redecorated at the same time as windows and doors. They may also be changed for, or covered with, PVC alternatives, which only require cleaning down rather than redecoration.

Garage floor
Floor paint is ideal for concrete floors, such as those commonly found in garages. It is hardwearing, has some decorative appeal, and is easily cleaned. New concrete floors must be allowed to dry out completely before paint is applied.

Internal wood-clad walls
Clad walls are best painted or given a natural wood finish. Interior specified coatings will provide the best finish.

Windows (exterior)
Wooden windows require either painting or the application of a natural finish. Redecoration should occur every 3–5 years, using only coatings recommended for exterior woodwork. Metal windows (steel or iron) will also require redecoration, although PVC and aluminium are best treated by regular cleaning down.

Preparing surfaces

TO ACHIEVE THE BEST POSSIBLE FINISH ALL SURFACES MUST BE ADEQUATELY PREPARED BEFORE THEY ARE DECORATED. THIS SECTION SHOWS YOU HOW TO GET THE BEST RESULTS ON LARGE AREAS SUCH AS WALLS AND CEILINGS, AS WELL AS TECHNIQUES FOR TREATING WOODEN SURFACES SUCH AS DOORS AND SMALLER AREAS OF EXPOSED DECORATIVE WOODWORK.

CEILINGS, WALLS, AND WOODWORK

Previously painted walls, in good condition, need little preparation before redecoration. Minor filling and sanding is usually all that is required. If a wall is papered, remove paper and tidy up the surface before redecorating. On a wooden surface good preparation is the basis for a professional finish. See pp.274–75 for preparing wooden elements or features.

TOOLS AND MATERIALS

Shave hook
Strips paint from a wooden surface, whether flat or ornate.

Wire brush
Used to remove debris and clean off flaky surfaces, such as a metal pipe.

Sandpaper
Paper with a rough face that smoothes surfaces and provides a key for coatings. Grades vary from the smooth to the very rough.

Wallpaper scorer
Perforates paper to let steam or water through. Essential for removing vinyl (waterproof) papers.

Heat gun
Blisters paint and makes it easy to remove from a wooden surface. Must be used with caution.

Steam wallpaper stripper
Electrically operated. Steam flows from a hot-water reservoir to a stripping pad, bubbles paper, easing its removal.

Sanding block
Easy to grip, with a sanding surface on one or more sides. You can make your own by folding sandpaper around a squared-off block of wood.

Steel wool
Cleans down metal surfaces and is used to apply wax. Comes in various grades of coarseness.

Place pad against wall to steam paper

Filler Powder filler is mixed with water into a stiff, creamy paste and used to fill holes in wood, plaster, and masonry surfaces. Once dry, you can sand it to a smooth finish and decorate. Ready-mixed fillers are also available. Most fillers designed for use with natural wood finishes are ready-mixed; other types accept the colour of stains or dyes. The other main type of filler is flexible filler (caulk), which is used along cracks in ceilings, walls, and woodwork.

Knotting solution Applied to knots in wood before primer or further coats of paint, to prevent sap weeping from the knot.

Sugar soap Powdered soap mixed with water and used to clean down surfaces before they are rinsed. Allow surfaces to dry before decoration.

Spray-on stain block Blocks out stains that show through normal coats of paint. Can also be bought as a "paint" in tins. May be water-based or solvent-based; water-based versions dry faster.

White spirit Solvent used for most oil-based paints.

Brush cleaner Restores brushes.

Hand cleaner For easy removal of paint, grime, and grease.

Stripping wallpaper
Dustsheets, steam stripper, warm water, refuse sacks

Washing down and filling
Sugar soap, hot water, sponge, oil-based undercoat (optional), brush, filler, filling knife, sandpaper

Filling cracks
Flexible filler, sealant dispenser, sponge, brush, oil-based undercoat*

* = optional

FOR BASIC TOOLKIT
SEE PP.24–25

STRIPPING WALLPAPER

Steam strippers work most efficiently when top layers of paper have been removed, exposing the more absorbent backing paper. The impermeable surface layer of vinyl papers often peels dry, relatively easily. Always follow the manufacturer's guidelines. Wear protective gloves, if the tool's manual recommends them, and goggles. Steam and drips may burn, so take all possible precautions to protect yourself. Never use a steam stripper to remove paper from a ceiling. Instead, simply soak the paper with warm water and then scrape the paper from the ceiling surface, an option that can also be used on a wall if you prefer.

Lay dustsheets over the room, and remove as much loose paper from the wall by hand as you can.

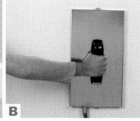

Fill the stripper with warm water before plugging it in. When it starts to steam, place it flush on the wall.

Hold the pad completely flush on the wall surface. After 15-30 seconds, move it along and scrape paper off the wall in the steamed area. The thicker the layer(s) of paper, the longer you will need to hold the pad in place. But do not hold it still for too long or plaster may crumble from the wall.

Work your way across the wall, steaming areas and removing paper.

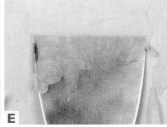

Carry on removing paper . Put it in a refuse sack as you remove it, so that it does not stick to the dustsheet or other surfaces.

WASHING DOWN A WALL AND FILLING HOLES

After a wall has been stripped, wash the surface thoroughly to remove all traces of adhesive. Mix sugar soap with hot water and sponge the wall with it. Then rinse with clean water. You can now repaper the wall. If you wish to paint the wall, apply an oil-based undercoat before a water-based emulsion. However well the wall has been cleaned, traces of adhesive may bleed through a water-based paint; oil-based undercoat prevents this. It is needed on a previously painted wall only if the wall is in a poor condition.

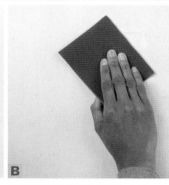

Deeper holes may need filling twice because filler contracts as it dries

Clean out the hole with a dusting brush. Apply filler by pressing it in place with a filling knife.

Once the filler has dried, sand it back to create a smooth surface flush with the surrounding area.

FILLING CRACKS

Cracks are best filled using flexible filler (caulk), which is supplied in a tube and requires a sealant dispenser to apply it along cracks or joins. It cannot be sanded, and must therefore be smoothed by hand before it dries. Some caulks may be overpainted when dry. Others need an oil-based undercoat to prepare them for water-based paints, which may crack if there is no undercoat. Caulk is also used on wood. A ceiling-wall junction is shown here.

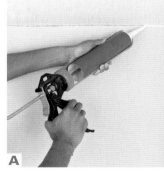

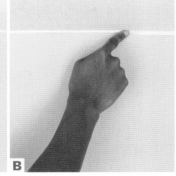

Dust out the joint . Prepare the sealant and gun as shown on p.81. Apply even pressure to the trigger, moving the gun along the join.

Gently smooth the sealant with a wetted finger. You may also use a damp sponge to smooth the caulk.

NEW WALL AND CEILING SURFACES

Plaster in a good condition can be directly overpainted with full-strength paint. Alternatively, first apply a mist coat of dilute emulsion (1 part water to 10 parts paint), which provides a base for further coats. Dry-lined walls and ceilings must be coated with a special sealer before emulsion is applied, otherwise paint may dry differently on the board to that on the jointing compound.

WORKING WITH WOOD

Woodwork provides the finer detailing in a home and its finish is a stamp of quality. To produce good results you must prepare surfaces, including doors, windows, and decorative woodwork for mouldings or panelling.

Stripping wood

A good finish is often achievable by recoating the existing surface. However, you may need to strip woodwork before redecorating – the existing coating may be so bad that it cannot be successfully recoated; it may be painted, but you want a natural wood finish; or it could have a natural finish but you want to paint it or apply a different finish. Beware of surfaces with lead-based paint, which is toxic and now found only in older properties. It is a health risk if heated with a heat gun, and fine particles created by sanding are also toxic. Paint-testing kits are available to identify lead-based paintwork.

TOOLS AND MATERIALS CHECKLIST

Using a heat gun
Shave hook

Solution stripping
Old paintbrush, scraper or shave hook, cloth, white spirit or water

Paste stripping
Filling knife or small trowel, stripper, covering cloth, cleaning cloth, neutralizing solution/white vinegar, water

Covering old paint
Oil-based eggshell paint, paintbrush, brush-cleaning

solution, mid-oak wood dye, dark or Jacobean wax, two cloths

Priming and filling before painting
Knotting solution, paintbrush, filling knife, sanding block, filler, primer

Filling for a natural wood finish
Filling knife, filler, sanding block

FOR BASIC TOOLKIT
SEE PP.24–25

USING A HEAT GUN

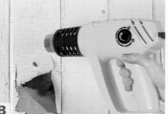

A **Turn the heat gun on** and direct the nozzle at the wood surface, leaving a gap of a few centimeters (inches) between the two.

B **After a few moments,** the paint will begin to soften and bubble, at which point use a shave hook or scraper to lift the old paint free.

C **Move the gun along** to the next area and repeat the process. Use a shave hook to remove paintwork in recesses, such as on panelling.

WORKING SAFELY

■ Take great care using a heat gun. Wear goggles and a respiratory mask, and perhaps gloves. Take any other precautions that are advised by the tool's manufacturer.

■ Do not hold the gun for too long over the wood, to avoid the risk of scorching it or even setting it on fire.

SOLUTION STRIPPING

Wearing gloves, a mask, and goggles, use an old paintbrush to apply the stripper. Use dabbing strokes to build up a good layer of the stripper on the wood's surface. Allow it to soak in and react with the paint. This may take only a couple of minutes or up to half an hour.

A

B **Once the paint** has bubbled up, scrape it off using a scraper and/or a shave hook.

C **Thoroughly clean the** surface afterwards. White spirit and cold water are best, but check the stripper manufacturer's guidelines.

PASTE STRIPPING

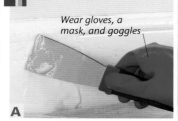

Wear gloves, a mask, and goggles

A **Apply the stripper** with a filling knife or small trowel to a depth of about 2.5mm (⅛in) – or deeper if there are many coats of paint.

B **If your manufacturer specifies** it, cover the entire surface with a proprietary cloth. Leave for 24 hours. Use a scraper to peel away the paste.

C **Thoroughly clean down** the area. If the manufacturer suggests it, use a "neutralizing solution"; or use white vinegar and then clean water.

DIPPING DOORS

Removable items such as doors can be "dipped" professionally. The whole item is submerged in a tank of powerful chemicals, which lift all traces of paint from the wood surface. Many companies offer a collection and delivery service.

COVERING OLD PAINT

Sometimes a natural wood finish may not be possible – if the wood is too rough, or the paint too ingrained to strip. Old beams may have stained finishes or may have been painted at some stage. You can have the paint sand-blasted away by a professional company but this is expensive, and extremely messy. An alternative is to apply the paint effect shown here.

A Completely paint the beam, using an oil-based white eggshell.

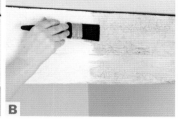

B Apply a wood dye over the top of the eggshell. A mid-oak colour is very effective.

C Rub dark or Jacobean wax across the whole surface to provide the effect of an oak beam.

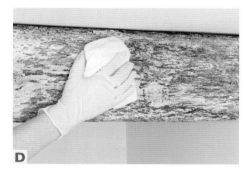

D After half an hour, buff off the wax with a clean cloth. Wax will remain embedded within the wood grain, resulting in the appearance of a natural wood beam.

PREPARING BEAMS

Natural wood beams are often tricky items to prepare for decoration, because of flaky surfaces and often very crumbly edges where the beam meets plaster. Trying to fill the edge is difficult and often ineffective, as the filler too crumbles and falls away.

One way to secure the edge is to apply a clear matt varnish to the beam, overlapping slightly onto wall or ceiling surfaces. The varnish both binds the surface and provides a natural look. The wall or ceiling paint may then be cut in along the edge to create a neat finish.

FILLING AND SANDING WOOD

Wooden surfaces are seldom completely smooth. Filling dents and sanding improves the finish. The type of filler to be used depends on whether the wood is to be painted or a natural finish applied. If it is to be painted, use powder filler (see pp.272–73) – flexible filler can be used in joints or cracks. If a natural wood finish is to be applied, use a "stainable" filler the same colour as the finish. See pp.282–83 for choosing a suitable primer.

PRIMING AND FILLING BEFORE PAINTING

Prime bare wood before using filler, to make it adhere better. Primer also makes it easier to see areas that require filling. If wood is painted, use primer only if there are large, bare patches, for instance on external woodwork. Any knots in bare wood must first be coated with knotting solution.

A

B Allow primer to dry. Mix up filler, and apply to holes, dents, or divots, using the flexibility of a filling knife blade to press in the filler.

C Allow filler to dry. Sand to a smooth finish. Deep holes may require refilling and sanding to provide the best finish.

FILLING FOR A NATURAL WOOD FINISH

A Apply stainable filler to holes in the wood surface with a filler knife. The filler colour should match the natural wood finish to be applied.

B Once the filler has dried, sand it smooth. Then apply coats of your chosen finish.

FURTHER INFORMATION

Sanding
Sandpaper should be chosen according to the condition of the surface. So, for rough surfaces, begin by using a rough paper. As the surface becomes smoother, reduce the coarseness of the paper
Remember that sanding produces dust. This should always be brushed away before a coating is applied.

A vacuum cleaner nozzle is ideal for removing dust from the base of skirting boards or the profiles of mouldings.
The best finishes are normally achieved when the wood has been wiped down with a damp cloth before coating, removing the finest residues. This is essential when sanding flat surfaces such as window sills.

Painting and finishing

PAINT AND NATURAL WOOD FINISHES ARE AN EFFECTIVE WAY TO PROTECT AND DECORATE SURFACES.
THE FOLLOWING PAGES SHOW YOU HOW TO CHOOSE A PRODUCT, USE THE RIGHT TOOLS, AND THE BEST
APPLICATION TECHNIQUE. PLAN IN WHAT ORDER YOU ARE GOING TO TACKLE A PAINTING PROJECT BEFORE
YOU BEGIN, AND PREPARE THE SURFACES BEFOREHAND AS SHOWN ON PP.272–75.

PAINT TYPES

Most paints fall into one of the general categories of emulsion, eggshell, or gloss (see below). You may also need to apply primer or undercoat, depending on the surface being painted. These basic paints will answer almost all of your needs but it is worth looking out for formulations that will perform better in specific situations (see box opposite). Always apply paint as recommended by the manufacturer.

BASE COATS

For a decorative topcoat to last and look as good as possible, the right base coats are essential. For interiors, a combined primer-undercoat is a good option.

Primer

Used on new, uncoated surfaces, primer protects the material beneath and provides a good base for further coats. If a surface has been previously painted you only need to patch-prime sanded and filled areas. Oil-based and water-based primers are available. Traditionalists prefer to use oil-based primer before oil-based paints, especially on exterior woodwork. Plaster and masonry are usually primed with a coat of emulsion diluted with 10 per cent water, known as a "mist coat", although a stabilizing primer or solution may be needed if the surface is very flaky or powdery. Special primers for other surfaces such as tiles or melamine are also available, which can be overpainted with normal paints.

Undercoat

A specially formulated paint used to build up opacity beneath oil-based topcoats, one or two coats of undercoat paint are usually required before the decorative topcoat is

USING WATER-BASED AND OIL-BASED PAINTS

Water-based paints are easy to clean from tools using water and detergent. If you have been using oil-based paints, wash your brushes in white spirit, then water and detergent (see p.283 for more information); discard pads and rollers. Tools used for oiling wood can be combustible in storage, so clean brushes well and store used cloths in water, or throw them out in a sealed container.

More environmentally friendly, or natural, paints and finishes are available. They are made of renewable materials such as plant oils, contain fewer chemicals, and their manufacture is less polluting. For more on greener paint options, see pp.278–79.

RECOMMENDED APPLICATION METHODS

Although many oil-based paints can be applied with rollers or pads as well as brushes, cleaning them afterwards is difficult and will require lots of white spirit or thinner.

Paint type	Brush	Roller	Pad	Sprayer
Primer	✓	✓	✓	
Undercoat	✓	✓	✓	
Emulsion	✓	✓	✓	✓
Eggshell	✓	✓	✓	
Gloss	✓			
Floor paint (on wood)	✓			
Floor paint (on concrete)	✓	✓		
Metal paint	✓			

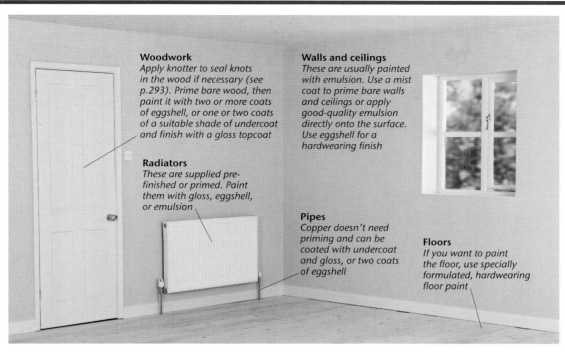

Woodwork
Apply knotter to seal knots in the wood if necessary (see p.293). Prime bare wood, then paint it with two or more coats of eggshell, or one or two coats of a suitable shade of undercoat and finish with a gloss topcoat

Radiators
These are supplied pre-finished or primed. Paint them with gloss, eggshell, or emulsion

Walls and ceilings
These are usually painted with emulsion. Use a mist coat to prime bare walls and ceilings or apply good-quality emulsion directly onto the surface. Use eggshell for a hardwearing finish

Pipes
Copper doesn't need priming and can be coated with undercoat and gloss, or two coats of eggshell

Floors
If you want to paint the floor, use specially formulated, hardwearing floor paint

Painting a room
New surfaces such as fresh plaster or stripped woodwork need an appropriate primer coat before undercoats or topcoats are applied. When decorating previously painted surfaces, you will still need to apply undercoats as well as topcoats. For information on applying natural wood finishes, see pp.290–91.

applied. Use pale undercoat beneath pale topcoats and a dark undercoat beneath dark topcoats. Although most oil-based undercoat is suitable for interior or exterior use, exterior undercoats are available that will last longer when exposed to the elements. Water-based paints are usually applied in as many coats as are required to provide an even coverage, so with these true undercoat is rarely used.

TOPCOATS
Once you have applied the base coats, or washed down previously painted surfaces with sugar soap and rinsed them thoroughly (see pp.272–73), you are ready to apply the decorative finish.

Emulsion
A water-based, versatile paint type, emulsion is normally used for walls and ceilings. Many types of finish are available — dead-flat matt, matt, a water-based eggshell (see also below), and silk. Some formulations contain vinyl to make them more hardwearing. Standard emulsion is only for interior use and suitable for plaster surfaces or previously painted plaster surfaces. Exterior emulsion is often called masonry paint and is available with a smooth or rough texture. Apply all emulsion using as many coats as are necessary for even coverage. For use in a sprayer, dilute emulsion with 10 per cent water.

Eggshell
An oil- or water-based paint, eggshell has a slight sheen. Always check the exact finish because the degree of sheen varies between manufacturers. Eggshell has particularly strong fumes, although there are now low-odour types. It is most commonly used on interior wood surfaces as an alternative to gloss, although some manufacturers will specify that the paint may be used on exterior surfaces. Eggshell can also be used on wall surfaces where a hardwearing finish is required. Two coats will usually give an even colour; use primer and undercoat as required.

Gloss and satin
A very hardwearing finishing paint, gloss is used mainly on wooden and metal surfaces. Satin is used in the same way as gloss but is slightly less shiny and is increasingly popular, especially for interior woodwork. Both oil-based and water-based versions of gloss and satin paints are available. Water-based paints are easier to apply and less prone to "yellowing" with age, but do not provide as high a shine or hardwearing a finish as oil-based paints. Almost all gloss and satin paints are suitable for interior or exterior use. Some glosses are formulated especially for exposed exterior surfaces. Gloss is generally applied as a single coat over one or two coats of undercoat.

SPECIALIST PAINTS
Good-quality paints will perform well in all domestic situations as long as they are used with the right base coats and on the surface they were designed for. However, sometimes it can be worth using paint formulated for a specific task.

Bathroom or kitchen paints
These emulsions resist fungal growth and moisture better than standard formulations, although if you have condensation you should consider improving ventilation, see pp.364–65.

Floor paint
Used on concrete and floorboards, floor paints are oil-based and very hardwearing. Gloss or sheen finishes are available. New concrete floors should be left to dry out completely before painting; check their progress with a moisture meter.

Metal paint
High-gloss, smooth, and textured (often hammered) metal paints are available. They can be used internally or externally; some types can be applied straight over rust. Thinner is generally required to clean brushes, rather than white spirit.

Traditional paints
Products such as distemper and limewash, as well as ranges of traditional colours, can now be purchased relatively easily.

Green paint, sometimes termed eco-paint or natural paint, is becoming a popular option for home decorating. The reason for choosing these paints over conventional ones is directly related to VOCs (see box, right). It has now been established that these compounds – which aid drying times and help with viscosity – can be harmful. Paint manufacturers have therefore been tasked with finding an alternative that still allows the paint to perform to product requirement. Usually, more natural raw materials, such as linseed oil, are used in paint production. In fact, many natural paints have been in existence for hundreds, if not thousands of years.

VOLATILE ORGANIC COMPOUNDS

Characterized by the often pungent fumes produced from drying paint, "volatile organic compounds" or VOCs (found in conventional paints and decorative coatings) are a major area of concern. There are many different types of VOCs, such as benzene and toluene, which can be harmful both to human health and the environment. Many countries are introducing legislation to greatly reduce VOC levels. In Europe, for example, all paints must comply with minimal VOC levels by 2010.

NATURAL PAINTS

All paints contain a binder, pigment, solvent, and sometimes a filler. Binders make up the main film-forming body of the paint, the pigment provides the colour, and the solvent essentially creates the paint's liquidity. Sometimes fillers are added to further thicken the mixture and increase its volume. With natural paints, it is straightforward to identify these different components as they are all naturally occurring – there are no synthetic parts. The following table provides information about the ingredients of natural paints – there are many variations on each type shown.

Making your own natural paint

It is possible to produce any of the paints shown in the table below, and there are numerous "recipe books" available, all offering different ideas on how to mix the perfect paint.

When making your own paints, the main concern is to produce the correct quantity for the job ahead – it is impossible to match colours so you won't be able to make a supplementary batch. The second problem can be with sourcing ingredients, as natural paints are not mainstream. You will need to source specialist local suppliers – a process that is far simpler than it once was thanks to the internet.

Paint type	Binder	Solvent	Filler	Comments
Limewash	Lime putty, non-hydraulic bagged lime, or hydraulic lime	Usually water, but some have a small oil content (typically linseed oil), particularly with external applications	Not required in pure limewash	A recommended system would be 3–4 coats for use indoors, and 4–5 coats for outside applications. Must be applied to a porous surface (not on top of other finishes) With casein limewash, casein (derived from milk curd) is also added for greater adhesion
Distemper (including milk paint and cheese paint derivatives)	Soft animal glue, casein (derived from milk curd), or natural oils	Water, linseed oil	Powdered chalk	A small amount of linseed oil is added, but the product is still water based While many milk paints only use the curd, more traditional types would simply mix skimmed milk directly with hydrated lime and pigment Oil-bound distemper may contain borax – an emulsifier that increases durability For interior use only
Flour paint (including clay paint)	Flour (not always used in clay paint)	Water	Clay	Clay often provides the colour, although further pigments may also be added
Natural oil paint	Natural oils such as raw linseed oil	Natural oils such as citrus oil	Not required	Natural oil paints have good all round application, both inside and out
Natural silicate paint	Potassium silicate	Water	Coloured rocks such as quartz	A more durable version of limewash that is well suited to exterior work
Egg tempera paint	Egg yolk or white	Water	None used	Not normally practical for large-scale work, but is extremely hardwearing and can be effective for the detailing in mouldings, for example

Natural pigments (not listed above) come from many different sources. Organic pigments can be derived from flowers and berries (although these tend to fade with light). More stable finishes are provided by natural earth pigments, such as ochre and umber. Most come in powder form, so precautions may be required to avoid inhalation of the powder whilst mixing.

LIMEWASH

A traditional paint, limewash is breathable and has anti-bacterial qualities. Its recent resurgence in popularity is due to its compatibility with eco-friendly building techniques, and to the move away from paints containing VOCs. It can be made from lime putty, powdered lime, and quicklime (although the use of quicklime is not advised as the reactions involved can be explosive).

PREPARING COLOUR

Natural pigments can be added to limewash, but first check they are compatible, as lime is a strong alkali. Pigments in powder form are best mixed with hot water to aid dispersal (see right). The amount of pigment needed depends on the required intensity of colour, with a ratio of 20:1 an average figure. With some earth pigments, it is best to soak them for 24 hours first (check manufacturer's instructions).

A Add powdered pigment to a jug of hot water.

B Using a hand whisk, mix the liquid to disperse the pigment. Add more of the same, or different-coloured pigments, to alter or intensify colour.

MAKING A LIMEWASH

The sequence shown here describes how to make limewash using lime putty. This method is thought to provide a superior finish to those made using a powdered lime (hydrated or hydraulic lime – see p.85).

A While the lime putty will have been pre-mixed, use a trowel to make sure it is sufficiently mixed before use. Aim for a thick, creamy consistency.

B Transfer three trowel-fulls of the lime putty to a clean bucket.

C Add water slowly to the lime putty. The ratio of water to putty may be 50:50, or even greater, depending on its original consistency.

D Mix the lime putty and water with a stirring paddle until the mixture is thin and creamy in consistency.

E You may add linseed oil, especially if the limewash is for exterior use (the oil aids adhesion and durability). As a guide, use a ratio of 12:1.

F Pour the mixture through a sieve and into a second bucket.

G Add any coloured pigment at this stage, again mixing it together with a stirring paddle.

H Mix the limewash again. It should have a thinner consistency (ideally milk-like) because of the dilution with the pigment.

I Give the limewash a final sieve and stir. Your homemade limewash is now ready to use.

APPLYING LIMEWASH

Limewash is applied in much the same way as most emulsion or water-based paints. It is important to keep a wet edge as the finish can become patchy where overlaps have occurred. Unlike conventional paints, limewash is always applied to a dampened surface (use a small hand-pumped spray) rather than direct to a dry substrate. It should not be applied in very cold, hot, or wet conditions. It is also essential to wear protective gloves and goggles.

PAINTING TOOLS

High-quality application tools are essential for an even paint finish. The tools you choose will depend on the size and type of job you are planning. The main options to consider are shown here. It is also necessary to protect surfaces you're not painting. Always wash away grease and dust with sugar soap or white spirit. For some jobs, further preparation is required. See pp.272–75 for more information.

BRUSHES

Paintbrushes are the most versatile and essential of all decorating tools. Ease of application and a successful finish are hugely affected by the quality of a brush. Remember, whether you choose natural or synthetic bristle brushes, a good brush is not cheap, and should have long bristles of equal length. It is normal for a brush to shed a few bristles when it is first used, however, this should not continue through the life of a brush.

Pure bristle brushes
Good-quality pure bristle brushes are expensive but will last for years if they are cleaned well and stored properly after each use, see p.283.

Pure bristles

Fitches
These are used for detailed work. The angled lining fitch (above left) is useful for straight lines.

Synthetic bristles

Synthetic bristle brushes
Although brushes made from pure natural bristle used to be considered superior quality, vast improvements have been made to synthetic bristle brushes and they are now used by most professionals.

MASKING UP MATERIALS

It is ideal to remove all the furniture and floor coverings from a room before decorating. However, this is often impractical so dustsheets and masking tape are used to prevent splashes and spillages damaging surfaces.

Masking tape
Use low-tack tape to protect surfaces and help you create clean, straight lines where areas with different finishes meet.

Fabric dustsheet
These sheets can be washed and reused, but large spills soak through. Plastic sheets are an alternative, but are easily damaged and slippery underfoot on floors.

PAINTING ACCESSORIES

Besides the more obvious painting tools such as brushes and rollers, there are other items that can be used to make the job easier, restore tools, and provide the best finish.

Steel pins

Paint kettle
Decant paint into a kettle so it is easier to carry and to keep debris such as dried paint on the brush from contaminating the main tin or tub.

Brush comb
Used to clean and shape brushes.

Dusting brush
Fine bristles remove debris from a surface before painting.

SPRAYING

Paint sprayers can be used to cover large surfaces quickly, or for intricate areas that are very time-consuming to paint with a brush. Small hand-held airless sprayers are most suitable for DIY work, although much larger airless or compressed-air sprayers can be hired. Sprayers can be dangerous, so always read the manufacturer's instructions very carefully. Wear any protective clothing specified and ensure good ventilation while you are spraying. For small jobs, it is better to buy aerosol paints.

PAINT SPRAYER

ROLLERS

There are several different designs of roller and frame. Large rollers can cover flat surfaces such as ceilings and walls quickly and efficiently, although be aware that very large rollers may be tiring to use. Mini-rollers are available for woodwork, although they tend not to provide as pleasing a finish as a brush. Rollers are best used with water-based paints. Cleaning a roller of oil- or solvent-based paints is difficult. It is best to simply throw away the sleeve and buy a new one. The best roller sleeves are pure sheepskin, although synthetic sheepskin also provides a good finish. Smooth, medium, and rough sleeves are available, and should be chosen to match the texture of the surface being painted. Other sleeve materials may produce a rough finish or shed fluff.

Roller cage
The cage holds the roller sleeve and is attached to a handle. Be sure when choosing a replacement sleeve that it fits the cage you are using.

Cage

Roller tray
A reservoir for holding paint that also has flatter, ribbed area adjacent to the reservoir, used for distributing paint evenly over the roller surface. The tray needs to be of the same width as your roller.

Extension pole
Attaches to the roller-cage handle to extend your reach. Buy a pole that is compatible with your roller.

Radiator roller frame
Used with mini-rollers. The long handle lets you gain access to wall surfaces behind radiators.

Roller sleeves
These fit onto the cage. Rough to smooth textures are available.

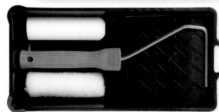

Mini-roller kit
A miniature roller cage, tray, and sleeve, designed for painting smaller surfaces and for using with a radiator roller frame.

PAINT PADS

These are designed to cover large, flat surfaces quickly and effortlessly. The flat pads have a painting surface composed of many tiny, tightly-packed bristles.

Pad holder

Paint pad frame
Holds the pad and provides a handle.

Paint pads
Replaceable pads of different sizes are attached to the frame for use.

Mini paint pad
Useful for more detailed work.

Paint pad tray
Similar to a roller tray. Some designs have a wheel that distributes paint evenly onto the pad.

PAINT EFFECTS TOOLS

These tools are used for different paint effects. As well as specialist tools like these, normal household items such as rags, and paper and plastic bags can be used, see pp.288–89.

Natural sponge
Used to apply or remove paint to make mottled, cloud-like effects.

Stencil brushes
For applying paint over a stencil.

Comb
Several different tooth sizes create straight or curved lines of different widths.

Rocker
Creates a wood-grain pattern in paint or glaze.

Softening brush
Smooth, fine-bristled brush for removing any hard paint lines.

Dragging brush
Extra long and coarse pure bristles create grained effect.

Stippling brush
Block-shaped brush with bristles of the same length, used for creating a velvet-like texture on surfaces.

Preparation and planning are the key to a good paint finish. All painting tasks are different, but using an efficient order of work will save time. The best ways to apply paint with other finishes are also described here. It is important to protect surfaces you are not working on because painting, especially with rollers or sprayers, is a messy job. Before you start, prepare surfaces, see pp.272–73. Preparing and painting external surfaces are shown on pp.292–93.

COVERING UP AND MASKING

Rooms should ideally be clear of all furnishings, fittings, and floor coverings before decoration. However, if this is not possible, ensure that you mask or cover anything you cannot remove. Plastic dustsheets are excellent for covering furniture, but have to be thrown away after a couple of uses and are slippery underfoot on floors. Fabric dustsheets will not protect against major spills, but provide a safer floor covering, and can be washed and reused many times. Use masking tape to protect any unpainted surfaces, especially around the edge of the floor. You can paint straight lines using the technique known as "cutting in" shown on p.284, but if you don't feel confident with this method, use masking tape at any junction.

Protecting flooring
Apply masking tape to the floor below the skirting boards and lay a fabric dustsheet so that it overlaps the tape. For carpet, use a scraper to push half the width of the tape right behind the carpet edge.

Combining paint with other finishes

As well as furniture and floors, any other decorative finishes in the room need to be protected while you paint, especially if you are using a roller or a sprayer. When combining painted surfaces with natural wood finishes, you need to consider which to apply first. Accuracy is impossible when applying waxes or oils with a cloth. It is usually easier to finish the wood before you paint and protect the woodwork with some masking tape (see below). Clean any smudges from the wall so that they don't affect the paint finish. Otherwise, paint before preparing and finishing the wood. If you are going to wallpaper the room, do any painting first because even low-tack tape may mark the paper.

Masking tape
Ideally, use low-tack masking tape when decorating. Other types of tape may pull away the finish when you try and remove them, or leave adhesive residue behind that is difficult to clean off.

PAINT COVERAGE

Paint coverage varies considerably depending on the surface you are decorating. Very porous or rough surfaces will need a lot of paint, so use the smaller figure in the estimated coverage range given; smooth, shiny areas need less so use the larger figure. Oil-based paints tend to cover less surface area than water-based types. When planning how much paint to buy, don't forget to take the number of coats needed into account. See pp.276–77 for requirements. Always check specific coverage guidelines on the container of the paint you are buying and overestimate rather than underestimate. Keep excess paint for touching up.

Paint type	Estimated coverage
Primer	5–15sq m per litre (245–734sq ft per gallon)
Undercoat	10–15sq m per litre (489–734sq ft per gallon)
Emulsion	10–20sq m per litre (489–979sq ft per gallon)
Eggshell	8–15sq m per litre (391–734sq ft per gallon)
Gloss	12–18sq m per litre (587–881sq ft per gallon)
Floor paint	7–15sq m per litre (343–734sq ft per gallon)
Metal paint	8–15sq m per litre (391–734sq ft per gallon)

ORDER OF PAINTING

If you are repainting a room, start from the top and work down. Cover the ceiling first, then the walls and finally the woodwork and other details. Complete the coats on one surface before moving on to the next, including the sealers, primers, and undercoats that are necessary (see p.276). Overlap onto the next surface slightly to ensure continuous coverage (see "cutting in" p.284), but brush out any thick areas of paint otherwise they will show through.

Order for painting a room:
1 Ceiling 2 Walls 3 Radiators if you are using the same paint as for the walls 4 Doors and windows, and the radiators if you are using the same paint as for the doors and windows 5 Architrave, skirting, and exposed pipework 6 Floors

PAINTING WINDOWS AND DOORS

Wedge open windows and external doors while painting and while the paint dries. Start early in the day to provide sufficient drying time. For both doors and windows, remove any handles and catches before painting for the best finish. For more on techniques see pp.284–85 and p.287.

Painting a window

The internal and external surfaces of windows are painted in the same order (see right). The hinged edge of an opening casement is considered an internal surface, and the opening edge an external surface. Wipe sills with white spirit before painting to remove dust.

Painting a door

Panel doors are divided into sections by their construction and are painted in the order shown far right. Mentally divide flush doors into sections and complete one section at a time. Begin in the top left corner, then work across, then down. Finish by painting the side edge that is exposed when the door is open. If the door opens outwards, the edge where the hinges are attached is seen. If the door opens inwards, you see the opening edge.

Order for painting a window:
1 Rails of opening casements
2 Outer rails of casements
3 Hinged edge (if painting the interior, shown here) or opening edge (if painting the exterior)
4 Rails of non-opening casements
5 Frame

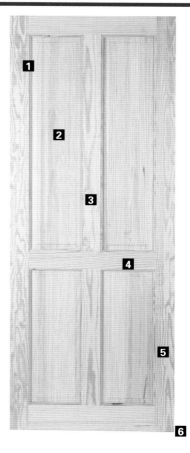

Order for painting a panel door:
1 Mouldings surrounding each panel
2 Panels
3 Central vertical stiles
4 Horizontal members
5 Outer vertical stiles
6 Door edge

STORING TOOLS

If you need to take a break midway through a job, store your tools in clingfilm. For long-term storage, thorough cleaning is essential. Water-based paints can be cleaned off of tools using water and mild detergent. Clean off oil-based paints using white spirit or thinner (see p.285), then rinse tools in water and mild detergent.

Temporary storage
During a break, you can wrap tools (here a roller) in clingfilm for up to two days before resuming painting.

Storing tools
When tools are clean and dry, wrap them tightly in paper so they stay dust-free in storage.

Reviving old brushes
If bristles of an old brush are stuck together with paint residue, use a brush comb to separate them.

TOOLS AND MATERIALS CHECKLISTS PP.284–95

Loading a brush; laying off; painting wood; cutting in p.284
Paint kettle

Using a roller p.285 Roller tray

Using a paint sprayer p.285
Basic toolkit only

Using a paint pad p.285
Paint pad tray

Painting a room pp.286–87
Roller, roller tray, extension pole, 100-mm (4-in) paintbrush, paint kettle, mini-roller kit, radiator roller cage, lining fitch,

25-mm (1-in) paintbrush

Stencilling p.288 Stencil, masking tape, stencil brush

Distressing p.288 Petroleum jelly*, PVA*, paints, sandpaper* hammer*, coloured wax*, glaze*, crackle glaze*, craquelure*

Applying "on" effects; creating "off" effects pp.288–89 Paints*, glaze*, clean dowel*, large paintbrush* or softening brush*, natural sponge*, rag*, bag*, stippling brush*, dragging brush*, graining tool*, white spirit*

Applying stain; applying dye p.291 Stain*, dye* brush

Applying wax; applying oil p.291 Wax*, oil*, cloth*, brush*

Applying varnish p.291 Brush, sandpaper, cloth

Cleaning old walls p.292 Stiff brush, paintbrush, fungicide, stabilizing solution*

Painting metal exterior pipework p.292 Stiff brush, paintbrush

Dealing with knots p.293
Heat gun, sandpaper, knotter, lining fitch

Using preservative pellets p.293 Fitch, wood hardener, exterior two-part filler, pellets, sandpaper, paints

Treating external door edges p.293 Paintbrush, wood preserver, paints

* = optional

FOR BASIC TOOLKIT SEE
PP.24–25

PAINTING TECHNIQUES

Many paints and finishes can be applied using whichever tool you prefer, although some have more specific needs (see pp.276–77 for paint and pp.290–91 for natural wood finishes). Tool choice is also governed by the size and roughness of the surface, and the accuracy needed. Brushes are fairly labour-intensive to use but give fine control over application and can be used on any surface. Rollers, pads, and sprayers cover large areas evenly, quickly, and easily but can be messy and are usually unsuitable for detailed work.

PREPARING PAINT

Open the paint tin using an old screwdriver or a lid-opening tool. Unless otherwise specified, use a clean wooden dowel or a power stirrer (see p.68) to mix the paint for at least a few minutes before use. Failure to do this can result in poor coverage and noticeable colour variation across a surface. If you are using a brush, decant some into a smaller container such as a paint kettle. This will be easier to carry and prevent the rest of the paint becoming contaminated.

LOADING A BRUSH

Good brush technique is essential to achieve even coverage. To avoid overloading the brush, only dip it into the paint to one-third of the bristle length for water-based paint, or one-quarter of the bristle length for oil-based paint. Then, scrape off the excess on the rim of the container. With the correct amount of paint on the brush you can begin covering the surface.

Ferrule

A

Hold the brush with your fingers at the top of the ferrule, or lower for a large brush. Small brushes can be held like a pencil.

B

Dip the bristles into the paint to one-third of the bristle length. Draw both sides of the brush across the rim to remove excess.

LAYING OFF

The majority of paints, especially if they have a sheen or are oil-based, require "laying off" to remove tool impressions from the finish. To do this, glide the unloaded painting tool very lightly over the wet paint, just touching the newly coated surface. Laying off with a brush is shown here but the principle is the same for rollers and, to a lesser extent, pads.

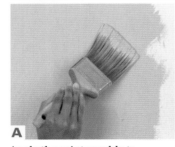

A

Apply the paint roughly to distribute the paint from the loaded brush. Use random strokes in differing directions.

B

Lay off the paint again using random strokes, allowing only the very tips of the bristles to glide across the freshly painted surface.

PAINTING WOOD

Woodwork is usually finished with a topcoat of gloss or eggshell. These types of paint need to be applied particularly carefully to achieve a good finish. On large, open surfaces such as flush doors, paint should first be applied at right angles to the grain, then brushed out and laid off in line with the grain. On narrow surfaces such as skirting board or panelled doors, the paint is easiest applied in line with the grain and brushed out and laid off in the same direction.

Coating a door
Paint each section separately. Take time to lay off the paint carefully, then cut in accurately along the construction joins for a neat finish (see below, and p.283 for orders of work).

CUTTING IN

The technique known as "cutting in" is used to create a precise dividing line. You need a brush to cut in accurately, although small paint pads can sometimes be used (see opposite).

Work in manageable sections along the division line. Load the brush, but take care not to overload it (see top), then position it with its bristles into the junction. Brush it steadily along and allow the bristles of the brush to make a neat "bead" – a tiny, slightly raised line created as the paint leaves the brush. Lay off the other side of the brush stroke to finish.

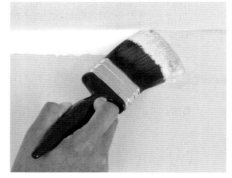

In a corner
A straight line between two areas of paint, especially a junction between surfaces, enhances the finish of a room.

Decorative woodwork
Carefully cut into the junction between the woodwork and adjoining surface.

USING A ROLLER

Rollers apply paint over flat surfaces very quickly and easily. Several different sizes and sleeves are available (see p.281). You should make sure you have the right kind of roller sleeve for the job. Rough roller sleeves can cope better with texture, smooth rollers are excellent for flat surfaces and applying paints with a sheen. Although you can apply most kinds of paint with a roller (see p.276), oil-based paint will be difficult to wash out. Rollers are not very accurate tools, so you will still need a brush to cut in to junctions and woodwork.

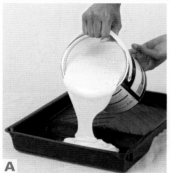

A

Tip paint carefully into the tray reservoir keeping the paint below the point where the ribbed section of the tray begins.

B

Push the roller along the ribbed section of the tray and then glide it over the paint surface – do not submerge it in the paint.

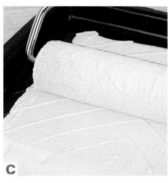

C

Move the roller backwards and forwards slowly over the ribbed section to distribute the paint evenly over the roller sleeve.

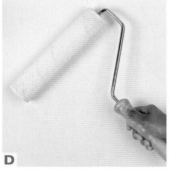

D

Apply the paint onto the surface in sections by rolling up and down, then "lay off" the paint with the roller (see opposite).

USING A PAINT SPRAYER

There are many variations of sprayer so you should carefully check the manufacturer's safety and operation instructions for the type you intend to use. Whether you are using a powerful compressed-air sprayer on a room or an aerosol can on a radiator, the aim is to build up several thin coats of paint. Spraying is a messy job so sprayers are most useful in rooms empty of furniture and floor coverings, or for exteriors. When spraying paint you should always wear a mask and goggles, and any other specified safety equipment.

A

Pour paint into the sprayer reservoir. Normal emulsion paint diluted with 10 per cent water, or paint designed for spraying is used.

B

Assemble the sprayer following the manufacturer's instructions.

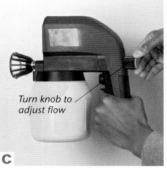

Turn knob to adjust flow

C

Try spraying on a sheet of scrap lining paper or similar. Adjust the flow until you can achieve a fairly even coat with no drips.

D

Spray back and forth over the surface. Apply a thin coat, allow to dry, then add more coats until you achieve good coverage.

USING A PAINT PAD

The most common design of paint pad is used in a very similar way to a roller. You can use a normal paint tray or a specially designed tray, some of which have a wheel to distribute paint evenly from the reservoir onto the pad.

Small pads are available for more detailed work. They can be used to cut in at a junction. Uneven surfaces are best finished using a brush to follow the slight contours. Cut in with a brush (see opposite), then lay off the brush marks as close as you can to the junction using the pad.

A

Dip the pad into the paint held in the reservoir, then move it across the ribbed section of the tray to remove the excess.

B

Apply paint to the wall surface with an up-and-down motion. The pad should create a very even coat without the need for laying off.

DISPOSING OF PAINT SAFELY

To thoroughly clean tools of water-based paints (including acrylic) you need a large amount of water. The waste water from this process must go into the mains drainage system and not into soakaways.

White spirit or thinners used to clean up oil-based paints, and old paint tins, must be disposed as advised by your local authority, often at a recycling facility. Never put them in the household waste.

PAINTING A ROOM

All surfaces must be prepared thoroughly before painting – any damage should be filled, sanded, and primed, and surfaces cleaned (see pp.272–75). Choose the right paint type for each surface. See pp.276–77 for your options. The order shown here is for undercoats or topcoats. Finish the ceiling and walls before tackling the woodwork. Details of the techniques needed to apply an even coat of paint with rollers, brushes, and other tools can be found on pp.284–85.

TOOLS AND MATERIALS SEE BASIC TOOLKIT AND P.283

1 PAINTING THE CEILING

A

Attach an extension pole to the handle of the roller. Decant paint into the paint tray and load the roller, taking care not to overload it (see p.285). Roll the paint onto the ceiling in sections, laying off each area before you reload the roller. When painting a ceiling it is important to wear goggles to protect your eyes from drips and spatters of paint.

2 PAINTING THE WALLS

A

Once the central area of the ceiling is coated, paint around the edge with a brush. Overlap slightly onto the wall surface.

B

Roll paint on in vertical sections. Use an extension pole to save bending when painting lower sections of the wall, and reaching for the higher areas.

C

Cut in at the junctions between the walls and the ceiling. A roller is not accurate enough so use a 100-mm (4-in) brush, or a small paint pad if your walls are straight.

D

Slightly overlap the wall colour onto the skirting board, or if your skirting has a natural finish, protect it with masking tape.

PAINTING AROUND OBSTACLES

Painting behind a radiator
Use a radiator roller to coat the wall behind the radiator. The long handle will reach down easily. An alternative is to remove the radiator while you decorate – see pp.504–05 for more information on how to do this.

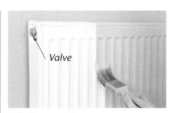

Valve

Painting a radiator.
Work from the top down. Take care not to paint over the valves because it will make them difficult to open.

Painting around a light switch
Use a lining fitch to paint carefully around plateswitches and plug sockets. Any slight overlaps can be cleaned off easily.

3 PAINTING THE WINDOW

A

Remove any window furniture before painting to make the job easier and to provide a neater finish.

B

Use a 25-mm (1-in) brush. Follow the order of work shown on p.283, starting with the glazing bars and the rails of the opening sections.

C

Open the window so that you can paint both the opening and the hinged edge, but avoid painting over the hinges themselves. Wedge the window open until the paint is completely dry.

D

Paint the glazing bars of any non-opening casements.

E

Create a neat dividing line between the window frame and the wall surface.

4 PAINTING THE SKIRTING BOARD

A

Mask floor surface if required

Begin to paint the skirting board, one manageable section at a time. Start by coating the middle of the board, then cut into the floor.

B

Cut in neatly at the skirting and wall junction. Lay off the paint carefully for an even finish then move on to the next section of skirting board.

5 PAINTING THE DOOR

If you stray onto the stiles or rails, brush out the paint to avoid lines

A

Remove the door furniture before you start painting. Begin by coating the panels and continue to paint the door according to the order of work outlined on p.283.

B

Follow the grain of the wood as you paint the stiles and rails. Where they cross, create a neat line along the join of the two pieces of wood.

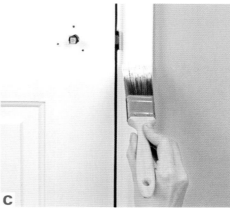

C

Finish by painting the architrave, cutting in precisely along the edge created with the wall surface. Paint the door lining (see p.160). For inward-opening doors paint the lining up to but not including the doorstop. For outward-opening doors, continue on to paint the doorstop. Wedge the door open while you paint the opening edge.

Some paint effects are used to add detail, such as stencilling, distressing, and some trompe l'oeil effects. Others are used to decorate whole walls or rooms, using a discontinuous topcoat of colour to create depth and texture. The topcoat is chosen to complement the base colour of the wall where it shows through. Traditionally a translucent glaze, known as scumble glaze, is used for the topcoat, although other paints are sometimes used. Once you are familiar with the key techniques of the effects shown here, you can experiment with colours, layers, and tools to create effects of your own.

TROMPE L'OEIL

Trompe l'oeil, translates as "trick of the eye" and includes all those paint effects that try to mimic a different surface. Examples include marbling, where paint and glaze are carefully applied to create the appearance of marble, and tricks such as recreating the look of old stone on a new plaster surface. To produce convincing trompe l'oeil takes practice, so hone your skills on some scrap lining paper before tackling a new project.

STENCILLING

Stencils are normally made from acetate or card and can be bought ready-to-use or you can cut your own. Any paint can be used for stencilling but water-based options dry quickly and are the most user-friendly.

Use a very small amount of paint on a special stencilling or small stippling brush and dab lightly into the stencil. Stencil crayons or aerosol paints can also be used. You can apply a coat of flat colour, or create a three-dimensional effect by concentrating colour around the edge of a design. This creates a central highlight. You can also apply more paint on one side to suggest directional light.

Using a stencil
Attach the stencil to the surface with low-tack masking tape. Use a stencilling brush in an up and down motion to apply the paint (see also Stippling, opposite). Remove the stencil carefully. Choose the next stencil location randomly, or create a regular pattern.

DISTRESSING

There are several techniques that can provide the illusion of age. Masking areas with petroleum jelly or PVA prevents paint adhering properly so that once the surface is painted and the area is sanded, the masked areas lose all their paint to provide a patchy, aged finish. Surfaces can also be physically distressed with strokes of a hammer or other objects. Accentuate the texture by rubbing some coloured wax into the surface or colourwashing (see opposite).

For a different effect use crackle glaze or craquelure. Used as directed they create a surface like cracked antique paint or varnish. You can enhance the finish with coloured wax.

Creating ageing effects
When using these effects, think carefully where you would expect to find natural wear, such as on the edges of a door, or on the area around a handle. The more layers of different coloured paint applied to that area, the greater the effect.

APPLYING "ON" EFFECTS

Glaze or emulsion can be applied over a flat coat of paint to create a textured effect. Translucent glaze, bought ready-to-use or mixed as shown for colourwashing (see opposite), gives a more subtle effect than emulsion. Here sponging on paint is described, although you can experiment with other "tools" – such as rags or bags. Whatever tool you use the general technique is similar.

The first step is to paint a base coat of emulsion or eggshell onto the wall. When this is dry, pour a small amount of your topcoat of paint or glaze into a roller tray. Dip in your chosen tool and make sure it is well coated. Remove the excess paint by dabbing it off on the ridged section of the tray, then on some newspaper, until a light touch produces a mottled mark rather than a solid block of colour. Begin to apply it to the wall in a random pattern, varying the side of the tool that you use for each mark. Build up the effect slowly rather than attempting a dense coat first time. Go over the whole surface with one very light coat first, then check it for even coverage. Apply subsequent layers until the desired result is achieved.

Creating a random yet even pattern is harder than it looks and you may want to practise on some scrap paper first. However, mistakes can be corrected and evened out by applying some of the paint you used for the base coat with the effect tool you are using.

Sponging on
A sponge is one of the easiest tools for a paint-effect novice to get to grips with. Build up the finish in layers until you achieve your desired density of colour. If different shades of the same colour are used then the final effect will be subtle; if contrasting colours are used then you will get a bolder result.

■ APPLYING COLOURWASH

A colourwash provides depth of colour and enhances textured and distressed surfaces (see opposite). Create the effect by applying translucent glaze over an opaque base coat.

Oil-based and water-based glazes are available and can be bought coloured, or you can colour them yourself using a special dye. For a greater range of colours, tint oil-based glaze with artists' oil paint, and use acrylic paint for water-based glaze. Apply a second coat of glaze if more colour is required, or work on the wet glaze to create one of the effects below.

A

Pour a small amount of dye into the glaze and mix it well with a length of clean dowel. Test the colour and adjust if required.

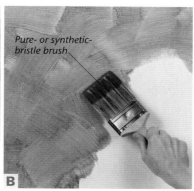

Pure- or synthetic-bristle brush

B

Spread glaze onto the wall, using random strokes. Work quickly because if you let the edges dry they will show on the finished surface.

CREATING "OFF" EFFECTS

The first step for these effects is a translucent colourwash of glaze that is applied over an opaque base coat. Use a vinyl silk or satin emulsion, eggshell, or even gloss for your base coat because this will prolong the drying time of the glaze while you work with it. You need to work quickly to complete a colourwash and create one of the "off" effects shown below before the glaze dries. If you are inexperienced at creating paint effects, or are tackling a particularly large area get some help so that one person can apply the glaze while the other follows behind creating the effect. When using these techniques, replace or wash your tool clean often and keep plenty of newspaper and water or white spirit to hand. Complete the whole wall surface before taking a break.

Sponging
Press a damp sponge into the glaze, and lift it off to leave a mottled impression. Move the sponge across the surface, pressing and removing the sponge in a random fashion. From time to time, rinse out the sponge to remove excess glaze.

Ragging
Press a dampened, crumpled cloth into the glaze randomly across the wall surface. Rinse the rag regularly or have a few ready for when the one you are using becomes too soaked with glaze. Vary the effect by using different types of cloth or even plastic and paper bags.

Rag-rolling
Crumple a rag and form it into a sausage shape, then roll it down the wall surface to create a subtle effect resembling tumbling material. Rinse or change rags often. You can also rag-roll glaze or emulsion onto a wall for a similar but more dramatic effect.

Stippling
By pressing the very ends of a specially designed stippling brush into the wet glaze you can create a very finely textured, almost velvet-like finish. Pat the brush into the wall surface in a random pattern and make sure that you go straight up and down with no drag.

Dragging
This creates a coarse-lined, textured finish running either vertically or horizontally. Hold a long-bristled dragging brush at a low angle, then draw it in a continuous stroke down or across the glazed surface. This effect can be used on wood as well as walls.

Graining
A wood-grain effect often used on MDF or melamine furniture, graining can be applied to any flat surface. Rock the special graining tool gently as you drag it down the wet glaze surface. Vary the pace of rocking to give different effects.

As their name suggests, natural wood finishes enhance rather than cover the grain of the wood. Some also offer protection. Transparent, translucent, and almost opaque finishes are available. There are several things to think about when choosing natural wood finishes – the range available is outlined below. Once you have chosen the finish you require, prepare the surface as shown on pp.274–75, then follow the application tips shown opposite for a perfect result.

TOOLS AND MATERIALS SEE BASIC TOOLKIT AND P.283

GREEN WOOD FINISHES

Natural oils and waxes are the most eco-friendly of wood finishes, although synthetic alternatives do exist. Beeswax and linseed oil are well known green finishes, but look out for safflower oil and carnauba wax as well. Water-based varnishes and stains also have good green credentials. Look at the manufacturer's label, check for any VOC content (see p.278), and determine exactly what ingredients have been used. For the application of eco-friendly products, follow the guide below.

WOOD FINISHES

Natural wood finishes, especially those that soak into the grain, are often difficult to remove, so take time to think about your requirements and choose the right product. Protection offered by natural finishes varies. Dye, for example, may offer no protection by itself. Always buy a suitable interior or exterior formulation. Consider if you want an almost invisible coat or would prefer some colour or gloss. Also, think about how much time you are prepared to spend on application – there may be one-coat options available. Finally, look out for eco-friendly options, such as water-based varnishes and stains, or products made from 100-per-cent natural ingredients.

VARNISH

STAIN

DYE

WAX

OIL

WOOD PRESERVER

FINISH AND EFFECT

Finish	Use	Application
Varnish Hardwearing, transparent or coloured, decorative, and preservative finish that highlights and protects the wood surface below. Matt and high-gloss versions are available. You can buy water-based and oil-based types.	For interior or exterior use as specified. Can be used on bare wood or to protect unsealed finishes, such as dye.	Covers 12–18sq m per litre (587–881sq ft per gallon). May need several coats. Apply with a brush for the best finish.
Stain Soaks into the wood to provide a decorative and sometimes preservative finish. Darkens or colours wood. Matt to gloss, water-based, and oil-based types are available.	For interior or exterior use as specified. Use as a finish or coat with varnish for extra durability. Apply to clean, bare wood for a true colour.	Covers 8–20sq m per litre (391–979sq ft per gallon). May need several coats. Apply with a brush for the best finish.
Dye Subtly enhances natural colour or evens out shades on different pieces of wood. Dyes can be mixed to match an existing colour. Gives a matt finish. Water-based and oil-based types are available.	Only for interior use unless specified, or protected with exterior varnish. Apply as a finish or beneath varnish or wax.	Covers 8–15sq m per litre (391–734sq ft per gallon). May need several coats. Apply with a brush for the best finish.
Wax Transparent or translucent decorative finish; some types can be buffed to a high gloss. Feeds and protects the wood but will not penetrate a sealed surface. Both water-based and oil-based types are available.	For interior use only. Apply to bare wood or over unsealed finishes such as dye.	Apply with a cloth. Brush-on waxes are also available. Needs several coats and regular maintenance.
Oil Transparent finish that nourishes and protects wood. External surfaces lose their finish but stay protected. Buff to achieve mid-sheen finish. Will not penetrate a sealed surface.	For interior or exterior use. Must be applied to unsealed wood.	Covers 8–15sq m per litre (391–734sq ft per gallon). Apply with a brush or cloth yearly. Highly flammable – see "cleaning tools" above.
Wood preserver Prevents rot and insect damage. Available clear or coloured with a matt or a semi-gloss finish. Both water-based and oil-based types are available.	Exterior use. Used alone, or as a base coat for another natural wood finish or paint.	Covers 8–20sq m per litre (391–979sq ft per gallon). Apply in sections as for stain (see opposite) or as specified.

APPLYING STAIN OR WOOD PRESERVER

Stain and wood preserver are applied in the same order as you would paint, see pp.282–83. You can apply coats to roughly finished wood quickly, but to get an even coat on smooth wood requires accuracy. Cover each surface without a break – if the stain or preserver dries midway then you will be left with a line.

Apply stain with the grain of the wood. Take care not to overload the brush and to brush out any drips before the stain dries.

Complete one section of wood before beginning the next. Where two sections join, ensure that strokes do not overlap each other.

APPLYING WAX

Wax is normally applied with a cloth, although some types are designed to be brushed on. Repeated application and buffing builds up depth of colour and sheen. It is not necessary to follow the grain of the wood, although this is considered to be the best way to efficiently penetrate and cover the wood surface.

Scoop some wax out of its container with a soft cloth and rub it evenly into the wood until there are no globules of wax left.

Leave the wax to dry, but not harden, for a few minutes. Buff the surface with a clean cloth to provide a smooth finish.

APPLYING OIL

All oils are applied using a similar technique. Pure tung oil is well suited to worktops and food preparation areas as it is non-toxic. Danish oil and teak oil are good for hardwoods, especially outdoor furniture; teak oil provides a glossier finish. If you choose traditional linseed oil, use boiled or double-boiled types because they are quicker to dry and not as sticky as the raw oil.

Apply liberally, using strokes of a soft brush in line with the wood grain to help ensure full coverage and aid penetration.

Allow the oil to soak in before removing excess with a cloth. Leave for half an hour, or as directed, then buff the surface with a dry cloth.

APPLYING VARNISH

Like stain, varnish must be applied in the direction of the grain, although you don't have to worry so much about accuracy. Because many varnishes are completely transparent, it is easy to miss areas during application. Good lighting and regular inspection of the surface is necessary to ensure good coverage.

Follow the grain of the wood. Finish one section before beginning the next.

Brush out the varnish to give an even coat. Use the technique shown for laying off paint, p.284.

Sand down the surface of the first coat because varnish, especially water-based varieties, tends to lift the grain of the wood.

Wipe the surface with a damp cloth to remove dust and let it dry before applying the next coat. Apply further coats as required.

APPLYING DYE

If you want to mix dyes to a specific shade, make sure they both have the same base – oil or water. Dyed wood needs a protective finish such as wax or varnish applied over the top.

Working with dye
Apply dye with the grain. Keep a wet edge where you work and take care not to overlap onto areas that have dried. Seal the dye with a protective finish. Check the manufacturer's specifications for compatible finishes.

MAINTAINING EXTERIOR SURFACES

Stained exterior woodwork needs only occasional maintenance. A single coat, applied every year or two, will keep wood protected and looking good.

Once a year, lightly sand and wipe exterior varnish before applying a maintenance coat, (see above).

The finish of exterior hardwoods treated with Danish or teak oil can fade quickly. Although the wood will remain protected, manufacturers often recommend that exterior oiled surfaces are recoated at least once a year.

PAINTING EXTERIOR SURFACES

Most of the tools and techniques for painting exterior surfaces are the same as those used for interiors. However, materials are often chosen for their greater durability. Painted masonry can last up to ten years, and wooden windows up to five years before recoating is necessary. Surfaces need to be filled and sanded before you paint (see pp.272–75). Additional preparation is often required. Vegetative growth and rot are more common problems on exterior surfaces and how to treat them is shown here. If you are working on the outside of your house, remember ladders and scaffolding will almost certainly be needed for access.

EXTERIOR PAINT

Items painted with light colours reflect the sun's heat. This reduces paint problems due to expansion so they need repainting less often. Exterior emulsion, also known as masonry paint, is used outside. Apply it in the same way as interior emulsion. Coverage is often less: 2–20sq m per litre (98–979sq ft per gallon). Coat woodwork and pipework with gloss. You can use specialist paint for rusty metal. See pp.276–77 for more on paint types.

PREPARING MASONRY FOR PAINTING

Remove any vegetative growth from masonry walls, and clean them down thoroughly. Small holes in masonry can be filled using all-purpose powder fillers as long as they specify exterior use. New render or masonry finishes should not need any further treatment.

Old masonry may need some more extensive repair (see pp.126–27). It will also benefit from an application of fungicide, and stabilizing solution if the surface is flaky (see cleaning old walls, below). Once the surface is clean and dry, fill any remaining holes and sand as normal.

When you come to paint walls the best choice is exterior emulsion, often called masonry paint. Apply a mist coat – the paint you are using diluted with ten per cent water – followed by two full-strength coats. Paint from the top down, covering the walls before woodwork and metalwork. Some deviation from this basic plan is often necessary because of access. You may find it easiest to paint roof details such as soffits, fascias, and bargeboards, followed by the top section of wall, before tackling the lower surfaces (see pp.26–27 for information on ladders and platforms).

CLEANING OLD WALLS

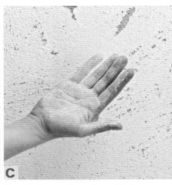

Wear any protective clothing specified

A Use a stiff brush to remove any loose paint, masonry, vegetative matter, or dirt from the wall.

B Apply fungicidal solution using the manufacturer's guidelines. Leave for 24 hours, then use a pressure washer to clean down the surfaces.

C Check the wall surface. If it is powdery to the touch you need to use a stabilizing solution.

D Apply the stabilizing solution with a large paintbrush. When it is dry, the wall is ready to fill, sand, and paint.

PAINTING METAL EXTERIOR PIPEWORK

Exterior pipework is usually made of metal or plastic. Exterior metalwork is treated in the same way as that inside the home, except that specialist exterior metal paints generally offer greater durability. Plastic items are simply cleaned when any dirt or vegetative growth accumulates. If you do wish to coat plastic pipes, apply two coats of gloss – there is no need for primer or undercoat.

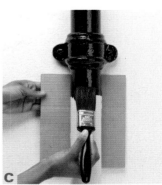

A Brush down the metal. Remove any flakes of paint and rust right down to bare, shiny metal. Some metal paints can be applied directly over rust.

B Prime patches of exposed metal using a metal primer specified for exterior use.

C Apply exterior-grade gloss paint, laying off the paint carefully as you work (see p.284). Shield the wall with a piece of card.

PAINTING AND TREATING EXTERIOR WOODWORK

Paint or a natural wood preservative finish (see pp.290–91) are essential for exterior woodwork because it is prone to damage from the elements. Maximize protection by using hardwearing fillers and exterior-grade paints. Problems can still occur. The heat of the sun can cause sap to bubble out of knots, blistering the paintwork. Use a heat gun followed by knotter (shown below) to prevent further damage. This technique can also be used on bare wood, prior to painting. Small cracks in paintwork can lead to minor damp and rot problems. Pellets of wood preservative are an excellent way to stop the rot spreading if the damage is caught early. Large areas of rotten wood need to be replaced (see p.154)

Wooden cladding is treated like any other exterior woodwork, but it must be washed down thoroughly in order to remove all signs of dirt. In some circumstances, fungicide may be required, which can be applied as shown for masonry walls, opposite.

▌▌ DEALING WITH KNOTS

A Scrape all the sap and excess paint away from the affected area.

B Use a heat gun to heat up the sap so that it bubbles out from the knot. Keep using the heat gun until the sap stops flowing.

C Sand the area to remove residue and provide a clean, smooth surface for painting.

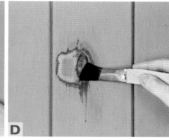

D Apply knotter to the knot using a lining fitch. Once this is dry you can prime and paint the area using exterior-grade paints.

▌▌ USING PRESERVATIVE PELLETS

A Scrape the rot back to sound wood. Allow the area to dry out, then apply wood hardener to the exposed wood.

B Use a two-part wood filler specifically for exterior use to repair the damage caused by the rot.

Drill bit size will be specified on pellet packaging

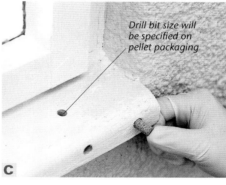

C

Drill holes around the rotten area. Push pellets into the holes, making sure they sit below the wood surface. You can then fill the holes with more exterior filler. Sand the treated area smooth before priming and painting. Like many preservative products, pellets contain toxins, so be sure to wear gloves when handling them.

TREATING WINDOWS AND DOORS

Wooden windows and external doors rely on paint or a natural wood finish (pp.290–91) for protection. Start work early in the day so you can close them before night. The order of work for painting the rest of the window or door is shown on p.283. Apply paint using the technique specified for wood on p.284.

▌▌ TREATING EXTERNAL DOOR EDGES

A Take the door off its hinges. Apply preservative primer to the top and bottom edges of the door.

B Prime and paint the edges when the preservative primer has dried using exterior paints.

Cracked puttywork can let down the finish of an otherwise well-painted window or glazed door. As long as the putty is sound, fill it with an all-purpose filler, then sand and paint with the wood. Take care not to allow the sandpaper to touch the glass surface, because it will scratch it. Where putty is very loose or missing, remove as much as possible, dust away any debris, and re-putty as shown on pp.150–51.

Plastic and metal windows and doors

UPVC doesn't require painting. It can be kept bright and clean with a non-abrasive cleaner. Some cleaners denature and degrade rubber seals or gaskets, so check the manufacturer's guidelines. When painting surrounding wall surfaces, take care to mask up UPVC as removing any paint overspray can be very difficult.

Metal windows or parts of windows are often factory-coated and so don't require painting. Old metal windows can be painted using a similar system to normal wooden windows, except an appropriate primer must be used to prevent rust damage.

REMOVING DRIPS

Drips are caused by poor technique – usually overloading the brush during application. See p.284 for the correct technique.

TOOLS AND MATERIALS
Scraper, sandpaper

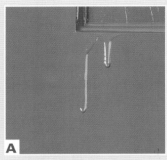

A Drips may look unsightly but can be easily removed.

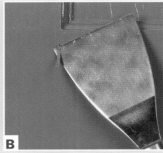

B Use a scraper to scrape back the paint drips.

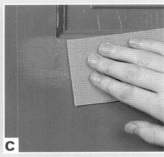

C Sand the area to a smooth finish. Repaint the sanded area.

HIDING A STAIN

Stains are caused by poor cleaning down before painting. The wall should always be washed with sugar soap. You can also treat stains caused by damp this way, provided the cause of the problem has been fixed.

TOOLS AND MATERIALS
Stain blocker or oil-based undercoat, paintbrushes, topcoat

A Clean the area thoroughly with sugar soap, then allow the surface to dry completely.

B Apply stain blocker or oil-based undercoat over the stain.

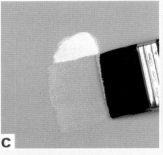

C Allow the stain blocker or undercoat to dry, then re-coat with spare topcoat.

SMOOTHING A GRITTY FINISH

Rough or gritty finishes are a result of poor preparation or impurities introduced into the paint during application. Always decant paint into a kettle when using a brush, and stir and sieve old paint before you use it again.

TOOLS AND MATERIALS
Sandpaper, cloth, paint, paintbrush

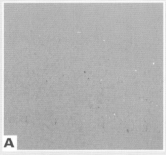

A A gritty paint finish spoils the appearance of a painted surface, as shown, but it is easily remedied.

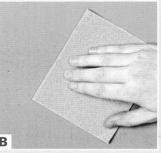

B Use sandpaper to sand the area back. Clean down with a cloth to remove dust.

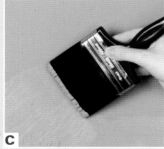

C Repaint the area with topcoat.

REMOVING WRINKLED PAINT

This effect is created by painting coats too quickly, and not allowing adequate drying time. It can also be caused by extremes of temperature while the paint is drying.

TOOLS AND MATERIALS
Chemical stripper or a hot-air gun, scraper, sandpaper

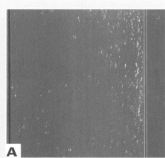

A This problem requires stripping, sanding, and repainting in order to get the desired finish.

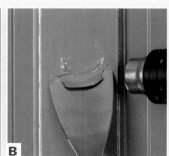

B Strip paint completely using chemical stripper or a hot air gun.

C Sand down the area and repaint.

REMOVING BRUSH MARKS

Prominent brush marks are caused by poor application technique. The problem is also common with natural wood finishes.

TOOLS AND MATERIALS
Sander, cloth, paintbrush, paint

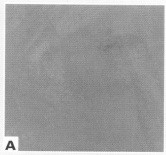

A

Obvious brush marks in different directions can make wood finishes look uneven.

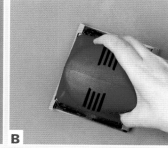

B

Machine sand the area. Wipe the area clean of dust with a damp cloth

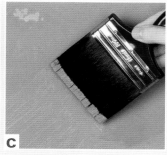

C

Repaint the area. If using a natural wood finish, take care to apply stain with the grain, keeping a wet edge at all times.

IMPROVING ON POOR COVERAGE

Poor coverage is caused by applying the wrong number of coats of paint. Sometimes this problem combines with prominent streaks in the paint caused by paint buildup on roller edges during application.

TOOLS AND MATERIALS
Sandpaper, roller

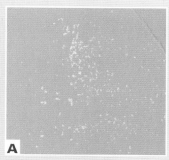

A

Poor coverage results in a patchy appearance, as shown above, and needs repainting.

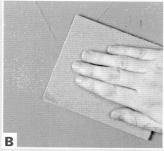

B

Sand the area to remove any paint ridges created by roller edge trails.

C

Recoat the area using the correct number of coats for the surface.

HIDING FILLER THAT SHOWS THROUGH

This problem sometimes occurs when filled areas are not primed before painting. It is always best to prime filler and/or apply an extra patch of paint to filled areas. This is especially the case for water-based paints.

TOOLS AND MATERIALS
Paintbrush, primer, roller, paint

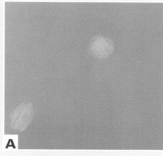

A

This problem can occur with some types of filler.

B

Recoat the patch of filler with a suitable primer, or if you are painting with emulsion, prime with full-strength emulsion.

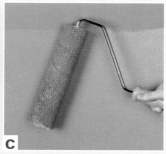

C

Recoat the entire wall.

DEALING WITH A BLEEDING KNOT

Where wood has not been knotted and primed, knots can continue to secrete resin that will show through coats of paint. See p.293 for proper preparation of knotted wood.

TOOLS AND MATERIALS
Scraper, sandpaper, paintbrushes, knotter, paint

A

Scrape back the paint from the knot and sand the area smooth.

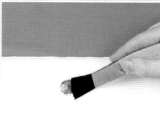

B

Apply some knotter.

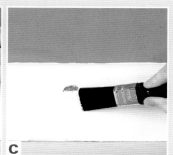

C

Apply primer, followed by the required paint finish.

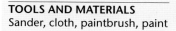

Papering

BEFORE APPLYING WALLPAPER, ALL WALL AND WOOD SURFACES SHOULD BE PREPARED IN THE USUAL WAY (SEE PP.272–75). IF ANY FEATURES NEED PAINTING, APPLY THE PAINT AFTER LINING THE ROOM; THIS FREES YOU TO OVERLAP ANY PAINT ONTO THE WALLS AND GIVES YOU A NEATER RESULT WHEN THE PAPER IS TRIMMED TO FIT. FOR MORE INFORMATION ON PAINTING SEE PP.282–83. WALLPAPERING IS ALWAYS THE FINAL JOB.

PAPERING TOOLS AND MATERIALS

This section only covers the application of new paper to stripped and prepared ceiling and wall surfaces. The tools and techniques required for stripping old wallpaper are shown on pp.272–73.

TOOLS

Aside from the general tools required for wallpapering, such as a tape measure, pencil, and craft knife, several specialist items are needed. The paperhanging brush, for example, is vital for creasing paper into corners.

Soft brush prevents damage

Bristles apply paste evenly

Paperhanging brush
Broad-handled brush for smoothing wallpaper.

Pasting brush
Large brush to apply paste to wallpaper.

Make sure you can read the scale

Steel rule
Used for drawing accurate guide lines, or for cutting with a craft knife.

Papering sponge
For cleaning paste off equipment and removing excess paste from wallpaper. Ideally you need more than one and plenty of clean water.

Keep the roller clean

Measuring jug
Essential for accurately mixing wallpaper paste.

Seam roller
Used to gently press wallpaper seams to ensure good adhesion. Do not use on embossed papers.

Handles have good grips

Paperhanging scissors
Long-bladed scissors for cutting wallpaper.

Pasting table
A long, narrow, foldaway table on which wallpaper is cut, pasted, and folded before hanging. Make sure you wipe down the surface with clean water after pasting each length.

Long, narrow reservoir

Wallpaper trough
Filled with water and used for dipping ready-pasted paper.

TYPES OF WALLPAPER

There are many types of wallpaper available. Your choice will probably be based on design. Textured paper hides uneven surfaces, as does lining paper. Vinyl-coated papers can be washed. Always buy rolls with the same batch number to avoid slight variations. Be aware that some papers are prone to fading in direct sunlight. Check the packaging for details on "colourfastness".

Standard types of wallpaper

Standard paper and vinyl-coated wallpapers are most commonly chosen, both can be used in most situations, but vinyl is more hardwearing. Paste-the-paper, paste-the-wall, and ready-pasted types are available (see below).

Specialist wallpapers

Unusual wallpapers such as flock or those with hand-printed designs may be subject to very specific handling and hanging procedures. Be sure to follow any guidelines from the manufacturer.

Embossed wall panels

Wall panels are hung in a similar way to standard wallpaper. They are thick and linoleum-based and are commonly used below dado rails in period properties. Embossed borders can be bought in a roll.

Lining paper
This provides a base for wallpaper or paint. For rough walls use a thicker gauge of lining paper.

Standard paper and vinyl paper
These two kinds of paper vary hugely in quality. Numerous patterns are available.

Woodchip paper
Several grades of texture can hide most rough or pitted walls. Can be painted.

Embossed paper
Disguises uneven surfaces. Hang gently to avoid flattening the relief. Vinyl-coated versions available.

Border paper
Strips used to divide or frame walls and features if required.

ECO-FRIENDLY WALLPAPER

There are a number of eco-friendly wallpaper options. Check labels for the FSC symbol (see p.75) and ensure that products are made from recycled paper. Look for non-toxic, water-based inks.
   The absence of vinyl as a component of "green" wallpaper raises some durability issues, but it is possible to find papers that use a water-based glaze to produce a wipeable finish.

TYPES OF ADHESIVES

There are various different types of adhesive associated with wallpapering and some types of wallpaper may require a particular adhesive. Wallpaper paste comes either ready-mixed or powdered, with the latter being mixed with water before use. Size is very diluted wallpaper paste used to prepare walls before lining paper or wallpaper is applied. Diluted with water, PVA is an alternative to size, and can be used to seal walls before wallpapering. Border adhesive is an extra-strong adhesive that ensures a good adhesion between borders and wallpaper. It is also used on overlapping wallpaper seams.

THREE METHODS OF ADHESION

There are three ways in which wallpaper is adhered to a wall surface. Paste-the-paper and paste-the-wall types require wallpaper paste. Ready-pasted paper is coated in a dry adhesive powder that is "activated" when submerged in water. Both paste-the-paper and ready-pasted types need to be left to soak after pasting or activation. Make sure you keep this soaking time consistent for each length of paper.

▌▌ PASTE-THE-WALL

To apply this type of paper, brush wallpaper paste onto the wall, then smooth the wallpaper into place. Ensure you apply an even coat. Unpasted patches will result in bubbles under the paper.

▌▌ PASTE-THE-PAPER

The aim is to create a loose concertina of paper, only allowing pasted faces to touch, with no paste on the patterned side. Leave the concertina for the recommended soaking period before hanging.

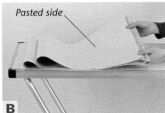
Pasted side

A Apply paste down the length, working from the centre of the paper out to the edges.

B Loosely fold up the pasted end of the paper. Paste the remaining length, then fold it up with the rest.

▌▌ READY-PASTED

Once you have wetted the paper (see below) you will need to loosely fold the length, as for paste-the-paper paper, although with the pasted side inwards to improve adhesive activation.

Keep the roll loose

A Roll up a length of the paper, pattern side facing inwards, and submerge it in the trough.

B Take the top of the roll length and draw it up onto the table, patterned-side down, then fold up loosely.

PAPERING PREPARATION

Before applying lining paper or wallpaper, it is important to consider the right order of work regarding the overall decoration of the room. Finish the lining first; then do any paintwork; then finally apply the wallpaper. When using wallpaper paste, always check the guidelines regarding "soaking" time. This refers to the length of time paste-the-paper (including wallpaper) and ready-pasted papers have to be soaked after pasting; for heavy-duty papers this can be 10 or 15 minutes.

CUTTING PAPER TO SIZE

Lengths need to be cut to an approximate size before they are applied to the wall surface. There are various ways of doing this to keep wastage to a minimum; the method you use will depend on the paper's pattern.

Free-match papers

Simply measure from the ceiling to the floor or the top of the skirting board and add a maximum of 100mm (4in) to allow for easy trimming.

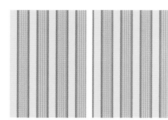

FREE MATCH

Straight-match papers

In addition to the trimming length, add the size of the paper's repeat pattern. If the pattern is very large this may cause a lot of wastage; an alternative is to hold a dry section of paper to the wall surface, cut it to an approximate length, and use this as a template for all the other "standard" lengths in the room.

STRAIGHT MATCH

Offset-match papers

Because of the offset, only every other length will be in the same "position" on the wall surface. You can use the same technique as employed for straight-match papers, but take alternate lengths from two rolls, each with a different starting point.

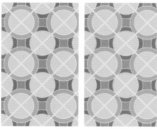

OFFSET MATCH

▌ CUTTING PAPER CORRECTLY

Unroll the paper on the pasting table. You will probably need to weigh down the end to stop it rolling back up. Measure the length of paper needed. If the table isn't long enough, fold the paper back on itself without creasing. At the required point, mark a pencil guide line, then cut the paper carefully.

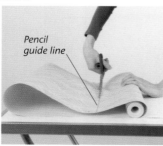

Pencil guide line

ESTIMATING QUANTITIES

To estimate how many rolls of wallpaper you need, add the height of the room to that of the paper's repeat pattern, if it has one (this measurement should be shown on the packaging). Multiply the total by the length of the room's perimeter. This is the total area of wallpaper needed. Divide this number by the area of a single roll of wallpaper (this may be on the packaging, or you should multiply the width by the length). Add an extra 10–15 per cent to this figure, depending on how many obstacles there are in the room. Round this up to the next whole figure to give you the number of rolls you need to buy.

LINING

Lining paper should be used on bare walls before any paper is hung. It creates an even surface for the paper, and prevents any wall colour showing through – use a thicker gauge of lining paper on very uneven or strongly coloured walls. Before applying lining paper, the wall surface must be "sized", or sealed. This has the effect of preventing the wall surface absorbing too much paste when the lining paper is hung. It also gives the surface a slight sheen that allows you to manoeuvre the paper more easily into position. Size is simply a diluted form of wallpaper paste, and it can be made by diluting any type of powdered paste.

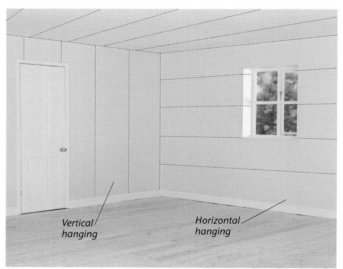

Vertical hanging

Horizontal hanging

Lining for ceiling and walls
Unlike wallpaper, lining paper can be hung horizontally or vertically. Which method you use depends on your surface. Hang it in the direction that uses the fewest lengths to cover the area. In either case you do not have to worry about patterns matching or obstacles – simply trim into every corner or edge with a craft knife as required.

FURTHER INFORMATION ON LINING

■ The techniques are similar to those for wallpaper (see pp.300–05). Try to be as accurate as possible, but any small gaps can be filled.
■ Treat each wall as a separate surface, and always cut and trim along joints at corners.
■ Work from corner to corner when lining vertically.
■ Work from the ceiling down when lining horizontally.
■ Lengths should always be butt-joined.

WHERE TO START PAPERING

Papers with large patterns should generally be centralized relative to any major features or symmetries in the room (see also tiling, p.311). For small patterns, centralizing is less important. In either case, it is essential to get the first hang dead vertical. Ideally choose a full ceiling-to-floor hang and use a pencil line drawn with a spirit level as your guide. In most cases you can choose an inconspicuous corner for the first hang because the dimensions of the room are unlikely to allow the final papers to match exactly. Draw your line about half a paper width away from the corner, rather than using the wall as your guide.

Ceiling with central light fitting
Start papering across the centre of the light fitting. Either trim the paper roughly around the fitting and tuck it under, or loosen the fitting so you can paper under it easily. Be sure to turn off the electricity in this case.

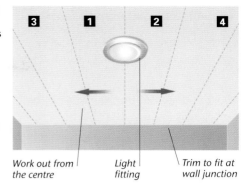

Work out from the centre / *Light fitting* / *Trim to fit at wall junction*

Starting from a corner
Draw a vertical line away from the corner. Try to position your starting point having calculated that there will be no tiny slivers required when cutting and trimming around doors and other obstacles. Hang the first length of paper against your guide line then work clockwise around the room.

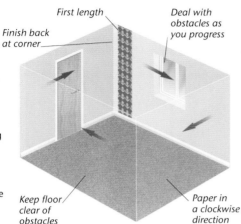

First length / *Deal with obstacles as you progress* / *Finish back at corner* / *Keep floor clear of obstacles* / *Paper in a clockwise direction*

Starting from the centre
If the room has a prominent feature such as a chimney breast, centralize a large motif in the pattern in the centre. Paper out from each side of the first length, then continue to paper clockwise around the room in the usual way.

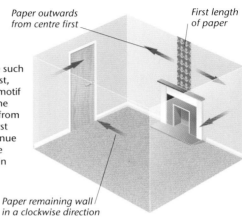

Paper outwards from centre first / *First length of paper* / *Paper remaining wall in a clockwise direction*

Papering around a window
Use the order shown right. Techniques are shown on p.302.
1 Hang the first length so that it overlaps the window.
2 Hang a short length at the top of the first. Then trim neatly to create flaps and fold these into the recess.
3 Hang a short length above the window and fold it into the recess.
4 Hang a whole length so that it overlaps the other end of the window.
5 Create flaps and fold them into the recess as before.
6 Fill in between the window sill and the floor. Trim the first and fourth lengths neatly around the sill.

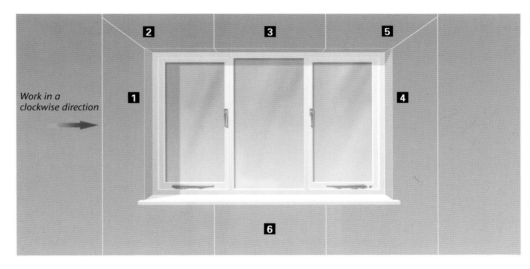

Work in a clockwise direction

TOOLS AND MATERIALS CHECKLIST PP.300–05

Basic papering (pp.300–01)
Wallpaper paste, pasting brush, paperhanging brush, sponge, paperhanging scissors, spirit level, seam roller

Papering a room (pp.302–03)
Wallpaper paste, pasting brush, paperhanging brush, sponge, spirit level, paperhanging scissors, cutting edge

Papering an external corner (p.304) Wallpaper paste, pasting brush, paperhanging brush, sponge, cutting edge, seam roller

Papering an internal corner (p.304) Wallpaper paste, pasting brush, paperhanging brush, sponge, spirit level

Working around radiators (p.304) Wallpaper paste,

pasting brush, paperhanging brush, sponge, paperhanging scissors, radiator roller

Working around sockets and plateswitches (p.305)
Wallpaper paste, pasting brush, paperhanging brush, sponge, paperhanging scissors

Working around ceiling lights (p.305) Wallpaper paste, pasting brush, paperhanging

brush, sponge

Applying borders (p.305)
Wallpaper paste, pasting brush, paperhanging brush, sponge

FOR BASIC TOOLKIT SEE PP.24–25

BASIC PAPERING

You will need to apply lining paper before wallpaper. Lining paper can be hung horizontally as well as vertically, depending on which technique will cover the wall fastest (see p.298). The horizontal technique is shown here; hang vertical lengths as for wallpaper. Use corners as guide lines and if walls undulate then allow the paper to overlap, then trim it back. Greater care must be taken with wallpaper; each sheet has to be hung perfectly vertical to achieve satisfactory results.

TOOLS AND MATERIALS SEE BASIC TOOLKIT AND P.299

1 LINING THE CEILING: THE FIRST SHEET

A

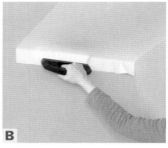

B

Take your concertina of pasted lining paper and hold it in position in line with the wall; you will need help with this.

Use the paperhanging brush to crease the paper into the junction between the ceiling and the wall.

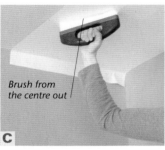

Brush from the centre out

C

D

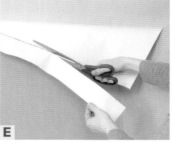

E

F

Smooth out the paper with the paperhanging brush; your helper should unravel the paper as you progress.

Brush out any bubbles trapped under the paper, then draw a pencil line along the junction between the ceiling and the wall.

Pull the paper gently back from the ceiling. Trim the paper along your line using scissors, then brush it back into position.

Use a damp sponge to remove any excess paste from the walls and the paper surface. Repeat steps D–F at the other end of the paper.

2 ATTACHING THE NEXT LENGTH

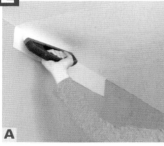

A

Make sure the join is tight

B

Take the next concertina of paper and repeat the process. Align the paper with the first sheet, then fold it into the junction as before.

Butt-join the paper length against the side of the previous sheet. Smooth the entire section before trimming and wiping down.

3 LINING THE WALLS

A

B

Position one end of a length of pasted lining paper into the corner of the wall, tight against the ceiling and overlapping into the corner.

Smooth the paper across the wall with a paperhanging brush, using the junction between the wall and ceiling as your guide.

C

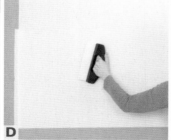

D

E

When the sheet is in place, return to the corner and crease the paper. Slice the sheet with a trimming knife or scissors to remove any excess paper.

Take the second sheet of pasted paper and position it below the first. Continue down the wall surface using the same techniques.

When you get to the bottom of the wall, trim the paper against the skirting board or floor using a craft knife. Wipe any paste from the skirting board. Before starting on the next wall, cast an eye across each hung length. Check for bubbles and smooth again if necessary.

4 HANGING WALLPAPER

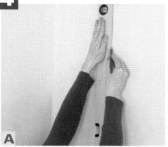

A

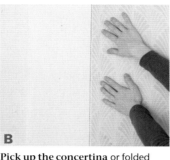

B

C

When you are happy that the paper is level, brush it down from the top and crease it into the junction. At the same time, ensure that the vertical edge of the paper is precisely aligned with the pencil guide line.

Draw a vertical pencil line on the wall surface at your chosen starting point (see p.291). Check and re-check this line using a spirit level.

Pick up the concertina or folded paper and unfold the top section. Position it against the guide line.

Unfold the concertina and work your way down the wall to the floor or skirting board. Be careful not to crease or tear the paper. Keep checking that the sheet is vertical.

D

Check the paper against the vertical guide

E

F

Use the brush to smooth the paper over the wall and remove any bubbles. Work from the centre of the paper to the edges.

At floor level, use the brush to crease the paper into the junction between the wall and skirting board.

5 TRIMMING AND JOINING THE NEXT LENGTH

A

B

C

D

Brush back up the paper to ensure good adhesion. Pay particular attention to the edges and to removing air bubbles.

Trim at the top and bottom of the length using whichever method you prefer. If you use scissors, mark the crease with a pencil line.

Brush the trimmed edges tight against the ceiling and skirting board.

Use a clean, damp sponge to wipe away any excess paste from wallpaper surface. Do the same for the ceiling and skirting board.

E

F

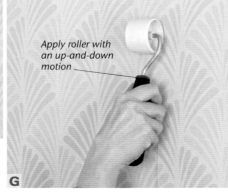

Apply roller with an up-and-down motion

G

Clean the joining seam with a wet sponge to remove any excess paste; do not apply too much pressure as this creates a shiny seam when the paper is dry. Finish off by gently running a seam roller up and down the seam.

Make sure that the pattern is matched at eye level; this keeps any pattern drop (or misalignments) at a high or low level.

Butt-join the edges together tightly, checking the join as you work your way down.

PAPERING A ROOM

Wallpapering a room is a methodical process. Plan the project carefully, making sure you have bought enough paper and are sure of your starting position (see pp.298–99). Clear the room of as much furniture as possible. This example shows how to tackle a typical room layout. Use the basic wallpaper-hanging instructions shown on p.301 in combination with the techniques described here to navigate around the room perimeter. Details of how to negotiate corners and other obstacles you might encounter are shown on pp.304–05.

TOOLS AND MATERIALS SEE BASIC TOOLKIT AND P.299

1 HANGING THE FIRST SHEET

A

Draw a vertical line half a width away from the starting corner and hang your first full length of pasted paper. If you are using patterned paper, try to choose an inconspicuous corner as the dimensions of the room are unlikely to allow an exact match when negotiating the final join (see opposite).

2 PAPERING THE SIDE OF A WINDOW RECESS

When you reach a window, hang the next length of paper so that it overlaps the recess. Make horizontal cuts in the paper and bend the resulting flap into the recess. If the paper doesn't reach the window, it will be necessary to insert a further length.

Trim around recess as if trimming around a door

A

B

Using a craft knife, finely trim the paper so that it fits perfectly around the sill.

C

After cutting the ends, brush the flap into place and crease the paper into the corner. Trim the edge so that the paper is flush with the window frame.

3 PAPERING THE TOP OF A WINDOW RECESS

A

Paste a short piece of paper on top of the existing sheet to create a flap to fold into the window recess. Make sure that the patterns on the two sheets match.

Flap to fill recess

B

After cutting the flap, use a cutting edge and a knife to cut a diagonal line through both sheets of paper from the corner of the recess to the edge of the top sheet.

C

Remove both pieces of paper, then peel away the bottom sheet and place the top piece onto the wall. As always, make sure that the pattern fits perfectly with the edge sheet.

Invisible diagonal seam

D

Fold the remaining flap of the new sheet into the window recess. Brush out any bubbles and trim any ends with the knife. Continue as shown on p.299.

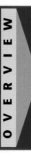

4 PAPERING AROUND A DOOR

Take care not to tear the paper on corners

A

When you get to a door, apply a sheet as normal. Cut out a rough area of the door with scissors, leaving plenty of excess paper.

B

Cut diagonally through the excess paper over the door to the corner of the architrave. Crease the top and side flaps into place, leaving the excess around the architrave.

C

Trim the excess paper from the top of the door frame, using a craft or trimming knife.

D

Continue trimming the paper down the side of the door frame. Use the edge of the architrave as a guide.

E

Smooth the paper around the architrave with the brush.

F

Hang a short length of paper above the door. When perfectly aligned, trim it against the ceiling and architrave.

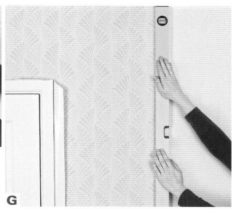

G

On reaching the other side of the door, use the same technique for the opposite edge, except do not trim along the vertical edge of the architrave until the next full length of paper is hung. In this way it is easier to maintain the precise vertical position of the lengths and to trim accurately along the architrave edge.

5 NEGOTIATING THE FINAL JOIN

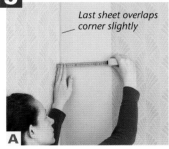

Last sheet overlaps corner slightly

A

Measure from the edge of the first length into the corner and add 20mm (¾in). Transfer this measurement to a length of pasted paper and cut along it.

Take care to brush the paper right into the corner

B

Take the measured strip and hang it against the first strip you hung, matching the pattern carefully. Brush the other edge into and around the internal corner.

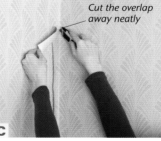

Cut the overlap away neatly

C

Carefully trim into the corner to remove the excess paper, and the top and bottom of the length. Smooth the ends when finished, adding extra paste if necessary.

D

The final edges may not match perfectly, but being in the corner this is hardly noticeable. Sponge any remaining paste from the paper to finish.

PAPERING AROUND OBSTACLES

Aside from the obstacles shown on pp.302–03, there are many other areas where precise measuring, cutting, and trimming are required. In most cases, it is simply a further application of the principles demonstrated on those pages. In others, however, some special techniques are needed; the most common of these are illustrated here. As always, remember to turn off the electricity before working around lights and switches, and drain radiators if removing them from the wall (see p.504).

TOOLS AND MATERIALS SEE BASIC TOOLKIT AND P.299

▌EXTERNAL CORNERS

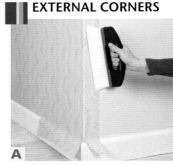

Overlap the first sheet

A

Hang the paper so that it bends around the corner. Slice the bottom to make two separate flaps, then brush the paper flat.

B

Hang a second sheet around the corner. Make sure it is vertical. Check that the pattern fits, then brush the second sheet flat.

Trim the top and bottom of both sheets in the usual way. Remove any excess paste from the paper surface. Use a roller to secure the join. You are now ready to hang the next sheet.

C

Use a straight edge (a steel rule is ideal) to cut through both layers of the overlap.

D

Pull back the overlap and remove the paper below. Then remove the excess from the top sheet. Smooth to reveal a precise butt join.

E

▌INTERNAL CORNERS

A

It is much easier to paper an internal corner with two vertical strips than with one. Start by folding a sheet into the corner.

B

Brush the sheet flat, then slice the paper 20mm (¾in) to the right of the corner to create two separate sheets.

C

Move the right-hand sheet to one side, then trim the top and bottom of the left-hand sheet. Move the right-hand sheet back across and trim.

D

Check the paper is at the right level by comparing points of the pattern with adjacent lengths.

▌WORKING AROUND RADIATORS

Radiators can always be removed before papering (see p.504), but it is also possible to simply work around them. Begin by securing the wallpaper as usual, pasting it to an inch or so above the radiator. Then allow the bottom section of the length to flap over the radiator surface.

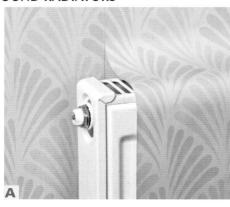

A

B

Cut the paper so that it will hang down slightly behind the radiator.

C

Use a radiator roller to push the paper behind the radiator.

WORKING AROUND SOCKETS AND PLATESWITCHES

A

Turn off the power. Hang a length of paper so that it covers the plateswitch. Mark the position of the corners of the plate.

B

Cut two diagonal slits from corner to corner, creating four triangular flaps. Fold the flaps out from the wall and cut along the folds.

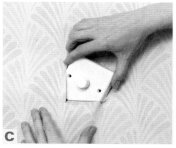

C

Loosen the plateswitch by removing its retaining screws. Rotate the plate and feed it diagonally through the hole in the paper.

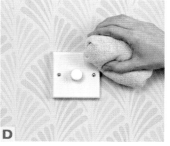

D

Smooth the paper under the plateswitch. Refix the plate and remove any paste with a sponge. Leave the electricity off until dry.

WORKING AROUND CEILING LIGHTS

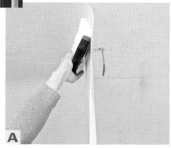

A

Turn off the power, then remove the light and light fittings and leave the cable hanging. Brush the paper across the ceiling to the cable.

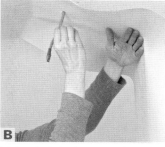

B

Make a hole in the paper where the cable joins the ceiling. Draw the cable through the paper, then continue smoothing down the length of paper.

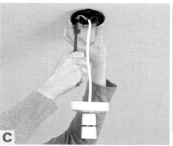

C

Finish hanging the paper, then re-attach the fittings. Screw the base back onto the ceiling, making holes in the paper where necessary.

D

Once the cable and base are secure, screw the final fittings into place. Leave the electricity off until the paper is completely dry.

APPLYING BORDERS AROUND A ROOM

A

Draw a pencil guide line on the wall at the height you wish the border to hang. Apply the border to the wall with a paperhanging brush.

B

Overlap around corners. Move the next length into place, ensuring the pattern matches. Trim overlap precisely in corner.

APPLYING BORDERS AROUND A FEATURE

Borders are often used to frame mirrors and other features. To make a frame they need to be joined at right angles. Use a level to make sure the strips are horizontal and vertical. Try to cross the pasted strips through the middle of a motif to get an approximate pattern match.

A

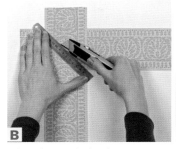

B

After placing the borders, use a straight edge and a trimming knife to cut through the overlap at 45 degrees.

C

Remove the excess paper from the end of each strip. You may need to lift the border to remove the paper from underneath.

D

Having removed the excess paper, flatten the borders against the wall and clean the final surface with a wet sponge.

STAIRWELLS

The most important consideration when papering a stairwell is to build a safe working platform. An example of this is shown on p.27, but the design can be varied, depending on your needs. Pad the tops of the ladders to prevent damaging the wall. You will need someone to help you when hanging long sheets.

PROBLEM SOLVER

FILLING BETWEEN CORNER EDGES ON LINING PAPER

A superior finish for lining is achieved by using caulk or flexible filler along all trimmed paper junctions. Caulk is applied using a sealant dispenser, and must be smoothed immediately after application.

TOOLS AND MATERIALS
Caulk, sealant dispenser, sponge

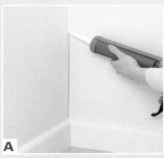

A **Apply caulk evenly**, creating a uniform bead along junctions.

B **Smooth** with a wet finger to remove ridges and surface imperfections.

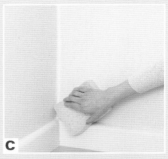

C **Use a damp sponge** to smooth caulk. Rinse regularly.

FILLING GAPS IN LINING PAPER

Imperfect joins on a lined surface may be improved by using some all-purpose decorating filler. Some manufacturers make ready-mixed "fine-surface filler", which is ideal for use here.

TOOLS AND MATERIALS
Filler, filling knife, sanding block, brush

A **Apply filler** using a filling knife.

B **Let the filler dry**, then use a sanding block to smooth any ridges.

C **Make sure the filler** is "sized" before any wallpaper is hung.

DISGUISING GAPS IN WALLPAPER JOINS

For a perfect finish, joints can be disguised in a wallpaper finish by painting the background a similar colour to the paper "base" colour.

TOOLS AND MATERIALS
Paint, paintbrush, pasting brush

A **Mark a line** on the wall where the papers will join. Paint over the line with the appropriate paint.

B **Allow the paint** to dry. Then hang the first sheet of paper and smooth down with a brush.

C **Hang the second sheet** next to the first. If there is space between the two sheets, the paint will disguise the gap.

REPAIRING TORN WALLPAPER

Paper is delicate and can sometimes be torn by a sharp object. You can often repair damage by carefully repositioning the torn section.

TOOLS AND MATERIALS
PVA adhesive, fitch, sponge

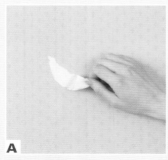

A **Carefully pull back** the torn section of paper.

B **Apply border or** PVA adhesive to the wall with a fitch (a small brush), taking care not to get it on the front of the paper.

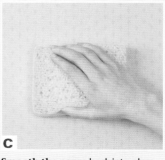

C **Smooth the paper** back into place with a damp sponge, removing excess adhesive.

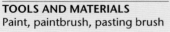

RE-STICKING PAPER THAT IS LIFTING OFF

Paper commonly lifts at its base, which is normally the junction with the skirting board. Poor initial application or moist air in a bathroom are the main causes.

TOOLS AND MATERIALS
PVA adhesive, fitch, sponge, silicone sealant

A

Peel back the lifted section of paper, and apply border or PVA adhesive to it.

B

Use a damp sponge to smooth the paper back into place.

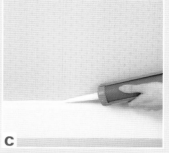

C

When the adhesive is dry, apply silicone sealant along the join between the paper and the wall.

GETTING A BUBBLE OUT OF WALLPAPER

Bubbles normally occur because of poor initial application. Where there are lots of bubbles, replace the paper. Where there are only a few bubbles, repair as shown.

TOOLS AND MATERIALS
Craft knife, PVA adhesive, fitch, sponge

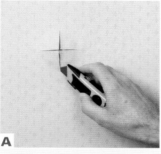

A

Using a craft knife, cut open the bubble with a cross cut.

B

Open out the four leaves of the cut and apply a small amount of PVA adhesive with a fitch.

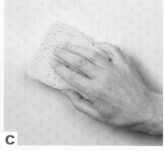

C

Use a sponge to smooth the leaves back into place, and allow to dry thoroughly.

REPAIRING A PEELING SEAM

Seams normally peel because of poor initial application, or because of an overlap. Overlaps are sometimes unavoidable, and (particularly with vinyl papers) they tend to peel easily if PVA adhesive was not used on the overlap during initial application. In either case, overlaps or peeling seams are easily repaired by using the following technique.

A

Sometimes when paper dries, the seams between sheets peel, and look unsightly.

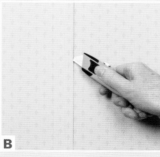

B

Carefully use a craft knife to lever back the overlap just enough to apply adhesive beneath it.

C

Apply a small amount of PVA adhesive, taking care not to get it on the front of the wallpaper.

D

Apply gentle pressure with a seam roller to flatten the seam edges together.

E

Wipe down the seam clean with a wet sponge.

F

Dry the seam with a cloth, working in one direction to smooth the seam.

TOOLS AND MATERIALS
Craft knife, fitch, PVA adhesive, seam roller, sponge, cloth

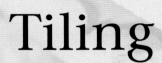

Tiling

TILES ARE WATERPROOF AND HARDWEARING, SO THEY ARE IDEAL FOR AREAS WHERE WATER IS USED, SUCH AS KITCHENS AND BATHROOMS. BEFORE APPLYING TILES, YOU WILL NEED TO PREPARE THE SURFACE THOROUGHLY. PLAN YOUR WORK CAREFULLY, AND TAKE TIME TO CHOOSE MATERIALS AND A WORKING METHOD TO SUIT, WHETHER YOU ARE TILING A NEW WALL, A PREPARED SURFACE, OR DIRECTLY ONTO OLD TILES.

PLANNING TILING PROJECTS

The type and size of tile you choose will affect your overall design and how you work. You can use larger tiles to cover an area more quickly, but you may find it more difficult to lay large tiles on uneven surfaces. In such cases, small tiles may be easier to use and be more forgiving. Consider whether to tile the whole room, just up to a border, or a specific area, like a splashback. Because of the grid pattern formed by tiles you need to spend time finding the best starting point in order to achieve a balanced overall effect and avoid thin slivers of tile. Use the next few pages to help you plan the project in its entirety first.

DESIGN OPTIONS

Tiles are usually applied in a regular grid pattern, but you can use other designs, for example, staggered or diamond patterns, or a combination of the two. For complicated designs, drawing a scale diagram will help you to plan your approach. See p.318 for the techniques needed for these effects.

Tiling patterns
The majority of ceramic tiles are square-shaped, and the most common design is to apply them in a grid pattern. However, tiles can be laid in a brickbond pattern or in more elaborate designs. Beware of using complicated arrangements in small spaces as the effect can be overpowering.

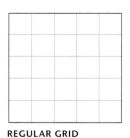

REGULAR GRID

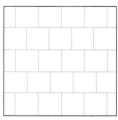

BRICKBOND

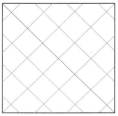

DIAMOND PATTERN

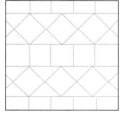

DIAMOND PATTERN IN REGULAR GRID

OCTAGONS WITH INSERTS

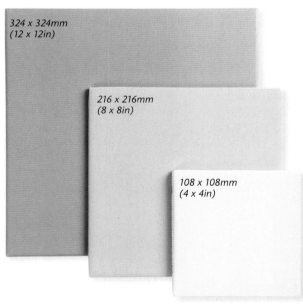

324 x 324mm (12 x 12in)

216 x 216mm (8 x 8in)

108 x 108mm (4 x 4in)

Choosing the right tiles
Size, shape, and colour are as important as the material from which the tile is made. The standard square sizes are shown above. When possible, buy tiles of one colour with the same batch number. Shuffle tiles of the same colour from different boxes, so that any slight colour variation will not show once the tiles are applied to the surface.

TYPES OF TILES

Most tiles are ceramic – they are made of clay, have a glazed, smooth surface that is easy to clean, and are very durable. Glazes are generally coloured to provide decorative options. Some glazed tiles are prone to crazing, which may affect their waterproofing properties, making them unsuitable for constantly wet areas such as showers. Non-ceramic tiles are made of materials such as marble or slate, with their natural texture, rather than a glaze, providing the finish. Tiles are a common object for reclamation (see pp.86–87).

MARBLE

SLATE   **LIMESTONE**

Natural tiles

Limestone, slate, and marble are common types of natural stone tile. Marble tiles are normally larger than standard-sized ceramic tiles, and are usually applied allowing for small grout joints to give a continuous marble effect. Natural stone is porous, so in areas where water is used, such as a bathroom or kitchen, natural stone tiles have to be treated with a waterproof sealant after application. Suppliers can provide appropriate sealants for the job.

Ceramic tiles

These are usually glazed and are available in many sizes, colours, and thicknesses. Ceramic tiles are also easy to cut to shape. Some manufacturers produce ceramic tiles that look like natural tiles (see top left), but are often cheaper than the real thing.

Plastic tiles

These are normally supplied in a sheet, and are applied to the surface with a tile adhesive. Never use plastic tiles in areas that will receive direct heat, such as close to an oven or hob.

GLASS   **STAINLESS STEEL**

Speciality tiles

Tiles made of glass, stainless steel, and some other materials can be considerably more expensive than ceramic tiles. Check that the material of your choice is suitable for the job. For instance, heat from an oven can crack some types of glass tiles.

Insert tiles

These tiles add a decorative detail to the main pattern of a larger design. They are usually small and square, but come in many shapes.

Mosaic tiles

Small ceramic or glass tiles are supplied in sheets on a net backing to control the space between tiles and to make them easier to apply. Some have a protective sheet of paper; it has to be soaked off after the tiling adhesive has dried. Sheets can be cut with scissors to size.

BORDER TILES, TILE EDGES, AND CORNER TRIMS

In addition to square tiles, you can buy border tiles to decorate the edges of the tiled area and trims to finish and protect the edges of the tiles. Both are available in a wide variety of finishes and designs. Quadrant tiles are a further option, creating a decorative edge where tiles join with a bath, basin, or work surface. They give a more finished look than regular tiles cut to fit a narrow space. Remember to include trims and border or quadrant tiles when estimating quantities (see overleaf).

CORNER PIECE FOR PLASTIC TRIM

SELECTION OF BORDER TILES

PLASTIC TRIM

Border tiles

Narrow border tiles provide a decorative band that runs through a design or along its top edge. Apply adhesive directly to thin border tiles. If the tile widths do not match exactly the width of the main tiles, use spacers cut down into T-shapes or apply cross-shaped spaces perpendicular to the wall, and remove before grouting. Apply full tiles first, leaving cuts until last.

Tile edging and corner trims

Regular, straight-edged tiles are straightforward to apply, whereas you may have to adapt your technique for those with irregular edges. Trims are usually plastic and applied along external corners. Where the design finishes in the middle of a wall surface they can be used to provide a neat finish and cover unsightly cut edges. Tile edges are often unglazed, and trims may be used to protect the edges of tiles.

PREPARING A SURFACE

New plaster must be sealed with PVA solution (five parts water to one part PVA). Old painted walls must be sanded and cleaned down. Wallpaper must be removed, and the surface below made good. Old tiled surfaces can be stripped of tiles and made good, but it is possible to tile over old tiles as long as they are still firmly attached to the wall. The grout joints of the new tiles should not coincide with those of the old tiles, so that if the old joints weaken and crack, the new tiled surface will not be affected.

CALCULATING HOW MANY TILES TO BUY

Follow the steps below to calculate the number of tiles you will need to buy.
1. Measure the height and width of the area you need to tile.
2. Multiply the height by the width to get the surface area.
3. Repeat for each surface. Remember to include small areas such as window reveals.
4. Add together all the areas to get a figure for the total area.
5. Subtract from that total any areas that do not need tiling (e.g. a doorway).
6. Add at least 10 per cent to your final figure to allow for wastage (broken tiles) and cutting. Then divide the surface area by the area of one of your chosen tiles to find out how many you need.

Using your supplier
If your design uses more than one type of tile, your supplier should be able to calculate for you how many tiles of each type you need. Where a relatively small number of tiles is needed it should be easier to give your supplier an accurate figure for the number of tiles you require.

▮▮ USING A TILING GAUGE

You can use a tile gauge – a length of marked-off wooden batten – to judge accurately the number of tiles you need. By marking the width of the tiles on the batten, you can "gauge" how many tiles are required for a particular area. It is particularly useful for visualizing the tiles in position. When you are calculating how many tiles are needed (see above), use the gauge to see how the different tile sizes will fit in the area you have to tile. If your tiles are rectangular, rather than square, you will need two gauges, one for vertical gauging, one for horizontal gauging.

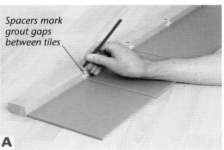

Spacers mark grout gaps between tiles

A

Cut a batten slightly shorter than the smallest width of the area to be tiled. Place the tiles along the batten with spacers between them. Mark the tile edges.

B

Hold the gauge against the surface of the wall and count the exact number of tiles. Use the gauge to plan the position of tiles around obstacles such as windows.

TILING A SMALL AREA

A stand-alone basin, sink, or hob may only require a small area of tiling above it. Plan the work so you only need to use whole tiles, with no cutting involved. Use the middle or edge of a tile as a central starting point to see if the tiles will look best centred in the space, or set either side of the starting point. A slight overlap at the end of a tiled section can look neat if evenly matched on both sides. For basins that have a slightly curved back edge, lay the first, central tile as before. Then, as you move out from the centre, use spacers or card supports to keep the tiles level. Check that the line of tiles is level as you progress.

TILING A SHOWER CUBICLE

You should tile a shower cubicle after tray installation, but before a screen is fixed. Standard-sized tiles will often divide exactly into the dimensions of the shower tray, so cuts are often unnecessary, but check with a gauge first. Start at the outside edge of the cubicle, with the tile extending slightly outside the screen.

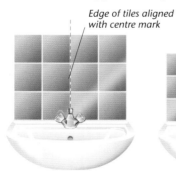

Edge of tiles aligned with centre mark

Option 1: Even tiling
If an even number of tiles will fit neatly above the basin, first use a pencil to mark a mid-point on the wall above the back of the basin. Line up the edge of the first tile with the centre mark and tile outwards.

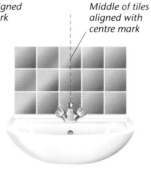

Middle of tiles aligned with centre mark

Option 2: Centred tiling
If an odd number of tiles lines up neatly above the basin, or you cannot fit the tiles without overlapping the edges of the sink, align the middle of the first tile with the centre point of the sink and tile outwards.

Option 3: Tiling behind a shaped back edge
If possible, loosen the retaining screws that hold the basin or shaped back section against the wall. Apply the first row of tiles behind the edge of the basin and re-fix it in place.

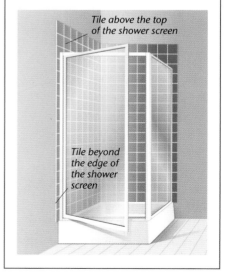

Tile above the top of the shower screen

Tile beyond the edge of the shower screen

PLANNING A TILE ARRANGEMENT

There is no single starting point that applies to all tiling jobs. In a small room it is a good idea to centre your tile layout on a small area, such as a basin or hob splashback, which is the area that you look at most often in the room. Use a tape measure or tile gauge (see opposite) to assess where the tiles would be positioned. Plan to site cut tiles in areas where they would be less noticeable, and avoid awkward, thin pieces. Although you should plan to start tiling at floor level, you will need to consider how columns and rows of tiles will be positioned in relation to focal points and level surfaces. If tiling from floor level, take into account the temporary batten you will use to provide a straight edge and support (see p.314). Eventually you will use cut tiles to cover the space left by the battens.

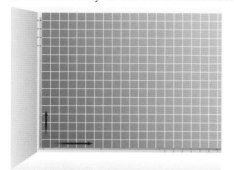

Start at floor level
Many floors and skirting boards are uneven, so you will need to fix temporary battens to the bottom of the wall to provide a straight edge. Aim to finish with any cut tiles in less conspicuous areas, such as around the floor or ceiling and in corners. You should always aim to start tiling from batten level.

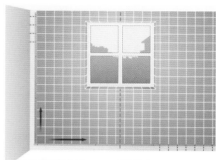

Plan around focal points
If your room has a focal point, such as a window, it is vital to consider this in your planning. Use a tile gauge to assess whether you can use whole tiles around it, or cut tiles to match on each side. Although you will start tiling at floor level, accurate planning will mean that the tiles around the window will be well positioned.

Consider level surfaces
A level surface, such as a worktop or bath, can sometimes act as a guide and support for the tiles above. Ideally, you should apply a row of whole tiles along the surface. Use a gauge to check how this will affect the positioning of tiles around other features. Even with a level surface, you should aim to start tiling from floor level.

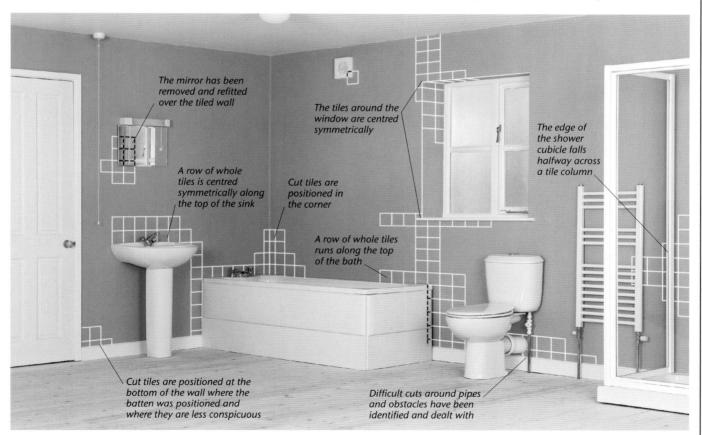

The mirror has been removed and refitted over the tiled wall

The tiles around the window are centred symmetrically

The edge of the shower cubicle falls halfway across a tile column

A row of whole tiles is centred symmetrically along the top of the sink

Cut tiles are positioned in the corner

A row of whole tiles runs along the top of the bath

Cut tiles are positioned at the bottom of the wall where the batten was positioned and where they are less conspicuous

Difficult cuts around pipes and obstacles have been identified and dealt with

Visualizing your room
If you are planning to tile a whole room, first you will need to consider some or all of the planning guidelines suggested opposite and above. In this example, the best possible tiling solution for each area of a bathroom has been visualized, and the overall tiling plan has addressed most of the practical and design issues that are covered here. However, in most cases, your design depends on room proportions and tile size. It is unlikely that you will be able to combine the ideal tile placement for each area of your room. In such instances, you will need to use a tile gauge to measure out possible combinations of tile placement and come up with a solution that offers the most acceptable compromise.

CUTTING TOOLS

For cutting straight tile edges, a score-and-snap cutter is usually the best option, but an electric one is worth considering if you need to do a lot of tiling, or are using floor tiles. To cut curves and irregular shapes you would normally use a tile saw, while special drill attachments are available for making holes in tiles.

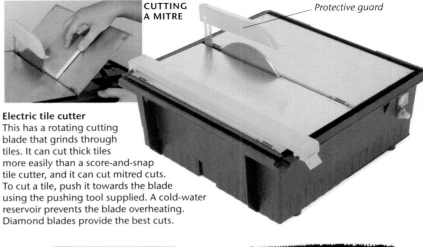

CUTTING A MITRE

Protective guard

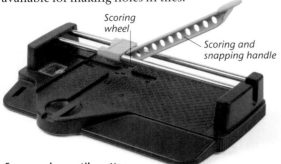

Scoring wheel

Scoring and snapping handle

Score-and-snap tile cutter

This cutter can cope with most cutting requirements. Cheaper models will be less accurate than heavy-duty cutters, and cannot be used for floor tiles. To cut a tile, place inside the central frame. Press the wheel onto the surface of the tile, and push it along to score its surface. Apply pressure on either side of this groove to snap the tile in two.

Electric tile cutter

This has a rotating cutting blade that grinds through tiles. It can cut thick tiles more easily than a score-and-snap tile cutter, and it can cut mitred cuts. To cut a tile, push it towards the blade using the pushing tool supplied. A cold-water reservoir prevents the blade overheating. Diamond blades provide the best cuts.

Tile spike

Use this to score a guide line along a tile before you snap it into two pieces.

Tile file

If a cut tile has a rough edge, use a tile file to get a clean, straight finish.

Cutting wheel and snapper

This hand-held cutter operates in the same way as the score-and-snap tile cutter. Once you have scored a guide line, place the tile between the tool's jaws. Applying downward pressure on each side of the line will break the tile in two.

Spring opens jaws when grip is relaxed

Tile nibblers

Used to remove small portions of tile. Score a guide line first.

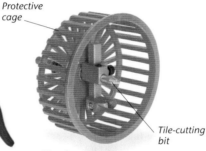

Protective cage

Tile-cutting bit

Circular tile cutter

This drill attachment cuts clean circles in tiles for pipework.

Blade wears quickly but is replaceable

Tile saw

Use a tile saw, preferably with a tungsten carbide blade, to cut curves in tiles.

OTHER TILING TOOLS

There is a large range of tools that are designed for measuring tiles, applying them to surfaces, and creating a neat finish. Decide which tools you need for your project using the checklist opposite.

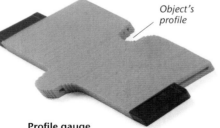

Object's profile

Profile gauge

Press the gauge against any profile or edge to make a guide that can be traced onto a tile.

An indelible pen
Use to mark cut lines on tiles. Best used with an electric cutter, so that the water used to cool the blade does not smudge the guide lines.

Grout spreader

The rubber blade presses grout into place, and the straight edge limits overspill onto the tiles.

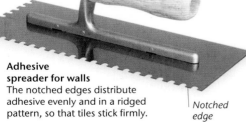

Adhesive spreader for walls

The notched edges distribute adhesive evenly and in a ridged pattern, so that tiles stick firmly.

Notched edge

Adhesive spreader for tiles

Use to apply adhesive to the back of tiles.

Grout rake

Scrape the blade along tile joints to remove old grout that you want to replace.

Blade

Grout shaper

Run along a grout line, after applying the grout, to create a smooth finish.

Sponge

Keep a bucket of water and a sponge to hand to wipe away excess adhesive, and to clean tools as you work.

USING SPACERS

Narrow spacer for tight fit

Wide profile for large tiles

Spacers
These small, plastic crosses are positioned between tiles to provide equal-sized joints. The size of the spacer will determine the thickness of the grout joints. Spacers can be positioned permanently, and covered by grout, but with some thinner tiles, you may need to remove them before grouting.

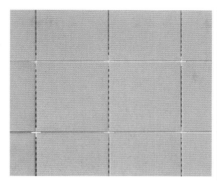

Using spacers flat against a surface
When tiling up from a firm batten with plastic spacers used flush to the wall surface, you can tile from batten to ceiling in a day. The spacers and batten prevent the tiles slipping.

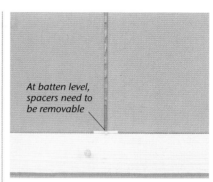

At batten level, spacers need to be removable

Using removable spacers or cardboard
When using removable spacers perpendicular to the wall surface, apply tiles to a maximum height of 1.5m (5ft) and leave the adhesive to dry before continuing with the next rows.

ADHESIVES AND SEALANTS

Good-quality adhesives and sealants are crucial for providing waterproof tiled finishes. Also pay particular attention to the grout you purchase, as some are more waterproof than others. Grout is available in a range of colours. White is the most popular, but you may choose off-white to match natural stone, for example. Natural tiles may also require sealing. Often it is best to apply one coat of sealant to the tiles before application, and one after. As sealants are often tile-specific, you should take advice from your supplier.

Adhesive
Powdered and ready-mixed varieties are available, but the latter are more expensive.

Adhesive and grout
This useful dual-purpose substance acts as both an adhesive and a grout. Close the lid between stages to prevent drying out. Good for small repairs.

Grout
Mix powdered grout with water to form a paste. Only mix as much as you can use in an hour, so that it does not dry out.

Epoxy grout
This is difficult to apply but makes a hygienic seal for joints on tiled kitchen worktops.

Grout protector
This liquid sealant stops the grout discolouring and keeps the finish clean. Leave grout to dry fully before application.

Grout reviver
Apply this paint-like substance to old grout to restore its finish. Available in white and a range of neutral colours.

Silicone sealant
Use this for a waterproof seal between tiles and a work surface, bath, wall, or floor.

TOOLS AND MATERIALS CHECKLIST PP.314–19

Basic tiling (pp.314–15) Wood battens, spirit level, tile adhesive, adhesive spreader, spacers, measuring jig*, indelible pen, tile cutter, sponge, grout, grout spreader, sponge, grout shaper

Tiling around a socket or switch (p.316) Pen, tile cutter, tile adhesive and spreader

Tiling an internal corner (p.316) Pen, metal ruler, tile cutter, tile adhesive, adhesive spreader

Tiling a recess (p.316) Wood battens, tile adhesive, adhesive spreader

Tiling an external corner (pp.316–17) Pen, tile cutter or saw, tile adhesive, adhesive spreader, corner trim*

Cutting a curve (p.317) Paper, scissors, pen or pencil, tile cutter or saw, profile gauge*

Tiling around a pipe (p.317) Pen, try square, ruler, tile hole cutter, tile adhesive, adhesive spreader

Using insert tiles (p.318) Spacers, tile adhesive, spreader

Creating a diamond pattern (p.318) Tile cutter, spirit level, tile adhesive, adhesive spreader

Laying mosaic tiles (p.318) Paint roller, scissors and/or tile nibblers, tile adhesive adhesive spreader

Creating a border (p.318) Spacers, tile cutter, tile adhesive, adhesive spreader

Other spacing effects (p.318) Pieces of thin cardboard, spacers

Using silicone sealant (p.319) Masking tape, silicone sealant, sealant dispenser

Sealing and unsealing a bath access panel (p.319) Silicone sealant, sealant dispenser

* = optional

FOR BASIC TOOLKIT SEE PP.24–25

BASIC TILING

Before you start tiling, ensure that you have planned your tile arrangement (see p.311). Generally you can tile from batten to ceiling in a day using the method shown here. If you do not use rigid plastic spacers flat against the wall, or have no batten support, you should tile to a height of 1.5m (5ft), then leave the adhesive to dry for at least 12 hours before continuing. Allow the adhesive to dry fully before grouting. See pp.316–19 for more advanced tiling techniques.

TOOLS AND MATERIALS SEE BASIC TOOLKIT AND P.313

1 ATTACHING THE BATTENS

Make sure you will be able to remove the batten easily

A

Nail the horizontal batten to the wall at your chosen starting point. Use a spirit level to keep it straight, and use a cable detector to check for cables before fixing the nails.

B

Place the vertical batten at the edge of your design, marking the start of the first vertical row of complete tiles. Nail the second batten at right angles to the first.

2 PLACING THE FIRST TILES

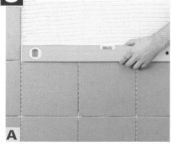

A

Apply the adhesive with a spreader, pushing it into the right angle created by the battens. Cover 1sq m (10sq ft) at most at a time.

B

Spread the adhesive by pulling the spreader's serrated edge through it, several times if necessary, to make sure it is even. This improves the adhesion of each tile.

Press firmly, with a very slight twisting motion

C

Place the first tile in the right angle of the two battens. Place the second tile beside it, remembering to leave a sufficient gap between them for the first spacer.

D

Place the spacer flat between the inside top corners of the two tiles. Stand a spacer at right angles to the wall at the bottom of the gap between the two tiles.

3 BUILDING UP THE TILE LEVELS

A

Add further tiles, building up the levels as you progress across the wall, adding spacers between the tiles. Use a spirit level to check regularly that the rows are straight.

B

As tiling progresses, check that the tile surface is even. Hold a batten with a straight edge across the tiles, and see if it lies flat on every tile.

4 MEASURING TO FILL GAPS AND CORNERS

A

Allow the completed area of tiles to dry fully – for at least 12 hours but ideally overnight. Then remove the horizontal batten by levering out the nails with a claw hammer.

B

Measure the remaining gap at every point where a tile will be placed, as widths may vary along the wall. Remember to allow space for grout joints.

OVERVIEW

ALTERNATIVE MEASURING TECHNIQUES

Measuring by hand
For pinpoint accuracy, turn the tile face inwards and mark the edges, allowing for grout joints.

Using a measuring jig
Tile cutters often have a measuring jig that quickly calculates widths plus grout space. This is then inserted into the cutter as a guide.

5 APPLYING CUT TILES

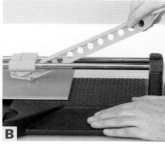

A

Mark the measurements on a tile using a felt-tip pen. If you have planned correctly, you will need approximate half tiles, rather than slivers.

B

To score the tile, grip it in your tile cutter, with the glazed surface facing upwards. Push the lever away from you to score along the marked guide line.

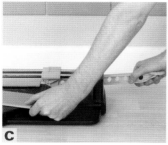

C

Depending on the cutter design, either position the tile in the cutter's jaws or below its mechanism, before applying downward pressure to the lever to split the tile in two.

D

Smooth any rough edges with a tile file. Before placing cut tiles, spread adhesive on the back of the tile. It is easier to add adhesive to a cut tile than to the wall space.

E

Position the tile on the wall. To complete the wall, continue along the row to fill the horizontal gap. Remove the vertical batten and repeat the process upwards. More information on dealing with internal corners is given on p.316.

6 GROUTING TILES

After tiling, let tiles dry for at least 12 hours. Then use a grout spreader to press grout into the joints between tiles to waterproof the wall and to give a neat finish. Remove any protruding spacers. Ensure that the grout covers spacers that lie flat against the wall.

A

B

Wearing a glove, use a damp sponge to wipe off any excess grout while it is still wet. Take care to avoid rubbing the grout out of the tile joins. Check that the spacers are covered.

Shape the grout to give a smooth, even finish

C

Use a grout shaper to neaten the grout line, then wipe again with a clean, damp sponge. After the grout has dried, polish the tiles with a dry cloth to remove any residue.

TILING AROUND OBSTACLES

Most surfaces have obstacles that interrupt the run of tiles and make tiling more complicated. Many of the problems that obstacles present can be dealt with by carefully planning your tile layout (see pp.310–11). Remove fittings if possible, and tile with just the supply pipes in place. Choose those techniques that are most suitable for your own project. Often there is more than one way of tackling some tasks, depending on which tools you have, or the circumstances you face.

TOOLS AND MATERIALS SEE BASIC TOOLKIT AND P.313

CONSIDERING TILE LAYOUT

When dealing with a number of obstacles, you will first need to plan the overall tile layout (see p.311) and work out a solution that addresses most problem areas.

Half tiles inside the recess

Tiles centred on window frame

Extend the tiles behind the extractor fan cover

Right-angled cut

Corner trim

Internal corner

Begin at centre of outer edge, and work towards window and corners

External corner

Fitting removed to facilitate tiling

◼◼ TILING AROUND A SOCKET OR PLATESWITCH

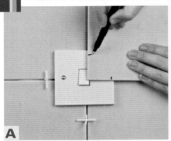

A Turn off the electricity supply and loosen the plateswitch. Hold a tile in place and mark it so that the cut edges will fit behind the plate.

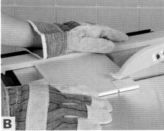

B Use an electric tile cutter to cut along the guide lines. Another option is to use a tile saw on the first line, then score and snap the second.

◼◼ TILING AN INTERNAL CORNER

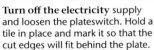

A Measure the space between the last full tile and the corner, allowing for grout gaps. The gap may be uneven, so measure at both ends.

B Mark your measurements on the tile. For an even gap, mark on one edge. For an uneven gap, or a large tile, draw a guide line right across.

C Cut the tile, placing it squarely in the cutter to cut for an even gap, or placing it at an angle in the cutter if the tile needs to fit in an uneven gap.

D Apply tile adhesive directly onto the tile, and fix it in position, using spacers as required. Repeat until the corner is completely tiled.

◼◼ TILING A RECESS

A Start tiling at the centre of the outer edge and work outwards towards the corners and up around the inner edge of the recess.

B Support tiles inside the top of a recess by wedging a piece of wood beneath them while the adhesive dries, to prevent them falling off.

◼◼ TILING AN EXTERNAL CORNER

A Measure the corner and cut the trim to length using a junior hacksaw. Fix the trim in place using adhesive.

B Position the edges of the adjoining tiles under the trim's support arm, remembering to use spacers.

ALTERNATIVE TECHNIQUES

There are various ways to finish tiling an external corner. In some cases, such as around a window reveal, a neater finish may be achieved by making mitred corners. For these you will need to use an electric tile cutter with a platform that can be angled (see p.312). Overlapping edges are a simple solution, but may be unattractive if the tile edges are unglazed. Corner profile strips are a neat and protective solution.

Mitred corner tiles
Press the angled edges neatly together at the corner. Leave a gap along the joint for grouting.

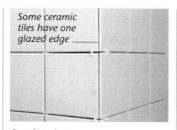

Some ceramic tiles have one glazed edge

Overlapping
Tile to the corner junction so that the tiles on one surface butt up hard over those on the other.

Using a strip
An L-shaped strip can be used to cover unglazed tile edges. Fix it in place with a silicone sealant.

CUTTING A CURVE

A Cut some paper to the size of a tile and place it up against the curved surface. Mark the profile of the curve on the paper with a pen.

B Cut along the pen line to create a template of the curve. Place the paper template over a tile and trace a guide line onto the tile.

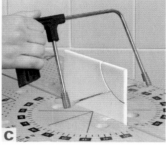

C Use a tile saw to cut along the guide line. This may take a while. Hold the tile in place to check the fit before fixing it in position.

ALTERNATIVE TECHNIQUE

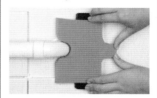

Cutting a curve
Press a profile gauge against the obstacle, and trace the curve onto the tile for a guide.

TILING AROUND A PIPE

A Remove the fixture, if possible. Hold a tile to one side of the pipe and mark the top and bottom edges of the pipe's diameter on the tile. Even if the fixture has not been removed, use this technique to measure where the hole will fall.

B Hold the tile below the pipe, in line with its column of full tiles, and mark on it the left and right edges of the pipe's diameter.

C Use a try square to join the marks, forming a square where the tile will fit over the pipe. Join opposite corners to find the centre.

D Adjust a tile hole cutter to the size setting you need.

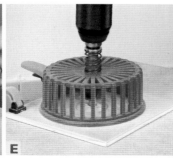

E Attach the hole cutter to a drill, sit its point on the mark in the centre of the square guide lines, and remove a circle of tile.

F Apply tile adhesive directly to the tile, and fix the tile in position over the pipe. If it has not been possible to remove the fitting, score and snap the tile along a line through the hole, so that you can fit the tile around the pipe.

USING OTHER TECHNIQUES

There are many different types of tiles and designs available, and, depending on your choice, you may need to adapt the basic application techniques or use alternative methods. Some designs will use regular square tiles in irregular grid arrangements, while other types of tiles, such as insert tiles, border tiles, and mosaic tiles each require a specific approach. Depending on the shape and size of the tiles you select, you may also need to improvise when applying spacers.

TOOLS AND MATERIALS SEE BASIC TOOLKIT AND P.313

USING INSERT TILES

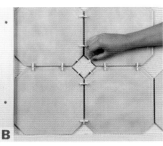

A **Before placing** insert tiles, build up a row of the larger tiles in your pattern, standing spacers on edge, as they will not lie flat.

B **Position insert tiles** as you build up subsequent rows, placing main and insert tiles alternately.

CREATING A DIAMOND PATTERN

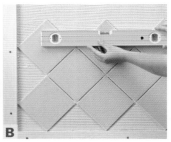

A **Buy extra tiles**, because this design requires cuts, and wastage may be high. Cut some tiles in half diagonally to fill in the design.

B **Keep diamonds even** by checking regularly, with a spirit level, that the corners are horizontally or vertically aligned, as required.

LAYING MOSAIC TILES

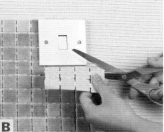

A **Treat each sheet** as a single tile, and use a paint roller to flatten it into place, considering the type of backing you have (see p.309).

B **To fit a sheet** around an obstacle, use scissors to cut through the backing. Use tile nibblers to remove parts of single tiles.

CREATING A BORDER

A border may run between rows of full tiles or across the top

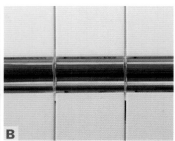

Mitring works well where border tiles meet at right angles

A **If your border** tiles are narrower than the main tiles, spacers may not sit flat. You will need to stand them on edge or cut them into a T-shape.

B **Apply border tiles** adjacent to the last row of main tiles, or at the required height within the main tiles. Leave any cuts until last.

C **Use an electric** cutter to make 45-degree cuts on two tiles. Press them neatly together using spacers on edge to maintain the mitred gap

ALTERNATIVE TECHNIQUE

Applying adhesive
Where it is difficult to apply adhesive to a wall, you can apply it directly to the back of the tile instead.

OTHER SPACING EFFECTS

Irregular tiles
Judge grout spaces by eye, or use pieces of thin cardboard, rather than trying to force spacers to fit irregular tile edges. Keep rows as level as possible.

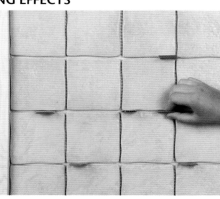

Brickwork
Align each row of tiles so that joints between tiles fall at the midpoints of tiles on the row beneath.

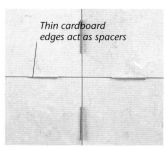

Thin cardboard edges act as spacers

Marble tiles
Create the illusion of a continuous marble surface by keeping grout gaps as narrow as possible.

SEALING A TILED AREA

A junction between a tiled area and another surface is a point of potential weakness, because grout can crack, or water seepage can cause damage to areas under tiling, including floors and ceilings. Silicone sealant reduces the risk of such damage. It is waterproof, flexible, so it will not crack, and is easily removed for access to concealed areas, such as the underside of a bath. Silicone fumes can be harmful, so open a window to keep the working area well ventilated.

TOOLS AND MATERIALS SEE BASIC TOOLKIT AND P.313

WHERE TO SEAL

Apply a waterproof seal to any area where tiling meets a bath, basin, sink, or kitchen worktop, and around the outer edge of a shower cubicle panel. You can also use sealant when installing flooring to waterproof areas where tiles meet a hard floor. This prevents water seeping into or beneath a floor. For more information on types of sealant, see p.81.

Apply sealant along this joint

▮▮ USING SILICONE SEALANT

Apply masking tape 2mm (¹⁄₁₂in) from each side of the joint. This will ensure that the sealant will have straight edges when finished. Cut the nozzle of the sealant tube at an angle, so that the diameter of the opening is slightly wider than the gap that needs sealing. Follow the instructions supplied to load the sealant tube into the dispenser.

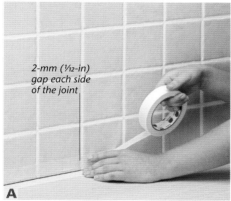
2-mm (¹⁄₁₂-in) gap each side of the joint
A

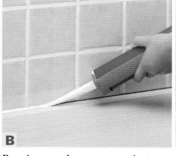
B

Pressing evenly, squeeze sealant into place, moving slowly along the joint. Apply a little at a time, so you can smooth it as you work.

C

Use paper tissues to remove any excess sealant from the nozzle. Smooth the sealant as you work by running a wet finger along the joint.

D

Remove the masking tape to reveal a straight sealant band along the extent of the joint.

E

If necessary, smooth over the sealant once more, pressing gently to avoid spreading it beyond the neat edges created by masking.

▮ SEALING AND UNSEALING A BATH ACCESS PANEL

A

A removable panel is needed for access (see pp.260–61), but it still needs waterproofing like any other tiled surface to avoid leaks.

B

Carefully apply sealant to the joint between the panel and the fixed tiles, trying to keep the joint invisible, if possible.

C

To access the cavity, carefully use a craft knife to cut away the silicone sealant. The panel will then pull free.

D

After replacing the panel, apply silicone sealant again to the joints between the panels, by repeating steps A and B shown here.

OTHER WAYS TO SEAL TILES

Grout protector
Simply applied with a brush, this is an option that can help to create a harder-wearing surface.

Tile sealant
Follow the manufacturer's advice on the selection and application of sealant for natural tiles.

REPLACING A BROKEN TILE

You will want to replace broken or cracked tiles to maintain the appearance of a room. It is also important to replace them because damaged tiles can lead to leaks in the room, which can damage walls and floors.

TOOLS AND MATERIALS
Gloves, goggles, grout raker, drill, club hammer, cold chisel, scraper, tile adhesive, adhesive spreader, spacers, grout

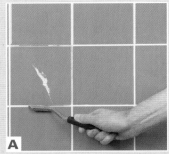

A Use a grout raker to remove the grout from around the edge of the broken tile. Check for electricity or water supplies using a detector.

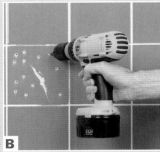

B Weaken the tile surface further by drilling a number of holes through it.

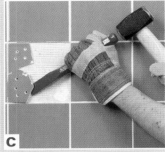

C Use a club hammer and cold chisel to remove sections of the broken tile. Be sure to wear gloves and protective goggles.

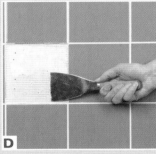

D Scrape any hardened adhesive off the wall surface, taking care not to damage any other tiles.

E Apply tile adhesive to the back of a tile using an adhesive spreader.

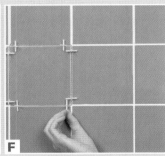

F Position the tile, checking that it sits flush. Use spacers to maintain grout gaps. When dry, remove the spacers and grout the joints.

REGROUTING

When grout deteriorates over time, it can lose its colour and waterproofing capability. Replacing grout can improve the appearance of a tiled room quickly and at low cost.

TOOLS AND MATERIALS
Grout raker, vacuum cleaner, grout, grout spreader, sponge

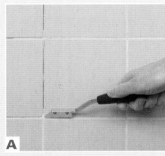

A Remove the old grout from the joints using a grout raker, taking care not to damage tile edges.

B Vacuum out the joints in order to remove all dust and debris.

C Regrout the joints, using a grout spreader as shown on p.315.

REVIVING TIRED GROUT

Where grout has deteriorated in terms of colour but not structure, a tube of grout reviver can be used to restore the grout to a clean, bright colour.

TOOLS AND MATERIALS
Sponge, sugar soap, grout reviver, cloth

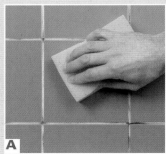

A Clean down the tiled surface thoroughly using a sponge and sugar soap solution.

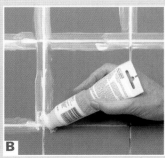

B When the grout is dry, apply grout reviver along the joints.

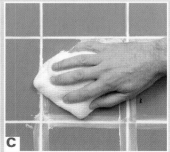

C Check the manufacturer's guidelines to see when to wipe off the excess grout reviver. Use a damp cloth.

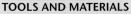

REPLACING SILICONE SEALANT

Junctions between tiles and other surfaces are normally sealed with silicone sealant, which can deteriorate over time. Once a seal begins to allow water penetration, it must be replaced.

TOOLS AND MATERIALS
Window scraper or sealant remover, masking tape, sealant

A Scrape away the old sealant. A window scraper is ideal, or use a proprietary sealant remover.

B Stick masking tape 2mm (1/12in) from each side of the joint. This will ensure that the sealant will have straight edges.

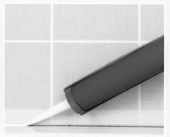

C Apply silicone sealant along the gap, and smooth with a wetted finger. Remove tape and smooth again if necessary.

REPAIRING A DAMAGED SHOWER CUBICLE

If water seepage has caused the wall around a shower cubicle to decay, tiles will start to become loose. The steps here are for repairs on a stud wall. If the studs themselves are decaying, you will need to remove sections of the wall and rebuild as required (see pp.104–09).

TOOLS AND MATERIALS
Craft knife, drywall saw, heater, claw hammer, water-resistant board, silicone sealant, sealant gun, glass fibre tape, tile adhesive, tiles, grout

A Remove any cubicle walls or shower screens before you start, so that you have full access to the tiles.

B Use a scraper to remove loose tiles, and any around which grout has decayed, until you expose a half-tile's width of sound plasterboard.

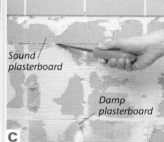

Sound plasterboard

Damp plasterboard

C Cut a line at this height using a drywall saw. Be careful not to cut through any concealed electrical or water supplies.

PREVENTION

In most cases, a shower cubicle leaks because of poorly grouted tile joints, or because of degraded silicone sealant around the shower tray or the shower screen.

Anywhere that a valve or pipe penetrates a tiled surface is also a potential point of weakness, and if even a small section of grout or sealant is missing, gradual water penetration may break down the wall structure and cause tiles to fall away from its surface.

The situation can deteriorate quickly if it goes unnoticed, so check these areas regularly for signs of damage or dampness. If you find any problems, tackle them immediately, using the techniques shown above.

D A craft knife may be helpful for cutting through plasterboard adjacent to studs.

E Use the claw of a hammer to remove old fixings. Leave studs exposed for a few days, to dry. A heater may speed up this process.

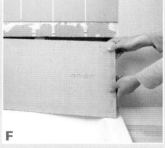

F Cut a piece of cement-based, water-resistant board to size, and screw it onto the studs.

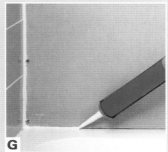

G Seal around the edges of the board with silicone sealant using a sealant dispenser.

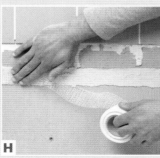

H Apply glass fibre tape to the joint between the new and old boards using tile adhesive.

I Apply tile adhesive and tile over the area to match the existing tiles then regrout. Re-apply silicone sealant to tray and corner joints.

Flooring

LAYING SHEET VINYL OR HESSIAN-BACKED CARPET REQUIRES QUITE A HIGH LEVEL OF SKILL. HOWEVER, COVERINGS SUCH AS TILES AND CLIP-TOGETHER WOODEN FLOORING ARE MORE STRAIGHTFORWARD TO LAY. IN SOME CASES YOU MAY NEED TO LAY A SUBFLOOR BEFORE THE FLOORING (SEE PP.327–28). BE AWARE THAT CLIP-TOGETHER FLOORING OR SANDED BOARDS MAY BE TOO NOISY FOR A FLAT.

ROLLED FLOORING

Hessian-backed carpet
Laid with an underlay. Needs to be stretched as it is fitted. It can be laid on nearly any type of subfloor, or directly on to floorboards if the boards are in good condition. Gripper rods are used around the perimeter to hold the carpet in place.

Foam-backed carpet
This does not require stretching or an underlay. It is normally stuck down with carpet tape. Some manufacturers suggest using an underlay, but it can then be difficult to stick the carpet and underlay to the floor surface.

Sheet vinyl
This is usually laid dry, on a subfloor (suitable floors include ply, self-levelled, and hardboard). Vinyl, especially if it is lightweight, can be stuck down.

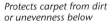

Protects carpet from dirt or unevenness below

UNDERLAY

Rubber-backed underlay
This creates a cushioning effect under the carpet. It also provides good heat insulation, and helps to absorb noise.

Felt underlay
An alternative to rubber-backed underlay. Comes in various thicknesses. Thicker, higher-quality examples are more expensive.

PREPARING TO LAY CARPET OR SHEET VINYL

Although carpet and vinyl are vastly different materials, they are laid in a similar way. Try to avoid joining lengths; if it is unavoidable, locate joins below any furniture or other fittings. For more on carpet and vinyl tiles, see pp.332–33.

TYPES OF FLOORING
Rolls usually come in set widths – 3m and 4m (10ft and 13ft 4in) are most common. This may dictate which way to run a design across a room.

Carpet This may be hessian-backed or foam-backed. The vast differences in quality and price are due to a carpet's make-up. It may be 100 per cent wool, a wool/acrylic mix, 100 per cent acrylic, or another man-made fibre. Texture and pile include smooth velvet, twist, loop, and shag pile. Most brands have a grading system for suitable use, such as light domestic (e.g. in a bedroom) or heavy domestic (e.g. hall and stairs). There are also natural-fibre floor coverings, e.g. jute or coir. How to lay them depends on their backing.

Sheet vinyl Since vinyl is hardwearing and easily cleaned, it is often used in bathrooms and kitchens. To increase its waterproof qualities, you may choose to run a bead of silicone around the edge. This also disguises rough edges.

Underlay Underlay acts as a shock absorber between the carpet and floor, provides greater comfort underfoot, protects the carpet, and reduces carpet wear.

Other types of sheet flooring Rubber and linoleum are durable and easily cleaned, but are more difficult to lay.

TOOLS AND MATERIALS

There is a variety of tools available for laying carpet and vinyl. Pictured below is a selection of the ones most commonly used for laying these types of flooring.

Napping shears
Used for trimming joins in a carpet. One blade is flattened and rests on the pile along the seam, acting as a guide for trimming.

Flattened section rests on seam

Carpet shears
Heavy-duty scissors used for cutting underlay as well as carpet.

Retractable blade

Cutting blade

Vinyl cutter
Precision tool for cutting vinyl.

Carpet knife
Heavy-duty craft knife designed for cutting all types of carpet and vinyl.

Serrated wheels grip carpet

Seam roller
Used to roll along seams when joining carpet with a seaming iron.

Seaming iron
Used with seaming tape and the seam roller to join lengths of carpet.

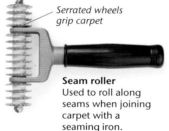

Carpet bolster
Tucks carpet behind gripper rods to secure it in place.

Double-sided tape
May be used for securing foam-backed carpet or vinyl in position.

Dial to set depth

Notch for gripping tacks

Knee kicker
Used to stretch and position hessian-backed carpet. The adjustable teeth can be set for different thicknesses.

Tack lifter
Acts in a similar way to the claw of a claw hammer. Shaped to deal with carpet tack removal.

Gripper rod
Thin length of timber, with razor-sharp teeth. Secured around the edge of a room to hold hessian-backed carpet.

Teeth grip hessian backing of carpet

ESTIMATING QUANTITIES FOR CARPET AND VINYL

Basic estimate	As a basic rule of thumb, base quantity estimates on the floor's area minus the area covered by fixed fittings – but see below for roll flooring.
Flooring supplied in rolls	For rolls, do not deduct permanent fittings from your calculations of the floor area.
Wastage and trimming	Allow about 10 per cent, whatever the material being used. It may be less if you have very specific dimensions for a sheet or carpet floor.
Gripper rods	Calculate requirement by measuring the perimeter of the room.
Underlays	Calculate requirement by measuring the actual floor area.
Extras	Consider subfloor requirements, which can add considerable expense to a flooring project.

GENERAL CONSIDERATIONS FOR FLOORING

Squaring patterned flooring
Patterns look best if "square" in a room. Walls may be uneven, so do not use them as a starting point to lay patterned flooring: any unevenness will make the design noticeably misaligned, because the effect becomes exaggerated across a whole room. To judge the best orientation for tiles, dry lay them as shown on p.334 and adjust as necessary. For sheet vinyl or carpet, allow a generous overlap when rough-cutting before laying (see p.330).

Adhesives
Many coverings – vinyl tiles, some cork tiles, and some sheet vinyls – can be stuck down with latex adhesive. Use double-sided tape or spray adhesive for foam-backed carpet or vinyl.

Threshold strips
These neaten the join between two kinds of flooring, usually between two rooms. The type used depends on which floorings meet. Those shown here are the most commonly used.

Wood finishing strip
A simple hardwood strip provides a decorative edge.

Carpet-to-carpet
Used where two hessian-backed carpets join in a doorway.

Carpet edge hidden by raised lip

Carpet-to-laminate
Joins hessian-backed carpet to rigid edges such as tiles, laminate, or wooden floor.

Finishing strip
Ends a floor covering, in this case hessian-backed carpet, at a threshold.

Teeth grip hessian-backed carpet

Flush strip
Joins vinyl to vinyl. Also available as carpet-to-carpet or carpet-to-vinyl strips.

The application methods for soft and hard floor tiles differ, but planning their layout is the same. The only difference is that hard tiles have grout joints, and soft tiles butt right up against each other.

TOOLS AND MATERIALS

Soft tiles are laid with the items in your basic toolkit and the extras listed opposite bottom. Hard tiles call for largely the same items as are used for wall tiles (see p.312), with a few key differences, as follows.

■ Tiles are very robust, so a cutter must be of a high quality. Check that a score-and-snap cutter, if you use one, is large enough for floor tiles.

■ Adhesive and grout must be harder wearing than on wall tiles, and some tiles need specialist additives in adhesive for sound adhesion. If you are laying tiles on a wooden subfloor, buy adhesive and grout with flexibility (check the packaging); additives may again be required.

■ Cross-shaped spacers, more heavy-duty than wall ones, lie flat on the floor and are covered with grout. If the tile depth is insufficient for this, position pieces of card vertically. Remove them after the adhesive dries.

TYPES OF TILES

Soft floor tiles
These may be self-adhesive, or laid with or without adhesive.

Carpet tile
Usually laid dry (i.e without any adhesive).

Vinyl tile
May be self-adhesive or may need adhesive.

Cork tile
May be ready-sealed, or need sealing once laid.

Hard tiles
These are available in various materials and sizes.

Porcelain
Laying porcelain tiles normally requires special adhesive or additives to standard adhesive.

Ceramic
A wide range of colours and designs is available, some mimicking natural tiles such as limestone.

Slate
A natural material. Apply sealant to the top surface before laying slate. This prevents excess adhesive soaking into the tile, making it easier to remove later.

Quarry
A natural material. Seal top surface before use.

Marble
Another type of natural tile.

Wooden tiles
These are usually patterned, and are another form of hard tiles.

Parquet tile
Gives appearance of traditional parquet design. Stuck down with adhesive. May be finished, or may need sanding and sealing after application.

Parquet tile (tongue-and-groove)
Tongue-and-groove mechanism locks tile in place. It is laid with adhesive.

LAYING A TILED FLOOR

Do not just start laying tiles against one wall: the wall may not be straight, and adjustments to allow for this will become exaggerated and unsightly as you progress across the room.

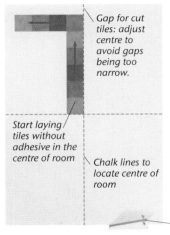

Gap for cut tiles: adjust centre to avoid gaps being too narrow.

Start laying tiles without adhesive in the centre of room

Chalk lines to locate centre of room

Door

First, find a starting point
Use the centre of the room as a base for the layout. "Dry lay" a few tiles, starting in the centre and working towards the walls. The last full tile before you hit the wall is at your provisional starting point. Adjust the gap between this and the wall to avoid the need to cut awkward thin slivers.

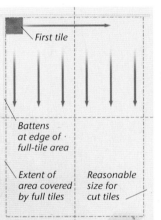

First tile

Battens at edge of full-tile area

Extent of area covered by full tiles

Reasonable size for cut tiles

Door

Lay the first tile
Consider how tiles will need to be cut to fit around any obstacles (see pp.332–35). If you can, tile with the fittings removed, so that cuts need not be exacting and the edges of tiles are hidden by the replaced fittings.

ESTIMATING QUANTITIES FOR FLOOR TILE

Basic estimate	As a basic rule of thumb, estimate quantities by calculating the area of the floor minus the area covered by permanent fittings.
Wastage and trimming	Buy about 10 per cent extra - maybe more if you are tiling a floor with many obstacles, because this results in a lot of cutting.
Adhesives	Manufacturers' guidelines for the necessary quantities tend not to be very generous, so it is worth buying a little more than is recommended.
Grout	Grout requirement depends on thickness of joints and size of tiles. There will be guidelines on packaging.
Extras	Remember to include spacers or sealant if necessary. Consider your subfloor requirements. These extras can add considerable expense.

Wood is an attractive and hardwearing option. Imitation wooden floors are broadly referred to as laminate floors. Real wooden ones are more expensive, but give a higher-quality finish. Real wooden floors can now be laid using clip-together techniques (ideal for DIY), as well as by more traditional methods such as gluing tongue-and-groove.

LAYING A WOODEN FLOOR

Do not lay timber or laminate where humidity will be high (e.g. the bathroom or kitchen) unless the manufacturer states that it is suitable. Wood can be laid on most subfloors that are level and in good condition.

Refer to the guidelines on p.323 for estimating quantities of underlay. Estimates for wood and laminate flooring should be made in the same way as those for floor tiles (opposite).

Technique

Most wooden flooring is laid "floating" (not attached to the subfloor). This allows some movement in the wood, aided by expansion gaps at the edge filled with cork and/or hidden by mouldings (fixed to skirting, not flooring).

Plan ahead, considering any fittings that will need boards to be cut to fit around them (see pp.338–39), and avoid awkward slivers. Try not to fix permanent fittings to or through a floating floor, which could restrict the floor's movement or cause cracks to appear.

Start laying boards at one wall and go across the room, staggering joints between boards for the most hardwearing and best-looking finish.

TOOLS AND MATERIALS

Plastic wedges
Used around the edge of the flooring, to keep expansion gap a consistent width during laying.

Hammer strikes raised section

Jemmy
Used in fitting end sections of floor, if space is too tight to use a hammer and/or knocking block.

Knocking block
Protects the edge of a laminate or wooden board when being positioned.

Strap threads into ratchet section

Ratchet floor clamp
Used to tighten joints when laying a floating floor, as shown on p.338.

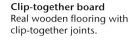

Clip-together board
Real wooden flooring with clip-together joints.

Laminate board
Wood-effect flooring connected by tongue-and-groove.

Tongue-and-groove wooden board
Real wooden flooring with tongue-and-groove fitting.

Pipe cover
Decorative cover to give neat finish at the base of pipe.

Edge beads
Moulding to cover expansion gaps around the edges of a floor.

Cork strip
Fills expansion gap. Needed only if manufacturer calls for it.

Roll underlay
Thin underlay positioned below floating floors.

Sheet underlay
Thick underlay supplied in small boards or sheets for use below floating floors.

TOOLS AND MATERIALS CHECKLIST PP.326–41

Laying ply or hardboard (p.328) Grab adhesive*, knee pads, ring-shank nails or staple gun and staples, metre rule*, paper*, scissors*, jigsaw*

Using self-levelling compound (p.328) Border for threshold, PVA, large brush, knee pads, power stirrer, plastering trowel, sanding block

Laying foam-backed carpet (p.329) Underlay*, carpet knife, double-sided tape, threshold strip

Laying vinyl (p.329) Vinyl cutter*, spray adhesive/double-sided tape, threshold strip

Laying hessian-backed carpet (p.330) Gripper rods, underlay, carpet knife, staple gun and staples, carpet bolster, knee kicker, threshold strip

Laying natural flooring (p.331) Gripper rods, underlay, craft knife, carpet shears*, adhesive, fine-notched spreader, carpet bolster

Laying soft floor tiles (pp.332–33) Sponge, straight edge, rolling pin, timber offcut, paper*, scissors*, profile gauge*, adhesive*, adhesive spreader*, paintbrush*, sealant*, threshold strip

Laying hard floor tiles (pp.334–35) Spacers, knee pads, timber battens, metal square*, floor fixings, adhesive, adhesive spreader, spirit level, score-and-snap cutter, electric cutter*, grout, grout spreader, grout shaper, mild detergent, sponge, threshold strip

Laying clip-together flooring (pp.336–37) Damp-proof membrane*, underlay or

combined DPM/underlay, masking or packing tape, plastic wedges, wood glue*, knocking block, jemmy, timber offcut*, jigsaw*, cork strip*, edge bead*, threshold strip, pipe cover*

Laying floating tongue-and-groove flooring (p.338) Underlay, damp-proof membrane* or combined DPM/underlay, plastic wedges, wood glue, knocking block, rachet floor clamp*, cork strip*, edge bead*, threshold strip, finish*

Gluing tongue-and-groove boards on concrete (p.338) Wood adhesive, adhesive, adhesive spreader, sponge, cloths, concrete blocks, timber finish*, edge bead or cork strip*, threshold strip

Laying nailed tongue-and-groove flooring (p.339) Pry bar, broom, self-levelling compound*, damp-proof membrane*, heavy-duty drill + bits, frame fixings, spirit level, battens, timber wedges, board nailer*, finish*, threshold strip

Laying parquet tiles (p.339) Timber, adhesive spreader, adhesive, jigsaw*, jemmy, cork strips*, threshold strip, sealant*

Sanding a floor (pp.340–41) Drum sander + paper, edging sander + paper, corner sander + paper, broom, vacuum, finish + required tools (pp.290–91)

* = optional

FOR BASIC TOOLKIT SEE PP.24–25

DECORATING AND FINISHING

To qualify as eco-flooring, a finish must be made from natural, sustainably sourced products. Many wooden flooring types fall into this category (see right), but this page concentrates on the soft types of flooring similar to carpet. The main options are listed below. For more on laying natural flooring, see p.331.

ALTERNATIVES TO VINYL

Linoleum is more environmentally friendly than vinyl flooring as its basic ingredient is linseed oil. It is is also popular for its non-allergenic qualities.

Traditionally, linoleum is laid in a similar way to vinyl (see p.329). It must, however, be stuck down, making it a harder job. Some linoleum can be bought on a wood-backing and is laid in a similar way to clip-together flooring (see pp.336–37).

WOOD FLOORING

Although wood is a natural product, for it to be an eco-friendly choice it is important to check that it is either reclaimed, sustainably sourced, or even made from recycled timber products. Eco-friendly alternatives to conventional wood flooring, such as bamboo, are increasingly viable. For more on wood flooring, see p.325.

Bamboo flooring
Bamboo is both durable and sustainable, and some bamboo flooring is similar in appearance to standard clip-together flooring. It can be laid floating, or stuck down, and can also be made into slats (as shown) – which are commonly used for rugs rather than fixed flooring.

FLOORING TYPE	Material	Properties	Where to use
Sisal	This is made from the leaves of the *Agave sisalana* plant. The leaves are crushed and soaked to extract the fibres, and then spun into yarn.	Probably the most versatile natural flooring for variety of design, comfort, and use. There is a wide range to choose from, varying from very tight to quite open-weave designs, in a choice of many colours.	Its hardwearing nature means sisal can be used in most areas of the home. Best avoided in bathrooms and kitchens, as water causes fibre to expand and contract, damaging the appearance.
Sisool	As the name suggests, this is a composite of sisal and wool, which creates a dual-fibre floor covering with two distinctive textures.	Combining sisal and wool makes for a more flexible material than raw sisal. The wool provides softness, while the sisal offers excellent durability.	Can be used in most areas of the home, but manufacturers tend to advise against kitchen and bathroom use. Natural floor coverings usually have a natural latex backing; sisool is normally backed with jute.
Paper	This is twisted to form a yarn that is then woven into a floor covering. Some manufacturers combine paper with sisal.	This has a very different look to other natural floor coverings. Resins are often added to make this flooring more hardwearing, and to protect the fibres.	Suitable for most areas, some paper flooring can even be used in bathrooms, as it is water repellent. However, exposure to standing water should be avoided.
Seagrass	There are a number of varieties of seagrass. Most commonly produced in paddy fields that are flooded with seawater, it is then harvested, dried, and made into yarn.	Seagrass offers a very strong yarn. It is hard to dye, and the colours are often limited, but its waxy surface makes it naturally stain-resistant. It gives off a very grassy smell.	Suitable for most domestic situations, seagrass is quite impermeable to water, making it possible to use in a bathroom. Standing water should be avoided.
Coir	Made from the husk of coconut shells, coir is removed from the shell, soaked, and pounded before being dried and woven into a wiry yarn.	Short, hard fibres give this a raw, unprocessed look. It is incredibly hardwearing and durable.	Ideally used in busy areas such as hallways and landing, this is not suitable for moist areas such as bathrooms and kitchens. It is commonly used for entrance mats.
Jute	A product of the *Corchorus* plant family and a close relation to hemp, the inner stems of jute are soaked, pounded, and then dried to provide a soft fibre for the yarn.	Jute is very soft to the touch, and comfortable to walk on. The softness allows it to be woven into a number of designs relatively easily.	Jute is hardwearing, but should not be used in bathrooms and kitchens, as humidity and damp damages fibres very quickly. It is often used in bedrooms, and other less busy domestic areas.

A subfloor provides the base for a floor covering. It is applied over the main floor structure, although in some cases the floor itself can provide the necessary base for the floor covering. The most common subfloors are made of ply, which is laid on a wooden floor, hardboard (also laid on wood), and self-levelling compound (on a concrete floor).

CHOOSING A SUBFLOOR

Existing floor	Suitable subfloor	Suitable flooring
Wooden	Thick ply	Hard tiles
Wooden	Thin ply	Soft flooring
Wooden	Hardboard: smooth side up	Soft tiles, or clip-together flooring
Wooden	Hardboard: rough side up	Carpet, or vinyl sheet, or floating wooden floor
Concrete	Self-levelling compound	Any

LAYING A SUBFLOOR FOR A WOODEN FLOOR

There are two options for a wooden floor: ply and hardboard. The information below will help you to choose the most suitable for your needs. A subfloor may raise a floor's height and stop a door opening smoothly. Do not trim a door until after you lay flooring: it may be possible to hide a slight step between rooms with a threshold strip (see p.305).

Choosing to use ply

Use thick ply as a subfloor for hard tiles, and thinner ply to provide a smooth surface for soft floor coverings such as vinyl, carpet, and soft tiles. Large sheets are ideal for large rooms, because they cover the surface quickly and with fewer joints. The order in which boards are fixed down is not important, except that joints between rows of ply boards should be staggered to avoid long joins.

◼ MAKING A TEMPLATE FOR CUTS

Make a paper template of any complicated areas, and trace a guide line along which to cut. Use a sheet of paper cut to size, positioned exactly where the board will be placed. Whether you are laying ply or hardboard, use a jigsaw to cut the board.

A

B

Cut slits along the edges of a sheet of paper. Press these slits against the obstacle, and crease them sharply around its shape.

Cut along the creases to create a template. Lay the paper on a board, use the cut edge to draw a guide line, and cut along the line.

Choosing to use hardboard

Decide what type of floor covering you wish to use before laying hardboard, because boards must be laid smooth-side up if the floor covering will be stuck down (vinyl tiles, for example), and rough-side up if the flooring will not (carpet, or sheet vinyl, for example). Before buying hardboard, check that it is of flooring grade. If it is not, it may expand or contract, depending on humidity, leading to lumps and bumps in the floor. To avoid unevenness, ensure that the hardboard is securely fixed down. Hardboard is available in large sheets, but smaller sheets of 1,200 x 600mm (4 x 2ft) are much easier to work with. Use a jigsaw for a curved cut, and make straight cuts as shown below.

◼ CUTTING HARDBOARD

A

To cut a straight line in hardboard, first use a craft knife to score the smooth side of the board. Take care not to let the blade slip.

B

Turn the board over, and lay a straight edge (such as a metre rule) along the scored line. Snap the board along the scored line. Separate the two pieces and neaten the cut edge with a craft knife.

LAYING A SUBFLOOR FOR A CONCRETE FLOOR

Self-levelling compound is a latex-based product which provides a very smooth subfloor. It is needed only if a concrete floor is in poor condition. Despite the name, some smoothing is needed for the best surface. The floor may be raised by the subfloor and flooring, so you may need to trim the lower edge of a door after laying flooring.

Preparing the surface

Thoroughly clean the floor. Do not lay compound over any residual bitumen-based products from a previous covering. Prime a dusty surface with diluted PVA solution (4:1 water to PVA). Fix a threshold strip across the doorway so that compound does not run into the next room.

Mixing the compound

Use a spotlessly clean bucket, because any impurities will affect the mix's integrity, and use a power stirrer to mix slowly, to avoid introducing too much air. Self-levelling compound sets relatively quickly, and will remain workable for no more than 30 minutes. Follow the steps shown for one bucket-load, and immediately mix and lay the next bucket while the wet edge is still workable. The coverage from a bag of compound depends on how thickly it is laid.

LAYING A SUBFLOOR

Read the descriptions on p.327 and decide which kind of subfloor is most suitable for your floor and, if relevant, chosen floor covering. Then follow the steps shown here for the method you need.

TOOLS AND MATERIALS SEE
BASIC TOOLKIT AND P.325

LAYING PLY

Sweep the floor, and check that all screws or nails sit below the surface. Knock in or countersink any protruding fixings, ensuring that they don't go right through the floorboards and into any cables or pipes beneath them.

B Check whether any floorboards are loose. If they are, screw them down securely, because a subfloor must be laid on a rigid floor surface.

C Pick a corner that is as square as possible for your starting point, and lay the first board. Use grab adhesive for extra rigidity.

An alternative to nailing thin ply is to use a staple gun

D Use ring-shank nails every 150mm (6in) around the edges of the board. Nails should go into floorboards but not through them.

E Apply nails every 150mm (6in) in a grid across the centre of the board, as well as around the edges, to keep the subfloor level and firm.

F Butt-join boards tightly. Continue laying boards. If boards need cutting to fit, use a panel saw for straight cuts, and a jigsaw for templated cuts.

LAYING HARDBOARD

Prepare the floor by sweeping and levelling it as shown in steps A to B for laying ply (above). If possible, choose a square corner in which to start laying boards. Stapling is the quickest way of securing hardboard, although ring-shank nails can be used. Position fixings at 150-mm (6-in) intervals.

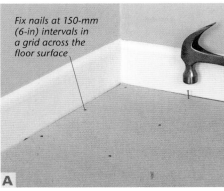

Fix nails at 150-mm (6-in) intervals in a grid across the floor surface

A

B Butt the second board hard against the first. When placing boards, keep them as neatly aligned as possible, so that later rows fit easily into place.

C Work across the room in rows, staggering the joints between boards on subsequent rows.

USING SELF-LEVELLING COMPOUND

A Block the threshold. Mix the compound, as detailed in the manufacturer's instructions, and pour it onto the floor.

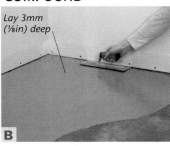

Lay 3mm (⅛in) deep

B Use a plastering trowel to spread the compound evenly across the surface, removing any peaks and redistributing it into depressed areas.

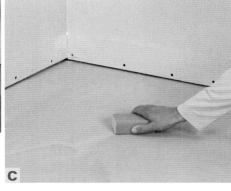

C

Mix and lay further compound until the floor is covered, smoothing it in with the damp edges of previously poured areas. Leave the compound to dry overnight before walking on it. Then use a medium grade of sandpaper to remove any ridges that were left by the trowelling.

LAYING FOAM-BACKED CARPET

Foam-backed carpet does not need an underlay or gripper rods. Lay the carpet roughly in place, allowing the overlap to run up the walls. Adjust the position until any pattern is aligned squarely within the room.

Make small cuts in the corners and any alcoves, to allow the carpet to sit flat on the floor.

Crease the carpet into the junction between wall and floor. Trim its edge at the base of the skirting, with a carpet knife, as precisely as possible.

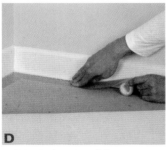

Pull back the edge of the carpet. Stick double-sided tape to the floor, all the way around the perimeter of the room.

Remove the backing from the top of the tape, in sections. Press the carpet down into place and smooth out any wrinkles.

For any joins between lengths of carpet, use double-sided tape along the edges to stick down both pieces of carpet. Slowly smooth the carpet into place by hand, making sure that it does not ripple along the join.

LAYING VINYL WITH ADHESIVE

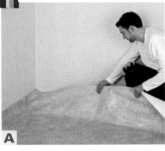

Lay the roughly cut vinyl on the floor, allowing the overlap to run up the walls. Adjust the position to get any pattern squared in the room.

Make small cuts at right angles to the corners and any alcoves to allow the vinyl to lie flat on the floor.

Crease vinyl into the joint between the wall and the floor. Thin vinyl creases quite easily. Thicker varieties can be made more pliable with gentle heating from a hairdryer (do not apply heat for long). Cut along the edges using a vinyl cutter or a craft knife. Take time to ensure that cuts are precise: you cannot correct errors later.

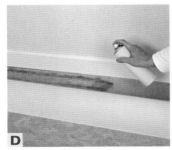

Fold back the edge of the vinyl. Spray adhesive on the floor, around the room's perimeter, or lay double-sided tape if you prefer.

Press down evenly on the vinyl, all around the room, to ensure it lies smoothly on the floor surface.

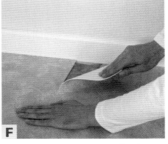

For any joins, use spray adhesive or double-sided tape along the edges between the lengths of vinyl.

THRESHOLD STRIPS

A threshold strip should be fitted at every doorway. The strip type will depend on the floor coverings being joined (see p.323). Some types of strip are screwed down to the floor surface before the floor covering is fitted into it. In other cases, the floor covering is roughly butt-joined before the strip is fitted over it.

LAYING HESSIAN-BACKED CARPET

For both carpet and vinyl, cut to at least 150mm (6in) larger than required, with an overlap along all edges. If possible, do the cutting where there is space to roll out the flooring. In dry weather, you may prefer to do this outdoors. With a large pattern, leave larger overlap areas so that the flooring can be adjusted to fit neatly. A hessian-backed carpet is stretched with a knee-kicker while being fitted, and is laid with underlay and gripper rods. A foam-backed carpet needs no stretching or gripper rods.

TOOLS AND MATERIALS SEE BASIC TOOLKIT AND P.325

⊞ LAYING HESSIAN-BACKED CARPET

For a concrete floor, use masonry nails or glue the rods in place

A

Nail down the gripper rods, their teeth pointing to the wall. Leave a gap between skirting and rod, a little less than the carpet thickness.

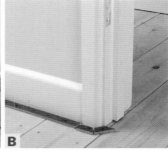

B

To fit the rods around an obstacle, such as a door frame, follow the shape of the obstacle's base and cut sections with a junior hacksaw.

C

Roll out the underlay across the floor, allowing it to lap over the tops of the gripper rod.

D

Cut along the inside edge of the gripper rods to remove any excess underlay. Leave a neat, flush fit.

E

Staple down the underlay to the floor, and tape any joins. Or, on a concrete floor, use a proprietary adhesive to stick down the underlay.

F

Position the roughly cut carpet, allowing the overlap to run up the walls. Adjust it to the required position, square within the room.

G

To allow the carpet to sit flat, make small cuts at right angles to the corners. Repeat for any other angles in the room, such as alcoves.

H

Trim the carpet around the edges, flush with the base of the wall or skirting board.

I

Use a bolster to secure the carpet to the gripper rods in one corner.

J

Using the knee kicker, stretch and position the carpet, and work towards an adjacent corner. Secure the carpet in this second corner.

Return to the first corner, and work with the knee kicker towards the other adjacent corner. Secure the carpet in this corner. Return again to the first corner, and work with the knee kicker diagonally across the floor to the opposite corner. Secure the carpet. If you need to reposition it at any time, unhook it from the gripper rod.

K

Check that the tension is even and there is no uneven stretching across pile lines

L

To complete the room, work around the edges of the carpet, fixing it in place behind the gripper rods.

SEAMS IN HESSIAN-BACKED CARPET

Joining lengths of hessian-backed carpet is best left to a professional (essential for expensive carpets). If you do decide to attempt it, you will need a hot seaming iron, a seam roller, and seaming tape. Take great care as you move along the join. Use napping shears to trim the pile along the join.

LAYING NATURAL FLOORING

Laying soft natural flooring, such as sisal or jute, differs slightly from laying hessian-backed carpet (see opposite) as most natural flooring is backed with latex. The laying process involves sticking the latex onto an underlay, which is itself stuck to the subfloor. The gripper rods used to secure the flooring around the perimeter have no upward teeth, as the flooring is glued down – the back edge of the rod is simply used to tuck in the flooring. As the flooring is stuck down, there is no need for a knee kicker to stretch the carpet. Check with your supplier for the best adhesive to use.

TOOLS AND MATERIALS SEE BASIC TOOLKIT AND P.325

LAYING NATURAL FLOORING

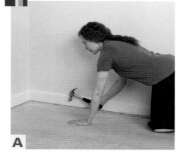

A Nail the blank gripper rods around the edge of the room, leaving a gap between the skirting and rod that is slightly thinner than the flooring.

B Ensure the square edge of the rods face into the room, with the slightly angled edge pointing towards the skirting board.

C Roll out the underlay, butting its straight edge directly up against the gripper rods where possible. This avoids excess trimming.

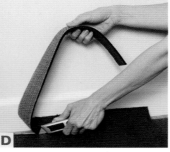

D Use a craft knife to cut the underlay to the edge of the gripper where needed. Roll out the underlay "dry" until the entire floor is covered.

E Roll back sections of the underlay to apply adhesive to the subfloor, using a fine-notched spreader. Follow any supplier's guidelines closely.

F Replace the underlay, smoothing it onto the adhesive below. You can kneel on the laid sections whilst positioning the rest of the underlay.

G Roll out the flooring across the underlay. Some manufacturers advise letting it settle for 24–48 hours before trimming.

H Allow an overlap of 2–4cm (1–2in) with the skirting board or wall. Trim with a craft knife or carpet shears, then smooth the flooring up to the wall.

I Roll back the flooring and apply adhesive directly to the underlay, again with a notched spreader. Aim for a smooth, even coverage.

J Having observed guidelines on drying times, roll the flooring back into place, flattening air bubbles and checking the positioning.

Hold a craft knife at right angles to the skirting board, and trim the flooring, leaving a small excess. Blades will blunt quickly, so be sure to have a supply of replacements, as the accuracy of this trimming is essential for a good fit. Once one area is glued and trimmed, move onto the next.

K

L Use a carpet bolster to finish the job by pushing the excess of flooring down behind the gripper rods.

BACKINGS

Although the majority of natural floorings are now laid using the technique shown here, it is possible to find other backings. Check with your supplier whether they use synthetic or natural latex backing. A synthetic version negates many of the arguments for choosing this flooring, as it will not be biodegradable.

LAYING SOFT FLOOR TILES

Soft tiles include vinyl, cork, and carpet tiles. Some are self-adhesive, others require a separate adhesive. Carpet tiles are laid dry (without adhesive). The sequence shown here relates to self-adhesive tiles. Your starting position will be the same whichever kind of tile is used (see p.324). If you are laying tiles on a hardboard subfloor, there will be no need to prime the surface. For ply or self-levelled subfloors, the surface needs sealing with dilute PVA solution, or a primer recommended by the tile manufacturer.

TOOLS AND MATERIALS SEE BASIC TOOLKIT AND P.325

1 GETTING STARTED

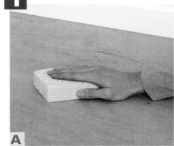

Laying self-adhesive tiles is straightforward. Start by thoroughly cleaning the floor: even the smallest particle may show through the tiles.

Draw pencil guide lines along the floor to indicate your chosen starting point (see p.324).

2 PLACING THE FIRST TILE

Remove the paper backing and position the first tile. Make sure that its edges align precisely with the guide lines. Press down firmly, and apply even pressure. Make sure the first tile is fixed securely before moving on. This will act as a fixed point that will anchor the positions for all the tiles that follow.

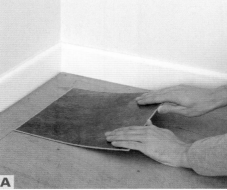

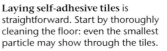
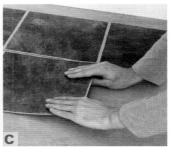

Build up the first row of tiles, butting their edges tightly together. A household rolling pin will help you to apply pressure evenly.

As you progress, make sure the tiles sit flat on the floor surface. A tile that is slightly out of position can throw out the whole design.

3 MEASURING SECTIONS TO CUT

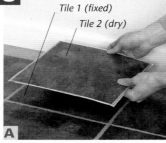
Tile 1 (fixed)
Tile 2 (dry)

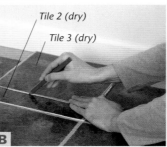
Tile 2 (dry)
Tile 3 (dry)

Cut the tile on a board (e.g. an offcut of MDF) to avoid damaging the floor

Mark off cuts in position, for the most accurate fit. On the last full row near the gap to a wall, lay a dry tile (tile 2) over a fixed one (tile 1).

Place another dry tile (tile 3) over the first, and slide it across so that it fills the gap. Where the edge of tile 3 overlaps tile 2, draw a line.

Remove the dry tiles, and cut along the guide line on tile 2, using a craft knife and a straight edge such as a metal rule.

Check that the cut section of tile fills the gap, before removing the paper backing and sticking the tile in place.

4 CREATING AN L-SHAPED TILE FOR A CORNER

Tile 2 (dry)
Tile 1 (dry)

Tile 2 (dry)
Tile 1 (dry)

Place two dry tiles on top of the closest fixed tile. Slide tile 2 across to one side of the corner. Mark the edge of tile 2 on tile 1 beneath.

Move tile 1, with its guide line, to the other side of the corner. Do not rotate it. Place it on the relevant fixed tile. Repeat the marking-off process.

Place tile 1 on a cutting board, and cut along the lines to remove the unwanted section of tile.

Check that the L-shaped section fits before removing the backing and fixing it down in place.

5 CUTTING CURVES (OR IRREGULAR CORNERS)

A For curves or unsquare corners, use a paper template to make a precise guide line. First, cut a piece of paper to the size of your tile.

B Cut a number of slits into the paper, slightly longer than the portion of tile to be removed.

C Place the paper tile in position, with its slits against the curve (here, a sink pedestal). Crease the slits against the curve, and draw a pencil line across.

D Remove the paper tile, and cut along the line. Place the template on a new self-adhesive tile, and draw around the guide line.

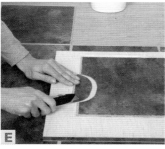

E Using a craft knife, cut the tile along the guide line, and remove the unwanted section.

F Check that the tile fits snugly around the curve. Remove the backing and stick the cut tile in position.

6 CUTTING IRREGULAR SHAPES

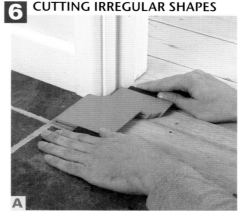

A

For irregular shapes, such as a door's architrave, a profile gauge gives the best guide line. If possible, place its corner where the tile's corner will go; or measure the gap from corner to profile gauge. Push the gauge into the irregular edge, keeping it flat on the floor and butted up completely into the irregular edge.

B Position the gauge on a tile, lining up the corners (or previously noted gap to the corner) for an accurate fit. Trace around the irregular shape.

C Cut carefully along the guide line, using a craft knife, and remove the unwanted section of tile.

D Check that the tile fits, and then remove the backing to stick the tile in place.

LAYING CARPET TILES

Some carpet tiles are laid dry, and can be regularly moved to even out wear. Planning and cutting is the same as for other soft tiles.

LAYING SOFT TILES THAT REQUIRE ADHESIVE

For soft tiles designed to be laid using adhesive, the principles shown above and on p.324 for planning the layout and for cutting sections of tile are exactly the same. The adhesive may be applied to the back of each tile, or to the floor. If you apply adhesive to the tile, do it carefully so that it does not spill over to the front of the tile surface.

The soft tile being applied to the right is cork. Before being laid, natural tiles such as cork should be left for 48 hours in the room where they will be laid, so that they acclimatize before being positioned. Once the floor has been completed, some cork-based tiles will require a sealant to be coated over the surface (the packaging will specify), as shown far right.

ADHESIVE BEING APPLIED TO THE FLOOR FOR CORK TILES

SEALANT BEING APPLIED TO LAID CORK TILES

LAYING HARD FLOOR TILES

Hard tiles must be laid on as flat a surface as possible - such as concrete, concrete with self-levelling compound applied, or a wooden floor that has been covered with a 19-mm (¾-in) ply subfloor. Flexible adhesive and flexible grout is needed on wooden floors and for some types of tile. Subfloors must first be sealed, using a dilute PVA solution (five parts water to one part PVA). Some natural or terracotta tiles are best sealed before application. This is to prevent adhesive and/or grout becoming ingrained in their surface during application.

TOOLS AND MATERIALS SEE BASIC TOOLKIT AND P.325

Fix the batten along the pencil line. In this example, the subfloor is ply so screws may be inserted. (For a concrete floor, drill pilot holes, using masonry bits, then plug the holes and insert screws.) Position a second batten at a precise right angle to the first batten. Here a metal square is being used for an accurate right angle.

B

FURTHER INFORMATION ABOUT ADHESIVE

Testing adhesive cover
Press tiles down just hard enough for the adhesive to make contact with the entire back face of the tile. Tap the tile to test – if there is a hollow sound, some areas are not in contact. This problem tends to occur with an uneven floor or with rustic tiles. Take up the tile, and add more adhesive to the hollow areas.

Adhesive drying time
Drying time depends on the type of adhesive, tile thickness, and porosity of the floor and tiles. Most adhesive will dry in 24 hours. If tiles are walked on before adhesive is dry, they may move, and the bond between adhesive and tiles will weaken. This would cause tiles to loosen, and grout joints may crack at a later date.

1 GETTING STARTED

Dry-lay a few tiles to mark your starting point, as explained on p.324. You may choose to use the edge and corner of the room as a rough guide. Mark the outer edge of the tiles. Draw a pencil line to mark where to position your wooden batten. This provides an accurate guide against which to lay the tiles (the wall or the corner may not be straight).

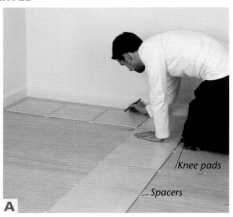

Knee pads

Spacers

A

2 APPLYING ADHESIVE

The spreader's serrated edge provides an even, grooved bed

A

B

Mix up adhesive with a power stirrer, as shown on p.68. Mix as much as you can use in about an hour. Apply the adhesive in the right angle made by the battens.

Position the first tile on the adhesive, butting it up against the two battens. Gently press the tile into position.

3 BUILDING UP ROWS

A

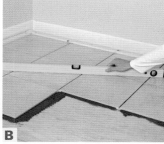

B

As you progress, insert spacers flat on the floor. The tile will probably be deep enough for spacers to be covered later with grout. Otherwise, use bits of card on edge as spacers.

Use a level to check that tiles lie flush with each other. Continue laying tiles until all the uncut ones are down. Allow the adhesive to dry, and then remove the battens.

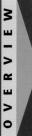

4 MAKING STRAIGHT CUTS

A

Measure the gap left by the batten between tile and wall, so that you can cut a tile to fit. Measure at each end of the tile to allow for variations in the width of the gap.

B

Subtract the grout gap, and mark off the resulting distances on the tile edge with a felt-tip pen. Place the tile in a score-and-snap cutter, aligning marks with the cutter's guides.

C

Push the cutting wheel away from you, across the tile, to score a line between the marks. Lower the handle to snap the tile along the line. Use a tile file on the cut edge.

D

Check that the cut tile fits the gap. Apply adhesive to the floor or back of the tile, and insert it into place.

5 CUTTING CURVES

A

Create a template, as shown on p.333. Draw a guide line. Wearing gloves and keeping hands clear of the blade, use an electric tile cutter to cut straight lines into the curve.

B

Continue with a series of straight cuts. Break off the unwanted section. Tidy up the curve by steering the tile around the blade.

6 MAKING A RIGHT-ANGLED CUT

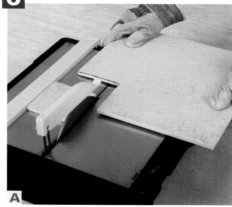

A

Mark the area of the tile that needs to be cut (see p.333 for measuring methods). Place the tile in an electric cutter. Wear gloves and keep your hands clear of the blade. Wear goggles. When the cut has reached the end of the first marked line, turn the tile around. Cut along the second guide line, to make the right angle.

CUTTING AROUND PERMANENT FIXTURES

There are three ways to cut around an architrave. If there is skirting board in the room, make a simple curved cut that follows the architrave's profile. When it is grouted, the inexact cut will be inconspicuous. If the skirting is to be fixed after tiling, there will be no grout gap to incorporate - in this instance, cut off the bottom section of the architrave and slip the edge of the tile underneath (see p.337). Or, remove the architrave, tile the floor area, and then refit the architrave over the cut edge.

Cutting holes for pipes can be done in the same way as for wall tiles (see pp.316–17). Some tiles will raise the floor level, so if you remove a fitting, check that the pipe will be the correct length to reconnect.

7 GROUTING THE TILES

A

Grout the tiles once adhesive is dry. Mix the grout to a smooth, stiff paste. Apply with a grout spreader and remove excess with a damp sponge. Finish with a grout shaper.

B

When grout is dry, use a mild detergent to clean off any powdery residue. Some natural tiles may then need sealing.

Most laminate and real wood floors are laid by dry-clipping boards together. Clipping mechanisms vary, but the principles are the same. Whether you need a damp-proof membrane or underlay will depend on the type of floor (see pp.174–81). If in doubt, lay one. Where possible, lay flooring before fitting skirting board or architrave so that they can cover the expansion gap. Wooden flooring needs to acclimatize for two or three days before being laid. Open packs and lay out the boards. Some flooring will need oiling after laying.

TOOLS AND MATERIALS SEE BASIC TOOLKIT AND P.325

1 PLACING THE UNDERLAY

A

B

Roll out the underlay across the floor's surface. Tape the joins together between the sheets of underlay.

Trim the underlay to size, ensuring that it fits precisely at the junctions between the walls and the floor. Use a craft knife to cut it.

2 LAYING THE FIRST ROW

Position the first board in a corner of the room. However, if your room has an architraved doorway, you may choose to start at the door. The information box opposite shows the different solutions to fitting the first board at an architraved doorway or the last board at the doorway. The steps shown here result in the last board being fitted in the doorway.

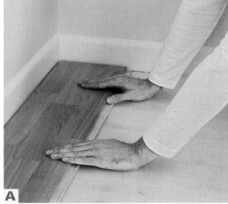

A

B

Make sure the grooved side of the boards is against the wall. Insert plastic wedges between the board and the wall.

C

To place the next board, engage it with the end of the first board by holding it at roughly 45 degrees to the first board.

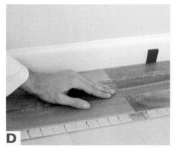

D

Press down on the second board, and lock it into place. Continue joining boards in this way to make the first row.

E

Insert wedges at regular intervals. As you near the end of the row, you will probably need to cut a board to finish: see next step.

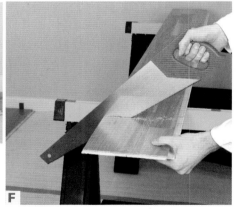

F

Place a new board on a workbench, and mark off the distance left to fill in order to complete the row. Allow space for a wedge. Use either a panel saw or a jigsaw to cut the board. Keep the board supported while cutting it, so that it does not chip as the saw nears the end of the cut.

3 LAYING SUBSEQUENT ROWS

A

Use the offcut piece from the end of the first row to start the second. Engage it at a 45-degree angle to the edges of the first-row boards.

B

Tap the board with a knocking block to tighten. Place another board beside it. Leave a slight gap so you can clip it to the first row, then knock fully into place. Repeat along row.

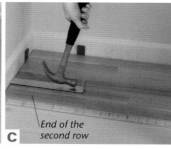

C

End of the second row

You may need a jemmy to tighten the joint for the last board in any row. Hook the jemmy over the end of the board, and knock its other end with a hammer.

D

Check the boards are "square" across the room. If not, adjust them by cutting the first row to fit against the wall, as below for a doorway. Carry on across the floor.

4 GOING AROUND A DOORWAY

In the doorway, boards should extend to the threshold. Keep laying boards until you near the final wall, and a whole board is too wide to fit. Cut some wood to the width of a board, and sharpen one end. Loosely position a board over the previous whole board fitted. Run the pointed end along the wall, using a pencil at the other end to draw the profile onto the unfixed board.

A

B

Cut along the guide line of the wall's profile with a jigsaw, then position the board in the doorway.

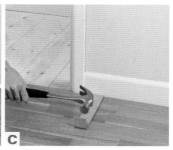

C

Fit the board, using a jemmy to knock in the clip-together mechanism. Use this method to cut and fit all boards against the wall.

D

Fix a threshold strip in the doorway. Choose a suitable one for the types of flooring that will meet here (see p.329).

E

Finish off the room with lengths of edging, pinned or glued (with contact adhesive) to the skirting. This is to cover the expansion gap.

FURTHER INFORMATION

Coping with an architrave
If you start at the doorway, trim the base of the architrave, as shown below, and slide the first board underneath it. Clip to the second board and work across the floor. If you finish at the doorway, you may need to

trim off the last board's tongue with a jigsaw or hammer and chisel so that it will fit against the wall. Then fit the board.

Cutting to go around a pipe
If the fitting is not in place, or can be removed, drill a hole in a board and slide it over the pipe. If the fitting is fixed, see p.335 for cutting to fit around an obstacle. Use a pipe cover to neaten the join at the base.

LAYING A WOODEN FLOOR

Although much wooden flooring is clip-together (see pp.336–37), you may prefer the older techniques shown here. Boards can be laid floating, nailed down, or with adhesive. On a timber floor, you can remove old boards and fix new ones to the joists (see pp.180–81), but not if a partition crosses the old boards. Check whether doors need trimming (see p.172). Remember that a damp-proof membrane (DPM) is important, especially on concrete. You may have to sand wooden boards after laying them.

TOOLS AND MATERIALS SEE BASIC TOOLKIT AND P.325

▮ FLOATING TONGUE-AND-GROOVE ON WOOD

A

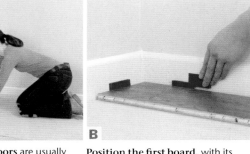

B

Glued wooden floors are usually laid floating, allowing for expansion and contraction. Lay a DPM if necessary, then roll out underlay.

Position the first board, with its tongue facing into the room. Use wedges to maintain an expansion gap against the wall.

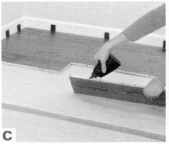

C

D

E

Apply glue to the board's grooved edge (avoid going deep into the recess, as less contact is made here with the tongue of the next board).

Tighten the joints as you proceed, by hitting a knocking block against the boards. Or you may prefer to use a ratchet floor clamp (see below).

Wipe away any excess glue that seeps out between joints after the boards are tightened. Continue adding rows, and stagger the boards in the normal way (see pp.336-37). Once adhesive has dried, add an edging bead to cover the expansion gap, or replace the skirting board if you removed it before laying the floor.

USING A RATCHET FLOOR CLAMP

A

B

C

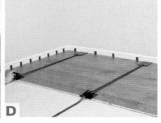

D

This is an alternative to step D above. Lip the clamp over the end board. Unroll the strap to beyond the nearest board.

Position the ratchet section over the edge of the board nearest to you. For a large floor area, you may need to position several ratchet clamps.

Thread the extended strap through the ratchet section, and clamp it down. You may wish to set up two across a section of flooring.

Move the ratchet backwards and forwards until the strap is taut and tightens the tongue-and-groove boards. Repeat every few rows.

▮ GLUING TONGUE-AND-GROOVE BOARDS ON CONCRETE

A

B

C

Glue joints between boards, using wood adhesive in the grooved edges. Avoid going too deep into the recess (see step C at top).

Spread a proprietary adhesive on the floor, using a spreader to groove it for better adhesion. Press the boards firmly in place.

Continue gluing the boards and pressing them into the adhesive. The weight of concrete blocks will help to push down the boards as they dry.

FLOOR FINISHES

Traditional unfinished boards will need a finish.
▪ Varnish provides a hardwearing coat, requiring little maintenance.
▪ Wax requires a number of coats, and needs to be regularly applied. However, it is often preferred as it allows wood to breathe, and over time increases the floor's depth of colour.

LAYING NAILED TONGUE-AND-GROOVE FLOORING ON CONCRETE

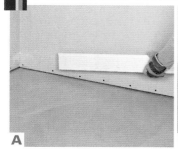

A **Remove skirting,** loosening it with a pry bar before pulling it from the wall. Sweep away debris. Apply self-levelling compound if required.

B **Lay damp-proof membrane,** with an overlap of 150mm (6in) up the wall. Fold it in the corners to allow it to sit flush on the floor.

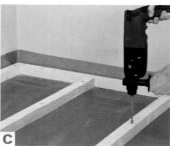

C **Fix battens** around the room with 100-mm (4-in) hammer-in fixings. Fix battens every 400mm (1ft 4in) at a right angle to the new boards.

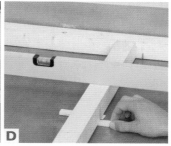

D **If battens do** not lie level, use small wedges or offcuts to pack out any indents and level the battens. If insulation is required, see p.360.

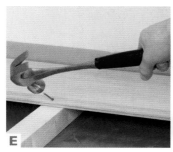

E **Start laying boards,** and fix with secret nailing into the battens. This is done by first positioning a nail at a 45-degree angle into the tongue.

F **Drive the nail** through the board and into the batten, so that the head is just beneath the board's surface. Or use a floor nailer (see p.181).

G **Continue laying** boards (as described on p.181, where tongue-and-groove is being fixed to joists). Once the floor is complete, apply any finish (e.g. wax or varnish) that may be required. Trim off the membrane overlap with a craft knife. Replace the skirting board to cover the expansion gap.

LAYING PARQUET TILE FLOORING

A **Fix two temporary battens** to the floor to mark your starting point (just as you would for laying hard floor tiles - see pp.324 and 334).

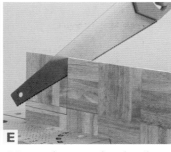

B **Spread enough adhesive** inside the angle of the battens for the first two or three tiles. Use a spreader, or the tool supplied with the adhesive.

Wood tile adhesive is solvent based, so make sure the room is well ventilated

C

Press the first tile into position, bedding it into the adhesive. (Some manufacturers specify that the adhesive should be allowed to become tacky before you position tiles.) Check that the edges of all tiles are precisely aligned as you work across the floor. As with other tiling jobs, lay all the full tiles first.

D **Remove the battens** with a claw hammer in readiness to work around the edges of the room. Then fill the gap with cut tiles.

E **Measure for cuts** as for other tiles (see pp.332-35). Wooden tiles are easy to cut with a fine-toothed saw. For curved cuts, use a jigsaw.

F **Apply adhesive** and place the cut tiles in the gaps to complete the floor and press them into position.

G **Finish off** by filling the expansion gaps with cork strips. Replace skirting or apply edge beads (see p.337). Seal the tiles if required.

SANDING A FLOOR

Floorboards can form an attractive finished floor but, unless the boards are very new, they will need sanding to remove old coatings and rough areas. Machine sanders are the ideal tools to carry out this work, but the job is still arduous and very messy. Sanders are also expensive, so hire them rather than buying (see below). Once sanded, the floor needs a decorative protection such as wax or varnish (see pp.290-91). Floor paint is an option, but a floor does not need to be sanded to such a high quality if it is to accept paint.

TOOLS AND MATERIALS SEE BASIC TOOLKIT AND P.325

PREPARATION

Order of work
The direction of sanding will depend on the floor's condition. If it is fairly flat, it may be possible simply to use the sander up and down the boards' grain. If the floor is uneven, or has a very thick coating of paint or varnish, start across the grain. Sanding at a right angle to boards may damage them, so sand at 45 degrees. Cross the room in one direction, then the other (see overview), before finishing along the grain. Reduce the coarseness of the sandpaper as you progress, finishing with the finest grade.

Protecting yourself and your home
Sanding is a very dusty, noisy, and messy job. Wear protective clothing, including ear defenders, earplugs, and a respiratory mask, and cover and mask around doors to prevent dust spreading throughout the house. Open all windows, so that you work in a well-ventilated room.

SEALING A DOORWAY

Sanders
You need three sanders: a heavy-duty drum sander (a drum wrapped in sandpaper that rotates at high speed); a heavy-duty edging sander; and a corner sander. Each requires sandpaper in a particular shape, which can be bought from the hire shop. The paper is expensive, and will tear if it is not correctly fitted. Do not allow nails to protrude from the floor and tear paper (see right). Disconnect the sander from the mains before changing paper, and allow it to cool if any parts have heated up in use.

CORNER SANDER
Pointed sanding pad reaches into corners

Dust bag

Has two handles for two-handed operation

Shaped to reach edges

EDGING SANDER

DRUM SANDER

---

1 PREPARING THE FLOOR

 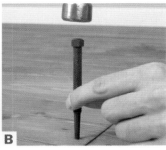

A   **B**

Fix down any loose floorboards, making pilot holes into joists (avoiding cables and pipes) before knocking nails into place. Punch the nail heads beneath the surface.

Check the floor for protruding nail or screw heads. If any are sticking out, knock them below the surface, again taking care to miss any pipes or cables.

2 READYING THE DRUM SANDER

A   **B**

With the sander disconnected from the mains, unscrew the retaining strip on the drum sander and feed a sheet of sandpaper underneath it.

Feed the sandpaper around the drum and secure the end under the retaining strip, aligning the cut sections with the retaining screws.

 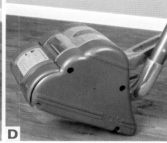

C   **D**

Check that the paper is taut and correctly positioned before you tighten the retaining screws.

Plug the sander into the mains, tilt it backwards so that the drum is raised off the floor, and start the machine.

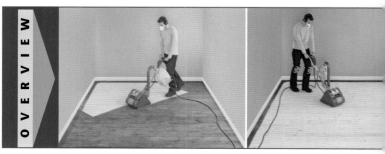

OVERVIEW

3 USING THE DRUM SANDER

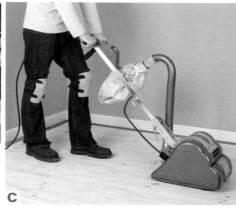

Then change direction again, and run the drum sander across the floor following the direction of the grain.

A **Lower the drum** onto the floor and make the first diagonal runs across the floor.

B **Sand the whole floor** in one direction. Then change direction and make the other set of diagonal runs across the floor, at a right angle to the first runs.

C

4 USING THE EDGING SANDER

Ensure that the sander is disconnected from the mains supply, then use the bolt key supplied with the edging sander to undo the retaining bolt, and remove the old disc of sandpaper. The key is often stored on a retaining clip on the underside of the sander.

A

B **Position a new disc** of sandpaper and retighten the retaining bolt to hold the disc securely in position. Ensure the retaining bolt head is well below the sandpaper surface level.

C **Take a firm hold** on the sander before starting it up, and work around the edges of the room. Take care to avoid heating pipes or electrical cables.

5 USING THE CORNER SANDER

A **To change the** sandpaper on a corner sander, simply take hold of the old paper and tear it off. Align a new sheet of paper with the pad's face and press it into position.

B **Use the corner** sander to deal with the room's corners, and to sand any awkward, otherwise inaccessible areas such as beneath a radiator.

6 FINISHING THE FLOOR

A **Sweep and then vacuum** the floor to remove any debris not held by the sanders' dust bags, and wipe with a damp sponge. If you find any rough areas, sand them by hand.

B **Apply your chosen finish.** Two coats of water-based varnish can be applied in a day (it dries quickly), but some light hand sanding is needed between coats (see p.291).

PROBLEM SOLVER

REPAIRING PARQUET FLOORING

Parquet flooring comprises rectangular blocks of wood that may be arranged in varying designs. Commonly, herringbone patterns are used. Over time, the blocks may become damaged through wear and tear, or they may become loose.

TOOLS AND MATERIALS
Hammer, chisel, scraper, wood adhesive, belt sander, wax, cloth

REVIVING PARQUET
To revive an old parquet floor, use a similar technique to that shown for sanding a floor (pp.340-41).
■ As long as the blocks are stuck fast, undulations can be removed by sanding. Work across the floor in the direction of the grain.
■ A traditional herringbone design would require diagonal runs, to deal with the orientation of the blocks.

A **Lever out the block.** If it remains firmly stuck, try breaking it up further, using a hammer and chisel.

B **Remove excess adhesive** from the back of the block, and from the floor surface, using a scraper.

C **Apply some wood** adhesive (latex-based) to the back of the block and to the floor surface.

D **Position a new block,** and press it firmly into place.

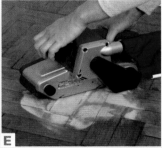

E **If the block** is not flush with the surrounding surface, sand the area until it is smooth. A belt sander is ideal for this.

F **Apply finish to the floor** surface. This may be wax or varnish, depending on the existing floor (see pp.290-91).

REPAIRING A LAMINATE FLOOR

If a damaged section is near the edge of a room, it can simply be replaced with a new piece. If this is not possible, a small dent or scratch can be repaired with a laminate repair compound kit, as shown here.

TOOLS AND MATERIALS
Scissors, repair compound kit, scraper

A **Cut off the nozzles** on the two-part syringe. Squeeze the repair compound into a tray, where the two elements will mix together.

B **Use the plastic scraper** included in the repair kit to press the repair compound into the damaged area.

C **Remove any excess** compound, with a metal scraper, from the area before it dries.

PATCH-REPAIRING CARPET DAMAGE

Aside from using cleaners, damage to carpet can be hard to remedy. But specks of paint can be removed with a craft knife, and a small area of damage can be replaced with a patch, if you have offcuts of the carpet.

TOOLS AND MATERIALS
Scissors, craft knife, metal lid or similar object, spray adhesive

A **Cut a patch** of carpet to a size that is larger than the area that needs to be repaired.

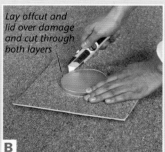

Lay offcut and lid over damage and cut through both layers

B **Find a metal lid** or other circular object, slightly larger than the repair area. Cut around it, down through the patch and the carpet below.

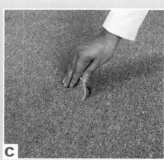

C **Remove the cut circle** of damaged carpet, and replace it with the circle of new carpet. You may wish to use spray adhesive.

PATCH-REPAIRING VINYL FLOORING

Although hardwearing, vinyl can be damaged by sharp objects or by heat, such as a cigarette burn. Re-covering an entire floor is expensive, but where vinyl has a pattern, such as "tiling", it can be used to aid the repair process. If you use this technique, be sure that the junctions between the patch and existing vinyl are firmly stuck down. Otherwise people may trip over them.

TOOLS AND MATERIALS
Scissors, tape, craft knife, double-sided tape, seam roller

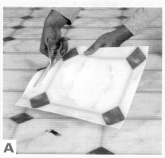

A **Cut a section** of new vinyl, to a size that is slightly larger than the damaged "tile" area.

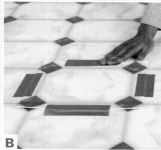

B **Tape this piece** loosely over the damaged area, making sure that it is aligned exactly with the pattern.

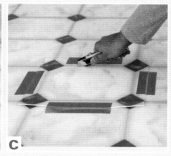

C **Use a craft knife** to cut through both layers of vinyl, using the "tile" edge as a guide line.

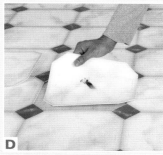

D **Remove both sections** of vinyl. As you lift out the damaged section, the cut shape will be revealed underneath.

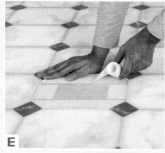

E **Apply double-sided tape** around all the edges of the revealed section of floor.

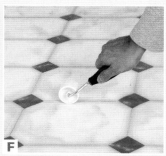

F **Position the new vinyl** section. Press down its edges, as well as those of the remaining old section. A seam roller is ideal for this.

REPLACING A BROKEN HARD TILE

Floor tiles can get cracked due to wear and tear, or through damage if a heavy object is dropped on them. Replacing a single tile is more cost-effective than re-tiling an entire floor. Wear goggles while drilling into the tile, in case any shards fly towards you. Wear gloves to protect your hands.

TOOLS AND MATERIALS
Grout raker, drill, goggles, gloves, club hammer, cold chisel, scraper, spirit level, tile adhesive, grout, grout shaper, sponge

A **Remove grout** from around the edge of the tile. A grout raker is ideal for this process.

B **Drill a series of holes** into the broken tile. This breaks it up, making it easier to remove.

C **With a club hammer** and cold chisel, remove the broken tile. It will come away in sections.

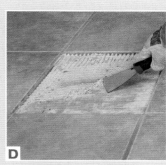

D **Scrape any hardened** old adhesive off the floor surface revealed by the tile's removal.

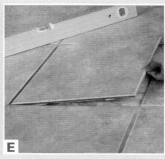

E **Apply adhesive** to the back of the new tile and position it. Use a spirit level to make sure it sits flush with the surrounding tiles.

F **Allow the adhesive to dry**, then grout the new tile. Clean off any excess with a sponge.

Finishing a room

ONCE THE MAIN DECORATION OF A ROOM IS COMPLETE, THERE IS NORMALLY A NEED TO "FINISH" THE ROOM BY ADDING WINDOW DRESSINGS, PICTURES, MIRRORS, AND OTHER ACCESSORIES. IT IS THEREFORE ESSENTIAL TO CHOOSE THE CORRECT FIXINGS FOR PARTICULAR WALL SURFACES (SEE PP.76-77) AND TO BE AWARE OF THE VARIOUS BRACKETS, CLIPS, AND FITTINGS THAT ARE AVAILABLE.

WALL FIXTURES

Wall fixtures such as curtains and blinds make up an important part of the final look of a room. For this reason it is important to choose the right materials, and to hang them in the appropriate way.

CURTAIN TRACKS

Most modern curtain tracks are made of plastic, though the traditional metal variety is still available. Light and flexible, plastic tracks are easy to install, and can be shaped to bend around curves and corners.

CURTAIN POLES

Curtain poles are secured by brackets that hold the pole away from the wall surface. Poles and brackets are normally made of wood (shown here) or metal, although other materials are available. For small windows, just two end supports should be sufficient to support the pole. For large windows, or when heavy curtains are being hung, a further centre support may be needed. Poles can be joined using dowel screws (see p.77).

FINIAL

Lock

Curtain track
Plastic curtain tracks are designed to be unobtrusive and to allow the curtain to hang close to the wall or window surface.

END SUPPORT   **TRACK BRACKET**

Curtain pole
These have certain decorative appeal and should therefore be chosen with some regard to the overall look of the room.

END AND CENTRE SUPPORT

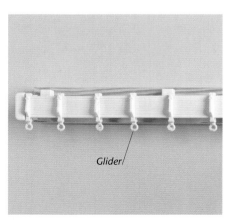

Glider

Curtain hook

TRACK HOOK OR GLIDER

Choosing a curtain track
Plastic curtain tracks have little decorative appeal and so are usually covered when the curtains are closed.

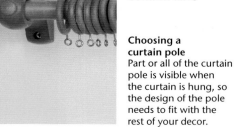

Eyelet screw

CURTAIN RING

Choosing a curtain pole
Part or all of the curtain pole is visible when the curtain is hung, so the design of the pole needs to fit with the rest of your decor.

RAIL FITTINGS

Other fittings to finish a room include the various racks and rails used for hanging clothes and towels. There are various types of bracket, and the type you use will depend on how you want to position them. The fittings themselves come in a range of materials; chrome is shown here.

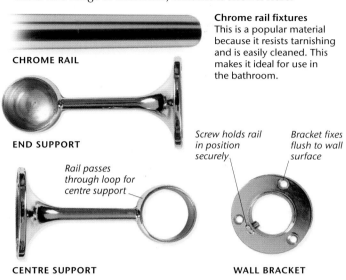

CHROME RAIL

END SUPPORT

CENTRE SUPPORT

Rail passes through loop for centre support

WALL BRACKET

Screw holds rail in position securely

Bracket fixes flush to wall surface

Chrome rail fixtures
This is a popular material because it resists tarnishing and is easily cleaned. This makes it ideal for use in the bathroom.

MIRROR FIXINGS

Mirrors can be hung in a variety of ways. The most important consideration is whether or not a fixing is strong enough to support the weight of a particular item. When fitting a mirror flush against a wall surface make sure that the wall has no undulations. If it does, be careful not to over-tighten the screws, otherwise the mirror may crack.

Head fixes over mirror

Mirror screws
These are ideal for fixing mirrors in place, if they have pre-drilled holes. If this is not the case, use adhesive or other specially designed brackets.

Use small screws or nails to fix to wall

Mirror corner brackets
Four brackets are fixed to the wall surface; each of these supports a corner of the mirror.

Peel off protective layer and stick to one surface first

Mirror pads (self-adhesive)
These should only be used for small lightweight mirrors. They are double-sided adhesive pads; one side attaches to the wall surface, the other adheres to the back of the mirror.

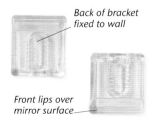

Back of bracket fixed to wall

Front lips over mirror surface

Mirror brackets (sliding)
Sliding brackets are normally combined with fixed brackets, both lipping over the front of the mirror surface to hold it securely in place.

PICTURE FRAME FIXINGS

Picture hooks can only be used for relatively lightweight items. For heavier frames, insert the fixings at a slightly downward angle. Greater strength can be achieved by using resin and heavy-duty fixings (see pp.77 and 80). In many instances, particularly when hanging extremely heavy frames, screw fixings (with the appropriate wall plug) or nails can offer the most secure hanging mechanism. Always take care to avoid fixing into pipes or cables below the wall surface.

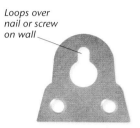

Loops over nail or screw on wall

Flush frame
These fixings are attached to the outside edge of a frame. Depending on the frame's size and weight, several may be needed. They allow the frame to sit flush against the wall surface.

Hold looped head firmly and twist to drive in

Eyelet screws
These screws have a looped head and are inserted into the back of the frame. For small frames, these eyelets can be used as a direct hanging point. Alternatively, one eyelet is attached to each side of the frame and picture wire is tied between the two and looped over a wall fixing.

Use a hammer to drive nails through

Hardwall picture hook
Modern design of hook that relies on a number of small tightly packed "nails" to penetrate the wall and provide strength.

Picture wire
Metallic wire suspended between eyelet screws on the back of a picture frame.

Front view

Side view

Lip loops over picture rail

Picture hangs from hook

PICTURE RAIL HOOK

Picture hooks
Traditional type of hanging mechanism designed to penetrate the wall at a slightly downward angle to increase fixing strength. Some hooks have two nails for increased strength. A more traditional design is provided by picture rail hooks. These are attached to picture rails, and pictures are hung either directly from the hooks or from wires looped between them. An advantage is that they leave no marks on the wall.

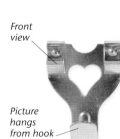

Front view

Picture hangs from hook

Side view

Drive nails into wall

PICTURE WALL HOOK

FITTING A CURTAIN POLE

Curtain poles are normally fixed outside a window recess. For the maximum amount of light, end brackets should be placed on either side of the recess, so that curtains can be drawn back completely; their exact placing will depend on the width of the gathered curtain. In the following example, only end supports are required. For larger windows, extra support also may be needed in the centre. Curtain weight and pole strength should also be considered when deciding on how much rail support is needed.

TOOLS AND MATERIALS SEE BASIC TOOLKIT, PP.24–25

BLINDS

Blinds are a popular alternative to curtains. When buying a set it is important to take note of the manufacturer's guidelines on how brackets are orientated so that the blind works efficiently. Many roller blinds are also supplied with an option to cut them down to your particular size requirements. The roller is generally made of wood or lightweight metal. Use a tenon saw to cut wooden rollers and a junior hacksaw to cut metal ones. Many blind manufacturers have proprietary fitting mechanisms that are manufactured according to design. Roller blinds tend to have two brackets that are fixed directly to the window frame or the immediate wall surface. Some blind systems also need to be tied to the frame or wall when opened; for this reason a small hook or cleat is fitted to the frame or wall surface. Some blind cords are a continuous loop; as these are a choking hazard for children, cut the loop to form an open-ended cord.

1 MEASURING UP

 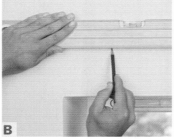  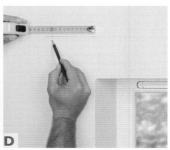

A

Make a mark above the window recess for the required height of the pole. This will depend on curtain length and aesthetic preference.

B

Use this mark to draw a level guide line above the recess; this should extend slightly beyond the recess width on either side.

C

Use a spirit level to make a mark on the horizontal line directly above the corner of the recess.

D

Measure back to mark the bracket position. This distance will depend on the width of the gathered curtain.

2 FIXING A CURTAIN POLE

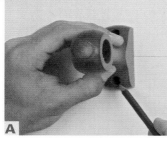 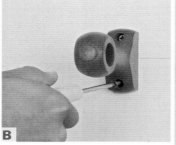 

A

Position the end support on the mark and use a pencil to mark off fixing holes. Remove the end support.

B

Plug fixing holes if necessary and screw into place. Repeat steps 1C, 1D, 2A, and 2B for the other end support.

C

Cut the pole to the required length. It must extend a few centimetres (a couple of inches) on either side of the end support brackets to accommodate end rings and finials. With supports in place, thread the pole through one end support.

3 ATTACHING RINGS AND END SUPPORT

  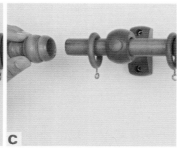 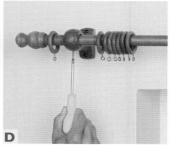

A

Position rings on the pole before threading the other end of the pole through the other end support.

B

Position one ring on the outer side of each of the end supports.

C

Position finials on the ends of the pole. Normally these are just pushed to fit; some are secured by a grub screw.

D

Finally secure the pole in place by securing screws through the supports and into the pole. You may need to pilot-drill these holes first.

FITTING A CURTAIN RAIL

Unlike curtain poles, curtain rails are often fixed directly to window frames, an arrangement which can hinder the opening of the curtain and thus reduce the amount of light that can enter the room. An alternative is to mount the track outside the window recess (as shown below), allowing you to draw the curtains well back from the recess and to admit the maximum amount of light. To provide secure bracket fixing points, mount the track on a wooden batten.

TOOLS AND MATERIALS SEE BASIC TOOLKIT, PP.24–25

1 FIXING A BATTEN

Batten mounting is a good idea if the wall surface is difficult to work with (e.g. an old lath-and-plaster wall). Use a spirit level to position the batten horizontally above the recess, then draw a guide line with a pencil.

Drill pilot holes and use the appropriate fixings to secure the batten to the wall surface. Use the guide line to ensure it is horizontal.

Draw a further guide line along the centre of the batten.

2 FITTING A CURTAIN RAIL

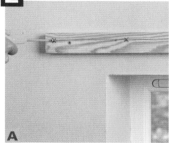

Position screws for rail brackets at regular intervals along the line.

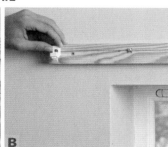

Position brackets on the screws. It may be necessary to adjust the screw depth to gain a tight fit.

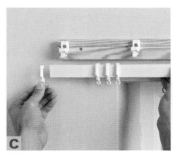

Position the required number of gliders on the rail.

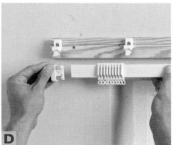

Fit the end support on the rail to prevent the gliders slipping off.

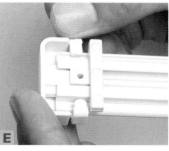

Positioning the end support will vary according to rail design. In this case make sure you position a final glider at the same time as the support.

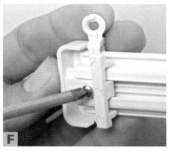

A grub screw is normally used to secure the support in place.

3 ATTACHING THE RAIL

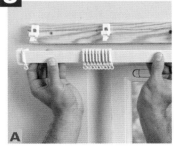

Clip the rail onto the brackets.

Most rails will have a clip on the brackets that needs to be closed off to secure the rail in place.

With the rail in position, space out the gliders to check that you have the required number. Most rails allow you to add further gliders without having to take down the rail and remove the end supports.

IMPROVING HOME PERFORMANCE

INSULATION AND VENTILATION
HOME SECURITY
CONSERVING ENERGY
USING SPACE

EFFICIENT HOME SYSTEMS

There are many ways in which you can improve your home structurally and decoratively. However, there are many other home-improvement methods you can use to boost the performance of your home and make it more efficient in terms of energy use, aspects of safety and security, and storage. Here we identify the areas of a home that may be improved in these ways.

ASSESSING YOUR PRIORITIES

When assessing your home's performance, you need to be able to prioritize the tasks at hand. Generally, matters of safety and security need to be placed at the top of your list, while other issues, such as improving storage space, can be tackled at your own pace. Not all issues and measures shown here will be relevant to every home. However, the aim of this section is to cover as many improvements in safety, security, storage, and energy efficiency as possible, some of which may be applicable to your home and lifestyle. Many of the technologies discussed in this section are new and will constantly develop and evolve. It pays to be aware of developments in all these areas, so that you can update your information and techniques for home improvement.

Using roof space for storage
Use decking and shelving to act as storage platforms in this otherwise unused area of the home (see pp.356–59).

Soundproofing floors and walls
Noise between floors or adjacent rooms can be drastically reduced by modern soundproofing techniques (see pp.362–63).

Loft insulation (cold roof)
A well-insulated loft is essential for saving energy (see pp.352–589). This is both environmentally friendly and cost-effective.

Fire escape route
All homes must have suitable fire escape procedures. In many cases an escape ladder can be fitted. Escape windows should also open wide enough to ensure it is possible for easy passage through them in the event of an emergency.

Using rainwater
Consider collecting and recycling rainwater. You can use it to water the garden or even channel it directly into your home plumbing system (see pp.386–87).

RECYCLING WATER

As well as recycling rainwater, it is now possible to install systems in your home that can recycle grey water (from sinks, baths, and washing machines), and black water (from toilets). Both systems can be expensive to install, but once fitted they are eco-friendly and cost-effective. Carry out research to ensure you fit a system appropriate to your needs. For more on the efficient use of water, see pp.384–87.

Floor insulation
Insulated floors not only save energy and household heating costs (see p.360) but also feel more comfortable underfoot.

Extractor fan
Make sure that extractor fans are used to take moist air out of the house where necessary.

Static ventilation
Make sure you have adequate ventilation for fuel-burning appliances.

Child safety: door catches
Use door locks to prevent children gaining unsupervised access to your fridge and cupboards.

Solar energy use
The use of solar panels is an increasingly viable, eco-friendly option for saving energy (see pp.380–81).

Tilt window
As well as providing daylight for a loft room, the window can be opened for extra ventilation when necessary.

Loft insulation (warm roof)
Insulation is essential at roof level when the loft is used as a living space (see pp.354–59).

ECO SOLUTIONS
Many of the improvements you can make to the efficiency of your home are also eco-friendly – loft insulation is an obvious example of this. For more suggestions on how you can increase home efficiency in tandem with environmental awareness, see pp.20–21.

Alarm system
This deters burglars and so offers a greater feeling of home security as well as lowering insurance-policy premiums.

Window locks
Burglars often use windows as points of entry. Therefore, ensuring that windows can be locked and secured is an important aspect of home security.

Extra storage
Make the best use of space wasted in alcoves by fitting shelves.

Security lighting
This not only offers an excellent deterrent to intruders, but also illuminates areas when you enter or leave home at night.

Child safety: stair gates
Prevent child accidents on stairs by positioning gates at both the top and bottom of a staircase.

Smoke alarms
These are among the most essential of all fittings in your home. If your house does not have smoke alarms fitted, you should treat it as a priority and fit alarms on each level of your home.

Draught-proofing
Doors and windows can be a major source of heat loss. You can make large energy and financial savings by fitting double glazing and draught excluders (see p.361).

Secondary door locks
Entry doors are generally fitted with some form of mortise lock and/or cylinder lock. Other secondary locks can further bolster this security.

Insulation and ventilation

YOUR HOME'S PERFORMANCE IS DEPENDENT ON THE QUALITY OF ITS INSULATION AND VENTILATION. HUGE AMOUNTS OF ENERGY ARE LOST THROUGH POOR INSULATION. THIS WASTES FUEL, DAMAGES THE ENVIRONMENT, AND COSTS YOU MONEY. NEW BUILDING REGULATIONS REQUIRE OWNERS TO IMPROVE INSULATION, VENTILATION, AND SOUNDPROOFING WHEN CARRYING OUT ALTERATIONS AND RENOVATIONS.

HOME INSULATION

Improving your home's insulation is one of the best overall investments of time and money you can make. Although the initial financial outlay may be quite high, the long-term savings on heating bills will make it worthwhile. You can insulate most parts of your home against heat loss, and even fairly modest measures can make a considerable difference. However, efficient thermal insulation must always go hand in hand with effective ventilation to prevent the buildup of condensation (see pp.364–65).

HOW INSULATION WORKS
Heat flows from warm areas to cold areas, and moves in any direction. In the home, warm air expands and circulates, escaping through walls, ceilings, roofs, windows, doors, fireplaces, and anywhere plumbing, ducting, or electrical wiring penetrates exterior walls. Thermal insulation acts as a barrier, reducing the amount of heat that escapes.

The term "U-value" is used when discussing thermal requirements in a house, especially in conjunction with insulation products. The aim is to achieve low U-values: this means that a house's insulation is efficient. In a new-build home U-values are governed by building regulations, and the type of insulation used will therefore need to meet certain requirements.

WHERE TO INSULATE
Insulating the walls, loft, floors, and windows of your home is the most effective way of reducing overall heat loss (see pp.354–61). However, there are many other parts of a home in which a few inexpensive and straightforward methods can make a dramatic improvement.

Thermal image of heat loss
On a thermal image of a house, the roof shows up as cool and blue, suggesting there is insulation present, but the red windows and wooden slats show heat escaping. Even if you have good loft insulation it is important to consider other areas such as walls and windows. If you are fitting new windows in your home, they must have double-glazed units.

If you have a cold-water tank in your loft, make sure that you buy a cover for it, or that you cover it with blanket insulation. To avoid possible water contamination, fit a secure seal underneath the insulation. You should also insulate any exposed loft pipes (see p.356).

Modern hot-water cylinders are usually sold with a layer of insulation pre-fitted. If yours does not have this, buy a cover and fit it over the cylinder.

You should cover any loft traps with a layer of insulation, otherwise all your efforts to insulate your loft or roof space may be undermined by leakage through the hatch or around its edges.

Heat emitted by the rear of a radiator can be lost into or through the wall it is fitted to. In the past, it was common practice to fit aluminium foil behind a radiator to reflect its heat back into the room, but now it is possible to buy purpose-made insulating kits to do this job.

Gaps between skirting boards and floorboards can cause unpleasant draughts and will lead to heat loss from your home. To avoid this, you can use filler or wood mouldings to close up any gaps.

INSULATING AND SOUNDPROOFING MATERIALS

When choosing insulation, take into account the material's cost, ease of use, suitability to your needs, and thermal properties ("U-value", see opposite). Bear in mind that greener materials are increasingly being used in this area. The effectiveness of a soundproofing material is based on what it is made of and how and where it is installed.

RECYCLED INSULATION

Recycled blanket insulation
This example, made from recycled plastic bottles, is both eco-friendly and non-itch.

Recycled loose-fill insulation
This is a wood-based cellulose fibre that mainly consists of recycled newspaper.

Blanket insulation
Versatile and easy-to-use, rolls are usually the same width as the space between joists or rafters.

Loose-fill insulation
An alternative to blanket insulation. It is easy to pour into awkwardly shaped spaces.

Framefoil
Retards heat transfer by reflecting heat back to its source and by trapping air in its multiple layers.

Pipe insulation
Use this in a cold roof to prevent pipes freezing, which may cause costly leaks and damage.

Damp-proof membrane
This waterproof polythene membrane is suitable for use below new concrete or wood floors.

Pipe lagging
Use to wrap around loft water pipes.

Flanking tape
Use to cover gaps along edges when soundproofing.

Vapour barrier
This polythene sheet plastic is used to prevent water vapour penetrating ceilings, and sometimes walls.

Acoustic underlay
Used under flooring instead of regular underlay, this helps to improve a room's sound insulation.

NATURAL INSULATION

Sheep's wool batt
Thermafleece made from 100 per cent sheep's wool. It is non-itch and is as easy to use as other forms of fibrous batt insulation.

Wood-fibre batt
Wood-based insulation primarily made from forestry waste and sawmill residues. Products are added for fireproofing.

Polystyrene board
A rigid board fitted below floors but also in roofs for insulation. Adjacent edges interlock using a tongue-and-groove design.

Insulating plasterboard
Plasterboard with an insulating layer of polystyrene. Ideal for converting a loft space into a warm roof area.

Foam board
A rigid board used to insulate concrete floors. It is also bonded under flooring sheets to make storage decking in a loft space.

Rigid board insulation
This comes in panels and provides a high level of insulation. It is more expensive than blanket or loose-fill insulation.

Insulated storage decking
Provides insulation for converting a loft to a cold roof area for storage purposes. Lay blanket or loose-fill insulation first, below the decking.

Acoustic mat
Used in a continuous layer below flooring, this densely packed material reduces the effects of airborne noise.

Acoustic slab
This dense soundproofing material is sold in slabs. It can be laid below floors, above ceilings, and within walls.

INSULATING A LOFT

One way to make huge energy savings is to insulate your loft. However, first you must decide whether you wish to create a warm roof or cold roof area. For a warm roof, the insulation is taken right up to just below the roof tiles, so that the loft space is kept warm. This process is mainly carried out when the loft area is being converted into a usable room. In cold roofs, the loft insulation is kept at floor level, and the loft space is left to be an open area that is prone to fluctuating temperatures. In this case, the loft is often used just for storage.

ROOFING FELT

The type of felt fitted in your roof affects your insulation options and influences how you ventilate your loft. Non-breathable felt creates an impermeable membrane that prevents moist air escaping. Breathable felt allows moist air to pass from the inside to outside, but not in the other direction. Breathable felt has only been used relatively recently, and usually has its properties written on its surface. Non-breathable felt is often black but do not assume that a felt of any other colour is necessarily breathable.

COLD ROOF

You must allow for efficient ventilation in a cold roof space so that moist air is able to escape into the atmosphere. If trapped in the roof space, the moisture will seep into the insulation and damage it, which will reduce its effectiveness. It is possible that trapped moisture will also rot timber, further damaging the fabric of the house. The type of ventilation required will depend on the type of roof felt used in your roof.

Cold breathing roof

A cold breathing roof has breathable felt below the tiles. This means that any residual moisture in the roof space can penetrate the felt and escape into the atmosphere. However, the felt will prevent external moisture penetrating the loft space.

Moist air escapes through ridge ventilation

Tiles

Moisture passes through felt and escapes through gaps in tiles

Breathable felt

Airflow below tiles helps to disperse moisture

Insulation

Most moisture is stopped by vapour barrier

Vapour barrier

Some residual moisture will always enter loft space

Cold ventilated roof

A cold ventilated roof is fitted with non-breathable felt, so it is essential to ventilate the roof directly through the eaves. Water vapour is then picked up and allowed to escape through a ventilated ridge or through ventilated tiles. Airbricks may also be used in gable walls.

Vented tiles (see p.201)

Non-breathable felt

Airflow allowed into roof at eaves

Moisture may enter through gaps around light fittings

Vapour barrier

Moisture may enter around pipes

Creating a cold roof

Check whether a vapour barrier has been installed on top of the ceiling on the surface visible between the joists. If not, you will need to lay one to prevent moisture rising through the ceiling and creating condensation damage. If the roof has breathable felt, moisture escapes through it. This is a cold breathing roof, shown above left, and here ventilation is less of a concern. If the felt is non-breathable, any moist air will be trapped inside the attic space. In this case, you need to ensure that there are ventilation gaps in the eaves. You may need to install vents at the ridge or through tiles. The cold ventilated roof is shown above right. Some modern ventilation systems are designed to be fitted retrospectively, while others are designed for new-build projects (see p.201).

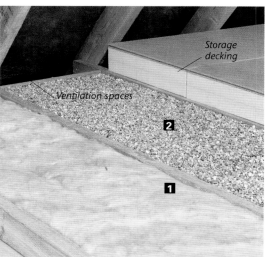

Storage decking

Ventilation spaces

2

1

Cold roof options

Choose one of the following options (see pp.336–37 for installation).

Option 1:
Lay a vapour barrier, then blanket insulation. Add another layer at right angles to this if regulations stipulate.

Option 2:
Lay a vapour barrier, then loose-fill insulation. Regulations may require you to build up loose-fill insulation above joist height (see box opposite).

In addition to option 1 or 2:
Place storage decking over the top of the joists. This creates a storage and walking area.

WARM ROOF

You may think of a warm roof as an insulated extension of your home, and in most cases you will be creating a warm roof in order to convert your loft space into a usable room. Like the main rooms in your home, the ventilation of this space mainly relies on windows and doors, although the entry to the loft may be through a stairwell or even still a hatch. As in the case of a cold roof, the ventilation design of a warm roof depends largely on whether your roof has been fitted with breathable or non-breathable felt.

Warm breathing roof

A warm breathing roof has breathable felt below the tiles. No gap is needed between the insulation and felt as long as the insulation is moisture-permeable. This allows moist air to pass through the insulation and then through the felt and out into the atmosphere.

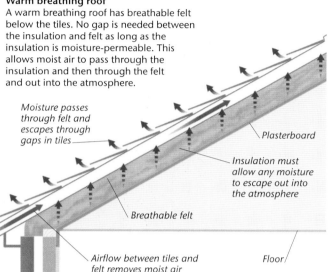

Moisture passes through felt and escapes through gaps in tiles

Plasterboard

Insulation must allow any moisture to escape out into the atmosphere

Breathable felt

Airflow between tiles and felt removes moist air

Floor

Warm ventilated roof

A warm ventilated roof has non-breathable felt below the tiles. Therefore it is essential to ensure that there is a ventilation gap between the underside of the felt and the insulation below. A vapour barrier should be used on the warm side of the insulation below the plasterboard surface.

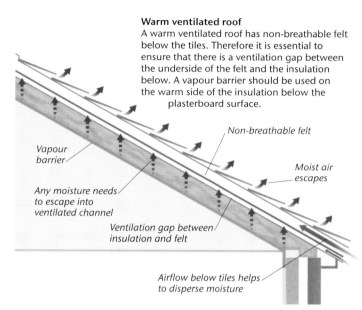

Vapour barrier

Non-breathable felt

Moist air escapes

Any moisture needs to escape into ventilated channel

Ventilation gap between insulation and felt

Airflow below tiles helps to disperse moisture

Creating a warm roof

Install blanket insulation between the rafters. You could also insulate below the rafters to stop them becoming a "cold bridge", an area that allows the cold in. If you are creating a warm roof to become a living area, such as an extra bedroom, it will almost certainly require planning permission and need to be overseen by a building control officer. In many circumstances you may wish to construct dwarf walls (shown right) that will make the area appear and feel more like the other rooms in your house. The area behind a dwarf wall should then be treated as a cold roof area (see opposite).

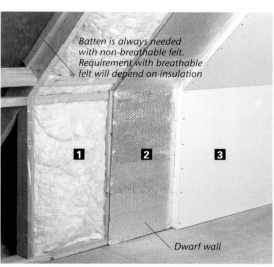

Batten is always needed with non-breathable felt. Requirement with breathable felt will depend on insulation

1 **2** **3**

Dwarf wall

Warm roof options

Choose one of the following options (see p.337 for a detailed guide).

Option 1:
Lay blanket insulation between rafters. This combines with option 3 and a vapour barrier.

Option 2:
Install framefoil with a ventilation gap behind. Specifications vary for this material. Always follow the manufacturer's guidelines.

Option 3:
Install thermal-check plasterboard. This should be used in conjunction with option 1 or 2.

INSULATION DEPTHS

Regulations on the required depth of loft insulation currently state that blanket insulation should be 270mm (10½in) deep. Therefore, you may need to increase joist or rafter depth before fitting insulation.

TOOLS AND MATERIALS CHECKLIST PP.356–61

Laying blanket insulation (p.356) Protective clothing, vapour barrier, staple gun, blanket insulation

Insulating pipes (p.357) Protective clothing, pipe insulation plus metal clips or tape, mitre block

Laying storage decking (p.357) Protective clothing, blanket insulation, loose-fill

insulation*, storage decking, woodworking adhesive

Laying loose-fill insulation (p.358) Protective clothing, blanket insulation, loose-fill insulation, plywood offcut

Insulating rafters (p.359) Protective clothing, battens, blanket insulation, vapour barrier, thermal plasterboard

Insulating a stud wall (p.360) Protective clothing, blanket insulation, plasterboard

Fitting brush and flexible seals (p.361) Basic toolkit only

* = optional

FOR BASIC TOOLKIT SEE PP.24–25

INSULATING LOFTS AND ROOFS

How you insulate your loft depends on whether you want a "cold" or "warm" roof space (see pp.354–55). A cold roof requires insulation at joist level to stop heat escaping through the unused roof space (see below and p.358). A warm roof is insulated between and under the rafters of the roof itself (see p.359). The recommended depth for insulation has been increased recently, so you may have to increase the depths of the joists or rafters if you want to create usable platforms of storage space.

RECYCLED INSULATION

Recycled insulation is a green and non-itch alternative to conventional blanket insulation. The techniques for laying this are the same, but non-itch insulation makes it a much more comfortable process. Check the instructions on the product to ensure that you fit it to the right depth requirement.

BLANKET INSULATION

One of the most widely used forms of loft-insulation, blanket insulation is simple to work with – although you should always wear protective clothing, as it can be uncomfortable to handle. Before starting, ensure that you have measured the surface area of your loft accurately, and that you bear in mind the recommended depth requirements and order accordingly (manufacturers supply blanket insulation in many different depths, so you must remember to order to the correct depth as well as to the necessary surface area). Always consider the recycled and natural alternatives to conventional blanket insulation (see boxes, above and opposite).

◼◼ LAYING BLANKET INSULATION

Sweep away any debris from between the joists. Determine whether a vapour barrier is needed. If the plasterboard surface is silver-backed, you won't need an extra membrane – if not, it is advisable to install one.

A

TOOLS AND MATERIALS SEE BASIC TOOLKIT AND P.355

Roll out the vapour barrier, cutting and laying lengths in between each pair of joists. Staple the barrier to the sides of the joists using a staple gun. Cut holes in the barrier to accommodate any electrical fittings.

B

C

Do not unpack the insulation blanket until you are in the loft. This will restrict the presence of insulation fibres to the work area.

D

Roll out the insulation blanket between the joists, taking care not to compress it. Tuck it in against the sides of the joists.

E

Butt the lengths of insulation up against one another, making sure that there are no gaps between each of the lengths.

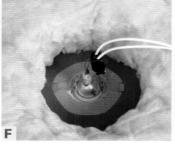

F

Cut a hole in the insulation blanket to allow for electrical fittings. This is an important step to prevent the fitting overheating.

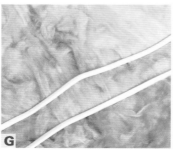

G

Lift any cables or wires above the insulation to stop them overheating. Any heat they do give off will rise harmlessly into the cold roof.

BUILDING UP LAYERS

Decking provides walking area

If required by regulations, run a second layer of insulation at right angles to the first to increase depth.

PIPEWORK AND STORAGE DECKING

The initial application of blanket insulation is only part of the job. Many loft spaces contain pipework that needs to be protected from freezing during winter months. Insulating warm water heating or supply pipes will also save energy.

Many people want to use part of their loft space for storage purposes. This often means you need to build up the joist height to accommodate building boards, which provide a base for storage. Alternatively, storage decking is a 2-in-1 application that combines extra insulation with a rigid board for storage (see below). Check the board sizes beforehand to make sure that they will fit through your loft hatch.

USING SHEEP'S WOOL

As with the recycled non-itch alternative shown opposite, sheep's wool is a more user-friendly alternative to conventional material. Build up depth by laying subsequent layers at right angles to the preceding layer. Check the instructional literature for depth requirements.

INSULATING PIPES

Custom-made pipe insulation is the best option. It can be bought in different diameters, depending on need. Split the pipe insulation along its length to slip over the pipe. Keep the join facing upwards. Although pipe insulation is non-itch, you should wear gloves to protect yourself from the blanket insulation.

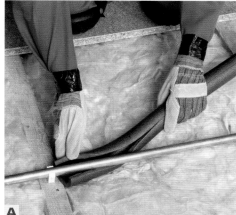

A

B

Take care that each length is tightly butt-joined to the next one, so that no part of the pipe is exposed.

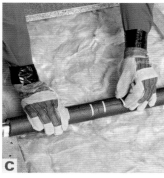

C

Hold the pipe insulation in position by taping it, or by using proprietary clips as shown here.

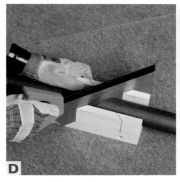

D

At corners, it is still necessary to keep a tight join. Use a mitre block and fine-toothed saw to make accurate 45-degree cuts.

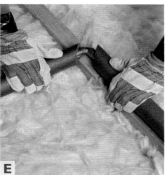

E

Make sure that the mitred sections of insulation meet precisely to avoid any gaps.

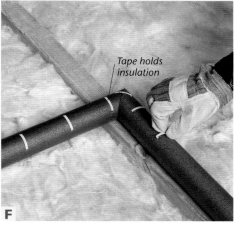

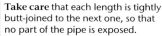

Tape holds insulation

F

Secure the insulation in position using tape or clips. Note how the corner has been secured with an extra clip across the mitre. For any valves or stop taps, wrap the pipe with insulation but leave the valve handle exposed.

LAYING STORAGE DECKING

A

Cut wedges of blanket to insulate the join of the roof rafters and floor joists, but with non-breathable felt leave a gap behind the wedge.

B

Lay the first board across the joists. Butt the edge of the board up against the rafters. Be sure not to close the gap behind the wedge of insulation.

C

To hold the deck in position, use one screw to fix each section to the joist below. Board ends should join on joists.

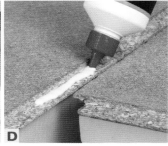

D

Glue the board edges with woodworking adhesive, then fit the boards together using their tongue-and-groove system.

IMPROVING HOME PERFORMANCE

LOOSE-FILL INSULATION

Loose-fill insulation can be used as a direct alernative to blanket insulation (see p.356). Which one you choose is a question of personal preference. Bear in mind that bags of loose-fill insulation are easy to handle and are simpler to transport into the loft than their blanket insulation equivalent. Also, where a loft is awkwardly shaped in its joist design and layout – it may have lots of noggings and inaccessible voids between the joists, for example – loose-fill insulation can provide a more user-friendly, easily installed alternative to common blanket insulation. Be aware that there are conventional and recycled alternatives (see box, right).

USING RECYCLED PAPER

Arguably, the greenest option in loose-fill insulation is shredded recycled paper. This is sometimes used in wall insulation, but can also be blown into loft spaces using a purpose-made applicator. Ensure that an adequate depth has been achieved to ensure thermally efficient results.

LAYING LOOSE-FILL INSULATION

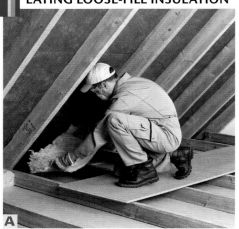

A

First, sweep the voids to remove any debris. To stop the loose-fill leaking out under the eaves, create a barrier where the joists meet the rafters using a small section of blanket insulation. If your roof is covered with non-breathable felt, leave a 50-mm (2-in) gap between the roof and the blanket to allow air to circulate freely.

B

Carefully pour loose-fill insulation into the areas between the joists. Pour in enough to reach the top of the joists. It is best to start at the eaves on one side of the roof and work across to the other.

C

Cut a section of plywood or MDF to the same width as the gap between the joists. Sweep the fill away from you, using the offcut to level it off. Move excess loose-fill to areas that need to be built up.

D

E

When levelled off, you should have an even coverage across the entire loft space. The blanket insulation at the eaves will prevent "creeping".

The depth of the loose-fill will determine any further requirements regarding regulations.

F

If you have an electrical fitting, such as a recessed light from the ceiling below, build a wooden frame around it to keep the loose-fill insulation out.

G

Should you require a deeper layer of loose-fill, you will need a platform from which to work, so that you can safely move across the loft space, as the insulation will obscure the joists from view. A further wedge of blanket insulation may be required at the eaves.

DEEP FILLING

Deep filling can be achieved with loose-fill, but a more practical alternative is to use decking boards above the loose-fill, combining the two to achieve regulation depth, and creating a useable storage space in the loft. Always think about combining insulation – even if you don't create a large storage area, the decking will provide safe access.

INSULATING RAFTERS AND WALLS

If you are converting the loft area into a living space, there are strict regulations on the amount of insulation required. Rafter depth is an issue, as there is often not enough depth to fit the required insulation – you may need to increase the depth of rafters by adding wood to their undersides. The plasterboard will probably need to be insulation-backed (see below); framefoil varieties will need to be stapled across the rafters before applying plasterboard. An air gap is generally required for this, which is achieved by battening of the framefoil – always pay close attention to a manufacturer's specifications. Remember to consider green insulation materials (see box, right).

USING RECYCLED BATTS

Recycled batts are a good alternative to blanket insulation for rafters and walls. They are more eco-friendly, and are often easier to position (blanket insulation can sag before it is secured in place by plasterboard). Either type may need to be cut to fit the exact space between rafters or studs.

INSULATING RAFTERS

In many cases, a dwarf wall is used to partition the eaves area. This makes a more practical space for positioning furniture and fittings. The area behind the wall is treated as a cold insulated roof even though it is a relatively small space. Insulation is laid at joist level to reduce heat loss from the floors below.

Fix lengths of treated timber along the inside edge of each rafter right up against the roof felt. These battens maintain the ventilation gap when non-breathable felt is in place. Even when using breathable felt, it is still good practice to leave this ventilation gap.

If necessary, increase the depth of the fill space by fixing 50 x 50mm (2 x 2in) wooden battens along the roof rafters. Screw them into position.

Infill the space by wedging the blanket between the battens but do not compress the insulation against the underside of the roof.

Wedge the insulation in the gaps between the studs in the dwarf wall. A tight fit is required to ensure that the insulation doesn't fall backwards. Nails can be tapped in along the back edge of the studs to prevent this. Alternatively, use a rigid insulation board instead of blanket insulation.

Cover the rafters and the lower dwarf wall with vapour barrier, then staple the sheets to the joists.

Fix thermal plasterboard to the dwarf wall, butting the boards up against one another.

Stagger the joins between subsequent boards to ensure you have complete coverage. Screw boards to the rafters as you go. For finishing the wall surface, see plastering (pp.128–37).

IMPROVING HOME PERFORMANCE

The ground floors of most modern buildings will have been insulated during construction, but insulating the floors of older buildings can noticeably reduce heat loss and increase energy efficiency – improving a home's green credentials. Some manufacturers specify that insulated floors should be laid "floating", that is, without battens and not secured in place. Similarly, the cavity walls of most modern houses are insulated on construction. Only internal walls tend to be insulated for soundproofing (see pp.362–63), but thermal insulation can be applied if required using the technique shown on p.363. The insulation of cavity walls in existing buildings should be carried out by professionals.

CAVITY-WALL INSULATION

Insulation between the outer and inner walls of a house is fitted in new houses as they are built. The cavity between inner and outer walls in older houses can be insulated by injecting insulation material through holes cut in the outer wall. This should be carried out by a certified contractor. Insulation materials can take the form of expanding foam, granules, or mineral-wool fibres.

INSULATING GAPS BETWEEN FLOORBOARDS

Rooms with bare floorboards are particularly prone to draughts because the boards can move away from each other or away from the walls as they contract and expand. Fill small gaps below the skirting board with a sealant (see pp.80–81). Cover larger gaps with a length of quadrant beading (see p.337).

Heat loss may also result from draughts entering between the boards themselves. Combat this by covering the gaps, perhaps with an underlay (see p.322). If the floorboards are fairly old and have a lot of gaps between them, consider laying a new boarded floor that will fit together more tightly (see pp.180–81).

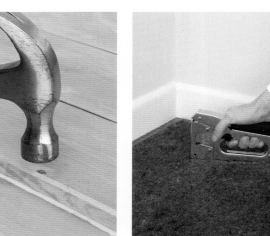

Wood strips
With wide gaps between boards, knock in strips of thin wood then plane them down.

Underlay
If your carpet is thin, or does not have underlay, consider laying underlay for extra insulation.

INSULATING A STUD WALL

Cavities in exterior walls should be filled by professionals (see box, above) but stud walls are normally insulated with blanket insulation. If you have access to the studs, this is a relatively simple task. Most internal stud walls are filled with blanket insulation not so much to prevent heat loss as to provide sound insulation between rooms (see pp.362–63).

A
Erect the studs and plasterboard on one side of the wall (see pp.106–108).

B
Wearing protective clothing, push insulation blanket into the space between the battens. The tight fit of the blanket should hold it in place.

C
When you have filled all of the gaps, screw panels of plasterboard over the top of the battens.

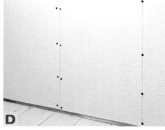

D
Once the plasterboard is in place, you can dry line or skim the wall to create a finished surface (see pp.128–41).

INSULATION BOARDS

You can insulate both concrete and wooden floors using insulation boards. The stage at which they are laid will depend on floor age and type. Damp-proofing membranes are always used in older properties, and help to prevent ground moisture getting into a wood floor.

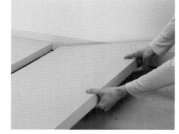

Laying a floating floor
On sound concrete you can lay insulation boards directly on the concrete surface.

Using fitted battens
Where you have battens at intervals across a floor, you can slot insulation panels between them.

Before laying concrete
Where concrete is still to be laid, lay the insulation panels first and then lay the concrete on top.

The slightest gap or crack around a door or window can admit draughts and undermine any insulation measures you have taken. Double-glazed windows and well-fitted frames reduce the risk of draughts, but may not eliminate them entirely. If you have draughts, try fitting excluders around the edges of your doors or windows; those shown here are the most common. Other areas that may let in draughts are keyholes, letterboxes, and fireplaces. An escutcheon will solve the problem with a keyhole, and letterbox draught excluders are available. Disused fireplaces can be blocked off but ensure you have adequate ventilation (see pp.364–65).

DRAUGHT-PROOFING MEASURES

■ Seal draughty fireplaces by boarding off the chimney. Ensure that the chimney is adequately ventilated, with a hit-and-miss vent for example (see p.343).
■ Attach brush seals to the sides of sash windows and rubber strips to where a window touches horizontal surfaces, both at the top and bottom.
■ Avoid losing heat through your windows by closing all curtains and blinds as dusk falls.

DRAUGHT-PROOFING DOORS AND WINDOWS

Both doors and windows settle with age and use, creating gaps that can admit draughts. Seals provide a cheap solution when you do not want the bother of refitting.

Butt up lengths of seal at corners

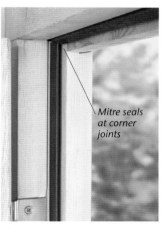

Mitre seals at corner joints

Flexible seal
This is the simplest form of draught excluder. Screw the seals to the bottom of a door. Although really only effective with smooth flooring, they are cheap and easy to install. They are also effective around the top of a door frame, so that the seal flaps onto the door surface when the door is closed.

Brush seal
Very effective at the foot of a door, you should fit a brush seal to the inside of an exterior door. Because they are flexible, brush seals are particularly effective where the floor is uneven, or where you have some form of textured floor covering. They are also good for sash windows and sliding doors.

Self-adhesive strip
Strip insulation is quick and easy to apply, and can be fitted around doors and windows. When the door or window closes onto the strip, the foam compresses to form a tight seal. Cut the foam with a craft knife or scissors, remove the backing tape, and stick it to the rebated edges of the frame.

Slot-fitting compression strip
When a door or window is closed, the compression of this strip creates a very tight, efficient seal. Designed for use with modern doors and windows, compression strips press into the groove in the rebate on a door or window. You can cut the strip with scissors or a craft knife.

FITTING SEALS

Fixing nylon flexible seals and brush seals is a quick and straightforward job. They usually come in standard lengths, and you will probably need to cut them to fit.

A Use a junior hacksaw to cut the seal to the required length. Pinch the plastic channelling with pliers to prevent the bristles falling out.

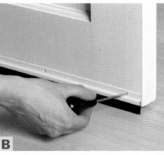

Position the excluder so that its bristles just touch and bend on the floor. Use a bradawl to mark where fixings are needed.

Screw the excluder to the door. Move the door backwards and forwards to check that the excluder is positioned correctly, and that there is a good seal, before securing the final screws.

SEALING FRONT DOORS

Front doors can be a major source of draughts, especially if your home does not have a porch. Ensure that in addition to sealing gaps around the edges of the door, you fit any openings with coverings.

Escutcheon coverplate
Choose an escutcheon (keyhole surround) with a coverplate.

Letterbox brush excluder
Keeps out draughts even when post is held in the letterbox.

SOUNDPROOFING A ROOM

Regulations on noise pollution are always tightening, so when planning any renovation or construction work, check the local regulations. Seek advice from a building control officer, as you may need to add soundproofing measures at the same time. Noise pollution comes in two forms – airborne and impact – and soundproofing products are often classified by the type of noise they affect. Airborne sound can be created by televisions, stereos, or speech. Impact noise travels as vibrations through solid materials, and includes footsteps or furniture being moved. Soundproofing a floor is easier than soundproofing a ceiling, but if you live in a block of flats you may not have a choice.

REDUCING SOUND TRAVEL

■ Sound travels on air. Making a room "airtight" reduces the amount of sound that can escape.
■ Using acoustically efficient materials to add mass to a structure increases its ability to absorb sound.
■ Structural elements carry sound, so creating a barrier between them prevents sounds travelling across a room.
■ Use acoustic sealant, flanking tape, or flanking strips to isolate a structural element.
■ Seal the edges of walls and floors to prevent sound travelling to the next room.

SOUNDPROOFING A FLOOR

Combining acoustic underlay with acoustic mats beneath a floor reduces the effects of both airborne and impact noise. If the problem is solely impact noise, underlay alone may suffice. Remove the coverings to reveal the floor (see Flooring, pp.322–43). If the floor is to be carpeted, leave the skirting board in place and proceed as shown below. For other floorings (see right), remove the skirting and lay out the acoustic underlay, butting the lengths up against one another and allowing them to lap a short distance up the wall. Tape all joints, and then lay acoustic mat, ensuring that any joins do not coincide with the joins of the underlay. Lay a floating tongue-and-groove chipboard floor over the top, and trim the edges of the underlay. You may then fit further floor coverings, such as laminated flooring.

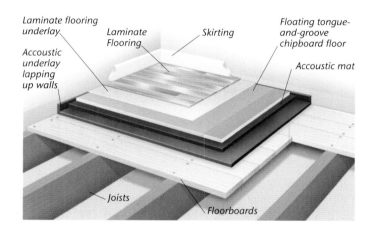

Laminate flooring underlay / Laminate Flooring / Skirting / Floating tongue-and-groove chipboard floor / Accoustic underlay lapping up walls / Accoustic mat / Joists / Floorboards

Skirting / Carpet / Gripper rod / Accoustic underlay / Accoustic mat / Batten / Floorboards / Joists

Soundproofing hard floors

A combination of acoustic underlay with acoustic mats and chipboard sheets is a very straightforward option for effective soundproofing. Here it is fitted below a floating chipboard floor, over which underlay and laminate flooring are laid.

Soundproofing carpeted floors

When soundproofing floors that are to be carpeted, first install battens around the room's perimeter, then lay acoustic mats and underlay between, and butting up against, the battens. Fit gripper rods to the battens and lay the carpet.

DOORS AND WINDOWS

■ Double glazing windows or glass doors improves sound insulation, as well as thermal insulation.
■ If noise from outside is a major problem, consider triple glazing.
■ Thermal insulation extruders fitted around doors and windows will insulate them against sound as well as heat loss.

Flooring materials and soundproofing

As soundproofing involves the building up of materials, thick floor coverings are more soundproof. For example, cushioned vinyl is more effective than regular vinyl. You can lay sheet vinyl over a soundproofed chipboard floor and fix it with double-sided adhesive tape. Similarly, high-quality hessian-backed carpets will prevent sound travel better than cheaper foam-backed carpets.

Do not add flanking strips to a carpeted floor. The fact that the carpet stretches across the gripper rods and makes contact with the skirting board should provide protection enough against flanking noise.

SOUNDPROOFING A CEILING

There are two main methods of soundproofing a ceiling. One is to use soundbreaker bars. These are lightweight metal channels that separate wall and ceiling surfaces, preventing airborne and impact noise from travelling through them. They provide a frame to which plasterboard can be fixed. The other method is to lower the ceiling by building a false ceiling beneath the existing one.

In both examples shown below, the plasterboard of the existing ceiling has been stripped away first. An alternative to these is to fit soundbreaker bars directly onto the ceiling, in a similar way to that shown for walls (bottom, left). Where the existing ceiling is high enough to permit it, the second technique may be used, but without removing the plasterboard on the existing ceiling.

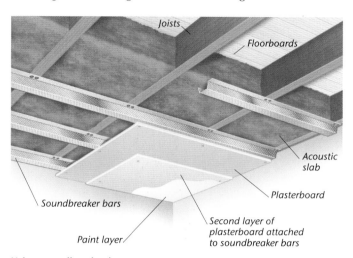

Joists

Floorboards

Acoustic slab

Plasterboard

Soundbreaker bars

Paint layer

Second layer of plasterboard attached to soundbreaker bars

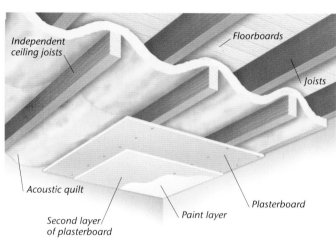

Independent ceiling joists

Floorboards

Joists

Acoustic quilt

Second layer of plasterboard

Paint layer

Plasterboard

Using soundbreaker bars
Remove the plasterboard from the existing ceiling and fix soundbreaker bars across the joists at intervals of 400mm (1ft 4in). Fit acoustic slabs 100mm (4in) deep above these bars, between the joists. Attach two layers of plasterboard, one 12mm (½in) thick, then one 9mm (⅜in) thick, staggering the joins. Twin-layered board is available, and is a quicker option, but ultimately would be more costly.

Using independent ceiling joists
Expose the existing joists and insert new ones between them. (The technique for fixing new joists is covered on p.101.) The lower faces of the new joists should be at least 55mm (2in) below the faces of the existing joists. You should then weave a layer of acoustic quilt between the two joist levels, as shown, before attaching two layers of plasterboard to the lower joists in the usual way.

SOUNDPROOFING A WALL

The principles for soundproofing ceilings and floors from below can also be applied to walls. For example, you can fit soundbreaker bars directly to the surface of an existing wall, as shown below left. If losing a little space in the room is not a problem, build a completely new, independent wall in front of the existing structure. This is most easily done with a metal stud wall (see p.109) as it is quick and creates little mess. Build it 25mm (1in) away from the original wall. You can then insert acoustic slab between the stud uprights to create a soundproof layer.

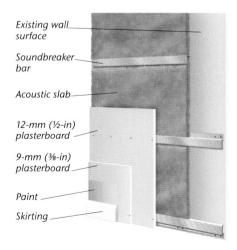

Existing wall surface

Soundbreaker bar

Acoustic slab

12-mm (½-in) plasterboard

9-mm (⅜-in) plasterboard

Paint

Skirting

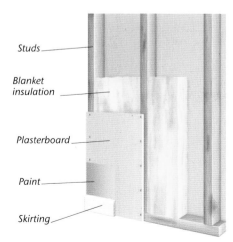

Studs

Blanket insulation

Plasterboard

Paint

Skirting

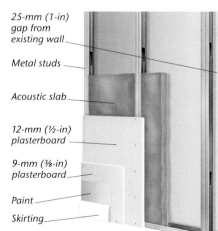

25-mm (1-in) gap from existing wall

Metal studs

Acoustic slab

12-mm (½-in) plasterboard

9-mm (⅜-in) plasterboard

Paint

Skirting

Using soundbreaker bars
Make sure that the open side of the ground-level soundbreaker bar is facing upwards. In the others it should face downwards.

Increasing mass
Adding to the mass of a stud wall will help it to absorb sound. Adding blanket insulation will also improve its thermal insulation.

Adding an independent wall
When creating a metal stud wall, make sure that the acoustic slab is rigid enough to remain vertical between the metal studs.

Efficient ventilation removes odours, dangerous fumes, and vapour-laden air trapped inside a home before they can cause any damage, discomfort, or harm. Condensation occurs when moist, warm air comes in contact with cold surfaces. It is easily visible on glass, walls, or ceilings, but it can also form on carpets and curtains. Damp surfaces may decay over time, and the resulting mould and fungus can cause an unhealthy living environment. Insulation, double-glazing, and heating can all lessen condensation but good channels for ventilation and the free flow of air must be fitted.

HEALTH AND SAFETY

When installing a fan, make sure that the extracted air is replaced by fresh air – especially in a room containing a fuel-burning appliance that does not have a balanced flue. Failure to provide fresh air can cause a fatal buildup of carbon monoxide in a room. Fuel-burning appliances should be regularly checked and serviced. If you have any doubts about how to ventilate an appliance, get professional advice before proceeding.

STATIC VENTILATION

A simple hole, usually at the top or base of a wall, with grills to let air in or out, provides static ventilation. Some interior grills can be closed, but others are fixed open for constant airflow. Static ventilation is mandatory in rooms with a fuel-burning appliance, and is often used for venting tumble driers. Disused chimneys also need static ventilation to circulate fresh air and prevent discolouring damp patches appearing on the chimney breast. "Trickle vents" in window frames provide ventilation even when the windows are closed.

Cutting ventilation holes

When a round hole is required, hire a core drill bit to cut through masonry (see below). This is an expensive tool that you are unlikely to use often. Use a drywall saw on timber. See opposite for the choice of vents and ducting.

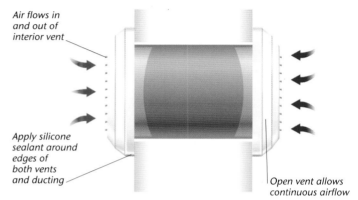

Air flows in and out of interior vent

Apply silicone sealant around edges of both vents and ducting

Open vent allows continuous airflow

Wall-mounted static vent
Ducting running through the wall connects grills fixed on the inside and outside of the wall.

▌▌ USING A CORE DRILL BIT ON A MASONRY WALL

Make sure you have a drill bit of the correct size for your ducting. Get advice on fitting the bit from the hire shop, as the system may differ from standard drills. Be prepared for the core drill to be heavy and arduous to work with. Protect yourself by wearing goggles, ear defenders, and a dust mask.

A

B

Draw a guide mark on the surface of the interior wall. Use the point of the masonry bit to begin drilling. This will direct the cylindrical core.

The cylindrical core section will cut the large hole needed. Keep the drill level or pointing slightly downwards as you progress.

Allow to cool before handling

C

D

Carefully remove the core. If it is a cavity wall, continue through the exterior section of the wall.

Insert ducting, as required. Here, a flexible length of ducting from a tumble drier is being inserted. Connect with a grill on the exterior wall.

EXTRACTOR FANS

You can ventilate most kitchens and bathrooms with a fan carrying air a short distance through a wall (an axial fan). Wall- or ceiling-mounted fans (below left) have their electric components directly behind a grill, and must not be used within reach of water. To ventilate a shower cubicle, use an in-line fan (below right), which is fitted with a length of ducting between the grill and the electric parts. Some kitchen fans are built into a cabinet or hood (see p.249). When choosing a fan, consider the sound it makes (you may want a "low noise" fan for an en suite bathroom), its power, and the manufacturer's advice for a specific fan's use. Most can be wired into the lighting circuit to run when a light is on (usually with a timer so that it continues for a while after the light is switched off), or operated separately with a pull-cord.

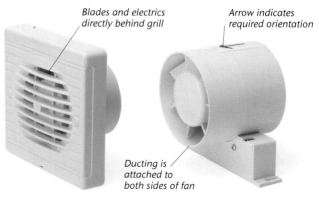

Blades and electrics directly behind grill

Arrow indicates required orientation

Ducting is attached to both sides of fan

WALL-MOUNTED FAN

IN-LINE FAN

Installing an in-line fan

The most common position for an in-line fan is near or above a shower cubicle. It is connected by ducting, which takes the air from the fan through a wall, roof, or soffit to an exit vent. The advantage of positioning this vent in a fascia or soffit board is that the hole for it can be cut with a drywall saw – as can the hole in the ceiling above the shower. If the hole must be through masonry, you will need to hire a core drill bit (see opposite). Make sure you have the correct power supply in place, and follow the wiring instructions closely (see pp.426–61 on working with electricity).

Installing a wall-mounted fan

Position the fan so that it is as high as possible in the wall opposite the main door. Ensure that you have the correct power supply and follow the wiring and safety instructions closely (see also pp.426–61). If you are mounting the fan in a pane of glass, check that the pane is at least the minimum thickness recommended by the manufacturer.

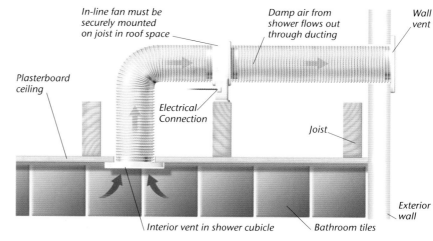

In-line fan must be securely mounted on joist in roof space

Damp air from shower flows out through ducting

Wall vent

Plasterboard ceiling

Electrical Connection

Joist

Interior vent in shower cubicle

Bathroom tiles

Exterior wall

In-line fan
In this set-up, the interior vent is in the ceiling over a shower cubicle with the fan in the attic at a safe distance from water.

Electrical connection

Exterior wall surface

Cowled vent protects fan from weather

Blades and electrics behind grill

Interior wall surface

Air exits here

Wall-mounted fan
Choose a fan by comparing the manufacturer's power guidelines to your needs. Power is usually measured in cubic metres of air extracted per hour.

VENTS AND DUCTING

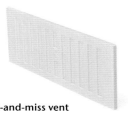

Hit-and-miss vent
Static vent that can be opened as required. Must not be used with any appliance that burns fuel.

Louvre vent
Standard grill is fixed open, making this type of vent suitable for use with appliances that burn fuel.

Plastic airbrick
Used under suspended floors (see p.177), or in attic gable walls. Also available in brick.

DEHUMIDIFIERS

Removing moisture from the air reduces dampness and condensation, and therefore helps to deal with their associated problems. An excellent way of doing this is to use a small, portable dehumidifier. You can move these around the home easily and place them in any room or space that has a damp or condensation problem. The dehumidifier collects water in a tank that is then emptied.

Plastic, flat, rigid channel ducting
Rectangular in cross-section, often used to vent kitchen extractor fans through or above wall units.

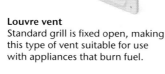

Round, rigid channel ducting
An alternative to flat, rigid ducting. Most rounded ducting is flexible (see right, and above).

Aluminium flexible ducting
Easy to use when installing in-line ventilation in a roof space. This is also made in PVC (see above).

Operating switches and "tank full" indicator

Make sure grill is not obstructed

Flat channel connector
Moulded to connect two lengths of flat channel ducting where a long length of ducting is required.

Flexible round-hose connector
Joins sections of flexible hose, but is also suitable for connecting rigid channel ducting.

Round-to-rectangular connector
Connects a length of rounded channel ducting to a length of flat channel ducting.

PORTABLE UNIT

Home security

INTRUDERS FEAR DETECTION, MAKING LIGHT AND SOUND EXCELLENT DETERRENTS TO UNWELCOME VISITORS. WITH AN INCREASE IN THE AVAILABILITY AND RELIABILITY OF BATTERY-OPERATED ALARM SYSTEMS, FITTING THEM YOURSELF IS NOW EASY AND QUICK. THIS SECTION DEALS WITH ISSUES OF SECURITY IN THE HOME AS WELL AS ISSUES OF SAFETY.

INSTALLING AN ALARM SYSTEM

The vast majority of alarm systems use sensors to detect movement or magnetic contact plates that set off the alarm when parted. The most commonly used sensors are called Passive InfraRed detectors (PIRs), which detect the movement of a heat source. The most important thing to consider when installing alarms is the positioning of these sensors, so that they can monitor all the necessary zones in your home.

SECURITY HOUSE PLAN

A sensor is placed at each access point to your house, which divides the area into zones. This lets you see at a glance where a zone has been breached, or where some maintenance is required. Front, back, and patio doors, windows, and fire escapes should be considered, although you may decide that some windows are inaccessible.

PIR POSITIONING TIPS

■ Know the detection range of your PIR.
■ Detection of movement across the detection arc is better than of movement towards or away from the sensor.
■ Do not position PIRs in direct sunlight or near a heat source, unless instructed to do so, or if solar power is required for operation.
■ Avoid areas of excessive vibration or where there are draughts.
■ If you live in a flat, you may only need to consider detection around the front door area, although you may need to consider window access in ground- and first-floor flats.

Remember that pets will have to be kept out of zones when the alarm is on unless you buy a system that can detect them by being sensitive to size. When you purchase an alarm it is worth checking for any extra features such as a panic button, or anti-tamper safeguards for sensors and the control panel.

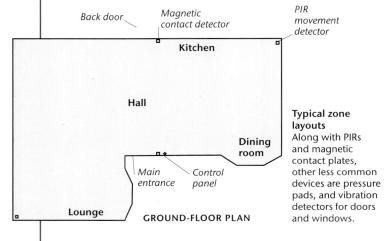

Back door — Magnetic contact detector — PIR movement detector

Kitchen

Hall

Dining room

Main entrance — Control panel

Lounge

GROUND-FLOOR PLAN

Typical zone layouts
Along with PIRs and magnetic contact plates, other less common devices are pressure pads, and vibration detectors for doors and windows.

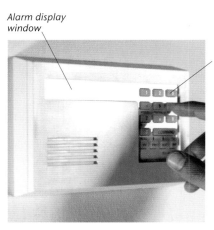

Alarm display window

Keypad

Arming and disarming alarm systems
Take time to study your instruction manual so that you fully understand how to arm and disarm the system. Large systems may allow you to alarm just some zones of the house as well as the whole house.

WIRED, PART-WIRED, OR WIRELESS?

Traditional alarms are hard-wired into the home's main electricity supply. However wireless or part-wired systems are now widely available.

Wired systems

Although these take longer to install there is no need to worry about replacing or recharging batteries. Professional installers tend to use hard-wired alarms.

Part-wired systems

Some alarms require the control panel to be wired into the mains electricity supply. However, many have the option to run off a built-in rechargeable battery and the panel can be removed and recharged at a power point when necessary.

Wireless systems

These can literally be set up in hours because there is no need for complicated cable routing and electrical connection. The PIRs, magnetic contacts for doors and windows, and the main control panel are all battery-operated, and the external bellbox is often solar-powered. The main drawback of wireless alarms is that batteries need replacing or recharging, although many systems give a prompt if maintenance is necessary.

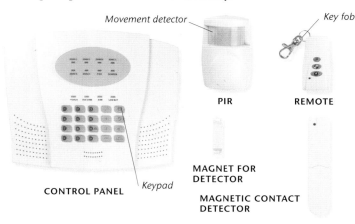

Movement detector — PIR — Key fob — REMOTE

MAGNET FOR DETECTOR

MAGNETIC CONTACT DETECTOR

CONTROL PANEL — Keypad

INSTALLING MAGNETIC CONTACT DETECTORS

The detector should be located on the fixed frame and the magnet on the door or opening light of the window. With the wireless example shown here, batteries must be inserted in the detector before it is fixed in place. Many contact detector kits are convertible in that they can be installed wired or wireless. The alignment and distance between the detector and contact is crucial, so the manufacturer's guidelines need to be closely followed.

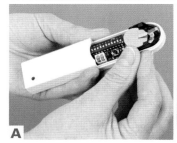

Insert battery into the main body of the detector.

Fix both detector and magnet in place on the door or window edge, ensuring that they are correctly aligned.

FITTING A BATTERY-OPERATED PIR

Once position has been decided, fixing a PIR in place is a straightforward task. For hard-wired systems, cable connection and routing becomes necessary, but for a wireless alarm, secure positioning and correct battery insertion is all that is required.

Remove the front cover of the PIR. You may need to undo a small grub screw in order to release the cover.

Some PIRs need to be set internally. This involves setting "DIP" switches inside the PIR.

Insert the battery and replace the front cover.

Hold the base plate in position and mark for pilot holes. Plug if necessary before fixing in place.

Refit front cover. In the example shown here a grub screw needs tightening on the underside of the PIR.

CCTV

These systems are becoming a more viable DIY installation task. Systems may either be linked up to a separate monitor, or directly to your TV and be connected to a video recorder. The majority of systems use PIR sensors, and wireless options are available. When the PIR senses a movement, the camera transmits the image to a receiver unit that is connected via a scart and socket cable to the monitor or TV. This automatic system can be bypassed by using the remote control. Follow the system manufacturer's instructions to plan and install a CCTV system.

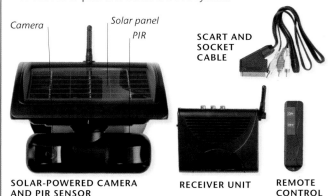

Camera — Solar panel — PIR — SCART AND SOCKET CABLE

SOLAR-POWERED CAMERA AND PIR SENSOR — RECEIVER UNIT — REMOTE CONTROL

All doors and windows are potential points of entry to a house and each must therefore be adequately secured. The primary security features for external doors are covered on pp.168–69. However there are also secondary systems that you can use in addition to these. Examples of many such systems are shown here, but be aware that there are many proprietary designs available. All have slight variations in the ways in which they are fitted and used; always follow any specific instructions that are provided.

PUSH-BUTTON LOCKS AND KEYPADS

It is now possible to add different types of push-button locks to your doors to provide a very secure entry system, eliminating the need for a key. These used to be a very expensive option, but they are now far more competitively priced. Keypad systems are similar, but require electrical connections. In this case, it is best to employ a specialist firm to install the system.

DOOR SECURITY

Items such as door limiters, security chains, and surface-mounted door bolts are straightforward to fit as they are simply positioned on the appropriate place on a door or frame and screwed into position. Items such as hinge bolts, mortise door bolts, and door viewers require a little more thought in positioning and installation. This is because slightly more involved woodworking techniques are required to ensure that they are fitted securely and correctly.

Door viewer
Allows you to check identity of a visitor before unlocking any part of the door. Versions with a viewer escutcheon provide even greater security.

Viewer escutcheon   *Thread*

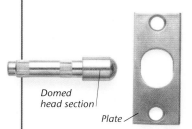

Hinge bolt
Adds greater security to the hinging edge of a door so that it cannot be forced open and/or off its hinges. Normally at least two are fitted.

Domed head section   *Plate*

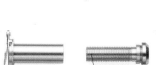

Door bolt key

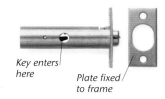

Key enters here   *Plate fixed to frame*

Mortise door bolt
Sometimes called a door security bolt or rack bolt. These are operated by a key and allow extra security along any edge of the door. Normally sited along the opening edge of the door.

Lock body   *Screws secure to door*   *Fit to frame*   *Fit in door*

Surface-mounted locking bolt
This differs from a standard surface-mounted bolt in that it is operated with a key and therefore offers greater security.

Patio door bolt
Specially designed bolt for use with most types of sliding patio door.

Bolt knob

Decorative door bolt
A design of bolt that provides security and decorative appeal. Some designs are rebated into the face or edge of the door.

Move to disengage

Security chain
Allows a door to be opened slightly to check identity, before the chain is disengaged allowing the door to open fully. A door limiter is similar to a door chain and offers a different design option.

▮▮ FITTING A HINGE BOLT

Hinge bolts should be fitted in pairs as a minimum requirement, one below the upper door hinge and one above the lower door hinge. For extra security a third and even a fourth bolt may be used.

A
Drill a hole into the door edge; its dimensions should be specified by the manufacturer.

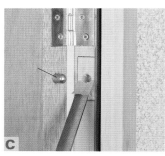

B
Hammer in the ribbed section of the bolt into this hole, leaving the smooth domed section protruding from the door edge.

C
Gently close the door to mark the frame. Position the plate, draw a guide line around it, and chisel out to a depth equal to the plate. Drill a central hole to house the bolt.

D
Screw the hinge bolt plate in place, and check that the door opens and closes smoothly. Use the same technique to fit further bolts as required.

FITTING A MORTISE DOOR BOLT

A Mark the position of the bolt on the door's edge, then drill a hole to accommodate the bolt; follow manufacturer's guidelines for depth.

B Remove any dust from the hole and insert the bolt.

C Draw a pencil line around the edge of the end plate.

D Chisel out the depth required to recess the plate.

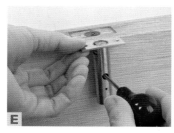

E Hold the bolt to the interior of the door and mark the point for the key hole. Drill through to the bolt hole using the recommended drill bit.

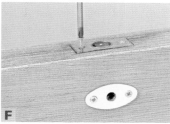

F Re-position the bolt, secure it in place, then fix the key cover plate into position.

G Turn the key to ensure that the bolt works.

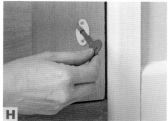

H Drill a hole in the door frame to accommodate the bolt. Fit the strike plate. Hang the door and turn the key to lock.

WINDOW SECURITY

Modern windows often have security features built in to their design. This may range from locking fasteners to multi-point mortise locks that are operated automatically as the window is fastened shut. The items shown here are additional features that may be used as secondary security options for windows.

Frame attachment

Window attachment

Casement window lock
Two-part lock for sealing casement windows (see below).

Screw

Window screw bolt
Two parts engage when casement is closed. Secured with key-operated screw.

Bolt

Metal window lock
Bolt screws down into the stay of the casement window.

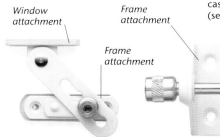

Window attachment

Frame attachment

Ventilation lock
Allows casement window to be locked open for ventilation.

Frame attachment

Window stay bolt
Screws over the stay on casement or pivot windows.

Key

Sash window lock
Fits through both sections of sash; when aligned, the bolt is screwed into place.

Upper sash attachment

Lower sash bolt

Key

Hole

Sash window press bolt
Plates align when sash window closes; the bolt is pressed into place.

Lower sash plate

Upper sash plate

FITTING A CASEMENT WINDOW LOCK

A With the window closed, use a bradawl to mark positions for the striking plate on the frame and the locking body on the casement.

B Pilot drill if necessary and then secure the locking body in place.

C Fix the striking plate in place.

D Close the window and check the lock using the supplied key.

Aside from the door and window security fittings discussed on pp.368–69, there are other areas of the home that can be improved with the addition of other types of locking system. These systems can supplement existing security, or they can also become the main burglar deterrent. Many of these systems are designed for security outside the house, in areas such as garages, sheds, and even for vehicle security. The options are always growing.

KEYLESS LOCKS

The disadvantage of any key-operated system is that the key can be lost. Combination locks are an alternative. They open when you enter the right number. With a combination padlock, you can change the combination number to one you will remember.

COMBINATION PADLOCK

CHOOSING LOCKS AND CHAINS

Numerous padlocks and chains are available for use in home security. The security rating of a padlock is generally related to its size and cost, and the same can be said for chains, which are generally used for looping through gates or securing movable items like ladders or motorcycles. The best use of each item is usually specified by the manufacturer.

Attach to frame
Attach to door

Pad bolt
This is much the same as a standard door bolt, except that it can be secured using a padlock.

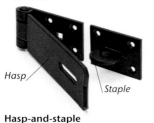

Hasp
Staple

Hasp-and-staple
A hasp-and-staple provides a reliable way of padlocking a door (see right).

Open-shackle padlock
Traditional padlock shape with the shackle in the form of an elongated loop.

Closed-shackle padlock
Here the shackle is flush with the main body of the lock, making it awkward to saw through.

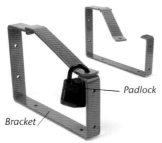

Padlock
Bracket

Security bracket
Brackets are useful for storing ladders; lock at least one bracket to the ladder.

Lock
Key

D-lock
This D-shaped frame is ideal for locking bicycles.

PVC covering

Security chain
Steel chains are commonly used for padlocking motorcycles and gates.

Keyhole

Locking cable
This hardened steel cable is perfect for locking down large items such as lawnmowers and motorcycles.

SECURING OUTBUILDINGS

Garages and sheds are particularly vulnerable to burglary and should always be well secured; not only do they contain valuable items, but some items can be used by burglars to gain access to the main house. Ladders are the most obvious aid, but any number of garden tools can be used to force entry. Most of the systems shown on the left are ideal for use in garages and sheds. Looks are not important with these items. Choose those that achieve the greatest level of security.

▌▌ FITTING A GARAGE HASP-AND-STAPLE

Padlock security is commonly used on outbuildings because the doors often do not have the thickness to accommodate cylinder locks or mortise locks. Where door design does allow, padlocks are often used as a second line of defence. The best way of using a padlock is by hanging it through a hasp-and-staple mechanism. When installing the latter, the plate of the hasp must be fitted so that it hides the fixings of both hasp and staple when locked. When choosing a padlock, be sure that it is suitable for outdoor use; "all-weather use" is a common manufacturer's specification. In the sequence below, a combination padlock is used. The main alternative to a hasp-and-staple is a pad bolt with a padlock.

A Mark out the fixing holes for the hasp. Make pilot holes for the screws.

B Screw the hasp to the door.

C Mark out the fixing holes for the staple. Make pilot holes for the screws, then screw the staple to the door.

D Secure the hasp-and-staple with a padlock.

VEHICLE SECURITY

Some security devices have been designed specifically with vehicles in mind. These provide a second line of defence to complement any features built into the vehicle itself. Some are portable, such as a wheel clamp, whereas others are permanently or partly fixed in place, such as a parking post. Although manufacturers are constantly improving vehicle security, the separate devices shown here can only help to discourage an opportunistic thief.

Hasp

Anchor bed

Ground anchor

This provides a secure anchoring for large, movable objects such as workshop equipment, trailers, and motorcycles. The anchor bed is fixed to the ground with large security bolts.

DETACHABLE POST

Padlock

BASE OF POST

CONCRETE BEDDING

Parking post

When locked in its upright position, a parking post provides an obstacle to moving a car. Designs vary, and include an electronic, remote-control version. Some installation work is needed as the post base needs to be set in concrete.

Wheel clamp

Fixed around wheels, this clamp ensures that a car or trailer cannot be moved. There are many different designs of this portable security system.

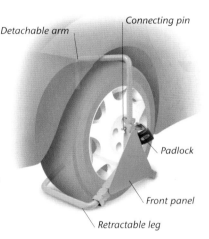

Detachable arm

Connecting pin

Padlock

Front panel

Retractable leg

USING A SAFE

A safe provides a last line of defence when securing items at home. Small safes must be secured in position to ensure that they cannot be moved. Their ideal location is on a concrete floor, although they may also be mounted on a wall. Fixings, normally coach bolts, are usually supplied by the manufacturer. The example shown below is just one option – there are many designs of house safe, with different features. Some may be disguised as electrical sockets, while others are bolted to the underside of desks, drawer systems, or behind paintings. The fire rating of a particular safe may also be something worth considering, especially if it is holding important documents.

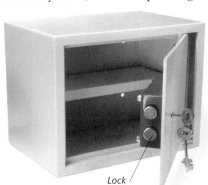

Lock

Using a safe

A safe is only secure if the keys for it are kept hidden in another part of the home. Push-button or keypad versions are also available.

OTHER WAYS TO KEEP YOUR HOME SECURE

In addition to conventional security devices, there are a number of other steps you can take to deter burglars. Many of these do not cost anything, but simply involve adapting your behaviour.

Alarms

Consider installing a burglar alarm. Some are linked up to the local police station. Before installing this type, check the local policy on false alarms, and that there is enough local manpower to respond to such systems. For alarm installation, see p.366–67.

Other deterrents

Lay a gravel driveway; it gives an excellent early warning system. Make sure you have good exterior lighting so that burglars cannot conceal themselves. Install a peephole in the front door so that you can see who is there before opening the door. Plant prickly shrubs in hedges to put off intruders.

Changing your routine

If you go on holiday, cancel all deliveries, including newspapers; the latter are often left in the letterbox. Arrange for a friend to clear any post from view. Install automatic light timers in your home; whenever you are away, set them to mimic your normal schedule.

Protecting young children around the home is an important consideration for many people. There are a number of different products available that can help to make your home more childproof, and most of these are shown here. Also outlined in this section are various precautions and tips that can create a safer environment for children to grow up in. When purchasing any child safety products, make sure that they have the relevant safety certification, and be sure to follow any instructions provided by the manufacturer. Never use second-hand safety equipment unless you are certain of its history.

EXTERIOR CHILDPROOFING

Make sure that walls and fences are regularly maintained to avoid children leaving the boundaries of your home. Remove any rough wood, or flaky paint (especially if it is lead-based paint), and cover ponds to prevent children falling in. Unstable bricks and blocks should be fixed or removed, and make sure that garden steps are in good condition. Any play areas are best laid with soft coverings such as grass or bark chippings.

SAFETY GUARDS AND GADGETS

The majority of safety fittings are quick and easy to fit – most can be adapted to fit a particular design. For example, toilet lid locks will generally fit the majority of toilets, but it is advisable to check dimensions first. It is very much an individual decision in terms of what are essential and what are non-essential items. However, there are various items, such as stair gates and fire guards, that the majority of parents consider a necessity.

Cooker and hob guard
Helps prevent a child getting too near to cooker surfaces.

Hob guard in position

A fire guard
This is placed in front of an open fire to keep children away. It may be necessary to screw in wall anchors to hold it in position.

Attaches to wall fixings

Folding sections

A corner protector
This is clipped on to a table corner to make it less sharp. It can also be used on other sharp corners around the home.

Normally self-adhesive

Glass safety film
Applied over glass, it prevents shards flying through the air if the window breaks or shatters.

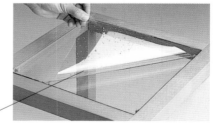

Smooth adhesive onto surface

Door slam stopper
Prevents a door slamming, reducing the risk of fingers being caught in the door.

Flexible shape

Fits on door edge

Stair gate
This is fitted to both the top and the bottom of the stairs, to prevent a young child climbing or descending unaccompanied. The gate may also be fixed across the entrance to a room to control access to a particular area in the home. Before buying a stair gate, check the dimensions of the stairway and/or entrance to ensure you get the correct design and size. Some designs are pressure-fitted to avoid the need for screw fixings to hold the gate in place.

Position gate at specified height

An electrical outlet cover
Clips over sockets to prevent children pushing their fingers or objects into the pinholes.

Push into socket

Stops fingers

SAFETY LOCKS AND CATCHES

Many gadgets are designed to prevent storage units being opened and to prevent windows being opened too wide. There are numerous designs on offer and therefore a wide selection to choose from. Keeping children out of cupboards or drawers prevents fingers being trapped and denies them access to fragile or dangerous items.

A fridge lock
Not only stops a child from raiding the contents of the fridge, but it also prevents the door being left open and the contents ruined.

Fits around corner of fridge

Release button

Cabinet slide lock
This lock clamps around cabinet doors and so prevents either door being opened.

Slides into place

Hooks over handle

Video lock
Stops children pushing items or hands into the video slot. Simple to fit.

Release button

Pushes into place

Drawer and cupboard catch
This stops drawers and cupboards being opened by a child. There are many types available.

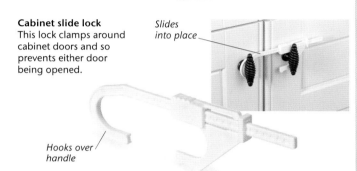

Used in drawers

Used on cupboards

A window limiter catch
This is designed to prevent a child opening a window wide enough to jump out. It needs to be screwed in place, with one part on the frame, and the other on the moving casement.

Stay release

Limited opening size

FITTING AN EMERGENCY-RELEASE DOOR LATCH

These latches are used to prevent a child being locked inside a room. Privacy door latches with a lever handle may be fitted using a similar technique to that shown for fitting a locking latch (p.168). If the handle is a knob design, the technique has to be altered to account for cutting a large access hole in the door to deal with the locking mechanism. Most such mechanisms are opened from the outside using a key inserted into the handle. Some designs simply have a lever that can be turned, or a large slotted screw that can be turned to undo the lock. Many also have a template to follow when fitting.

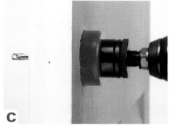

A

B

Measure exact central point for access hole, on both sides of the door. If supplied, use a template.

Attach a hole cutter to a cordless drill; the correct size will be specified by the latch manufacturer. Drill into one door face.

C

D

Stop drilling when the bit exits the opposite door face.

Change to the opposite side of the door, drilling until the cutter reaches the cut on the other side.

Large hole to accommodate handles

E

F

Drill or cut out the edge of the door to accommodate the latch mechanism (see p.162).

Chisel a recess for the latch plate, then fit the latch into the hole.

G

H

Position the handles, threading the spindle through the latch mechanism as shown.

Tighten the screws, then close the door to check that the mechanism works.

The effects of fire can be devastating, and it is therefore necessary to take precautions to prevent fire in the home. Be sure to have adequate early warning systems, as well as effective escape routes should a fire occur. The first port of call for further advice on fire security should be your local fire safety officer. They can provide help and advice relevant to your particular circumstances and can also advise on any fire safety stipulations that are part of your building regulations. This is essential when any major renovation or building work is being carried out.

MAINS OPERATION
Mains-operated alarms are wired up to a dedicated permanent supply that cannot be accidentally turned off by the average user. They should also have battery back-up in the event of power failure. Mains-operated systems are more common in newly built premises. All electrical safety guidelines must be followed (see pp.432–33) before installing mains-operated systems.

ALARMS AND HEAT DETECTORS
One of the most effective early warning systems is the smoke alarm. The terms "smoke alarm" and "smoke detector" have become the generic terms for these devices, although some react to heat rather than smoke.

Smoke alarms
The two main types of smoke alarm are battery operated and mains operated (see above right). The former are easy to install and need regular battery checks. The alarm should have a warning system to indicate when power is low, and should be checked according to the manufacturer's guidelines. Most are tested by pressing a button that sounds the alarm. At the very least, smoke detectors should be located on every floor of your home.

BATTERY-OPERATED SMOKE ALARM

MAINS-OPERATED ALARM

Heat detectors
Heat detectors are often slightly smaller in appearance compared to smoke detectors. They tend to be used in areas such as kitchens where a smoke detector may be too sensitive to cooking fumes.

Carbon monoxide alarms
These are now essential fittings for homes. They look similar to smoke detectors, and are located close to fuel burning appliances and sleeping areas. Carbon monoxide is an odourless gas emitted by fossil fuels during combustion. When fittings are not vented correctly or are functioning incorrectly, carbon monoxide builds up in the home; high levels may be fatal. Alarms are normally located on walls between 1m and 1.5m (3ft and 4ft) above floor level.

HEAT DETECTOR *Battery warning light*

CARBON MONOXIDE DETECTOR

FITTING A BATTERY-OPERATED ALARM

Mark off fixing points on ceiling surface. Ideally fix into a ceiling joist; use the wall plugs and fittings that are supplied.

A

B

Use pilot hole fixings if fixing directly into joist, or use cavity wall plugs if fixing into plasterboard.

C

Screw plate into position, ensuring it is secure.

D

Fit the battery into the alarm, checking the connection carefully.

E

Close up the hinged alarm casing.

F

Press the test button on the alarm to check that it is working.

TACKLING A FIRE

As a rule you should never try to tackle a major fire on your own. However, it is important to know how to deal with minor fires, and for this a fire blanket and a fire extinguisher are essential. Another possibility is to have a sprinkler system installed. If in any doubt as to what equipment to buy, contact your local fire service for advice.

Hose

Water fire extinguisher
Water extinguishers are designed for use on paper, wood, and textile fires.

Pressure gauge

Foam fire extinguisher
Like water, foam removes heat by absorption. Can also be used on flammable liquid fires.

Operation levers

Horn

Carbon dioxide fire extinguisher
This takes away the oxygen needed for combustion. Not to be used in confined spaces.

Hooks over window sill

Stand off

Valve

Operation lever

Powder fire extinguisher
The powder smothers the fire, preventing oxygen from fuelling the flames.

Blanket folded in bag

Pull straps to remove blanket

Fire blanket
This is designed for covering chip-pan fires, or wrapping someone up if they are on fire. A fire blanket is best located in the kitchen.

Escape routes
It is essential to have planned escapes routes for use in the event of a fire. For upper floors this may mean having an escape ladder or two; these can be bought in various lengths.

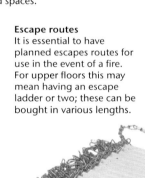

Chain stiles

Ladder compacts into small storage area

FIRE DOORS AND WINDOWS

The type of doors and windows you have can make the difference between life and death during a fire. Both can be adapted to maximize your safety.

Fire doors
These are very effective for hindering a fire and providing extra time for escape. They are more commonly found in commercial premises, but they can be a regulation in domestic premises, especially in multi-storey dwellings and properties with integral garages. They are hung using the same techniques as for normal doors, but in addition they need to be fitted with some form of door closer (see p.165). As well as the door having a fire rating, the hinges are also fire rated. Intumescent strips can be used around the door perimeter. These swell up under the effects of heat, sealing around the edge of the door. Intumescent paint is also available; on heating, this produces a char layer that insulates the door from fire.

Windows
Most windows afford vital escape routes during a fire, so it is important to ensure that they open and close properly and that any security keys are readily available.

Modern UPVC windows have friction-stay hinges that limit the degree to which the window can be opened. To ensure that the window can be used as an escape route, install egress friction-stay hinges; these allow the window to be opened to its full extent.

Conserving energy

ENERGY CONSERVATION IS AN EMOTIVE SUBJECT THAT TOUCHES MANY AREAS OF DIY AND HOME IMPROVEMENT. ALTHOUGH THESE PAGES PRESENT MANY ALTERNATIVE OPTIONS AND ECO-FRIENDLY IDEAS, THE EXTENT TO WHICH YOU LEAD AN ECO-FRIENDLY LIFE, AND WHAT MEASURES OR CHANGES YOU ARE PREPARED TO MAKE, WILL ALWAYS COME DOWN TO PERSONAL CHOICE AND CONSCIENCE.

ENERGY EFFICIENCY

Being energy-efficient means assessing your home and lifestyle and deciding in which areas you might save resources. Although some of the measures outlined in these pages may take some effort, for most, this will be outweighed by the rewards of a more eco-friendly and cost-effective lifestyle.

REDUCING POWER REQUIREMENTS

The demands of modern living require power to supply appliances, provide heat, and run all the consumer items that fill our homes. However, reducing the amount of power you use may not require a major lifestyle change. You can make a huge impact simply by being a little more careful about the items you buy, being aware of their power use, and finding ways of using less power in your home.

Insulation

The best way to reduce the power requirements of your home is to ensure that it is well insulated. Even in very large houses, a loft can be insulated quickly and at relatively low cost. Some local authorities even subsidize loft insulation. In fact, the reduction in heating costs that result from improved home insulation far outweigh the initial expense of installation. For more information on insulating your home, see pp.350–65.

Smart meters

These are devices that show you how much electricity is being used by household appliances, encouraging you to be more vigilant about energy consumption and allowing you to monitor individual appliances. Variations include a direct smart-meter link to your electricity supplier that enables them to inform you about your power usage during the day and, consequently, where potential savings can be made.

USING THERMOSTATS

Thermostats play a vital part in regulating heating and air temperature throughout your home. Make sure that water-heating thermostats are not set too high. As well as wasting energy, this is potentially dangerous in terms of scalding. Make sure that radiators are fitted with thermostats so that their temperature is kept under control.

Energy-efficient appliances

Many product lines now have standardized labelling systems that denote how energy-efficient an appliance is, how much energy it consumes, and even how much noise it makes. This labelling has made it much easier for consumers to have some control when choosing products that are more efficient and therefore "greener".

US ENERGY STAR®
Products with this label meet the US Department of Energy's strict efficiency guidelines.

Australian Energy Rating
A star rating from one to six stars indicates energy-efficiency levels.

EU Energy Label
This label is a compulsory notice that is applied to all domestic appliances sold within European Union countries. It allows consumers to see clearly the efficiency and energy consumption of a product.

ELECTRICAL EFFICIENCY TABLE

Electrical power is rated in watts, and all electrical appliances will carry labels stating how many watts are required for them to run. If this is not the case, they may state volts and amps, and wattage can be worked out by multiplying the volts by the amps.

The table below gives an approximate guide to the amount of electricity (in watts per hour) that is used by common household appliances. Quite simply, the higher the figure, the larger the amount of energy the appliance uses.

Appliance	Energy used (watts per hour)	Comment
Tumble dryer	4,000–6,000	Exceptionally high consumption
Oven	3,000–6,000	In general, the larger the oven, the more energy it uses
Air-conditioning unit	1,000–6,000	Larger units use more energy
Electric space heater	2,000–4,000	Huge user when in constant use. Electrical storage heaters provide a more economical option
Immersion water heater	2,000–4,000	Make sure that its thermostat is working well and timing is controlled at efficient levels for household use
Fan heater	2,000–3,000	Use as a backup or emergency heating source, rather than on a daily basis
Kettle	1,500–2,500	Fast boilers use up more power
Hob	1,000–2,000	Rapid heating elements use more power
Iron	1,000–1,500	Try to limit ironing to only those items you consider essential
Computer system	1,000–1,500	Screen size is important in determining power usage
Toaster	1,000–1,500	Choose one with an option to toast one slice
Dishwasher	1,000–1,500	Figure represents energy used per cycle
Hairdryer	700–1,500	Large variations in consumption are due to size differences
Microwave	500–1,500	Size is the determining factor here
Washing machine	400–1,500	Figure represents energy used per cycle
Fridge	500–1,000	Make sure you monitor and adjust the temperature level
Freezer	500–1,000	Defrost regularly to maintain efficiency
Vacuum cleaner	200–1,000	Make sure that filters are clean and it is working efficiently
Stereo system	250–750	Size of the system and speakers will affect consumption
Television	50–400	Screen size largely determines power use. Switch off completely when not in use
Video/DVD/Satellite receiver	50–400	As with televisions, switch off completely when not in use
Extractor fan (cooker)	100–200	Use will depend on size, but essential for removing fumes
Towel rail	100–200	Keep on a timer so it is not in constant use
Extractor fan (bathroom)	20–200	Use a timer linked to the light switch to prevent overuse
Regular light bulb	40–150	The brighter they are, the more power they use
Low-energy light bulb	10–20	More expensive than standard bulbs, but require less power for the same amount of light produced
Fluorescent tube	10–20	Provide good, even light at reduced power requirement levels compared to standard bulbs

PASSIVE SOLAR POWER

Solar power is central to the issue of renewable energy. As an energy source, it is in abundant supply, and ready and waiting to be harnessed. Categorized as either "active" (see pp.380–81) or "passive" (described below), both types of system make use of the sun's light and heat to reduce the requirement for more conventional energy supplies. Passive solar systems involve the addition of solar features to old or new houses to maximize the use of sunlight, reducing energy usage.

(see pp.380–81)

TRIPLE GLAZING

When discussing the insulating properties of glass, it is important to mention triple glazing (for its soundproofing benefits, see p.362). While the arguments for its superior thermal efficiency – in comparison with double glazing – are far from clear cut, it does have clear benefits when it comes to minimizing and maximizing solar heat gain.

see p.362

CHOOSING THE RIGHT GLASS

The right type of glass is crucial to the process of making passive solar modifications to a house. The decision about which type of glass to use in a design should be based on several factors. For example, the absorbtion of heat from the sun may not be desirable during the summer months, as it may require air conditioning to keep temperatures down, increasing energy costs rather than lowering them.

The use of solar-control glass in this situation will reduce heat gain inside the building. Conversely, where you wish to maximize heat gain, low-emissivity glass will let more heat in and less heat out (see p.150). Many manufacturers will combine glass coatings in an attempt to meet your specific needs, but it is an area that you should research carefully to optimize your benefits.

see p.150

GLASS HOUSE EXTENSION

If you are planning a glass extension, effective positioning of glass within the design is essential for capturing heat and light (see diagram below). Remember that while you will want to use the heat of the sun to increase the warmth of your home during the winter, you will want to minimize the impact of the sun's heat during the summer. This can be achieved by orientating windows to be sunny during the winter and shady during the summer.

You can make the roof of your extension from glass (as shown below). However, having a traditional opaque roof structure over glass walls may be more suitable, as a glass roof can make the room too hot during the summer months.

TROMBE WALL

Thermal mass is the expression of a wall's capacity to store heat. Trombe walls combine thermal mass with insulated glazing and vents (for the convection of warm air into a room) to create an effective thermal heating system in the winter, without overheating the room in the summer. During hotter periods, the roof design (as shown in the diagram below) offers increased shade compared with that available during the winter months. This significantly reduces the heating process described above. Garden design is an important issue here – it is crucial to the effectiveness of the system that the wall is not shaded during the winter by large shrubs or trees, as this detracts from the heat absorbed.

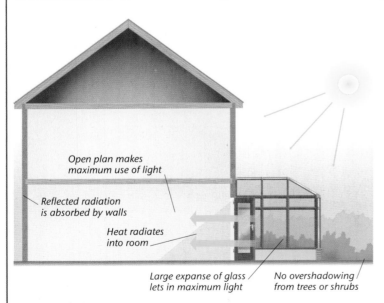

Open plan makes maximum use of light

Reflected radiation is absorbed by walls

Heat radiates into room

Large expanse of glass lets in maximum light

No overshadowing from trees or shrubs

Summer sun

Roof overhang

Warm air in

Winter sun

Airflow

High thermal mass wall

Glass

Cool air out

Wall absorbs heat and conducts it into room

Single-storey building design

Extension design
Any extension can be a demanding project, but if you intend to make the most of solar power in the design, then even greater thought than usual is required. For example, an open-plan design will probably mean significant changes to wall structure, including the removal of loadbearing walls (for more information on this, see pp.102–03). Outside the house, it may be necessary to alter garden design, as any shade provided by trees and large shrubs will affect the amount of sunlight that is utilized in this design.

see pp.102–03

Thermal mass
Determining the potential thermal mass of a new or existing wall is crucial to the design of a successful trombe wall. Concrete has a very high thermal mass, but for something with a greener production process, you could consider a rammed-earth wall. Sometimes, combinations of material are the best solution – excellent insulation is offered by a straw-bale wall, for example, while plaster layers will increase its thermal mass.

SUN PIPES

A good way of using solar power to light the home is with the use of sun pipes. These channel the sun's rays through a highly reflective tube into a dark area of the home in need of illumination. Sun-pipe size varies, with the light created being directly proportional to the diameter of the pipe. The size you can use will often be governed by the gap between the ceiling joists or roof rafters. Both joists and rafters are normally set at 40cm (16in) or 60cm (24in) intervals, from one centre to the next. Larger sun pipes are better suited to situations where joists or rafters are spaced at larger intervals.

Suppliers sell sun pipes in kit form. When purchasing a kit, find out what comes as standard, and whether you need an extra roof flashing assembly. The latter depends on whether you have a flat roof or pitched roof, and whether the tiles are flat or undulating.

Installing a sun pipe requires access to the room it is intended to illuminate, the roof, and the void through which the pipe will travel (normally a loft space).

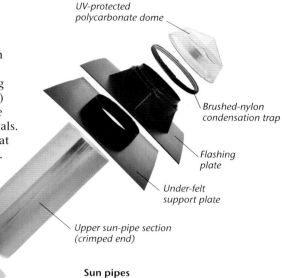

UV-protected polycarbonate dome

Brushed-nylon condensation trap

Flashing plate

Under-felt support plate

Upper sun-pipe section (crimped end)

THINGS TO CONSIDER

- It is vital to plan a good route for the sun pipe, taking into account obstacles such as ceiling joists.
- Consider the exact position of the interior lens to maximize the light in the room. The centre of the room is the most logical place, but if you are installing more than one sun pipe, a suitable pattern must be designed.
- The length of the sun pipe, and the number of angles in the pipe, will directly affect the amount of light provided – the shorter the pipe, and the fewer the angles, the better.
- Efficiency will also be improved by ensuring that all joints in a sectional pipe are taped to ensure no light leakage.
- The void through which the pipe will travel before it gets to the roof is normally a loft space, so check the access. You will need to get on the roof to install the pipe. This may be simple, but if scaffolding is required, build the cost of this into your budget.
- Although you can install a pipe on your own, it is a difficult job; it can be made much easier with the presence of a second person.
- The interior of the pipe is likely to be inaccessible once fitted, so ensure it is cleaned thoroughly after installation. Pay special attention to any gaskets or seals, which allow for ventilation and reduce the risk of condensation clouding the dome.

Adjustable elbow

Lower sun-pipe section (plain end)

Ply backing panel and template

Fixing ring

Short ceiling connection section

Ceiling trim and diffuser

Sun pipes

Most sun pipes have a round dome, although other styles are available, such as those that replicate the design of a roof window, for example. Rather than a sectional pipe, as shown, some manufacturers produce a flexible pipe that can be simply cut to the required length. This can make the process of routing the pipe through the ceiling, void (loft space), and roof significantly easier.

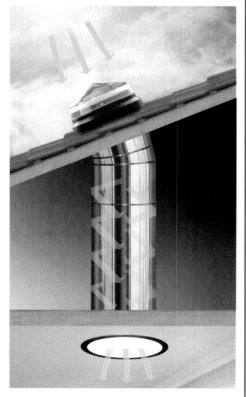

LIGHT PRODUCED BY A TYPICAL SUN PIPE

Available sunlight	Equivalent output (watts)
Overcast winter sky	130
Clear winter sky	200
Overcast summer sky	300
Clear summer sky	500+

WORKING SAFELY

Never look directly inside the pipe during installation, as sun bouncing off the interior can damage your eyes. The inside of the pipe is normally covered with a layer of plastic to dull the glare. Remove this as each section of pipe is added.

How sun pipes work
Solar rays are reflected off the highly polished, mirror-like interior of the pipe. This produces a concentrated light source in the room below.

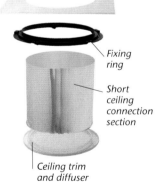
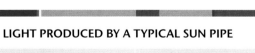

ACTIVE SOLAR POWER

"Active" solar power can be defined as any system that uses a mechanical device to harness and transform the energy of the sun (for more on "passive" solar power, see pp.378–79). For many people, active solar power is exemplified by the large, roof-mounted panels seen on some buildings. These panels differ in both design and function, depending on whether they use solar energy thermally (to heat water) or photovoltaically (to make electricity). Supposed drawbacks of these systems are that they are costly, unattractive, and unreliable, but prices are falling, and panel efficiency is improving.

Evacuated-tube collectors
Although they are heavy and may dominate the appearance of a roof, evacuated-tube collectors are a very efficient option.

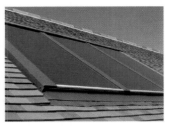

Flat-plate collectors
While flat-plate collectors may look sleeker than tube collectors, more are required to produce the same amount of energy.

THERMAL SOLAR ENERGY (SOLAR HOT WATER)
In a thermal solar energy system, the energy of the sun is used to heat water. There are two principal types of panel to choose from with this system – evacuated-tube collectors and flat-plate collectors (a third category incorporates unglazed plastic collectors, but these are normally only used for heating water for swimming pools).

Evacuated-tube collectors
With this design, each panel contains an arrangement of vacuum tubes that are connected in a manifold (a network of pipes for redirecting a gas or fluid) that can be connected to other panels if required. Designs vary, with different types of tube and heat-exchange fluid being used. Commonly, each vacuum tube contains a fin of light-absorbent material past which a flow-and-return loop (a smaller tube) runs. This smaller tube contains a heat-exchange fluid that is warmed by the sun's rays, and which may then be used to heat the flow-and-return loop to the hot-water cyclinder.

Climatic conditions influence the preferred choice of system. In colder climates, the heat-exchange fluid normally contains antifreeze, and the water is indirectly heated – this is known as a "closed system". In warmer climates, the water is heated in the tubes and fed directly into the hot-water supply – this is an "open system". Tube collectors are harder to install than flat-plate collectors (see right), but they are arguably more efficient, meaning they can be smaller.

Flat-plate collector
Flat-plate collectors contain an absorber plate through which thin tubes of fluid run. This type of system may operate in a closed or open system, similar to evacuated tubes (see left). They are much thinner, lighter, and simpler to install than evacuated tubes, although they are considered less efficient than tube collectors, so it may be necessary to install a larger surface area of panels. However, manufacturers are constantly improving the efficiency of plate collectors.

Gravity versus pump-operated systems
Both evacuated-tube and flat-plate systems can function soley under the force of gravity, but it is standard to fit a pump that moves fluid around the system. The pump is regulated by a central control unit.

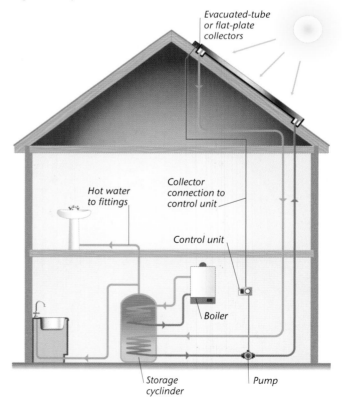

Evacuated-tube or flat-plate collectors

Hot water to fittings

Collector connection to control unit

Control unit

Boiler

Storage cyclinder

Pump

Thermal solar power system
It is usually possible to modify an existing heating system and install a solar-powered one with relative ease, although it is always simpler to plan a system in the context of a new-build.

THINGS TO CONSIDER
■ In most cases, a thermal solar power system requires a storage tank for hot water. This means that houses with combi-boilers are often unable to use this form of heating. However, some manufacturers are now producing combi-boilers that can be used in conjunction with a solar system.
■ Before installation, consider the structural implications of fitting a system for thermal solar energy; if roof-mounting is not a viable option, panels may be used at ground level as long as they still receive enough sunlight.
■ To generate a useful amount of power for an average home, panels need to occupy 2–4sq m (21½–43sq ft) of space.
■ The proportion of domestic hot water that can be produced by such a system is debatable. Clearly, a larger amount of hot water is produced during the summer than the winter; over the course of a year, however, the thermal contribution to the overall hot-water supply ranges from 30–70 per cent.
■ Check your system's maintenance and servicing requirements with the supplier.

Photovoltaic panels
For a worthwhile system, you may need a large number of photovoltaic panels. Make sure the panels interlock easily for a neat finish.

Photovoltaic roof tiles
Many manufacturers now produce panels in the form of roof tiles, which will maintain a consistent appearance to the roof.

USING MINIATURE PANELS

Photovoltaic panels are commonly used for exterior lighting. By harvesting and storing the sun's energy during the day and releasing it at night to provide illumination, small solar panels are used to power lights. Two examples of solar-powered lighting are pictured here.

Photovoltaic panels can be used on fixed or moveable lighting. Small panels are also an excellent source of renewable power for appliances with relatively small energy requirements, such as a CCTV system (see p.367).

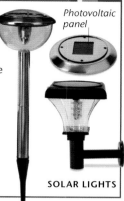

Photovoltaic panel

SOLAR LIGHTS

PHOTOVOLTAIC SYSTEM (SOLAR ELECTRICITY)

Photovoltaic systems are used to generate electricity rather than to heat water. Consequently, the composition of the panels is very different to that used for thermal solar energy systems (see opposite). Photovoltaic panels are made up of a large number of interconnected cells (although in some designs a single cell can make up the entire panel layer). These cells are comprised of semi-conductive materials, typically silicone. Having absorbed sunlight, the silicone releases electrons that create an electrical current, which can then be utilized. The cells are light-sensitive, not sun-sensitive, and are therefore capable of producing electricity even on cloudy days. It is true, however, that the more light there is available, the more electricity the system will generate. The electricity produced is DC (direct current), which needs to be channelled through an inverter and changed into AC (alternating current) to provide a form of electricity that can be used in the home.

Photovoltaic systems offer the possibility of a link-up with the national grid, which allows you both to benefit from the generated electricity yourself, and to feed back any unused power to your supplier. This can lead to further savings, as you can effectively make your electricity meter run backwards. The alternative to this is to have an off-grid system, in which banks of batteries are used to store the power you don't use.

Power output

It is difficult to estimate how much power you can expect to gain from photovoltaic panels. Manufacturers' figures for panel efficiency (the amount of light converted to energy) are normally quoted in percentages, with 10–15 per cent being a standard figure. The output of most domestic systems is measured in "kilowatts peak" (kWp), which is the amount of energy that a panel will produce under peak operating conditions. An average installation of around 8sq m (86sq ft), for example, could be expected to produce 1kWp. This will provide 20–30 per cent of the electrical requirements of an average home.

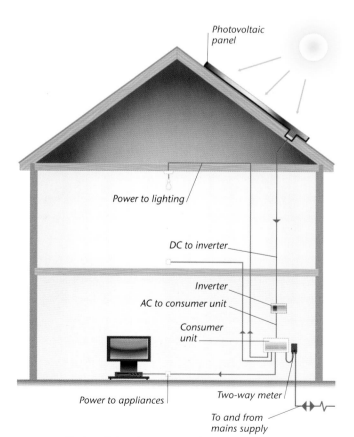

Photovoltaic panel

Power to lighting

DC to inverter

Inverter

AC to consumer unit

Consumer unit

Power to appliances

Two-way meter

To and from mains supply

Photovoltaic solar power system
Most of the hardware in a photovoltaic system sits on the roof, meaning that the only internal additions to the electricity system are a current inverter and a meter.

INSTALLING SOLAR ELECTRICITY

■ As with thermal solar power, the positioning of your panels is vital to the efficient functioning of your system. Carefully consider the pitch and exact latitude of your roof and ensure that the installer takes this into account.

■ To generate a large amount of electricity you will need a lot of panels. The average area of 2–4sq m (21½–43sq ft) for thermal panelling (see opposite) will need to be doubled to produce significant results. This will increase initial outlay, and delay the point at which your system yields a financial reward.

■ Photovoltaic panels present less complications than thermal collectors – there are no issues concerning boilers, for example – and they usually require less maintenance. However, you will still need to research your options thoroughly with regard to panel design. The aesthetic qualities of photovoltaic panels are being improved all the time.

■ If you want to connect to the national grid, make sure that your energy supplier is compatible.

■ Contact your local authority regarding planning consent.

■ If you install a system not connected to the national grid, consider the number of batteries you require, and how often they need to be replaced (typically every 6–10 years).

WIND POWER

Wind power is a way of generating electricity using a natural resource that emits no greenhouse gases. As with photovoltaic energy (see p.381), the bigger the equipment, the more power generated. However, unlike solar panels, which can still generate electricity on cloudy days, wind turbines cannot produce power without wind. Good positioning is therefore a critical factor in their use; most commercial systems are found on hills, shores, or off-shore, to increase the amount of wind to which they are exposed. You need to consider this issue on a domestic scale: if you do not live in a windy area, then wind power may not be for you.

DOMESTIC WIND POWER

Wind-generated energy is increasingly being used to supply the national grid, and it is now possible to consider using it to some effect on a domestic level. Although wind turbines provide a "clean" power source, there is a considerable environmental impact in terms of their appearance, which means you will need to seek the relevant permissions. Small, domestic turbines can produce several hundred watts of power, while using larger ones may increase this figure to two or three kilowatts.

Commercial wind farm
Although the wind provides a clean source of energy, wind farms on a massive scale can dominate a landscape, and have a clear visual impact on their surroundings.

Domestic turbine
Wind-turbine-driven domestic power systems have become an increasingly viable option. Turbines are often roof-mounted, like satellite dishes.

Wind-turbine design

There are two main designs of turbine, which are dictated by the axis on which the turbine spins – horizontal or vertical. Horizontal axis wind turbine (HAWT) designs are characterized by large blades rotating like a giant propeller – these are by far the most common type and are considered to be the most efficient. Vertical axis wind turbines (VAWT) are less efficient but much quieter – they have shorter towers, can operate closer to the ground, and can theoretically produce electricity at very low wind speeds. These pages focus on the HAWT design.

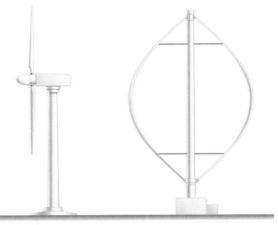

HORIZONTAL AXIS   **VERTICAL AXIS**

Levels of electricity produced

Domestic wind turbines come in a number of different sizes and their power output is measured in terms of wattage, i.e. how many watts of power they can produce in an hour (see p.377 for more details).

Small increases in the diameter of the blades make large increases in the surface area of the rotating blade. Therefore, doubling the diameter of a blade will in fact quadruple its output. The other important issue to consider is the wind speed required to produce the output. Most turbine manufacturers suggest a minimum operating requirement of around 3–4m/s (10–13ft/s), and a doubling in wind speed can cause output to increase by eight times, but it is claimed that optimum performance is achieved at around 12m/s (39ft/s). It is also worth considering the maximum speed the blades can reach before damage begins to occur; safety mechanisms are built into the equipment to prevent this. However, just as output increases significantly when wind speed goes up, it lowers dramatically as wind speed falls, meaning it can be difficult to assess the overall benefit of utilizing wind power.

HYDROELECTRIC POWER

Hydroelectric power has become a major source of electricity. Although it is seen as clean energy, there is clearly an environmental impact when large dams are built to create the reservoirs that supply the power stations. While in some areas people can choose to take their mains electricity from hydroelectric sources, it is also possible to produce your own hydroelectric power. Of course, you will need to have a sufficiently powerful source of running water but, with the correct permissions, you can feasibly set up your own systems.

WIND-TURBINE POWER OUTPUT

Rotor diameter	Wattage	Typical appliances
1-m blade	up to 0.3 k/w	Three lightbulbs
3-m blade	up to 1.5 k/w	Television and stereo
6-m blade	up to 6 k/w	Over half average household requirement

Anatomy of a wind turbine

As with photovoltaic power, it is possible to link up your turbine with the national grid so that excess power can be fed back to your supplier, bringing down your own electricity bills – check with your supplier that they are compatible with the two-way metering required for this. Aside from the turbine itself, a charge regulator or controller is required if you are also using batteries in the system – this item monitors battery charging and prevents battery damage (not needed for a turbine working solely on a grid system). An inverter is required to change DC to AC, and you will also need a meter to measure the amount of electricity you need in addition to your turbine, and how much excess you are feeding back.

Installing wind turbines

For ground-secured wind turbines, the assembly and installation of the tower is an important consideration – it requires bolting down to a concrete foundation. Some turbine designs incorporate guy ropes to aid the tower's stability. For smaller roof- or wall-mounted turbines, ensure that the entire assembly is secured and bolted down correctly. It is important to bear in mind that factors such as vibration can loosen anchoring points over time and damage the turbine, reducing its lifespan.

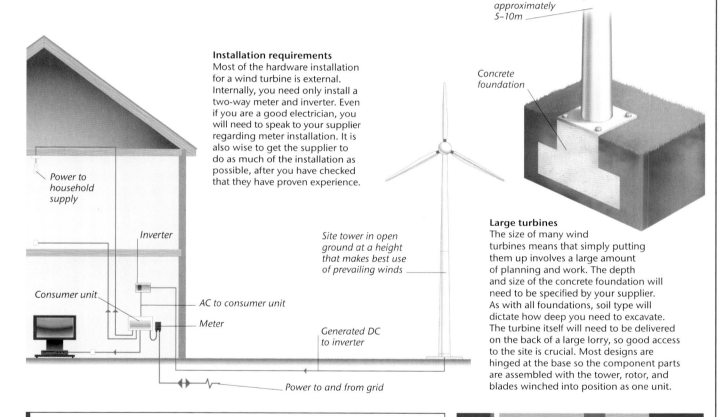

Rotor blade

Generator

Rotor

Gearbox

Tower

Height of tower varies between approximately 5–10m

Concrete foundation

Installation requirements
Most of the hardware installation for a wind turbine is external. Internally, you need only install a two-way meter and inverter. Even if you are a good electrician, you will need to speak to your supplier regarding meter installation. It is also wise to get the supplier to do as much of the installation as possible, after you have checked that they have proven experience.

Power to household supply

Inverter

Consumer unit

AC to consumer unit

Meter

Site tower in open ground at a height that makes best use of prevailing winds

Generated DC to inverter

Power to and from grid

Large turbines
The size of many wind turbines means that simply putting them up involves a large amount of planning and work. The depth and size of the concrete foundation will need to be specified by your supplier. As with all foundations, soil type will dictate how deep you need to excavate. The turbine itself will need to be delivered on the back of a large lorry, so good access to the site is crucial. Most designs are hinged at the base so the component parts are assembled with the tower, rotor, and blades winched into position as one unit.

THINGS TO CONSIDER

■ The most important factor to consider is whether there is enough wind in your area to make installing a wind turbine worthwhile. There are now websites that provide information of this nature – you can use these to help gauge the suitability of any proposed system.
■ Try to assess the time period within which you can expect to recoup any financial outlay. A large turbine, and the accompanying equipment, are expensive purchases.

■ Discover how often the turbine requires servicing, and whether you will need to replace any moving parts.
■ Local authority permission will probably be required for the installation of a turbine, especially for a larger one.
■ Wind turbines make some noise as the blades rotate – the product literature will normally display a decibel rating. As you might expect, larger wind turbines are liable to make more noise than smaller ones.

HYBRID SYSTEMS

Due to the changeability of their effectiveness, a commonly asked question is how different green technologies can be combined to increase efficiency, with one system taking over from another during lean periods. Wind power and solar power are fairly compatible in this regard, and people often combine both systems to good effect. On a windy, cloudy day, for example, a wind turbine can generate most of your power needs, whilst on a still, sunny day, the solar panels can take over the responsibility for generating power.

IMPROVING HOME PERFORMANCE

Levels of water consumption in the home largely depend on individual habits, but by far the heaviest consumers of household water are toilets, washing machines, baths, and showers. While there is a wide range of simple measures that you can take to ensure more efficient water usage in these and other areas, a more active effort may include water recycling and water treatment methods.

HOUSEHOLD APPLIANCES

There are many measures you can take, of varying extremes, to improve the efficiency of household appliances that use water. When buying appliances, choose energy-efficient models and look out for items that have been designed to reduce an appliance's water use. Changing your boiler for a condensing boiler is seen as one of the best ways to improve the efficiency of your heating system. However, looking backwards – in technological terms – may sometimes prove beneficial. For example, using a conventional mixer shower rather than a pumped power shower may save water and energy, while you might also question the whole concept of the flushing toilet. Although the idea of composting toilets may seem anachronistic, over recent years the developments in their design and efficiency have meant that they are increasing in popularity. Although they are unlikely to come into mainstream use, it is conceivable that composting toilets may become viable alternatives to mains-connected toilets.

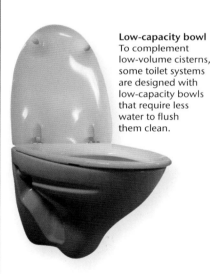

Low-capacity bowl
To complement low-volume cisterns, some toilet systems are designed with low-capacity bowls that require less water to flush them clean.

Dual-flush valves
Cisterns with dual-flush valves give the option of low-volume flushes.

Flow-reducing attachment
For more efficient water provision, taps may be fitted with a range of flow-reducing attachments.

WATER TREATMENT

Home water treatment systems can vastly improve water efficiency. It is becoming much easier to treat most of the water that you use in your home on site, rather than letting it drain away into municipal sewerage systems or soakaways.

All water can be treated. Blackwater – from the toilet – can be used more efficiently by creating a reed bed (see opposite). Greywater – all domestic waste water, excluding that from the toilet – can be recycled and used as shown opposite. Rainwater can also be harvested and reused – methods for this are demonstrated on pp.386–387.

IMPROVING APPLIANCE EFFICIENCY

Where hard water is a problem, a water softener is a good long-term investment. Hard water scales up all appliances, making them much less efficient and more costly to run. Water softeners are fitted in the water mains supply, but do not affect the kitchen or any other drinking-water taps.

Other water treatment devices include magnetic and electrolytic scale inhibitors that are designed to reduce scale in the system but do not soften the water.

Water softener
Domestic water softeners can improve the efficiency of your home's water system and any appliances that use water.

Scale inhibitor
This device helps prevent scale appearing in the water system by passing a series of electric currents around the mains water pipe.

SAVING WATER IN THE HOME

The following is a list of simple ways in which you may reduce your household water consumption.

■ Leaks in your water system can be a key source of wastage. If you have a water meter, turn off your water and take two readings several minutes apart. If they are different, you may have a leak.

■ When buying new appliances that use water, choose those that are energy-efficient. This saves on water as well as electricity (see pp.376–77).

■ A five-minute shower uses about one-third of the water that a bath does. However, power showers can use more water than a bath in less than five minutes.

■ Toilet cisterns may use as much as 9 litres (2 gallons) of clean water with every flush. Reduce your cistern's capacity by placing a brick or filled bag in the cistern.

■ Burst water pipes are a major cause of damage as well as of water wastage, so ensure that your water pipes and external taps are well lagged.

■ Water butts in your garden will collect rainwater that may be used on plants, saving large volumes of treated water.

■ Dripping taps can waste huge volumes of water. Make sure that you regularly replace worn tap washers (see pp.486–87).

■ Try not to leave the tap running while you brush your teeth, shave, or wash your hands, as this can waste up to 5 litres (1⅓ gallons) of water per minute.

■ Swap your hose pipe for a bucket of water when you wash your car.

Greywater recycling systems range from the small (see below) to the large (see right). A small-scale greywater system can be easily installed without professional help. These systems come in kit form with clear instructions. In addition to a filtration unit, you will need to buy extra waste pipe and the right connections, as well as a compatible water butt. This system is ideally suited for connection to bath or basin wastes.

TOOLS AND MATERIALS SEE BASIC TOOLKIT

LARGE-SCALE SYSTEMS

It is now possible to buy large tank storage and treatment systems that can cope with the majority of greywater produced in the home. This can then be fed back into the domestic system for most uses, except drinking water. A relatively complex system of filters and pumps cleans the water, discarding sediment and debris; the water is also treated with UV to kill off the most harmful bacteria. These tanks can be underground, similar to those for rainwater (see p.387). Generally, however, upright tanks situated in the house are used. Some dual-sytems recycle rainwater and greywater.

■ ADDING A GREYWATER SYSTEM

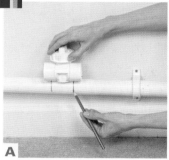

A

Mark on the waste pipe where you will fit the combination outlet. Allow space for the cut ends of the pipe to fit into the sockets of the outlet.

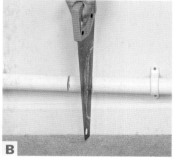

B

Use a fine-toothed saw to cut out the section of pipe, following the guidelines as accurately as possible.

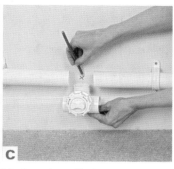

C

Mark on the wall where you want to route the drainage pipe outside. Do this by temporarily fitting the outlet, or by holding it in the correct position.

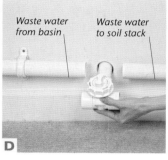

Waste water from basin   *Waste water to soil stack*

D

Drill a hole at the marked position, using a core drill bit (see p.364). Fit a piece of waste pipe long enough to extend through the wall.

Seal with silicone sealant

E

Cut back the pipe on the exterior wall to a suitable length for connecting an elbow. Position the elbow on the cut section.

F

Fit lengths of waste pipe from the connecting elbow down to a point above, and adjacent to, the water butt. Screw in brackets to fix the pipe.

G

Assemble the filter unit and place it on the water butt, following guidelines about filter alignment. Fit the hose tail adaptor to the base of the waste pipe.

Secure hose with jubilee clip

H

Use the hose to join the pipe to the filter. For all waste-pipe joints, use solvent cement to secure them in place (see p.481).

REED BEDS

In addition to a composting toilet (see opposite), a reed bed is an eco-friendly way of getting rid of blackwater. The toilet functions conventionally, except that the discharge runs into an underground primary chamber. Solid waste settles at the bottom of it (and needs to be pumped out periodically), while an overflow at the top takes the liquid waste onto a planted reed bed. The root system "treats" the water by filtering out potentially harmful bacteria, and oxygenating it to help beneficial micro-organisms thrive. Another pipe takes the treated water away, normally for garden irrigation.

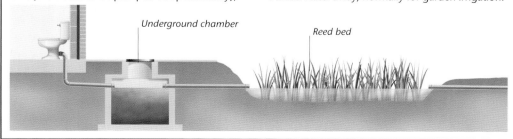

Underground chamber   *Reed bed*

Multiple benefits
Reed beds are not only effective; they also provide an aesthetically pleasing feature that can host a large variety of wildlife.

Rainwater is a free resource, and it makes sense to harvest it for use in the home. Although it cannot normally be used for drinking water, it can be collected and used for watering the garden or, at a more sophisticated level, to supply household fittings and appliances such as toilets and washing machines (see opposite). The simplest way to harvest rainwater is to install a water butt. Rain from gutters runs through a downpipe where a diverter channels water into the butt. Once the butt is full, water flows down into the ground drainage system as normal.

TOOLS AND MATERIALS SEE BASIC TOOLKIT

DIVERTING RAINWATER

This is a typical rainwater diverter. The main body of the unit has a leaf trap and an overflow to divert water back to the downpipe when the butt is full. Different sizes of diverters or adaptors are used for different types and diameter of downpipe.

Coupling for connection to water butt

Linking pipe

Body of diverter

RAINWATER DIVERTER KIT

FITTING A WATER BUTT AND RAIN DIVERTER

A

Position the water butt adjacent to a downpipe. Here, the butt has a specially designed base that needs to be levelled when in position.

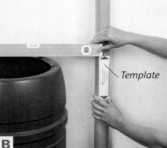

B

Place the butt on the base and determine where to cut into the downpipe. Most manufacturers will supply a marking template.

Template

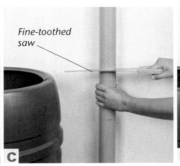

Fine-toothed saw

C

Use a fine-toothed saw to cut through the downpipe, following the guidelines as closely as possible.

D

Remove the cut section of pipe and insert the main body of the diverter, using any adaptors that are required.

E

Use a hole cutter to make a hole in the water butt. Again, use a template to measure the correct position.

F

Fit the coupling in the hole, making sure any washers supplied are used to create a watertight fit.

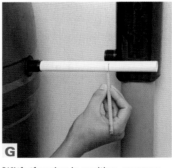

G

With the pipe in position, measure it to the correct size, then remove it again to cut. Here the pipe is rigid, but some may be flexible.

H

Fit the linking pipe in place, first pushing it into the socket section of the diverter, and then into the water-butt coupling.

I

When the fitting is completed, wait until it rains to test that everything is working correctly. Remember that the diverter unit should be disassembled from time to time to remove any debris from the filter. It is always best to try to prevent debris getting into the pipe in the first place by using leaf guards (see right).

PREVENTING BLOCKAGES

When harvesting rainwater, it is important to take precautions to prevent pipes from becoming blocked with vegetation and debris. Gutters, and the outlets into downpipes, will need attention, and leaf guards are designed to protect these areas.

This is an example of a leaf guard that can be pushed into the running outlet at the top of the downpipe. Leaves should be cleared from it periodically.

DOWNPIPE LEAF GUARD

USING LARGER TANKS

With large rainwater collection systems, it is most common to situate tanks underground (see below). However, the expense of this option means it may be worth considering a surface collection tank. It is also easier to identify leaks, or other problems, in an above-ground tank. A disadvantage with this system, however, is that water can overheat and become a host environment for algae and bacterial growth. In addition to this, large tanks can also be an unattractive feature in your garden, although a range of designs is available to cater to specific space and positioning requirements.

Above-ground tanks
These tanks have been integrated into the design of a development of new houses – a viable option for new-build projects.

LARGE-SCALE RAINWATER COLLECTION

Domestic systems on a large scale involve the use of large storage tanks, which may be above ground (see box, above) but are more commonly buried underground. The advantage of a subterranean tank is that it saves space, is more aesthetically pleasing, and is shielded from direct sunlight so that the water maintains a more constant temperature (meaning there is less likelihood of algae growth or bacterial build up). Correct placing of the tank requires careful planning, as you may need to adjust gutters and downpipes to maximize the amount of water delivered to the tank.

How does the tank work?

Water enters the tank through a "calmed inlet", which means that sediment at the bottom of the tank and residue on the surface of the water is not stirred up. Once collected, the rainwater is pumped back into the house. The pump may be located in the tank itself, which reduces noise but is less accessible for maintenance. Conversely, you can site a suction pump inside the house, which is more accessible but may prove noisy.

Topping up water levels

When the tank level is low, mains water is used to top it up so that the tank does not run dry. With this type of system, it is important to ensure that there is an air gap between the rainwater supply and the top-up supply to prevent contamination. This can also be achieved by non-return valves – check with your local authority regarding regulations. Similarly, the overflow from the tank to the mains drains must not allow any backflow of material. Monitoring systems may also be purchased and installed as part of a large-scale rainwater tank system.

Maintenance and treatment

The only significant maintenance required for a rainwater tank is to ensure that filters are regularly cleaned and gutters and downpipes are unblocked. Be aware that there are moving parts in this system, such as pumps and valves, which may need occasional servicing. Some domestic systems use UV filtration to make the water drinkable, although this does require more advanced hardware.

Tank size
Consider the size of tank you require before installation. Typical domestic sizes range from 5,000–10,000 litres (1,320–2,640 gallons). You can make a more precise estimate by calculating the roof size of your home, balanced against the annual rainfall in your area, in relation to your estimated water consumption. Most suppliers will help you with this calculation before you order.

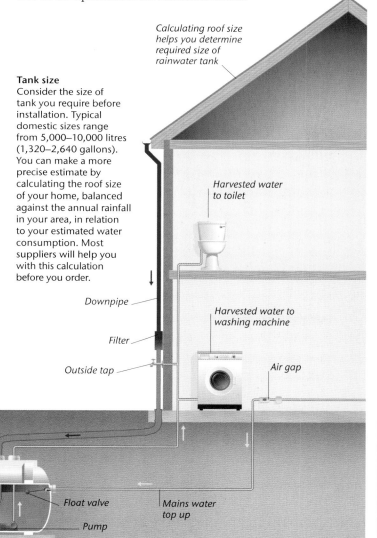

Calculating roof size helps you determine required size of rainwater tank

Harvested water to toilet

Downpipe

Harvested water to washing machine

Filter

Outside tap

Air gap

Inspection chamber

Overflow to ground water drainage system

Rainwater harvesting tank

Float valve

Mains water top up

Pump

Using space

SPACE IS ALWAYS AT A PREMIUM IN THE HOME, SO USE WHAT YOU HAVE EFFECTIVELY. CONSIDER BOTH SHELF AND CUPBOARD SPACE – THERE ARE MANY EXCELLENT READY-MADE UNITS AVAILABLE. ALTERNATIVELY, WITH SOME SIMPLE WOODWORKING SKILLS OR THE USE OF ADAPTABLE SUPPORT SYSTEMS, YOU CAN CONSTRUCT ATTRACTIVE UNITS TAILOR-MADE TO FIT YOUR HOME AND YOUR NEEDS.

PREPARING TO PUT UP SHELVES

Shelves – whether flatpack or custom-made – can be fitted almost anywhere, as a major feature or in an otherwise disused corner such as an old fireplace, or under the stairs. You can increase storage options by adding hooks or storage boxes, and doors can enclose part or all of the shelving. How you combine types of shelves and their supports depends on chosen shelf position, level of support needed, and the style of your home. "Floating" shelves have invisible fixings, and are an attractive option but can only be used on masonry.

SHELVING BRACKETS

There are many brackets and support systems for shelves; some are fixed in position and some are adjustable. Styles vary, so a system can be found to fit most requirements. To prevent a shelf sagging, position brackets every 600mm (2ft) along its length. If the shelves are to store heavy items such as books, put the brackets slightly closer together.

Adjustable shelves

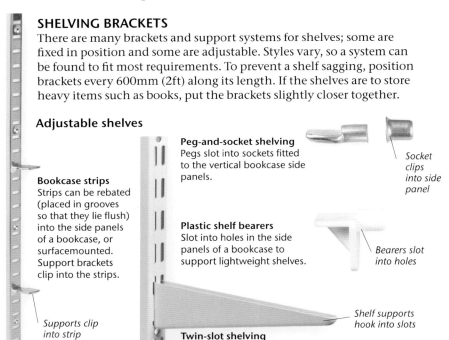

Bookcase strips
Strips can be rebated (placed in grooves so that they lie flush) into the side panels of a bookcase, or surfacemounted. Support brackets clip into the strips.

Supports clip into strip

Peg-and-socket shelving
Pegs slot into sockets fitted to the vertical bookcase side panels.

Socket clips into side panel

Plastic shelf bearers
Slot into holes in the side panels of a bookcase to support lightweight shelves.

Bearers slot into holes

Shelf supports hook into slots

Twin-slot shelving
A versatile adjustable system that can be used in many situations.

Fixed shelves

Utility brackets
Utility brackets come in a range of sizes and designs. Simple ones are a basic L-shape.

Shelf slots in here

Glass shelf bracket
Brackets fix to a wall, and a glass shelf fits into the slots.

Rod goes into holes in wall and shelf

Threaded metal rods
These provide invisible support to a "floating" shelf on a masonry wall.

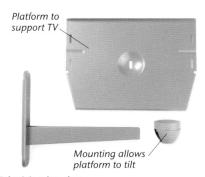

Platform to support TV

Mounting allows platform to tilt

Television bracket
Some manufacturers produce speciality brackets and shelves suitable for supporting particular items. A common example is a TV bracket.

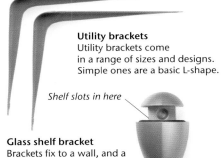

CONSIDERATIONS WHEN PLANNING SHELVES

As well as choosing suitable materials, make sure that your shelves are strong enough for whatever is to be stored on them, and that they are level so that nothing rolls off.

Supporting heavy weights

Shelving needs to support its own weight as well as the items you wish to store or display. A few lightweight items will cause little difficulty, but a full shelf of books can be very heavy. Fixings must be strong enough to prevent shelves collapsing – to support books, screws should penetrate masonry walls or timber studs by at least 50mm (2in), and supports should extend across two-thirds of a shelf's depth. Fixings for floating shelves are not designed to support heavy loads, although if you can sink metal rods into a solid wall to a depth of two-thirds that of the shelf, you may be able to support greater weights (see p.391).

Coping with undulating walls

Brackets must be precisely vertical and shelves horizontal. Use a spirit level to assess all shelves' positions before securing them in place. If the wall surface is not level, pack slivers of wood behind shelf supports so that they lie square and support shelves on the level. For the best finish, scribe shelves so that they sit neatly against any undulations in a wall without leaving gaps (see p.221). This can be difficult in alcoves, in which case consider using a card template.

FLATPACK PREPARATION

Shelving and storage "flatpack" systems are usually cheap, easy to transport, and simple to assemble. Good preparation will prevent problems arising during or after construction.
■ Check the dimensions of the finished item and the space it needs to fit into before buying it. If it is a tight fit, in an alcove for example, check the width in several places.
■ Consider whether the assembled item will be sufficiently sturdy and spacious for its intended purpose.
■ The packaging should state if any additional fixings and tools are needed for assembly: check it before starting.
■ Check that all parts are in the box and are undamaged – at the point of purchase, if possible, or soon afterwards.
■ Lay out the components in the order they fit together and check that you understand the manufacturer's instructions.

TOOLS AND MATERIALS CHECKLIST PP.390–95

Using batten or ladder supports in an alcove (p.390) Spirit level, fixings suitable to wall type, shelf material, paint*, paintbrush*, wood finish*, decorative moulding*, panel pins*, filler, sandpaper

Assembling twin-slot shelving (p.391) Spirit level, fixings suitable to wall type, timber offcuts*, paint*, paintbrush*, wood finish*, decorative moulding*, panel pins*, filler, sandpaper

Invisible fixings on an open masonry wall (p.391) Threaded metal rods, thick shelving material, try-square, spirit level, masonry drill and long bit, resin, paint*, paintbrush*, wood finish*, decorative moulding*, panel pins*, filler, sandpapers

Building a flatpack cupboard (p.395) Spirit level, fixings suitable for wall/ceiling/floor, timber offcuts*, tenon saw

* = optional

FOR BASIC TOOLKIT SEE PP.24–25

SHELVING MATERIALS

Ready-cut shelves can be bought in a range of materials, the most common of which are shown below. Shelving is also a feature of the reclamation industry (see pp.86–87). Check with the supplier that your chosen material is strong enough to provide the required support – usually, boards or timber should be at least 18mm (1in) thick. If you want a material with a veneer or laminated edge, use a standard sheet size so as not to have to cut it, or plan to hide the uncovered cut edge.

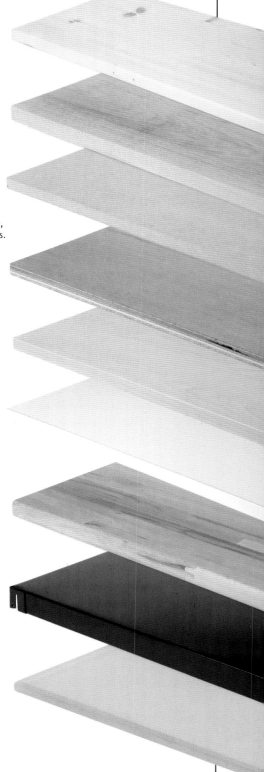

Softwood
Can be painted or have a natural wood finish applied. Avoid very cheap wood, which may be low quality and may warp.

Hardwood
The appeal of hardwood is in its colour and grain, but it is more expensive than softwoods.

Medium-density fibreboard (MDF)
This versatile material can cater for all manner of shape, depth, and size requirements. Can be finished with paint.

Ply
Very strong, but is usually used for shelves where a decorative finish is not important.

Veneered chipboard
Looks like solid hardwood but at a fraction of the price. Use a standard sheet size to retain veneer.

Melamine
Cheap, strong chipboard laminated with coloured, textured, or wood-effect plastic. Use a standard sheet size.

Kitchen-worktop offcuts
The thickness makes this ideal for floating shelves, because it is easy to drill into the edges.

Metal
Pressed metal shelving is a hardwearing option which does not need any kind of finish before use.

Glass
Use toughened glass for shelving – its packaging will indicate what it can support. Standard clear glass is not strong enough.

MADE-TO-MEASURE SHELVING

A good place to put up shelves is in an alcove, as shown here. Ladder shelving is stronger than the batten method and can be used across a wider span because shelves are more rigid. Twin-slot brackets can be used anywhere. Invisible fixings can be used with thick wood (such as a kitchen worktop) to make floating shelves, but only on a masonry wall, and not to support heavy loads. Check the wall with a detector for wires and pipes before drilling. If the wall is a stud wall, fix into the studs themselves.

TOOLS AND MATERIALS SEE BASIC TOOLKIT AND P.389

USING BATTEN SUPPORTS IN AN ALCOVE

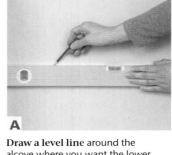

A

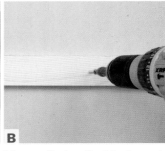

B

Draw a level line around the alcove where you want the lower edge of the first shelf. Start with either the top or the bottom shelf.

Measure the length of the line and cut a 50 x 25mm (2 x 1in) batten to fit. Hold its top edge against the line and drill pilot holes. Fix it in place.

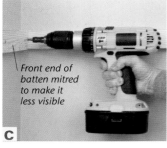

Front end of batten mitred to make it less visible

C

D

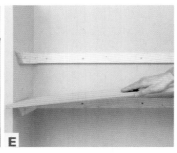

E

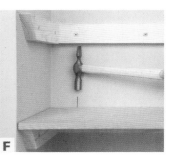

F

Measure and cut two battens to extend from the ends of the back one to at least two thirds of the shelf's depth. Fix them in place.

Measure down (or up) to where you want the next shelf, and mark guide lines for it. Cut and fit battens in the same way as for the first shelf.

Cut and position shelving material (see p.389) on the battens. If walls are not square, scribe shelves to fit against them (see p.72).

Nail each shelf to the battens every 250mm (9¾in) along the back and side edges.

USING LADDER SUPPORTS IN AN ALCOVE

Measure for battens as above, but cut two long battens – one for the back and one for the front of the shelf. Cut short battens to fit between them at each end and roughly every 250mm (9¾in) in between to create a ladder-like frame. Build the frame using butt joints (see p.392), countersinking all the screws.

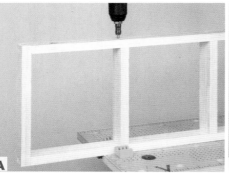

A

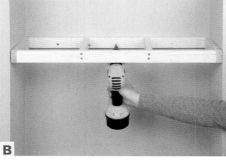

B

Attach the frame to the wall at the back and along the sides of the alcove. Use fixings suitable to the wall's type every 250mm (9¾in). Then attach the shelf to the frame by nailing it onto the battens at regular intervals. Hold a spirit level across the shelf in between inserting fixings, to ensure that the shelf is level.

FINISHING SHELVES

MDF is the ideal shelf material for DIY use because it is so easy to work with, but it usually needs decorating after construction. A decorative wooden moulding or veneer can be fixed along the edges of shelves to make them look like solid wood (see p.215). The example here shows putting a moulding on the front of a shelf in an alcove. For simple back-and-side supported shelves, mitre the fronts of the side supports to make them less obvious.

The edges of shelves can be filled and sanded. If there are gaps between any shelves and the wall, use a flexible filler on them. Do not use white filler if you are going to apply a natural wood finish (see p.290); use stainable filler to match the finish.

If you paint shelves, leave them to dry for several days before using them; the usual 24 hours is not long enough to prevent items on a shelf sticking to new paint.

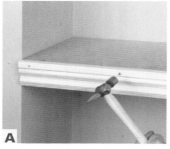

A

B

Fix moulding in place with panel pins every 100mm (4in). Punch the pins' heads below the surface.

Fill all fixing holes in the shelves with filler, then sand smooth, and decorate as required.

USING SPACE

ASSEMBLING TWIN-SLOT SHELVING

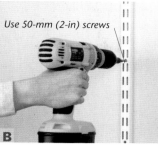

Use 50-mm (2-in) screws

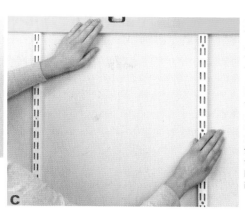

Hold the next bracket in place. Rest a spirit level across the tops of both brackets to get them level. You may find it helps to have someone hold the bracket. Adjust the position of the bracket until it is completely level with the first, fixed one. Pilot drill through the top fixing hole, then secure in place.

Draw a vertical guide line, using a spirit level, where you want the first support. Hold a bracket against the line and mark the fixing holes.

Drill pilot holes and plug them (see p.77), then fix the first bracket in place. Use timber pieces to fill behind the bracket if the wall is uneven.

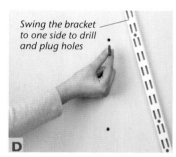

Swing the bracket to one side to drill and plug holes

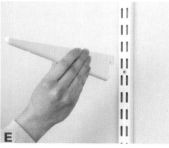

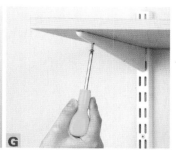

Mark for other pilot holes, then swing bracket to one side. Drill the pilot holes, plug them, and loosely fix the bracket in place.

Check that the bracket is vertical, then fix it securely. Hook the shelf supports into the wall brackets, taking care that they are level.

Mark the position and depth of the brackets on the back of a shelf. Cut out this area with a chisel so that shelves will sit flush against the wall.

Place shelves on the supports, and secure them by inserting small screws through the support into the underside of the shelf.

INVISIBLE FIXINGS ON OPEN MASONRY WALLS

The thicker the shelf material, the easier this system is to apply. Use rods one-third longer than the shelf's width. Measure and mark for fixing points on the back of the shelf roughly near the ends, and at similar intervals in between if spanning a wide space.

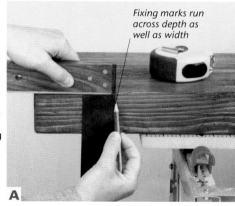

Fixing marks run across depth as well as width

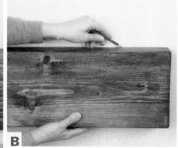

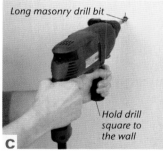

Long masonry drill bit

Hold drill square to the wall

Use a level to draw the shelf's position on the wall. Hold the marked shelf up to it and mark the fixing points from the shelf on the wall.

Drill into the wall to a depth that equals two-thirds the width of the shelf. Use a bit slightly larger than the diameter of the threaded rods.

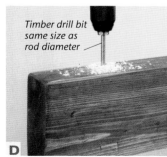

Timber drill bit same size as rod diameter

When the resin has set, slide the shelf onto the rods. Sit a spirit level on the shelf – if it is level, it does not need to be permanently fixed onto the rods. (This will allow it to be removed with ease for future redecoration.) If the shelf wobbles, insert resin into the holes to fix it onto the rods.

Clamp the shelf securely. Drill at the fixing points to the depth of the holes in the wall, ensuring that the drill stays square to the timber.

Inject resin (see p.80) into the drilled holes in the wall, and insert the rods. Use a spirit level to ensure that they are exactly straight.

WOODWORKING JOINTS

A knowledge of joining wood will allow you to design and construct customized shelving or other forms of storage. Understanding how to make common woodworking joints will also enable you to carry out repair jobs on items such as doors, windows, stairs, kitchen cabinets, and other furniture. Choosing which joint to use in any situation involves weighing up strength, looks, and ease of construction. Biscuit jointers (see p.64) give the option of easily making joints with a power tool.

CHOOSING A SUITABLE JOINT

The complexity of any joint is determined by the strength and quality of finish required. Joints hidden from view do not need to be decorative, and a butt joint will usually do.

Some joints are made for strength: for example, a halving joint is much stronger than a butt joint, and a mortise-and-tenon joint is stronger still. Your skills and experience may also affect your choice of which joint to use.

BUTT JOINTS

To make these simple joints you need only be able to measure lengths accurately, and make clean, straight cuts. Nails or screws should be slightly angled so that they cannot pull apart. Butt joints are commonly used in hidden frameworks such as stud walls (see pp.104–07).

Dowelled butt joint
Strengthen butt joints by inserting ready-made dowel pegs into the joint. Mark and measure carefully, so that the dowel aligns with the hole: one option is to knock pins into one side of the joint, at the dowel positions, and use them to create an impression in the other side of the joint. Drill holes half the depth of the peg, then glue and insert the dowel.

Dowel holds joint together

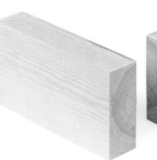

Simple butt joint
In the most simple type of butt joint, the face of one piece of timber meets the face of another at a right angle.

Mitred butt joint
This is similar to the other butt joints, but the ends of both lengths of timber join at an angle, normally 45 degrees. This gives a more visually pleasing finish. Cutting guides can help you make angled cuts easily and accurately (see p.35).

HALVING JOINTS

A halving joint is stronger than a butt joint. Each piece of timber has half its depth removed so that it overlaps and interlocks with the other piece. A cross-halving joint (see below) creates a cross or T-junction rather than a right angle. For both, accuracy in measuring and marking up is essential.

◼ MAKING A HALVING JOINT

A Use a marking gauge to make identical cutting guides on each section of timber to be joined.

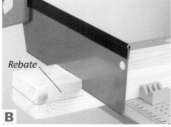

Rebate

B Cut a rebate with a tenon saw, making the cuts first across the grain, and then along the grain.

C Fix the joint as required; screws are used here. Use wood glue as well if you want extra strength.

◼ MAKING A CROSS-HALVING JOINT

A Mark the dimensions and position of the joint. Make several cuts across the grain, to the required depth, in the marked area.

B Chisel away the waste wood from between the cuts, working slowly and carefully.

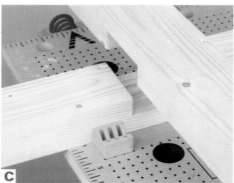

C Slot the two notched lengths of wood together. Fix them with wood glue and/or nails or screws.

HOUSING AND LAP JOINTS

These two joints are useful for cabinet and shelving construction. Both are easiest achieved with a router, a power tool that cuts a rebate to a set size (see pp.66–67).

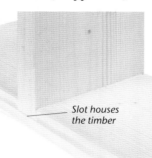

Housing joint
This is used to create a T-junction between wide boards, often in shelf construction. Cut a slot with a router or use a tenon saw and chisel as shown opposite bottom. Push the timber into its slot and fix with glue and screws.

Slot houses the timber

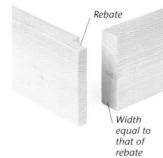

Rebate

Width equal to that of rebate

Lap joint
This is similar to a housing joint but the lengths of timber are joined at their ends. It can also be used to join wide boards at a right angle. Cut a rebate at the end of one length with a tenon saw (opposite bottom). Glue and screw the joint.

MAKING A MORTISE-AND-TENON JOINT

Mortise-and-tenon joints join pieces of wood very strongly and neatly. The end of one length of timber is cut away on two, or all four, sides to make a peg. A peg-sized hole is then cut out of another timber, and the peg is inserted. Joints connecting the stiles of doors with the rails are often made in this way.

A

Mark the cuts needed for the peg and slot on two lengths of timber. Cut the peg with the wood grain as shown for a halving joint.

B

Drill overlapping holes to the depth required for the slot with a flat bit. Remove as much of the waste wood as possible with the bit.

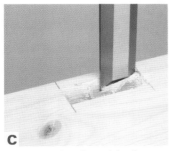

C

Neaten up the edges of the slot hole using a hammer and chisel.

D

Insert the peg into the slot to check the fit. Then apply wood glue to the inside of the slot, and make the joint.

JOINT BRACKETS AND BLOCKS

There are a number of fittings and fixing plates that can be used to repair existing wooden joints, or create new joints. To fit a bracket or block flush with wood, draw around it, and use a chisel and hammer to create a shallow rebate.

Plates

Tee plate
Flat plate used to strengthen a tee-shaped joint.

Angle plate
Strengthens any right-angled joint. Often used as a repair option on the corner of window casements.

Corner plate
Used to strengthen corner joints.

Mending plate
Straight, strengthening plate.

Stretcher plate
For internal joints. Has elongated fixing holes used to adjust position.

Braces

Corner brace
Flat plate bent to form a right-angled brace to strengthen a joint.

Angle brace
Small corner brace, commonly used to fix down kitchen worktops.

Joints

Assembly joint (joint block)
Used to strengthen a right-angled joint, commonly in kitchen units.

KD joint
Used to strengthen a right-angled joint. Comes in two sections.

Dowel fits into lock *Lock*

Cam dowel and lock
Used in flatpack units for joining flat sections or panels.

Insert dowel into lock *Lock*

Cross dowel and insert
Used to create joint between panels or sections of a framework. Commonly used in self-assembly furniture such as beds.

A custom-built cupboard can be built in an alcove, in a corner of a room, against a wall, or freestanding. To put up flatpack cupboards and wardrobes, follow the manufacturer's instructions, and the advice on p.389. See opposite for the steps to erect a typical flatpack cupboard with sliding doors. If you wish to produce custom-built storage, see below for further details on the options and advice on planning it. Making a cupboard of any size requires a considerable number of materials, and much careful planning and measurement.

THINGS TO WATCH OUT FOR

■ Aim to get the cupboard square even if walls, floors, and ceilings are not dead straight. Use a spirit level, and pack out sides with battens or wedges if necessary to get them square. Hide any gaps with decorative mouldings (see pp.214–17).
■ Use factory-cut straight edges on any boards to their best advantage – where they will be seen.

■ Use brackets to keep corners square and rigid (see p.393).
■ Support long-span shelves along their length, with extra brackets, or with dividers.
■ Consider buying ready-made doors, because making your own doors is difficult. Attach doors with simple flush hinges (see p.159) unless they are particularly heavy or large, in which case you should use butt hinges (see p.161).

PLANNING A CUSTOM-MADE CUPBOARD

Whatever your planned cupboard or wardrobe, you will need lengths of timber to provide the framework, and sheet materials – such as MDF (see pp.72–73) – to construct the sides, backs, tops, shelves, divisions, and doors. You may also need sheet materials for a fascia and plinth, and you can embellish the unit with decorative wooden mouldings (see pp.214–17). When drawing up your design, consult the preceding pages on woodworking joints (see pp.392–93). Think also about the type of wall (see pp.96–97), suitable fixings (see pp.76–79), and locating pipes or cables in the wall before you drive in nails or screws (see pp.104–05).

Planning the design

Creating a cupboard inside a preexisting alcove is illustrated below. This is probably the most straightforward of designs, as there is no need to build any side panels. A cupboard can also be fitted into a corner, against a wall, or it can be freestanding. Design complications such as this are one reason why custom-made, flatpacked kits such as

the one shown opposite are becoming more popular – there are many variations with nearly all possible options catered for in their designs. If you wish to create your own side panels for a custom-made cupboard, then building board such as MDF is a good material to use. Depending on the thickness of the board and the size of the panel, you may need to construct a framework in which to fix the MDF side panels. Alternatively, you may be able to use stretcher plates or angle braces (p.393) at both ceiling and floor level.

Fitting sliding doors to an alcove

Sliding doors can be easily positioned across the front of an alcove, to section off a cupboard or wardrobe area. Several widths are available – decide what size, and how many, will best fit your alcove and design. If the ceiling is too high for your chosen doors and frame, it may be necessary to use some studwork to effectively lower the ceiling height so that the cupboard can be installed, providing a custom-fitted appearance.

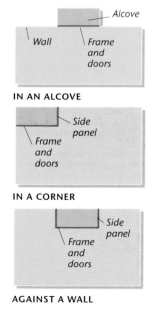

IN AN ALCOVE

IN A CORNER

AGAINST A WALL

Easy cupboard structures
These illustrations show three ways of using a room's shape to make a cupboard. The red line represents the basic frame shown to the right; the green lines are side panels.

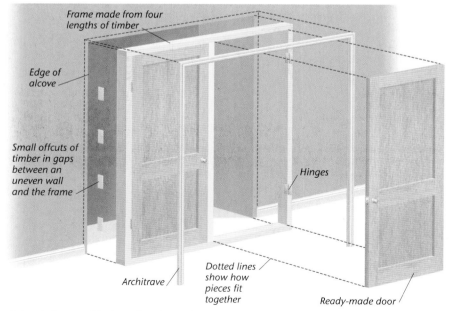

A simple frame with doors fitted to an alcove
Build a timber frame to fit in the front of the alcove (as shown) or to your chosen size (if the cupboard is to be in a corner or against a wall), and fix it to the walls. If a wall is uneven, it may leave small gaps – fill these with timber offcuts. Attach doors and architrave.

BUILDING A FLATPACK CUPBOARD

These are typical steps to construct a flatpack cupboard. Study the instructions in case you need other techniques, for instance, to fit the doors. If possible, get someone to help hold the sections in position.

TOOLS AND MATERIALS SEE BASIC TOOLKIT AND P.389

1 FITTING THE SIDE

A

Use a spirit level to get line vertical

B

This example needs scribing around skirting

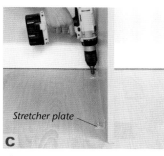

Stretcher plate

C

Measure from the corner of the room to where you want the cupboard's side panel. Draw a vertical guide line on the wall.

Hold the side panel in place. It will not sit flush if the wall is uneven; if this is the case, scribe it to fit (see p.72). Cut the panel to size.

Check with a try square that the angle between wall and panel is 90 degrees. Then use stretcher plates to secure the panel to the floor.

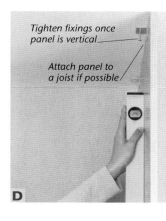

Tighten fixings once panel is vertical

Attach panel to a joist if possible

D

Attach the panel loosely to the ceiling with stretcher plates. Use a spirit level to check that it is vertical. If necessary, use the slots in the stretcher plates to adjust its position. Then secure it. At the cupboard's other "side", draw a guide line on the wall for the cupboard's front edge. The lining will sit against this line.

2 FITTING THE LINING

Section of skirting to be removed

Guide for front edge of lining

A

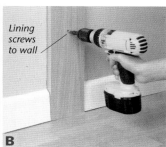

Lining screws to wall

B

Cut a section from the skirting board (see p.106) to allow the lining to sit flush against the wall.

Cut the lining to size. Then fix it to the wall. Use a spirit level as you work, to check that the lining is vertical.

3 FITTING THE RUNNERS AND DOOR

Measure the distance between the inside edges of the side panel and the lining. Check that the cupboard is "square" by measuring at the top and bottom of the opening, and adjust if necessary. Use a hacksaw to cut the top rail of the sliding door mechanism to fit the opening.

A

B

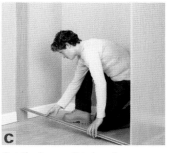

C

Following the manufacturer's guidelines on positioning, fix the rail to the ceiling. Use plugged fixings as required for the type of ceiling.

Cut the base rail to length. Position it loosely between the side panel and lining, but do not fix it down at this stage.

D

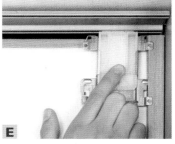

E

F

Hang the doors on the runner mechanism, paying close attention to the manufacturer's instructions.

Once the doors are hung, adjust the runners to allow the doors to hang correctly. Check that they operate smoothly.

With the doors and rails in the best position for smooth operation, use a detector to find out whether there are any cables or pipes below the floor. Secure the base rail to the floor. The length of screw needed depends on the type and thickness of the flooring.

OUTDOOR ALTERATIONS AND REPAIRS

HARD LANDSCAPING
WOODEN STRUCTURES

GARDEN LANDSCAPING

The principles of garden landscaping apply to the smallest back yard just as they do to more substantial outside areas around a home. In all cases, consider what options are available, and how they may best suit your needs. The pages that follow show you how to carry out hard landscaping as well as building wooden structures outside. They also demonstrate the most effective ways of creating both practical and attractive finishes to the space outside your home.

Trees
To avoid problems with subsidence, always plant trees away from the house.

Decorative garden walls
Garden walls are generally non-structural and are used as boundaries, or decorative screens in a garden design. They may be constructed from different brick, block, or stone materials.

Steps
These may be wooden, masonry-based, or a combination of both. See p.415 for information on how to construct steps.

Gates
Used as entrances to drives, paths, or sectioned-off areas of a garden, gates are usually made of wood or metal. Manufacturers supply a number of standard sizes, but anything specific needs to be custom-made. The main gates for a drive can now have remote-control opening and closing mechanisms built in. This increases security as well as being very convenient.

Garden shed
Small outbuildings and garden sheds are ideal storage areas for all garden tools and leisure items. They are supplied in easy-to-build kit forms, but must be raised off ground level on a good foundation. Concrete blocks or slabs can be used to provide solid piers for the shed. Wooden bearers laid across these "piers" will provide a good surface on which to situate the shed base.

Retaining walls
Where there is a change in level in a garden or where you require a raised bed, you may need a retaining wall. These walls therefore require greater structural strength than other garden walls because one side will have material piled against it.

Pavers
Paving blocks or pavers are ideal for paths, drives, and any exterior walkway. Patterns, colours, and the options for how they are laid to create particular designs, are wide and varied. Purpose-made paving blocks can be used, or bricks are another option to create this effect.

Fences
Normally used as boundaries, fences are commonly made of wood, although concrete and metal posts are also used. Wire mesh is sometimes used in a fence, especially if the fence is used to retain animals.

OTHER FEATURES

Not all features are included on every garden. Others not illustrated here that may be relevant to you include:

Asphalt

This is an ideal material for paths of drives. A large-scale task is a job for the professionals. Good edging will prevent the sides of an asphalt drive deteriorating.

Pergola

Decorative features such as pergolas and arches are more common in gardens today. They can be built to your own design or you can buy kits for home construction.

Water features

Small pumps, reservoirs, pond liners and water-feature systems are now readily available. A supply of water is not needed as the pump recirculates the initial supply.

ASPECT

When building any new feature outside your home, consider where light will come from during the day and whether the feature will cast shadow across the house, or parts of the garden. In the UK, the east side of your home will receive light during the morning, and the west in the afternoon and early evening. Outbuildings or trees to the south of your home may cast shadows across the surface of your home, and block light to parts of the garden.

Concrete
Often used for outbuilding bases, drives, and paths, concrete offers a very hardwearing surface for outside areas.

Slabs
Commonly used for patio areas, slabs provide a decorative hard-landscape surface that is exceptionally durable. Designs and slab type vary.

Gravel
This may be used on drives, paths, or soakaways, and is a relatively cost-effective option in all these circumstances. Colours and size vary considerably.

Edging
Used in many areas in the garden, edging can be placed around patios, along the side of flowerbeds, or to create the edge to a drive. Tailor-made kerb stones or edging blocks can be used for this purpose, or bricks, pavers, and other types of building block. Wooden edging planks are commonly used along the side of paths and patio areas.

Decking
This is the wooden alternative to patio slabs, pavers, and other hard-landscaped surfaces. As long as the wood is treated, and maintained regularly, it can last for years.

GREENER GARDENS

There are a number of possibilities for making your outside space more environmentally friendly; it is always worth considering harvesting rainwater (see pp.386–87), composting (see pp.400–01), and using reclaimed materials, such as slabs, wherever feasible (see pp.86–87).

COMPOSTING

Composting is the natural breakdown of organic matter to produce a crumbly nutrient-rich soil. The resulting compost can be added to other soil types as a fertilizer, forming an excellent growing medium for plants. By managing this natural process in your own garden, you can dispose of waste, and produce an agent that will improve the look and yield of any plants and flowers. Regardless of the size of your outdoor space, there will be a composting solution to suit your needs.

WORMERIES

A wormery performs the same task as a compost heap, but on a smaller scale. Worms are kept inside a suitable container, where they eat organic matter; their waste products are then used as a fertilizer. Tiger worms are best for the job, as they live and feed on decomposing compost (unlike common earthworms, which prefer to burrow in soil). You can make your own wormery, or buy a kit that comes with a supply of tiger worms.

MAKING COMPOST

Theories vary on how to produce the perfect compost, but there are some general rules. Firstly, a suitable container or store is required. Different types and designs are shown here, including homemade, shop-bought, and recycled varieties. As the natural process of composting generates heat, storing compost in a container enables the heat to be retained more easily, and allows for the efficient breakdown of material. It is best to keep a compost heap covered to retain this heat, and to prevent rain from making the compost too wet. While some moisture is needed, it is usually supplied in the form of moist grass cuttings and other green waste.

Building up layers

A system of layering different materials will aid the composting process and enhance the finished product. A layer of coarser, more fibrous material, for example, will introduce air to the centre of the heap, which is vital as composting is an aerobic process. However, this may not always be a straightforward task. In the height of summer, for example, the majority of layers are likely to be grass clippings, so it is important to make sure you break up large amounts of one material with other layers – perhaps from the kitchen.

The process of composting takes between two and nine months. You will need to gain access to the base of the heap to take out the crumbly, fully decomposed compost for use on the garden. Some containers have an access hatch at the bottom of the container, while others may need one side to be disassembled so that the bottom level of compost can be dug out. In larger gardens, you may have space for two or three heaps, with each at a different stage of composition.

Plastic bin
Purpose-built plastic bins are fitted with a hatch at the bottom for easy access of composted material.

Slatted wooden bin
This design of bin encourages greater air circulation, improving the ventilation of the heap.

Wooden sectioned bin
This bin design can be disassembled in layers, allowing the heap height to be raised or lowered as required.

Hurdle-style compost bin
As well as looking attractive, this bin offers good ventilation. The heap is accessed by removing one side.

Top layer of green clippings

Bottom layers are well rotted

Cross-section of a slatted wooden bin
Slatted bins are great for gaining access to the bottom of the heap. The sides are easily disassembled, and the compost is normally integrated enough not to spill out.

Concrete bin
This type of bin may have a block or slatted structure. Unlike its wooden alternatives, it will not rot.

Recycled bins
Large recycled containers, such as those used to deliver building materials, make ideal compost bins.

MATERIALS THAT CAN BE COMPOSTED

The complete list of items that can be composted is extensive, but it can be categorized generally as either "brown waste" or "green waste". Examples of specific items included in each category – as well as some exceptions – are detailed in the table below. Although all organic matter will compost, it is advisable not to compost items that may attract vermin or disease (outlined at the bottom of the table).

HOUSEHOLD WASTE **GREEN WASTE** **BROWN WASTE**

COMMON ITEMS FOR COMPOSTING

Type of waste	Example ingredients	Comments
Green waste As the name suggests, this category includes all types of green leafy garden waste. Other types of fast-rotting waste material is also included in this group. All these items have a high nitrogen content	Fresh grass clippings	A plentiful summer supply should be layered with other items
	Flowers	Ensure stems are chopped up; do not use diseased plants
	Nettles	These act as good natural activators
	Vegetable and fruit peelings	Can be added straight to heap from kitchen
	Vegetable crop residue	Such as potato and tomato plants
	Young weeds	Take care with some weeds – perennials are best avoided
	Herbivore manure	Such as that from horses, cows, and rabbits
	Tea leaves	Bear in mind that tea bags will take longer to break down
Brown waste This category refers to the slower-rotting items that have a high carbon content	Dead or autumn leaves	Only small amounts should be used
	Paper	Make sure it is shredded first
	Coffee grounds and filter	Use only paper filters
	Cardboard	This should be torn into small pieces
	Woody hedge clippings and twigs	Ideally these should be put through a shredder
	Sawdust	Mix well with more aerated material
	Herbivore bedding	Such as hay and straw
Other items There are a number of other items that are not immediately obvious candidates for composting but that are nevertheless suitable	Egg shells	These need to be washed and crushed up
	Hair	Either human or animal hair can be added – both are high in nitrogen
	Wool and cotton	Must be 100-per-cent wool or cotton, and cut into small pieces. Tumble-dryer lint can also be composted
	Vacuum-bag contents	Common sense is required depending on what has been picked up
	Wood ash	Only use small quantities

ITEMS NOT TO COMPOST

Although all organic material breaks down, avoid the following as they may attract vermin and harbour potential pathogens	Meat and fish (cooked and raw)	Can harbour disease and attract vermin
	Dog and cat faeces	Harbour disease
	Cat litter	Will normally contain faeces
	Glossy magazines	Contain too many inorganic chemicals
	Barbecue coals and coal ash	Contain harmful sulphur oxides

Hard landscaping

PATIOS, PATHS, AND BRICK WALLS PROVIDE THE FRAMEWORK FOR OUTDOOR AREAS AROUND THE HOME. CREATING HARD SURFACES AND BUILDING SMALLER BRICK WALLS REQUIRE SOME PLANNING AND SKILL, BUT CAN BE CARRIED OUT BY MOST COMPETENT HOME-IMPROVEMENT ENTHUSIASTS.

HARD LANDSCAPING MATERIALS

Materials for hard landscaping include a wide range of masonry products that can be used for building many different types of flat, stepped, or vertical construction. The range of materials available is increasing, but the ways in which new products are used follow a number of basic principles.

SLABS

Slabs used in hard landscaping are normally made of either concrete or natural stone. Size and shape can vary considerably. Like other paving materials, they can be laid in many different patterns.

Concrete slab
Made in a mould, concrete slabs tend to be regular in shape and depth. They may be textured and coloured to mimic natural stone slab or other masonry finishes such as brick paving.

Stone slab
Types of stone often used for paving include yorkstone, granite, and slate. Natural stone slabs are often irregularly shaped making laying more difficult. Some have very straight, machine-cut edges although they usually still vary in depth.

PAVERS

Pavers and paving blocks are smaller, and generally thicker than slabs. They can be laid in many different ways to create any number of different patterns (see p.410).

Paver
Paving blocks are often brick shaped, and bricks themselves can be used as pavers. Round-edged and many other shapes of paver are also available.

EDGING

Most designs of hard landscaping, such as paths, patios, and driveways are improved by some form of edging. In some cases the edge is created by a building or wall, but otherwise use edging blocks to provide a neat, retaining edge. Treated timber is also an option (see p.410). If you are laying any edging next to a lawn, lay it slightly lower so that you can mow over the top.

Edging block
Bricks, or concrete or natural stone blocks such as granite sets, are commonly used to provide an edge. More substantial blocks, called kerbs, are designed for large driveways rather than edging a path, for example.

Edging strip
This consists of a number of blocks or sets joined together. It makes laying much faster.

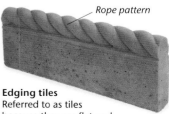

Rope pattern

Edging tiles
Referred to as tiles because they are flat and often made of terracotta, these often have a decorative edge.

AGGREGATES

Many types of aggregate are used in exterior landscaping. Cements, sands, and mortar are discussed in greater detail on pp.70–71. Below are two of the more common sizes of decorative aggregate used outside.

Cobbles
Used for paving or edging, cobbles can also be used with other materials to create pattern or texture. Many sizes and colours are available.

Decorative gravel
A huge variety of sizes and colours of natural and synthetic gravels are available, suitable for creating paths and driveways.

TARMAC

Tarmac can provide an excellent surface for a large driveway. Laying an even, well-compacted tarmac surface that is a good depth, drains effectively, and does not have any unsightly joins requires considerable skill and is a job best left to the professionals. You can make simple repairs to an existing tarmac surface. Fill potholes with cold, ready-mixed tarmac and tamp it down into the hole using a rammer or wooden post (see p.424).

CONCRETE

Concrete forms part of many exterior hard-landscaped areas. Laying a relatively small pad of concrete – as the base for a shed, for example – is a viable DIY project (see p.411). To create a level surface you will need to construct a level wooden frame (a formwork) to hold the wet concrete in place, then remove air bubbles and level the surface across the top of the formwork to produce a flat pad (called screeding, see p.29 for screed machines). If the surface is to support an outbuilding such as a shed, lay a damp-proof membrane over the compacted hardcore under the concrete pad.

If you want to lay a large area of concrete such as a path or driveway, it will require contraction and expansion strips, such as those shown in the path illustrated on the right. Ply is commonly used as a material for expansion strips.

Expansion strips help prevent concrete cracking

CONCRETE PATH

GARDEN WALL MATERIALS

Normal bricks, blocks, and stone are all commonly used to build garden walls, as well as specially designed blocks. Different types of bricks and blocks are shown on pp.82–83. For more on reclaimed materials, see pp.86–87. When choosing materials, check that they are frost-resistant. Choosing bricks with a low salt content will prevent efflorescence (salt crystals forming on the finished wall).

Bricks and blocks

Below are commonly used brick and block materials used in hard landscaping. There are many design variations.

Common brick
For garden walls, common bricks provide a simple decorative option.

Screen wall block
Concrete blocks with holes can be used to create a see-through wall (see p.409).

Garden walling blocks
These are designed specifically for garden-wall construction and are completely frost-resistant.

Wall-feature block
Reconstituted stone blocks are shaped to mimic a number of laid blocks.

Coping stones

The coping is the top layer of a wall that prevents water penetrating the brick- or stonework of the main structure. Specially designed coping stones are available, although you can also use bricks.

Pier cap
Finishes off the top of each pier in a screen-block wall.

Coping stone
Also known as capping stones, coping stones are positioned along the top of some walls and may be purpose-made from concrete or natural stone.

Screen-wall coping stones
Specifically designed to finish off along top of screen-wall blocks.

PREPARING TO BUILD A WALL

When building a wall, the height and style will determine the foundations required. The depth of foundation is relative to wall height and width. If you want a wall higher than 1.2m (4ft) the excavation work needed will be more extensive, so seek professional advice on design and foundations. If you are building a retaining wall, you will also need to build in damp-proofing, and drainage channels to remove the water from the soil behind the wall. With all construction, sound planning and preparation are essential.

PLANNING PERMISSION

You will not normally require planning permission to build a decorative garden wall. However, if the wall is structural or goes above a certain height – normally regulations start at about 2m (6ft) – you may need permission. It is always best to contact your local planning officer if you are in any doubt about regulations or whether permission is needed.
Permission is also required if any wall over 1m (3ft 3in) high is to be built next to a road and/or footpath.

LAYING BRICKS

Bricks can be laid with their long side (stretcher face) or their short side (header face) facing outwards. How stretchers and headers combine in the wall structure is known as the bond.

Brick bonds

Most brick bonds are designed to ensure that joints are always staggered between each course, maintaining the strength of the wall. Stretcher, English, and Flemish bonds are the most popular, although there are many variations. Laying bricks end to end creates a thin "single-skin" wall, whereas other bricklaying patterns result in a thicker "double-skin" wall.

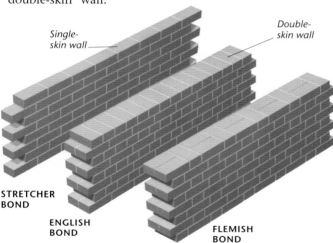

Single-skin wall

Double-skin wall

STRETCHER BOND

ENGLISH BOND

FLEMISH BOND

Corners and piers

The bond has implications when it comes to features such as corners because if bricks are not laid in the correct pattern, the wall will be weak. Pillars, called piers, can be purely decorative but are essential to strengthening single-skin walls over 400mm (15¾in)in height. They should be positioned evenly along the wall at least every 3m (9ft 10in), and can bisect the wall or be offset to one side. The foundations need to be wider at pier position. See p.408 for more details on corner and pier construction.

Making a gauging rod

A gauging rod is a useful tool for keeping a consistent size of mortar joint (see p.408). Simply lay out some bricks flat on the ground one above the other, stretcher-face up. Make a gap of 10mm (½in) between each brick to represent a mortar joint. Hold an offcut of batten against the bricks and mark off the necessary position of each mortar joint.

FOUNDATIONS

The foundations for a garden wall are known as strip footings and consist of concrete laid in a trench. The depth of concrete required depends on wall height and soil type. As a basic guide, for walls up to 1m (3ft 3in) in height, the footing should be at least 150mm (6in) deep for a single-skin wall, and 250mm (10in) deep for a double-skin wall. For clay subsoil, add a further 100mm (4in) to the depth of each footing. The footing should finish 150mm (6in) below ground level, more in extreme climates, to protect the footing from frost damage and allow planting to occur right up to the edge of the wall. Footing width should normally be 200mm (7¾in) wider than the wall or pier– 100mm (4in) on each side. Footings should be 400mm (1ft 4in) wider than the wall in loose, sandy soils.

If the wall is only three or four courses high, a shallower strip footing or even concrete blocks can be used. If you hit bedrock, or you are building off an existing concrete pad, you will not need footings. If you dig a deep footing and the subsoil is still uncompacted, dig down a little further and infill to the footing base with compacted hardcore.

Setting out

Once you have decided on the design of the wall and worked out what size the strip footings need to be, you need to ensure that levels and angles across the sight are correct. Use string lines and wooden pegs for setting out. Even better, construct some profile boards that can be used for marking out the foundation trench and the first course of bricks. You need a profile board at both ends of every straight section of wall. For the easiest possible construction it is worth dry-laying a course of your chosen bond with mortar gaps and adjusting the layout so you do not have to cut more bricks than necessary. Once you are happy with the trench layout, mark the edge of it using a spade to cut into the soil below the lines. Excavate the trench to the required depth.

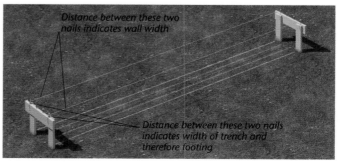

Distance between these two nails indicates wall width

Distance between these two nails indicates width of trench and therefore footing

USING PROFILE BOARDS

LAYING STRIP FOOTING

Knock in a stake at each end of the trench down to footing depth, and at intervals of 1–2m (3–6ft). Make sure that they are vertical.

Rest a spirit level across the top of adjacent stakes to ensure they are level.

Pour concrete into the trench up to the top of the stakes.

Use a metal float to smooth the concrete. The footings should be left to dry for a few days before building the wall.

BUILDING ON A SLOPE

If you need to build a wall on sloping ground the foundation widths and wall thicknesses need not vary, but the way in which the foundations are laid may need to be modified. If the slope is very shallow, simply excavate a level foundation – it will be deeper at one end than at the other. However, if the drop is more than a few courses of bricks then the foundations need to be stepped.

In order to create steps in the footings, some temporary wooden shuttering is used to hold the concrete in position while it dries. Plan the step height to be divisible by brick size so you will not have to cut bricks in order to maintain the bond.

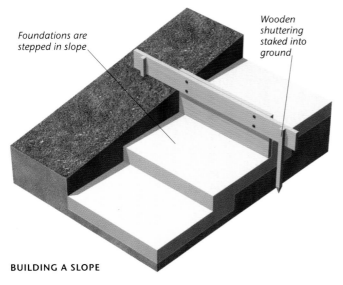

Foundations are stepped in slope

Wooden shuttering staked into ground

BUILDING A SLOPE

MIXING CONCRETE

Use a cement mixer for mixing concrete, because mixing by hand is an arduous task. If you have a large concrete requirement – several cubic metres – hire the services of a ready-mix company. To work out how much concrete you need multiply the depth by the area (width x length). For more on concrete see pp.70–71. Below is a rough guide to quantities.

Foundation concrete
To mix 1cu m (35⅓cuft) of foundation concrete you need 300kg (661lb) of cement; 600kg (1,323lb) of sharp sand, 1,000kg (2,204lb) of course aggregate.

General concrete
In extreme climates and on the coast, increase the proportion of cement to make a stronger mix.

RETAINING WALLS

If a wall is going to hold back soil for a terrace, or be used to create a raised bed, it needs to be especially strong. A single-skin wall is unsuitable, although two skins of stretcher bond can be tied together using wall ties (see p.83). You can reinforce the wall by sinking steel bars into the footings and building a skin on each side of them. You will need a waterproof membrane to protect a retaining wall from damp and frost damage. Build drainage channels or pipes into the wall above the second course of mortar to allow excess moisture to escape. Plastic or copper pipes are ideal. Either drill holes in the bricks to house the pipes, or position the pipes in mortar joints. Infill behind the wall with gravel to aid drainage.

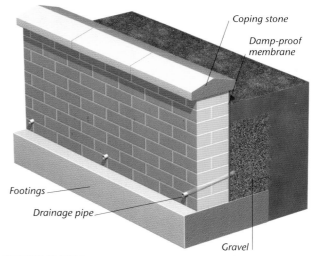

Coping stone

Damp-proof membrane

Footings

Drainage pipe

Gravel

RETAINING WALL

TOOLS AND MATERIALS CHECKLIST PP.406–09

Building a wall (pp.406–07)
Pegs, strings, profile boards, bricks, mortar, brick trowel, spirit level, gauging rod, pins, brick jointer

square, spirit level, brick trowel, mortar, bricks, gauging rod

Turning a stretcher bond corner (p.408) Pegs, strings, profile boards, builder's

FOR BASIC TOOLKIT
SEE PP.24–25

BUILDING A WALL

Lay the footings for the wall and allow them to dry for a few days before starting to build (see p.405). Use a single-skin stretcher bond to hone your basic bricklaying technique. Laying walls with different bonds is simply a case of modifying the pattern in which you lay the bricks (see p.404). The technique here shows racking, which involves building up the ends of the wall, like a flight of steps, and infilling the central area. Getting the first course of brickwork in the right position is essential. Keep checking it using your profile boards and a spirit level.

TOOLS AND MATERIALS SEE BASIC TOOLKIT AND P.405

1 LAYING THE FIRST BRICKS

A Attach lines to the nails on your profile boards to provide a guide for the first course of bricks.

B Dry lay the first row of bricks allowing for mortar joints of 10mm (½in). Cut half bricks to maintain the bond (see p.83 for cutting bricks).

C Mix up some mortar (see p.71) and lay a bed just over 10mm (½in) deep for the first three bricks at the start of the first course.

D Use the point of the trowel to make some furrows in the mortar along its central line.

E Lay the first brick, applying a little pressure to bed it into the mortar. Use a spirit level to check its alignment with the string lines above. In this example, simple piers are being constructed at each end of the wall. More complex pier designs are shown on p.409.

2 COMPLETING THE COURSE

A Butter the end of the next brick and position it next to the first on the bed of mortar.

B Lay a spirit level across the top of the bricks to check they are level. Apply more pressure to the top of the bricks where required in order to get them level.

C Cut away excess mortar from around the brick bases, and remove excess mortar from the vertical joints. Check and re-check their position, using the spirit level across the top.

D Continue along the course, positioning two or three bricks at a time and then tidying the joints. Remove the profile boards and lines when the course is complete.

3 RACKING THE ENDS

Start building up the pier and the end of the wall by three more courses. This is the best practice and will make it easier to infill the rest of the bricks later. Use a spirit level to check the pier is vertical and level.

Use your gauging rod (see p.404) to keep the mortar joints even.

Add two more courses so you have a series of stepped bricks leading up to the top of the pier. Keep checking levels using the gauging rod and spirit level.

4 INFILLING THE COURSES

Repeat the racking procedure at the other end of the wall. Use a spirit level as shown to check bond and levels.

Knock line pins into the mortar joint above the first course of bricks at each end. Tie a line between them. Use this as a guide to infill bricks for the second course.

Infill all the way to the top if the wall is to extend no higher than you have racked. Otherwise, rack back each end once you have infilled two or three courses.

Lay the top course of the wall frog (indent) down. Alternatively, you can lay other types of coping to finish the top of the wall (see p.403).

5 POINTING THE JOINTS

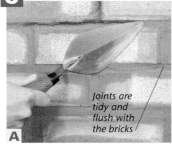

Joints are tidy and flush with the bricks

Fill any areas of missing mortar in the wall. Let the mortar begin to go off but do not let it harden too much. How long this takes will vary, so start checking after one hour.

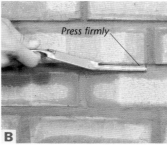

Press firmly

When the mortar is firm, tidy up the joints. A brick jointer (shown here) can be used to create a v-shaped profile.

Helps shed water

Garden wall joints can be pointed in a number of other ways. Here weatherstruck joints are created by using a pointing trowel to angle the mortar joint so that it is recessed at the top and flush with the brick at the bottom. This helps the wall to shed water.

BUILDING OTHER TYPES OF WALL

Once you have mastered the basic technique for laying bricks to form a low, straight wall (see pp.404–07) you can tackle more demanding projects. Shown opposite are more complex designs for piers, and the techniques required to build walls from materials other than brick. Other types of corner are shown below. When building any corner, it is essential that a "square" guide line for the corner is established (see right). The technique shown here is for building a single-skin stretcher bond wall with a corner.

A BUILDER'S SQUARE

In order to turn a corner at precisely 90 degrees, a builder's square is required. This is basically a large carpenter's square (see p.45). You can make a builders square by nailing pieces of batten together into a triangle that has sides in a ratio of 3:4:5. The square shown below is lightweight and can be folded away for easy storage.

CORNERS AND PIERS

These more complex structures are based on the techniques shown on pp.404–07. See p.404 for information on the different types of bond.

Corners

When turning a corner with a wall, ensure the turn is at the correct angle – usually 90 degrees – and that the bond is correctly maintained so that the wall does not lose strength. In both English and Flemish bond walls you need queen closers (bricks cut in half lengthways) to maintain the bond round a corner. See p.39 for information on how to cut bricks. Apart from the different bond, the preparation, the techniques for laying the bricks themselves, and the racking up each end then infilling is the same as for a stretcher bond wall, see pp.406–07.

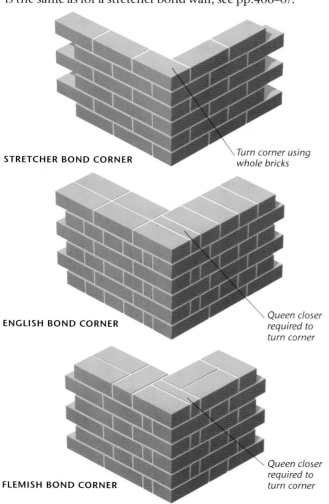

STRETCHER BOND CORNER

Turn corner using whole bricks

ENGLISH BOND CORNER

Queen closer required to turn corner

FLEMISH BOND CORNER

Queen closer required to turn corner

TURNING A STRETCHER BOND CORNER

A Having laid out the footings, mark out the corner accurately using four profile boards and a builder's square.

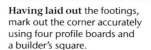

B Lay a bed of mortar and position three stretchers along what will be the front edge of one wall. Use the string lines as guides.

C Continue to lay bricks from the corner to create the first course of the adjacent wall.

D Lay the second row of bricks with the first brick overlapping the corner join of the first row to maintain the bond.

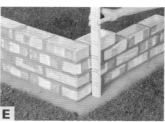

E As you build up further rows, check that the mortar courses are even with a gauging rod.

F Rack up the corner as shown for building a brick wall (see pp.406–07).

G Fill in the rows of bricks as for a straight brick wall. If you are using indented bricks, remember to turn the top course indented-side down (frog down). Point the joints as for a straight wall (see p.407).

Piers

You need piers every 3m (9ft 10¾in) to support single-skin stretcher bond walls over 400mm (1ft 3¾ in) tall. Flemish or English bond walls below 1.2m (3ft 11¼in) in height don't need piers. Seek building advice for walls higher than this.

END AND CENTRAL PIERS ON STRETCHER BOND WALLS

OFFSET END PIER AND CENTRAL OFFSET PIER ON STRETCHER BOND WALLS

BUILDING OTHER TYPES OF WALL

Bricks are not the only material used in garden-wall construction and there are variations in technique required for different types of wall. As well as the three types of wall construction discussed here, different walling materials can be mixed in a design. A brick wall could have a screen wall-block section within it for example, and walls can also be combined with fences.

Screen walls

Available as a kit, screen walls are laid on the same foundations as a brick wall. The main difference in laying technique is that the blocks tend to be laid in a stack bond. In other words, joints between blocks are not staggered. Steel reinforced pillars, called piers, are an integral part of their structure. Expanded steel mesh is used between courses to strengthen the construction. Pier caps and coping stones then protect the wall structure.

Wall blocks and natural stone

A wide range of exterior wall blocks are available, often designed to mimic expensive natural stone. Blocks of differing size can be married together to form a random

MAKING A SCREEN WALL

The stack bond design of a screen wall is very weak. You must use the mesh reinforcement supplied between each course of screen blocks, and the reinforced piers that the blocks slot into. Ensure that the blocks are laid level, using the same techniques as for any wall structure. Make sure you take time to position the pier blocks accurately before you infill with the screen. They will help to align each course correctly.

A **Build up the piers** using the specially designed blocks. Infill screen blocks. Use the strips of mesh reinforcement between the courses.

B **Finish the wall** with coping stones and pier caps. Make sure they are precisely level.

pattern. The challenge is to maintain a vertical line, even though the block surface is irregular. Levels can only be used when laying single blocks because there are no defined courses.

Natural-stone walls are more challenging to build than brick walls. Stone heights vary, as do the roughness of their facing side, and their depth. No stone will be the same size as another. Keeping levels and maintaining a vertical build requires skill. Producing consistent mortar joints and pointing them to a good standard can also be problematic.

Wall features

Statues, alcoves, and arches can be used to provide interest in an otherwise plain wall. Statues of any size should always have a mortar base when positioned on a wall or patio, or a concrete foundation should be dug out of bare earth. Alcoves must have support above them. Their size will dictate what is required so seek professional advice. Brick arches are popular features in many gardens. You will need to build a wooden former to support an arch whilst it is being built (see below).

Building an arch
The arch is built using a ply former with strutting. The former is supported by lengths of timber. Once dry, the former is removed and joints pointed.

Just as walls require sound foundations for construction, surfaces such as patios, paths, and driveways also require a firm base. Foundation depth and type is purely dependent on whether the area will be used only for walking on, or whether cars will be driving or parking on it. Other considerations include the need for adequate drainage, so that water is channelled away from the surface, and away from any walls (see opposite). As well as being functional, paths and patios have a role in garden design, and are often made of decorative materials laid in a pleasing pattern.

MANHOLE COVERS

Never seal over any manhole covers or other access points to underground services with any kind of hard landscaping. Either build around them, or if they are set very low, create an easily removable and well-marked panel in the surface above, or raise the cover itself on a course of bricks. Engineering bricks (see p.82) are ideal for building up the level of a manhole cover because of their strength.

DESIGNING PATHS AND PATIOS

You may already have a clear idea of where you want a path to lead or a patio to be situated, but take time to consider your options. As well as taking into account the hard landscaping itself, think about how the layout and materials fit in with the overall design and style of your house and garden. If your garden has an informal style consider including some cracks and crevices for planting, and staggering paving materials to soften straight lines. For a more formal area choose neat, geometric shapes to carry on the theme.

Patios

Privacy is a key concern when planning a patio because both you and your neighbours will probably prefer not to be overlooked. The aspect of a seating area is also important – a south- or west-facing area receives the most sun during the day and early evening.

Paths

You can use garden paths to lead the eye to a focal point and to create interest, or they can be purely for access. Your choice will influence your design – a decorative path might take a winding route, while an access route is more likely to follow a straight line. You can use a single material to create paths, or mix different surfaces (see below, right). Consider laying slabs or pavers in different patterns – a few are illustrated on the right.

Edging

Hard-landscaped areas are generally designed with some form of edging. If you are making a gravel path, or using slabs or pavers laid dry on a sand bed, the edging will help prevent any lateral movement of the surface. Even if the slabs or pavers are bedded into mortar, an edge of some nature provides the neatest finish. If a hard-landscaped area abuts a lawn, the edging should be lower than the lawn, so that you can mow over it. Treated timber can be used, or edging blocks bedded into a mortar strip (see p.402). Treated timber is the most straightforward to work with, does not require mortar, and provides instant guidelines for levelling across a site (see p.412).

DAMP-PROOF COURSES

The top of an area of hard landscaping that abuts the house must be at least 100mm (4in) below the damp-proof course in the house wall. Any higher than this and splashes from falling rain can bridge the course and cause damp problems inside.

LAYING PAVERS AND SLABS

The pattern chosen for laying slabs or pavers is very much a personal choice. Manufacturers often provide good displays or brochures showing the various options. Some simple types of paver and slab design are shown below. Also remember that bricks (see p.82–83) can be used for paving. You can also buy cut or curved slabs to create alternative designs (see bottom right). Cutting such a curve yourself is practically impossible. Don't forget you can also pave areas with any combination of pavers, slabs, gravel, and cobbles.

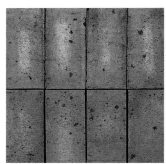

STACK BOND PAVERS

HERRINGBONE PAVERS

BRICKBOND PAVERS

BASKETWEAVE PAVERS

COMBINED PAVERS AND SLABS

CURVED SLABS AND COBBLES

DRAINAGE

You will need drainage around the edge of large hard-landscaped areas. Standing water near the house may soak into walls and cause damp. Water on a paved surface can lead to the growth of algae and vegetation making it slippery and dangerous – a problem for paving laid on a concrete slab, or if mortar has been used. If pavers have been bedded onto sand, some water will drain down through joints and into the subsoil below. Always lay paths and patios with a very slight slope running away from adjacent walls (see below).

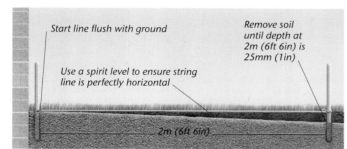

Start line flush with ground

Remove soil until depth at 2m (6ft 6in) is 25mm (1in)

Use a spirit level to ensure string line is perfectly horizontal

2m (6ft 6in)

Establishing a fall
Over a small area you can establish a fall to aid drainage by reducing the amount of mortar or sand under slabs or pavers as you move away from the house. For larger areas of hard landscaping establish the correct fall in the foundations. A fall of 25mm (1in) in 2m (6ft 6in) is sufficient.

PLANNING FOUNDATIONS

Paths and paved areas that will take the weight of vehicles will need more extensive foundations than those used only by people. When planning a major project like a new driveway, seek professional advice about the foundations.

Slabs

If you are laying slabs for a path or patio that will not be driven on then they can be laid directly on a compacted subsoil base. If the base has been recently disturbed by excavation work – for example, if an extension has been recently built – lay a hardcore base on the compacted soil. The slabs may then be dry laid onto a sand layer or laid on mortar. The excavation depth will vary. Ideally hardcore should be 100mm (4in) deep. Slabs can also be laid on an old concrete surface such as a yard without any excavation.

Pavers

Foundation requirements for pavers are similar to that of slabs for paths and patios. However, for driveways and parking areas, pavers do not need a concrete base. They can be laid on compacted hardcore covered with a sand layer.

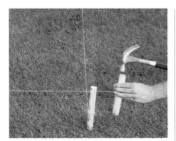

Square paths and patios
Use strings and pegs to lay out an area for a square patio area (see following pages).

Planning a path
For straight guide lines use string and pegs. A garden hose is ideal for planning curves in a design.

LAYING A CONCRETE PAD

A

Level pegs around the site to the depth of the concrete pad plus the foundations – usually a depth of 200mm (8in). Nail boards into the pegs. Insert further level pegs and boards to divide the slab into manageable strips. This wooden frame is known as the formwork.

B

Lay a 100-mm (4-in) layer of hardcore in the bottom of all the formwork sections and compact with a roller.

C

Slide the batten across the formwork

Pour foundation concrete (see p.405) into the first section. Use a batten in a chopping motion to compact it, then level the surface.

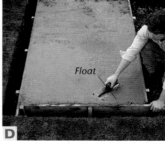

D

Float

Use a float to smooth the surface of the concrete. For large areas, consider hiring a power float or screed (see p.29).

E

Cover the pad with a plastic sheet to protect it from the weather. You can remove the formwork once the concrete has hardened.

TOOLS AND MATERIALS CHECKLIST PP.412–15

Laying a patio pp.412–13
Mallet, pegs, string, builder's square, spade, edging boards, spirit level, wheelbarrow, hardcore, plate compactor, slabs, angle grinder, sand, mortar, rubber mallet, batten offcuts, brick trowel, brick jointer, paintbrush

Laying a paver path p.414 Pegs, string, spade, wooden mallet, edging boards, sand, batten, block splitter*, lump hammer, bolster chisel, blocks, rubber mallet, spirit level, compactor, brush

Creating a gravel path p.415
Edging boards, pegs, rubber mallet, spirit level, weedproof membrane, shovel, hardcore, rammer, gravel, rake

Making steps p.415 Pegs, post, string, spade, hardcore, brick trowel, mortar, bricks, slabs, spirit level

* = optional

FOR BASIC TOOLKIT SEE PP.24–25

LAYING A PATIO

Laying slabs requires considerable planning. The foundations required will depend on its intended use (see p.411). Before calculating the exact area that needs to be excavated, think about the paving design and how to minimize cut slabs. Decide whether to lay slabs butted directly up against each other or with pointing (shown here). You may need to allow space for an edging material. In this example treated timber is being used. You will need two people to manoeuvre large slabs into place.

TOOLS AND MATERIALS SEE BASIC TOOLKIT AND P.411

1 SETTING OUT

A Knock pegs into the ground and tie string lines between them. If possible use a house wall to act as the initial guide line for measuring out the patio.

B Use a builder's square (see p.408) to ensure that the area has 90-degree corners. Adjust pegs and lines if necessary.

2 EXCAVATING FOR FOUNDATIONS

A Mark the edge of the area with a spade, cutting down into the grass. Once the patio is marked out, remove the string lines.

B Dig down to the required depth. Include slab depth, hardcore, and the mortar base in your calculations (see p.411). The patio surface should be lower than any surrounding grass.

3 POSITIONING THE EDGING

A Cut treated timber edging to the same depth as the excavations for the patio. Lay it in position around the edge and check it is square.

B Adjust the timber so that the patio slopes away from the house at a gradient of 1:50, using a gradient level or the peg method shown on p.411.

4 LAYING THE HARDCORE BASE

Knock pegs into ground at 1-m (3ft 3-in) intervals along the outside of the edging. Nail through the face of the edging timber into the pegs to hold the edging in an upright position.

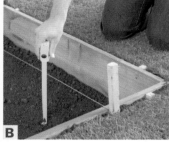

B Run string lines from pegs on one side to those opposite. Measure down from various points along the string line to the excavation base to check depth and gradient.

C Distribute hardcore across the floor of the excavation to an approximate depth of 100mm (4in). Rake it level.

Compact the hardcore using a hired plate compactor. Re-fix the string lines and measure down to check the level of compacted hardcore across the site. Add and compact more hardcore where required to give a reasonably smooth surface that slopes very slightly away from the house.

D

5 PLANNING THE SLAB LAYOUT

A

B

Dry lay the slabs, starting from a corner and working down the edges for a straight design. Remember to allow for mortar joints. Here a brickbond pattern is being laid.

Cut any slabs necessary for the design using a stone saw or angle grinder (see p.61). Dry lay them to check you have a good fit.

6 MORTARING THE SLABS IN PLACE

A

Tap the slab with a rubber mallet to bed it in place

B

C

Scrape away some mortar if a slab sits proud of the others

D

Lay a bed of mortar for the first slab 2–3cm (¾ –1¼in) deep.

Insert spacers made from offcuts of thin batten between the slab and edging to keep pointing consistent. Lay the second slab. Insert spacers between the first and second slab.

Continue laying slabs according to your design. Lay a spirit level across the slabs to check the position, and maintain the fall away from the house.

Lay the rest of the slabs, adjusting the amount of mortar where necessary to maintain an even surface.

7 FINISHING THE PATIO

Once the patio is complete, it should not be walked on for at least 24 hours while the mortar sets. If rain or frost is forecast, cover the area with plastic sheeting held down with spare slabs or bricks. Once the base mortar has set, press more mortar into the joints between slabs using a pointing trowel. Remove excess mortar from the slab surfaces as you progress.

A

B

C

Smooth the mortar along the joins using a brick jointer, or leave flush according to personal preference. Flush joints will drain better.

Tidy up the pointing mortar with a clean paintbrush.

CREATING PATHS AND STEPS

Paths can be created from any number of materials – slabs, pavers, or gravel for example. The preparation of the ground is shown on pages 410–11. Remember to establish a gradient away from the house. Because paths are usually quite narrow, setting them out accurately is much more straightforward than for patios or larger paved areas. If you have a lot of pavers to cut, hire a block splitter before you start. This makes the job much quicker and is therefore a very cost-effective option.

TOOLS AND MATERIALS SEE BASIC TOOLKIT AND P.411

Compact the soil with a rammer. Pour sharp sand into the excavated area and use a wooden batten notched out at each end to level off the sand surface to the depth required for the pavers.

Check boards on both sides are level

C

1 PREPARING TO LAY A PAVER PATH

A

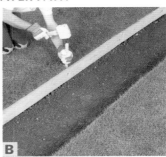

B

Lay out pegs and string lines along the edges of the path. Dig out the path area to a depth of paver height plus a 50-mm (2-in) sand bed.

Put treated timber edging into the excavated area. Knock in wooden pegs on the external side of the board to keep it in place.

2 CUTTING PAVER BLOCKS

A

B

Position the paver between the jaws of the block splitter. Align the point you wish to cut.

Lower the handle of the splitter to break the paver in two.

3 LAYING A PAVER PATH

A

B

C

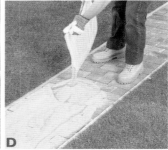

D

Lay blocks in your chosen design. Butt each end up against the next.

Use a rubber mallet to bed blocks into place. Infill cut blocks to finish the design.

Lay a spirit level across the pavers as you finish a row to check that it sits level. If the pavers are uneven, remove them and re-level the sand.

Pour kiln-dried sand over the laid path, making sure that it covers the gaps between the pavers.

Use a compactor over the entire path to ensure the pavers are well bedded. A layer of sand on top of the pavers prevents the compactor from marking the pavers.

E

F

G

Go over the surface once again with a brush once you have finished with the compactor. Brush sand into the spaces between the pavers.

Allow the path to settle for a few days, and go over the surface once more with some sand, filling any gaps.

CREATING A GRAVEL PATH

Excavate your path area to a depth of at least 100mm (4in), then lay treated timber edging boards held in place with wooden pegs. Use a spirit level to check that both sides of the path are level. If not, bed the edging boards down with a rubber mallet.

Fix the edging boards to the pegs with a drill-driver.

Trim with a craft knife

Lay the weedproof membrane on the soil base. If it is necessary to join lengths of membrane, overlap lengths by at least 100mm (4in).

Shovel in hardcore over the membrane surface. Distribute it as evenly as possible, making a layer of about 50mm (2in).

Rake the hardcore level before using a rammer to compact it. Use a roller if you have one.

Pour the gravel into the path area. Make sure you take care when lifting bags.

Rake the gravel level. Once the path has settled for a few weeks, it may be necessary to add some more gravel to top up the level.

MAKING STEPS

Calculate the number of steps by dividing the height of the slope by that of one riser (including slab and mortar). To measure slope height, place a peg at the top of the slope and a post at the bottom. Tie string between the two so that it is level with top of the slope; measure the distance between the string and ground level.

Use string and pegs to mark the sides of the steps and along the fronts of the treads. Dig out the steps and compact the earth for each tread.

Make a footing 150mm (6in) deep and twice the brick width; fill with concrete over a 100-mm (4-in) base of hardcore.

Lay bricks for the first riser on the set concrete footing; use string to check that the bricks are level (see bricklaying technique, p.406–07).

Fill risers with hardcore to the height of the bricks and tamp down Set slabs on 10mm (½in) of mortar. Leave a small gap between them.

Mark the position of the second riser on the slabs; mortar bricks in place. Fill in and set treads. Mortar between the slabs as you lay them.

OTHER TYPES OF STEPS

You can also create steps using concrete or gravel and edging boards, using a similar method to that shown for creating a gravel path, above. Excavate the site and position boards around each step as shown. Then infill with 100mm (4in) of hardcore, and lay concrete or gravel on top to create the treads.

Wooden structures

AS WELL AS FEATURING IN THE HARD LANDSCAPING OF MANY GARDENS, WOODEN STRUCTURES ARE ALSO COMMONLY USED TO CREATE FENCES AS WELL AS DECORATIVE FEATURES IN THE GARDEN. ALL WOOD USED IN GARDENS MUST BE TREATED AND IF IT IS IN CONTACT WITH THE GROUND IT MUST BE TANALIZED (SEE P.75). WOODEN STRUCTURES CAN ALSO BE STAINED, VARNISHED, OR PAINTED (SEE PP.290–91).

WOODEN GARDEN MATERIALS

Wood can be used to build garden structures such as fences, features, or decking. Wooden structures can be combined with masonry or metal components for decorative effect, extra strength, or ease of construction. Kits are often available for you to construct yourself, or you can use ready-made components such as sawn timber, posts, and brackets to create your own design using basic woodworking joints (see pp.392–93).

FENCE CONSIDERATIONS

Most fences need a gate. These are usually hung between two fence posts. Some open fences, such as post and rail designs (see below) can be given a mesh backing if you need a barrier for animals.

FENCE TYPES

There are several traditional designs of fence often used as boundaries or screens within a garden design. Some have panels or boards fixed between posts to form a solid boundary, whilst other designs are more open, being simply constructed of vertical and horizontal members. When choosing a fence, consider how well it will fit with the style of house and garden, and what level of security and privacy you require.

Panel
Large manufactured wooden panels fixed between posts provide a solid barrier. Different sizes and designs of panel are available, but the most common are overlapping horizontal boards housed in a square frame.

Close-board
A solid fence built from separate components, easily adapted to your specifications. Overlapping vertical timbers are fixed to horizontal rails (arris rails) running between fence posts. Featherboards are often used.

Palisade
Similar in construction to a close-board fence, this decorative, partially see-through fence has gaps between the uprights. The uprights may be rounded or pointed for decorative effect.

Post-and-rail
A simple, open design. Horizontal members run between posts. Wire mesh can be used across the framework to provide a less penetrable barrier if necessary. The mesh is attached to the posts and rail using staples (see p.79).

FENCING POSTS

The type of fence post you use will partly be determined by the type of fence you are constructing. In domestic gardens, wood is the most common material used, although metal and concrete posts are also an option.

Square or rectangular in cross-section

Round wooden
Can be used to provide a more rustic appearance than a sawn, square post. Often used with half-round horizontal members in a post-and-rail fence.

Square wooden
A simple design that can be made from a variety of different woods.

Concrete
Pre-cast posts are made for a variety of different fence types. They may have slots in to house fence panels or fit into pre-drilled holes for chain-link fencing.

▮ PUTTING IN POSTS

Excavate a hole for each post, approximately 300mm (12in) square and 500mm (20in) deep to allow for infill around it.

A

Pack hardcore into the base of the post hole to a depth of 100mm (4in).

B

Fill the hole with post mix. Tamp the mix down, making sure the post remains vertical.

C

Check the post is vertical using a spirit level.

D

Use a watering can with a spray head to water in the post mix, which will dry quickly to hold the post securely in position.

E

Nail a wooden batten to the post to keep it upright while the post mix sets. Concrete can be used as an alternative to post mix.

F

FENCE ACCESSORIES

Along with fence timbers, there are a number of accessories that are used to aid fixing and help repair these structures. The brackets and clips shown below provide a few examples of the types of systems that are available.

Post spike
Metal spike that has a square socket at the top to house the base of a post so no excavation or foundation is necessary.

Post clip
Small clip that fixes to post and fence panel, holding the panel in place.

Bolt-down post bracket
Socket that houses a post on concrete or other masonry surfaces.

Driving tool
Specially shaped tool to aid knocking a post spike into the ground. It fits into the cup of the socket to provide a firm surface to strike with a sledge hammer.

Post cap
Decorative cap fixed to the top of wooden post. Also prevents water penetration into the end grain of the post.

Triangular or trapezoid in cross-section

Arris rail
Runs horizontally between fence posts behind a close-board fence (see opposite).

Arris rail bracket
Connects the triangular arris rail used in a close-board fence to the post. Saves having to form a mortise joint.

WOODEN WALKWAYS AND DECKS

Wood is also used underfoot in garden construction for paths and steps, and patio areas. Decking has become increasingly popular as it offers a clear alternative to hard-landscaped areas.

Small ridges provide grip underfoot

Reversible decking board
Some manufacturers produce decking boards with different textures on opposite sides.

Widely spaced channels provide good drainage

Rough-sawn decking board
Decks can also be made from rough-sawn, treated timber which will not necessarily be sold as a "decking board".

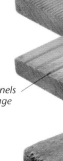

ERECTING A FENCE

To set out for a fence, secure a string line with pegs at the starting and finishing point of each straight run of fence. If you are using manufactured panels it is best to plan to use whole ones. With other types of fence it is easier to adjust the design to your specifications where necessary. Once you have marked out the position it is a case of firmly fixing the posts before filling in the fence between them.

PLANNING THE FENCE

Once you have marked the run of the fence with a string line, you need to work out the post spacing. The distance between posts will vary according to fence type. For a panel fence, the distance is governed by panel size, which is commonly 1.8m (6ft). A similar distance may be used for close-board fences, although this can be adjusted depending on the type of boarding used. Fence posts can be set in concrete, held in place by sockets bolted to a concrete surface or sunk with the aid of a post spike (see p.417 and box top right). When a fence is positioned on or next to a wall, the posts may be bolted directly to the wall, so there is no need for an attachment at ground level.

Securing posts

Once the post position has been marked out, the next step is to dig post holes. Alternatively you can drive in or bolt down post sockets. If you are digging post holes, a 1.8-m (6-ft) fence will need posts secured in holes approximately 500mm (20in) deep, and 300mm (12in) square. The holes need a 100-mm (4-in) layer of compacted hardcore in the bottom. Soak the cut ends of the posts in wood preserver before they are positioned in the holes. They can then be secured with concrete mixed to a stiff foundation consistency (see p.71) or a specially formulated post mix as shown on p.417, which is more expensive but quicker to use.

ERECTING A PANEL FENCE

Fence panels can be nailed into place, but clips give a neater finish. You need to make sure that the bottoms of the panels don't touch the ground – they must never sit in standing water. You can use gravel boards below the panels (as shown for the close-board fence, right). Alternatively, as shown here, fix fence panels so that they are slightly above ground level.

Fix clips to post, one at the top, one in the middle, and one at the bottom of the post.

Slot the edge of the panel into the clips and secure it in place.

POST SOCKETS

Post spikes (see p.417) can be driven below ground level to hold a post invisibly, although you can leave the socket section of the spike above ground and screw through the slots in it and into the post for extra security. Bolt-down post brackets (see p.417) can be used on hard surfaces. You will need to drill pilot holes using a suitable masonry bit and insert plugs before screwing down the sockets. Slip the post into the socket and tighten the bolts across the socket corner so it grips the post tightly.

ERECTING A CLOSE-BOARD FENCE

Traditional close-board fences have arris rails mortised into the posts. However, it is much easier to fix rails to the post using specially shaped brackets. These brackets are also ideal for making repairs (see p.425). Another option is to nail specially shaped rails to the posts and fix the boards to these. The number of arris rails needed will depend on fence height. In the example shown here, two are sufficient.

Use a drill-driver

Fix a length of gravelboard to the base of the post. Use a spirit level to check that it is level.

Fix one arris rail bracket close to the bottom of the fence post, and another near the top of the post.

Slot an arris rail into each bracket. Hold the rails level to fix brackets for their other ends on the next post. Fix the rails into the brackets.

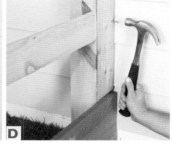

Nail the first featherboard to the end post. Make sure it is vertical.

Use a nail gun for speed (see pp.52–53)

Overlap the featherboards as you continue along the fence. Check that they are vertical with a spirit level.

Nail a fence cap to the top of each post to protect the end grain.

Decking provides an attractive outdoor seating area and can also be used to cover up an old concrete yard or patio without needing to excavate it. Decking is quicker to install than paving and can be easily adjusted to almost any size and situation. Installing a deck is easier with some help. Before installation check local building regulations (see right). Ensure that your chosen spot will not be overlooked, or that you do not overlook your neighbours. You may also want to consider when an area gets the sun.

DECKING REGULATIONS

Check with your building control office before constructing a deck, especially for a listed property or if the deck is raised high enough to overlook any neighbours. Regulations regarding steps and balustrades are similar to those for staircases (see pp.184–89). If you are building a large or very high deck, get professional advice on timber specifications.

FOUNDATIONS

Generally the higher the decking is off the ground, the deeper the foundations need to be. For ground-level decking the slab method shown overleaf is usually sufficient.

Ground-level decking

On soft ground you may need to create footings. Strip the turf or soil surface to take concrete blocks or slabs. On uneven ground, if you need to raise a slab, excavate 30–40mm (1–1½in) of soil below the slab and infill the hole with compacted hardcore. On very uneven ground use concrete blocks instead of slabs to build up levels.

Raised decking

Post holes should be at least 300mm (12in) deep, or up to 500mm (20in) in disturbed ground (see p.417). On a concrete surface use bolt-down post sockets (see box opposite, top). When building a large deck, or one raised by more than 600mm (2ft), get professional advice on timber and footing specifications.

BUYING TIMBER

Timber for decking must be pressure-treated to resist weathering and any cut ends must be treated with preservative. Plan the support layout on paper beforehand so that you can work out how much timber you need to buy. You can also buy decking systems of notched bearers

that slot together quickly to form a frame for ready-made decking panels. These are even quicker to put up than the decks shown in the following pages.

◼ ADAPTING DECK DESIGN

Deck shape can be easily adjusted to any requirement with minimal woodworking skills. The decking boards themselves can be straight, run diagonally, or you can create more complex chevron or square designs. Trim edges with a power saw to create curves (see below). You may need to use double joists to enable you to fix more complex designs.

A — **Where you want** a curved edge to a deck, run the framework in steps around the curve. Use a pencil and string tied to a nail to draw a smooth curve across the boards.

B — **Use a jigsaw** to cut around the edges of the boards. Treat the cut ends with preservative.

Decking with rails and steps

Even small-scale decks such as that shown left are governed by regulations. Check with your manufacturer that you have sufficient supports for the size of deck.

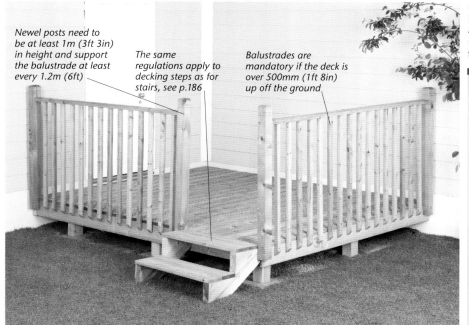

Newel posts need to be at least 1m (3ft 3in) in height and support the balustrade at least every 1.2m (6ft)

The same regulations apply to decking steps as for stairs, see p.186

Balustrades are mandatory if the deck is over 500mm (1ft 8in) up off the ground

TOOLS AND MATERIALS CHECKLIST
PP.420–23

Laying ground-level decking, (p.420–21) Bearers, decking boards, fascia boards, joist hangers, decking screws, batten, mitre saw, try square, spade, paving slabs, trowel, gravel, scissors, weedproof membrane, preservative, paintbrush

Laying raised decking, (p.422–23) Bearers, decking boards, fascia boards, joist hangers, decking screws, batten, blocks and bricks, trowel, spade, hardcore, foundation mix, gravel, weedproof membrane, frame fixings, nuts, bolts, preservative, paintbrush

FOR BASIC TOOLKIT SEE PP.24–25

LAYING GROUND-LEVEL DECKING

Building a ground-level deck is a relatively straightforward process. Make sure you use treated timber and screws designed for the purpose. On a concrete base such as a yard or old patio, there is no need for any foundation work. Simply pack out the bearers that do not sit flush with the surface using thin offcuts of treated timber. On soft ground such as an old lawn use paving slabs to support the deck slightly off the ground. Bed down the slabs on gravel as shown below. Always lay a weedproof membrane to prevent weeds growing up through the deck.

TOOLS AND MATERIALS SEE BASIC TOOLKIT AND P.419

1 CONSTRUCTING A FRAME

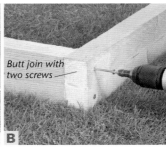

Butt join with two screws

A

Cut all bearers to the required length. A power saw such as a mitre saw is ideal for this purpose.

B

Lay out the four bearers that form the outside of the square and butt join them at the corners. Fix using 150-mm (6-in) screws suitable for outdoor use.

Attach the struts to the frame formed by the bearers. Fix them in position with 150-mm (6-in) wood screws from the outside of the frame.

C

To ensure the framework is square, position a batten brace across the corner of the framework to form a triangle with sides in a 3:4:5 ratio.

D

Mark off fixing points for further struts at 400-mm (1ft 3½-in) intervals on opposite bearers.

E

2 PREPARING THE GROUND

A

Mark the four corners of the frame. Put the frame to one side and strip the turf or 5mm (2in) of topsoil from the deck site to give a level surface. Reposition the frame.

B

Slip paving slabs underneath each corner of the frame and midway down each bearer, or every 1.2m (4ft 3in)for large decks. Move the framework to one side.

C

Mark around a slab with a brick trowel. Lift it to one side so that you can remove 25mm (1in) of soil from beneath it.

D

Pour a layer of gravel into the slab bed you have created. Repeat for all the slabs.

3 LEVELLING AND FINISHING THE GROUND

Cut away the membrane and trim around the slab edge. Repeat for the rest of the slabs so they are all free from the membrane. This will prevent vegetation growing through the decking. Lay gravel to cover the membrane and brush it level around the slabs.

A **Rest a level** on a batten between slabs. If slabs need to be lowered to give a level surface, remove more soil or gravel as necessary.

B **Once the slabs** are levelled, roll out weedproof membrane over the slabs. Feel for the slab's position and cut the membrane around each slab.

4 FIXING THE FIRST BOARDS

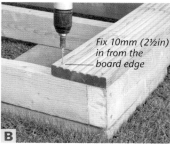

Fix 10mm (2½in) in from the board edge

A **Position the first** board along the edge of the deck farthest from the wall. Make it flush with the framework edge.

B **Fix the board** with two decking screws (see p.77) into each bearer.

C **Position the next** board using screws or wooden offcuts to give a gap of 3–10mm (⅛–⅓in) between the two lengths.

D **Continue placing** boards towards the wall. If you find the boards are splitting as you drive the screws in, you can drill pilot holes for them to reduce the problem.

5 FINISHING THE DECK

A **The finishing board** on the deck will probably need to be cut along its length. Scribe it to fit the wall if necessary (see p.72 for technique).

B **Treat the cut edges** by painting on preservative with a brush. Treat any other cut edges on the decking.

C **Slot the final board** into place and fix as before.

D **Cover the bearer** framework and the board edges with a fascia of treated timber. Fix it into the bearers around the edge of the deck.

LAYING RAISED DECKING

The frame for raised decking is constructed in the same way as for ground-level decking (see pp.420–21) then raised on posts. On a concrete base, posts can be secured to the ground using bolt-down post brackets; on soft ground, some excavation work is required to bed the posts securely on a solid foundation. Take time to remove vegetation and put down a membrane and gravel beneath a deck on soft ground, as for a gravel path (see pp.414–15). A raised deck will require a handrail.

TOOLS AND MATERIALS SEE BASIC TOOLKIT AND P.419

1 MARKING OUT

A Position the framework at ground level, then raise it on blocks and bricks to the required height. Use a spirit level to check that it is level.

B Hold the base of a post inside a corner of the frame. Cut soil from around its base using a trowel. Mark out the other post holes in the same way. Remove the framework.

2 EXCAVATING THE POST HOLES

A Dig a foundation hole for each post 300 x 300mm (1ft x 1ft) square and to at least the same depth. Put the framework back on to check their position.

B Compact hardcore into the bottom of the holes to serve as footings. Lay weedproof membrane as for the ground-level deck (see p.421). Pour a thin layer of gravel over the top.

3 FIXING THE FRAME IN PLACE

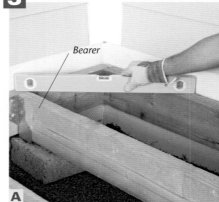

Bearer

Use blocks and bricks at each corner to support the deck temporarily at the correct height. If you are fixing the frame against a wall, as shown here, it should be fixed below the damp-proof course. Hold a spirit level across the corner of the frame. Pack out one end to get it level if required.

B Mark fixing positions and drill pilot holes through the bearer for frame-fixing screws. Tap the plugs and screws into place. Then fix the frame to the wall.

C Position the posts, using a spirit level to check that they are vertical. Drill a hole through bearer and post. Then screw them together with a nut and bolt.

D Infill the base of all posts with foundation-mix concrete (see pp.70–71). Check the frame is level again before the concrete dries. Alternatively use post mix (see p.417).

E Use a panel saw to cut the posts, so that they are flush with the framework.

4 FIXING THE BOARDS

Once the concrete has dried, place a board along the edge of the deck farthest from the wall perpendicular to the bearers. Make it flush with the frame edge. Fix the board with two decking screws at each bearer. You may wish to use pilot holes to prevent boards splitting as you drive the screws in.

A

B

Fix a screw into the bearer at the edge of each board. Then fix the next board in place as on a ground-level deck (see p.421). Continue laying boards across the frame.

C

Scribe and cut a final board to fit (see pp.72–73). Then fix it in place as before.

5 ATTACHING THE HANDRAIL AND STEPS

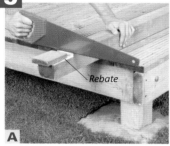

A

Rebate

Cut a rebate in the base of the newel post to a depth of 20mm (1in).

B

Drill two holes through the rebated section of the post and the frame beneath. Screw the post to the frame using nuts and bolts. Repeat with the other newel posts.

C

Cut the handrail to size, then fix it to the post with wood screws. Use a spirit level to check that it is level.

D

Spindle

Cut a piece of wood to the length required between spindles (not more than 100mm (4in) long). Use this to position the first spindle and fix the spindle to the handrail.

E

Use your piece of cut wood to space the bottom of the spindle. Then fix the spindle to the frame of the deck. Continue fitting spindles around the deck.

F

Fix the side supports of the steps to the edge of your frame. Step kits can be bought specially made for decks, or you can make your own.

G

Fix trimmed decking boards to form the treads of the steps. Remember to treat all cut ends with preservative. On soft ground you may wish to bed paving slabs under the bottom of the steps, bedding them on gravel, as shown on p.420.

OUTDOOR ALTERATIONS AND REPAIRS

REPLACING A BROKEN SLAB

Slabs can become unstable, or may crack due to poor laying technique, frost, or a fault introduced during manufacture. In whichever case, the slab needs to be lifted and relaid. Laying slabs on a bed of sand is a more straightforward procedure than shown here, where they have been laid on mortar.

TOOLS AND MATERIALS
Gloves, goggles, pry bar, block of wood, lump hammer, cold chisel, mortar, trowel, spirit level, rubber mallet, batten, new slab

Block of wood provides leverage

A **Use a pry bar** to lift the old slab. If it is concreted in place, break it with a lump hammer and cold chisel. Wear protective goggles and gloves.

B **Chip away** any old mortar and remove debris from the slab bed.

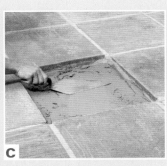

C **Lay a new bed** of mortar, levelling it off with a trowel.

D **Position the new slab**, checking that it is level with those around it. Tap it into place with a rubber mallet.

E **Repoint the slab** with mortar, or a dry mix as required (see pp.70–71 for mixing information).

MAINTAINING PAVING
Paving along with other exterior surfaces such as decking can become covered in algae, this is very slippery and potentially dangerous. Pressure washing these areas at least once or twice a year should keep the problem at bay. In some cases, particularly in damp or shady areas, fungicidal washes may be useful to prevent algae quickly regrowing.

LEVELLING BLOCK PAVING

Block paving can often sink if it has not been laid correctly. Because it is generally laid on sand, rectifying the problem involves lifting the sunken blocks and re-seating them on more sand.

TOOLS AND MATERIALS
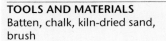
Batten, chalk, kiln-dried sand, brush

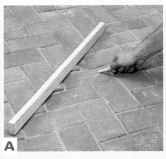

A **Hold a batten** across the area, and mark with chalk any blocks that do not sit flush with the underside of the batten.

B **Prise up the blocks** with old flat-head screwdrivers. Add more sand with a trowel, levelling off with a batten.

C **Reposition the blocks**, checking that they are level, and brush kiln-dried sand into the joints.

PATCHING TARMAC

Relaying a tarmac drive is a job for the professionals, but patching holes is relatively straightforward. Use cold-mix tarmac that can be bought by the bag.

TOOLS AND MATERIALS

Brush, cold-mix tarmac, trowel, wooden post or rammer

A **Remove any loose debris** from the damaged drive.

B **Trowel in** some cold-mix tarmac, leaving it slightly proud of the surrounding surface.

C **Tamp it down** using a wooden post offcut, or a rammer if you have one.

RE-SEATING A CAPPING STONE

Coping and capping stones can loosen over time. Re-seat them so that rain cannot penetrate the top part of the wall.

TOOLS AND MATERIALS
Gloves, goggles, lump hammer, cold chisel, bricklaying mortar, trowel, spirit level

A Remove the loose stone from the top of the wall.

B Chip out old mortar with a lump hammer and cold chisel. Mix up some mortar (see pp.70–71). Lay it across the top of the brick course.

C Reposition the capping stone using a spirit level to check position. Re-point the joints.

RELAYING GRAVEL PATHS

The main problem with a gravel path is weeds. They can be controlled by weedkillers, but a longer-lasting solution is to use a weedproof membrane.

TOOLS AND MATERIALS
Polythene sheets, shovel, weed membrane, rake

A Move the gravel out of the path. Pile it up alongside the path, ideally on polythene sheets.

B Roll out a proprietary weed membrane along the path base, cutting as required. Overlap joins by at least 100mm (4in).

C Move the gravel back onto the membrane, and distribute evenly using a rake.

REPAIRING CONCRETE

Hairline cracks in concrete pads are no problem, but larger cracks should be filled. Excavate the crack to a reasonable depth, to give the repair more surface area to stick to. Repairs to the edge of a slab are shown here.

TOOLS AND MATERIALS
Brush, PVA, plank, bricks, mortar

A Remove loose debris and dust out the hole as necessary. Apply some dilute PVA to the rough concrete surface.

B Use two bricks to support a section of plank that will hold the concrete in place while it dries.

C Fill the crack with concrete until it is level with the surrounding area. Allow the mortar to dry before removing the bricks and plank.

REPAIRING FENCES

Rotten wooden fences are generally best replaced but damaged sections can be strengthened using clips or brackets. If a joint is loose, consider inserting wedges around the joint to strengthen it.

TOOLS AND MATERIALS
Hammer, wedge, joint-repair bracket, drill, screwdriver

Loose fences
Stabilize loose panels by knocking wooden wedges into the joints.

Mending broken rails
Brackets may also be used. Here, an arris-rail bracket connects the rail securely with the post.

OTHER WOODWORK JOINTS

The brackets shown here are fairly specialist in terms of shape. There are also many other types of plate and bracket that can be used to strengthen different types of joint found in wooden constructions in the garden (see pp.392–93). Technique and procedure will therefore have to be tailored to the type of damage you have.

ELECTRICS

ELECTRICAL SYSTEMS
COMMUNICATIONS SYSTEMS

HOME WIRING SYSTEMS

The wiring system in your home is almost totally concealed. All you can see are light fittings, switches, the socket outlets that allow you to plug in your appliances, and the box of tricks that controls the whole system – the consumer unit or fuse box. Here is what each of these visible components does.

A GUIDED TOUR

It is worth taking a little time to find your way around your home's wiring system. On the following pages you will find full details about how the system is controlled and how the various circuits are run. This illustration will help you to identify all the electrical components you can see in your home. Some of them will be more familiar than others, and your system may not have all of them. Note the special switches controlling the cooker, the shower, and the immersion heater in the hot-water storage cylinder. Look too for two-way switching – control of lights from more than one switch position – and for unswitched socket outlets behind kitchen appliances which are controlled by switches above the worktop.

Fused connection unit (FCU)
Square, wall-mounted fitting allowing a small, fixed appliance such as an extractor fan to be connected to the power circuit cables directly, rather than via a plug and socket outlet. It may be switched or unswitched. The removable fuseholder contains a 3- or 13-amp cartridge fuse.

Socket outlet
Square or rectangular, wall-mounted fitting allowing portable appliances to be connected to power circuit cables concealed within walls. The fitting may offer one, two, or three outlets, and is usually switched. It may also feature a neon on-off indicator.

Ceiling rose
Round, ceiling-mounted fitting where a pendant lampholder's flex is connected to the lighting circuit cables running in the ceiling void.

Outdoor socket outlet
Weatherproof socket outlet fitted on the house wall. It may contain a high-sensitivity residual current device (RCD) to protect users of garden power tools from the risk of electric shock.

Cooker connection unit
Square wall-mounted fitting installed behind a freestanding cooker, allowing its cable to be connected to the cooker circuit cable.

Double-pole (DP) cooker switch
Square or rectangular, wall-mounted fitting controlling a cooker, oven, or hob and rated at 40 or 45 amps. It may also contain a switched socket outlet.

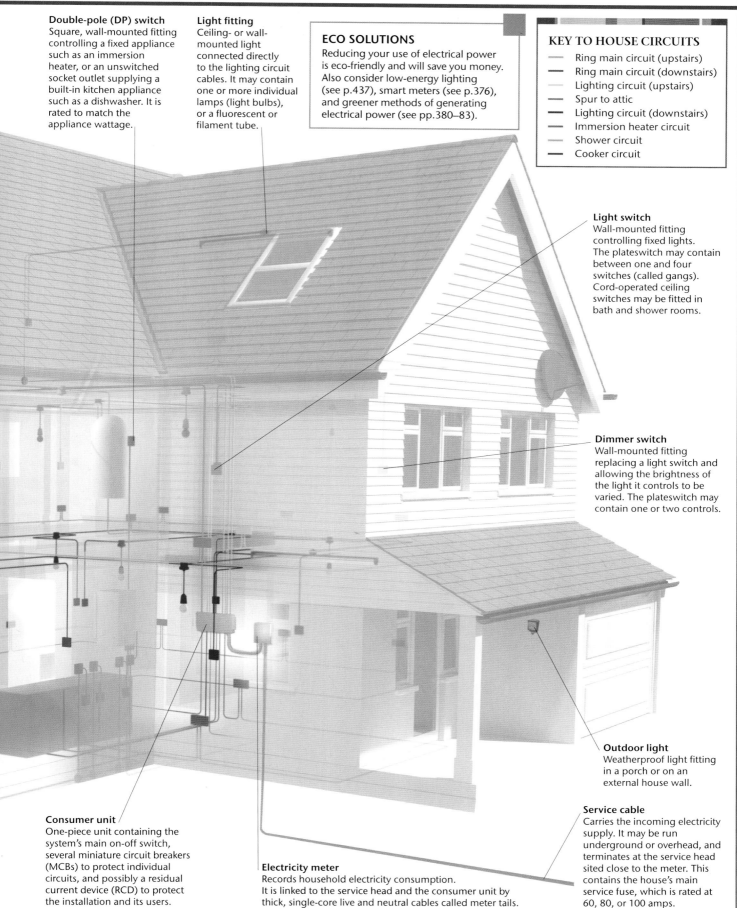

Double-pole (DP) switch
Square, wall-mounted fitting controlling a fixed appliance such as an immersion heater, or an unswitched socket outlet supplying a built-in kitchen appliance such as a dishwasher. It is rated to match the appliance wattage.

Light fitting
Ceiling- or wall-mounted light connected directly to the lighting circuit cables. It may contain one or more individual lamps (light bulbs), or a fluorescent or filament tube.

ECO SOLUTIONS
Reducing your use of electrical power is eco-friendly and will save you money. Also consider low-energy lighting (see p.437), smart meters (see p.376), and greener methods of generating electrical power (see pp.380–83).

KEY TO HOUSE CIRCUITS
— Ring main circuit (upstairs)
— Ring main circuit (downstairs)
— Lighting circuit (upstairs)
— Spur to attic
— Lighting circuit (downstairs)
— Immersion heater circuit
— Shower circuit
— Cooker circuit

Light switch
Wall-mounted fitting controlling fixed lights. The plateswitch may contain between one and four switches (called gangs). Cord-operated ceiling switches may be fitted in bath and shower rooms.

Dimmer switch
Wall-mounted fitting replacing a light switch and allowing the brightness of the light it controls to be varied. The plateswitch may contain one or two controls.

Outdoor light
Weatherproof light fitting in a porch or on an external house wall.

Service cable
Carries the incoming electricity supply. It may be run underground or overhead, and terminates at the service head sited close to the meter. This contains the house's main service fuse, which is rated at 60, 80, or 100 amps.

Consumer unit
One-piece unit containing the system's main on-off switch, several miniature circuit breakers (MCBs) to protect individual circuits, and possibly a residual current device (RCD) to protect the installation and its users.

Electricity meter
Records household electricity consumption. It is linked to the service head and the consumer unit by thick, single-core live and neutral cables called meter tails.

Electrical systems

WHEN YOU WORK ON YOUR HOME WIRING SYSTEM, YOU NEED TO KNOW HOW THE VARIOUS CIRCUITS AND WIRING ACCESSORIES HAVE BEEN INSTALLED. THIS NOT ONLY HELPS YOU TO UNDERSTAND HOW TO ALTER OR EXTEND THE SYSTEM, BUT ALSO GIVES YOU EXAMPLES OF CORRECT WIRING PRACTICE THAT YOU SHOULD COPY IN YOUR OWN WORK. FOR INFORMATION ABOUT OUTDOOR CIRCUITS, SEE PP.452–55.

TYPES OF CIRCUIT

There are several different wiring circuits inside the typical home, supplying electricity to socket outlets for portable appliances, to lights and light switches, to large fixed appliances such as a cooker, shower, or immersion heater, and possibly to outdoor lights and socket outlets. A standard modern home is likely to have at least two socket outlet and lighting circuits, usually one on each floor.

POWER CIRCUITS

These circuits supply electricity to socket outlets where portable or movable appliances are plugged in, and also to fused connection units (FCUs) for small fixed appliances such as cooker hoods and waste disposal units.

AVOIDING OVERLOAD

Every circuit is fitted with a protective device (a fuse or circuit breaker – see p.432) that stops it being overloaded if too many appliances or lights are connected to it. A power circuit can supply a maximum of about 7,000 watts (7 kilowatts/kW), and a lighting circuit up to about 1,200 watts. The maximum load for a circuit to a single large appliance such as a cooker depends on the cable size used to wire it, and on the rating of the fuse or circuit breaker. Before you extend an existing circuit or fit a more powerful appliance, check that what you plan to do will not overload it.

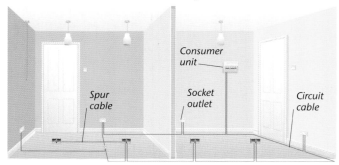

Ring main circuit

The circuit cable runs from socket outlet to socket outlet, with its live core starting and terminating at the fuse or miniature circuit breaker (MCB) in the consumer unit. This allows the current to flow in either direction around the ring. The circuit can supply an unlimited number of socket outlets or FCUs on the ring. Each outlet on the ring can also supply a spur cable running on to one single- or double-socket outlet or FCU. The floor area of the rooms served by the circuit must not exceed 100sq m (1075sq ft).

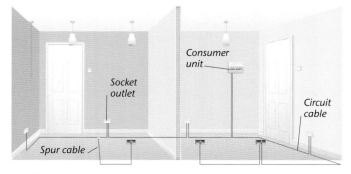

Radial circuit

The circuit cable runs from the circuit MCB to each socket outlet or FCU in turn, terminating at the most remote one. A radial circuit is used in two situations: to supply a long building where a ring circuit would double the amount of cable needed, and for a home extension where extending an existing ring main circuit would exceed the floor area limit. The floor area served by a 20-amp radial circuit wired in 2.5mm² cable must not exceed 50sq m (540sq ft). It can supply an unlimited number of socket outlets.

LIGHTING CIRCUITS

These circuits supply electricity to all the fixed lighting points in the home. They are wired up as radial circuits, terminating at the most remote light on the circuit.

Loop-in wiring

The circuit cable runs into and out of a series of loop-in ceiling roses, each containing three sets of terminals. The switch cable is wired into the rose terminals, as is the flex to a pendant lampholder or decorative light fitting.

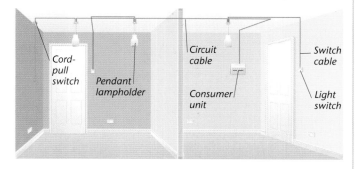

Cord-pull switch
Pendant lampholder
Circuit cable
Consumer unit
Switch cable
Light switch

Junction-box wiring

The circuit cable runs into and out of a series of junction boxes, each containing four terminals. Separate cables run from each box to a ceiling rose and to its switch. Junction boxes are used on modern wiring circuits either to extend an existing circuit, or to make more economical use of cable.

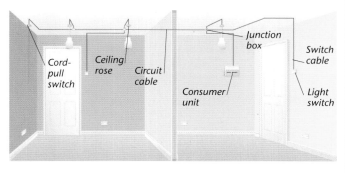

Cord-pull switch
Ceiling rose
Circuit cable
Junction box
Consumer unit
Switch cable
Light switch

Two-way and intermediate switching

These types of switches allow the control of a light fitting from two switch positions. They are frequently used to control stairwell lighting. The switches are linked using special three-core-and-earth cable (see p.438). Intermediate switches can be fitted between a pair of two-way switches to provide additional control points.

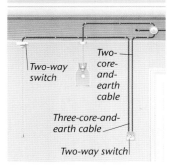

Two-way switch
Two-core-and-earth cable
Three-core-and-earth cable
Two-way switch

STANDARD TWO-WAY SWITCHING

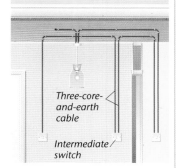

Three-core-and-earth cable
Intermediate switch

TWO-WAY SWITCHING WITH INTERMEDIATE SWITCH

COOKER CIRCUITS

The circuit runs from the consumer unit to a double-pole (DP) isolating switch close to the cooker position. As a general guide, the circuit to a cooker rated at up to 12kW should be wired in 6-mm² cable and protected by a 30- or 32-amp MCB. The circuit to one rated at over 12kW should be wired in 10-mm² cable and protected by a 40- or 45-amp MCB. If separate built-in components are installed, cable runs directly from the switch to the terminals on the oven and hob. Both must be within 2m (6ft 6in) of the switch.

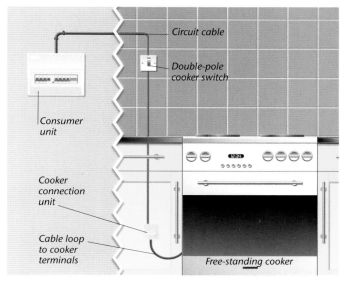

Circuit cable
Double-pole cooker switch
Consumer unit
Cooker connection unit
Cable loop to cooker terminals
Free-standing cooker

SHOWER CIRCUITS

The circuit cable is run from the consumer unit via a high-sensitivity 30-milliamp residual current device (RCD) and then on to a DP switch – usually ceiling-mounted near the shower cubicle – and on to the shower unit. For a shower rated at up to 8kW, 6-mm² cable is adequate, but 10-mm² cable is a better option in case an existing shower is upgraded in the future to a more powerful one. The MCB and switch should be rated at 40 or 45 amps.

Power showers are driven by a low-voltage pump, which can be supplied via a spur from a power circuit.

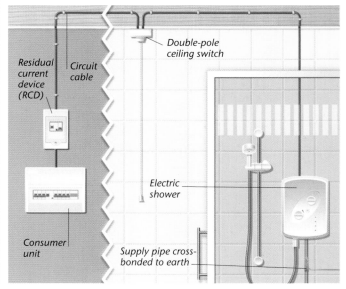

Residual current device (RCD)
Circuit cable
Double-pole ceiling switch
Electric shower
Consumer unit
Supply pipe cross-bonded to earth

WORKING SAFELY

If you decide to tackle your own electrical work, you must first find out how your wiring system is controlled. This ensures that you can isolate the part of the system that you want to work on from the mains supply, so that you can repair or extend it in complete safety. You must also be aware of the rules and regulations that govern domestic wiring work.

ELECTRIC SHOCK: WHAT TO DO

■ If someone receives a major electric shock and is still connected to the current source, turn it off. If you cannot, either grab clothing or use a non-conductive object, such as a broom handle, to drag the casualty away from it.
■ See pp.514–15 for what to do next, depending on whether the casualty is conscious or unconscious.

UNDERSTANDING THE CONTROLS

The consumer unit (or the fuse box on an unmodernized wiring system) is the main control point. Here you can switch off the entire system, or isolate individual circuits.

Modern consumer unit

This one-piece enclosure (below) contains a row of switches called miniature circuit breakers (MCBs). The MCBs control the power supply to individual circuits. There may also be an extra circuit breaker called a residual current device (RCD). This provides additional protection to some at-risk circuits. Alternatively, some circuits may be protected by a combined MCB-RCD called a residual current breaker with overcurrent protection (RCBO).

The RCD or RCBO trips off and isolates the protected circuit from the mains supply if it detects a fault caused by current leaking to earth. This occurs if someone receives a shock from touching something live, or if insulation breaks down somewhere on the circuit. The RCD or RCBO cannot be switched on again until the fault has been cleared.

Consumer unit with RCD isolator

For some years after the introduction of RCDs, it was common to install one as the system's main isolating switch, along with an array of circuit MCBs. This had the effect of switching off every circuit in the house (including lighting circuits, which do not need RCD protection) if a fault developed. Such an arrangement is no longer allowed on new installations, and existing ones should be altered to include a main on-off switch and a separate RCD.

Consumer unit with rewirable fuses

The first one-piece consumer units contained circuit fuses rather than MCBs. They have a main isolating switch, and circuit fuseways that are colour-coded for identification – white for lighting circuits, red for circuits to socket outlets, and yellow, blue, or green for circuits to individual appliances.

Each fuseholder contains either a cartridge fuse (larger than a plug fuse), or a length of fuse wire held between two terminals. If an overload or short circuit occurs, the fuse blows and must be replaced to restore the power supply.

Separate fuse boxes

Old, unmodernized wiring systems will have a series of separate enclosures rather than a one-piece consumer unit. One will contain the main isolating switch; others will house a fuseholder and replaceable fuse (see above) protecting an individual circuit. This system should be replaced by a qualified electrician.

Modern consumer unit
Most modern consumer units are the split-load type, with some circuits – typically to socket outlets and an electric shower – protected by an RCD.

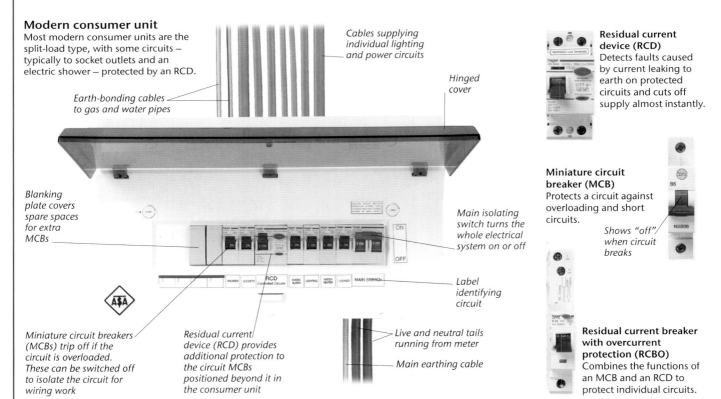

Cables supplying individual lighting and power circuits

Hinged cover

Earth-bonding cables to gas and water pipes

Blanking plate covers spare spaces for extra MCBs

Main isolating switch turns the whole electrical system on or off

Label identifying circuit

Miniature circuit breakers (MCBs) trip off if the circuit is overloaded. These can be switched off to isolate the circuit for wiring work

Residual current device (RCD) provides additional protection to the circuit MCBs positioned beyond it in the consumer unit

Live and neutral tails running from meter

Main earthing cable

Residual current device (RCD)
Detects faults caused by current leaking to earth on protected circuits and cuts off supply almost instantly.

Miniature circuit breaker (MCB)
Protects a circuit against overloading and short circuits.

Shows "off" when circuit breaks

Residual current breaker with overcurrent protection (RCBO)
Combines the functions of an MCB and an RCD to protect individual circuits.

IDENTIFYING CIRCUITS

In a modern consumer unit, each circuit should be labelled for identification. If not, identify each circuit as follows:

■ Each lighting circuit will be controlled by a fuse or MCB rated at 5 or 6 amps. Turn on all the lights in the property, then remove each fuse or switch off each MCB in turn so you can mark on the label which rooms are on each circuit.

■ Each socket outlet circuit is controlled by a fuse or MCB rated at 30 or 32 amps. Plug an appliance into each socket and repeat the procedure above. You may find one or two outlets in a room wired on a different circuit to the others; this may have been done to avoid having a long cable run to a remote outlet. Label the fuses or MCBs as above.

■ Identifying circuits to individual appliances is more straightforward. A 15-, 16-, or 20-amp fuse or MCB controls an immersion heater, and a 30-, 32-, 40-, or 45-amp one will control an electric cooker or shower. Remove the fuse or switch off the MCB to check which is which.

SHOWER	SOCKETS	RCD Controlled Circuits	SMOKE ALARM	LIGHTING	WATER HEATER	COOKER	MAIN SWITCH

Circuit labels
A label identifying each circuit in the consumer unit makes it easy to spot which circuit has been affected by a fault, or to isolate any circuit from the mains so that you can carry out wiring work on it safely.

EARTHING FOR SAFETY

Every part of your home wiring system must be linked to earth, via a continuous electrical conductor that runs round each circuit and is connected to the property's main earthing terminal at the consumer unit. Whenever you make alterations or extensions to the wiring system, you must ensure that the earth continuity is maintained. Check that all cable earth cores are connected to their respective terminals and that metallic accessory faceplates are earthed.

The only exception to the earthing rule involves the use of all-plastic lampholders and double-insulated portable appliances such as hairdryers and power tools. These do not need earthing, and are connected to the mains supply using two-core flex.

RULES AND REGULATIONS

Since the introduction of Part P of the Building Regulations in 2005, all DIY wiring work must now comply with the Building Regulations throughout Britain. This means it must meet the requirements of British Standard BS7671, entitled "Requirements for Electrical Installations" and better known as the Wiring Regulations. All the instructions given in this section comply with BS7671.

Getting approval
DIY wiring work is still allowed, but any work you do must now be tested and certified by a qualified electrician when you have completed it. For some major jobs such as installing new circuits or carrying out new work in a kitchen or bathroom, you have to notify your local authority's Building Control department before you start work. This involves submitting a Building Notice, and paying a fee to have the work inspected and tested when you have completed it. You will then receive a certificate stating that the work complies with the Building Regulations.

Some minor works do not have to be notified. These include replacing existing wiring accessories and their mounting boxes, replacing damaged circuit cable, adding new socket outlets or fused spurs to an existing power circuit, and adding new lighting points and switches to an existing lighting circuit. However, they must still be inspected and tested by an electrician, who will issue the certificate of compliance.

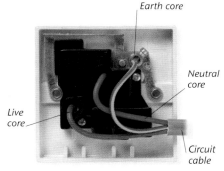

EARTHED SOCKET FACEPLATE

Earth core

Neutral core

Live core

Circuit cable

The earth conductor
Every domestic wiring accessory is connected to the main earthing terminal in the consumer unit via the earth core in the circuit cables. This is a bare copper wire and must be covered with a length of green-and-yellow PVC sleeving whenever it is exposed to make a connection within an accessory or other component.

SAFETY IN BATHROOMS

The Wiring Regulations (see box above) place particular restrictions on wiring in bath and shower rooms, because of the potentially dangerous proximity of electricity, water, and exposed skin. They define four zones within the room, and specify what electrical equipment can be installed in each zone:

■ Zone 0: no equipment allowed;

■ Zone 1: instantaneous shower, power shower or water heater and the wiring to it;

■ Zone 2: as zone 1, plus a light fitting, extractor fan, space heater, shaver supply unit, shower or whirlpool bath pump and the wiring to the fitting or appliance;

■ Zone 3: as zones 1 and 2, plus any other fixed appliance so long as it is protected by a high-sensitivity RCD.

The space beneath the bath is regarded as being outside any zone so long as the bath is panelled in and tools are needed to remove the panelling.

It is best to have all electrical work in a bathroom carried out by a qualified electrician.

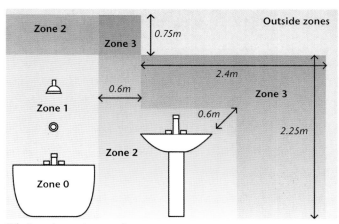

What equipment goes where
The Wiring Regulations specify dimensions for each zone. Zone 1 extends above the bath or shower tray to a height of 2.25m (7ft 6in), and is as wide as the bath or tray. Zone 2 extends for 600mm (1ft 11in) beyond the bath or shower tray; if there is a basin, bidet, or WC in the room, it extends to 600mm (1ft 11in) beyond them as well.

WIRING ACCESSORIES

Many different types of wiring accessory are used in home wiring systems. Some are switches and safety devices, while others allow lights and appliances to be connected to the system – either permanently, or temporarily as in the case of appliances plugged into socket outlets. A permanent connection is useful for kitchen appliances that are in constant use, such as a cooker hood. Here are some of the accessories most widely used in domestic wiring.

LIGHT SWITCHES

Every light in the home is controlled by a switch, which may be wall- or ceiling-mounted. A wall switch, known as a plateswitch, may have up to six rockers (gangs), but in most homes switches with just one, two, or three gangs are used. The faceplate may be flush- or surface-mounted. Most switches have two terminals on the back, plus an earth terminal if they are made of metal; these are known as one-way switches. Two-way switches have an extra terminal, and are used for two-way switching (see p.446) where a light is controlled from two switch positions – in a stairwell, for example.

Cord-operated ceiling switches are usually made as two-way switches, but can be wired for one-way use.

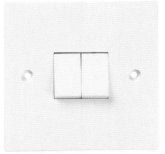

One-gang plateswitch
A single switch used to control ceiling or wall lights, available in one-way and two-way versions.

Two-gang plateswitch
Allows control of two lights from one switch position. Each gang usually has three terminals.

Architrave switch
Slimline plateswitch with one or two gangs (arranged vertically), used where wall space is limited.

Dimmer switch
Allows the brightness of the light to be varied. Two- and three-gang versions are also available.

Cord-operated ceiling switch
Used in bathrooms when the switch is near a bath or shower, or wherever a pull cord is convenient.

Outdoor switch
Waterproof switch designed for use outdoors, with the rocker sealed or covered by a flexible membrane.

LIGHT FITTINGS

The ceiling rose is the commonest light fitting in the home. It provides the connection point between the lighting circuit in the ceiling void and a pendant lampholder. It consists of a circular baseplate fixed to the ceiling, and a screw-on cover through which the flex to the lampholder passes. A batten lampholder is a utility light fitting consisting of a baseplate with an attached lampholder.

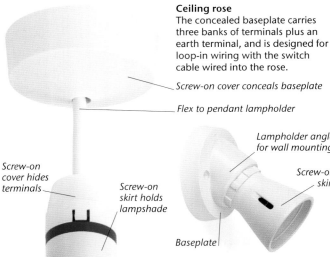

Ceiling rose
The concealed baseplate carries three banks of terminals plus an earth terminal, and is designed for loop-in wiring with the switch cable wired into the rose.

Screw-on cover conceals baseplate

Flex to pendant lampholder

Screw-on cover hides terminals

Screw-on skirt holds lampshade

Lamp socket

Lampholder angled for wall mounting

Screw-on skirt

Baseplate

Batten lampholder
One-piece utility light fitting with straight or angled lampholder, often used in a loft or garage.

TRANSFORMERS

Extra-low-voltage (ELV) light fittings are becoming increasingly popular in the home. They are supplied by small transformers that are concealed in the ceiling void. When choosing one, it is important to match its output to the lighting load it will supply to ensure optimum performance.

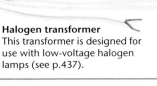

Halogen transformer
This transformer is designed for use with low-voltage halogen lamps (see p.437).

APPLIANCE SWITCHES

Switches are used to control the power supply to a fixed electrical appliance such as a cooker, shower, or heater. They may also control a socket outlet supplying a built-in appliance, such as a dishwasher, that has a concealed socket outlet. The double-pole (DP) switch mechanism breaks both the live and neutral side of the circuit when it is switched off, enabling repair work to be carried out safely.

Cord-operated ceiling switches are designed mainly for bathroom use. The higher-rated types have a mechanical on-off indicator flag as well as a neon light.

Wall-mounted DP switch
Available in 20-, 32-, 40-, and 45-amp ratings to match appliance current demand. The 20-amp type also comes with a front flex outlet.

Ceiling-mounted DP switch
Cord-operated for bathroom use. Choose a 15- or 16-amp switch for a wall heater, and a 40- or 45-amp one for an electric shower.

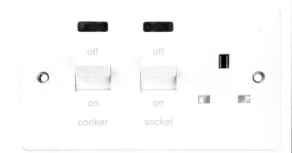

Cooker control unit
Combined 40- or 45-amp DP cooker switch and switched socket outlet. Plain DP switches (see left) are usually used to control a separate split-level oven and hob.

APPLIANCE OUTLETS

A socket outlet provides a connection point for a portable appliance, which is connected to it with a three-pin plug. The outlet may be switched or unswitched, and may have a neon on-off indicator. Faceplates can be flush or surface-mounted, and may have one, two, or three outlets (gangs).

A fused connection unit (FCU) provides a permanent connection for an appliance such as an extractor fan, and may be switched or unswitched. The flex runs into the FCU through a hole in its faceplate. The appliance fuse is housed in a removable fuse carrier next to the switch.

Cable-in cable-out FCUs with no front aperture are used to wire-fused spurs, mainly for lighting sub-circuits.

Socket outlet
13-amp socket outlets have three slots, each guarded by a safety shutter that lifts when a plug is inserted, but resists other objects.

RCD socket outlet
Installed indoors to provide a safe RCD-protected power supply for appliances used outdoors. Contains a high-sensitivity (30-mA) RCD.

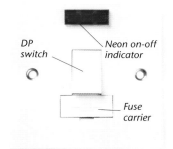

DP switch / Neon on-off indicator / Fuse carrier

Fused connection unit (FCU)
Provides a permanent connection for the flex from an appliance such as an extractor fan, or for the cable to a lighting subcircuit.

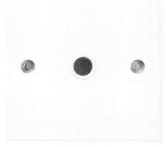

Flex outlet plate
Used in a bathroom to connect the flex from a wall heater or towel rail. The outlet plate is supplied by a spur cable from a remote FCU.

ADAPTORS

Block adaptors can take two or three plugs, but the weight may physically strain the socket outlet terminals and lead to poor contacts and sparking. Strip adaptors have a flex and separate plug, and are available with up to six gangs. Computer adaptors contain a surge protector, to prevent equipment being damaged due to variations in mains voltage.

Strip adaptor
Can be wall-mounted for convenience. The strip accepts several plugs.

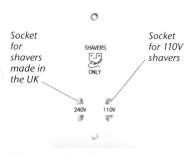

Socket for shavers made in the UK / Socket for 110V shavers / SHAVERS ONLY / 240V / 110V

Shaver supply unit
Contains a transformer to provide a safe, earth-free power supply for an electric shaver in a bathroom. Offers two voltage outputs.

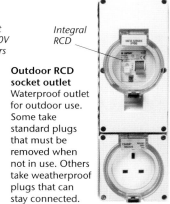

Integral RCD

Outdoor RCD socket outlet
Waterproof outlet for outdoor use. Some take standard plugs that must be removed when not in use. Others take weatherproof plugs that can stay connected.

There is more to your wiring system than the equipment you can see on the surface. Key elements include the mounting boxes that contain all the wiring connections, and the conduit and trunking that protect the circuit cables. This page also looks at the tools you will need to do your own wiring work, and includes a guide to some of the lamps and tubes you can use to light up your home.

Insulation

Brass terminal

Terminal connectors
Used mainly for connecting cable to flex in light fittings. Sold in strips of 10 or 12 from which you cut the number of separate terminals you need.

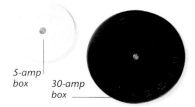

Earth clamp
Use to connect an earthing cable to metal pipework.

CONNECTING CABLES

The connections between circuit cables and wiring accessories must be made within a non-combustible enclosure, and this is the job of mounting boxes and junction boxes. Other cable connections are sometimes made using small, insulated brass terminal connectors.

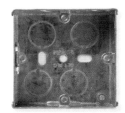

Flush metal mounting box
Single or double, galvanized-metal box for flush-mounting accessories in masonry walls.

Clip-in plastic mounting box
Single or double box for flush-mounting accessories in timber-framed partition walls.

5-amp box

30-amp box

Junction boxes
Use to connect lighting circuit and switch cables, and for wiring spurs from ring main circuits.

CABLE MANAGEMENT

Your wiring work may involve extending your existing system. For ease of installation, you can run the new cables on the surface and use cable clips to secure them, but it is safer and neater if they are concealed.

Masonry nail

Cable clip
Fixes cable to masonry or woodwork. Made in various sizes to match common cable types.

Mini-trunking
Conceals and protects new surface-mounted cable runs. Available in various sizes. May be self-adhesive.

Flat, oval PVC conduit
Conceals and protects new cable runs concealed in chases cut in the plaster. Held in place with nails.

WIRING TOOLS

You will need a range of specialist tools to cut cable and flex to length and to prepare the cores inside for connection to wiring accessories. It is a good idea to store these separately from your ordinary DIY tools, so they are easy to find when you need them. Note that although these tools have insulated handles, you must not use them to work on live parts.

SIDE CUTTERS

COMBINATION PLIERS

LONG-NOSE PLIERS

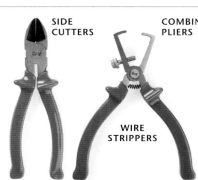

WIRE STRIPPERS

Insulated blade and handle

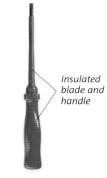

Cutters and strippers
Use side cutters to cut cable and flex to length, and wire strippers to remove core insulation neatly.

Pliers
Use combination type for bending cable cores, and long-nose type for inserting them into terminals.

Terminal screwdriver
Use to tighten and loosen terminal screws in wiring accessories.

OTHER TOOLS

There are several other tools that may be worth investing in if you are doing a lot of wiring work.

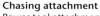

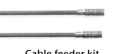

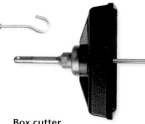

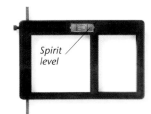

Spirit level

Chasing attachment
Power tool attachment used to chop out chases in plaster to accommodate cable runs in flat, oval conduit.

Cable feeder kit
Screw-together rods and end hook used to pull cables through ceiling voids.

Box cutter
Power tool attachment that cuts a recess in masonry to receive a flush, metal mounting box.

Drilling jig
Guide for marking and drilling out recesses for single or double flush mounting boxes.

TESTING EQUIPMENT

Now that Part P of the Building Regulations requires all new DIY wiring work to be tested and certified on completion by a registered electrician (see p.433), you may feel that you do not need to test any work you do. However, it is well worth buying the three testers shown in the top row, right. They are inexpensive, and will save you time by enabling you to check a variety of electrical situations and locate potential faults as you work.

The multimeter and insulation test meter are more advanced tools, and worth buying only if you are planning any large-scale wiring work.

Remember that visual inspection is always the first level of testing you should use – making sure that cores are wired into the correct terminals, for example, and that terminal screws are fully tightened.

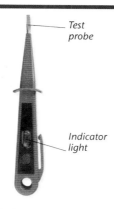

Test probe

Indicator light

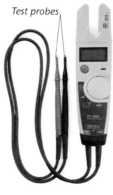

Test probes

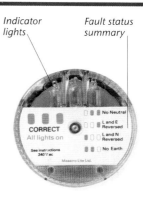

Indicator lights

Fault status summary

Mains (voltage) tester
Screwdriver-like tool used to check for the presence of live voltage at terminals or components.

Continuity tester
Checks for a continuous electrical path between points on a circuit, or in a flex or cartridge fuse.

Socket tester
Plug-in tester with neon indicators, used to check that socket outlets have been wired up correctly.

Test probes

Multimeter
Multi-purpose meter used to check for live voltages in components and circuits, and to carry out continuity testing.

Insulation tester
Battery-powered tool that applies a DC test voltage to check insulation resistance.

LAMPS AND TUBES

Known in the trade as general lighting service (GLS) lamps, mains light bulbs come in standard pear and mushroom shapes with a clear-, pearl- (translucent), white-, or coloured-glass envelope. Other shapes include pointed candle lamps, small pygmy lamps and round decor lamps intended to be on show in a lampshade or light fitting.

Mains halogen lamps are becoming more widely used for display lighting. They give a clear, white light that is brighter than a GLS lamp.

Reflector lamps are used in spotlight fittings where you want a high-intensity beam rather than a diffuse source of light.

Tubes may be fluorescent or tungsten filament types, and are used mainly in concealed lighting effects.

Bayonet end cap

Edison screw end cap

GLS lamps
Mains-voltage light bulbs have bayonet cap (BC) or Edison screw (ES) end caps. Outputs range from 25 to 150 watts.

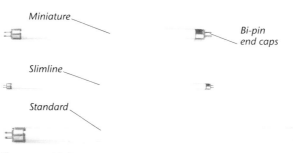

Miniature

Slimline

Standard

Bi-pin end caps

Fluorescent tubes
Mains-voltage lamps in tubular form. Available in standard, slimline, and miniature sizes, and in various wattages.

Halogen lamp
Mains-voltage spotlight bulbs have two contact pegs (above) or an Edison-screw end cap. Most are rated at 50 watts.

LOW-ENERGY BULBS

Contact pegs

LED lamp
Spotlight LED bulbs offer the most energy efficient option as they use the least power and outlast other types of bulb.

Bayonet or Edison screw end cap

Low-energy spotlight bulb

Compact fluorescent lamps
Use about one-fifth of the energy of a comparable GLS lamp, and can last up to eight times as long.

Cable is used for all the fixed wiring in your home.

It has a flattened, oval cross-section, and the metal conductors inside (called cores) that carry the current are surrounded by a protective PVC sheath. The cores are covered in PVC insulation and colour-coded for ease of identification. Cable is available with conductors of different sizes, described by their cross-section in square millimetres (mm²).

CABLE AND FLEX
You must use the correct type of cable or flex (used for connecting appliances and lampholders to their supply circuits) for any wiring work you carry out. You will need 1-mm² cable for work on lighting circuits, and 2.5-mm² cable for work on power circuits. Choose flex sizes to match the wattage of the appliance they are connecting.

Two-core-and-earth cable
The most widely used cable for home wiring work has three cores. Two carry the current, while the third core is a bare copper wire. This acts as the circuit's earth continuity conductor (ECC, or "earth"), providing a path along which current can flow to earth if a fault develops anywhere on the circuit. It is also commonly known as "twin-and-earth" cable.

Neutral
Earth
Live (or "phase")

OLD TWO-CORE-AND-EARTH

Neutral
Earth
Live

NEW TWO-CORE-AND-EARTH

Three-core-and-earth cable
Cable with four cores – three insulated and one bare – is used for wiring two-way light switches. The insulated cores are at present colour-coded red, yellow, and blue for identification purposes only; any or all may be a live core, depending on how the switches are configured. New three-core-and-earth cable has cores coloured brown, grey, and black.

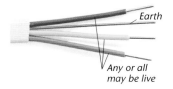

Earth
Any or all may be live

OLD THREE-CORE-AND-EARTH

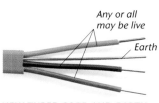

Any or all may be live
Earth

NEW THREE-CORE-AND-EARTH

Three-core flex
Flex (short for flexible cord) also has an outer sheath. The type used for most domestic appliances has three cores, each covered in coloured PVC insulation – brown for live, blue for neutral, and green-and-yellow for earth.

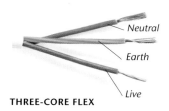

Neutral
Earth
Live

THREE-CORE FLEX

Two-core flex
This has no earth core, and is used for wiring light fittings with plastic lampholders, and also for small, portable appliances such as hairdryers and power tools which are double-insulated and need no earth connection.

Neutral
Live

TWO-CORE FLEX

▮▮ PREPARING CABLE CORES

To connect a cable to a wiring accessory such as a light switch or socket outlet, or to a fixed appliance such as a cooker, you have to remove some of its outer sheath and then strip away a little of the core insulation to expose the bare metal conductors, ready for connection to their terminals. To do this, you will need a sharp trimming knife and some wire strippers.

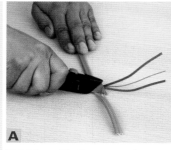

A

Hold the cable flat on a cutting board and slit the sheath along the centre line. Pull out the cores and cut off about 100mm (4in) of the sheath.

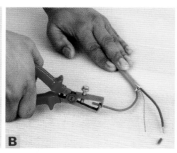

B

Set the wire strippers to match the core's diameter. Remove about 10mm (½in) of insulation from both insulated cores.

C

Cut a piece of PVC earth sleeving to cover all but the last 10mm (½in) of the core, leaving this exposed ready for connection to its terminal.

LAYING CABLE UNDER FLOORS

When your house was built, many of the circuit cables will have been installed in the floor voids, running parallel to or across the line of the floor joists. You can use these voids to run new cables out of sight across rooms when you want to extend your existing wiring. However, unless you are working in a loft, this will involve lifting floorboards (and possibly fitted carpets or other floorcoverings too). It is therefore best to plan any major rewiring work to coincide

with a full-scale room makeover, so that the inevitable disruption becomes part of a larger project.

If your house has solid ground floors, you will not be able to run cables within the floor as cutting channels in the concrete risks disturbing the damp-proof membrane and any pipes concealed within it. Instead you will have to run cables down from the floor above in chases cut in the wall to supply any new wiring accessories you are fitting.

▌▌RUNNING CABLE THROUGH JOISTS

Select a floorboard that follows the best route for the cable. Remove any screws, or prise up the floorboard using a crowbar.

Use a 10-mm (½-in) flat wood bit to drill a hole in the centre of each joist. Drill at a shallow angle if your drill will not fit between the joists.

Feed the cable through the holes in the joists, leaving a little slack between each pair of joists.

Replace the floorboards . Write CABLE BELOW on the boards to remind you of its presence.

▌▌RUNNING CABLE PARALLEL TO JOISTS

 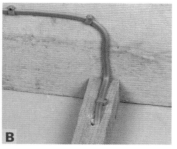

Lift every fourth floorboard and feed the cable through the floor void. Fix it to the joist with cable clips where it is exposed.

If the cable feeds a new lighting point positioned between two joists, fix a batten to support it and run the cable through a hole in the batten.

FEEDING CABLE UNDER BOARDS

Use some stiff wire to "fish" cable through floor voids. Lift a board at each side of the room and feed the wire through.

Attach the wire to one end of the cable. Retrieve it at the other side of the room and use it to pull the cable through the floor void.

TOOLS AND MATERIALS CHECKLIST PP.440–53

Running cable down an architrave (p.440) Cable clips, pin hammer

Running cable along skirting board (p.440) Cable clips, pin hammer

Using mini-trunking (p.440) Mounting box for socket outlet, PVC mini-trunking

Running cable in a solid wall (p.441) Club hammer, brick bolster, oval PVC conduit, mounting box, galvanized nails, plaster, filling knife, glasspaper

Running cable in a stud wall (p.441) Padsaw (drywall saw)

Running cable in a new stud wall (p.441) Padsaw (drywall saw)

Surface-fitting a mounting box on a solid wall (p.442) Basic toolkit only

Flush-fitting a mounting box in a hollow wall (p.442) Padsaw (drywall saw), clip-in mounting box

Flush-fitting a mounting box in a solid wall (p.443) Drilling jig or box-chaser attachment,

club hammer, brick bolster, oval PVC conduit, flush mounting box, rubber grommet, filling knife, plaster, glasspaper

Replacing a single socket with a double (p.444) Padsaw (drywall saw), new double mounting box (clip-in or flush metal type) and socket outlet

Running a spur from an existing socket outlet (p.445) Length of 2.5mm² two-core-and-earth cable, PVC earth sleeving, cable clips or mini-trunking, new socket outlet and mounting box, side cutters, wire strippers

Replacing a light switch (p.446) New switch faceplate, brown PVC tape, PVC earth sleeving

Preparing a new lighting point (p.448) Basic toolkit only

Installing a security light (p.453) Masonry drill bit, new switch, junction box, switched FCU*, brown PVC tape, PVC earth sleeving

* = optional

FOR BASIC TOOLKIT
SEE PP.24–25

RUNNING CABLE IN WALLS

Any extension or alteration work you carry out on your electrical system will involve routing cable to new lights, switches, socket outlets, and other wiring accessories. How you tackle this depends on whether you want to conceal the cables completely. In general, your aim will be to cause as little disruption to existing decor and furnishings as possible. You can do this by surface-mounting the cables initially, and then hiding them in channels in the wall surface (or within hollow walls) next time you redecorate the room.

TOOLS AND MATERIALS SEE BASIC TOOLKIT AND P.439

PERMITTED ZONES

The Wiring Regulations specify permitted zones within which new cables should be run, to minimize the risk of damaging them when fixing things to walls. You can run cables vertically above or below a wiring accessory, and within an area 150mm (6in) wide next to an internal corner of a room. You can run them horizontally to the left or right of an accessory, and within a horizontal area 150mm (6in) wide immediately below the ceiling.

SURFACE-MOUNTING CABLE

The easiest way to run cable to a new wiring accessory is to mount it on the wall surface, and to use a surface-mounted plastic box for the accessory. To make the installation as unobtrusive as possible, use cable sheathed in white rather than grey PVC, and secure it in place with white cable clips. The cable can be run horizontally along the top edge of skirting boards to socket outlets, and vertically down the sides of door architraves to new light switches. Surface-mounting cable across a ceiling to a new light position is not generally recommended, however. It is better to lift floorboards in the room above so you can gain access to the ceiling void, and to install the cable run to the light position there (see p.439 for more details).

RUNNING CABLE DOWN AN ARCHITRAVE

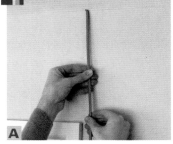

Position light switch 1.2m(4ft) from the floor, next to the architrave

A **To run cable** to a new light switch, drill a hole in the ceiling above one side of a doorway. Draw the cable down through it.

B **Run the cable** vertically down to the switch position. Clip it to the wall or to the edge of the architrave at intervals of 400mm (1ft 4in).

RUNNING CABLE ALONG A SKIRTING BOARD

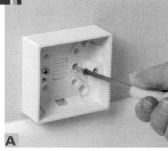

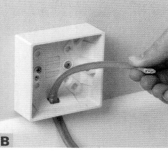

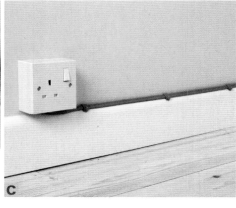

A **Remove a knockout** from the mounting box. Attach the box to the wall using screws and wallplugs or cavity fixings as required.

B **Feed one end** of the new cable into the box through the knockout. Remove 100mm (4in) of the sheath and prepare the cores for connection.

Run the cable along the top of the skirting board with its flat face against the wall. Secure it with cable clips every 400mm (1ft 4in). Shape the cable around any external or internal corners, and secure it there with clips 25mm (1in) away from the corner. Connect the cores to the accessory faceplate, fold them into the box and attach the faceplate.

USING MINI-TRUNKING

White PVC mini-trunking looks neater than bare cable, and gives the cable run extra protection against accidental damage. Use 16mm (⅝in) square mini-trunking for a single cable, and the 25mm x 16mm (1in x ⅝in) size for two or three cables. As with surface-mounted cable runs, the cable can be recessed in a chase cut into the wall surface when the room is next redecorated.

A **Fit a surface-mounted** box to the wall at the required position. Clip a connector for the mini-trunking into a knockout in the box.

B **Cut the trunking** to length with a hacksaw. Peel off the backing strip and stick it in place. Non-adhesive types must be pinned or screwed.

C **Place the cable** in the trunking and fit the cover strips and corners. Prepare the cable, connect it to the accessory, and fit the faceplate.

RUNNING CABLE IN A SOLID WALL

The neatest way of installing new cable runs if you have solid walls is to hide them in vertical or horizontal channels (called chases) chopped into the masonry. To protect the cable from accidental damage by drills and nails, you must enclose it in oval PVC conduit, fitted into the chases and covered with plaster. Use a cable detector first to check for any existing cables where you plan to cut the chase.

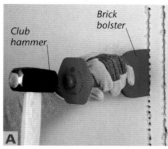

Club hammer   Brick bolster

A Mark guide lines on the wall and drill a series of holes along them 25mm (1in) deep. Chop out the plaster and masonry.

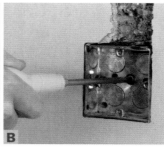

B Mark the outline of the mounting box on the wall. Chop out a recess deep enough for it to fit flush, and secure it with screws and wallplugs.

C Remove a metal knockout from the box next to the chase, and insert a rubber grommet in the hole. This stops the cable chafing on the metal.

Cut oval conduit to length using a junior hacksaw. Feed the cable into the conduit and then position it in the chase so it butts up against the mounting box. Secure it by driving in galvanized nails at intervals down the sides of the conduit so their heads trap the conduit in position.

D

E Plaster over the conduit and around the mounting box. Prepare the cable, connect it to the accessory faceplate and screw this to the box.

POWER CHASING

If you have a lot of chases to cut, it is worth considering using a power tool. You can either buy an attachment for a power drill (it fits only drills with a 43-mm collar), or you can hire a wall-chasing machine, which uses twin diamond discs to cut the chase neatly and effortlessly. You still have to chop out the masonry, however.

RUNNING CABLE IN A STUD WALL

If your rooms have timber-framed stud partition walls, you may be able to hide the cables within the wall. How easy this is depends on where you want to fit the wiring accessory, and on whether there are horizontal braces or blanket insulation in the way. To gain access to the cavity you will have to drill a hole through the head or sole plates at the top or bottom of the wall framework.

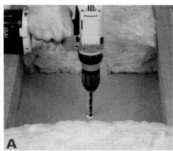

A Locate the wall position and lift floorboards or remove insulation to reveal the ceiling. Drill a 10-mm (½-in) hole through the head plate.

B Feed the cable down through the hole and into the wall cavity. It will drop freely if there are no noggings or insulation inside the wall.

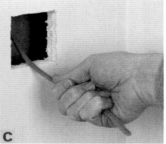

C Cut a hole in the wall at the new accessory position. Fish out the cable, feed it into a clip-in mounting box, and fit this into the hole.

RUNNING CABLE IN A NEW STUD WALL

A Clad one side of the wall. Drill a 10-mm (½-in) hole through the head or sole plate and draw in the cable from above or below.

B Drill 10-mm (½-in) holes through the studs and thread the cable through until you reach the position of the new wiring accessory.

C

Clad the other side of the wall. Then mark and cut a hole for the new clip-in mounting box and draw the cable out through the hole.

FITTING MOUNTING BOXES

Every switch, socket outlet, or other wiring accessory is attached to a mounting box that is either fixed to the wall surface or recessed into it. The box provides an enclosed space within which the cable supplying the accessory can be connected to its faceplate. Surface-mounted boxes are quicker to install than flush ones, but because they project from the wall surface they are prone to accidental damage. Flush boxes look neater.

TOOLS AND MATERIALS SEE BASIC TOOLKIT AND P.439

CEILING MOUNTING BOXES

Most of the wiring accessories fitted to a ceiling, such as a pull-cord switch, are surface-mounted. To ensure that they are securely fixed, screw them to a ceiling joist if possible.
If you cannot do this, use strong cavity fixings such as expanding metal anchors rather than plastic plugs. If you need to provide a recessed enclosure, for example, to install a light fitting with no room inside its baseplate for the wiring, use a clip-in, circular, plastic mounting box. This fits into a hole cut in the ceiling with a padsaw, and is locked in place by lugs (see p.451).

■■ SURFACE-FITTING A MOUNTING BOX ON A SOLID WALL

Use surface-mounted plastic boxes for ease of installation, especially if the new cable run is surface-mounted or run in mini-trunking. Different sizes are available to take different-sized accessories. Select the box depth to match the accessory. You need a 16-mm deep box for light switches, a 25- or 30-mm box for socket outlets, and a 47-mm box for cooker switches. Metal boxes are also available, for use in garages and outbuildings.

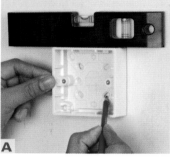

A

Hold the box in position with a small spirit level on top to ensure that you fix it level. Mark, drill, and plug the fixing holes.

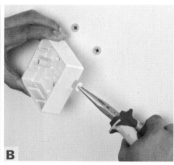

B

Choose the cable entry point and use a screwdriver to remove a knockout. If necessary, nibble away any jagged bits of plastic with pliers.

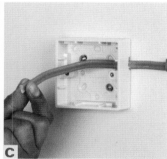

C

Screw the box to the wall and feed the cable in through the knockout, ready to be connected to the wiring accessory you are installing.

■■ FLUSH-FITTING A MOUNTING BOX IN A HOLLOW WALL

Clip-in dry-lining boxes make light work of flush-mounting wiring accessories in timber-framed partition walls and plasterboard ceilings. Some have spring-loaded lugs that grip the rear face of the plasterboard; others have to be pushed out to clip the box in place. They are available in square and rectangular versions for wall-mounted accessories, and as circular boxes for ceiling mounting (see box above).

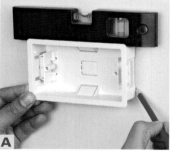

A

Hold the box in place and draw around its outline with a pencil. Use a spirit level to check that it is level.

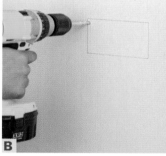

B

Drill a hole big enough to admit a padsaw blade inside each corner of the marked outline.

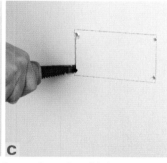

C

Insert the padsaw blade into each hole in turn and cut along the lines to remove the plasterboard.

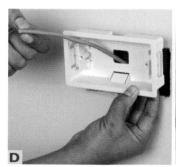

D

Remove a knockout from the back of the box, offer it up to the cut-out in the wall, and feed the cable through it.

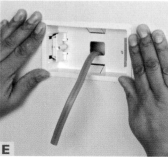

E

Push the box into the cut-out until its flange fits flush with the face of the plasterboard and conceals any uneven edges to the cut.

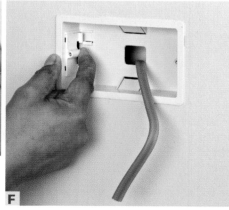

F

Engage the lugs on the inside of the mounting box. Spring-loaded lugs should snap into position as you push the box in, but with the example shown here you have to push the lugs out to lock them into place. You can now prepare the cable for connection and fit the accessory faceplate to the box.

▮▮ FLUSH-FITTING A MOUNTING BOX IN A SOLID WALL

Flush-mounted accessories look neater than surface-mounted ones, and are less prone to physical damage. To fit a flush box in a solid wall, you need to remove some of the masonry behind the plaster to create a recess for a galvanized-metal mounting box to which the accessory faceplate is attached. This is relatively easy in blockwork, but harder if the wall is built in brick.

Hold the box against the wall in the required position. Use a small spirit level to check if it is level, and mark the box outline on the wall.

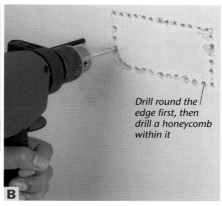

Use a masonry drill bit to drill a honeycomb of holes in the wall. Drill within the marked outline to a depth a little greater than the depth of the box.

Drill round the edge first, then drill a honeycomb within it

Use a brick bolster and a club hammer to chop out the masonry. Then test-fit the mounting box to check that the hole is deep enough.

Wear thick work gloves to protect your hands

AIDS FOR CUTTING RECESSES IN SOLID WALLS

Plastic template
Hold the template against the wall, and mark the cut-out you require. Use only the left-hand cut-out for a single socket.

Box chaser attachment
Fit it to your drill to cut a recess neatly and quickly. It is quite expensive to buy, but useful if you need to fit many sockets.

Fit a rubber grommet into the cable entry point to prevent it chafing, then cut the chase for the cable run to the mounting box.

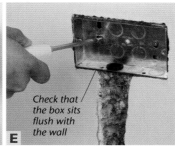

Check that the box sits flush with the wall

Fit the box in the recess and mark the positions of the fixing screws. Remove the box, drill and plug the holes, and screw the box to the wall.

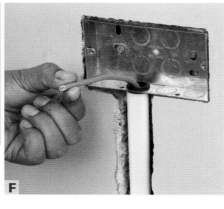

Feed the new cable through a length of oval PVC conduit and secure this in the chase. Prepare the cable end ready for connection.

CONVERTING A SOCKET OUTLET

If you have a lot of single socket outlets on your system, a simple way of providing more outlets is to convert these to double or triple outlets. There are four conversion options:

Surface-mounted to surface-mounted
Remove the single mounting box and replace it with a double or triple one. Reconnect the existing cable cores to the new outlet faceplate and fix it to the new box.

Flush to surface-mounted
Remove the single outlet and fix a new surface-mounting box over the old flush one. This minimizes damage to existing decorations, and the new outlet can be converted to a flush one when the room is next redecorated.

Surface-mounted to flush
Remove the existing outlet and mounting box, and cut a recess (see above) for the new flush outlet. This may involve some damage to decorations, but results in a much neater installation.

Flush to flush
Remove the old outlet and mounting box, and enlarge the existing recess so that it will take a larger flush mounting box. As you do this, take care not to damage the incoming cable(s). On solid walls, it is generally best to enlarge the recess equally at each side; on plasterboard walls, simply enlarge the cut-out on one side, and press the new box into place (see overleaf).

Few homes have enough socket outlets for all the electrical equipment that householders want to plug in, and existing outlets are often not in convenient places. Fortunately, providing extra outlets and positioning them where you want them are relatively straightforward jobs. These pages show you how to convert existing single sockets, and how to add a new outlet to your ring-main circuit. For information on fitting mounting boxes and the options available for different types of socket outlet conversions see pp.442-43.

TOOLS AND MATERIALS SEE BASIC TOOLKIT AND P.439

RING MAIN CIRCUIT RESTRICTIONS

The Wiring Regulations allow you to have an unlimited number of socket outlets on each ring main circuit. However, the circuit can only serve rooms with a total maximum floor area of 100sq m (1,075sq ft). If you are adding spurs to new socket outlets in rooms that are not served by the circuit you will be extending, check that the total floor area of all the rooms that will be served by the extended circuit does not now exceed 100sq m (1,075sq ft).

CONVERTING A FLUSH SINGLE SOCKET TO A FLUSH DOUBLE ONE

The quickest way to increase the number of socket outlets in a room is to convert any existing single outlets to double (or triple) ones. The example shown here is on a stud partition wall. If you are working on a solid wall, it is best to enlarge the existing recess by half the required amount at each side. In either case, take care not to damage the circuit cables as you enlarge the recess.

A

Turn off the power. Unscrew the existing single-socket faceplate from the wall. Then disconnect the cores from the faceplate terminals.

B

Release the lugs in the old box and ease it carefully out of its recess. Hold the new double box against the wall and draw lines round it to indicate the size of the cut-out. Drill a hole in each new corner to admit a padsaw blade. Push the cable to one side and use the padsaw to cut neatly along the lines. Remove the off-cut of plasterboard.

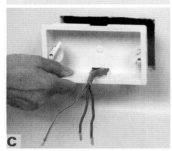

C

Remove a knockout in the new box and feed in the cable. Fit the box in its cut-out and push out the lugs to lock the box in place.

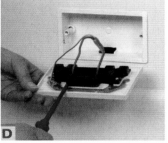

D

Connect the cable cores to their terminals on the new socket faceplate. Screw it to the box, restore the power, and test the outlet.

Look for a moulded letter identifying each terminal on the outlet faceplate. The live cable core (red or brown) goes to the terminal marked L, the neutral core (black or blue) to the one marked N, and the earth core to the one marked E or ⏚.

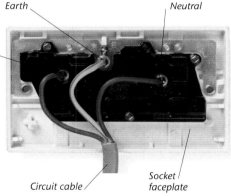

Earth *Neutral* *Live* *Circuit cable* *Socket faceplate*

ADDING A NEW SOCKET OUTLET

To install a new socket outlet, you need to run a spur cable from the new outlet's position to a suitable connection point on the ring main circuit. Usually the easiest place to do this is at an existing socket outlet. However, you must first check the status of the outlet you choose for this.

The Wiring Regulations allow you to connect a spur cable to any outlet on the main circuit, but you cannot use one if is supplying a spur already. You can easily eliminate any outlet that is doing so, because there will be three cables connected to it. You are also not allowed to connect a spur to an outlet that is already on a spur, so that eliminates any outlets with just one cable present.

That leaves one further possibility to check out. An outlet with two cables present will probably be on the ring main circuit, but it might be the intermediate outlet on a two-outlet spur. These were once permitted, but are now no longer allowed; you may still find one in an older house. You can decide which it is with a simple test.

Testing an outlet's status

The best way to check an outlet with two cables present is to turn off the power to the circuit and to remove the faceplate from the outlet you want to use for your spur connection. Disconnect the two live cores from their terminal and separate them, then restore the power to the circuit. Check whether other outlets on the circuit still have power by plugging an appliance into each one in turn.

If all outlets on the circuit are now dead, you know that the disconnected outlet is on the main circuit, and you can safely connect the spur cable to it. Do this and restore the power to the circuit.

If only one other outlet is dead, you have found the intermediate outlet on an old two-outlet spur, and you may not connect a new spur cable to it. In this case, you must either find another outlet that is on the main circuit, or connect the new spur directly to the circuit cable using a 30-amp three-terminal junction box (see opposite, bottom).

RUNNING A SPUR FROM AN EXISTING SOCKET OUTLET

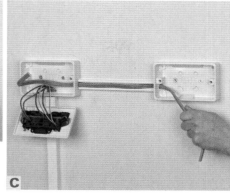

Measure the length of cable needed to reach the new outlet position, and allow extra for making the connections. Feed it along the route between the two outlets - either surface-mounted as here, or run in oval PVC conduit concealed in a wall chase (see p.441).

Turn off the power and unscrew the socket faceplate. Remove a knockout from the mounting box to admit the spur cable.

Screw a mounting box to the wall at the new outlet position. Prepare the route for the spur cable. Here it is to be run in mini-trunking.

Prepare the spur cable cores at the existing socket outlet and connect them to the live, neutral, and earth terminals (see below for details of the connections). Note that on (older) existing wiring, the two circuit cables may have red live and black neutral cores rather than brown and blue ones shown here.

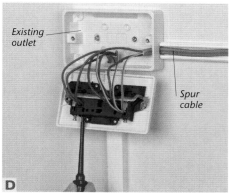

Existing outlet

Spur cable

Repeat the process at the new socket outlet to connect the spur cable to its terminals (see below for details of the connections).

Fold the cable cores into the two mounting boxes and attach the faceplates. Conceal the spur cable and restore the power.

FACEPLATE AT EXISTING OUTLET

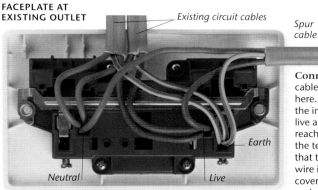

Existing circuit cables

Spur cable

Spur cable

FACEPLATE AT NEW SOCKET

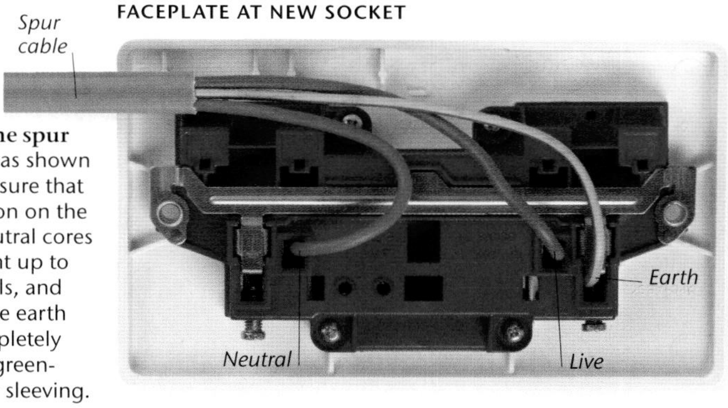

Connect the spur cable cores as shown here. Make sure that the insulation on the live and neutral cores reaches right up to the terminals, and that the bare earth wire is completely covered in green-and- yellow sleeving.

Earth

Neutral

Live

Earth

Neutral

Live

TAKING A SPUR FROM A CIRCUIT CABLE

If your house has suspended timber floors, it may be easier to locate the main circuit cable beneath the floorboards and connect the spur cable directly to it. You will need a round, 30-amp, three-terminal junction box, which you screw to the side of a joist once you have made the cable connections. To locate the circuit cable, lift floorboards close to existing outlets. Turn the power off and cut the cable at a convenient connection point. Remove part of the sheath from each cut end and prepare the cores for reconnection. Run the spur cable from here to the new outlet position. Install the new mounting box and connect the spur cable to the new outlet faceplate. Fit the faceplate onto its box. Connect the spur cable to the junction box terminals as shown (right). Screw the box baseplate to the side of a nearby joist and screw on its cover. Restore the power and test the new outlet.

CONNECTIONS IN JUNCTION BOX FOR SPUR OFF RING MAIN

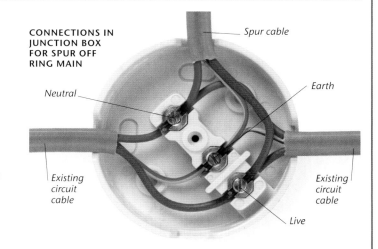

Spur cable

Earth

Neutral

Existing circuit cable

Existing circuit cable

Live

ELECTRICS

WORKING ON A LIGHTING CIRCUIT

There are several simple jobs you can do on your existing lighting system, including replacing old switches, lampholders or ceiling roses, and fitting dimmer switches in place of existing on-off switches so you can vary the lighting level in the room. None of these jobs involves any alterations to the existing circuit wiring.

One slightly more complicated lighting circuit job you may want to tackle is providing two-way switching for a particular light, for example, so you can control the landing light from both a hall and landing. This does involve some new wiring work, but it will give you useful experience of running cables and mounting accessories.

ISOLATING THE CIRCUIT

■ Before carrying out any work on a lighting circuit, you must always cut off its electricity supply at the main fusebox or consumer unit. Either turn off the main on-off switch and remove the circuit fuse, or switch off the MCB if you have a modern consumer unit.
■ Turning the light off at the wall switch does not isolate the light fitting, which means that the fitting is still live even when the switch is off.

LIGHT SWITCHES

Most light switches in the home are plain white plastic. You can replace them with a different design for cosmetic reasons, or because you have accidentally damaged the faceplate. It is important to use the correct type of switch. You can use a new two-way switch for both one-way and two-way switching, but a one-way switch can accept only one switch cable. New, metallic faceplates must be earthed to their mounting boxes if they are flush-mounted. This involves linking the earth terminals on the faceplate and in the box with a short length of PVC-sleeved earth core. You can obtain this from an offcut of cable.

▌▌REPLACING A LIGHT SWITCH

If the switch you are removing has two terminals on the back and a single cable running to it, it is a one-way switch and you can replace it with either a one-way or two-way switch. The same applies if it has three terminals but just one cable. If it has three terminals and a cable core is connected to each one, it is a two-way switch and must be replaced by a new two-way switch (see right).

A **Isolate the circuit.** Run a sharp knife round the plateswitch to cut through any paint or wallpaper stuck to its sides, then unscrew it.

B **Ease the plateswitch** away from the wall and make a sketch of the wiring connections. Then undo the terminal screws to release the old plateswitch.

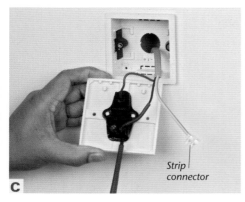

C

Strip connector

Reconnect the cable cores to the new switch, using your sketch as a guide. Wrap PVC tape round the neutral core to show it is live (use red tape on a black core, brown on a blue one). If the mounting box is plastic, the earth core should be wired into a plastic strip connector.

ADDING TWO-WAY SWITCHING

If you want to control an existing light from two switch positions instead of just an existing one, you need to install two-way switching. This involves replacing the existing one-way switch with a two-way one, adding a second two-way switch at the new switch position, and connecting the two together using special three-core-and-earth cable. Run this cable up the wall from the first switch, then take it through the ceiling void to a point above the new switch position, and run it down the wall to its mounting box. Make the connections to the new switches as shown here (note that the existing cable may have red and black cores).

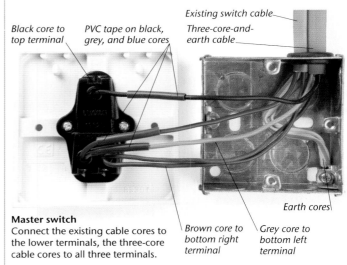

Black core to top terminal   *PVC tape on black, grey, and blue cores*   *Existing switch cable*   *Three-core-and-earth cable*

Earth cores

Master switch
Connect the existing cable cores to the lower terminals, the three-core cable cores to all three terminals.

Brown core to bottom right terminal   *Grey core to bottom left terminal*

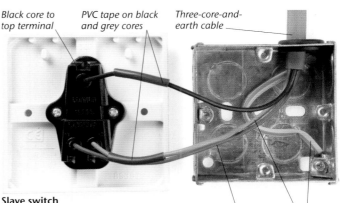

Black core to top terminal   *PVC tape on black and grey cores*   *Three-core-and-earth cable*

Slave switch
Connect the three cores to the same terminals at this switch as you used at the master switch.

Brown core to bottom right terminal   *Grey core to bottom left terminal*   *Earth core*

FITTING A DIMMER SWITCH

A dimmer switch allows you to vary the brightness of a light. It replaces an existing switch, and is easy to fit. You can buy one- and two-gang versions.

To fit a dimmer switch, turn off the power, remove the existing plateswitch, and disconnect the cores. Follow the instructions supplied with the new dimmer switch to reconnect the cores to its terminals. The earth core(s) will be terminated in a strip connector if the mounting box is plastic, and in the earth terminal in the box if it is a flush metal one.

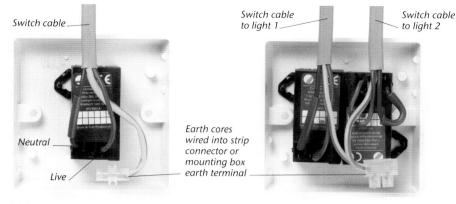

Switch cable

Neutral

Live

ONE-GANG DIMMER SWITCH

Switch cable to light 1

Switch cable to light 2

Earth cores wired into strip connector or mounting box earth terminal

TWO-GANG DIMMER SWITCH

REPLACING A PENDANT FLEX AND LAMPHOLDER

Before you start, turn the power off at the consumer unit and check that the light is isolated. Unscrew the rose cover and let it slide down the flex. If it is stuck to the ceiling with paint, run a knife round it first. Disconnect the flex cores from the rose terminals.

Cut some new flex to the same length and prepare the ends (see p.438). Connect one end of the flex to the lampholder terminals. Hook each core over its anchor, thread the flex through the lampholder cover, and screw this on.

Thread the flex through the rose cover and connect the cores to the two outer terminals on the rose baseplate. Again, hook the cores over their anchors at each side of the baseplate. Screw on the rose cover, restore the power supply, and switch the light on to test it.

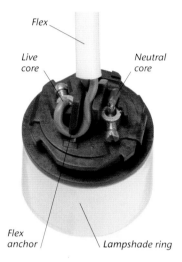

Flex

Live core

Neutral core

Flex anchor

Lampshade ring

Connections at the lampholder
The terminals on the lampholder are not labelled, and it does not matter which way round you connect the flex cores to them.

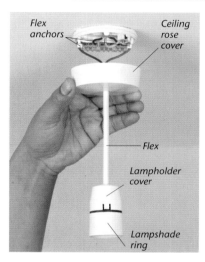

Flex anchors

Ceiling rose cover

Flex

Lampholder cover

Lampshade ring

Connections at the ceiling rose
Connect the cores to the outer terminals on the rose baseplate. Don't forget to thread the flex through the rose cover first.

REPLACING AN OLD CEILING ROSE

Ceiling roses can become discoloured over time, and may be encrusted with paint or Artex. To replace one, you have to disconnect the circuit cables.

Turn off the power and unscrew the rose cover. Identify and label the switch cable if you have loop-in wiring (its neutral core goes to the same terminal as the flex live core – see right). Disconnect all the cable cores from their terminals. Unscrew the rose baseplate from the ceiling and discard it.

Remove a knockout from the new rose baseplate, feed the cables through it, and screw it to the ceiling. You should be able to use the same screw holes to do this. Reconnect the cable cores to the terminals on the new baseplate (see right for the two wiring options). Cover any bare earth cores with PVC sleeving. Screw on the cover, restore the power, and test the light.

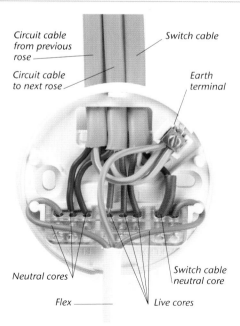

Circuit cable from previous rose

Circuit cable to next rose

Switch cable

Earth terminal

Neutral cores

Switch cable neutral core

Flex

Live cores

CEILING ROSE WITH LOOP-IN WIRING

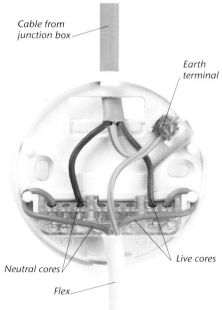

Cable from junction box

Earth terminal

Neutral cores

Live cores

Flex

CEILING ROSE ON A JUNCTION BOX SYSTEM

EXTENDING A LIGHTING CIRCUIT

If you need extra lights in new positions, you can extend an existing lighting circuit by connecting a spur cable to it. You will need access to the ceiling void to do this, either through a loft space, or by lifting floorboards. You can connect the spur at an existing ceiling rose (if you have loop-in wiring) or junction box, or you can fit a new junction box at a convenient place on the circuit cable. Choose whichever option is the easiest to wire up. An alternative is to run a spur from a power circuit (see opposite).

OVERLOADING A CIRCUIT

Each lighting circuit can in theory supply a maximum of about 12 lighting points, each rated at up to 100 watts. In practice this is usually limited to eight, to allow for the use of multiple or higher-wattage lamps. If you cannot add another light without the risk of overloading the circuit, wire the new light as a spur from the power circuit instead.

PREPARING A NEW LIGHTING POINT

Decide where you want to install the new ceiling rose or light fitting, and investigate where the nearest existing lighting circuit runs so you can find the most convenient connection point for the spur cable. If there is a lighting point in the room already, gain access to the ceiling void above it so you can see how it is wired up, where the circuit cables are, and how the spur cable will run in relation to the direction of the floor joists. Move more insulation aside in a loft, or lift more floorboards as necessary, to gain access to the ceiling above the new light position. You will then be able to plan the spur cable route to it – either between the joists, or across the joist line through a series of holes drilled in them (see p.439). Measure the distance from your chosen connection point to the new light position, cut the cable to length, and feed it into position.

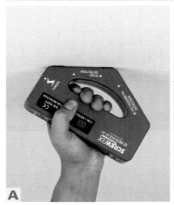

A Use a stud detector to find the joist nearest to the new light position. Alternatively drill a hole next to it from above the ceiling.

B Drill a larger hole to one side of the joist for the spur cable to pass through. You can then screw the rose or light fitting to this joist.

C Working above in the ceiling void, feed the spur cable down through the hole. Pull 150mm (6in) through from below the ceiling.

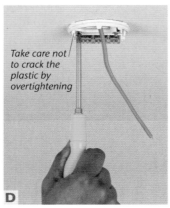

Take care not to crack the plastic by overtightening

D Thread the cable through a knockout in the rose baseplate. Drill pilot holes through the ceiling into the joist and screw on the baseplate.

CONNECTING A LOOP-IN ROSE

With the spur cable laid along its run and the new rose fixed in place, you can make a start on the wiring work. The simplest option is to add a new rose to the end of the existing lighting circuit, and to provide a new light switch to control it. The illustrations below show how to connect the spur cable at the existing rose (top), and how to wire the spur and switch cables into the new rose (bottom).

You can also add a spur to an intermediate rose, but in this case there will already be three cables present. This means you will have to make space for a fourth cable, and also double up the core connections in one of the terminal blocks. Old existing cables may have live red and neutral black cores, rather than the brown and blue shown here.

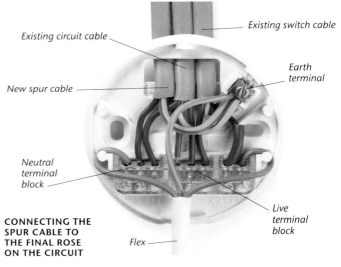

Existing circuit cable
Existing switch cable
New spur cable
Earth terminal
Neutral terminal block
Live terminal block
Flex

CONNECTING THE SPUR CABLE TO THE FINAL ROSE ON THE CIRCUIT

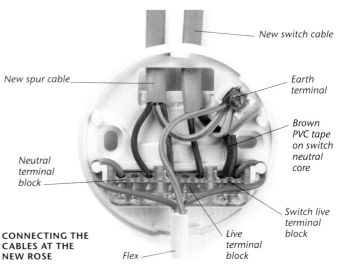

New switch cable
New spur cable
Earth terminal
Brown PVC tape on switch neutral core
Neutral terminal block
Switch live terminal block
Live terminal block
Flex

CONNECTING THE CABLES AT THE NEW ROSE

CONNECTING AT AN EXISTING JUNCTION BOX

If your wiring system uses junction boxes, you can connect your spur cable into any existing box. Turn off the power and unscrew the box cover so that you can identify the existing cables. If you want the new light to be controlled by its own switch, connect the spur cable cores to the terminals containing existing live, neutral, and earth cores as shown below. Run your spur cable to the new ceiling rose and connect it and its new switch cable as shown opposite.

If you want the new light to be controlled by the switch that is connected to this junction box, connect the spur cable cores to the same terminals as the cable supplying the existing ceiling rose or light fitting.

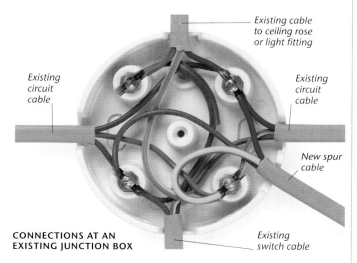

Existing cable
to ceiling rose
or light fitting

Existing
circuit
cable

Existing
circuit
cable

New spur
cable

**CONNECTIONS AT AN
EXISTING JUNCTION BOX**

Existing
switch cable

CONNECTING AT A NEW JUNCTION BOX

If it is more convenient to make the spur connection directly into the lighting circuit cable, you can use a new four-terminal junction box to make all the connections. Check that the cable you plan to use is a lighting circuit cable, not a switch cable. Turn off the power to the circuit and cut the cable. Prepare its cores and connect them to the junction box. Then prepare and connect in the new spur and switch cables as shown below. Screw the junction box baseplate to the side of a nearby joist and fit its cover. Run the cables to the new light and switch positions and connect them up, then restore the power supply.

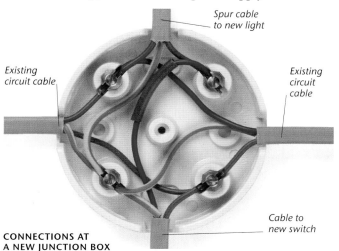

Spur cable
to new light

Existing
circuit cable

Existing
circuit
cable

Cable to
new switch

**CONNECTIONS AT
A NEW JUNCTION BOX**

TAKING A FUSED SPUR FROM A POWER CIRCUIT

If extending an existing lighting circuit is inconvenient, or if it is already at full capacity, it is possible to create a subcircuit for the new lights by connecting a spur cable into a power circuit.

The connection to the circuit is made at a suitable socket outlet, or at a 30-amp junction box cut into the circuit cable (see p.445 for details). From there, a length of 2.5-mm² cable is run to a switched fused connection unit (FCU), which must be fitted with a 5-amp fuse. From the FCU, use 1-mm² cable to run the subcircuit wiring onto the new ceiling- or wall-light position.

The FCU can be used as the on-off switch for a single light. If there will be several lights on the subcircuit, it is better to use an unswitched FCU on the spur and to provide a separate switch for each light. If you are installing wall lights, connect the supply and switch cable cores at each light using strip connectors (see p.451 for how to connect the cable and flex tail cores to the terminals).

Single-light extension

Arrange the cable run to the new light so that it runs vertically up the wall to the light position, and fit the mounting box for the FCU below it. Fit a flush mounting box in the wall behind the light position to contain the strip connectors that will link the subcircuit cable to the light fitting's flex tails (see p.451). When you have made all the wiring connections, screw the light fitting to the wall so that its baseplate covers the mounting box.

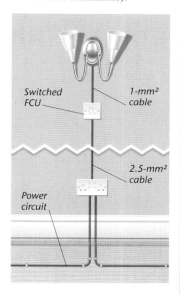

Switched
FCU

1-mm²
cable

2.5-mm²
cable

Power
circuit

Multiple-light extension

Run the subcircuit cable vertically or horizontally to the new light positions, and fit a mounting box in the wall at each one. Connect the circuit and switch cables and the fitting's flex tails as before using strip connectors (see p.451).

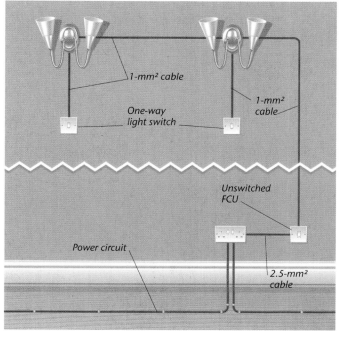

1-mm² cable

1-mm²
cable

One-way
light switch

Unswitched
FCU

Power circuit

2.5-mm²
cable

INSTALLING A LIGHT FITTING

If you are happy to have the new light fitting in the same location as an existing ceiling rose, you can use its wiring to supply it, and its switch to control it. The way you connect it up will depend on the type of wiring you find at the existing rose, and on the wiring in the new fitting. See below for the various options.

ASSESSING YOUR LIGHT-FITTING OPTIONS

Before starting, switch off the lighting circuit's miniature circuit breaker (MCB) or remove the circuit fuse, and check that the existing light no longer works when switched on. Remove the screw-on cover from the old ceiling rose, then disconnect it and unscrew its baseplate from the ceiling (see p.447 for how to do this).

Fitting with fixed terminals

If the fitting has fixed terminals and there is just one cable at the ceiling rose, you can connect it up directly as shown below. Otherwise you must use a block of strip connectors to wire in the circuit and switch cables. If there is no room within the baseplate of the fitting for these connectors, you must use a mounting box (see opposite).

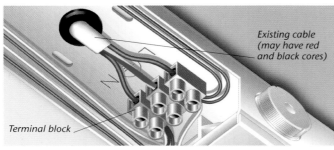

Existing cable (may have red and black cores)

Terminal block

FITTING WITH FIXED TERMINALS

Fitting with a hollow baseplate

Many light fittings have two- or three- flex cores (called tails) emerging from the lampholder. You need to connect these to the circuit cables using strip connectors. If the fitting is designed to be mounted directly against the ceiling, there may be room for them within its baseplate (see below). Connect the cable cores to the flex tails as shown opposite.

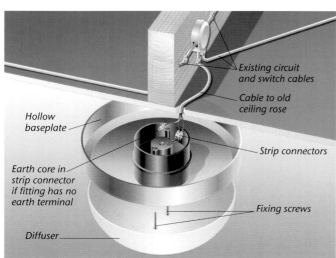

Existing circuit and switch cables

Cable to old ceiling rose

Hollow baseplate

Strip connectors

Earth core in strip connector if fitting has no earth terminal

Fixing screws

Diffuser

FITTING WITH HOLLOW BASEPLATE

REPOSITIONING THE NEW LIGHT

If you want to install the new fitting in a different position to the existing ceiling rose, you will have to run a spur from there to the new light. You will need a four-terminal junction box to replace the ceiling rose, and a length of 1-mm² two-core-and-earth cable. You will also need access to the ceiling void from above, which may involve lifting floorboards.

With the power off, identify and label the various cables present. Then disconnect and discard the old rose. Draw the cables up into the ceiling void and connect their cores into the junction-box terminals. Connect the spur cable into the junction box. Screw the box base to the side of the joist and fit its cover. Run the spur cable to the new light position and connect it to the fitting. It will be controlled by the original switch. Secure the new fitting and patch the ceiling at the original rose position.

Installing recessed fittings

Recessed downlighters and spotlights are designed to be installed between the ceiling joists. After removing the old ceiling rose, gain access to the space above the ceiling through a loft space or by lifting the floorboards. Draw the existing cable(s) up into the ceiling void. If more than one cable is present, identify and label the switch cable. Then free the cables from any clips holding them to the joists, so you can route them to the new light position nearby. There should be enough play on them to allow this.

Mark the outline of the light fitting on the ceiling from below. Drill a hole inside the circle so that you can insert the tip of a padsaw blade, and cut out the circle. Feed the cable(s) down through the hole, and make the connections to the fitting's flex tails using strip connectors as shown opposite. Feed the cable(s) back into the ceiling void and push the light fitting up into the hole so the spring-loaded clips hold it securely. Restore the power and test the light.

If there is an unboarded loft above the fitting, pull back the insulation from around it to stop it overheating, and screw a board offcut to the joists above it to give it some protection from accidental damage.

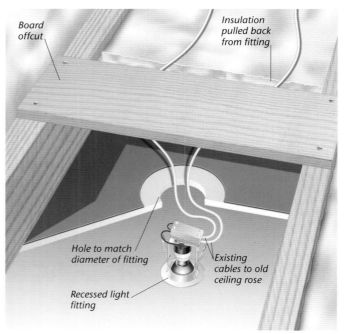

Board offcut

Insulation pulled back from fitting

Hole to match diameter of fitting

Existing cables to old ceiling rose

Recessed light fitting

RECESSED FITTING

INSTALLING A MOUNTING BOX

If there is no room within the light fitting's baseplate for strip connectors, you must provide an enclosure to contain them. The easiest way is to use a round mounting box, which fits in a hole cut in the ceiling and is held in place by two retractable lugs. It requires a hole about 63mm in diameter, and has threaded fixing lugs at 51-mm centres to which some light fittings can be screwed directly.

Hold the box against the ceiling and draw a pencil line round it. If you have a holesaw of the correct diameter, use this to cut the hole. Otherwise drill an entry hole within the waste area and use a padsaw to cut round the circle. Draw the cables down through the hole and feed them through a knockout in the base of the box. Push the box up into the hole and push out or rotate the fixing lugs to lock it in place. Check that it is secure. Its flange will cover any roughness round the edges of the cut-out.

Work out how to fix the fitting before making the wiring connections. If the fitting has fixing holes at 51-mm centres, screw it to the mounting box. If you can screw the fitting to a joist, mark the screw positions and drill pilot holes through the ceiling. If you need cavity fixings, drill holes and insert them at the screw positions. With the fixing positions prepared, you can screw the fitting in place as soon as you have made the connections.

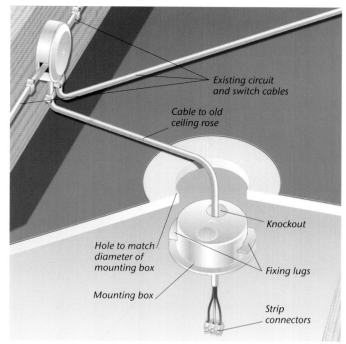

INSTALLING A ROUND CEILING BOX

CONNECTING CABLES TO FLEX TAILS

Strip connectors are used to connect circuit cables to light fittings with flex tails. How many you need depends on how many cables there are at the existing light position.

If there is just one cable, you need three connectors. Link the cable and flex live cores in the first, the neutral cores in the second, and the earth cores in the third. Remember to sleeve the cable earth core. If there is no earth flex tail, terminate the cable earth core in a connector anyway.

If more than one cable is present, you will need four connectors. Identify the switch cable so that you can connect its neutral core to the live flex tail in the first connector. Connect all the cable live cores in the second. Link all the cable neutral cores and the neutral flex tail in the third, and all the earth cores in the fourth.

Make sure that the core insulation reaches right up to the connector, and that the terminal screws are tightened fully.

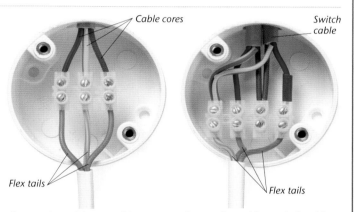

Connecting with one cable
Connect like cores using three strip connectors. There may be no earth flex tail on some light fittings.

Connecting with a switch cable
Use four connectors, linking the switch cable neutral and the live flex tail in the extra connector.

EXTRA-LOW-VOLTAGE (ELV) LIGHTING

ELV light fittings are powered by a 12-volt transformer, which takes its mains supply from an existing lighting or socket outlet circuit. The fittings use small halogen bulbs that give up to three times as much light as a conventional filament lamp, yet consume much less electricity. Lamp life is also longer than on normal light fittings. However, the lights perform best when left on for long periods; regular on-off switching can significantly reduce lamp life.

The transformer may be contained within the baseplate of an integral fitting such as a track or spotlight unit, or may be separate and placed in the ceiling void near the fitting. In the latter case it may power one or more ELV lights. One of the most popular (and easy-to-install) systems consists of a single transformer, a wiring harness, and a number of individual recessed downlighters (right).

Note that installing ELV lighting other than CE-approved integral fittings must be notified to Building Control.

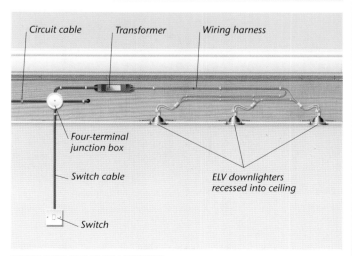

EXTRA-LOW-VOLTAGE LIGHTING

INSTALLING OUTDOOR LIGHTING

Outdoor lighting helps to show visitors the way to your front door after dark, and is an excellent burglar deterrent. Lighting down the garden simply adds an extra dimension to your enjoyment of this outdoor space. The wiring work involved in carrying out the jobs described here is quite straightforward, but you must take great care to ensure that any work you do outside the property is correctly installed and is electrically safe.

TOOLS AND MATERIALS SEE BASIC TOOLKIT AND P.439

BUILDING REGULATIONS APPROVAL

Under Part P (Electrical Safety) of the Building Regulations, you must notify your local authority Building Control department of your intention to install any new circuits or electrical equipment outside the house. You must do this before you start the work, and pay a fee to have it tested and certified on completion.

The only job described here for which your local authority does not need to be notified is installing a light on a house wall, unless it is controlled by an outside switch. However, you must still have the work tested and certified by a qualified electrician to ensure that it is safe. Installing low-voltage lighting may also be exempt from notification, depending on the type of fittings being installed. If in doubt, check with your local authority.

INSTALLING A LIGHT ON THE HOUSE WALL

The light fitting must be suitable for outdoor use, even if it will be under cover. You can supply it via a direct spur from an indoor lighting circuit, or as a fused spur from a ring main circuit. Drill a hole through the wall at the installation point and feed the cable through (see opposite). Inside the house, route the spur cable towards the connection point, then turn off the power supply to the circuit.

Using a lighting-circuit spur

For a lighting-circuit spur, cut the circuit cable and strip all the cable ends for connection to the junction box. Run another length of cable from here down to the new switch position. Connect the circuit, spur, and switch cables to the junction-box terminals as shown (bottom left).

Using a ring main spur

To use a spur cable from a ring main circuit, run the new cable to a point near the socket outlet where you will connect in the spur (see p.444 for details about selecting a suitable outlet). Use an upstairs outlet, so that the spur cable can run in the ceiling void. This is also the best place for you to fit the junction box. Wire the spur and switch cables into the junction box, then add a length of cable to connect the junction box to the FCU. Mount this close to the socket outlet, then connect in the cable from the junction box. To complete the job, connect the 2.5-mm² cable from the FCU into the socket outlet terminals, and fit a 5-amp fuse in the FCU. Restore power to the circuit and test the light.

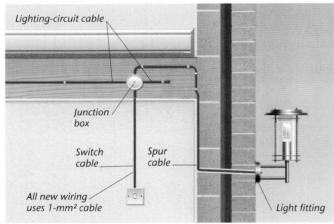

SPUR FROM A LIGHTING CIRCUIT

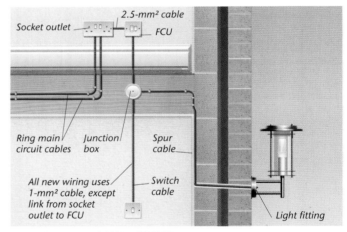

SPUR FROM A RING MAIN CIRCUIT

MAKING CONNECTIONS

For a spur from a lighting circuit (above), wire the four cable cores into a four-terminal junction box (right).

For a spur from a ring main circuit (above right), only one circuit cable is wired into the junction box. Wire the spur cable from the FCU into the socket outlet, as shown, far right. Existing circuit cables may have red live and black neutral cores.

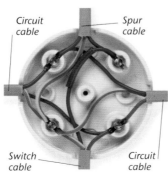

CONNECTIONS AT FOUR-TERMINAL JUNCTION BOX

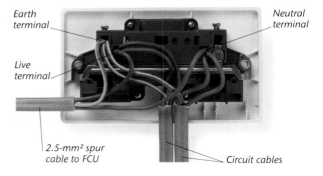

CONNECTIONS AT SOCKET OUTLET ON RING MAIN CIRCUIT

INSTALLING THE LIGHT FITTING

In some light fittings, you can connect the spur cable cores directly to the lampholder terminals, as shown here. In others, you must use a block of strip connectors to link the cable to the flex tails inside the fitting. If the fitting does not need earthing, terminate the earth core in a single strip connector as shown. Run some silicone mastic round the fitting's baseplate to seal it to the wall and keep water out.

A **Drill a 10-mm (½-in) hole** from outside, angled upwards to prevent water penetration. Feed the spur cable through from inside.

B **Hold the new light** over the cable exit point and mark the positions of its fixing screws. Drill and plug the holes and fit the light on the wall.

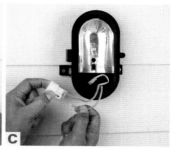

C **Feed the cable** through the light's baseplate and connect the cores to the lampholder. Use heat-resistant sleeving on live and neutral cores.

INSTALLING GARDEN LIGHTS

Remote garden lights must be supplied by their own circuit, run from the consumer unit if there is a spare fuseway available, or else from an additional small consumer unit. The new circuit must be protected by a high-sensitivity residual current device (RCD), and should be controlled by a double-pole (DP) isolating switch.

Decide where you want the lights and mark out the cable route. You can use ordinary 1.5-mm² PVC-sheathed cable for the circuit to the lights, but it must be protected by rigid PVC conduit. Dig a trench along the cable route (see p.454) and feed the cable into the conduit. Use solvent-welded connectors to link the lengths, and add a T fitting at each light position to bring the cable run up to the surface, ready for connection when you have installed the lights.

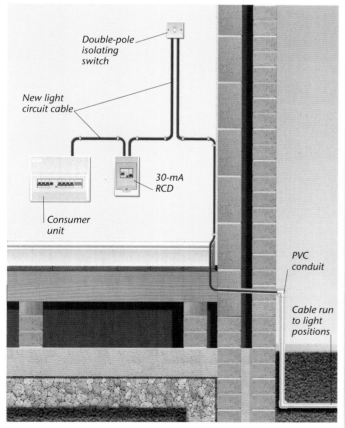

Double-pole isolating switch

New light circuit cable

30-mA RCD

Consumer unit

PVC conduit

Cable run to light positions

REMOTE GARDEN-LIGHT CIRCUIT

INSTALLING EXTRA-LOW-VOLTAGE (ELV) LIGHTS

Extra-low-voltage garden-light fittings are powered by a 12-volt transformer. Because of this safe voltage, there is no need to bury the cables underground. They can simply be run on the surface across flower beds and through shrubberies to the light positions. This arrangement allows you to move the light fittings around easily if you wish; they are usually mounted on spikes to facilitate this.

The transformer is sited indoors, where it is plugged into a conveniently-located socket outlet. The ELV cable passes through a hole drilled in a wall, window frame, or door frame, and should be clipped to the house wall where it drops down to ground level.

The only drawback of ELV lighting is that the maximum cable length is restricted by the relatively high current it carries, so unless you use several circuits (each with its own transformer) you cannot illuminate a very large area of the garden. A typical garden lighting set includes three or four light fittings plus 8–10m (26–30ft) of cable – enough to light up a patio or deck.

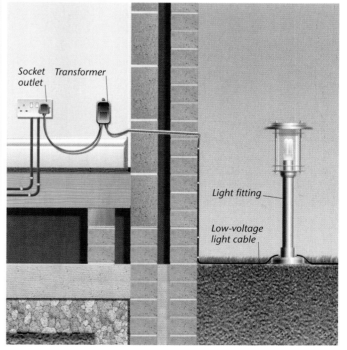

Socket outlet Transformer

Light fitting

Low-voltage light cable

EXTRA-LOW-VOLTAGE LIGHT CIRCUIT

There are two projects that are well worth carrying out to add convenience and safety to your use of electricity out of doors. The first is installing an outdoor socket outlet for your garden power tools, and the second is taking power to a garden shed or other outbuilding. The wiring work required is quite straightforward, but you must notify your local authority Building Control department before you start so that it can be inspected and certified.

FITTING OUTDOOR SOCKET OUTLETS

Having a dedicated outdoor socket outlet on the house wall for garden power tools saves trailing long flexes through open windows. It also provides the safety of RCD protection for anyone using electrical equipment out of doors. All you need is a weatherproof outlet with a built-in high-sensitivity RCD, plus a length of 2.5-mm² two-core-and- earth cable and a conveniently-sited indoor socket outlet to which to connect the spur cable. Alternatively you can install an ordinary outdoor outlet, and connect it to a separate RCD indoors.

Position the outdoor socket outlet so that you can drill a hole through the house wall and feed the spur cable in close to the indoor outlet. Fit the mounting box over the exit hole, draw in the cable and connect it to the outlet terminals. Fit the faceplate on the box, making sure that the weatherproof seals are correctly positioned. Indoors, run the spur cable to its connection point, via a separate RCD if necessary.

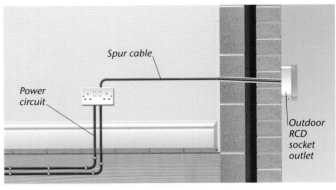

FITTING AN OUTDOOR RCD SOCKET OUTLET

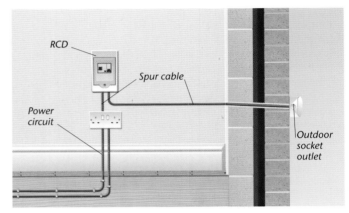

FITTING AN OUTLET WITH SEPARATE RCD

RUNNING CABLE OUTDOORS

If you need to take a power supply to any point outside the house, you have to decide whether to run it overhead – easier to do, but ugly and prone to accidental damage – or to take it underground – trickier to install, but far safer.

Running cable overhead

You can use ordinary PVC-sheathed cable if the span between the two buildings is 3m (10ft) or less. Longer spans must be supported by a tensioned catenary wire and cable buckles, and this wire must be earthed to the house's main earthing point. The span must be at least 3.5m (12ft) above ground over a path, and 5.2m (17ft) above ground over a drive or other area with vehicular access.

Running cable underground

Underground cable runs must be protected by continuous solvent-welded PVC conduit, which should be buried in a trench at a depth of 450mm (1ft 6in) beneath paths or patios, and at 750mm (2ft 6in) beneath lawns and flower beds.

Make up the run of conduit using straight connectors and elbows. You can cut conduit to length with any fine-toothed saw. Feed the cable in and assemble the entire run dry to check the fit. When you have completed it, go back to the start and solvent-weld all the connections before laying the conduit in place on a bed of sand with a row of bricks at each side. For maximum protection, lay small paving slabs or roof tiles over the conduit run as shown, and place a length of special black-and-yellow warning tape on top. Add a layer of soil and another strip of tape. Then back-fill the trench and tamp the soil down firmly.

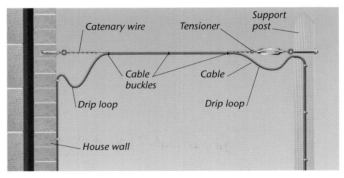

RUNNING CABLE OVERHEAD USING A CATENARY WIRE

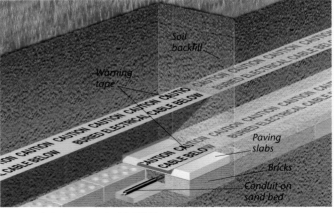

RUNNING CABLE UNDERGROUND

TAKING A POWER SUPPLY TO AN OUTBUILDING

The new circuit is run through a 2.5-mm² cable from a 30-amp MCB in the consumer unit, or from a new second consumer unit installed next to it if there is no spare on the existing one. The circuit must be protected by a high-sensitivity RCD.

The circuit cable can be run overhead or underground (see opposite). Within the outbuilding, connect it to a small consumer unit. This should contain a main switch so you can isolate the circuit, a 30-amp MCB to protect the subcircuit to socket outlets, and a 5-amp MCB to protect the lighting subcircuit. Alternatively, you can provide a single 30-amp circuit with a fused spur via an FCU supplying the lighting.

Do not connect the circuit cable's earth core to the consumer unit earth terminal. Instead, run a 6-mm² single-core earth cable from this earth terminal to an earth electrode driven into the ground beneath the building.

Use metal-clad surface-mounted wiring accessories rather than plastic ones.

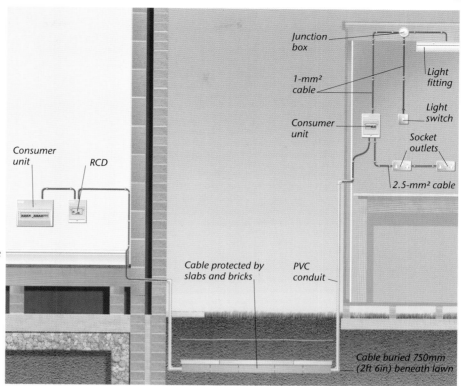

TAKING A POWER SUPPLY UNDERGROUND TO AN OUTBUILDING

PROVIDING POWER FOR WATER FEATURES

If you want to provide a power supply for a water feature, or for a fountain and underwater lighting in a garden pond, the safest and easiest way of doing so is to use extra-low- voltage (ELV) equipment powered from a transformer. Install this indoors, plugged into a conveniently sited socket outlet (or wired into a fused connection unit for a more permanent installation). Feed the cables out through a hole drilled in the house wall, then run them in a shallow trench to wherever the ELV equipment is to be installed. Protect the cable from accidental damage by enclosing it in PVC conduit. Use waterproof connectors to link the cable to the flex tail from the pump or light.

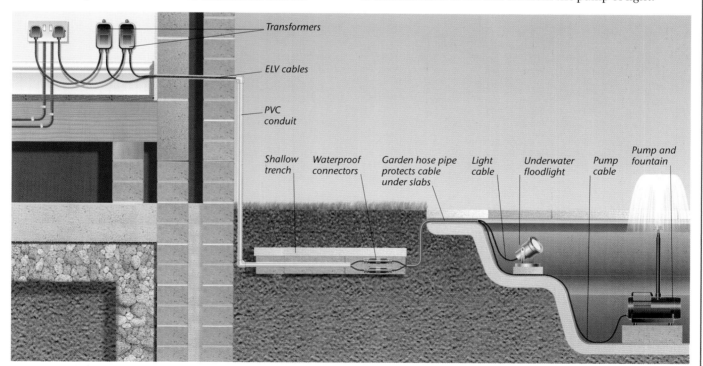

PROVIDING POWER FOR WATER FEATURES USING ELV EQUIPMENT

REPLACING A DAMAGED PLATESWITCH

If a wiring accessory's faceplate is cracked or broken, make it safe temporarily by patching it with PVC insulating tape. Buy and fit a replacement as soon as possible.

TOOLS AND MATERIALS
Terminal screwdriver, paper and pencil, plateswitch

A Turn off the power supply to the circuit concerned. Undo the plateswitch fixing screws and ease it away from the wall.

B Make a sketch showing which coloured core goes to which terminal, and how the earth core is connected or terminated.

C Disconnect the old plateswitch. Reconnect the cores to the new one, screw it to the mounting box, and restore the power.

REPLACING A BROKEN PULL-CORD SWITCH

If the cord breaks below the acorn connector, unscrew this and fit a new length of cord. If it breaks above the acorn, replacing the switch is easier than trying to replace the broken cord.

TOOLS AND MATERIALS
Terminal screwdriver, replacement pull-cord switch

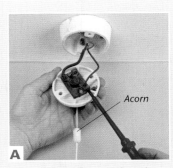

Acorn

A Turn off the power supply to the switch. Unscrew its faceplate and disconnect the cable cores from their terminals.

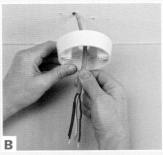

B Unscrew the old baseplate from the ceiling and remove it. Fit the new switch baseplate in its place after feeding the cable through it.

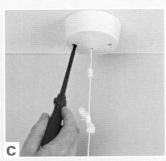

C Connect the cable cores (see p.446) to the terminals on the new switch faceplate and screw it to the baseplate. Restore the power.

REPLACING A DAMAGED LAMPHOLDER

The plastic lampholder below a ceiling rose can crack or become discoloured over time, due to heat rising from the light bulb. Fitting a replacement is a simple task. A plastic lampholder needs no earth connection, and is wired using two-core flex. If you want to fit a metallic one in its place, you must replace the two-core flex with a three-core flex containing an earth core. This is connected to the earth terminal on the lampholder and to the earth terminal on the ceiling-rose baseplate. See p.447 for more information on replacing pendant flex.

TOOLS AND MATERIALS
Terminal screwdriver, slip-joint pliers, new lampholder

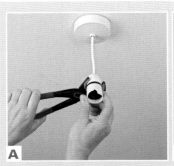

A Turn off the power supply to the lighting circuit, then undo the lampholder cover. Grip it with slip-joint pliers if it is stuck.

B Slide the cover up the flex to expose the lampholder terminals. Undo the screws and release the flex cores.

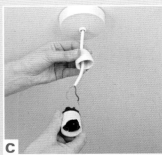

C Pull the old lampholder away. Slide off the flex grip (if present) and the old lampholder cover, then discard them.

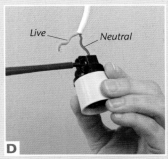

Live   Neutral

D Thread the flex through the new lampholder cover (and the flex grip if supplied). Then reconnect the cores to their terminals.

E If no separate flex grip is supplied, hook the flex cores over the support lugs to prevent any strain on the terminals.

F Screw the cover to the body of the lampholder. Fit a light bulb and restore the power supply so that you can test the light.

REPLACING A DAMAGED PLUG

All new appliances are now supplied with a factory-fitted plug that cannot be opened. To replace a damaged plug you must cut off its flex and reconnect this to a new plug.

TOOLS AND MATERIALS
Side cutters, wire strippers, terminal screwdriver, new plug

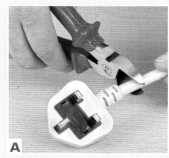

A

Use side cutters to sever the flex close to the damaged plug. Discard it immediately.

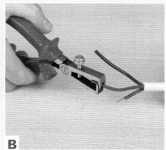

B

Cut off about 50mm (2in) of the flex sheath with a sharp knife. Then trim 12mm (½in) of insulation from each core with wire strippers.

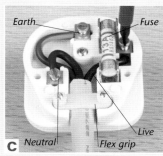

Earth *Fuse*

Neutral *Live* *Flex grip*

C

Open the new plug, release the flex grip and connect the cores as shown. Replace the flex grip and screw on the plug cover.

RE-THREADING A MOUNTING BOX

If faceplate fixing screws were cross-threaded when originally driven into their fixing lugs, the threads will have been damaged. If so you may have difficulty in undoing and replacing the existing plateswitch. You will need re-thread the holes.

TOOLS AND MATERIALS
Re-threader

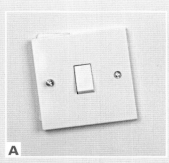

A

Turn off the power supply to the switch. Use a screwdriver to undo the existing plateswitch fixing screws. Force them if necessary.

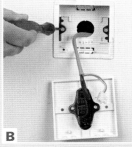

B

Ease off the plateswitch. Rotate the re-threader inside each lug to cut a new internal thread. Re-attach the plateswitch using new screws.

DEALING WITH BROKEN LUGS

Flush metal mounting boxes contain one fixed and one adjustable lug, allowing accessory faceplates to be fixed level even if the box is not. Forcing cross-threaded screws out may shear off one of both of these lugs. If this happens, you have no alternative but to remove the damaged mounting box and replace it with a new one.

RESETTING A LOOSE MOUNTING BOX

Surface-mounted boxes are prone to knocks that can pull them away from the wall, especially if this is hollow and the original fixings were poorly made. If this happens, remake the fixings to secure the box.

TOOLS AND MATERIALS
Drill and drill bit, new wall fixings to suit wall type

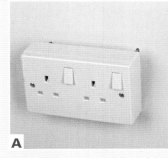

A

Turn off the power supply to the damaged accessory. Unscrew the faceplate and ease it away from the mounting box.

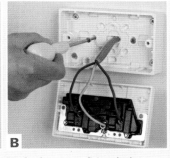

B

Undo the screws fixing the box to the wall and remove the old fixings. Reposition the box slightly and drill new fixing holes.

C

Insert new wall fixings and screw the mounting box securely to the wall. Re-attach the faceplate and restore the power supply.

USING ADAPTORS AND EXTENSION LEADS

If you need extra socket outlets, use a strip adaptor rather than the block type, which can pull out of the socket and cause sparking and overheating if several appliances are connected.

TOOLS AND MATERIALS
Strip adaptor, extension lead, RCD adaptor, surge protector

Strip adaptor
Fitted with a 13-amp fuse. Use this to plug in several low-wattage appliances such as TVs and stereos.

Extension lead
Always unwind to prevent overheating. Add an RCD adaptor to plug in equipment used outdoors.

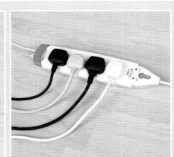

Surge-protected adaptor
Adaptor with surge protection to connect up your computer, which can be damaged by current surges.

Communications systems

YOUR HOME IS LIKELY TO CONTAIN AN INCREASINGLY COMPLEX SYSTEM OF TELECOMMUNICATIONS AND HOME-ENTERTAINMENT EQUIPMENT. PARTS OF THESE SYSTEMS WILL BE VISIBLE, ESPECIALLY IF THEY HAVE BEEN INSTALLED SINCE THE HOUSE WAS BUILT, BUT MUCH OF THE WIRING WILL BE CONCEALED. HERE IS AN OVERVIEW OF THE SYSTEMS, AND AN EXPLANATION OF HOW EVERYTHING IS INTERCONNECTED.

SYSTEMS TYPES

Communications and home entertainment systems consist of similar components. These include a signal collector or a piece of electrical equipment that generates a signal, and cables of one sort or another to transmit the signal to the receiving equipment that makes the signal visible or audible to the user.

HOME ENTERTAINMENT SYSTEMS

In a typical home, the heart of the entertainment system is the television set. The family set is likely to be connected to an aerial socket outlet which is wired to an external or loft TV aerial, while other sets will probably rely on portable aerials. Video or DVD equipment may also be connected to the TV set as alternative signal sources.

Most radio sets in the home are likely to be portable, but the tuner in a home entertainment ("hi-fi") system may be connected to a separate FM aerial for better reception. The hi-fi system also allows CDs or other audio sources to be accessed. You can easily provide additional TV- and FM-aerial socket outlets in the home by extending the aerial system you have already.

Increasing numbers of homes now receive TV and FM signals from a satellite dish, which gathers analogue or digital signals broadcast via a stationary satellite, or from a local cable network. These incoming signals can also be channelled to other TV sets or tuners.

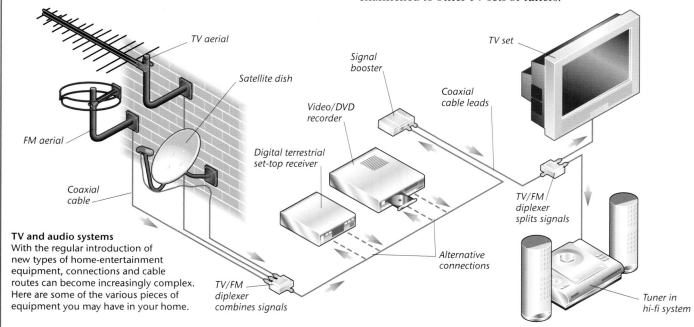

TV and audio systems
With the regular introduction of new types of home-entertainment equipment, connections and cable routes can become increasingly complex. Here are some of the various pieces of equipment you may have in your home.

TV aerial

Satellite dish

FM aerial

Coaxial cable

TV/FM diplexer combines signals

Video/DVD recorder

Digital terrestrial set-top receiver

Signal booster

Alternative connections

TV set

Coaxial cable leads

TV/FM diplexer splits signals

Tuner in hi-fi system

WORKING WITH COAXIAL CABLE

If you are installing a new aerial download, plan the route of the coaxial cable with care. To minimize signal losses, always use good-quality "screened" cable, and keep the route as short as possible. Avoid sharp bends which could kink the cable, and avoid crushing it when driving in cable clips.

It is generally easiest to run the cable down the outside of the house wall and take it into the room to be served through a hole drilled in the wall or a window frame. The cable can run directly from an external aerial, and can be fed from a loft aerial out through the eaves soffit board.

If the cable is to be run internally, drop it inside timber-framed partition walls or down service ducts such as the one housing the soil pipe. It can then be run in floor voids as necessary to reach wall-mounted aerial outlet positions.

A

To prepare coaxial cable, slit the sheath with a sharp knife. Then cut round it about 50mm (2in) from the end and remove the offcut.

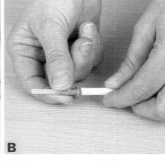

B

To fit a connector, slip the screw cap over the cable. Push the copper braid mesh back to expose the insulation round the central core.

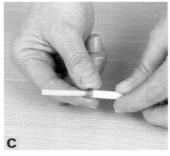

C

Gather the mesh into a neat bunch round the end of the outer sheath. Trim off any stray strands with side cutters.

D

Cut away all but 3mm (⅛in) of the inner core and slip the metal claw gripper over the braid. Pinch it with pliers to tighten it.

E

Fit the plug pin over the central core and push it up against the claw gripper. Trim off the excess core so it is flush with the end of the pin.

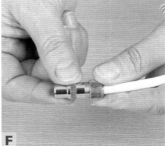

F

Slip on the plug body so it fits over the plug pin, and tighten the screw cap onto it to complete the assembly of the connector.

INSTALLING AERIAL OUTLETS

Aerial outlets can be flush or surface-mounted. A single outlet is shown here. A twin outlet is fed by two separate downloads – usually one from a TV aerial and one from an FM aerial. A diplexed outlet has one TV and one FM socket. It is fed by a single aerial download (see opposite), and contains electronic circuitry that splits the signal to the two sockets. A second diplexer is fitted (usually in the loft) to combine the feeds from the TV and FM aerial.

For satellite or cable services, outlet plates with threaded (F-type) connections are used, allowing the coaxial link to the TV set to be physically secured to the outlet instead of having a push-fit connection. Twin TV outlets are also available with one F-type socket and one coaxial socket.

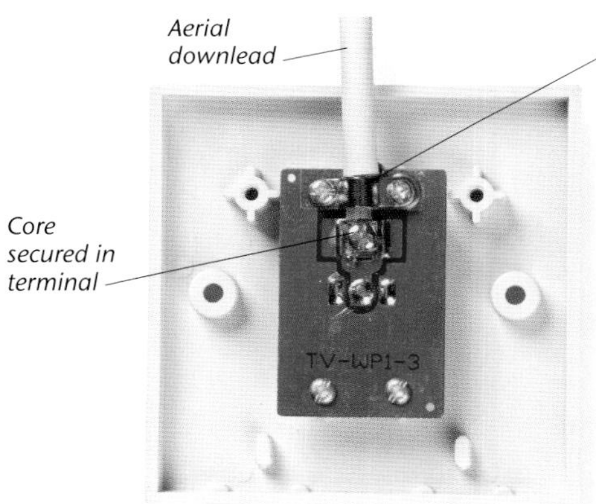

Aerial download

Braid trapped beneath clamp

Core secured in terminal

Single aerial outlet
This type is fed by a download from a TV or FM aerial. Prepare the cable as shown above. Pass the central core through the braid clamp and connect it to the single terminal. Trap the bunched braid beneath the clamp.

TELECOMMUNICATIONS SYSTEM

Unless you have a broadband internet connection (see below), your home's telecommunications system will be based on the master telephone socket outlet, which will have been fitted by your telecoms supplier. You can increase the versatility of your system by adding any number of extension outlets (see p.461), so you can plug in up to four phones (see pp.460–61) or connect your computer to the phone network via a modem.

If you have a broadband internet service in your area, your internet service provider (ISP) will install all the necessary cabling and the modem when you sign up for the service. All you have to do is plug in your computer for a permanent "always-on" connection.

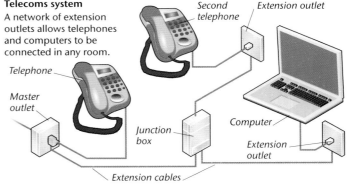

Telecoms system
A network of extension outlets allows telephones and computers to be connected in any room.

Second telephone
Extension outlet
Telephone
Master outlet
Junction box
Computer
Extension outlet
Extension cables

EXTENDING A TELEPHONE SYSTEM

Despite the massive growth in the use of mobile phones, it has usually been cheaper to make and receive calls in your home using a conventional landline. You can install a telephone extension outlet in every room except the bathroom if you wish, but you must not plug in more than four telephones at once, otherwise none will ring properly. The incoming line will be connected to a master socket outlet (also known as a linebox) installed by your telecoms supplier. There are two ways of extending a system from here: by wiring new cable into a BT NTE5 outlet if you have one, or by plugging in an adaptor and extension cable otherwise.

CABLE CONNECTING TOOL

An IDC cable connector tool is used to push telephone cable cores into the screwless brass blade terminals that are used in some extension phone outlets.

PLANNING YOUR REQUIREMENTS

You can buy the components needed to extend your system individually or in kits from telecoms equipment suppliers and DIY stores. Plan your requirements and work out how your extended system is to be wired up. You can either wire the new outlets in series, looping the extension cable into and out of each one in turn, or use a junction box to wire in up to three extension cables if this makes for more economical use of cable. The total circuit length should not exceed 100m (330ft). Extension (slave) outlets are available as flush and surface-mounted units, in single and twin types.

A one-piece master outlet must be fitted with a plug-in adaptor to extend the system.

A BT NTE5 outlet has a removable section of the faceplate, allowing you to wire in the extension cable.

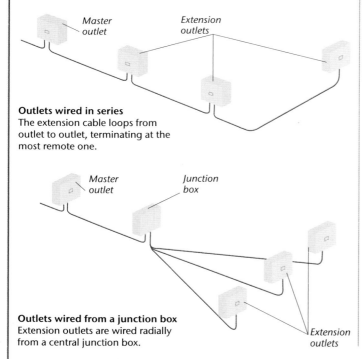

Outlets wired in series
The extension cable loops from outlet to outlet, terminating at the most remote one.

Outlets wired from a junction box
Extension outlets are wired radially from a central junction box.

RUNNING CABLE

The best place to conceal telephone cable is by running it in the gap beneath skirting boards. The section of cable running up to a flush outlet can then be passed up through a hole drilled behind a skirting board. Alternatively, if you are happy with a surface-mounted installation, you can clip the cable to the top of the skirting boards. At doorways, run the cable up and over the edge of the architrave moulding; do not conceal it under floor coverings at door thresholds. Pass it from room to room through holes drilled through the wall, or up and down via the ceiling void.

You can also enclose cable in slim surface-mounted PVC mini-trunking, or conceal it in flat oval conduit in chases cut in the plaster. You must not run it in the same trunking or conduit as any mains circuit cables, which should be at least 50mm (2in) away to minimize interference.

PREPARING CABLE

Prepare the phone cable for connection by slitting its sheath lengthways for about 50mm (2in) and trimming off the waste. Inside are four or six thin cores, colour-coded as detailed below. The number refers to the terminal in the phone outlet to which that core is connected. Four-core cable contains only cores 2 to 5. Cores 1 and 6 in six-core cable are not needed on simple domestic installations, so you should cut them off flush with the outer sheath before connecting the other cores to an outlet or junction box.

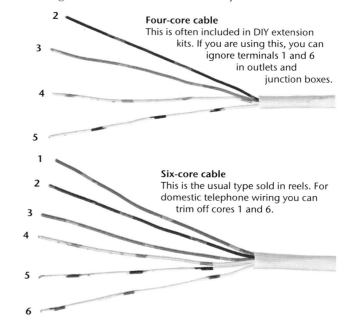

Four-core cable
This is often included in DIY extension kits. If you are using this, you can ignore terminals 1 and 6 in outlets and junction boxes.

Six-core cable
This is the usual type sold in reels. For domestic telephone wiring you can trim off cores 1 and 6.

CONNECTING CABLE

Connect each cable core to its numbered terminal on the back of the outlet faceplate. Some outlets have standard screw-down terminals; others have screwless brass blade terminals, and you need a special IDC cable connector tool (see opposite) to push in and connect the cable cores. For screw-down terminals, strip about 5mm (¼in) of insulation from each core and trap the bare metal securely beneath its terminal screw. For blade terminals, do not strip the insulation. The terminal contains small metal jaws that cut through the insulation and make an electrical contact as you push the core in with the connector tool.

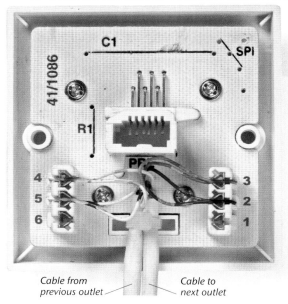

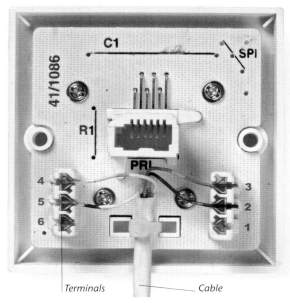

Screwless brass blade terminals
Make sure that you push the connector tool as far into the terminal as possible so that the cores make a good electrical connection.

Screw-down terminals
Trap the bare end of each core securely beneath its terminal screw, tighten the screw, and tug on the core to check that it is secure.

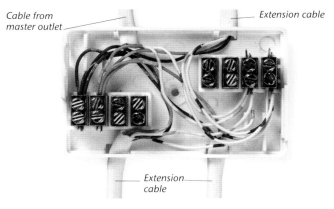

Cable from previous outlet

Cable to next outlet

Connecting cable at extension outlets
To wire a second outlet in series from the first one, connect the next length of cable to it at the same terminals. Repeat for other outlets in turn, terminating the cable at the final outlet.

Cable from master outlet

Extension cable

Extension cable

Connecting cables at a junction box
Again, connect like cores together, as shown above. Each set of terminals will accept two sets of cable cores, allowing you to wire in one feed cable and three extension cables.

Connecting to the master outlet

Run the extension cable back from the first extension outlet or the junction box to the master outlet. If you are using an adapter, simply plug it in and test each new outlet in turn by plugging in a phone and making a call. If you have a BT NTE5 outlet, unscrew the front cover, feed in the extension cable and connect its cores to the numbered terminals using the connector tool. Secure the cable in the cable grip, replace the cover, and test the installation.

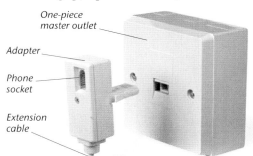

One-piece master outlet

Adapter

Phone socket

Extension cable

Master outlet
You can still plug a phone in at the master outlet - either into the extension adaptor as shown here, or into the original outlet if it is a BT NTE5 type.

PLUMBING

PIPE CONNECTIONS

TAPS AND VALVES

PLUMBING SYSTEMS

Your plumbing system consists of water supply and waste disposal. The water supply may run direct to each point of use, or the system may store cold and/or hot water. The waste-disposal system carries used water from appliances via waste and soil pipes to the drains. For information on re-use of water, see pp.384–87.

NON-MAINS DRAINAGE

If a house doesn't have mains drainage, waste water flows into a cesspool or a septic tank.

Cesspool

This is simply a large storage tank – holding up to 18,000 litres (4,000 gallons) – that has to be emptied on a regular basis by a specialist contractor. Most existing cesspools have been replaced by a septic tank (see below), or have been filled in when local mains drainage was eventually provided in the vicinity.

Septic tank

This is a chamber that works like a miniature sewage plant, treating waste water from the property by a combination of filtration and bacterial action so that the treated water can be safely discharged into the ground. The sludge remaining in the chamber has to be removed periodically.

Cold-water storage cistern

Metal (obsolete) or plastic tank that provides a reservoir of stored water for indirect supply systems (see p.467). New tanks must have a lid, an insulating jacket, and several special fittings to comply with Water Byelaw 30.

Gate valve

Isolating valve on each supply pipe from cold-water storage cistern. It allows the supply to the cold taps or hot-water storage cylinder to be shut off for maintenance.

Shower pump

Boosts hot and cold water pressure to provide power shower.

Toilet cistern

Ceramic or plastic tank that provides a reservoir of stored cold water for flushing the toilet. It may have an external or internal overflow.

Supply pipework

Lead (obsolete), copper, or plastic pipes carry water to taps, float valves, and storage cisterns.

Soil stack

Appliances discharge waste water via a large-diameter vertical plastic pipe vented above eaves level and running into an underground drainpipe.

Appliance trap

Plastic or metal fitting that traps a water seal in the waste pipe leading from appliances such as baths and sinks, to keep drain smells out.

Gully

In-ground waste-water collector with internal trap.

FEED-AND-EXPANSION CISTERN

You may find a second, smaller cistern in your loft, close to the larger cold-water storage cistern. This is called the feed-and-expansion cistern, and its job is to top up the water content in the primary pipe circuit between the boiler and the hot-water storage cylinder. It also accommodates the expansion in the primary circuit that takes place when the system heats up. It should be about one-third full when the system is cold. The cistern has a mains-pressure water supply and is refilled when necessary via a float valve, like the one in the cold-water storage tank. The vent pipe curving over the top of the tank acts as a safety valve if the primary circuit overheats. For more details, see p.497.

OVERFLOW WARNING PIPES

Both the cold-water storage and feed-and-expansion cisterns have an overflow pipe. Each is connected to the cistern just above the level of the float valve, and runs to the roof eaves, where an overflow caused by malfunction of the float valve will be immediately noticeable. Toilet cisterns also have an overflow pipe, which may discharge externally or back into the toilet pan.

EARTH BONDING CABLES

For electrical safety, all exposed metalwork such as copper pipes must be linked to the house's electrical earthing system with single-core earth cables. These conductors must have a cross-sectional area of at least 10mm² and must be attached to the pipes with special metal earth clamps. If you have no bonding conductors, call in an electrician to install them without delay.

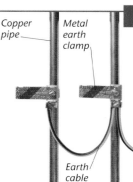

Copper pipe

Metal earth clamp

Earth cable

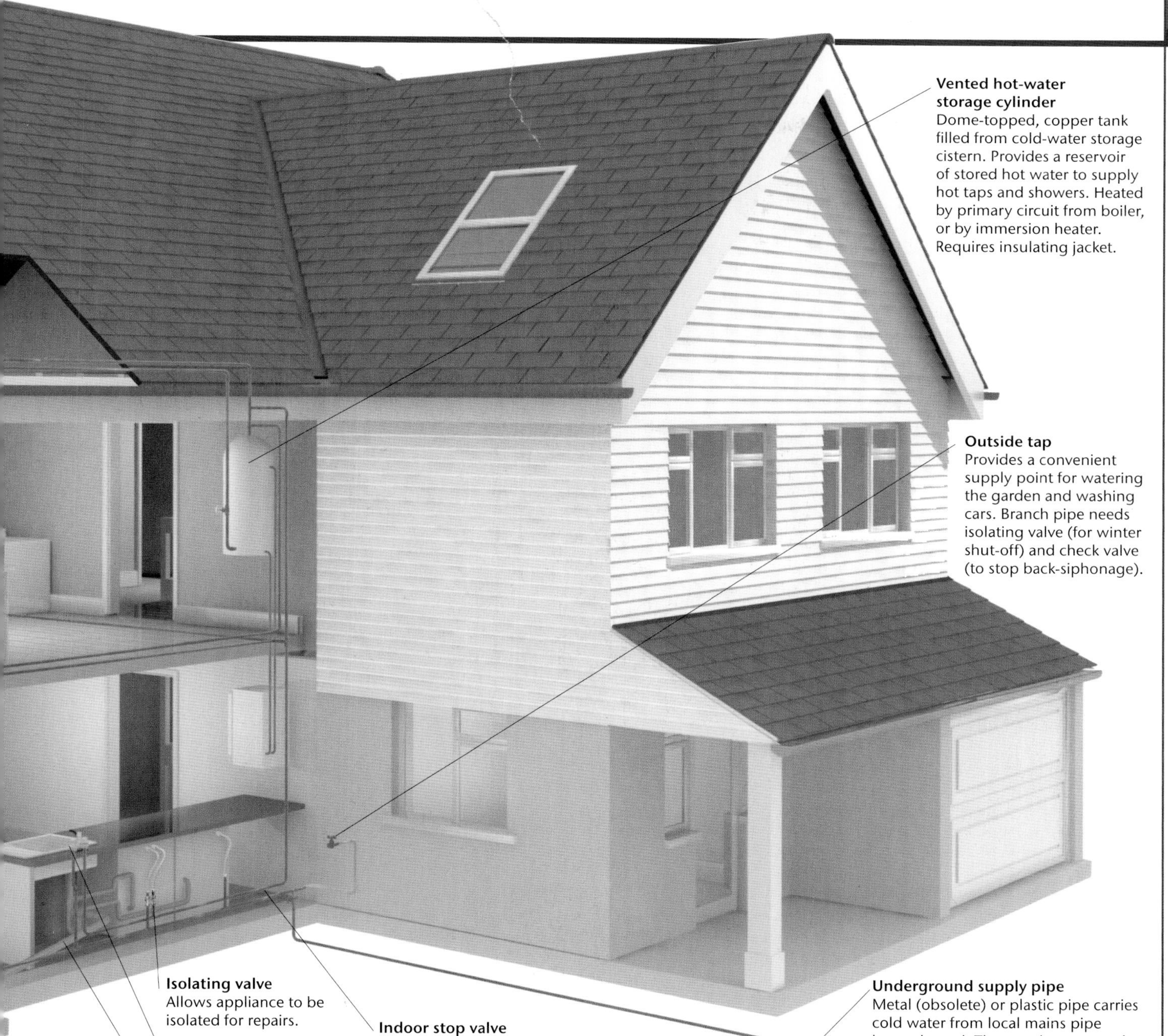

Vented hot-water storage cylinder
Dome-topped, copper tank filled from cold-water storage cistern. Provides a reservoir of stored hot water to supply hot taps and showers. Heated by primary circuit from boiler, or by immersion heater. Requires insulating jacket.

Outside tap
Provides a convenient supply point for watering the garden and washing cars. Branch pipe needs isolating valve (for winter shut-off) and check valve (to stop back-siphonage).

Isolating valve
Allows appliance to be isolated for repairs.

Kitchen sink tap
Supplies pure cold water for drinking and cooking.

Waste pipe
Metal or plastic pipes carry waste water away from appliances to a gully or soil stack.

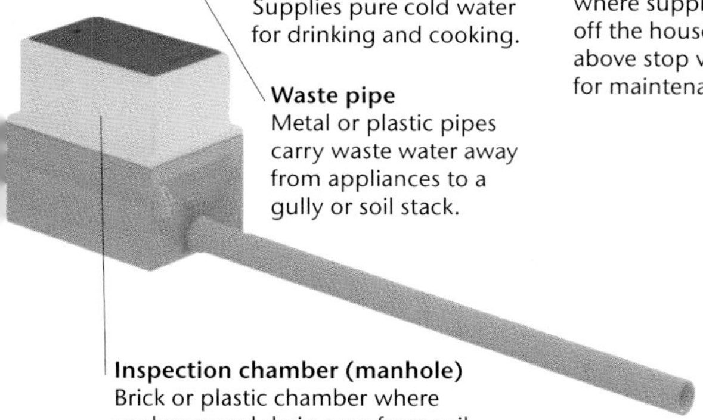

Indoor stop valve
Mains-pressure isolating valve located near where supply pipe enters the house. Shuts off the house water supply. Drain valve above stop valve allows pipe to be drained for maintenance.

Underground supply pipe
Metal (obsolete) or plastic pipe carries cold water from local mains pipe beneath road. The supply company's underground stoptap (and a water meter, if fitted) will be located on the pipe near the property boundary, under a metal cover plate for access.

Inspection chamber (manhole)
Brick or plastic chamber where underground drain runs from soil stacks and gullies connect to the main drain run. Fitted with a removable metal cover, allowing access to drain pipes for cleaning if a blockage occurs. Also installed where a drain changes direction.

UNVENTED HOT WATER STORAGE CYLINDER
Some homes have a mains-pressure hot-water system, rather than the low-pressure system shown here. This may be supplied directly from a combination boiler, or via an unvented hot-water storage cylinder that is heated by a conventional or condensing boiler or by an immersion heater. The mains-pressure cylinder is a flat-topped steel tank rather than a domed copper cylinder. In such a system there is no cold-water storage cistern or open vent pipe, and a range of safety devices protects the system from the risk of overheating. See pp.496–501 for more details about this type of hot-water system.

WATER SUPPLY SYSTEMS

The cold-water supply system in your property will be one of two types: a direct system, with all points of use supplied by mains-pressure water, or an indirect system, which relies chiefly on supplies from a cold-water storage tank. It is important to find out which type you have, as this affects how the system works and what you have to do to carry out maintenance or repairs.

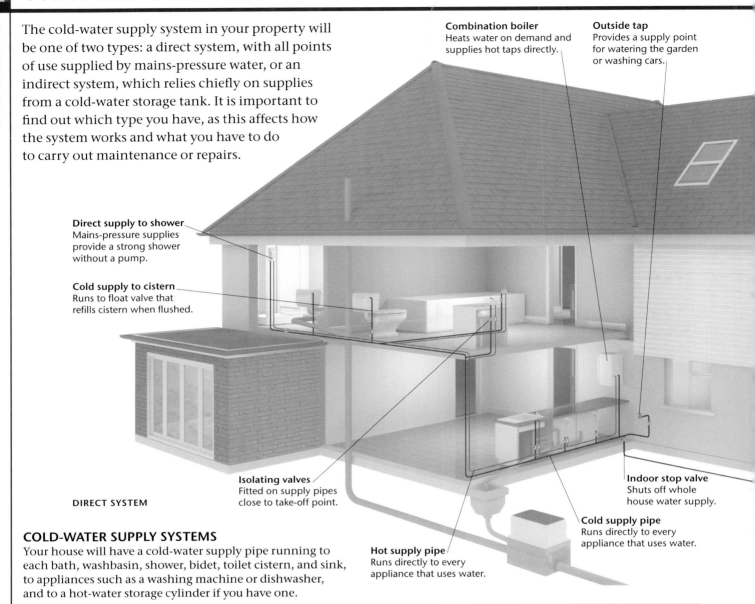

Combination boiler
Heats water on demand and supplies hot taps directly.

Outside tap
Provides a supply point for watering the garden or washing cars.

Direct supply to shower
Mains-pressure supplies provide a strong shower without a pump.

Cold supply to cistern
Runs to float valve that refills cistern when flushed.

Isolating valves
Fitted on supply pipes close to take-off point.

Indoor stop valve
Shuts off whole house water supply.

Cold supply pipe
Runs directly to every appliance that uses water.

Hot supply pipe
Runs directly to every appliance that uses water.

DIRECT SYSTEM

COLD-WATER SUPPLY SYSTEMS

Your house will have a cold-water supply pipe running to each bath, washbasin, shower, bidet, toilet cistern, and sink, to appliances such as a washing machine or dishwasher, and to a hot-water storage cylinder if you have one.

Direct supply system

Many new properties have a direct supply system. From the builder's point of view, this is cheaper and quicker to install than an indirect system. For the householder, there are two main benefits and one slight drawback. The benefits are having drinking-quality water at every cold tap, and not having tanks and pipework in the loft that could freeze up or leak. The drawback is that the system may rely on a combination boiler for its hot water supply (see p.498), and this may not be able to provide a generous supply of hot water to more than one tap at once. But there are ways round this (see below and pp.500–01).

With a direct system, the incoming supply pipe runs first to an indoor stoptap, which usually has a drain valve fitted immediately above it. From there, a branching network of pipes takes cold water directly to each tap, WC cistern, shower, and also to either a combination boiler or a multi-point water heater, either of which will supply the system's hot water needs. Taps, shower valves, and float valves in toilet cisterns are all high-pressure types – a point to remember when you need to repair or replace them.

PLUMBING RULES AND REGULATIONS

A variety of official rules and regulations apply to work done on your plumbing and heating systems.

■ The Water Supply Byelaws aim to prevent waste, undue consumption, contamination, or other misuse of the water supply. They apply to any new work you carry out. You must give your supply company five days' notice if you plan to install or alter a bidet, a flushing cistern, a tap or valve to which a hose may be connected, or any fitting through which contamination of the water supply could occur. In Scotland, you must give

notice of work to alter or install any water fitting.
■ The Building Regulations cover the disposal of waste water from appliances within the property, but not the water supply. They also cover the installation of any new fuel-burning appliance, especially those involving unvented systems (see p.501).
■ The Gas Safety Regulations make it illegal for anyone to carry out any work on the house gas supply, fittings, and equipment unless competent to do so. In practice this means using engineers who are GAS SAFE registered.

POWER SHOWERS AND BIDETS

■ Power showers use a pump to increase the pressure of cistern-fed (but not mains-fed) water supplies. To prevent the pump starving other appliances that use water when it is on, it must have its own supply pipes. The cold pipe is taken directly from the cold-water storage tank, and the hot supply from the storage cylinder via a connector called a Sussex flange. This helps to eliminate the tendency for the pump to suck air in from the cylinder vent pipe.
■ Bidets with a douche spray must also have separate water supply pipes with no branches off them. This is because the spray nozzle is submerged when the bidet is full, and so there is a potential risk of back-siphonage of used water into the supply.

Indirect supply system

Most older homes have an indirect supply system. Its chief advantage is that if the mains water supply is interrupted for any reason, a supply of stored water is still available (although stored water used for drinking or cooking should be boiled for complete safety). They are also quieter in use, because most of the take-off points operate at low pressure. Their main drawback is their relative complexity. They have more components, pipes, and connections, so there are potentially more things that can go wrong.

As with a direct system, the incoming supply runs first to an indoor stoptap and drain valve. It then runs vertically - this section of the system is called the rising main – to the main cold-water storage cistern, which is usually sited on a platform in the loft to give a reasonable water pressure for upstairs taps and showers.

A branch off the rising main supplies drinking-quality water to the kitchen cold tap. Other branches may also be fitted to supply a washing machine and dishwasher in the kitchen, and also an outside tap.

Outlet pipes from the cold-water storage cistern supply water to toilet cisterns and all other cold taps in the house. A second pipe supplies the hot-water storage cylinder (see pp.497 and 501). Each of these pipes should be fitted with an isolating valve called a gate valve, which allows that section of the system to be shut off for maintenance or adaptation. Each pipe running to a tap, toilet cistern, or shower mixer should also have a small in-line isolating valve fitted just before the point of use. These valves allow the supply to be shut off for local maintenance work without the need for the system to be drained (see p.489).

KEY TO PIPE FUNCTIONS
— Boiler flow and return pipes
— Hot supply pipes
— Cold supply pipes

Supply pipe
Brings house supply from mains supply.

Vent pipe
Discharges over storage cistern

Water to hot cylinder
Cold supply to hot-water storage cylinder

Cold-water storage cistern

Gate valve

Cold supply to power shower

Rising main

Cold supply to upstairs fittings

Hot-water storage cylinder

Flow pipe from boiler

Hot supply to upstairs fittings

Return pipe to boiler

Hot supply to power shower

Cold supply to downstairs fittings

Hot supply to downstairs fittings

Boiler

Isolating valves

Outside tap

Indoor stop valve

Underground mains supply pipe

INDIRECT SYSTEM

PLUMBING TOOLS AND MATERIALS

Along with a basic toolkit, there are a number of tools that will be necessary to carry out plumbing jobs. Not all the tools shown here may be required for every job; the checklist opposite shows which tools are needed for key tasks. Material requirements are also shown and explained over the next few pages.

SPANNERS AND WRENCHES

Multipurpose gripping tools are used for holding fixtures and fittings in position and for tightening or loosening various types of joint.

Adjust spanner width here

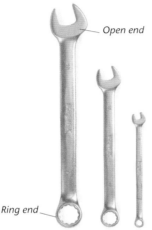

Open end

Ring end

Adjustable spanners
A set of adjustable spanners can accommodate most domestic nut or bolt sizes. These sets are commonly sold as three spanners in different sizes.

Set of spanners
A standard spanner set is also essential. Sets with both open and ring ends are advisable. Ring ends are less likely to slip, open ends are better in tight spaces.

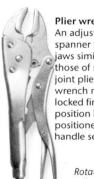

Plier wrench
An adjustable spanner that has jaws similar to those of slip-joint pliers. The wrench may be locked firmly in position by a lever positioned on the handle section.

Rotate screw to adjust jaw size

Stillson wrench
A heavy-duty adjustable spanner that has serrations along the jaws to provide greater grip. When pressure is applied to the handle, the jaws grip even tighter to the object being held.

Basin wrench
A specially designed spanner that allows for access in particularly tight areas, such as under basins, baths, or sinks. Available with either fixed or adjustable jaws. A fixed-jaw version is shown here.

Slip-joint pliers
Adjustment by dislocating the joint to widen or narrow the distance between the two jaw sections. The jaws are usually serrated and concave for extra grip on nuts, bolts, or rounded fittings.

PLUMBING ACCESSORIES

As well as pipes, there are a number of materials required for installing or working on a plumbing system. The most commonly used materials are shown below. There are also many other products used in plumbing systems such as the descalers, cleaners, and the various inhibitors used to maintain efficient central heating systems.

Washer selection box
Useful for washers, O-rings, and other small items.

Small compartments to store assorted washers

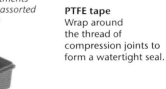

PTFE tape
Wrap around the thread of compression joints to form a watertight seal.

Solder wire
An alloy, supplied as a wire coil, which melts at a temperature lower than the metal pipes being joined. It may contain lead or be lead-free. Lead wire is not suitable for drinking-water pipes, so always choose the lead-free option.

Tube-cleaning brush
Wire brush to clean the inside of a pipe joint.

Gas blowtorch
Used to heat pipe joints when soldering. Always store upright.

Soldering mat
Used to protect surrounding surfaces from the heat generated when soldering a joint.

KEYS

There are some specially shaped spanners and keys that are designed for specific plumbing jobs. The three used most often are shown here.

Attaches to radiator bleed valve

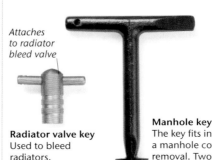

Radiator valve key
Used to bleed radiators.

Manhole key
The key fits into a hole in a manhole cover for easy removal. Two keys are normally required.

Stop valve key
Shaped to fit over the handle of a tap or stop valve. The long handle provides easy access to a stop valve.

UNBLOCKING TOOLS

Blocked toilets and drains can be expensive to fix if you call out an emergency plumber; for this reason it is worth attempting to clear the blockage yourself first.

Plunger
Handle with cup section on one end. The cup section is fitted over the drain outlet. Pump up and down to build suction and release the blockage.

Rubber cup section

PLUNGER

Grip support

Concertina cup for greater suction

MODERN PLUNGER

Fits over sink waste outlet

Hydraulic plunger
Uses pumping action to force a high-pressure jet into the blockage in order to dislodge it.

ROD SECTIONS

PLUNGER   **CORK-SCREW**

Drain rod set
Used to unblock exterior drainage systems. Once a manhole cover is lifted, rod sections are fed into the sewerage system, with extra lengths added as required. A plunger or corkscrew are attached to the end of the first rod and used to push into the blockage to break it up and allow free flow.

Corkscrew coil

Auger
The wheel of the auger is turned to allow the coiled section to burrow into the blockage and dislodge material.

ADDITIONAL MATERIALS

There are many different compounds and substances used for adhesion and lubrication when plumbing in pipes. The properties of the most commonly used are detailed below.

Flux compound is used on joints before soldering to ensure that the joint is totally clean.

Jointing compound is used as an alternative to PTFE tape and in conjunction with it to create a watertight compression joint. Should not be used on pipes containing drinking water unless specified by the manufacturer.

Solvent cement adhesive is used to join solvent-weld pipe systems. Different types are available to suit different plastic types.

Plumbers putty is a non-setting putty that creates a waterproof joint. It is used for bedding in sinks and sanitary ware, and around socket joints in sanitary ware.

Silicone spray is used to ease push-fit plastic pipes into joints.

Soft paraffin paste is an alternative to silicone spray. Use for easing push-fit joints into position.

TOOLS AND MATERIALS CHECKLISTS PP.470–89

Pipe bending (p.470) Pipe bender, bending spring

Boxing in surface-mounted pipes (p.475) Battens, paint or tiles, paintbrush, ply

Running flexible pipes through joists (p.475) Basic toolkit only

Running flexible pipes between joists (p.475) Basic toolkit only

Running pipes across joists (p.475) Carpet felt, metal plates

Cutting copper pipe (p.476) Pipe cutter, metal file, tube-cleaning brush

Making a compression joint (p.476) Compression joint

Making a solder-ring capillary joint (p.477) Gas blowtorch, wire wool, non-corrosive flux paste, cloth, small paintbrush

Making a solder end-feed joint (p.477) Gas blowtorch, wire wool, non-corrosive flux paste, solder wire, cloth, brush

Cutting plastic pipe (p.478) Plastic pipe cutter

Making a push-fit joint (p.478) Pipe insert, push-fit joint

Disconnecting a colleted push-fit joint (p.479) Demounting tool

Disconnecting a grab-ring, push-fit joint (p.479) Side cutters

Joining plastic and metal pipes (p.479) Plastic push-fit joint or metal compression joint, metal insert

Cutting drainage pipes (p.481) Sheet of paper, metal file, cloth

Making a solvent-weld joint (p.481) Solvent cement, fine brush, solvent-weld joint, cloth

Making a compression joint (p.481) Compression joint

Making a push-fit joint (p.481) Silicone spray, push-fit joint

Extending a pipe to plumb an appliance (p.482) Compression fittings, pipes, solder-ring tee, solder wire, gas blowtorch

Teeing off to plumb an appliance (p.482) Pipe cutter, compression fittings

Connecting to a main waste pipe (p.483) Hole cutter, solvent cement, boss, waste pipe

Fitting a self-cutting external tap (p.483) Basic toolkit only

Repairing taps (p.487) Washer or ceramic-disc valve or inlet seals or disc cartridge

O-rings, glands, and reseating taps (p.488) Reseating tool

Replacing gland packing (p.489) Slip-joint pliers

FOR BASIC TOOLKIT SEE PP.24–25

PLUMBING PIPES AND CUTTERS

Plumbing systems in the home may incorporate metal and plastic pipes. Traditionally, all hot and cold water pipes were metal, but various types of plastic pipe are now commonly used in domestic situations. The most common varieties of pipe are shown here, along with pipe bending and cutting equipment. Many manufacturers refer to pipe as tube or tubing.

METAL PIPES

Copper pipe is the most commonly used type. It resists corrosion well and is relatively easy to work with. In older homes, lead and iron pipes still exist. Brass and stainless steel pipes are generally used for aesthetic considerations.

Copper pipe
Half-hard copper pipe or tube is the most commonly used copper tubing for domestic systems. It can be used for both heating and hot and cold wate r supply. Diameters include 15 and 22mm (⅜ and ¾in). It is often sold in 2- and 3-m (6- and 9-ft) lengths.

Chrome-plated copper pipe
A copper tube that has a chrome coating for aesthetic reasons.

Micro-bore copper pipe
Small-bore copper tube can be bent by hand. Common diameters include 8 and 10mm (¼ and ⅜in). It is usually sold in 10- and 25-m (30- and 75-ft) coils.

OTHER METAL PIPES

Galvanized-iron pipe
Once used for domestic water pipes, iron is more susceptible to corrosion than copper. It is also much more difficult to work with than copper, and is therefore not recommended for any new installation.

Lead pipe
This was once used for both supply and drainage pipes in many homes. However, the health risks associated with lead mean that it is now no longer used in new installations.

PIPE BENDERS

Pipes normally require cutting to size and, in many cases, bending, in order to change direction in the pipe run. Metal pipes can be bent using a spring or a pipe bender. If you need to route plastic pipe, use flexible pipe. Pipe bending in itself is not difficult, but there is a lot of skill required in measuring and bending the pipe at the right point. It is better to bend a pipe before cutting it; greater accuracy is achieved by this, rather than by trying to cut precisely first.

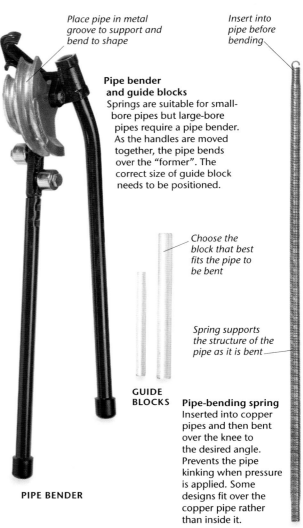

Place pipe in metal groove to support and bend to shape

Insert into pipe before bending

Pipe bender and guide blocks
Springs are suitable for small-bore pipes but large-bore pipes require a pipe bender. As the handles are moved together, the pipe bends over the "former". The correct size of guide block needs to be positioned.

Choose the block that best fits the pipe to be bent

Spring supports the structure of the pipe as it is bent

GUIDE BLOCKS

PIPE BENDER

Pipe-bending spring
Inserted into copper pipes and then bent over the knee to the desired angle. Prevents the pipe kinking when pressure is applied. Some designs fit over the copper pipe rather than inside it.

◼◼ MACHINE BENDING

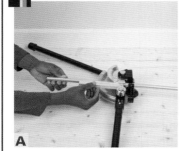

A

B

Set the former curve. Place the pipe against the curved former. Support with the guide block.

Pull the handles together to bend the pipe between the guide block and curved former, then remove.

◼◼ SPRING BENDING

A

B

Insert the bending spring into the area of pipe you want to bend.

Protect your knee with a cloth, then bend the pipe carefully to the required angle.

PLASTIC SUPPLY PIPES

When first introduced, plastic pipe was used mainly for drainage. However, in recent years it has become much more common for supply and heating pipes. It is much easier to work with than metal equivalents as no soldering tools or special materials are required. It also doesn't corrode and has the further advantage of not building up with scale in hard-water areas.

Plastic pipes cannot be used for gas or oil supplies. A plastic hot or cold water pipe run also needs more regular support than rigid copper to prevent pipes sagging. Plastic pipe may also have limitations in the heat it can withstand, so check specifications before use. Most plastic pipes should not be used within 1m (3ft 4in) of a boiler. The first metre (3ft 4in) of pipe from the boiler should normally be metal.

Chlorinated polyvinyl chloride (CPVC) pipe
A rigid form of plastic pipe used in both hot and cold water pipes and waste systems. Its use as a supply pipe is limited by some local authorities, so check before use.

Polybutylene (PB) pipe
A very flexible pipe that can be used in domestic hot and cold water pipes.

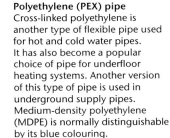

Polyethylene (PEX) pipe
Cross-linked polyethylene is another type of flexible pipe used for hot and cold water pipes. It has also become a popular choice of pipe for underfloor heating systems. Another version of this type of pipe is used in underground supply pipes. Medium-density polyethylene (MDPE) is normally distinguishable by its blue colouring.

PLASTIC WASTE AND DRAINAGE PIPES

Commonly 32mm (1¼in) or 40mm (1¾in) in diameter, drainage pipes are larger than those used for general plumbing. Drainage pipes take waste water from fittings to the mains drainage system. Soil and vent pipes are even larger – most commonly 110mm (4in) in diameter. In older properties, it is still possible to find clay or cast-iron pipes used for drainage systems. Both these materials are now rarely used on new installations.

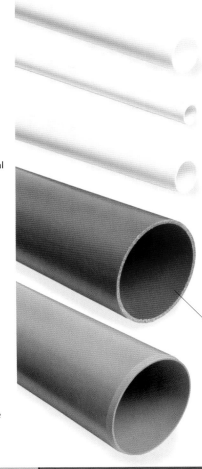

Acrylonitrile butadiene styrene (ABS)
This was one of the first rigid plastics used commonly in drainage systems, including soil and vent pipes.

Polyvinyl chloride (PVC)
This is a more modern version of ABS pipe and, with UPVC, is used for the same purposes.

Polypropylene (PP)
Flexible version of ABS and PVC used often in waste systems. Needs push-fit joints; cannot be solvent-welded.

Unplasticized polyvinylchloride (UPVC)
Used mainly for underground drainage. Available in 110-mm (4-in) diameter.

Brown pipes are generally used for drainage, grey for soil stacks

Unplasticized polyvinylchloride (UPVC)
Used mainly for soil pipes. Available in 110-mm (4-in) diameter.

PIPE CUTTERS AND FILES

Like the pipes themselves, pipe cutters come in various types and sizes. Some are adjustable, to cope with more than one size. Shown here are three types of cutter used for cutting supply pipes. Those used for metal (mainly copper, although most will cut brass, chrome-plated, or aluminium pipe) have small cutting wheels located in their jaw design. Plastic supply-pipe cutters simply have a straight blade to cut through the pipe. For metal pipes and some plastic pipes, a metal file is required to smooth the edges once cut. For file types, see p.41.

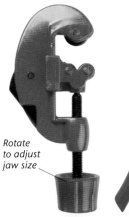

Blade

Rotate to adjust jaw size

Cutting wheel

Groove holds deburrer in place

METAL-PIPE CUTTER   **VINYL-PIPE CUTTER**

Size-specific cutters
Some cutters are sized to the most common diameter of pipe. Shown left is a 22-mm (⅞-in) cutter. This saves adjustment time as the cutter is simply clamped directly onto the pipe.

Plastic-pipe deburrer
Removes the rough edges from plastic pipe after it has been cut.

PIPE CONNECTORS AND JOINTS

All plumbing systems consist of more than just the pipes themselves. Connections, joints, valves and a selection of other fittings are required to complete a pipe run. As well as establishing the type and design of fitting that can be used with the different types of pipe, it is also important to identify the various ways in which these connections can be made. The most commonly used connectors are shown on the table here.

CONNECTOR ACCESSORIES AND VARIETIES

The most common designs of pipe connector and joint are shown in the table on the right. However, there are many other accessories that may be needed to make joints, as well as variations on those standard designs. A few of these extras are shown below.

Extra O-ring seal

PLASTIC INSERT

Metal body

METAL INSERT

Pipe inserts
Pipe systems may or may not need inserts at each joint. When plastic pipe is being used with plastic joints, some manufacturers suggest using inserts to create an extra seal. When plastic supply pipes are used with metal fittings it is almost certain that inserts will be required.

Connects small- and large-bore pipes

Push-fit variety

Combined plastic and metal joint

45-DEGREE ELBOW **REDUCING TEE** **TAP CONNECTORS**

Miscellaneous joints
Not all joint types are shown on the table (right), and all systems have a number of other different joints to cope with different requirements. A selection of joints are shown here.

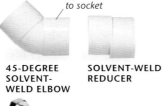

Pipe connects to socket

45-DEGREE SOLVENT-WELD ELBOW **SOLVENT-WELD REDUCER**

Flexible connectors
Flexible hoses or connectors are one of the great plumbing inventions. Making connections between rigid pipes and fittings requires accurate measurement and skilled joining techniques, often in inaccessible areas. Flexible connectors have practically eliminated this problem.

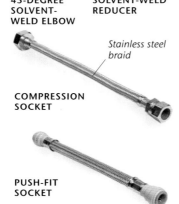

Stainless steel braid

COMPRESSION SOCKET

PUSH-FIT SOCKET

CONNECTION

Elbows change a pipe's direction

End-feed
These joints require solder to be added to the joint during the heating and jointing process. Along with solder-ring joints, they offer the most unobtrusive form of connection.

Solder-ring
Solder-ring joints already have the correct amount of solder around the inner surface of the joint section. This makes them easier to use than end-feed joints as no extra solder is required.

Brass push-fit
These fittings do not require heat. Pipes are simply pushed into the joint where a stainless steel grab-ring secures the pipe in position. A demounting tool is needed to disassemble pipe runs.

Brass compression
Metal compression fittings may be made of brass or chrome-plated brass. No solder and therefore no heat is required. The threaded sections of the joint fit onto the pipe and as the nuts of the joint are tightened, olives within the joint create a watertight seal.

Grab-ring push-fit
Pipes are pushed into the joint and held in position by a grab-ring. Joints may be unscrewed and a demounting tool used to disassemble the joint. Inserts are normally used when connecting plastic pipes.

Colleted push-fit
These designs may have a straightforward collet design that secures the pipe in place, plus an additional twist-and-lock mechanism. Pipe inserts may or may not be used; check the manufacturer's guidelines.

Solvent-weld
Solvent cement is used to seal the joints. It may be used to join PVC and ABS pipes. Make sure that the cement specified is suitable for the particular pipe you are using; some are multipurpose.

Push-fit
Rubber seals within the jointing section of a push-fit drainage system create a watertight seal. The pipe is simply pushed into the joint and the seal fits tightly against the side of the pipe.

Plastic compression
These work on a similar principle to metal compression joints except that the materials are plastic and a rubber seal is used instead of an olive. Hand-tighten only.

Reducers connect pipes of different size	**Straight tees** join pipes at 90 degrees	**Straight couplers** join horizontal pipes	**Stop ends** terminate pipe runs	**Joint interiors** vary in appearance	**Tools needed** for fitting connection
					Pipe cutter, blowtorch, flux, soldering wire, tube-cleaning brush, file, soldering mat
					Pipe cutter, blowtorch, flux, tube-cleaning brush, soldering mat, file
					Pipe cutter, tube-cleaning brush, file
					For copper pipes: spanners, pipe cutter, tube-cleaning brush, file. For plastic pipes: vinyl-pipe cutter, spanners, inserts
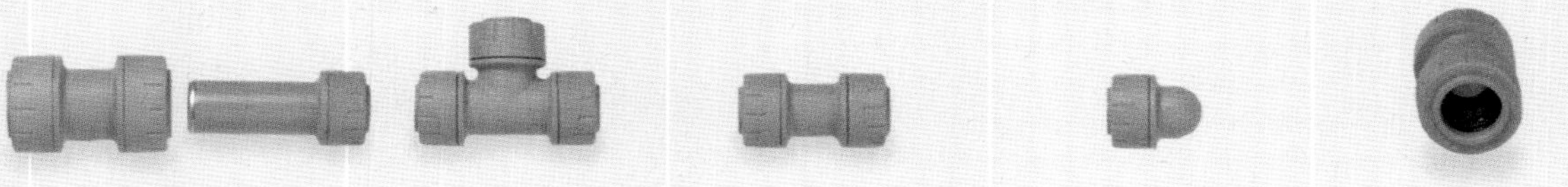					For plastic: vinyl-pipe cutter, inserts. For copper: pipe cutter, tube-cleaning brush, file
					For copper: pipe cutter, tube-cleaning brush, file. For plastic: vinyl-pipe cutter, possibly inserts
					Solvent cement, panel saw or junior hacksaw, deburrer, file
					Silicone spray, panel saw or junior hacksaw, deburrer, file
					Panel saw or junior hacksaw, deburrer, file

Pipe connections

IF YOU WANT TO MOVE AN EXISTING FIXTURE, OR PLUMB IN A NEW RADIATOR, BATHROOM, OR KITCHEN, YOUR PROJECT WILL BENEFIT FROM CAREFUL PLANNING. TO ACHIEVE THE BEST RESULT, THINK ABOUT HOW BEST TO ROUTE WATER IN AND TAKE IT AWAY SO THAT THE PIPEWORK IS UNOBTRUSIVE. YOU WILL ALSO NEED TO CONSIDER WHETHER PLASTIC OR COPPER PIPES ARE APPROPRIATE FOR THE TASK.

ROUTING PIPES

Supply and drainage pipes are usually hidden, but they need to be easy to access for repair or maintenance work. For supply pipes, the best option is to run pipes through floors or ceilings. If you have a solid floor you can surface-mount pipes, then box them in if you wish.

PLANNING PIPE RUNS

Once you have decided on the location of a new fixture you need to find the best way of getting water to and from it. This will involve investigating your existing water supply and waste systems (see pp.464–67). If you are laying a concrete floor, pipes must be laid in channel ducts with a plywood cover so that there is easy access for repair or maintenance work. With a suspended wood floor, lift the floorboards and run the pipes across or between the joists (see right).

Waste pipes

Unlike clean water, waste water is not under pressure, so to get the water to run away, the pipes need to drop at least 20mm (¾in) for every metre (3ft 4in), but not more than 50mm (2in) in a metre (3ft 4in). It is best to keep new installations close to the existing waste-pipe system, making connecting easier.

Supply pipes

The neatest solution for routing a water supply is usually to run the pipes under floorboards. Other options are to go through the ceiling or loft space and then drop a surface-mounted pipe down to the correct point. If you are surface-mounting pipe, it is usual to route it in corners and along skirting so it is easy to disguise by boxing in later (see right). Hot water pipes expand as they warm up. If your route includes any very long straight runs, fit expansion loops to absorb the movement.

CLIPS

Pipes are secured in place by clips. These come in a number of designs and sizes according to the pipe diameter. Clips may be nailed or screwed into place, depending on their design. Three of the most common types of clip are shown below.

Copper two-screw fixing
Simple copper bracket with two pre-drilled holes for fixing to wall or beam.

Copper loop

Nail inserted to secure

Nail-in fixing
A plastic loop holds the pipe in position; the fixing is then secured to the wall or beam by a nail.

Screw inserted here

Single-screw fixing
A screw is used to secure the bracket. The pipe is then clipped into the bracket.

PIPE SUPPORT CLIPS		
Pipe type	**Pipe width**	**Spacing intervals**
Copper pipes Vertical pipes:	15mm (½in) 22mm (⁹⁄₁₀in)	1.8m (5ft 11in) 2.4m (7ft 11in)
Horizontal pipes:	15mm (½in) 22mm (⁹⁄₁₀)	1.2m (4ft) 1.8m (5ft 11in)
Plastic pipes Vertical pipes:	10–15mm (²⁄₅–½in) 22mm (⁹⁄₁₀)	50cm (1ft 7in) 80cm (2ft 7in)
Horizontal pipes:	10–15mm (²⁄₅–½in) 22mm (⁹⁄₁₀)	30cm (1ft) 50cm (1ft 7in)

RUNNING PIPE THROUGH WALLS

If running a pipe through a solid masonry wall, the pipe should be protected with sleeving – another pipe of slightly wider diameter is ideal. When routing a pipe through a solid wall, choose a drill and bit size that make a tight hole.

Try to avoid running pipes through stud walls, as it can weaken the strength of the wall. If unavoidable, position pipe holes in the centre of a stud, and not at the edge. The diameter of the hole should be no greater than one-quarter of the stud depth, and holes should also be no closer to each other than 300mm (1ft).

SURFACE-MOUNTING PIPE

The least disruptive way to install new pipes on a wall or floor surface, this offers access for repair and maintenance. Mark the path of the pipes on the surface. Measure and mark where pipe clips need to be fixed along the line. Drill and plug the wall and screw the clips in place. Push the pipework into the clips to secure it in place.

Surface pipe runs can be hidden in a plywood box, and decorated in the same way as the wall behind. You will need: 50 x 25mm (2 x 1in) battens, plywood, screwdriver or drill, screws, hammer, nails, and decorating materials. Shown right is a straightforward boxing-in technique that may need to be varied depending on the type of pipe run.

BOXING IN SURFACE-MOUNTED PIPES

A **Attach a batten** either side of a vertical pipe (shown here), or to the wall above and the floor below a low horizontal pipe run.

B **Measure and cut** ply or MDF to size for the vertical sheet of the boxing. Fix it to the appropriate batten with screws or nails.

C **Measure and cut** the ply for the top of the box and screw it into the wall batten. Nail or screw the sheets of ply together where they meet.

D **Paint or tile** the box to match the surrounding decoration. Remember to allow for emergency access.

WORKING WITH JOISTS

Plastic pipe is normally run between or through joists, whereas copper is run either between or across them. When running across joists, you will need to make notches in the wood to hold the pipe. These should be no deeper than one-eighth of the joist depth, and should not be positioned any closer to the wall than 0.07 times the joist length. They should also be no further away from the wall than one-quarter of the length of the joist, because the middle of the joist is its weakest point. Below are three of the most common ways of working with joists.

RUNNING FLEXIBLE PIPES THROUGH JOISTS

If using flexible plastic supply pipe, you can drill holes through joists. Drill holes in the middle of the joist, and slightly larger in diameter than the pipe.

A

RUNNING PIPES BETWEEN JOISTS

This is best avoided because maintenance would require many floorboards to be lifted. If unavoidable, screw supporting battens between the joists at the same intervals needed for supporting a horizontal pipe run (see left). Fit clips onto each batten.

A

RUNNING PIPES ACROSS JOISTS

A

B *Notches should be slightly deeper and wider than the pipe diameter*

C *If you are laying more then one pipe, ensure they do not touch*

D

Mark the position of the pipe run on the joists.

Use a hammer and chisel to make notches. Make sure they are not deeper than one-eighth of the depth of the joist.

Lay a thin, soft pad, such as carpet felt, at the bottom of the notched-out area. Use clips to hold them in position.

Fix thin metal plates over the pipes to protect them. Replace the floorboards and mark where the pipe runs below.

By far the most common water pipes in the home are those made of copper. They can be cut with a hacksaw or a pipe cutter, and can be joined by either solder-ring, end-feed, push-fit, or compression joints. Compression joints are more expensive than soldered joints, but are handiest when doing small jobs and repairs. The most popular sizes of copper pipe are 15mm (½in) and 22mm (⅞in). The techniques shown here relate to both sizes.

TOOLS AND MATERIALS SEE BASIC TOOLKIT AND P.469

CUTTING COPPER PIPE

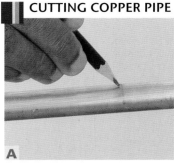

A Carefully measure the length of pipe you need, taking the size of any joints into account. Mark the pipe with pencil where you need to cut.

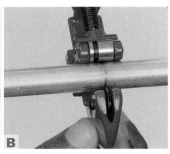

B Position the cutter so that the cutting wheel is aligned with the mark. In this example, an adjustable pipe cutter is used.

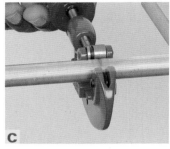

C Rotate the blade as indicated on the side of the cutter.

D Keep rotating until the copper is cut right through; do not be tempted to snap the pipe.

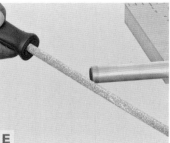

E Prepare the cut edge for cleaning by filing away any rough burrs from the rim of the pipe using a metal file.

F Clean the outside of the pipe using wire wool and clean inside with a tube-cleaning brush to help ensure a watertight seal.

COMPRESSION JOINT

A compression joint requires no solder and therefore no heat. The joint is made watertight by compressing two olives (soft metal rings), which provide seals on either side of the joint. Pipes are held in sockets in the joint body, and nuts are tightened onto the body to secure the olives in place. When creating a compression joint, do not overtighten as this may damage the olive. Although not a necessity, PTFE tape or jointing compound are often used with compression joints. PTFE tape is especially useful for making a repair (see p.493). Generally, joint compound should not be used on joints that may be used to carry drinking water.

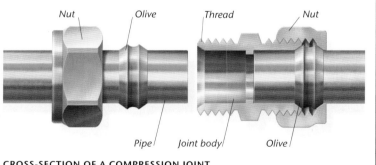

Nut *Olive* *Thread* *Nut*

Pipe *Joint body* *Olive*

CROSS-SECTION OF A COMPRESSION JOINT

MAKING A COMPRESSION JOINT

A Unscrew the nuts from each end of the joint body.

B Slide a nut onto the end of each of the copper pipes to be joined.

C

Position one olive on the end of each pipe. Always check that you have the right size olive. If you are not sure, replace it with another of the correct size rather than risking a leak.

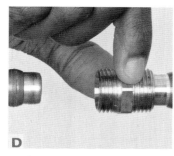

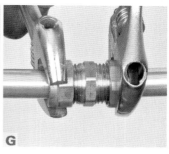

D Fit the compression joint onto the first pipe end, then fit the second pipe end into the joint and push both pipes together.

E Slide both olives up to the joint ends until tight against the joint.

F Screw the nuts carefully onto the threaded sections of the joint. Tighten them by hand, checking that the pipes do not move out of position.

G Use a pair of spanners to finish tightening the joint. Do not over-tighten; between one and two full turns of each nut should suffice.

MAKING A SOLDER-RING CAPILLARY JOINT

A Light a gas blowtorch, adjust the flame, and allow to warm up in an upright position. Be sure to keep the flame clear of any walls or ceilings. Protect adjacent surfaces with a soldering mat, and never leave the blowtorch unattended. Follow manufacturer's guidelines for blowtorch use precisely.

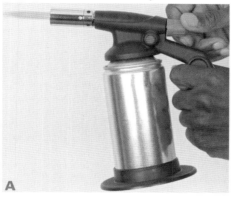

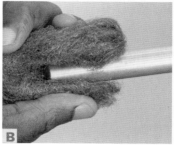

B Use wire wool to deburr and clean the outside of the pipes and joints until they are shiny.

C Apply flux paste to the pipe end and the inside of the joint. This ensures a totally clean joint is made.

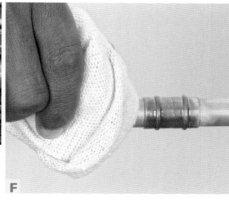

Remove the heat as soon as solder appears around the joint. This indicates that the solder inside the capillary joint has melted and is now ready to set. Allow the joint to cool before cleaning off any excess flux with a cloth.

D Push and twist each pipe into the joint as far as possible. Mark a line across the joints using a pencil so that you can keep them in position.

E Heat the pipe and the joint over a soldering mat, moving the flame around to heat evenly. This melts the internal solder-ring to form a joint.

MAKING A SOLDER END-FEED JOINT

A Clean the pipe and the joint and brush both with flux. Push the two pipe ends into the joint.

B Heat one end of the joint, working around the pipe. Periodically touch some solder on the joint to see if it is hot enough to melt.

C When hot enough, apply the end of the solder wire between the pipe and the fitting. The solder will melt around the joint to create a neat seal.

D Repeat on the other end of the joint. Allow the joint to cool before cleaning off any excess flux from the joint using a cloth.

JOINING PLASTIC PIPES

Plastic pipes are extremely versatile and can be used for most types of plumbing, subject to limitations discussed on p.471. The connection techniques shown here relate mainly to supply pipes. Techniques for plastic waste pipe are shown on pp.480–81. Supply pipes should always be cut using a vinyl-pipe cutter. Their main drawback is that they sag easily and so require lots of support (see p.474). They can also be used in conjuction with metal pipes (see opposite).

TOOLS AND MATERIALS SEE BASIC TOOLKIT AND P.469

CUTTING PLASTIC PIPE

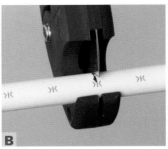

A **Measure the length** of pipe you require, taking into account the size of the joint. Mark the cutting point on pipe with a felt-tip pen or a pencil.

B **Position the pipe** in the jaws of the cutter. Squeeze the handles together and slice through the pipe.

DESIGN VARIATIONS ON PUSH-FIT JOINTS

There are a number of push-fit joint designs. Shown to the right is a colleted push-fit joint that also has a twist-and-lock mechanism. How these joints are assembled and disassembled is shown below and right. Some designs will not have a twist-and-lock mechanism; these designs are most likely to use another type of sealing device, such as grab-rings. Colleted joints contain a plastic collet with stainless-steel teeth that grip the pipes when pulled. They may also use a collet clip between the collet collar and the joint. Grab-ring fittings assemble in a similar way to colleted ones, though disassembly is somewhat different (see opposite).

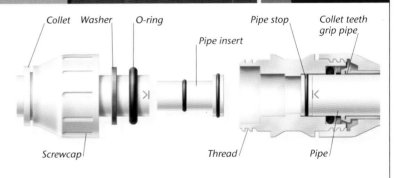

CROSS-SECTION OF A PUSH-FIT JOINT

MAKING A PUSH-FIT JOINT

Push plastic inserts into the ends of the pipes to be joined. The marked-off points on the side of this pipe show how far the pipe needs to be inserted into the joint to provide a sound joint.

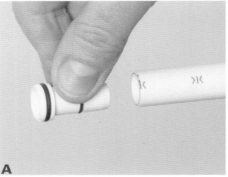

B **Push both pipes** into the fitting until they reach the marked-off points on the pipes.

PIPE INSERTS

Plastic supply-pipe systems may or may not need inserts at each joint. When plastic pipe is being used with plastic joints, some manufacturers suggest using inserts to create an extra seal. When plastic supply pipes are used with metal fittings it is almost certain that inserts will be required.

MAKING A TWIST-AND-LOCK JOINT

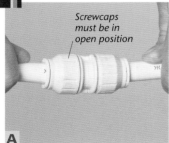

Screwcaps must be in open position

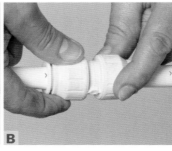

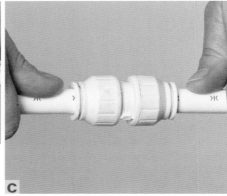

Give both pipes a final pull to check that the joint is secure. Some types of joint will require a collet clip to be positioned between the head and the main joint body.

A **Pull on both** pipes to allow the collet to grip. This joint also has a twist-and-lock function to improve the seal on the O-rings.

B **Tighten the** screwcaps on the joint to create a lock function and to make a completely water-tight seal.

C

DISCONNECTING A COLLETED PUSH-FIT JOINT

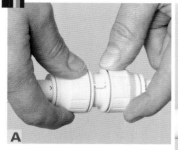

A

If the joint has screwcaps, these must first be unscrewed into an open position.

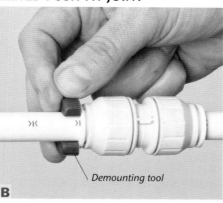

Remove collet clips (if joint uses them), then use a special demounting tool to push down on the collet on either side of the pipe.

Demounting tool

B

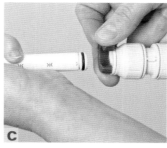

C

Pushing down releases the grip of the collet teeth, allowing the pipe to be pulled free.

DISCONNECTING A GRAB-RING PUSH-FIT JOINT

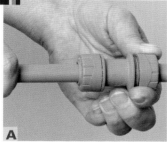

A

Unscrew the screwcap on the joint.

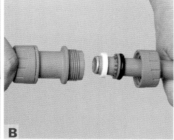

B

Pull the pipe from the fitting to reveal the O-ring and grab-ring mechanism.

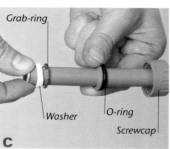

Grab-ring

Washer

O-ring

Screwcap

C

Move the O-ring and screwcap aside to reveal the grab-ring.

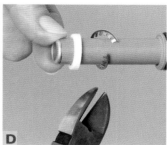

D

Slice the grab-ring with cutters and discard. Renew the grab-ring when reconnecting the joint.

JOINING PLASTIC AND METAL PIPES

To join a copper pipe with a plastic pipe, use either a plastic push-fit joint, or a metal compression joint (shown here). Press a metal insert into the end of the plastic pipe that will meet the joint. This helps to ensure that the pipe shape does not distort under pressure.

A

B

Unscrew the nuts on the joint. Position the nut and olives onto both the plastic pipe and the copper pipe.

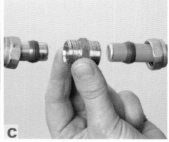

C

Place the joint onto the copper pipe adjacent to the olive.

D

Push the plastic pipe with its insert into the joint, slide the olive down the pipe to meet the joint, then tighten the nut by hand.

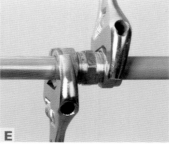

E

Use two spanners to finish tightening the joint, taking care not to overtighten it; one or two turns should be sufficient.

FURTHER INFORMATION

Electrolytic action
An advantage of using plastic pipework is that plastic cannot be corroded through electrolytic action. Two different types of metal (e.g. steel and copper) joined together would eventually corrode. If you need to join two different metals, use a plastic joint so that both metals are kept separate from each other.

Bonding pipes (see also p.464)
All pipework in a house must satisfy earth-bonding requirements. Clamps are attached to metal pipes and a single-core earth cable is attached to the clamps and run back to the main earthing terminal on the consumer unit. Two metal pipes joined by a plastic connector will also therefore need to be bonded.

Plastic pipes are the main material used in modern waste systems. They have three main types of joint; push-fit (which have rubber ring seals instead of grab-ring collets), solvent-weld, and plastic compression. Adhesive can be used on PVC and ABS pipes, but not on PP pipes (see p.471). The latter are always joined using push-fit or compression fittings. Bear in mind that as with plastic supply pipes, brackets are required to support pipe runs. Traps are also an essential part of a waste system; various types are illustrated below.

TOOLS AND MATERIALS SEE BASIC TOOLKIT AND P.469

HOW TRAPS WORK

The example here shows a simple P-trap. Most traps are designed so that they are held in position by plastic compression fittings. This makes access simple if unblocking is required (see p.266). Because traps in toilets or outside gulleys cannot be accessed like this, augers, plungers, and rods may be required to move any blockage.

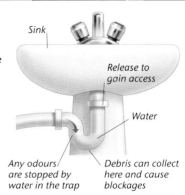

Sink
Release to gain access
Water
Any odours are stopped by water in the trap
Debris can collect here and cause blockages

TRAPS AND THEIR USES

All waste systems have traps, some of which are integral to a fitting (e.g. a toilet trap), and some of which are sold separately (e.g. a basin or sink trap). Traps have a U-shaped section that provides a barrier that separates fittings from the drainage system. The U-shaped design means that whenever water is discharged through a trap, some remains in the U-section. This creates the barrier that stops smells and bacteria entering the house through the drainage system.

Basin and sink traps are made in a variety of designs that are aimed at making installation and connection to the drainage system as simple as possible. Because traps are often positioned in relatively inaccessible areas, such as in a basin pedestal or in a cabinet below a sink or basin, it is important to choose a design that fits your needs. Below is a selection of common trap designs. Each of these has variations that may better suit your requirements.

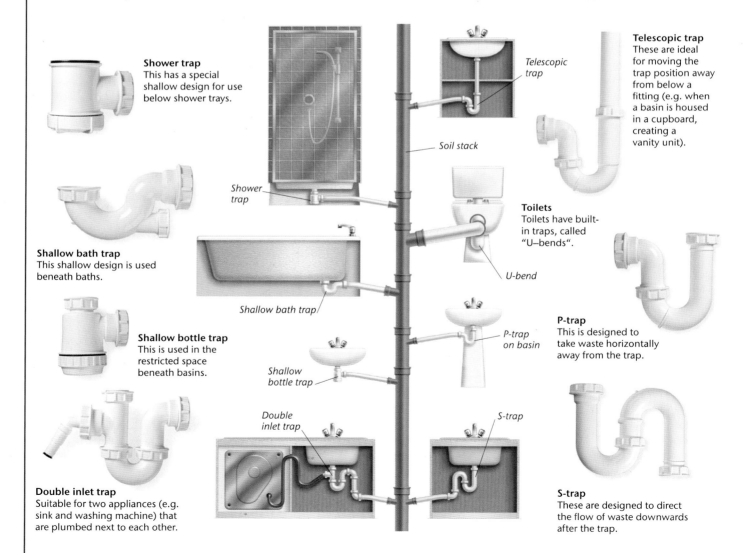

Shower trap
This has a special shallow design for use below shower trays.

Shallow bath trap
This shallow design is used beneath baths.

Shallow bottle trap
This is used in the restricted space beneath basins.

Double inlet trap
Suitable for two appliances (e.g. sink and washing machine) that are plumbed next to each other.

Soil stack
Shower trap
Shallow bath trap
Shallow bottle trap
Double inlet trap
Telescopic trap
U-bend
P-trap on basin
S-trap

Telescopic trap
These are ideal for moving the trap position away from below a fitting (e.g. when a basin is housed in a cupboard, creating a vanity unit).

Toilets
Toilets have built-in traps, called "U–bends".

P-trap
This is designed to take waste horizontally away from the trap.

S-trap
These are designed to direct the flow of waste downwards after the trap.

CUTTING WASTE PIPES

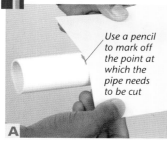

Use a pencil to mark off the point at which the pipe needs to be cut

A

After marking the point to cut, wrap a sheet of paper around the outside of the pipe so that its edge is against the marked point.

Junior hack saw

B

Check that you are cutting square to the pipe, using the paper as your guide. For the pipes to join well, the edges must be square.

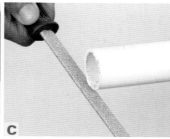

C

Use a fine metal file to deburr the edges of the pipe. A plastic pipe deburrer can be used on the inside of the pipe.

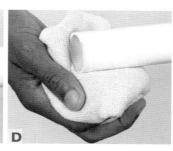

D

Use a soft, damp cloth to wipe away any fine plastic dust from the pipe. A dust-free edge is important when using solvent to join pipes.

MAKING A SOLVENT-WELD JOINT

Establish where you want the joint to be. Place it over the end of the pipe and mark the distance required using a pencil. Remove the joint, then apply solvent cement with a brush.

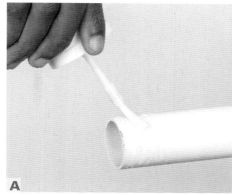

A

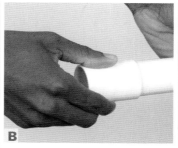

B

Push the joint onto the pipe until it reaches the pencil mark. Insert a second length of pipe that has been filed and glued in the same way.

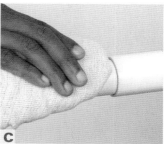

C

Wipe away any excess solvent using a soft cloth. The solvent will react with the plastic pipes to form a solid, waterproof joint.

MAKING A COMPRESSION JOINT

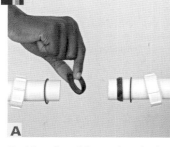

A

Position the rubber seals on both pipe ends. If your joint is supplied with additional washers or O-rings, thread them onto the pipes.

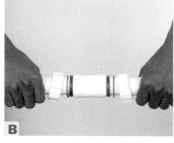

B

Push both pipe ends into the main body of the joint, taking care to keep the pipes straight.

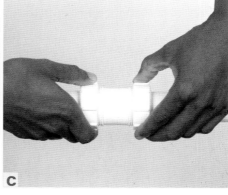

C

Twist the threaded nuts until tight on the joint. There is no need to use a spanner for this joint; it is designed to be fastened by hand.

MAKING A PUSH-FIT JOINT

Cut the pipe following the instructions above. Apply silicone spray around the end of the joint. This is essential for large diameter pipes, but is not always required for small pipes.

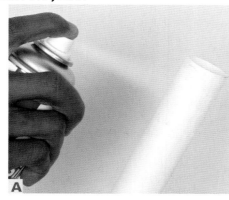

A

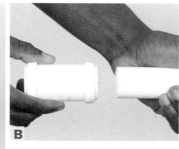

B

Push the joint onto the end of the pipe. Push firmly as far as it will go; the pipe will meet the internal socket of the joint.

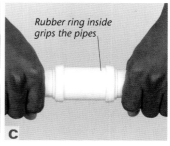

Rubber ring inside grips the pipes

C

Push in the second length of pipe, again making sure that it goes right into the internal socket of the joint.

ADAPTING A SYSTEM

Existing plumbing systems often need to be adapted when a new appliance such as a dishwasher or washing machine is installed. When a kitchen or bathroom is being renovated, the supply and waste pipes may need to be altered to accommodate new designs. In most instances, this involves cutting into an existing pipe, teeing off from it, and changing direction. These techniques are best illustrated in the examples shown below. If installing a new basin, make sure to fit an isolating valve into the pipework (see p.489). This enables you to turn off the water flow when needed without turning off the main water supply.

TOOLS AND MATERIALS SEE BASIC TOOLKIT AND P.469

BEFORE YOU START WORK

■ Before working on any supply pipes make sure that the water has been turned off.
■ To turn off the water, you may need to shut off a particular isolation valve or to drain an entire system. The latter may involve locating valves in the pipe runs to turn water off, and/or may mean shutting down the main stop valve to drain the supply (see pp.464–67 and p.489).
■ If soldering copper pipes, protect any nearby areas with a heat-resistant mat.

■ Read the instructions supplied with your washing machine or dishwasher to establish whether your machine is cold-water feed only, or requires both hot and cold water.
■ Any work on plumbing pipework is governed by certain rules and regulations. Seek professional advice if in doubt (see p.467).
■ Remember that pipe runs need the appropriate support. Make sure you have clips and brackets (see pp.474–75).

ADAPTING PIPES FOR WASHING MACHINES AND DISHWASHERS

Appliances are often positioned in close proximity to sinks – commonly the kitchen sink. In such cases, it is best to connect directly into the sink waste. The washing machine and/or dishwasher hose is clamped directly to an adaptor socket on the sink waste. If you are fitting a new washing machine or dishwasher direct into the waste pipe, rather than the sink trap, you will need to fit a new trap into the pipe run. Telescopic traps are commonly used for this purpose.

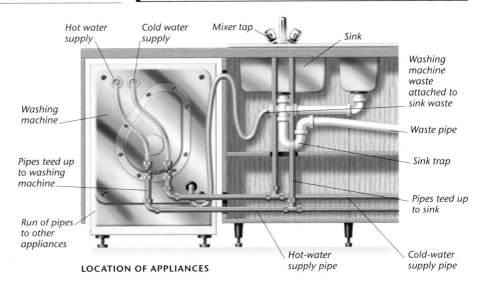

LOCATION OF APPLIANCES

Hot water supply · Cold water supply · Mixer tap · Sink · Washing machine waste attached to sink waste · Waste pipe · Sink trap · Pipes teed up to sink · Washing machine · Pipes teed up to washing machine · Run of pipes to other appliances · Hot-water supply pipe · Cold-water supply pipe

▌▌ TEEING OFF TO PLUMB IN AN APPLIANCE

When installing a washing machine or dishwasher, it will be necessary to tee off from the cold water supply. You may also need to connect to the hot water supply (as shown below). If the standard hose supplied with the appliance can reach the back of the machine easily, it is possible to use a tee that contains a valve and a threaded compression joint for connection. These are secured onto the cut pipe ends with compression fittings. Make sure that supply pipes have been drained before starting work.

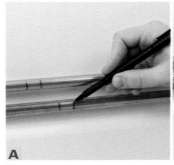

A Measure and mark the position to tee off from the pipe. Using a hacksaw, cut out a section measuring 18mm (⅞ in).

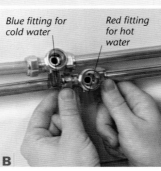

Blue fitting for cold water · Red fitting for hot water

B Fit joints as shown on pp.476–77. Attach hoses and connect to washing machine.

▌▌ EXTENDING A PIPE TO PLUMB IN AN APPLIANCE

In some cases it may be necessary to extend the pipe when teeing off from the supplies. Again, compression joints can be used for this purpose (see above), as can push-fit fittings or soldered joints as shown in the example here. In this case, end-feed joints have been used (see p.477). Also, note that a "crossover" has been used to keep both pipes close to the wall surface. This short length of pipe contains an arch just large enough for a second pipe to run beneath it. Here the crossover is soldered into its pipe run.

A Cut pipes as shown in the previous example (left). Prepare and fit tees, then solder into place as required.

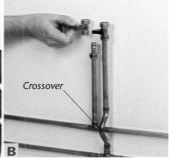

Crossover

B Attach compression valves to the new pipes. Use red for the hot water supply and blue for the cold water. Attach the hoses to the fittings.

WASTE WATER PIPES

When changing old waste pipes for a new system, the process is normally very straightforward. Usually the ideal pipe route has been established for the existing system. When adding a new fitting such as a basin, it may be possible to tee into an existing drainage pipe using a special type of tee called a "swept tee". Alternatively, it may be more practical to connect directly to the soil stack. This may be possible using an adaptor (shown right) or by using a strap-on boss (shown below).

Attach to soil stack

Connect to waste pipe

Remove discs to attach waste pipes

MANIFOLD ADAPTER **SOCKET ADAPTER**

▌▌ CONNECTING TO A MAIN WASTE PIPE

A

Use a hole cutter to make a hole in the mains stack. Choose a bit to cut a hole that will accommodate the boss size.

B

Apply solvent cement around the hole. Place the boss over the hole, allowing the collar to fit around the entire pipe.

C

Tighten the nut and bolt on the opposing side of the stack. Insert the black rubber adaptor section supplied with the boss.

D

Finally, insert the new waste pipe into the socket section of the boss. Ensure the new waste pipe is fixed at the correct gradient (see p.474).

▌▌ FITTING A SELF-CUTTING EXTERNAL TAP

Kits are available that allow you to cut straight into a copper pipe. The self-cutting tap allows you to tee off from the mains cold supply without having to turn off the water or drain any pipes. The self-cutting tap has to be positioned after the mains stop valve. The steps below show how to use a self-cutting connection kit to connect to an outside tap. The external tap is supplied from the mains water system. You can then attach a hose pipe to the external tap to supply water to the garden. Self-cutting valves can also be used as a way of making the necessary connections for washing machines or dishwashers, rather than using the techniques shown left. Again, these connections are often supplied in kit form. If you install an outside tap with exterior pipework, be sure to drain it down during winter months to prevent the pipe freezing. If not, the pipe may crack and need replacing.

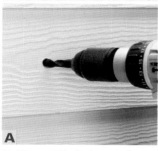

A

Drill a small hole through the outside wall using a power drill. The drill bit used will depend on the wall structure.

B

Feed the connection pipe through the hole and attach the external wall bracket.

C

Screw the tap wall bracket to the wall surface. Screw the tap in place. Tighten the locking nut between the tap and the hole using a spanner to make the tap secure. If the outside tap does not have an integral check valve, fit a separate one to it.

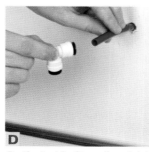

D

On the inside, fit an elbow joint. In this case a push-fit joint is being used.

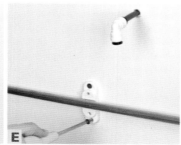

E

Attach the self-cutting tap bracket to the internal wall. It should fit snugly around the copper supply pipe.

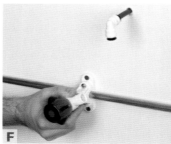

F

Attach the tap bracket to the wall bracket. Turn the tap section, allowing it to cut into the supply pipe.

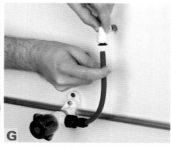

G

Connect a further section of pipe between the tap and the elbow. Turn the inside tap on. The exterior tap is now ready to use.

Taps and valves

TAPS AND VALVES CONTROL WATER FLOW THROUGHOUT THE HOME. BOTH ARE ESSENTIALLY "VALVES" BUT TAPS ARE FOUND AT THE END OF A PIPE, WHEREAS VALVES ARE SITUATED IN THE MIDDLE. THE CONTROL OF THE WATER FLOW, AND THE WAY IN WHICH THE TAP IS FITTED, VARIES WITH THE DESIGN. ALWAYS CHECK COMPATIBILITY WHEN REPLACING TAPS. FOR MORE ON EFFICIENT PLUMBING AND RE-USE OF WATER, SEE PP.384–87.

TAP CONNECTIONS AND REPAIRS

Designs for taps vary considerably and may be determined by where they are used in the home. They can either be fixed within the fitting – such as on the rim of a bath – or in a worktop or wall next to the fitting. When fitting taps you need to know how a particular design is fitted and the connections required. A detailed understanding of the internal operation of taps (see pp.486–87) is crucial only where tap repairs are required, usually only after they have been in use for some time.

BUYING TAPS

Apart from appearance, consider also:
■ Do the number of access holes match the fitting? Taps can require up to three access holes (see opposite and below).
■ The easiest way to connect taps is to use flexible hoses. Hoses are sometimes supplied with the taps. There are two main types: push-fit connections or compression-joint connections (see p.472).
■ It is also possible to purchase reducing connectors joining a 15-mm (⅜-in) pipe to a 22-mm (⁹⁄₁₀-in) fitting, for example.

SINGLE-HOLE TAP

Pillar taps supply either hot or cold water, therefore, generally, one of each are used on a basin or sink. Single taps are commonly used for outdoor garden taps, supplying only cold water. A mixer tap can have a single access hole for both the hot and cold water supply.

Spindle

Tap body

Pillar
For a basin, sink, or bath, you need two pillar taps; one to supply cold and one hot water.

Access hole

Monobloc mixer
Hot and cold supplies feed through one access hole into the tap body. The lever determines the flow rate and the mix of hot and cold water.

Pop-up waste rod

Tap body

Access hole

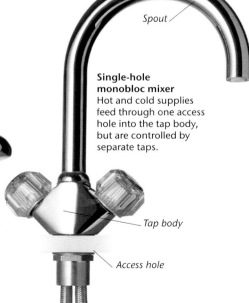

Spout

Single-hole monobloc mixer
Hot and cold supplies feed through one access hole into the tap body, but are controlled by separate taps.

Tap body

Access hole

TWO-HOLE MIXER TAP
Hot and cold supplies feed into the tap body through two access holes. This type of tap is most commonly seen in kitchens, particularly where the spout needs to be movable, and swing between two sinks. Sometimes further attachments are included in the design – shower heads for baths (see right), and an extra hole may be required for spray-head attachments with a kitchen sink.

Spout

Two-hole mixer tap with shower attachment
In a bathroom, two-hole mixer taps may have a shower attachment.

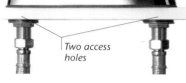

Two access holes

Two-hole mixer tap
Water enters the tap body through separate access holes. Hot and cold water mix together as they flow through the spout.

THREE-HOLE MIXER TAP
The three holes are needed for hot and cold water supply and the spout. Designs vary according to whether the hot and cold water supplies come together below the fitting or above it. A three-hole mixer may also combine with a spray-head attachment creating a four-hole system (the hole for the spout, one for the attachment, and two holes for the hot and cold water supply).

Three-hole mixer
The water is not mixed in the tap body, but in the pipework before it emerges into the visible spout.

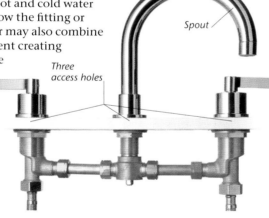

Spout

Three access holes

WALL-MOUNTED TAPS
There is very little difference between the taps mounted on a horizontal surface, as shown above, and wall-mounted taps (right and below). The main difference regarding operation is that the water supply is routed through the wall surface. You need to plan access behind the wall for maintenance. When plumbing new taps, allow space to tile to achieve a flush finish.

SIDE VIEW

Spout

FRONT VIEW

Three-hole pipework
Wall-mounted taps require extra planning when installing to ensure they are set at the right height for the bath, basin, or sink.

DIVIDED FLOW
Some mixers keep the hot and cold water separate, so that they mix outside the tap spout. This system is often used when there are different pressures between hot and cold supplies. Water byelaws can stipulate the need for divided flow when the hot-water system is fed by a cold-water storage tank to prevent contamination of the mains cold-water supply.

WATER SUPPLY PIPES
Traditionally, water supply pipes would feed directly into the tap, but in modern homes a shut-off valve is positioned on the pipe, to enable easy control of the water supply when maintenance work is needed, such as changing washers, or when taps need to be changed. Where there is no valve, work is more difficult because water supplies need to be shut off to larger areas of the home, and in many instances, complete systems drained.

Pipe junction
If there is an isolating valve near a fitting, you can stop the water here rather than shutting off the entire system.

POP-UP WASTE SYSTEMS
Commonly used in mixer-tap design, a pop-up waste system works using a small lever that moves the stopper or plug. The lever is connected to a rod, that connects under the sink or basin to the plug.

Lever

Tap body

Remote lever
Pop-up waste systems are normally fitted when you install the taps. Waste systems are a standard size to fit all basins.

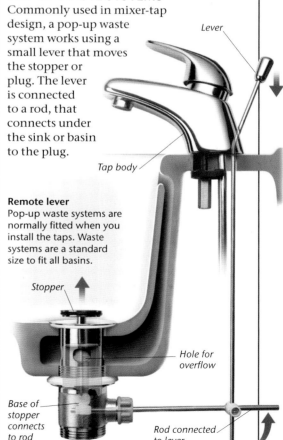

Stopper

Hole for overflow

Base of stopper connects to rod

Rod connected to lever

The mechanism that operates a tap is concealed, but you need to understand it before you start any repairs. There are three main types of tap mechanism: compression-valve taps, ceramic-disc-valve taps, and ceramic-disc-cartridge taps. Shown opposite are ways to gain access to the inside of the most common tap models, something that is not always related to the valve or cartridge type used by the tap. The sequences below right show steps for dismantling different taps and for replacing washers and seals.

TOOLS AND MATERIALS SEE BASIC TOOLKIT AND P.469

BEFORE YOU START

- Assess what is causing the leak. If water is dripping from the spout, you may need to replace the washer. If water drips from beneath the handle, the O-ring needs replacing.
- When buying a replacement ceramic disc, check whether it is for a right- or left-handed tap.
- Turn off the water supply pipe.
- Turn the tap to full-on to ensure that any water in the spout or pipes runs off before you start.
- Put the plug in the sink to avoid losing any small part of the tap down the plughole.
- As you remove tap components, lay them out in order on a convenient flat surface, so that you can put them back correctly.
- Smear the components with silicone grease before re-assembling the tap.

TAP OPERATING MECHANISMS

Manufacturing and design differences mean that there are huge variations in the appearance of different taps, but the vast majority of taps will fall into three main types of tap operating systems.

Handle cap

Handle screw

Handle

Shroud

Control insert

Spindle

O-ring

Washer

Compression valve

Handle cap

Handle screw

Handle

Spindle

O-ring

Ceramic disc valve

Handle cap

Handle nut

Handle washer

Handle

Shroud

Cartridge-retaining nut

Ceramic disc cartridge

Compression-valve tap
Taps with this mechanism usually have separate hot and cold handles. A rubber washer at the base of the tap valve creates a seal with the tap seat when the tap is closed. If the seal is broken, drips will occur. This style of washer is the most traditional tap operating system, but is still common.

Ceramic-disc-valve tap
The top sections of ceramic disc valves appear similar to the headgear of a tap that uses compression valves, so a similar technique is used for removal. Ceramic discs tend not to wear out, but their function may deteriorate over time in a hard-water area. Ceramic valve taps are sometimes known as "washerless".

Ceramic-disc-cartridge tap
Single-lever taps also use ceramic disc technology but, unlike two-handle tap systems, both flow and temperature are controlled by the same mechanism, in this case, a cartridge. There are many different designs of cartridge, so take care to find the correct type for your particular tap when looking for a replacement.

GETTING INSIDE A TAP

There is a vast range of tap designs and styles available, but all can be dismantled to reveal the inner operating mechanism. The most common ways of access are shown here. On different models, search for concealed screws or Allen key holes under the handle or lever. As you remove parts of a tap, lay out each part in order nearby for easy re-assembly.

Concealed grub screw

Unscrew removable cap

Hole for Allen key

Flip caps
Handle caps can be prised up using the flat edge of a screwdriver to reveal the screw below.

Grub screws
Small grub screws on the side undo to remove the handle. Remove the shroud to access headgear.

Screw cap
Unscrew by hand to reveal the main handle screw.

Allen key
Similar to grub screws, use an Allen key to take off the tap handle.

REPAIRING A COMPRESSION-VALVE TAP

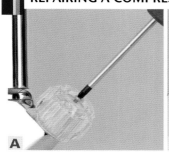
A

B

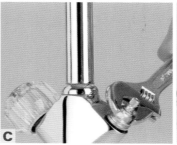
C

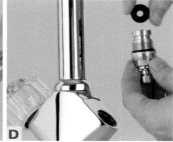
D

Remove the handle cap, if there is one (see top), to expose the handle screw. Unscrew this to remove the handle.

Remove the tap handle and shroud, if there is one, to expose the tap valve.

Using an adjustable spanner, unscrew the tap valve. Then remove the valve from the tapseat.

Use the flat end of a screwdriver to remove the washer. Position a new washer in place and reassemble the tap by following the steps in reverse.

REPAIRING A CERAMIC-DISC VALVE TAP

Lift off the handle cap and unscrew the handle screw. Lift off the tap handle to expose the valve beneath.

A

B

C

Unscrew the tap valve, using an adjustable spanner.

Lift out the body of the valve. Inspect the ceramic disc valve, clean it, and replace it if it is worn. Re-assemble the tap.

REPAIRING A CERAMIC-DISC CARTRIDGE TAP

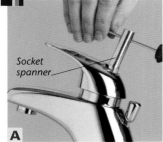
Socket spanner
A

B

C

D

Remove the handle cap. Fix a socket spanner to the handle nut. Thread a screwdriver through the shaft to remove the nut.

The tap handle will lift off easily to expose the top of the cartridge.

Remove the shroud (if there is one). Then remove the cartridge-retaining nut.

Remove the cartridge. Replace the inlet seals on the underside of the cartridge or replace the entire cartridge. Re-assemble the tap.

Although the anatomy of a tap may seem complex, most problems occur either through worn washers or cartridges, or a worn tap seat in the body of the tap (the part at the base where the valve sits). The main techniques for washer, valve, and cartridge replacement have been shown on pp.486–87. Below are other areas in which leaks may occur. Spout O-rings can cause leaks as well as O-rings on valve bodies. In certain cases, tap reseating may also be necessary.

TOOLS AND MATERIALS SEE BASIC TOOLKIT AND P.469

GLAND PACKING

Most modern taps do not have gland packing; inside the valve there is a threaded section with an O-ring. This creates the gland seal. To replace gland O-rings, see below. If your taps do have gland packing, use PTFE tape and follow the technique shown opposite for replacing packing in a stop valve.

When gaining access to gland O-rings it may be necessary to remove a circlip (a type of seal) positioned around the spindle of the valve. It is normally a case of trying to remove the washer unit first, without removing the circlip.

If this doesn't work, try removing the circlip to see if that allows the washer unit to be unscrewed. On a traditional gland, plumber's putty can be used to seal leaks, though PTFE tape works best.

▊▊ SPOUT O-RINGS

A **If you are replacing** an O-ring at the base of the tap's spout, remove the grub screw at the back of the spout, then twist the spout to release.

B **Lifting the spout** off allows you to gain access to the O-ring at the base of the spout.

C **Identify the worn-out** O-ring, then cut it off or prise it off with a slot-headed screwdriver.

D **Roll on a replacement** O-ring to renew the seal. Align the marker with the groove in the tap body for re-assembly.

▊▊ GLAND O-RINGS

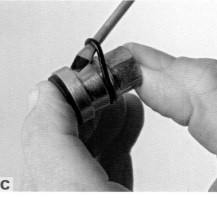

A **Remove valve** as shown on p.487. Damaged O-rings on the visible part of the valve can simply be cut away and replaced.

B **To gain access** to gland O-rings, turn the spindle and valve body in opposite directions. This should allow the washer unit to unscrew.

C **On the washer** unit there will be a further O-ring or O-rings that may need replacing. Cut away damaged rings with a craft knife or break free with a slot-headed screwdriver. Roll on a replacement and re-assemble the valve. Fit the valve back in the tap body and re-assemble the tap.

▊▊ RESEATING TAPS

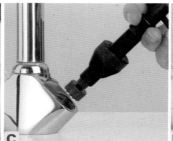

A **Remove the valve.** If you can, remove the seat, using a valve-seat spanner. Replace with a new one.

B **In many cases,** seat replacement is not possible, so screw a reseating tool into the thread of the tap body.

C **Be sure to insert** the tap reseater carefully so that you do not damage the thread for the valve.

D **Slowly turn the** handle of the reseating tool to grind until the surface is smooth. Replace the valve and re-assemble the tap.

There are a number of different types of valves found in domestic pipe runs. They are used to control water movement around the house, isolating areas as required for maintenance, or as an emergency mechanism to stop water flow. The most important valve is the stop valve, which controls the main water supply into the home. It is important that you know where to locate the stop valve in case of emergency. Others include gate valves and the various types of non-return and isolating valves.

TOOLS AND MATERIALS SEE BASIC TOOLKIT AND P.469

ISOLATING VALVES

Used as shut-off valves for the smaller areas of a plumbing system, isolating valves come in a number of different designs and should be located throughout a plumbing system. For example, an isolating valve may be fitted close to a tap. If the tap needs replacing, it is then only necessary to turn off the water supply to that tap rather than shut down a larger part of the water system. Isolating valves normally have an arrow on their outer casing to show that they must be fitted in the same direction as the directional flow of the water. They may have a handle, or are closed and opened using a slot-headed screwdriver.

The valve is open when the orientation of the groove in the grub screw that opens the valve is in line with the pipe. A quarter turn is all that is required to close down the water supply. Many plastic fittings are only suitable to hold water up to a certain temperature. This should be indicated on the side of the fitting along with the directional arrow.

Open/close valve with a screwdriver · *Push-fit socket* · *Screw thread*

PLASTIC PUSH-FIT

COMPRESSION FIT

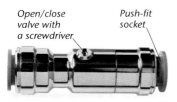

Open/close valve with a screwdriver · *Push-fit socket*

METAL PUSH FIT

Push-fit socket · *Threaded end*

PLASTIC PUSH-FIT/THREADED WITH HANDLE

GATE VALVE

Similar to stop valves, gate valves are used to isolate areas. However, they should only be used in low-pressure runs. Gate valves do not have a right or wrong way round in terms of fitting in relation to the directional flow of water. They are identified easily by their wheel handles.

Wheel handle

GATE VALVE

STOP VALVE

All homes should have one main stop valve that controls the flow of the main water supply into the home. On large systems a number of stop valves may be used to isolate various areas of a supply or system. If installing a stop valve, be aware that it must be fitted correctly in relation to the directional flow of the water. This is indicated by an arrow on the outer casing. Stop valves are normally fitted in a pipe run with compression fittings. Typically they have a handle with a traditional shape.

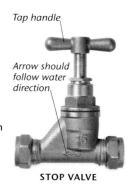

Tap handle

Arrow should follow water direction

STOP VALVE

DRAIN VALVE

Drain valves are positioned on a pipe run as the point to attach a hose pipe when an area of plumbing requires draining. Use a drain valve key to operate the valve.

Thread to attach to pipe run · *Attach key here* · *Attach hose here*

DRAIN VALVE

▌ REPLACING THE GLAND PACKING

Valves rarely fail because they are not used as often as taps, and so parts do not wear out as quickly. The most likely problem with a valve is that it may seize in an open position because of lack of use. It is worthwhile opening and closing valves periodically to prevent seizures. Some lubricating oil will also keep them in good condition. If a stop valve or gate valve leaks around the gland, try tightening the gland nut to see if that stops the leak. If this does not work, the gland packing will need replacing with PTFE tape (see below).

A Turn the valve into a closed position, and undo the gland nut.

B Remove any old packing material with the end of a screwdriver.

C Wind PTFE tape around spindle. Push down with a screwdriver. Replace nut and handle.

NON-RETURN VALVES

Check valves or non-return valves only allow water to flow in one direction. They are used mainly on outside taps and mixer taps/valves and are usually built into the design. Their function is to prevent the back siphonage of water down a supply pipe, which would contaminate the water supply.

There are two types of domestic cold-water tank or cistern; loft storage tanks that store water for parts of the plumbing system (not all homes have these), and toilet cisterns. The latter provide the flush-water supply for the toilet. Cisterns have two elements; a float valve, to control inflow, and a siphon or equivalent valve for outflow. Repairs are often simple and rarely require a plumber. See pp.384–87 for more on the efficient use of water.

TROUBLESHOOTING: WATER INFLOW

■ Water flowing continuously into the cistern is caused by a deteriorating diaphragm or washer in the valve. With Part 1- and Part 2-type valves (see below), turn off the water supply to the toilet, remove the split pin holding the float arm in place, and remove the cap on the valve body to reveal the piston. Designs vary, but the washer or diapraghm will be positioned behind the piston. Replace and re-assemble. With Torbeck and Part 3-type valves, simply undo the screwcap to reveal the diaphragm.

■ To make adjustments because water is constantly overflowing, see p.267.

INLET VALVES

Most inlet valves are termed float-pattern or float-arm valves, and they control the flow of water into the cistern. The float drops when the toilet is flushed. As the float descends, a valve in its arm opens to allow water into the cistern. Then, as the cistern refills, the float arm rises and returns to its original position, shutting off the valve.

Brass lever arm with ball float

In this traditional design the float is positioned on a float arm which itself may be of two types. Part 1 types are straight and the float is screwed to the end of the arm, while Part 2 types are right-angled and the float screws to an adjustable clamp attached to the float arm. Part 1-type valves contain a piston that can be removed to change the washer. The split pin can also be removed to release the float arm. This kind of valve is commonly used in water tanks in lofts.

Torbeck Valve

This is a plastic valve that has a proprietary float design and is quieter and smaller than ball valves. Because it is plastic, parts do not corrode. Again, they may be fitting to both side-entry or bottom-entry inlet pipes. To adjust the water level, the drum-shaped float is screwed up or down within the float arm frame. The inlet valve has a diaphragm (a disc-shaped flexible membrane) rather than a washer (a rubber ring); both are seals that stop the flow of water. Access is gained by undoing the retaining cap. A silencer tube may also be attached to the water outlet.

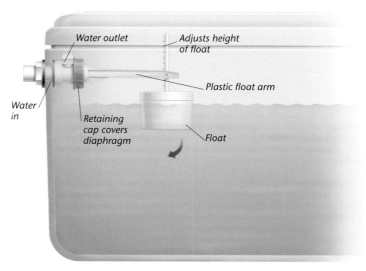

SIDE-ENTRY TORBECK VALVE

Diaphragm valve with ball float

This is a more modern version of the traditional brass valves and is made from plastic components. Where brass Part 1-type and Part 2-type valves are both side-entry, Part 3-type plastic ball valves have both side- and bottom-entry versions. Again, a diaphragm rather than a washer is used to close off supply. To adjust the water level, the plastic screw next to the valve assembly is screwed in or out, depending on the level at which you wish to position the float arm.

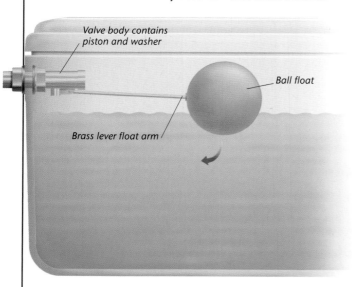

SIDE-ENTRY BRASS VALVE

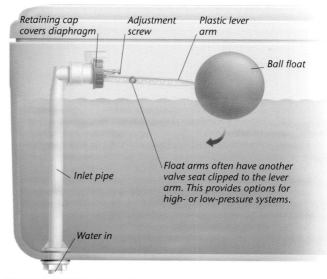

BOTTOM-ENTRY PLASTIC VALVE

SIPHONS AND FLAPPER VALVES

Siphons are the traditional type of outlet valve, and there are many variations available. There has also been progress in the development of other types of outlet valves (such as flapper valves). Some common examples of outlet valves are shown below.

Traditional toilet siphon

These have a flap valve that is opened when the flushing handle is depressed. The flap valve can be replaced when worn; this will be evident when there is a continual flow of water into the toilet pan.

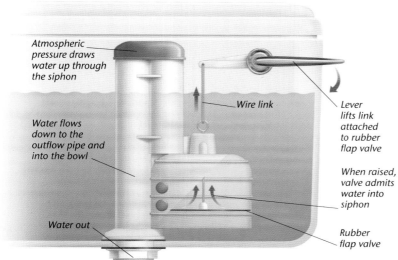

Atmospheric pressure draws water up through the siphon

Water flows down to the outflow pipe and into the bowl

Water out

Wire link

Lever lifts link attached to rubber flap valve

When raised, valve admits water into siphon

Rubber flap valve

TRADITIONAL TOILET SIPHON

TROUBLESHOOTING: WATER OUTFLOW

■ If the lever is not working, this generally means that the link between lever and the valve is broken; simply replace the link.

■ If the toilet is not flushing first time, this usually means that the flap valve isn't working (if you have a siphonic valve). This can be replaced, but it usually involves removing the entire siphon; some models allow you to detach the valve section only. A flushing problem with a drop valve normally relates to the flush volume controls. These have two options; one for total flush and one for partial flush. Some trial and error with these adjustments should solve the problem.

■ Any type of outlet valve can leak around the washer seals that connect it to the outflow pipe. To replace these seals you will need to turn off the water supply, drain the cistern, and remove the siphon or valve. The water supply can be stopped by turning off the isolating valve on the pipe supplying the toilet. The cistern can then be flushed until empty. Alternatively, the float arm of the inlet valve can be tied up to stop it opening and allowing water in after the flush. Simply remove the cistern lid, position a wooden batten across it and tie the arm to the batten so that it closes off supply.

■ It is possible to adjust the volume of flush with some recent siphonic models. This is achieved by plug removal in the siphon body (as shown left); different sizes of flush are created by different plugs.

Drop Valve

Drop valves are a modern replacement for traditional siphons. They use dual-button technology so that you have a choice of full or partial flush. They also have an internal overflow.

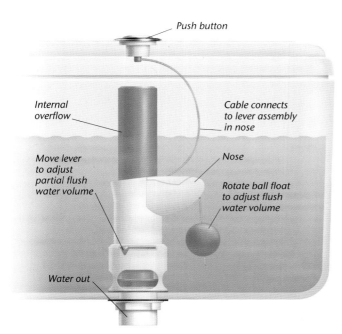

Push button

Internal overflow

Move lever to adjust partial flush water volume

Cable connects to lever assembly in nose

Nose

Rotate ball float to adjust flush water volume

Water out

DROP VALVE FOR PUSH-BUTTON TOILETS

Flapper flush valve

An alternative to the siphon valve is the flapper flush valve. When the toilet handle is operated, a simple flap lifts to allow water to flow into the toilet pan. Most models also have an internal overflow connected to the outflow pipe rather than the external overflow that is still prevalent in some toilet designs.

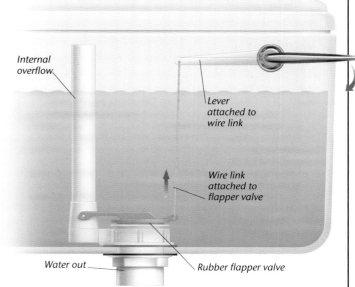

Internal overflow

Lever attached to wire link

Wire link attached to flapper valve

Water out

Rubber flapper valve

FLAPPER FLUSH VALVE

TEMPORARY REPAIR OF A HOLE

You might decide to make a temporary repair to a pipe before getting professional assistance. Shown here is a temporary repair for a hole in a pipe accidentally made by a screw or a nail.

TOOLS AND MATERIALS
Self-tapping screw, PTFE tape, screwdriver

A This type of accident occurs when replacing a floor. This is why it is important to check fixing positions before working on floors.

B Effect a temporary repair to a hole by wrapping PTFE tape around the self-tapping screw and inserting it in the hole.

TURNING OFF THE WATER

When a leak is detected, always turn off the water supply. It is important that everybody in the house knows the location of the mains stop valve. Depending on your system, it may only be necessary to shut off supply to a particular area. This in turn will depend on the frequency and position of isolating valves.

TEMPORARY REPAIR OF A HOLE OR CRACK

If water is allowed to freeze in a pipe, it may lead to cracks or splits, which can cause a leak when the water thaws. This method can cover a length of pipe.

TOOLS AND MATERIALS
Jubilee clips, section of hose pipe, screwdriver

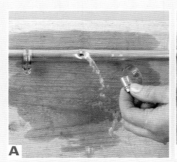

A Place jubilee clips on the damaged pipe, either side of the hole or crack. Do not tighten at this stage.

B Cut out a section of hose to cover the hole or crack. Open the section along one side.

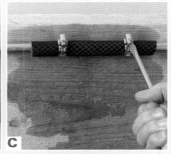

C Place the piece of hose pipe over the area of pipe that is leaking. Clip into place with the jubilee clips, and screw them tight to secure.

SHUTTING OFF A SECTION

This method can be used on a section of pipe that, if closed down temporarily, would not affect the whole plumbing system in the house. An example might be the cold feed to a basin tap.

TOOLS AND MATERIALS
Junior hacksaw or pipe cutter, push-fit stop end

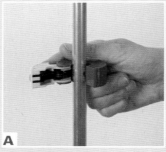

A Turn off the water supply. Cut through the pipe with a pipe cutter, below the damaged section.

B Bend the damaged section away from the undamaged pipe section to provide space to work.

Damaged section

C Position a stop end on the cut end of the undamaged pipe. A push-fit stop end is quickest and easiest to fit.

REPAIR USING A PUSH-FIT HOSE

A simple way to repair a damaged pipe is to use a length of flexible hose with push-fit sockets on each end.

TOOLS AND MATERIALS
Junior hacksaw or pipe cutter, push-fit flexible hose

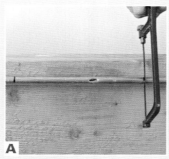

A Turn off the water. Cut out the damaged section of pipe; you need to remove about three-quarters of the length of the flexible hose.

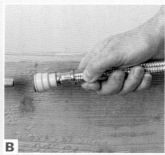

B Push one end of the flexible hose onto one end of the pipe. The rubber socket will grip the pipe.

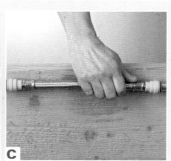

C Push the second end section in place. A slight bend in the hose will not affect flow, but make sure that it is not kinked.

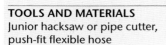

REPAIR USING A SLIP COUPLING

Slip couplings are useful for repairing small, damaged sections of pipe when the pipe is in a fixed position where space is restricted. If it is possible to move the pipe easily, you could make a sprung repair with compression fittings instead (see below).

TOOLS AND MATERIALS
Junior hacksaw or pipe cutter, slip-coupling fitting, adjustable spanners

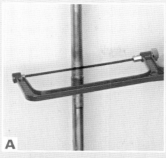
A **Turn off the water.** Cut out the damaged section of pipe. Use a junior hacksaw or pipe cutter.

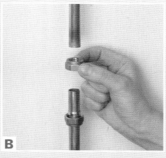
B **Position both nuts** and olives on the cut-end sections of pipe.

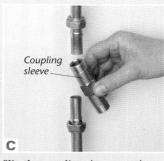
C **Slip the coupling** sleeve over the top piece of pipe.
Coupling sleeve

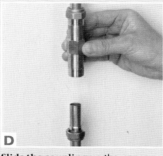
D **Slide the coupling** up the upper section of the pipe.

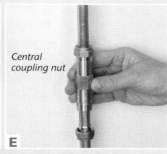
E **Align the coupling** with the lower section of pipe and lower it into place.
Central coupling nut

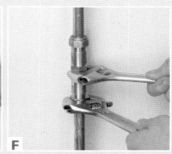
F **Tighten the coupling** nuts using spanners to make the fitting and pipe watertight.

REPAIR USING A COMPRESSION FITTING

If there is movement in the pipe, the leak may be repaired with a standard compression fitting. The new section springs into position.

TOOLS AND MATERIALS
Marker pen, junior hacksaw or pipe cutter, compression fitting, adjustable spanner

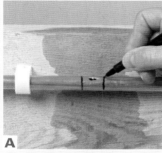
A **Turn off the water,** then mark around the damaged section of pipe. Cut out the section using a junior hacksaw or pipe cutter.

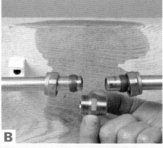
B **Detach the pipe** from its clips. Place the nuts and olives on the pipe ends. Slide the compression fitting between the pieces of pipe.

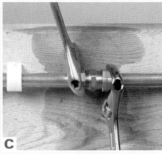
C **Tighten the nuts** onto the compression joint to make the repair watertight.

REPAIR USING PTFE TAPE

Joints with threaded sections can corrode over time, and small movements in the joint over time can create a leak. The best solution is to take the joint apart and re-assemble with PTFE tape.

TOOLS AND MATERIALS
Adjustable spanners, PTFE tape

A **Turn off the water,** then undo the joint to expose the threaded section. If the olive is misshapen, replace it.

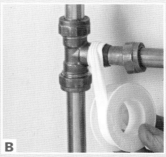
B **Wrap PTFE tape** around the male section of the thread. Make sure the tape is not kinked or folded during this process.

C **Tighten the olive** back on by hand to check that the tape is staying in position. Tighten with a spanner.

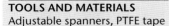

HEATING

HEATING SYSTEMS

Heating systems

TODAY MOST HOMES ARE WARMED THROUGHOUT AND PROVIDED WITH HOT WATER BY SOME KIND OF HEATING SYSTEM. SOME OF THE PROS AND CONS OF DIFFERENT SYSTEMS ARE DISCUSSED HERE, WITH MORE DETAILS GIVEN LATER IN THE CHAPTER. INSTALLING A NEW SYSTEM IS BEST LEFT TO THE PROFESSIONALS. HOWEVER, YOU CAN USUALLY EXTEND, UPGRADE, OR MAINTAIN AN EXISTING SYSTEM YOURSELF.

CENTRAL HEATING

The most popular home-heating system – wet central heating – is discussed opposite. It warms the whole home, provides hot water, and is fully adjustable to your needs. However, there are other options for heating your home and you might want extra heating in some areas, or a different system in a new extension.

CHOOSING A HEATING SYSTEM

If you are having a new system installed, your choice will be influenced mainly by the fuel you intend to use, and by ease of installation. When upgrading all or part of an old system, it will often be easiest to replace like with like. Your installer will be able to advise you about replacing major components such as boilers, hot cylinders, and radiators with modern, energy-efficient versions. The advantages and disadvantages of the main systems are shown below.

DIFFERENT HEATING SYSTEMS

Type of heating system	Advantages	Disadvantages
Wet central heating with radiators in every room (see pp.497–509)	Reliable, economical to run, easy to control, suits all types of property. Provides hot water supply to storage cylinder or direct to taps (combination boilers only)	Disruptive and expensive to install, needs mains gas supply or space to store alternative fuel (see p.499)
Storage heaters using off-peak electricity (see p.507)	Easy to install and relatively economical to use with cheap, night-rate electricity. Off-peak immersion heater can also provide hot water supply to storage cylinder	Needs separate meter and consumer unit. Can be inflexible to use, and backup heating using expensive day-rate electricity may be needed. Heaters can be obtrusive
Electric heaters using peak-rate electricity (see pp.500 and 506)	Instant room and fast water heating. Flexible, often used to back up other systems	Expensive
Open fires burning solid fuel (see pp.190–91)	Attractive focal point in the room, can use various fuels including logs	Only heats one room, chimney needs regular sweeping, space needed for fuel storage
Underfloor heating (see pp.508–09)	Economical to run, provides very even heat distribution with no visible heaters. Can be powered by electricity or run off existing wet central heating system. Electric under-tile kits easy to fit in bathrooms or kitchens	Full underfloor heating is expensive to fit retrospectively, so it is a more viable option in new-builds or extensions. System takes time to heat rooms after being switched on
Heat pumps (see pp.510–511)	Very cheap to run and an environmentally friendly option	Expensive to install. May need back-up to supply enough heat for water and/or space heating
Biofuel-based systems (see p.511)	Carbon-neutral – and therefore eco-friendly – way of producing energy. Biomass boiler is cheap to run	Biomass boilers are the only viable option – other biofuels largely untested for home use

WET CENTRAL HEATING

Most homes in the UK have a wet central-heating system. Water is heated by a boiler and is pumped round a series of wall-mounted radiators to heat individual rooms. The boiler also provides a stored or direct hot water supply. There are two main types of system in use – open-vented and sealed.

Open-vented system

In this type of system, the boiler (see p.498) feeds heated water into two circuits – one to the hot-water storage cylinder, where it heats the house's hot water supply (see p.500), and one to a series of radiators (see p.503). The radiators are supplied by a two-pipe circuit, with each radiator inlet connected to the flow pipe and each outlet connected to the return pipe. A valve on each pipe controls the flow of water into and out of each radiator.

A small water tank in the loft, called the feed-and-expansion tank, automatically tops up any losses from the system, and also accommodates the expansion in its water content as it heats up. An open vent pipe from the boiler terminates over the tank, providing a safe discharge point for boiling water if the system overheats.

In older systems, water in the circuit to the hot cylinder circulates by gravity, while the flow of water round the heating circuit is driven by a pump. In more modern systems, the circulation in both circuits is pumped, and a motorized valve switches the flow from one circuit to the other, according to the system's demands. These are detected by room and cylinder thermostats (see p.502).

Sealed system

This type of system is an alternative to the usual open-vented type. The circuits are basically the same, but there is no feed-and-expansion tank. Instead, the boiler circuit is filled to the required pressure (and topped up if necessary) from the mains water supply via a filling loop with a non-return valve, and a pressure vessel on the circuit takes up the expansion that occurs when the system heats up. A safety valve operates if the system overheats, and an air-release valve automatically vents any air in the system.

Since the heating system is sealed, there is less risk of corrosion. It runs hotter than an open-vented system, so radiators can be smaller for the same heat output, and can be sited at any level in the house. However, high-quality components are essential to ensure that the system is completely watertight, and also to prevent pressure loss.

Instead of a conventional vented hot water cylinder, as shown here, the cylinder may be unvented and supplied with mains-pressure water, thus doing away with the need for a cold-water storage tank and vent pipe. Both hot and cold taps run at mains pressure. In this case, there is an additional pressure vessel and safety valve on the hot water side of the system as well. Alternatively, if a combination boiler is used, there is no need for a storage cylinder either; instead, the hot taps are supplied directly from the boiler.

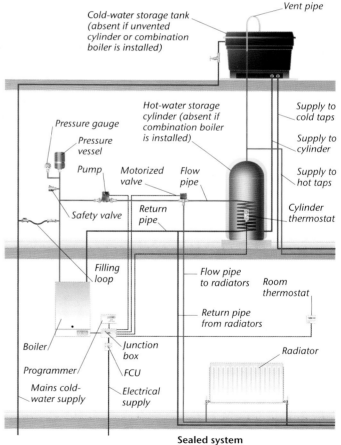

Sealed system
This type of system (above) is popular in flats, smaller homes, and conversions. However, it is a more expensive system to install, and a high level of plumbing skill is needed on the part of the installer to ensure that it performs well.

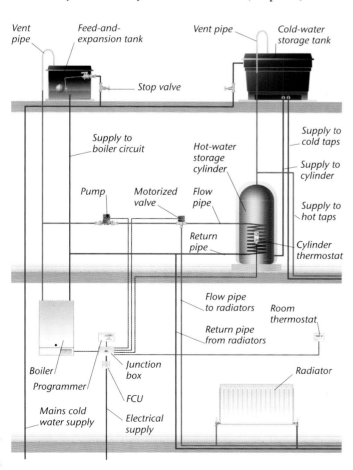

Open-vented system
This traditional system (left) is still installed in many homes because it is a tried-and-tested arrangement with which plumbers and heating engineers are familiar.

If you are selecting a boiler as part of a complete new heating system, you have maximum flexibility when it comes to deciding what fuel to use and what type of boiler to install. Your choices are more restricted if you are simply replacing an ageing boiler on an existing system. This is because you are unlikely to want to consider changing the type of fuel you use, and the system may impose other requirements that only certain boiler types can satisfy. In either situation, it is best to ask for advice from a heating engineer before placing your order.

BOILER TYPES AND SPECIFICATIONS

If you have a mains gas supply, then a new gas-fired boiler is the obvious choice. There is a wide range of models and heat outputs available, installation is simple, and the latest models are extremely compact and quiet in operation. The three main types are illustrated here.

If you do not have mains gas, you will have to consider whether to opt for oil or liquefied petroleum gas (LPG), both of which require on-site storage facilities and the installation of fuel lines.

The heat output you need depends on the number of rooms to be heated, their size, the way the house is built, and the room temperature you want to achieve. Your boiler supplier may offer to do the calculations, or may supply you with computer software so you can do it yourself.

Lastly, consider where you intend to site the boiler, whether you prefer a wall-mounted or floor-standing model, and whether a new flue will be required. The boiler should ideally be fitted against an external wall, although fan-assisted boilers can be mounted up to 3m (10ft) from the flue outlet, giving greater flexibility as far as siting the boiler is concerned.

RULES AND REGULATIONS

■ The installation of a new or replacement boiler requires Building Regulations approval, as does the fitting of a new flue. The Regulations specify minimum energy efficiency ratings for all boiler types.

■ The Gas Safety Regulations make it illegal for anyone to carry out any work on the house gas supply, fittings, and equipment unless competent to do so. In practice this means using engineers who are GAS SAFE registered.

■ Oil safety regulations apply to the installation of fuel storage facilities and supply lines for oil-fired heating boilers. Your oil supplier will ensure that your installation complies with the regulations.

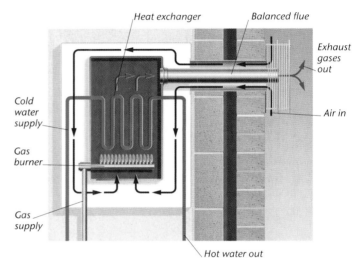

Conventional boiler
Latest models have aluminium or stainless-steel heat exchangers. Most are designed for use on fully pumped vented systems, but some will also work with older gravity systems. Modern conventional boilers are reasonably efficient and very reliable.

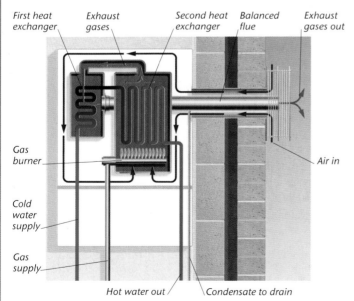

Condensing boiler
This type provides heating and stored hot water more efficiently than a conventional boiler because it uses the heat in the exhaust gases to warm up the incoming cold water before releasing it through a balanced flue. They are more expensive to buy and fit, but are eco-friendly and can save up to 30 per cent on fuel bills compared to an old conventional boiler.

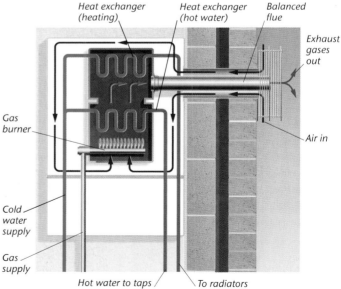

Combination ("combi") boiler
This is a combined central heating boiler and multi-point water heater. Separate pipe circuits pass through the heat exchanger, with one supplying radiators in the usual way and the other delivering hot water on demand when a hot tap is turned on. The flow rate to the taps can be slow if more than one is turned on. Condensing types are also available.

ECO-FRIENDLY BOILERS

Manufacturers are constantly trying to upgrade and improve boiler efficiency. Of the examples shown opposite, a condensing boiler is undoubtedly the most efficient – and therefore greenest – option. Bear in mind that there is also a condensing combi boiler, which is an excellent option for those who prefer combi-boiler set-ups to more conventional systems. Biomass boilers (see p.511) are another area of growing interest in this market.

TYPES OF FLUE

All boilers need an unlimited source of air to ensure that they burn their fuel safely and efficiently, and an outlet known as a flue to discharge their exhaust fumes outside the building. Older boilers usually have open flues; more modern ones have have room-sealed balanced flues.

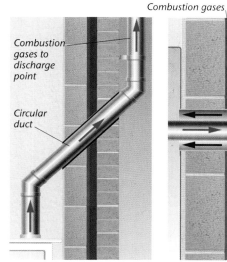

Combustion gases to discharge point

Circular duct

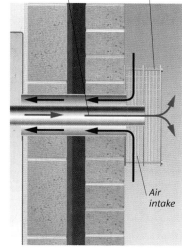

Combustion gases   Protective grille

Air intake

Open flue
This can be an existing chimney with the correctly specified liner, or a purpose-built external flue. It is essential that the air intake in the room where the boiler is situated provides sufficient ventilation to ensure that combustion is complete.

Balanced flue
The flue exits through an external wall immediately behind the boiler casing. It not only lets out the exhaust fumes but incorporates the air intake as well. Fan-assisted types allow the boiler to be mounted up to 3m (10ft) away from the external wall.

DIFFERENT FUELS FOR HEATING

Most boilers run off natural gas or oil. Even if you have central heating, it is common to also have electric or solid-fuel fires in some rooms. In homes without a modern boiler, there might be a "back boiler", which sits in a fireplace behind a room heater and warms water, or a traditional cast-iron range – both use solid fuel.

Mains gas
The largest range of boiler types and heat outputs is available for use with natural gas, which burns very cleanly. The latest models are compact and efficient, and there is no need to store fuel.

Liquefied petroleum gas (LPG, also called propane)
This is an alternative to mains gas. There are planning rules that you must follow about where to site the outdoor tank needed to store LPG, and how large it can be – usually about 1,200 litres (264 gallons). Your fuel supplier will provide the tank and fit the supply pipe. LPG is comparatively expensive and is best bought and delivered in bulk. That said, it is efficient with lower CO_2 emissions than oil or solid fuels.

Oil
Like LPG, oil is stored in a large outdoor tank – ideally with a capacity of at least 2,700 litres (594 gallons). Check local planning requirements about siting and tank size. Your fuel supplier will provide the tank and install the supply pipes. You must check your oil levels regularly – an engineer will need to restart the boiler if you run out of fuel.

Solid fuel
New boilers are rarely powered by solid fuel, but open fires in addition to central heating are still popular. Plenty of space is needed to store the fuel and keep it dry. The heat given out is difficult to control, and solid fuels are bad polluters in terms of smoke and CO_2 emissions.

Electricity
Although electricity is very rarely used to fuel boilers, it is a water- and space-heating option. Off-peak electricity is inflexible but relatively cheap; peak-rate electricity is convenient but expensive. Although electricity is efficient and clean to use, its generation releases huge amounts of CO_2 into the atmosphere.

ECO-SOLUTIONS – BIOFUELS

With the exception of biomass (see p.511), biofuels – such as those derived from plant oils – are used mainly in large-scale energy supply and transport. However, some countries are researching how biofuels can be used in domestic heating situations.

AT-A-GLANCE GUIDE TO BOILER TYPES

Boiler type	Efficiency	Hot water	Heating system	Property size	Flue	Fuel	Notes
Conventional	New models good	Stored	Any	Any	Open or balanced	Gas, LPG, oil	Cheap to buy and maintain, versatile, reliable, although old boilers are inefficient. Needs hot-water storage cylinder
Condensing	Excellent	Stored	Fully pumped	Any	Balanced	Gas, LPG, oil	Expensive to buy, but a green option and efficiency will pay for itself in lower fuel bills. Needs hot-water storage cylinder unless you choose a condensing combination boiler
Combination	Good – very good	Direct to hot taps	Any or sealed	Most	Balanced	Gas, LPG, oil	Conventional and condensing types available. No need to store hot water. Hot water can be slow to come through; most can only supply one tap at a time

HEATING WATER

HEATING SYSTEM

Unless your home has a combination boiler, you will have a hot water cylinder. This is a cylindrical copper tank where water is heated and stored so that it is available when it is needed. If you do not have central heating, the water in the cylinder will be heated by an immersion heater. If you do have central heating, most of your hot water will be heated by the boiler (see pp.498–99), but an immersion heater is usually fitted for use as a summertime or supplementary heat source. Electric point-of-use water heaters are another supply option, and are often used in cloakrooms and showers.

HEALTH AND SAFETY

If the hot cylinder is in the bathroom, the circuit to the immersion heater must be protected by a high-sensitivity residual current device (RCD). The double pole (DP) switch controlling it must be at least 600mm (2ft) away from the bath or shower. If this is not possible, install a 20-amp ceiling-mounted, cord-operated switch and run cable on to a flex outlet plate next to the cylinder to supply the heater.

An unvented cylinder must comply with both the Building Regulations and the water byelaws. Installation must be carried out by a qualified fitter.

TYPES OF IMMERSION HEATER

An immersion heater is a long, U-shaped element which may be folded back on itself. It is screwed into the top or side wall of the hot cylinder (see opposite).

Single-element heaters are available in lengths from 280mm (11in) up to 800mm (2ft 7½in), and are rated at 3kW. The shorter models are designed to be installed in the side of the cylinder, one above the other, to heat either the whole cylinder or just the upper part, depending on which element is switched on. Each element has its own thermostat. This arrangement is known as a dual-element heater.

Twin-element heaters have one short and one long element, usually rated at 2kW and 3kW respectively. The longer element heats the whole cylinder, the shorter one just the upper part. Both are controlled by the same thermostat. Twin- and dual-element heaters are often installed to satisfy variable water demands at different times of the day.

An immersion heater is supplied by its own radial circuit, run in 2.5-mm² cable from a 15– or 16–amp MCB in the consumer unit. The circuit cable terminates close to the cylinder at a 20–amp double-pole (DP) switch with a flex outlet, to which the heater (or a timer if you have one) is connected with 2.5–mm², three-core, heat-resisting flex. See p.512 for details of how to replace a failed heater element.

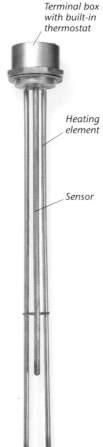

Terminal box with built-in thermostat

Heating element

Sensor

SINGLE-ELEMENT IMMERSION HEATER

Off-peak electricity

If your home has night storage heaters (see p.507) rather than a central heating system, you can use their cheap night-time electricity supply to run your immersion heater too. You need a well-insulated tank, large enough to satisfy your daily demand for hot water. The best arrangement is to install dual-element heaters. Connect the lower element to the off-peak supply so you have a full cylinder of hot water in the morning. Wire the upper element from the main consumer unit so you have the option of heating up more water during the day if you need it.

ADDING AN IMMERSION HEATER TIMER

If you rely on the immersion heater for your hot water supply, and you do not have a night-rate electricity supply, it is a good idea to fit a timer. This allows you to set the heating periods you want, so that the heater comes on automatically before times of high hot water demand and is off at other times. Special immersion heater timers are available which are wired in between the DP switch and the immersion heater using three-core heat-resisting flex. You will need a length of new flex to complete the connections.

Check that flex will reach timer

A

Turn off the power supply to the immersion heater at the consumer unit. Mount the timer backplate on the wall next to the switch.

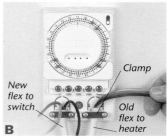

Clamp

New flex to switch

Old flex to heater

B

Disconnect the flex from the DP switch and take it to the timer's OUT terminals. Fit new flex in the other clamp, next to the IN terminals.

C

Connect the cores, following the timer's wiring instructions. Connect the other end of the new flex to the DP switch terminals.

D

Fit the timer cover to its baseplate, and re-attach the plateswitch to its mounting box. Restore the power supply, switch on, and set the timer.

POINT-OF-USE WATER HEATING

If you have a cloakroom that is remote from the rest of the house's hot water supply, it may be more economical to provide hot water for washing hands by installing a small point-of-use electric heater beside its washbasin. This heats water on demand by passing mains-pressure cold water through a small heat exchanger. The heater can be supplied via a switched fused connection unit (FCU) on a spur from a ring-main circuit (see p.445), to which it is connected using three-core flex. The FCU must be at least 600mm (2ft) away from the basin.

TYPES OF HOT WATER CYLINDER

The type of hot water cylinder you have will depend on the design (and age) of your hot water system. Older homes often have an open-vented system and a low-pressure water supply, where a vented direct or indirect cylinder is supplied with cold water from a storage tank in the loft. Newer homes are more likely to have a mains-pressure hot supply.

This may come from a combination boiler (see p.498), or from one of two special types of storage cylinder. Both are more expensive to install than a conventional vented cylinder, because their higher operating pressure requires a range of safety devices to be fitted. Unvented cylinders need Building Regulations approval (see box, opposite).

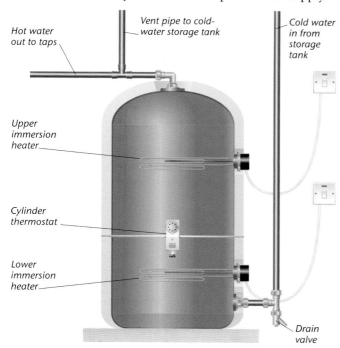

Hot water out to taps

Vent pipe to cold-water storage tank

Cold water in from storage tank

Upper immersion heater

Cylinder thermostat

Lower immersion heater

Drain valve

Vented direct cylinder

In homes with no central heating system, hot water is provided from a storage cylinder that is heated directly by one or two electric immersion heaters. Cold water enters the cylinder near the bottom, and heated water is drawn off to taps through a pipe at the top.

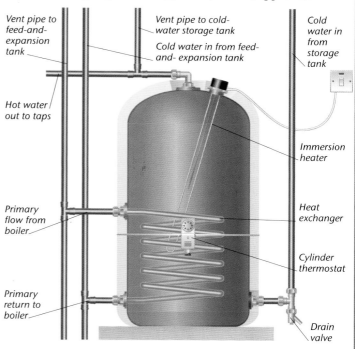

Vent pipe to feed-and-expansion tank

Vent pipe to cold-water storage tank

Cold water in from feed-and-expansion tank

Cold water in from storage tank

Hot water out to taps

Immersion heater

Primary flow from boiler

Heat exchanger

Cylinder thermostat

Primary return to boiler

Drain valve

Vented indirect cylinder

In homes with a conventional wet heating system (see p.497), the boiler also heats the hot cylinder. The primary circuit from the boiler passes hot water through a copper coil inside the cylinder, and this heats the water indirectly. An immersion heater may also be fitted to the cylinder.

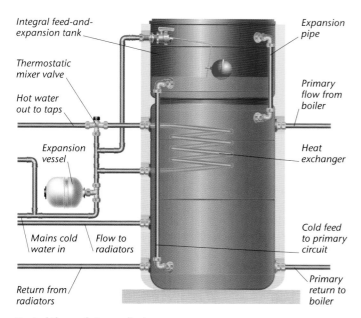

Integral feed-and-expansion tank

Expansion pipe

Thermostatic mixer valve

Primary flow from boiler

Hot water out to taps

Expansion vessel

Heat exchanger

Mains cold water in

Flow to radiators

Cold feed to primary circuit

Return from radiators

Primary return to boiler

Vented thermal store cylinder

The primary circuit from the boiler flows into and out of the cylinder, and also supplies the radiators. The water in the cylinder heats mains-pressure cold water flowing through the heat exchanger. As the extremely hot water leaves the cylinder, a thermostatic mixer valve adds cold water to it.

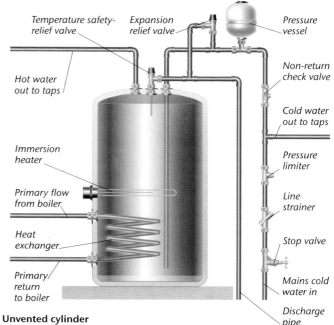

Temperature safety-relief valve

Expansion relief valve

Pressure vessel

Hot water out to taps

Non-return check valve

Cold water out to taps

Immersion heater

Primary flow from boiler

Pressure limiter

Line strainer

Heat exchanger

Primary return to boiler

Stop valve

Mains cold water in

Discharge pipe

Unvented cylinder

Mains-pressure water is heated by a heat exchanger, as in an ordinary indirect cylinder. However, the expansion in the system is accommodated by a pressure vessel instead of an open vent and tank. An immersion heater may also be fitted to the cylinder.

HEATING CONTROLS

Modern heating systems rely on a range of controls to provide space heating and hot water and to run the system efficiently. Existing controls can be upgraded as required, and additional controls can be installed to improve the system's performance and versatility. The controls divide into three main groups: operational controls such as timers and programmers, temperature sensors (thermostats), and flow controllers (motorized valves).

ELECTRICAL SAFETY

Before adding, replacing, or working on any existing or new controls, turn off the electricity supply to the junction box into which they are wired. It is usually supplied via a fused spur from a power circuit. If this is the case, switch off the fused connection unit (FCU) and remove its fuse while you carry out the work. Otherwise find which circuit in the house is supplying the junction box, and isolate it at the consumer unit. Then use a voltage tester to check that the box is no longer live. See pp.430–33 for more information on working with electricity.

INDIVIDUAL CONTROLS

A typical set of controls for a pumped central heating system is shown in the diagram. Here is what each one does.

Timers and programmers

The most important control is a timer that switches the system on when heating or hot water is needed, and off when it is not. Basic timers offer two on and two off settings for a single day. The settings can be altered or overridden when different times are required.

Programmers are more sophisticated, offering a wider range of timer settings for heating and hot water that can be set individually for each day of the week.

Thermostats

There are four main types of thermostatic controls on a typical heating system.

The boiler thermostat controls the boiler's heat output, and its setting is seldom altered once the system has been installed.

The room thermostat senses the air temperature in the area where it is installed, and turns the heating on or off as required to maintain the temperature at the same pre–set level in every room in the house. If different temperatures are required in different rooms, a thermostatic radiator valve may be fitted to each radiator to control its heat output and regulate that room's air temperature.

The cylinder thermostat senses the temperature of the stored water in the hot cylinder, and diverts more hot water from the boiler to heat the cylinder up when the water temperature drops below the pre–set level, usually 60°C (140°F).

Lastly, a frost thermostat may be fitted if your boiler is in an unheated area. It switches on the heating system if temperatures drop to stop the boiler from freezing.

Motorized valves

These control the flow of hot water to the heating or hot water circuits, as directed by the other system controls. They can also be used to divide the house into two or more separate zones, so that each one can be heated at different times of the day.

Typical system controls for a pumped heating system
Individual controls are wired into a central junction box. This is usually connected to the mains via a spur from a power circuit (see p.445). This runs to a switched fused connection unit (FCU), which should be fitted with a 3-amp fuse.

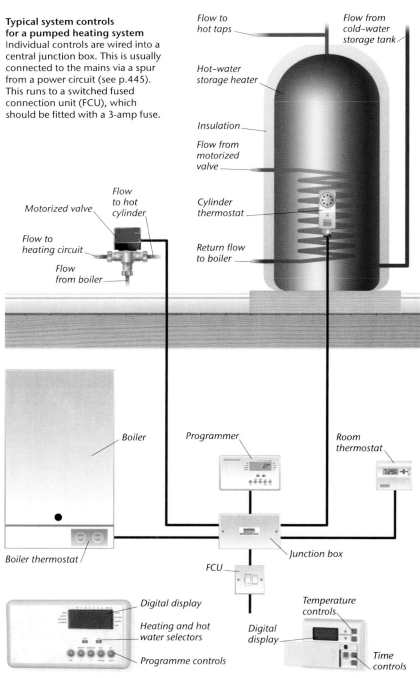

Flow to hot taps

Flow from cold–water storage tank

Hot–water storage heater

Insulation

Flow from motorized valve

Cylinder thermostat

Return flow to boiler

Motorized valve

Flow to hot cylinder

Flow to heating circuit

Flow from boiler

Boiler

Programmer

Room thermostat

Boiler thermostat

FCU

Junction box

Digital display

Heating and hot water selectors

Programme controls

Temperature controls

Digital display

Time controls

Programmer
Controls water and space heating independently, and can store different time settings for each day.

Room thermostat
Programmable types allow several different time and temperature settings to be entered for each day.

Radiators in a wet central–heating system always follow the same basic design. They rarely need much maintenance, although a few of the more common problems and their solutions are identified below. For information on replacing a radiator and fitting new valves, see pp.504–05. You will need to drain your heating system before replacing radiator valves.

BALANCING RADIATORS

When a system is installed, the flow rate through each radiator is set using the lockshield valve so that the radiators farthest from the boiler are as hot as those nearest to it. When you close a lockshield valve to remove a radiator, it is important to note how many turns of the valve spindle were needed, so you can re-open the valve later by the same number of turns.

PARTS OF A RADIATOR

A standard panel radiator is made from pressed steel. It may have a single or double panel, and convector types have fins on the back to increase heat output. The size of a radiator is selected to provide the right heat output for each room. Every radiator has a threaded inlet at each corner, into which various fittings are screwed. You may need a special radiator spanner to fit some of them. Many radiators have a handwheel valve for manual temperature control rather than the thermostatic valve shown here.

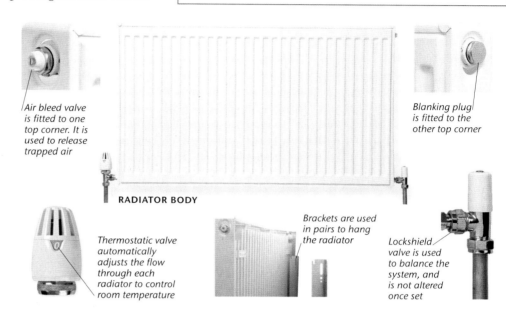

Air bleed valve is fitted to one top corner. It is used to release trapped air

Blanking plug is fitted to the other top corner

RADIATOR BODY

Thermostatic valve automatically adjusts the flow through each radiator to control room temperature

Brackets are used in pairs to hang the radiator

Lockshield valve is used to balance the system, and is not altered once set

DRAINING THE HEATING SYSTEM

Turn the system off and locate the drain valve (usually at the lowest point on the circuit pipework, near the boiler if it is a floor–standing model, otherwise on the supply pipe to a downstairs radiator). Fit a length of garden hose to its outlet and lead the other end to a gully or drain outdoors. If you have an open vented system, turn off the stop valve on the supply pipe to the feed–and–expansion tank (or tie its float arm up to a batten resting across the tank if there is no stop valve). Turn off the mains supply to a sealed system. Open the drain valve plug with a small spanner. As water flows out of the pipework, open the air bleed valves – first on the upstairs radiators, then on the downstairs ones – to drain the system completely.

Refilling the system

Close the drain valve and all the radiator air bleed valves. Restore the water supply to the feed–and–expansion tank, or turn on the supply to a sealed system. As the system fills, bleed the downstairs radiators, then the upstairs ones. When the system has refilled completely, check for any leaks and turn the system back on.

If the system does not seem to be refilling properly, check whether water is entering the feed–and–expansion tank. If it is not, the float valve that should refill it automatically may have jammed shut through lack of use. Move the float arm up and down several times to free the valve, and check that it is refilling the tank. If it does not shut off properly when the tank is about one–third full, it is best to remove it and fit a new one in its place; you need to be able to rely on it to operate automatically without regular inspection.

IDENTIFYING RADIATOR PROBLEMS

Problem	Solution
Leaking connection	Tighten the nut slightly (see p.504)
Leak from either valve	Replace the valve (see p.504)
Leaking radiator seams due to corrosion	Replace the radiator (see p.505) Add corrosion inhibitor to the system
Cold area at top of radiator	Bleed air from the radiator (see p.512) Check level in feed–and–expansion tank
Cold area at bottom of radiator	Remove radiator, take outside and flush with hose, then replace (see pp.504–05)
One or more radiators completely cold	Check that valves are open and heating is on. Check pump (see p.513). Check motorized valves; if jammed, operate the lever on the valve body to free them

TOOLS AND MATERIALS CHECKLISTS PP.504–05

Fitting a new radiator valve Wrenches, hacksaw, PTFE tape, radiator spanner

Temporarily removing a radiator Dustsheet, bowl, wrenches, small spanner or pliers, radiator bleed key

Replacing an old radiator with a new one Dustsheet, bowl, wrenches, radiator spanner, PTFE tape, radiator bleed key

FOR BASIC TOOLKIT SEE PP.24–25

FITTING RADIATORS

Radiators need occasional maintenance. Most often, an old radiator valve may develop a leak. Consider fitting a thermostatic valve (see p.503) when you replace it. If you are decorating, you can temporarily remove a radiator to make hanging wallpaper easier. Or you might want to update a room by replacing an old radiator with a modern design. Buy one as close in width as possible to the old one to avoid modifying the pipework. See pp.474–79 for if you need to alter the existing pipework.

TOOLS AND MATERIALS SEE BASIC TOOLKIT AND P.503

FITTING A NEW RADIATOR VALVE

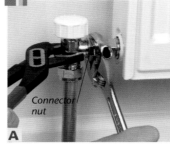

A Connector nut

Drain the central heating system (see p.503). Brace the old valve with a wrench and loosen the connector nut with an adjustable spanner.

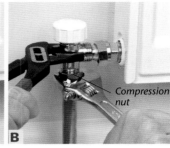

B Compression nut

Keep bracing the valve while you loosen the compression nut on the pipework below with the adjustable spanner.

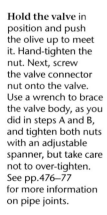

C Olive — Slip off the compression nut

Carefully cut through the old olive. If you damage the pipe you will need to replace it. Remove the olive and the compression nut.

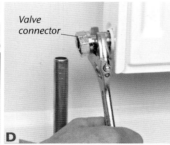

D Valve connector

Remove the valve connector from the radiator outlet. Use an adjustable spanner. For some types of valve you might need a radiator spanner.

E

Wrap PTFE tape around the threads of the new valve connector. Screw it into the radiator outlet and tighten with an adjustable spanner.

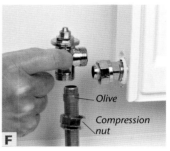

F Olive — Compression nut

Slip the compression nut from the new valve onto the supply pipe, followed by the olive. Position the new valve.

Hold the valve in position and push the olive up to meet it. Hand-tighten the nut. Next, screw the valve connector nut onto the valve. Use a wrench to brace the valve body, as you did in steps A and B, and tighten both nuts with an adjustable spanner, but take care not to over-tighten. See pp.476–77 for more information on pipe joints.

G

H

Position the valve head on the body and adjust the thermostat to your requirements, using the manufacturer's instructions.

I

Refill the system (see p.503). If the compression or connector nuts leak, tighten them slightly. Turn the heating back on.

TEMPORARILY REMOVING A RADIATOR

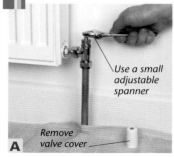

A Use a small adjustable spanner — Remove valve cover

Close the lockshield valve, keeping note of exactly how many turns it takes. Shut the thermostatic or handwheel valve.

B

Place a container under the radiator. Undo the lockshield valve connector nut, then open the bleed valve (see p.503) to drain the water.

C

Undo the connector nut to the other valve so that you can lift the radiator off the wall brackets. Carefully tip out the remaining water.

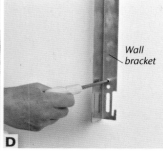

D Wall bracket

Remove the wall brackets. If you are hanging wallpaper, replace the screws so that it is easy to find the fixing points later.

Replace the wall brackets and the radiator. Hand-tighten the connector nuts onto the valves. Brace each valve with a wrench, as shown in steps A and B of fitting a new valve, and tighten the nuts. Take care not to over-tighten them. See pp.476–77 for more information on pipe joints.

E

F

Open the lockshield valve by exactly the same number of turns that it took to close it in step A. Open the thermostatic or handwheel valve.

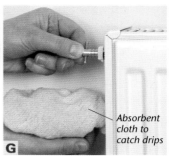

G *Absorbent cloth to catch drips*

Hold a cloth under the bleed valve and open it using a radiator bleed key. Close the valve when water appears (see also p.512).

REPLACING AN OLD RADIATOR WITH A NEW ONE

A

Disconnect and remove the old radiator and the wall brackets, as shown in steps A to D of removing and refitting a radiator (opposite).

B

Unscrew the valve connectors from the bottom corners of the radiator. Clean the threads and reuse them in the new radiator.

Adaptors can be fitted between the radiator and valve connector if required

C

Fit the valve connectors into the new radiator (see step E, Fitting a New Radiator Valve). Use adaptors to avoid small pipework alterations.

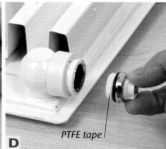

PTFE tape

D

Fit a new bleed valve into one top corner of the new radiator, and a new blanking-off plug into the other top corner.

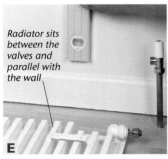

Radiator sits between the valves and parallel with the wall

E

Position the radiator as far from the wall as the valve outlets are above the floor. Mark lines on the wall, opposite the radiator brackets.

F

Measure from the skirting board to the bottom of the bracket. Measure and mark the same distance on the wall on the vertical line.

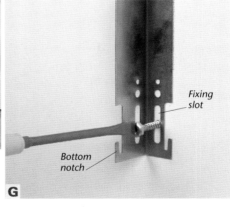

Fixing slot

Bottom notch

G

Position the first bracket against the vertical line, so the mark you have made and the bottom notch align. Mark the centre of the two fixing slots. Remove the bracket. Mark out the second bracket in the same way. Drill pilot holes and plug them if necessary, then reposition and screw both brackets into the wall.

The connector and valve should be aligned

H

Position the radiator. Match up the valve connections by removing the radiator, loosening the bracket screws, and sliding the brackets.

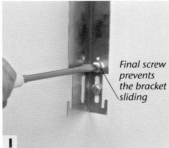

Final screw prevents the bracket sliding

I

Mark one of the round fixing holes in each bracket when it is correctly positioned. Drill and plug pilot holes, then replace and fix both brackets.

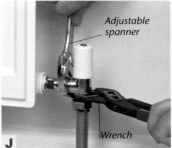

Adjustable spanner

Wrench

J

Hang the radiator on the brackets, and tighten the connectors onto the valves. Brace each valve with a wrench as you tighten the nut fully.

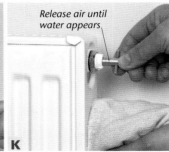

Release air until water appears

K

Open both valves by the number of turns it took to close them. Bleed the radiator using a radiator bleed key (see also p.512).

Electric room heaters are often used on their own, or to supplement central heating, especially when a quick temperature boost is required. In a bathroom, where the heater must be permanently wired in, this extra heat is often needed only for short periods, so the relatively high running cost is not important. In other rooms, you can use a range of portable heaters.

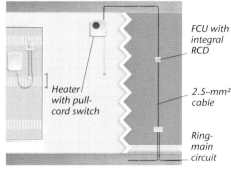

BATHROOM HEATING

A wall-mounted electric heater must be installed at least 600mm (2ft) away from the bath or shower (see also p.433). It is supplied via a flex outlet plate in the bathroom, which is in turn connected to a switched fused connection unit (FCU) outside the room. The subcircuit used to supply the heater must be protected by a 30-mA residual current device (RCD), and the simplest way of providing this is to use an FCU with an integral RCD. The circuit layout is shown above right.

To comply with Part P of the Building Regulations, you must notify your local authority Building Control department before installing the heater, and you will have to pay a fee to get it tested and certificated afterwards.

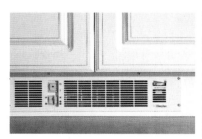

Heater with pull-cord switch

Wall-mounted heater
The heater is supplied by a fused spur from a nearby ring-main circuit. If this is already protected by a 30-mA RCD in the consumer unit, the FCU need not contain an RCD. The heater must be cross-bonded to earth in the same way as other bathroom equipment.

FCU with integral RCD
2.5–mm² cable
Ring-main circuit

Towel rail
Flex outlet plate
FCU
2.5–mm² cable
Ring-main circuit

Electric towel rail
You can use a switched FCU without an RCD to supply a towel rail, but it must still be situated outside the bathroom. The supply cable runs from it to a flex outlet in the room, where the towel rail flex is connected.

KITCHEN HEATING

In fitted kitchens, finding wall space for a radiator can be difficult. It must often be sited some distance away from the fitted area of the room, which can feel cold as a result. A neat solution is to warm the room using small electric convector heaters mounted behind the plinths under the base units. The Part P rules (above) also apply to this installation. You can also fit this type of heater in other rooms where fitted furniture takes up valuable wall space.

Kitchen plinth heater
The heater flex is wired into a flex outlet plate concealed behind the kitchen base unit. This is linked by 2.5-mm² cable running in a chase up the wall to a switched FCU mounted above the worktop. This allows convenient on-off control of the heater. The FCU should be fitted with a 13-amp fuse.

OTHER ROOM HEATERS

Other rooms may occasionally benefit from the extra warmth provided by a portable electric heater. A wide variety of heater types is available, providing either radiant or convected heat, with outputs ranging up to 3kW.

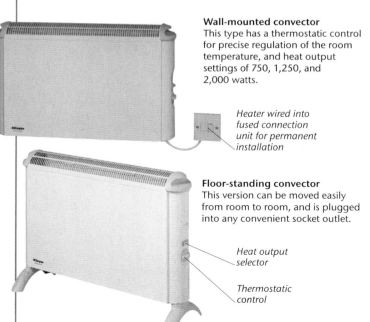

Wall-mounted convector
This type has a thermostatic control for precise regulation of the room temperature, and heat output settings of 750, 1,250, and 2,000 watts.

Heater wired into fused connection unit for permanent installation

Floor-standing convector
This version can be moved easily from room to room, and is plugged into any convenient socket outlet.

Heat output selector

Thermostatic control

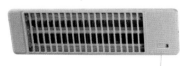

Wall-mounted radiant heater
This infra-red bathroom heater provides a comforting radiant heat. It has an integral pull-cord switch.

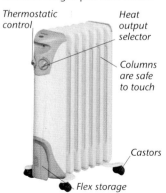

Thermostatic control
Heat output selector
Columns are safe to touch
Castors
Flex storage

Oil-filled radiator
This type is ideal for use in a child's bedroom, where the noise of a fan convector could be intrusive.

Neon on-off indicator

Downflow heater
This compact wall heater provides a powerful airflow and has a step-down thermostat which cuts heat output if it is left unattended.

Pull-cord switch

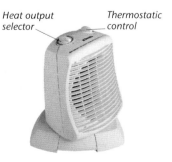

Heat output selector
Thermostatic control

Fan heater
Small but powerful fan heaters are an ideal standby for providing extra heat in any room in the house.

STORAGE HEATERS

If you have no existing central heating, installing storage heaters is less disruptive than plumbing in a traditional wet system. Each room has its own heater, sized to deliver the required heat output. The heaters are powered by cheap off-peak electricity (see box, right), which makes them more economical than running ordinary electric heaters on full-price daytime electricity. Once the supply is installed, you can also use it to heat your hot cylinder and even to run your washing machine and dishwasher at night.

OFF-PEAK ELECTRICITY

Storage heaters are supplied from a separate consumer unit which is connected to a special off-peak timer and meter; these control the night-time supply and record the amount of electricity used. The unit contains a main on-off switch and an MCB for each heater, plus one for your immersion heater. You need 16-amp MCBs for standard heaters, and 32-amp ones for fan-assisted heaters. The number of heaters that can be run on the off-peak supply depends on the size of the main service fuse on your house wiring system. A 60-amp fuse can supply a total load of up to 13.8kW, a 100-amp one up to 23kW. Your electricity supplier will advise you on selecting the optimum mix of heater ratings.

TYPES OF STORAGE HEATER

Each heater contains an insulated heat-retaining core that is warmed during the night. It then discharges the stored heat gradually during the day, with the rate of heating controlled by dampers and fans, which can be thermostatically controlled.

Standard heaters are available with output ratings from 1.2kW up to about 3.4kW, while more powerful fan-assisted ones are rated at up to 6kW. This type contains an additional fan heater that can be used during the day if the stored heat is exhausted. The fan heater uses more expensive day-rate electricity.

If you want to install storage heaters, contact your electricity supplier who will install the necessary equipment – the off-peak meter and timer – and will advise on heater selection. Ask what charging tariffs are available; some suppliers now offer cheap-rate electricity for periods during the afternoon and evening as well as overnight, allowing you to recharge the heaters during the day if necessary.

The heaters are normally delivered with the storage blocks packed in separate containers. Because these are very heavy, you need to position each heater cabinet before you place the blocks inside it. The cabinets are floor-standing, but must be secured to the wall for safety. The blocks have heating elements embedded inside them, and once they have been fitted in place you have to connect them to a series of terminal blocks within the heater cabinet. Be sure to follow the instructions supplied by the heater manufacturer to ensure correct installation.

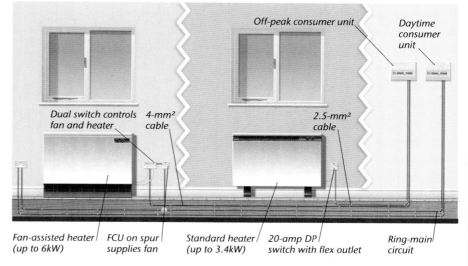

Off-peak consumer unit   Daytime consumer unit

Dual switch controls fan and heater   4-mm² cable   2.5-mm² cable

Fan-assisted heater (up to 6kW)   FCU on spur supplies fan   Standard heater (up to 3.4kW)   20-amp DP switch with flex outlet   Ring-main circuit

Wiring up storage heaters
If you install the heaters yourself, you must notify your local Building Control Office before you start, and pay a fee to have the work certificated when it is complete. You may prefer to leave the entire installation to an electrician, who will carry out the testing and certification as well.

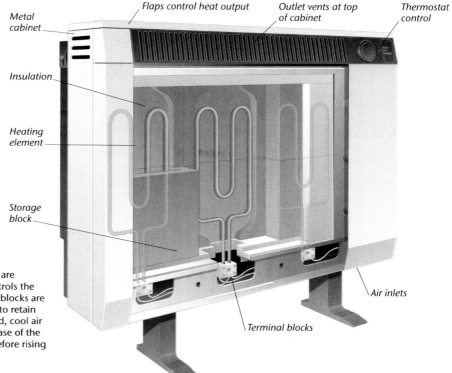

Metal cabinet   Flaps control heat output   Outlet vents at top of cabinet   Thermostat control

Insulation

Heating element

Storage block

Air inlets

Terminal blocks

Inside a storage heater
The built-in elements heat the storage blocks, which are insulated to retain the stored heat. A thermostat controls the level of heat that is supplied to the blocks. While the blocks are heated, the flaps at the top of the cabinet are closed to retain the heat until it is wanted. When the flaps are opened, cool air from the room is drawn in through air vents in the base of the cabinet and is warmed as it passes over the blocks before rising through the top vents.

UNDERFLOOR HEATING

The main advantage of underfloor heating is that there are no radiators or other heat sources cluttering up wall surfaces, and the heat it provides is particularly even and comfortable. You can embed plastic heating pipes or electric cables in a solid floor screed, but this is a realistic option only for new-build projects such as home extensions or conservatories. If you want to warm an existing floor, it is easier to use electric underfloor heating kits, which are designed to be laid on an existing floor surface and then covered with ceramic floor tiles. These can be laid on concrete or timber floors, and do not raise the existing floor level significantly.

HEALTH AND SAFETY

Buildings Regulations approval

Following the recent introduction of Part P of the Building Regulations, which deals with electrical safety, you must now notify your local authority Building Control department if you plan to install electric underfloor heating. You will also have to pay a fee to have the work inspected, tested, and certified by an electrician when it is complete.

You do not need approval to install a hot water system. However, since the pipework will be buried, it is important to ensure that the installation is designed and carried out to the highest standards.

BUILT-IN UNDERFLOOR HEATING

Systems that use pipes or cables buried in concrete floors cannot easily be installed into an existing house because of the upheaval involved in excavating the existing floor to avoid raising the floor level. However, these systems can be easily built in during construction, are efficient and reliable, and can be used with any type of floor covering. The heat provided by the system is even from floor to ceiling – there are none of the hot and cold spots that are created by wall-mounted radiators. Once the floor slab has warmed up, its temperature is thermostatically controlled, and it needs very little extra energy to keep it warm. For this reason, and because the initial warming takes some time, underfloor heating tends to be left on throughout the day (and night, if needed).

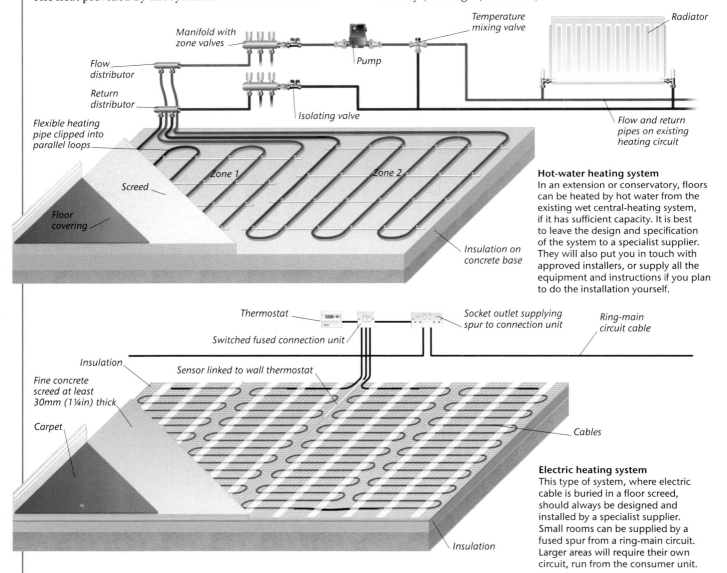

Manifold with zone valves

Temperature mixing valve

Radiator

Flow distributor

Pump

Return distributor

Isolating valve

Flow and return pipes on existing heating circuit

Flexible heating pipe clipped into parallel loops

Screed

Zone 1

Zone 2

Floor covering

Insulation on concrete base

Hot-water heating system

In an extension or conservatory, floors can be heated by hot water from the existing wet central-heating system, if it has sufficient capacity. It is best to leave the design and specification of the system to a specialist supplier. They will also put you in touch with approved installers, or supply all the equipment and instructions if you plan to do the installation yourself.

Thermostat

Socket outlet supplying spur to connection unit

Ring-main circuit cable

Switched fused connection unit

Insulation

Sensor linked to wall thermostat

Fine concrete screed at least 30mm (1¼in) thick

Carpet

Cables

Electric heating system

This type of system, where electric cable is buried in a floor screed, should always be designed and installed by a specialist supplier. Small rooms can be supplied by a fused spur from a ring-main circuit. Larger areas will require their own circuit, run from the consumer unit.

Insulation

DIY UNDERFLOOR HEATING KITS

Two types of heating kits are available for DIY installation. Both are designed to be laid beneath ceramic tiled floors only. They cannot be used with other types of flooring.

Heating cable

This system uses coils of heating cable that you tape to the floor in parallel loops after applying a special primer, so it takes a little longer to lay out than a heating mat (see below). However, using cable allows more flexibility than a mat when you are planning the layout in an awkwardly-shaped room. The cable kits come in three sizes. The 300-watt kit will warm an area up to 2.2sq m (24sq ft), the 500-watt kit an area up to 4.4sq m (47sq ft), and the 1,000-watt kit an area up to 10.9sq m (117sq ft). You can use two or more kits to warm larger floor areas.

Once the cable has been laid and the temperature probe positioned, tile adhesive is spread over the top ready to receive the floor tiles. The system is controlled by a wall thermostat and can be wired as a fused spur from a ring-main circuit unless the total load will exceed 3kW. Larger floor areas with power consumption in excess of 3kW require their own circuit, run from a 30- or 32-amp MCB in the consumer unit.

Mesh mats

This system uses heating cable fixed to pre-assembled mesh mats in parallel loops. The mats are available in a range of sizes covering from 1 to 10sq m (11 to 108sq ft), and one or more mats can be laid side by side to cover the required floor area. The mat is laid on a bed of flexible tile adhesive and is covered with more adhesive, into which the floor tiles are bedded. If the mat is to be laid over a suspended timber floor rather than a solid concrete one, special thermal boards are put down first to direct the heat output upwards. The temperature sensor is placed in the centre of the heated floor area, concealed in flat oval conduit, and is connected to the wall-mounted thermostat that controls the heat output of the mat(s). A mat area of up to 24sq m (258sq ft), with a heat output of 3kW, can be supplied via a fused spur from a ring-main circuit, since its power consumption is no more than a standard electric heater.

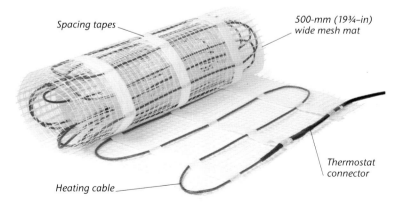

Spacing tapes

500-mm (19¾-in) wide mesh mat

Thermostat connector

Heating cable

Mesh heating mat
The mat is 500mm (19¾in) wide, and is available in lengths from 1 to 20m (3 to 65ft). Each mat has a connection to the wall-mounted thermostat at one corner, so the mat should be orientated to allow easy connection to it. You can trim the mesh to fit the floor area, but you must not cut the heating cables or overlap adjacent mats.

INSTALLING A HEATING MAT

As well as the right size of mat, you will need enough flexible tile adhesive to cover the floor to a thickness of about 5mm (¼in), plus a similar quantity to cover the mat when the tiles are laid over it (see pp.314–15 for more on tiling). You will also need oval PVC conduit to protect the power leads and the sensor cable, and a switched fused connection unit (FCU) to control the power supply to the mat. If you are laying the mat on a timber floor, you will need cement-based thermal boards to cover the mat area. Lay these first, using the fixings supplied, and tape over the joints.

If you are installing the mat in a bath or shower room, it must be protected by a high-sensitivity residual current device (RCD). The neatest way of providing this is to run the spur to the mat via a 13-amp FCU containing its own 30-milliamp RCD.

A digital multimeter is supplied with the kit so you can check the mat's insulation reading. Take a reading before you install it to confirm that the mat is undamaged, and repeat once the mat has been laid in its adhesive bed, and again before its power supply is finally connected. See pp.438–45 for more on electrics.

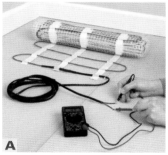

A

Do an insulation test on each mat to begin with. Then, lay out the mats side by side, and trim the mesh backing if necessary.

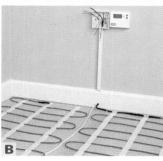

B

Plan the power supply to the mats, so you can decide where to site the FCU and thermostat. Run the cables up the wall to this position.

C

Spread tile adhesive on the floor to a depth of about 5mm (¼in) using a notched trowel, and unroll the mat on top of it.

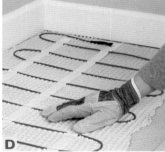

D

Press the mat into the adhesive by hand, or use a board offcut. Enclose the sensor cable in oval conduit and place it in the centre of the mat.

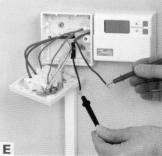

E

Connect up the FCU and the thermostat, following the wiring instructions supplied. Carry out the second insulation test on the mat.

F

Cover the mats with more tile adhesive, and bed the floor tiles in place. Allow the floor to dry out for 14 days before using the heating.

HEAT PUMPS AND BIOMASS BOILERS

In recent years, the search for greener, more sustainable ways of producing heat has intensified interest in heat pumps and biomass boilers. Although they function differently, they are often grouped together, as they both extract stored solar energy from natural sources – the former exploits water, soil, and air, while the latter uses crops. These pages explore both heat pumps and biomass boilers, and offer guidance on their potential for use in a domestic heating system.

TYPES OF HEAT PUMP

Heat pumps encompass air-source, ground-source, and water-source systems. They are energy efficient, as the amount of energy required to power them is far less than the energy they can produce. The type of heat pump you choose depends on a number of variables – a water-source pump is only viable if you have a suitable water supply, while the type of ground-source heat pump you choose depends on the amount of land you have. Consequently, air-source heat pumps tend to be the most popular, as they are not subject to the same limitations. However, they are arguably the least efficient of the three options, because air temperatures tend to fluctuate much more than ground temperatures. Consequently, choosing the correct system for your needs can be complex, making the need for professional help essential. However, the effectiveness of these systems is proven, and their popularity has increased correspondingly.

HOW HEAT PUMPS WORK

Heat pumps extract heat from water, the ground, or the air, and process that heat until it can be used domestically. Details about each system are described below and opposite, but all three have common components: a heat source (the ground, for example) and a tool for extraction (the pump); a circulation fluid that carries the heat, such as water and antifreeze; and a means of distributing that heat through the house, such as underfloor heating.

A heat pump has an evaporator, a compressor, a condenser, and an expansion valve (the illustration below depicts their relationship in a ground-source pump for heating water). A gaseous compound called a "refrigerant" absorbs heat from the air loop, or fluid from the ground loop, and is compressed, causing its pressure and temperature to rise. The gas is cooled in a condenser, forming a warm liquid. This liquid has its pressure lowered in an expansion valve, before being passed through an evaporator, which turns it into a gas, beginning the cycle again. The heat released during this process can be used domestically.

A reversing valve allows heat to move in both directions – in the summer, the system can cool rather than heat. The output depends on the system, but a ground-source heat pump could change a soil temperature of 5°C to 35°C as air or water heating.

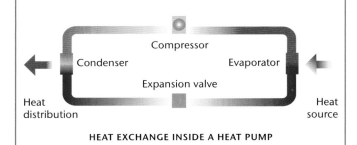

Compressor

Condenser

Evaporator

Expansion valve

Heat distribution

Heat source

HEAT EXCHANGE INSIDE A HEAT PUMP

Air-source pumps

An air-source heat pump consists of an outdoor unit and various indoor components, the design and configuration of which depend on whether you are heating water or air. The external part of the pump uses a refrigerant to extract heat from the air (see box, above). The evaporated refrigerant is compressed, and its temperature is increased. It then passes inside, where it enters a wall-mounted unit that distributes warm air throughout the house (often through ducting). For heating water, the exterior process is the same as it is for heating air, but the interior set-up involves a water-pump unit, in which the refrigerant heats water; this heated water then passes through to a hot-water cylinder, which can be used to provide hot water, or underfloor heating. A typical arrangement is shown below.

Positioning components
The close proximity of components shown here is purely illustrative. The indoor unit can be positioned almost anywhere in the home, as refrigerant pipework can be up to 30m (98½ft) in length for most system designs.

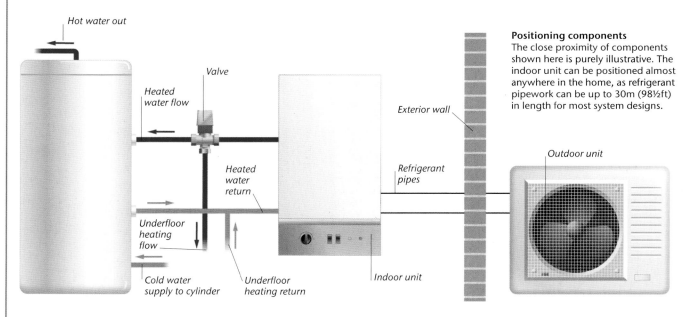

Hot water out

Valve

Heated water flow

Heated water return

Exterior wall

Refrigerant pipes

Outdoor unit

Underfloor heating flow

Cold water supply to cylinder

Underfloor heating return

Indoor unit

Ground-source pumps

Ground-source pumps use a system of undersoil pipes that extract heat from the earth and convey it to the heat pump, where the refrigerant heating cycle begins (see box, opposite). Again, air or water can be heated. This system is the most efficient, because of the consistency of ground temperature – output control is therefore very simple. The main consideration in design is whether the pipework runs horizontally or vertically outside the home. The three examples below depict typical systems, but there are further variations.

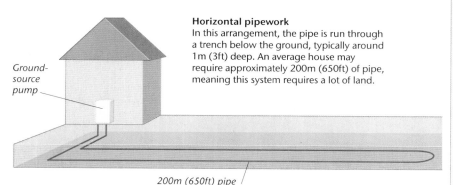

Ground-source pump

Horizontal pipework
In this arrangement, the pipe is run through a trench below the ground, typically around 1m (3ft) deep. An average house may require approximately 200m (650ft) of pipe, meaning this system requires a lot of land.

200m (650ft) pipe

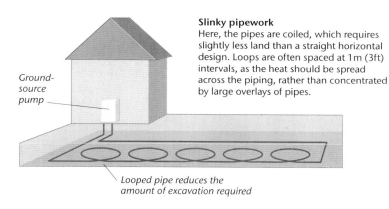

Ground-source pump

Slinky pipework
Here, the pipes are coiled, which requires slightly less land than a straight horizontal design. Loops are often spaced at 1m (3ft) intervals, as the heat should be spread across the piping, rather than concentrated by large overlays of pipes.

Looped pipe reduces the amount of excavation required

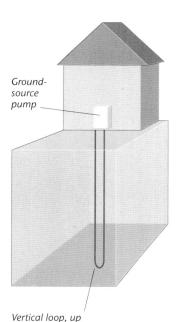

Ground-source pump

Vertical pipework
This system requires the least exterior space, as the pipe goes straight down. This involves some drilling into the ground, and can be expensive, depending on depth – drilling to 70m (230ft) is not uncommon. Clearly, a geological survey will be required to determine the suitability of drilling to such great depths.

Vertical loop, up to 70m (230ft) in depth

WATER-SOURCE PUMPS
Water-source pumps may operate as an open- or closed-loop system. In a closed system, flexible pipes are used to carry circulation fluid through water, and back to the heat pump; in an open system, the water supply acts as the circulation fluid. It is drawn up into the pipes, passing through the heat pump, where the warmth from the water is extracted, and is then discharged again. Both systems rely on proximity to a river, or an underground water source, for example. You will need to contact your local authority about permissions, especially in an open system, where uptake and discharge is taking place.

Flue

Hopper access hatch for fuel

Combustion chamber

BIOMASS SYSTEMS
Although using organic materials for fuel is not a new concept, biomass systems generate electricity by burning specially planted trees and crops, and a variety of by-products from industry, agriculture, and forestry. While burning biomass produces similar amounts of carbon dioxide as burning fossil fuels, the trees and crops that are incinerated extract carbon dioxide from the atmosphere during their life, and are replenished as they are used. In this way, biomass is seen as a "carbon-neutral" energy source.

Biomass, also known as biofuel, or bioenergy, generates electricity and heat at custom-built plants that feed power to the national grid. However, it is possible to fit domestic biomass burners that use specially produced fuels and logs to power home-heating systems.

Waste products
As well as specially grown crops, biomass is also sourced from waste products generated by agricultural and industrial processes. This includes waste wood produced by forestry.

Types of fuel
The most common fuels are woodchips and pellets. They are easily stored and loaded into the hopper as required.

Woodchips
Normally suitable for a domestic biomass boiler, woodchips require more storage space than pellets.

Pellets
Made of compressed wood shavings and sawdust, pellets have a high combustion efficiency.

BLEEDING A RADIATOR

If a radiator feels cool along the top but hot elsewhere, the most likely cause is a pocket of air (or of gas produced by corrosion within the system) trapped inside the radiator. To get rid of it, you will need to open the air vent at one of the top corners of the radiator, using a bleed key (widely available from DIY stores). If this does not cure the problem, if you have a feed-and-expansion tank in the loft that tops the system, check if it is empty. This can happen because its float valve has jammed shut. Free it and fill the tank about one-third full, then bleed any cold radiators and check that the tank has refilled.

TOOLS AND MATERIALS
Radiator key, absorbent cloth

A **Feel if the radiator** is cool at the top and hot at the bottom when the heating is turned on.

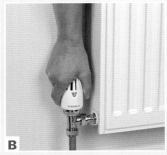

B **Open the handwheel** valve fully, or turn the thermostatic valve to its highest setting.

C **Fit the key over** the vent plug and open it to release the air. Hold a pad of cloth below the vent to catch any escaping water.

D **Open the valve** a little more, but be ready to close it quickly as soon as water starts to splutter out. The water may be dirty.

E **Tighten the vent** plug fully and wipe away any drips. Check that the radiator is now hot all over. Then reset the valve position.

VENTING PROBLEMS
- The plug has been painted over. Chip away the paint with a small screwdriver or the point of a sharp knife.
- The key does not turn the plug. Fit it in and grip its crossbar with pliers to increase your leverage. If this fails to free it, apply penetrating spray oil and leave it to soak in for a while. Then try opening the plug again.

REPLACING AN IMMERSION HEATER

The commonest cause of immersion heater failure is a burnt-out element. Check whether you have a top-fitting element (as here) or a side-fitting one, and buy a suitable replacement. Switch off the heater at its nearby double-pole switch. Next, prepare to drain the cylinder to just below the level of the heater boss. Turn off the gate valve on the cold-water supply pipe to the cylinder, and attach some garden hose to the drain valve near to its base. Lead the other end to the bath, then open the valve with pliers or a small spanner. Close it when you have let out enough water.

TOOLS AND MATERIALS
Pliers or small spanner, terminal screwdriver, immersion heater spanner, penetrating spray oil, knife, PTFE tape, new heater

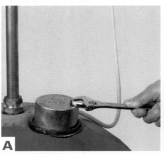

A **Undo the nut** that secures the heater cover using pliers or a small spanner. Check that the power supply to the heater is switched off first.

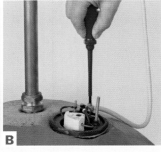

B **Make a note** of which flex core is connected to which terminal, then disconnect the cores and loosen the flex grip screws to free the flex.

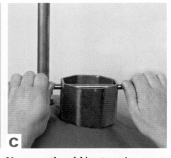

C **Unscrew the old** heater using an immersion heater spanner. Apply penetrating spray oil if it will not undo easily. Do not force it; you may buckle the cylinder wall.

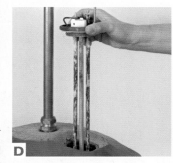

D **Lift out the** old heater and discard it. Clean old sealant from the threads inside the heater boss using the point of a knife.

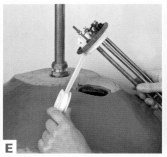

E **Wrap PTFE tape** round the threads of the new heater and fit the sealing washer. Insert it in the cylinder and tighten it.

F **Reconnect the flex** cores to the new heater terminals and set the thermostat. Replace the cover and switch the heater back on.

REPLACING A PROGRAMMER

You may be able to mount a new programmer onto the baseplate of the existing one if they are the same brand. If this is possible, simply set the switch on the back of the new programmer to suit the type of system you have, and clip it on.

If the new programmer is incompatible with the existing baseplate, you will have to disconnect its wiring and remove it, then fit and reconnect the new one in its place. Use the steps shown here and the detailed wiring instructions that are supplied by the manufacturer of the programmer to make the changeover.

TOOLS AND MATERIALS
New programmer, paper, pen, terminal screwdriver

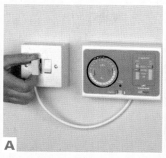

Switch off the FCU providing power to the programmer (or to the system wiring centre) and pull out the fuseholder.

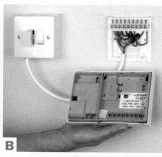

Locate the small screw that secures the old programmer to its baseplate. Unscrew it and lift the programmer away.

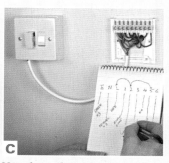

Note down the wiring layout and label the cable cores. Disconnect the cores and remove the old baseplate.

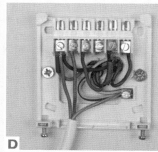

Feed the cables through the new baseplate and screw it in place. Connect the cores using your notes and the instructions.

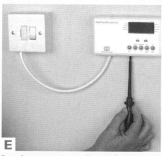

Set the switch on the back of the programmer to suit your system, then mount it on the baseplate. Restore the power.

BOILER NOT WORKING
- Check that its pilot light is on. If it has gone out, re-light it by pressing the ignition switch.
- Check the boiler and room thermostat settings. Move the programmer to the next "on" setting.
- Turn the room and boiler thermostats to a higher temperature setting.
- If the boiler still does not fire up, call in a heating engineer to fix the fault.

REPLACING A THERMOSTAT

A room thermostat may need replacing, or you may simply want to fit a more modern one. Before you start, switch off the power at the FCU supplying the heating system's wiring centre.

TOOLS AND MATERIALS
Terminal screwdriver, new thermostat

Remove the thermostat cover and undo the screws securing the body of the thermostat to its baseplate.

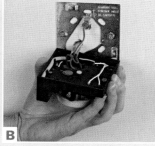

Ease the thermostat away from the wall. Note how the cable cores are connected to it, then disconnect them.

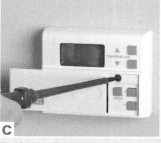

Fix the new baseplate in place and reconnect the cores to the new thermostat. Fit it on the baseplate and restore the power.

FIXING A FAULTY PUMP

Two common problems affect central heating pumps. An airlock in the pump means that the radiators do not heat up properly. A jammed pump impeller means they do not heat up at all.

TOOLS AND MATERIALS
Screwdriver, cloth

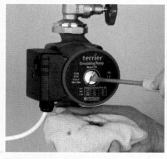

Fixing an airlock
With the pump off, loosen the screw-in bleed valve to let the air out. Use a cloth to catch any drips.

Freeing a jammed impeller
Remove the bleed valve to reveal the slotted end of the impeller. Rotate it with the screwdriver to free it.

REPLACING THE PUMP
Turn off the boiler and close the isolating valves at either side of the pump. Drain the system if there are none. Turn off the power supply to the pump an d disconnect the flex. Undo the connecting nuts securing the old pump and remove it. Fit the new pump, tighten the nuts, and reconnect the power supply. Open the isolating valves and bleed the pump.

However carefully you work, accidents can happen during DIY projects, and when they do, a little knowledge of basic first aid can be very useful. In all cases of serious injury you should of course call an ambulance or get to a hospital as soon as possible. Even with minor injuries it is wise to seek advice from a doctor, but the notes on this page may help you to deal with an immediate emergency. Keep a well-stocked first aid kit somewhere close at hand and whenever possible get someone else to help you treat an injury.

BASIC FIRST AID KIT

A good first aid kit should contain the following:

- Bandages
- Scissors
- Tweezers
- Safety pins
- Antibiotic ointment
- Iodine or similar prep pads
- Alcohol prep pads
- Butterfly bandages
- Medical adhesive tape
- Pain relievers
- Eye drops
- Burn medication

BLEEDING

Cuts and grazes are among the most common injuries. If the cut is minor, the bleeding will soon stop on its own, but it is still wise to clean and dress the wound, especially considering the dirt generated during DIY work. Rinse the wound under cold running water, then clean around it with a sterile swab or antiseptic wipe, removing any foreign objects embedded in it. Dry the area around the wound, and cover it with a plaster or wrap it with a sterile dressing. In any situation where the skin is broken, bear in mind the danger of tetanus. Most people have been immunized at some point, but the effect wears off without a "booster shot" every ten years. If your immunization is out of date, visit your doctor for a new shot.

PLASTERS

OTHER COMMON INJURIES

If an object becomes embedded in your skin, you may be able to remove it yourself. Splinters are relatively simple – clean the wound, and pull the splinter out using tweezers sterilized over a naked flame and allowed to cool. If the object is larger, go to a hospital, pinching the wound together if necessary to prevent bleeding. Whenever you or anybody else touches an open wound, make sure to use sterile gloves or at least freshly washed hands. If an object enters the eye, seek a doctor's help as soon as possible. For a broken bone, call an ambulance and do not move the casualty. Try to support the injured limb (or the head and neck if you suspect a spinal injury).

TWEEZERS

SCISSORS

CHEMICAL BURNS

Many domestic chemicals, and especially those used in DIY, can cause serious damage to the skin. Act quickly to wash the chemical off, then cover the burn with a sterile dressing and seek advice at a hospital immediately. If possible, make a note of the chemical that caused the burn, or take it with you to the hospital.

DIY CHEMICALS

ELECTRIC SHOCK

Never touch an electrocuted person who is still in contact with the electric current – you risk electrocuting yourself. Break the current by switching off at the mains or meter point, removing the plug, or wrenching the cable free. If you cannot do this, stand on dry insulating material such as a wooden box, rubber mat or pile of newspaper. Push the casualty's limbs away from the source of electricity using a wooden broom, stool, or chair. Call an ambulance immediately. If the casualty is unconscious and you know how to, put them into the recovery position.

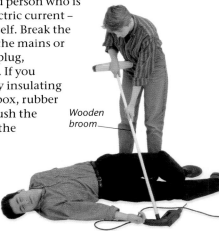

Wooden broom

ELECTRIC SHOCK

TREATING MINOR BURNS

Cool the burn with copious amounts of cold water for at least ten minutes or until the burning feeling stops. Use a running tap if possible, but any source of cold, clean water will do. Raise the limb to reduce swelling.

A

B

Try not to touch the burn itself, but protect it from the surroundings. If necessary, wrap it in a clean polythene bag or cling film.

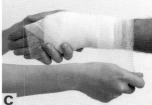

C

Alternatively, cover the burn with sterile gauze, and bandage it loosely before going to a hospital as soon as possible.

EMERGENCIES

The sections in this book offer solutions to many problems involving leaks, breakdowns, or malfunctions of home systems and appliances, but this page offers some brief advice on what to do in an emergency. However, many situations will call for professional help. You should certainly not attempt to fix a gas leak yourself, for example. The table to the right may be a useful way to keep a record of emergency and contact numbers.

GAS

If you smell gas, try to determine whether it is coming from a leak, or whether an appliance has been left on, or turned on accidentally. Extinguish any naked flames, do not turn lights on or off, and avoid using any other item that could create a spark. After checking that gas appliances are off, turn off the gas at the mains. These are normally located by the meter. Open windows and doors, evacuate the house, and keep people away from the building. If you suspect a leak, telephone your gas supplier from outside the property, at a safe distance.

PLUMBING

Leaks are dealt with comprehensively in the plumbing chapter, but in the event of a major leak, remember that turning off the main stop valve prevents any more water entering the system. If you cannot find any other way to isolate the leak, run all the cold taps in the house. This will help empty pipes if it is a supply pipe problem. Flushing toilets will also help empty the system. If the problem lies in the central heating or hot water pipes, shut down the boiler or water heater, make sure the immersion heater is off if you have one, close the radiator valves, and turn on hot water taps. Call a plumber, and if a leak is near any electrical appliance, turn off the electricity at the mains.

ELECTRICITY

If you lose all power in your home, first check that the main trip switch on the consumer unit has switched to the off position. Check whether your neighbours have the same problem, and therefore whether it is a generalized power cut or a problem for you alone. If just one circuit switches off, this could be due to overloading – check how many appliances are being used at one time. If the main isolator switch or circuit breakers trip persistently, call an electrician to deal with the problem.

EMERGENCY EQUIPMENT

It's important to have easy access to some vital equipment in case of emergencies. Most of the equipment you may need is listed under the basic toolkit (see pp.24–25), and some suggestions for a basic first aid kit are listed opposite, but you should also check that you have the following around the house:

- Spare plugs
- Fuses
- Torch
- Spare batteries
- Candles and matches
- Light bulbs
- Bucket or large bowl

IN THE EVENT OF AN EMERGENCY, GO TO THE NEAREST TELEPHONE AND DIAL 999. ASK FOR THE POLICE, AMBULANCE, OR FIRE BRIGADE

EMERGENCY CONTACTS

Emergency services   **999**

Local hospital ....

General Practitioner ....

Local police station ....

Local authority helpline ....

Floodline ....
....
....

Gas supplier ....

Telephone ....

Gas engineer ....

Telephone ....

Mobile ....

Location of gas tap ....
....
....

Water supplier ....

Telephone ....

Plumber ....

Telephone ....

Mobile ....

Location of mains stop valve ....
....
....

Electricity supplier ....

Telephone ....

Electrician ....

Telephone ....

Mobile ....

Location of fuse box/consumer unit ....
....
....

GLOSSARY

This glossary provides quick definitions of some commonly used terms in the book, as well as some definitions of building terminology that you may find helpful. Knowledge of these terms can help in both understanding structural issues, but can also make ordering materials easier, as well as explaining requirements and describing needs to suppliers.

Abutment
Joint between two surfaces. Commonly used in roofing terminology to describe the joint between a roof and a wall, for example.

Acoustically efficient
A technical term for materials that have soundproofing qualities.

Actual
The actual size of a member, as opposed to the nominal one.

Adhesive
Substance that joins surfaces, objects or materials together, for example, wood glue.

Architrave
Decorative moulding used around a wall recess or opening, such as a doorway.

Attic
The room directly under the roof.

Balloon framing
Traditional method of timber-frame house construction where single vertical members stretch from ground level up to the height of the eaves.

Baluster
Vertical member of a balustrade that fits beneath the handrail, offering support.

Balustrade
Collective term for the handrail, balusters, and baserail of a staircase.

Bargeboard
The fascia board that follows the line of the verge at the edge of a gable roof.

Bat
A brick or block cut across its shortest dimension – a quarter of a brick is a quarter bat. Used to create a particular type of bond. Also the name of rigid sections of insulation material.

Batten
Thin, square-edged timber.

Bead
A thin line of sealant, thin moulding, or technique used to cut paint in accurately at a junction.

Bearer
Supportive member. Beams are the bearers that support a raised wooden deck, for example.

Bespoke
Handcrafted work that is made to measure.

Birdsmouth
A section of the base of a rafter that is cut out in order so that it can fit/connect with the wall plate on an exterior wall.

Bond
The strength of adhesion between two materials or the arrangement of junctions between building materials. A brick bond refers to staggered vertical joints between courses, and also to wall tiles or rows of patio slabs, for example.

Bracket
Projecting supportive fixture or fitting.

Butt
To join pieces together forming a butt-join or joint.

Butter
Technique of applying mortar to the end of a brick or block before positioning it.

Capping stone
Stone laid on the top of a wall to protect the wall from the weather. Normally edges are flush with the wall, and do not overhang.

Caulk
Flexible filler used for filling cracks and joints when decorating.

Cavity
Gap between the inner and outer leaf of a cavity wall.

Cavity wall tie
Shaped bracket or connector that links the structure of the inner leaf of a cavity wall to the outer leaf.

Cement
Adhesive that is also used to bind other materials (aggregate) to make concrete. Dries to a very hard finish.

Cladding
The covering of another surface for decorative, fireproofing, or weatherproofing purposes. Wood,

stone, concrete, or tiles can be used.

Coping stone
Stone laid on top of a wall to protect the wall from the elements. The edges normally overhang the wall slightly.

Counterbatten
Double layer of battens, secured at right angles to each other. Commonly used in roofing or timber-frame wall structure to provide a cavity for ventilation and/or water runoff.

Countersink
To recess the head of a fixing (normally a screw) to below surface level.

Course
A row of building components, such as bricks.

Cutting in
Term used for painting a precise line at a junction or joint between two surfaces.

Coving
Decorative moulding used at the junction between ceiling and walls.

Dado
Lower area of a wall surface.

Dado rail
Rail that divides the dado and the upper wall. Commonly positioned 1m (3ft 3in) from floor level.

Damp-proof course (DPC)
Strip of impervious material built into the lower level of a wall that prevents ground moisture rising into the house structure. Also applies when a wall is impregnated with damp-proof chemicals to stop the upward movement of moisture.

Damp-proof membrane (DPM)
Sheet of impervious material positioned under floors to prevent moisture rising into the house structure. Edges can be built into surrounding walls to act as a DPC.

Dowel
Small peg, normally wooden, partially inserted into two adjacent surfaces strengthening the joint. Also a thin strip of wood that is round in cross-section.

Drip groove
Small channel in the underside of sills, thresholds, and other exterior projections, that prevents water running back to the wall surface by making it drip down to the ground.

Dry laying
Laying bricks or tiles, for example, using no adhesive or mortar, in

order to plan the best positions and order of work.

Edge cutter
Type of bit used with a router to create decorative profiles along the edge of a board.

Fascia
Plank-shaped member used to cover the ends of rafters, and to which guttering is normally fixed.

Female
The joining part of a fitting that the male part fits into. A male thread screws into a female thread.

First-fix
The early stages of a construction job. For example, first-fix carpentry includes erecting studs and fixing rafters. First-fix plumbing or electrical work involves routing the pipes or cables to where fixtures or fittings will be placed.

Flashing
Waterproofing layer used at joints on a roof, for example, where a flat roof meets a wall.

Float
Type of trowel with a rectangular blade used for finishing a render or plaster coat.

Flush
Level with an adjacent surface.

Foundation
The base on which to build or support a structure.

Frog
The wedge-shaped depression in the surface of a brick.

Gasket
Shaped piece of sealing material that prevents liquid or gas leaking from joined surfaces.

Gluelam
Laminated sections of timber used to create structural elements such as beams and lintels.

Go off
The gradual process by which an adhesive or wet substance dries to a hard finish, a substance that has "gone off" is not yet fully dry.

Hand/handed
When a fixture or fitting is designed to work in one direction by rotating one way, or opening from one edge. For example, it is possible to buy handed ceramic-disk valves for taps, and handed rising butt hinges for doors.

Lath
Thin, wooden strip nailed to studs or joists used in old buildings to create a framework for the application of

lime plaster. Also a small sheet of plasterboard.

Laying off
Technique of using a tool such as a paintbrush to lightly skim a surface, creating a flat, even finish.

Making good
Putting right any flaws or problems with a finish after a job.

Male
The joining part of a fitting that inserts into the female side. For example, a male screw thread fits into a female thread.

Mastic
Sealant that retains a very rubbery and flexible consistency, even when fully dry.

Member
Structural element or section in a building.

Mitre
A joint using angled cuts. Most mitres consist of two members with ends cut at 45 degrees so they form a right-angled joint.

Mortar
Mixture of cement, sand, and sometimes other materials to create an adhesive for masonry and constructional members.

Mortise
Rectangular cavity in wooden joints or in security devices such as locks and latches.

Newel post
Upright post in a balustrade that supports a handrail and provides structural strength.

Nogging
Short, wooden members used as strengthening for stud walls and in timber floor structure.

Nominal
A size of a member that may not be completely accurate in terms of measurement, but is informative in terms of estimation for building purposes. The nominal size of a brick, for example, includes mortar on the short and long side to make estimation of quantity requirement easier. The nominal size of timber cross-section may not be its actual size because it has dried out or been planed down from its actual size.

Nosing
Front edge of a staircase tread.

Offering up
Holding a fitting or material in place to check for appropriate fixing points, level positioning, or aesthetic appeal.

Olive
Metallic ring used to create a watertight seal in a compression joint between pipes.

Opaque
Describes a surface or substance through which light cannot pass.

Packing
Material (often wooden wedges or slivers) used to fill in a gap during construction or to wedge a member or fitting into position, normally so that it is level or securely fixed.

Padstone
A dense block or stone that is positioned under the ends of beams helping to support and spread weight.

Parapet
A low wall around the edge of a roof, above the eaves.

Partition wall
Internal wall that divides rooms or a space.

Party wall
A wall that is shared between neighbours, such as the wall that divides semidetached houses.

Pier
A supportive pillar common in garden-wall construction.

Pilot hole
A guide hole made for a fixing (normally a screw).

Platform frame
Timber-frame house construction where panelled timber frames are erected in storeys. Each floor forms the base for the next storey.

Plug/wall plug
A plastic or metal sleeve used in masonry or cavity walls to provide a secure insertion point and housing for a fixing.

Plumb
Exactly vertical.

Profile board
A batten nailed to two wooden stakes, with nails positioned along its top edge to indicate foundation and/or wall width. String is attached between the nails of opposing boards to provide guide lines for foundation and wall width.

Prop
Adjustable, heavyweight pole used to support the weight of structures during construction.

PTFE tape
Tape used on the male threaded plumbing joints to create a watertight seal.

Polytetrafluoroethylene may also be supplied as a paste.

Purlin
Supporting beam positioned at right angles to and below rafters.

PVA
Polyvinyl acetate, a synthetic resin used as an adhesive in its neat form, or, when diluted with water, as a sealer for porous surfaces.

PVC
Polyvinyl chloride, a type of thermoplastic often used in the production of electrical wire insulation, roofing sheets, and soft floor tiles. Unplasticized PVC is used for more rigid articles such as windows and drainage pipes.

Racking/racking back
Building up the corners first when constructing a brick or block wall.

Rafter
The sloping joists on a roof that normally run from the ridge to the wall plates.

Rebate
A groove or step cut into the edge of a piece of wood.

Reducer
A connection that joins pipes of different diameters.

Render
A mortar used as an undercoat for further plaster coats on the interior of the home. May be a finishing coat on exterior walls.

Ridge
The apex created by the joining of two pitched roofs.

Sarking
Sheathing boards fixed to rafters before felt and battens, although the term is sometimes used to refer to the felt layer alone.

Screed
Layer of mortar laid over a concrete floor pad for a smooth finish.

Scribing
Method of creating a cutting guide line on a material so that it will perfectly fit against a surface. A pointed wooden offcut is used with a pencil to "trace" a guide line that matches the profile of the surface.

Sealant
Flexible substance used to create a waterproof seal along a junction, or a liquid painted onto a surface to seal it.

Second-fix
The final stages of construction. For example, a carpenter fitting skirting boards, a plumber fitting radiators,

or an electrician fitting switches and sockets.

Sheathing
Boards used on roofs before felt, battens, and tiles. Also the boards fixed to timber-frame walls in timber-frame house construction.

Skim
The process of applying topcoats of plaster to a wall.

Solvent
The base of a substance. Water is the solvent for emulsion paint. The solvent of a substance is also used as the cleaning agent.

Square
Describes the position of an object that is exactly aligned so that it is level, vertical, parallel, or at right angles to a surface.

Stud
Wooden (or metal) member used in the construction of walls.

Subfloor
Floor material below decorative flooring, for example, plywood sheets below ceramic floor tiles.

Subsidence
Movement of the ground below or around a building that can lead to foundation and structural damage.

Tank
Technique of creating a waterproof layer or layers on a wall or floor to prevent the ingress of damp.

Topcoat
Final coat of a material e.g. plaster or gloss paint.

Translucent
Allowing a proportion of light to pass through. Transparent materials allow all light through.

Trap
Water-filled U-bend shape found in drainage systems that prevents the ingress of bad smells and odours

Undercoat
Preparatory coat for topcoats.

Underpinning
Building or adding strength to the existing foundations of a building, normally to counteract subsidence.

Vermiculite
Granular material used as loose-fill loft insulation. Also mixed with cement to make a lightweight concrete with fireproof qualities, commonly used as backfill behind the fireback in a fireplace.

Wainscoting
The use of wooden panelling at dado level.

Author acknowledgements for this revised edition

Thank you to Stephanie Farrow and Lee Griffiths for getting this edition up and running. Everybody knew it was a good idea, but it always requires a lot of work behind the scenes and we greatly appreciate their efforts on our behalf.

In producing this second edition, we would like to thank all of those companies listed in the suppliers section who supplied products and offered advice on their use. It was also great to work once again with some of the original team; Sharon Spencer was our leading light in amalgamating the new material into the original design – a huge task in itself – and we thank her for putting up with us again, and for producing more stunning-looking work. Gary Ombler returned to pick up the camera where he left off, and has clearly managed to re-capture the style and look of the original work – we thank him for that, and also for keeping us entertained on photo shoots in his usual manner. Many thanks to Julia Barnard who looked after us magnificently on the photo shoots once more, happily feeding and watering us at incredibly regular intervals. On the illustrative side, we appreciate Patrick Mulrey coming back to produce his beautiful artworks, which marry so well with the existing material. A big thank you to Barbara Hunt and Daniel Perret, models from the first edition, who also returned for more, which helped greatly with continuity.

The new editorial team, including Bob Bridle and Ed Wilson, were superbly efficient in flowing in the new material and dealing with the mass of editing problems that seems to keep multiplying when working on a book of this size. Many thanks. Indeed, to all of the people at DK who we never meet, but know are beavering away on our behalf – thank you once again.

...and of course, last, but not least, thank you to our families, who had to go through it all again!

Author acknowledgements for the original edition

When writing an illustrated book, there are always a number of people that authors like to thank for their efforts and contributions. However, when writing an illustrated book of this size, there are a truly enormous number of people to thank for work over several years.

Firstly, we will always be indebted to Stephanie Jackson, who engineered the transformation of ideas into reality. She was backed up along the way by Adele Hayward and Karen Self. In these initial stages we would also like to thank Tim Ridley, Jude Garlick, and Carole Ash for photographic, editorial, and design contributions that helped to get initial ideas off the ground.

Once the preliminaries had been sorted out, the full-time work on this book began in the autumn of 2003. Up to its completion in the autumn of 2005, many people contributed and to those in sales, marketing, production, and all those areas of publishing that authors tend not to come into contact with, thank you for all your efforts.

The day-to-day team that handled this project gradually grew and grew as more and more material was gathered. To those that were involved along the way – including Becky Alexander, Karen Constanti, Marghie Gianni, Miranda Harrison, Linda Martin, Constance Novis, and Corinne Roberts – thank you for your contributions.

All books have managerial tiers that guide and oversee progress. Stephanie Farrow, Lee Griffiths, and Bryn Walls all helped to guide us ever nearer the finish line. Later additions to the team that finished the book included David Ball, Vânia Cunha, Sunita Gahir, Phil Gamble, Jörn Kröger, Monica Pal, Matt Schofield, Giles Sparrow, David Summers, and Andrew Szudek. All had to deal with two battle-weary authors nearing the end of a long journey. Thank you for dealing with our mood swings and moans.

For most of the project Letty Luff and Suzanne Arnold took on the many editorial challenges, along with Peter Jones who oversaw everything and everybody. We would like to thank Letty for making so much sense of so many pages in so many parts of the book – her editorial mind is one of the best we have ever come across. We want to thank Suzanne for the endless days of rejigging phrase after phrase, and managing to fit what we needed 100 words to say into a perfectly concise 10. We would like to thank Peter for being the linchpin in this project – an incredibly tough task, and we have enormous admiration for the way in which he managed this book to the end, ensuring that it got to print on time. Throughout the many arguments, stand-offs, and disagreements, he kept the show moving, and we are extremely grateful for all his hard work.

On the illustrative side, we would like to thank the small army of illustrators who turned our reference material into various diagrams throughout the book. Special thanks to Patrick Mulrey who contributed the most in number, and experimented with all sorts of effects to produce some stunning images. Thanks also to Julian Baker, Peter Bull, Richard Burgess, Andrew Green, Adam Howard, Andy Kaye, Tim Loughhead, and Matthew White.

The greatest challenge on this project was undoubtedly photographic, and it was in this area that we developed our closest relationships in the team. Gary Ombler shot the majority of images, but a significant minority were from Steve Gorton. Over an 18-month period, they were guided at all times by designers Phil Gilderdale, Su St. Louis, Sharon Spencer, and Michael Duffy. We would like to thank Phil for initially setting up the style and the look of photography. Thank you to Michael for his attention to detail, and his dry sense of humour that helped the course of many shoot days, and his later help on styling the artworks in the book. An enormous thank you to Gary and Steve who were always there, ready to take the first frame come rain or shine, good health or poor health, and always managing to complete the task that was put before them. Steve takes the meaning of being easy to work with to another level, and we must thank Gary for enriching our lives with his incredible knowledge of worldwide culinary cuisine (specializing in cheeses). Art direction on the majority of shoots was the responsibility of Sharon and Su, which meant they had to navigate the precarious path of keeping us, the photographers, and their bosses back at Dorling Kindersley all happy. We thank them both for being such great fun to work with, and for making such a contribution to the look of this book. The photographic and design team are also owed a considerable thank you for their custom from most of the restaurants, inns, bed and breakfasts, and pubs of Somerset, Dorset, and Wiltshire. We think they frequented most on the 20 or so weeks of photographic shoots that they stayed in the West Country. If ever a publisher needs a holiday or eating guide for the area, this team could certainly supply the top 10s in any subject, from the pubs that provided the best cooked steaks to the guest houses that provided the most comfortable mattress.

There were many, many other contributors to the success of the photography. We would like to thank the many models who came through our doors and were often asked to sit, stand or lay in the most uncomfortable of positions for hours on end whilst the rest of us contemplated the merits of changing a shirt colour or the fractional movement of a little finger. Particular thanks to Jakki, Barbara, and Heath for tackling all our demands with such good humour.

During every day of photography we were extremely luck to have Julia Barnard or her daughter Rose (and even Helena once) to keep everybody topped up with coffee and food. That was their job description, but in reality they did so much more, ranging from cognitive therapy to simply making us all smile. We owe them a huge thank you on both our behalf and on behalf of the Dorling Kindersley team.

ACKNOWLEDGEMENTS

On a technical level, we were aided on shoots by Mike O'Connor with his always inimitable plastering work, Steve Hearne and Dave Reakes with their building and block work, and Vince Macey who steered us through the maze of wiring during the electrical shoots. We also had help at the end of a phone from Craig Rushmere, Dave Norris, Steve Cuff, Alan Berry, Andy Mainstone, and Ed Humphris of Henry James masonry (who also supplied us with a fireplace). Further supplies and help were from Martin Cole, Shaun McConnell and John and Susannah Deverell – thanks for the "German" hammer. Steve and Johnny at the "yard" were also there to help lift

a "wall" or "set" at any time of day, whilst Bert and Sue Read were our ever-understanding landlords. We are incredibly grateful to you all.

We would also like to thank another DIY guru, Mike Lawrence. He took the electrical and heating section from our initial framework, and worked a very difficult brief to provide such great sections for the book. It was a real pleasure working with him once again, and we wholeheartedly thank him for all his work and advice.

Our greatest debt of thanks goes to Phil Gilderdale. Any success that this book may have has much to do with his ideas

and hard work. We could not have wished to work with anyone more professional, and amenable at all times. His good humour and encouragement kept us going throughout the project, we are sincerely grateful to him.

Lastly, but most importantly, thank you to our families for dealing with our mood swings, late nights, and ups and downs over the years this book has taken to complete. To Adele, Emmanuelle, Jack and Rebecca, Sam and Leo, we love and thank you all.

Step Editions would like to thank the following companies for supplying materials for this revised edition:

Renewable energy
Special thanks to all at United Heating for their help with photography and advice on all aspects of renewable energy systems.

United Heating Ltd
Unit B5, Southgate,
Commerce Park,
Frome, Somerset BA11 2RY
Tel: 01373 452300
www.unitedheating.co.uk

Smartenergy UK ltd
Technology House
Haven Road, Colchester
Essex CO2 8HT
Tel: 0800 2300239
www.smartenergyuk.com

www.sunpipe.co.uk

Natural building and decorating products
Back to Earth
Jubilee House,
Cheriton Fitzpaine,
Crediton, Devon EX17 4JH
www.backtoearth.co.uk

Mike Wye & Associates Ltd
Buckland Filleigh Sawmills,
Buckland Filleigh, Beaworthy,
Devon EX21 5RN
Tel: 01409 281644
Fax: 01409 281669
www.mikewye.co.uk

Crucial Trading
PO Box 10469,
Birmingham B46 1WB
Tel: 01562 743747
www.crucial-trading.com

www.vanessacoopernaturally.co.uk

Water saving and recycling
Laundry Company Ltd
Tel: 01827 874100
www.laundrycompany.co.uk

The Bin Company (UK) Ltd
The Colin Sanders Innovation Centre,
Mewburn Road, Banbury,
Oxfordshire OX16 9PA
Tel: 0845 6023630
Fax: 01295 817601
www.thebincompany.com

Aquastore Filters Ltd
Authorised Distributors,
BLF Group
Tel: 01288 331733
Fa: 0871 2390745
www.blfgroup.co.uk

Insulation Products
Second Nature UK Ltd
Soulands Cate, Dacre,
Penrith,
Cumbria CA11 0JF
Tel: 017684 86285
Fax: 017684 86825
www.secondnatureuk.com

YBS Insulation
The Crags Industrial Park,
Creswell, Derbyshire S80 4AJ
Tel: 01909 721662
Fax: 07909 721442
www.ybsinsulation.com

Excel Industries Ltd
Maerdy Industrial Estate
Rhymney, Gwent NP22 5PY
Tel: 01685 845200
Fax: 01685 844106
www.excelfibre.com

Ecomerchant Ltd
Head Hill Road, Goodnestone,
Faversham, Kent ME13 9BU
Tel: 01795 530130
Fax: 01795 530430
www.ecomerchant.co.uk

Step Editions would like to thank the following companies for supplying materials for the original edition:

Screwfix Direct Ltd
Meade Avenue,
Houndstone Business Park,
Yeovil, Somerset BA22 8RT
Tel: 0500 414141
www.screwfix.com

Access, hire, and heavy equipment
Belle Group
Sheen, Nr Buxton,
Derbyshire SK17 0EU
Tel: 01298 84606
Email: sales@belle-group.co.uk
www.bellegroup.com

Bomag GB Ltd
Sheldon Way, Larkfield,
Aylesford, Kent ME20 6SE
Tel: 01622 716611
Fax: 01622 718385
www.bomag.com

Hewden Hire
Tel: 0161 8488621

Hire Technicians Group Ltd
Chalk Hill House,
8 Chalk Hill, Watford,
Hertfordshire WD19 4BH
Tel: 01923 252230
Fax: 01923 238799
www.hiretech.biz

HSS Hire
25 Willow Lane, Mitcham,
Surrey CR4 4TS
Tel: 08457 282828
www.hss.com

Kubota (UK) Ltd –
Construction Equipment
Dormer Road, Thame,
Oxfordshire OX9 3UN
Tel: 01844 214500
www.kubota.co.uk

Omega Wolf Ltd
Interex House, Prospect Close,
Lowmoor Business Park,
Kirkby-in-Ashfield NG17 7LF
Tel: 01623 758666
Fax: 01623 723994
www.omegawolf.com

STIHL
www.stihl.com

Strongboy
Unit 25, Kingspark Business Centre,
Kingston Road, New Malden,
Surrey KT3 3ST
020 8288 1005

Titan Ladders Ltd
Mendip Road, Yatton,
Bristol BS49 4ET
Tel: 01934 832161
Fax: 01934 876180
Email: sales@titanladders.co.uk
www.titanladders.co.uk

Adhesives, sealants, and abrasives
Building Adhesives Ltd
Longton Road, Trentham,
Staffordshire ST4 8JB
Tel: 01782 591100
www.building-adhesives.com

PC Cox Limited
Turnpike Industrial Estate,
Newbury, Berkshire
RG14 2LR
Tel: 01635 264500
www.pccox.co.uk
www.cox-applicators.com

Saint Gobain Abrasives Ltd
Doxey Road, Stafford, ST16 1EA
Tel: 01785 222000
Fax: 01785 213487
Email: orders.stafford.uk@saint-gobain.com

Bathrooms
CRAMER U.K. Ltd
www.cramer-gmbh.de
Ideal Standard
The Bathroom Works,
National Avenue, Hull HU5 4HS
Tel: 01482 346461

Decorating products
Cuprinol and Dulux Wood Finishes
Wexham Road, Slough,
Berkshire SL2 5DS
Tel: 01753 550555
www.cuprinol.co.uk
www.dulux.co.uk

HallsBeeline Group
Homebright House,
Hillview Road,
Belfast BT14 7HP
Tel: 02890 351707
Email: sales@hallsbeeline.net
www.hallsbeeline.net

LG Harris & Co. Ltd.
Stoke Prior, Bromsgrove,
Worcestershire B60 4AE
Tel: +44 (0)1527 575441
Fax: +44 (0)1527 570522
Email: sales@lgharris.co.uk
www.lgharris.co.uk

Polyvine Ltd
Severn Distribution Park,
Burma Rd, Sharpness,
Gloucestershire GL13 9UQ
Tel: 0870 787 3710
Fax: 0870 787 3709
www.polyvine.co.uk

Today Interiors
Hollis Road, Grantham,
Lincolnshire NG31 7QH
Tel: 01476 574401
www.todayinteriors.com

Decorative mouldings and stairparts
Richard Burbidge Ltd
Whittington Road, Oswestry,
Shropshire SY11 1HZ
Tel: 01691 655131
Email: info@richardburbidge.co.uk
www.richardburbidge.co.uk

Doors and windows
Crittall Windows Limited
Springwood Drive, Braintree,
Essex CM7 2YN
Tel: 01376 324106
Fax: 01376 349662
Email: hq@crittall-windows.co.uk
www.crittall-windows.co.uk

Eden House Ltd
COLONY shutters by Eden House
Elveden, Kennel Lane,
Windlesham GU20 6AA
Tel: 01276 470192
www.internalshutters.co.uk

Laird Lifestyle Products Ltd
Unit 5/6 Judson Road,
North West Industrial Estate,
Peterlee, Co. Durham SR8 2QJ
Tel: 0191 518 5200
Fax: 0870 242 1846
www.lairdlifestyle.com

Paragon Sales Centres Ltd
Systems House, Eastbourne Road,
Blindley Heath, Surrey RH7 6JP

PremDor
Gemini House, Hargreaves Road,
Groundwell Industrial Estate,
Swindon SN25 5AJ
Tel: 0870 990 7998
Email: ukmarketing@premdor.com
www.premdor.com

VELUX Company Ltd
Woodside Way, Glenrothes,
Fife KY7 4ND
www.VELUX.co.uk

Fireplaces
Henry James Stone Masonary
Brook House, Meade Lane, Wanstrow,
Shepton Mallet, Somerset BA4 4TF
01749 850 896

Winther Brown & Co Ltd
75 Bilton Way, Enfield,
London EN3 7ER
Tel: 0845 612 1893
Fax: 0845 612 1893
Email: sales@wintherbrowne.co.uk
www.wintherbrowne.co.uk

Flooring
Axminster Carpets Ltd
Axminster, Devon EX13 5PQ
Tel: 01297 630650
www.axminstercarpets.co.uk

Kahrs (UK) Ltd
Unit 2 West, 68 Bognor Road,
Chichester, West Sussex PO19 8NS
Tel: 01243 778747/784417
Fax: 01243 531237
Email: sales@kahrs.co.uk
www.kahrs.com

Western Cork Ltd
Penarth Road, Cardiff CF11 8YN
Tel: 029 2037 6700
www.westcofloors.co.uk

General construction materials
Bradfords Building Supplies Ltd
Head Office, 96 Hendford Hill,
Yeovil, Somerset BA20 2QT
Tel: 01935 845245
Fax: 01935 845242
www.bradfords.co.uk

James Hardie Building Products Ltd
7 Albemarle Street,
London W1S 4HQ
Tel: 0800 068 3103
Fax: 0800 917 5424
www.JamesHardieEU.com

Hye Oak Group Ltd
Tel: 01474 332291
Fax: 01474 564491
www.hyeoak.co.uk

Lafarge Plasterboard Ltd
Marsh Lane, Easton-in-Gordano,
Bristol BS20 0NF
Tel: 01275 377773
www.lafargeplasterboard.co.uk

Marshalls plc
Tel: 0870 120 7474
www.marshalls.co.uk

Supreme Concrete Ltd
Coppingford Hall,
Coppingford Road,
Sawtry, Huntingdon,
Cambridgeshire PE28 5GP
Tel: 01487 833300
www.supremeconcrete.co.uk

ACKNOWLEDGEMENTS

Trus Joist
East Barn, Perry Mill Farm,
Birmingham Road, Hopwood,
Worcestershire B48 7AJ
Tel: 01214 456666
Fax: 01214 456677
www.trusjoist.com

Wickes
Wickes House,
120–138 Station Road, Harrow,
Middlesex HA1 2QB
Tel: 0800 106068
www.wickes.co.uk

General tools and materials
Irwin Industrial Tool Company Ltd
Parkway Works, Kettlebridge Road,
Sheffield S9 3BL
Tel: +44 0114 244 9066
www.irwin.co.uk

Rollins & Sons (London) Ltd
Rollins House, 1 Parkway,
Harlow Business Park, Harlow CM19 5QF
www.rollins.co.uk
The Spot Board Company Ltd
Tel: 01252 821007
www.spotbord.co.uk

Stanley UK
Europa View,
Sheffield Business Park, Europa Link,
Sheffield S9 1XH
Tel: 0114 244 8883
www.stanleyworks.com

TOOLBANK
Tel: (UK) 0845 658 0357
(Overseas) +44 1322 321 495
Email: info.ecommerce@toolbank.com
www.toolbank.com

Guttering
Coppagutta
8 Bottings Industrial Estate,
Hillsons Road, Botley,
Southampton SO30 2DY
Tel: 01489 797774
Fax: 01489 796700
www.coppagutta.com

Lindab Ltd
Building Products Division,
Shenstone Trading Estate, Bromsgrove Road,
Halesowen, West Midlands B62 8TE
Tel: 0121 585 2780
Fax: 0121 585 2782
Email: buildingproducts@lindab.co.uk
www.lindab.co.uk

Insulation and draught-proofing
dBan
Interfloor Ltd,
Edinburgh Road, Heathhall,
Dumfries, DG1 1QA
Tel: 01387 240815
Email: info@dBan.co.uk
www.dBan.co.uk

Knauf Insulation
PO Box 10, Stafford Road, St Helens,
Merseyside WA10 3NS
Tel: 01744 766666
www.knaufinsulation.co.uk

Minelco Specialities Ltd
Raynesway, Derby, DE21 7BE
Tel: 01332 673131
Fax: 01332 677590
Email: minelco.specialities@minelco.com
www.minelco.com

Slottseal Group
Fleming Road, Earlstrees, Corby,
Northamptonshire NN17 4TY
Tel: 01536 200555

Kitchen appliances
Glen Dimplex Home Appliances
Stoney Lane, Prescot,
Merseyside L35 2XW
Tel: 0870 458 9663
www.gdha.com

Plants
Crestmoor Garden and Leisure
Bruton, Wincanton,
Somerset BA9 8HA
Tel: 01963 33134

Plaster accessories and coatings
Aristocast Originals Ltd
2 Wardsend Road, Sheffield S6 1RQ
Tel: 0114 2690900
Email: sales@troikaam.co.uk
www.plasterware.net

Artex-Rawlplug Ltd
Pasture Lane, Ruddington,
Nottingham NG11 6AE
Tel: 0115 984 5679
Fax: 0115 940 5240
Email: info@bpb.com
www.artex-rawlplug.co.uk

Plumbing supplies
JG Speedfit Ltd
Horton Road, West Drayton,
Middlesex UB7 8JL
Tel: 01895 449233
Fax: 01895 425314
Email: info@johnguest.co.uk
www.speedfit.co.uk

Yorkshire Fittings Ltd
PO Box 166,
Leeds LS10 1NA
Tel: 0113 270 1104
Email: info@yorkshirefittings.co.uk
www.yorkshirefittings.co.uk

Power tools
ITW Construction Products
29 Blair Court, 100 Borron Street,
Port Dundas Business Park,
Glasgow G4 9XG
Tel: 0141 342 1660
Fax: 0141 332 7489
www.itwcp.co.uk

Roofing products
John Brash and Company Ltd
The Old Shipyard, Gainsborough,
Lincoln LN3 4ES
Tel: 01427 613858
Fax: 01427 810218
www.johnbrash.co.uk

DIY Roofing Ltd
Hillcrest House, Featherbed Lane,
Hunt End, Redditch,
Worcestershire B97 5QL
Tel: 0800 783 4890
www.diyroofing.co.uk

Lafarge Roofing Ltd
Regent House, Station Approach,
Dorking, Surrey RH4 1TG
Tel: 08705 601000
Fax: 08705 642742
www.lafarge-roofing.co.uk

Ruberoid Building Products
Appley Lane North, Appley Bridge,
Wigan, Lancashire WN6 9AB
Tel: 01257 255771
Fax: 01257 252514
www.ruberoid.co.uk

Web Dynamics Ltd
Moss Lane, Blackrod,
Bolton BL6 1JB
Tel: 01204 695666
Fax: 01204 674739
www.webdynamics.co.uk

Samples
Longpré Furniture
The Claddings, Station Road,
Bruton BA10 0EH
www.longpre.co.uk

Pilkington Building Products – UK
Prescot Road, St Helens,
Merseyside WA10 3TT
Tel: 01744 692000
Fax: 01744 692880
Email: pilkington@respond.uk.com
www.pilkington.com

Security and safety products
Mothercare
Cherry Tree Road, Watford,
Hertfordshire WD24 6SH
Tel: 08453 304030

Response Wireless Alarms
Tel: 01372 450960
Email: Info@wireless-alarms.net
www.responsewirelessalarms.com

Yale
www.yale.co.uk

Tiles and tiling accessories
Fabriform Neken Ltd
Station Road, Liphook,
Hampshire GU30 7DR
Tel: 01428 722252
Email: sales@neken.co.uk
www.neken.co.uk

H & R Johnson Tiles Ltd
Harewood Street, Tunstall,
Stoke-on-Trent ST6 5JZ
www.johnson-tiles.com

World's End Tiles
Silverthorne Road,
London SW1 3HE
Tel: 020 7819 2100
Email: sales@worldsendtiles.co.uk
www.worldsendtiles.co.uk

Windmill Extrusions Ltd
Whitley Way,
Airfield Industrial Estate,
Ashbourne, Derbyshire DE6 1LG
Tel: 01335 344554
www.windmill-unilux.com

Wardrobe system
Home Decor Innovations
Home Decor GB Ltd
Tel: 01142 764099
Fax: 01142 764091

Waterproofing products
Leadplus (UK) Limited
Unit 2, Oasthouse Way,
Orpington,
Kent BR5 3PT
Tel: 01689 898844
Fax: 01689 898804
www.leadplusltd.com

Safeguard Europe Ltd
Redkiln Close, Horsham,
West Sussex RH13 5QL
Tel: 01403 210204
Fax: 01403 217529
www.safeguardchem.com

Sealocrete PLA Ltd
Greenfield Lane,
Rochdale,
Lancashire OL11 2LD
Tel: +44 (0)1706 352255
Fax: +44 (0)1706 860880
Email: bestproducts@sealocrete.co.uk
www.sealocrete.com

Dorling Kindersley would like to thank the following:

FOR THIS REVISED EDITION
Thank you to Aparna Sharma, Garima Sharma, Balwant Singh, and Arunesh Talapatra at DK Delhi for their assistance with updating the existing material for this edition. Thanks also to Adam Brackenbury for digital retouching, Jillian Burr for design assistance, and Ian D. Crane for indexing.

FOR THE ORIGINAL EDITION
Adele Hayward, Karen Self, and Stephanie Jackson for the initial set-up of this book.

Illustrators: Julian Baker, Peter Bull Art Studio, Richard Burgess, Adam Howard (Invisiblecities), Tim Loughhead, Patrick Mulrey, and KJA-artists.com

Design assistance: Mark Cavanagh, Hiren Chandarana, Robin Hunter, Ted Kinsey, Jörn Kröger, Peter Laws, Jenisa Patel, Matt Schofield, and Alison Shackleton

DTP Design assistance: Julian Dams and Janice Williams

Editorial assistance: Liz Coghill, Antonia Cunningham, Jude Garlick, Richard Gilbert, Constance Novis, and Monica Pal

Photographic assistance: Julia Barnard, Helena Beer, Rose Beer, Molly Browne, and Ruth Jennings

Additional photography: John Freeman, Tim Ridley, Howard Shooter, and Colin Walton

Models: Scott Andrews, Caroline Boulton, Tom Bowman, Matthew Bowman, Caroline Cordery, Ziggy Davies, Andy Grazette, Jakki Gregory, Daniel Hatcher, Tom Hatcher, Barbara Hunt, Victoria Keene, Shahid

Mahmood, Heath Okley, Kenny Osinnowo, Daniel Perret, Steve Redwood, Kimberley Rimmer, Duncan Smith, Edmund Tapfield, Dave Tinsell, Fiona Watson, Howard Watson, Catriona Watts, Michael West, Alison Webb, Rochele Whyte, Lamarr Wilder-Gay, and Ben Woolrych

Proofreader: Constance Novis

Index: Margaret McCormack

With additional thanks to:
Blue Ball Hotel, Brue House, Sally Snook at Clanville Manor, Hillview Farm, Lower Farm, New House Farm, Andrew and Lisa Pickering at The Cottage, and Jean Constantine at The Pines

For providing visual material:
American Standard
www.americanstandard.com

Anglian Home Improvements
www.anglianhome.co.uk

AVS Fencing Supplies Ltd
www.avsfencing.co.uk

Artex-Rawlplug Ltd
Tel: 0115 984 5679
www.artex-rawlplug.co.uk

Bell Flow Systems Ltd
www.bellflowsystems.com

Belle Group
Sheen, Nr Buxton,
Derbyshire, SK17 0EU,
Tel 01298 84606
www.bellegroup.com

Bird & Moore Ltd
birdandmoore@btinternet.com
Blackdown Horticultural Consultants Ltd
www.greenroof.co.uk

Bomag GB Ltd
www.bomag.com

BSH Home Appliances Ltd
www.boschappliances.co.uk

BSH Bosch und Siemens Hausgeräte GmbH
www.bsh-group.com

Challis Water Controls UK
www.alchallis.com

Chug Tugby
www.strawbale-building.co.uk/

Cope and Timmins Ltd.
www.copes.co.uk

Dimplex UK Ltd
www.dimplex.co.uk

ENERGY STAR®
www.energystar.gov

Excel Industries Limited
(Excel Building Solutions)
Maerdy Industrial Estate,
Rhymney, Gwent NP22 5PY

Warmcel
www.excelfibre.com

FSC (Forest Stewardship Council)
www.fsc.org

Garador Ltd
Bunford Lane, Yeovil,
Somerset, BA20 2YA
01935 443700
enquiries@garador.co.uk
www.garador.co.uk

Genersys plc
37 Queen Anne Street,
London W1G 9JB
www.genersys-solar.com
www.genersys.com (US only)

ACKNOWLEDGEMENTS

Green Building Store www.
greenbuildingstore.co.uk

Hydro International
www.hydro-international.biz

Ideal Standard (UK)
www.ideal-standard.co.uk

Kubota (UK) Ltd
www.kubota.co.uk

The Loft Shop Ltd
National Telephone Sales (UK):
0870 604 0404,
www.loftshop.co.uk
Mothercare
www.mothercare.com

NAEEEC (National Appliance and
Equipment Energy Efficiency Commitee)
www.energyrating.gov.au
Pella Corporation
www.pella.com

Philips Lighting
www.lighting.philips.com

Pozzani Pure Water plc
www.pozzani.co.uk

STERLING a KOHLER Co. brand.
www.sterlingplumbing.com
www.kohler.com
STIHL
www.stihl.co.uk

Thermascan Ltd
www.thermascan.co.uk

Today Interiors
www.todayinteriors.com

VELUX
www.VELUX.com

Windsave Ltd
27 Woodside Place, Glasgow, G3 7QL
0141 353 6841
(fax: 0141 353 6842)
windsave.com,
www.windsave.com

PICTURE CREDITS

The publisher would like to thank the following for their kind permission to reproduce their photographs:

28 STIHL (tr, cr); Belle Group (br).
29 Bomag GB Ltd (rca); Belle Group (tl, cl, tr); Kubota (UK) Ltd (bl).
75 © 1996 FSC A.C. (cr).
123 Corbis (tr).
141 Artex-Rawlplug Ltd (bl, bcl, bcr, br).
144 Pella Windows & Doors (bl, cr, br).
170 Garador Ltd (tl, tcl, tcr, tr).
171 Garador Ltd (cr).
184 Getty Images: Peter Gridley (tl).
185 The Loft Shop Ltd (tl, tc, tr).
191 Dimplex UK Ltd (cl, bl, cra, cr, br).
193 The Loft Shop Ltd (cr, bl, br).
210 VELUX (bl, bc); The Loft Shop (tr, br).
211 Zefa Visual Media UK Ltd: D Rose (ca);
VELUX (tc, cr); The Loft Shop (br).
228 Corbis (bl), (cl).
231 Corbis: Michael Pole (bl).
232 FLPA – Images of Nature:
Derek Middleton (cb); G E Hyde (c);
Hugh Clark (bc).
252 American Standard (bl); Ideal Standard (UK) (bc, br).
253 Ideal standard (UK) (tl, tc, tr, cl, cr, cfr, clb, bl); Dimplex UK Ltd (br).

262 Ideal Standard (UK) (tc, tr, cl, c, cr, bl, bc, br).
263 Ideal Standard (UK) (tc, tr, c);
Dimplex UK Ltd (cr).
352 Thermascan Ltd (c, cr).
358 Excel Building Solutions (tr)
366 Corbis (br).
372 Mothercare (tc, c, bc, tr, cra, crb, br).
373 Mothercare (tc, ca, c, cb, bc).
376 ENERGY STAR® (bl); NAEEEC (bcr); BSH
Bosch und Siemens Hausgeräte GmbH (br).
379 www.sunpipe.co.uk (br).
380 Smartenergy UK ltd (tc);
© Genersys Ltd (tr).
381 www.solarcentury.com (tl, tc).
382 Corbis: Kevin Schafer (cl);
Windsave Ltd (bl).
384 Green Building Store (bl);
Sterling, a Kohler Co. brand (c);
Challis Water Controls UK (bc);
Pozzani (cr, br).
385 Peter Parham (br); permission to
photograph reed bed www.carymoor.org.uk
387 Tom Parham (tl).
403 Corbis (bc).
416 AVS Fencing Supplies Ltd (bl, bcl, bcr, br).
506 Dimplex UK Ltd (c, bl, bla, bc, bca, br, bra).
514 Corbis (bl).

All other images © DK

Every effort has been made to trace the copyright holders. Dorling Kindersley apologizes for any unintentional omissions and would be pleased, in such cases, to add an acknowledgement in future editions.

Also thanks to:
Bosch Home Appliances Ltd,
Bell Flow Systems Ltd, Hydro International,
Blackdown Horticultural Consultants
Limited, Anglian Home Improvements, Bird
& Moore Ltd, Philips Lighting, Cope and
Timmins Ltd.

THE AUTHORS
Julian Cassell (right) and Peter Parham (left) are the authors of titles covering all aspects of DIY. Their books have sold more than one million copies worldwide. Having run their own successful property renovation business for over 20 years, these award-winning authors offer technical know-how combined with an innovative approach to DIY. They are the authors of DK's *Decorating Hints & Tips*.